INSPIRING CRIMINAL JURISPRUDENCE

Inspired by the work of distinguished criminal justice scholars, this volume explores the methodological commitments and distinctive research agenda of 'criminal jurisprudence'.

It comprises ten essays on jurisprudential topics written over a period of twenty years. Presented here for the first time as a coherent body of work with a new thematic Introduction and concluding chapter, the volume highlights recurrent issues, debates and methodological principles in the disciplinary constitution of criminal jurisprudence.

Criminal jurisprudence combines theorising about criminal law with intimate engagement with its institutional fabric and primary juridical sources. It overlaps with the theoretical ambitions of philosophical approaches to criminal law and justice, but equally encapsulates the traditional research programmes of doctrinal legal scholarship. Criminal jurisprudence takes domestic law seriously, but is cosmopolitan in its outlook and topical inclusivity, as befits the condition of modern legality.

The essays in this book traverse criminal law theory, substantive criminal law, criminal procedure, evidence law, comparative criminal process, international criminal justice, criminology and legal pedagogy. In addition to their legal-doctrinal content, they draw on moral and political philosophy, penal theory, epistemology, history, sociology, international relations, jurisprudence and comparative legal studies.

Inspiring Criminal Jurisprudence

Festschrift Essays

Paul Roberts

•HART•
OXFORD • LONDON • NEW YORK • NEW DELHI • SYDNEY

HART PUBLISHING

Bloomsbury Publishing Plc

Kemp House, Chawley Park, Cumnor Hill, Oxford, OX2 9PH, UK

1385 Broadway, New York, NY 10018, USA

Bloomsbury Publishing Ireland Limited, 29 Earlsfort Terrace, Dublin 2, D02 AY28, Ireland

First published in Great Britain 2026

A catalogue record for this book is available from the British Library.

A catalogue record for this book is available from the Library of Congress.

Library of Congress Control Number: 2026936549

ISBN: HB: 978-1-50998-618-7
ePDF: 978-1-50998-620-0
ePub: 978-1-50998-619-4

Typeset by Compuscript Ltd, Shannon
Printed and bound in Great Britain

For product safety related questions contact productsafety@bloomsbury.com

To find out more about our authors and books visit www.hartpublishing.co.uk. Here you will find extracts, author information, details of forthcoming events and the option to sign up for our newsletters.

For my inspirational parents

Keith Roberts (1943–2025)

Sandra Roberts (1942–2020)

ACKNOWLEDGEMENTS

This book draws on my experiences and intellectual formation in legal research and scholarship over what is now – all too quickly – approaching forty years, as undergraduate, postgraduate, researcher, lecturer and professor. A roll-call of every teacher, scholar and student from whom I have learnt over the course of a career is clearly out of the question. I cannot even attempt to list all of my major influences, including collaborators and coauthors, past and present, from whom I continue to learn and take inspiration. They know who they are, and don't doubt the extent or sincerity of my gratitude for their fellowship.

The influence of the nine honorands for whom the *festschrift* essays reproduced in this volume were originally written will be self-evident in the following pages. I mention here, with renewed thanks, those whose encouragement, advice and editorial feedback contributed directly to the contents of this volume: Anthony Amatrudo; Rabeea Assy; Peter Bartlett; Paul Behrens; Neil Boister; Emma Breeze; Fiona Briden; Lynne Chave; Antje du Bois-Pedain; Andrew Higgins; Jeremy Horder; Jill Hunter; John Jackson; Dino Kritsiotis; Máximo Langer; Michael Lobban; Hemi Mistry; John Riddell; Julian Roberts; Andrew Simester; Gerry Simpson; Dirk van Zyl Smit; Matt Thomason; and Lucia Zedner.

At Hart Publishing, Kate Whetter was brave enough to take on this idiosyncratic project despite the increasing unfashionability of edited collections, and Sasha Jawed worked wonders on production, including securing permission to reproduce the cover image I particularly wanted. The text was expertly copyedited by Chris Harrison. Three anonymous reviewers for Hart quite properly forced me to articulate the volume's ambitions and parameters with greater clarity and coherence. The book has been materially improved by all of these various sources of critical feedback, and doubtless would have been still better if I had followed more of the advice I was given. Independent thinking and contrarian attitudes go hand-in-hand with a certain bloody-mindedness, and I do not shirk sole responsibility for what they produce under my name. To the extent that these character traits are genetic or nurtured through the early years, I suppose I have my parents to thank for them, too.

PR

Welton le Marsh,
9 November 2025

CONTENTS

1

Inspiring Criminal Jurisprudence

I. Motivational Agenda

This book is concerned with inspiring criminal jurisprudence in two complementary senses. It contains essays which were inspired by my university teachers, academic colleagues and intellectual sparring partners; and – channelling etymological derivation[1] – it aims to breathe life into the disciplinary orientation I call 'criminal jurisprudence' by encouraging other scholars, researchers and students (proto-scholars) to engage with its topics, themes, questions, arguments and normative recommendations.

Criminal jurisprudence is not a recognised disciplinary sub-field of criminal justice scholarship and probably never will be.[2] This is no cause for regret. Let me immediately foreswear any imperialist territorial ambitions or desire for reputational immortality as the pioneering scholar who planted a flag. Coining new terminology is an irritating academic habit that should not be overindulged, especially when combined with tendentious claims to novelty. My special pleading for criminal jurisprudence boils down to the claim that the style of scholarship and the research programme it represents are not reducible to established disciplinary categories such as Criminal Law, Criminal Justice, Criminal Process, Penology or Criminology,[3] or even to more specialist chapters of scholarly inquiry such as Criminal Law Theory, Jurisprudence, Penal Theory, the Philosophy of Punishment, or any of the many adjectival criminologies[4] now on offer in the bustling marketplace of disciplinary conceptions. Related to and in significant ways overlapping with each of these disciplinary spheres, criminal jurisprudence has a distinctive character and function, which this book sets out to describe,

[1] Latin *in-spiro*, to blow into. In Greek mythology, Prometheus steals fire from the gods in order to 'inspire' (animate) clay men.

[2] I am sometimes introduced at international (especially, interdisciplinary) conferences as '*a* professor of criminal jurisprudence', as though that is the most natural thing in the world to be. I can only presume a mixed audience reaction of incomprehension, exasperation ('Criminal jurisprudence' is it now? *Whatever* next …?), bemusement and disinterest.

[3] Designations of disciplinary fields are proper nouns, and thus capitalised, not as affectation, but because the difference matters. For example, the disciplinary specialism called Criminal Law is concerned with (substantive) criminal law, but the two are very far away from being coterminous. If you doubt this, compare popular Criminal Law textbooks with *Blackstone's Criminal Practice* (LexisNexis UK).

[4] I will explain in Chapter 10.

exemplify and promote. I assume that more scholars will be inspired to engage with this programme and to contribute their own labours to it if they appreciate its value, which in turn presupposes that scholars are cognisant of criminal jurisprudence and know it when they see it. Hence the desirability of a distinctive label for criminal jurisprudence, if only for advertising purposes, and notwithstanding the risk of alienating readers with a well-warranted phobia of gratuitously proliferating terminology. The agenda is flying a flag – or raising a standard – not planting one on somebody else's turf.

Two further points about this agenda and its motivations should be stressed at the outset. First, I am not making any far-reaching or extravagant claims to theoretical innovation. Much existing criminal law scholarship, which was catalysed by renewed interest in normative theorising during the late 1980s and the early 1990s when I was a student,[5] would qualify as criminal jurisprudence in my terms. I would just like to see more of it, as well as greater awareness (including reflexive self-awareness) of its scope, methods and value. My understanding of criminal jurisprudence, prominently combining various branches of philosophy, social theory and comparative legal studies, has been influenced in particular by the inspiring scholarship of Nicola Lacey (who taught me as an undergraduate at Oxford),[6] Tony Bottoms (who taught me as a postgraduate at Cambridge),[7] David Nelken[8] and William Twining,[9] in addition to the nine scholars for whose *festschriften* the essays reproduced in this book were originally written.

[5] Catalytic texts include RA Duff, *Intention, Agency and Criminal Liability* (Blackwell, 1990); Nicola Lacey, *State Punishment: Political Principles and Community Values* (Routledge, 1988); John Braithwaite and Philip Pettit, *Not Just Deserts: A Republican Theory of Criminal Justice* (OUP, 1990); Stephen Shute, John Gardner and Jeremy Horder (eds) *Action and Value in Criminal Law* (OUP, 1993); A P Simester and A T H Smith (eds), *Harm and Culpability* (OUP, 1996). A longer 20th-century tradition traces an unbroken line back through George P Fletcher, *Rethinking Criminal Law* (Little, Brown, 1978); H L A Hart, *Punishment and Responsibility* (OUP, 1968; 2nd edn John Gardner ed, 2008); Herbert L Packer, *The Limits of the Criminal Sanction* (Stanford University Press, 1969); and Glanville Williams, *Criminal Law: The General Part*, 2nd edn (Stevens & Sons, 1961).

[6] Nicola Lacey, *In Search of Criminal Responsibility: Ideas, Interests, and Institutions* (OUP, 2016); Nicola Lacey, 'Philosophy, History and Criminal Law Theory' (1998) 1 *Buffalo Criminal Law Review*, 295; Nicola Lacey (ed), *A Reader on Criminal Justice* (OUP, 1994); Nicola Lacey, Celia Wells and Dirk Meure, *Reconstructing Criminal Law: Critical Perspectives on Crime and the Criminal Process* (Weidenfeld & Nicolson, 1990). And see Iyiola Solanke (ed), *On Crime, Society, and Responsibility in The Work of Nicola Lacey* (OUP, 2021).

[7] Anthony E Bottoms and Jonathan Jacobs (eds), *Criminology as a Moral Science* (Hart Publishing, 2023); Anthony Bottoms, 'The Philosophy and Politics of Punishment and Sentencing' in Chris Clarkson and Rod Morgan (eds), *The Politics of Sentencing Reform* (OUP, 1995); Anthony E Bottoms, 'Reflections on the Criminological Enterprise' (1987) 46 *Cambridge Law Journal* 240. And see Alison Liebling, Joanna Shapland, Richard Sparks and Justice Tankebe (eds), *Crime, Justice and Social Order: Essays in Honour of AE Bottoms* (OUP, 2022).

[8] David Nelken, *Comparative Criminal Justice: Making Sense of Difference* (Sage, 2010); Esin Örücü and David Nelken (eds), *Comparative Law – A Handbook* (Hart Publishing, 2007); David Nelken, 'Criminal Law and Criminal Justice: Some Notes on Their Irrelation' in I H Dennis (ed), *Criminal Law and Justice* (Sweet & Maxwell, 1987).

[9] William Twining, *Rethinking Evidence: Exploratory Essays*, 2nd edn (CUP, 2006; Blackwell, 1st edn, 1990); William Twining, *Globalisation and Legal Theory* (Butterworths, 2000); William Twining, *General Jurisprudence* (CUP, 2009); William Twining, *Law in Context: Enlarging*

A second contextualising stipulation concerns disciplinary boundaries and membership. I am content for qualification as 'criminal jurisprudence' to be a matter of degree and, to some extent, authorial self-identification. I do not propose any dichotomous litmus test; pluralism and inclusion are my methodological default settings. Join me in this endeavour if you are persuaded by the positive case, but if not, fine by me: you do you. This capacious big tent does not imply that anything goes for criminal jurisprudence. Some combination of foundational theorising and intensive engagement with institutional facts, processes, and normative resources is an essential ingredient; interdisciplinarity is a further characteristic dimension. Whilst scholarship within criminal jurisprudence may range across a spectrum from the relatively theoretical to the relatively doctrinal, if your work is pure theoretical speculation, experimental science, or technical legal commentaries on the latest (often, yesterday's) pronouncements of the Court of Appeal,[10] then you are not engaged in criminal jurisprudence on my terms.

An important distinction should be observed between employing disciplinary categories as ideal-typical paradigms in order to orientate oneself within the flow of ideas or to highlight meaningful comparisons and treating disciplinary membership as a badge of tribal affiliation. The first approach can be illuminating, as when distinctions are drawn between 'socio-legal studies' and 'sociology of law'[11] or between 'jurisprudence' and 'legal philosophy'.[12] I employ this contrastive technique in Chapter 10 to differentiate between the distinctive disciplinary orientations of Criminal Justice and Criminology, as I interpret them.[13] The second approach, in my estimation, has less to do with scholarship and more to do with dividing the academic world into friends, fellow travellers, opponents and enemies. If your jam is debating whether sociology of law really – *really*? – qualifies as socio-legal studies, or whether this or that publication or research programme is really – *really*? – mainstream or critical criminology, good luck with that. I've moved on.

The essays in this collection traverse criminal law theory, substantive criminal law, criminal procedure, evidence law, comparative criminal process, international criminal justice, criminology and legal pedagogy. In addition to their legal-doctrinal

a Discipline (OUP, 1997). And see David Sugarman, 'William Twining: The Man Who Radicalised the Middle Ground' (2021) 16 *International Journal of Law in Context* 475; Upendra Baxi, Christopher McCrudden and Abdul Paliwala (eds), *Law's Ethical, Global and Theoretical Contexts: Essays in Honour of William Twining* (CUP, 2015).

[10] There is no disparagement of legal journalism to appraise it *as* legal journalism, distinct from legal scholarship.

[11] Roger Cotterrell, 'Socio-Legal Studies, Law Schools and Legal and Social Theory' (2018) 2 *Journal of the Oxford Centre for Socio-Legal Studies* 19. Cotterrell's work was not a major formative influence on my thinking, but I am very sympathetic to his mature theoretical orientation. He envisages, ibid 30, 'jurisprudence as deeply receptive to social scientific insight and not confined by the disciplinary protocols and intellectual bounds of philosophy'. Insert 'criminal' before 'jurisprudence' and I entirely concur.

[12] Roger Cotterrell, 'Why Jurisprudence is Not Legal Philosophy' (2014) 5 *Jurisprudence* 41.

[13] Note that concept-construction always takes place within a purposive context of motivation, and in this threshold (thin) sense there are no 'value-free' or 'innocent' concepts in practice. Chapter 3 expounds on this caveat.

content, they draw on moral and political philosophy, penal theory, epistemology, history, sociology, international relations, jurisprudence and comparative legal studies. Such breadth of scope inevitably entails trade-offs in terms of depth and sustained focus. A drilling rig can bore deeply in one place, whereas a cultivator operates across the field but closer to the surface. All disciplinary formations and methods (advertently or otherwise) confront this basic choice between range and penetration. Criminal jurisprudence self-consciously sacrifices some microscopic details and any (dubious) aspirations to comprehensiveness as a fair price for cultivating more holistic, interdisciplinary perspectives.

II. Virtuous Recycling

The ten essays comprising this volume were written over the past 20-odd years since I was appointed to a personal chair in Criminal Jurisprudence at the University of Nottingham in January 2003. All but one have been published previously. They appear here with some minimal editing for style and essential updating. Why bother re-issuing – much less forking out cash money to buy – previously published work, when nowadays everything is available on the internet anyway? I offer three reasons, in ascending order of importance.

First, with one exception, these essays were written for edited collections over an extended period of time and were published in disparate locations with multiple disciplinary audiences. They are not readily available on the open internet and may not be accessible even behind paywalls (I offer no guarantees, since publishers are forever adding more items to packaged bundles of electronic resources, and it is near-impossible to keep track of re-released back-catalogue, sometimes indexed only under the names of editors rather than of individual authors).

The second reason for relaunching afresh would be cogent even if all of this material *were* already floating somewhere out there in cyberspace. There has been a veritable explosion in published legal scholarship over the last several decades, mirroring the exponential growth of information of all kinds generated in a digitally enhanced, globally networked modern world. What we used to call 'the information superhighway' has metastasised into all-encompassing virtual worlds. In its largely well-motivated embrace of 'open access',[14] UK higher education has increasingly exposed itself to this very imperfectly regulated free market in knowledge-production and exchange, with barely imagined – let alone properly mitigated – moral, political and epistemic implications. Once information becomes detached from expertise or responsibility for its production and dissemination, questions of trust and pedigree loom large. Who is telling me this alleged fact? How do I know whether it is true or false? Can I rely on what I am being told and the reasons advanced as its justification? How can I select what is

[14] Discussed in Chapter 11.

worth reading from the oceans of dross and disinformation swamping the internet, given that (ostensibly) salient new material is being generated in volumes and at a rate far outstripping the capacity of any human being to filter and process it all in real time? In this precarious epistemic environment, knowledge *curation* to ensure relevance, quality and credibility becomes an essential task and service. Responsibility for curating legal scholarship has traditionally fallen to university libraries, academic publishing houses, journal editors and referees, research communities and their academic societies, and individual scholars. What happens when this essential work of selection, evaluation and quality control is ceded to state-funded research councils, university bureaucracies, Twitter/X and the open internet is anybody's guess. This book's final chapter embroiders some plausible implications for legal scholarship. What I can confidently say on my own account is that I prefer to curate my own scholarship, rather than leaving it to an AI chatbot or a predatory internet 'journal' to turn it into word-soup. Readers may assess for themselves whom they would rather trust to make the best sense of it.

The third reason for bringing these essays together in a single volume, in the physical legacy format, is that I intend the value of the whole to be greater than the sum of its individual parts. In particular, this volume develops the case for 'criminal jurisprudence' as a distinctive method in legal scholarship. This term was already in standard use in the nineteenth century,[15] but largely as a prosaic noun referring to the law applied by criminal courts,[16] and it later fell out of fashion.[17] I don't recall ever hearing it as a student, and when I took it as the title for my chair at Nottingham, there was, to the best of my knowledge, only one other professor of criminal jurisprudence in the world.[18] There are now possibly two more,[19] but mine

[15] See, eg, *R* v *Middleton* (1872–75) LR, 2 CCR 38, 54 ('It is a good rule in criminal jurisprudence not to multiply crimes, to make as few matters as possible the subject of the criminal law …'); *Winsor* v *R* (1866) 6 Best and Smith 143, 169; 122 ER 1150, 1160 ('We are here dealing not with one of the fundamental principles of our criminal jurisprudence … but with a question of practice, which has fluctuated at various times, and even now may not be considered as finally and conclusively settled'). The oldest citation on Westlaw is to a colonial Court of Criminal Jurisprudence: *R* v *Captain Roche* (1775) 1 Leach 134, 168 ER 169. In *R* v *England* (1796) 2 Leach 767, 168 ER 483, Erskine and Garrow appearing for the defence are reported to have argued against 'introducing a new and dangerous practice into the criminal jurisprudence of the country'.

[16] *Cf* K J M Smith, *Lawyers, Legislators and Theorists: Developments in English Criminal Jurisprudence 1800–1957* (OUP, 1998) (offering 'an analytical account of the intellectual and institutional forces promoting and driving core developments in English criminal jurisprudence from 1800 to 1957'). For Scottish exemplars, see Robert S Shiels, 'The Literature of Scots Criminal Law and John Macdonald's Textbook' [2017] *Juridical Review* 247; Anon (attributed to Lord Cockburn), 'Art VII: Scottish Criminal Jurisprudence and Procedure' (1846) 83 *Edinburgh Review* 196 (reviewing Bell's *Supplement to Hume's Commentaries on the Law of Scotland respecting Crimes* (1844)).

[17] Not entirely. Contemporary judicial usage remains infrequent but persistent: see, eg, *R* v *Maunders* [2025] EWCA Crim 579, [12] ('the appellant met the test for *dangerousness* in the criminal jurisprudence'); *R* v *Jauvel* [2018] EWCA Crim 787, [46]: '"Finding out the truth" in criminal jurisprudence … is the function of the judge sitting with the jury, and it is critical that nothing is done to create the impression that the judge has taken sides'.

[18] In 2003 Kathleen F Brickey was the incumbent of Washington University School of Law's James Carr Professorship of Criminal Jurisprudence.

[19] In 2018, Liz Campbell was appointed by Monash University's Faculty of Law as its inaugural Francine McNiff Chair in Criminal Jurisprudence. Professor Brickey sadly died in 2013, and subsequently the

remains the only UK professorship. What's so special or different about 'criminal jurisprudence' compared, say, to criminal law theory or vanilla criminal law scholarship? The essays in this volume are meant to provide their own, fuller answer to that question, but some general themes can usefully be extrapolated by way of preliminary overview in this introductory chapter.

Now, recycling – a polite term for self-plagiarism – is a routine facet of academic publication. More so today than ever, it may be motivated by performance targets and incentives rewarding ostentatious productivity in a world of citation counts and other 'metrics'. When it is not spurious double-counting, recycling may be a legitimate way of incorporating previous publications into larger, more holistic and considered works, especially textbooks and monographs. But collections of essays that have not undergone significant revision stand at the least credible end of this justification. Is a book like the present one, then, the lazy scholar's excuse for a properly worked-up monograph? Not necessarily, and not in this instance.

I think it important to retain a variety of publishing formats in legal scholarship, even whilst institutional incentives become increasingly coercive in demanding (only) 'four-star pieces' for the REF.[20] Different kinds of publication perform different, complementary functions in the legal publishing ecosystem, which draws strength and vitality from pluralism and diversity. People learn in different ways: some prefer florid narrative, others formalistic logic. I find myself switching between the two, according to mood and current preoccupations. Moreover, I have taken inspiration from books which I have found particularly illuminating over the years which do not conform to the model of the standard-issue academic monograph. These include biographies[21] and autobiographies,[22] interviews with scholars,[23] scripted debates,[24] text and materials books,[25] instruction manuals,[26]

WashU chair may have been converted into the James Carr Professorship of International Criminal Law, currently held by Leila Sadat. If I have that right, we are back down to just two professors of criminal jurisprudence worldwide.

[20] Lucky for you if you don't already know what the REF is. Chapter 11 will have much more to say about the UK's Research Excellence Framework (REF).

[21] Nicola Lacey, *A Life of HLA Hart: The Nightmare and the Noble Dream* (OUP, 2006); Ray Monk, *Ludwig Wittgenstein: The Duty of Genius* (Cape, 1991).

[22] Daniel C Dennett, *I've Been Thinking* (Penguin, 2025); Bertrand Russell, *My Philosophical Development* (Spokesman, 2007 [1959]).

[23] Michel Foucault, *Power/Knowledge: Selected Interviews and Other Writings, 1972–1977*, Colin Gordon ed (Pantheon, 1980).

[24] Daniel C Dennett and Gregg D Caruson, *Just Deserts: Debating Free Will* (Polity Press, 2021); Jeffrie G Murphy and Jean Hampton, *Forgiveness and Mercy* (CUP, 1988); J J C Smart and Bernard Williams, *Utilitarianism – For and Against* (CUP, 1973).

[25] The two most instructional books I used as an undergraduate were C M V Clarkson and Heather M Keating, *Criminal Law: Text and Materials* (Sweet & Maxwell, 1984); and J C Smith, *Smith & Thomas: A Casebook on Contract*, 8th edn (Sweet & Maxwell, 1987).

[26] Peter Boghossian and James Lindsay, *How to Have Impossible Conversations: A Very Practical Guide* (De Capo, 2019); Elliot Sober, *Ockham's Razors: A User's Manual* (CUP, 2015); Daniel C Dennett, *Intuition Pumps and Other Tools for Thinking* (Penguin, 2014); Joel P Trachtman, *The Tools of Argument: How the Best Lawyers Think, Argue, and Win* (CreateSpace Independent Publishing, 2013); Terrance Anderson, David Schum and William Twining, *Analysis of Evidence*, 2nd edn (CUP, 2005).

popular non-fiction,[27] fictionalised jurisprudential parables[28] and, of course, edited collections, including those reproducing previously published material.[29] The latter can be especially convenient for multi-disciplinary audiences, who retain topical interest but cannot be expected to keep up with specialist literatures in every cognate field. Edited collections helpfully consolidate and synthesise disciplinary developments for periodic consumption at more leisurely pace. As a co-creator and editor of four collections publishing new essays,[30] I have found the entire process, from original conception through work-in-progress seminars to editorial feedback on drafts and final production, highly educational, collegial and rewarding.

In the present instance, the justification for recycling previously published work rests on more intellectually sturdy foundations than convenience and effective communication. Long-form academic monographs lend themselves to the presentation of a single idea, elaborated argument or project-specific research report. In theoretical work, the prototypical format is 'A theory of …' this or that. It is not my intention to present 'a unified theory of criminal jurisprudence', partly because I don't have one, but more pertinently because I don't see how one could usefully be constructed. In fact, mindful of our old friend spurious novelty now in cahoots with our new frenemy the REF, I would be quite sceptical of any claim to offer such a theory.[31] Criminal jurisprudence, in my conception, is a method, perspective

[27] The Secret Barrister, *Stories of the Law and How It's Broken* (Picador, 2019); Jay Heinrichs, *Thank You for Arguing: What Cicero, Shakespeare and The Simpsons can Teach Us About the Art of Persuasion* (Penguin, 2017); Nassim Nicholas Taleb, *The Black Swan* (Allen Lane, 2010); Philippe Sands, *Torture Team* (Allen Lane, 2008); Julian Baggini, *The Pig that Wants to be Eaten – and Ninety-Nine Other Thought Experiments* (Granta Books, 2005); Robert Kee, *Trial & Error*, 2nd edn (Penguin, 1989); Ludovic Kennedy, *Ten Rillington Place* (Gollancz, 1961).

[28] Norval Morris, *The Brothel Boy and Other Parables of the Law* (OUP, 1992) (with thanks to Rob Canton for this recommendation). It is only a short step to learning directly from fiction. See, eg, Peter Singer and Renata Singer (eds), *The Moral of the Story: An Anthology of Ethics Through Literature* (Blackwell, 2005); Christopher Brooker, *The Seven Basic Plots: Why We Tell Stories* (Continuum, 2004).

[29] A *very* selective sampling of recycled collections I have found particularly illuminating: William Twining, *Rethinking Evidence: Exploratory Essays*, 2nd edn (CUP, 2006; Blackwell, 1st edn, 1990); Susan Haack, *Defending Science – Within Reason: Between Scientism and Cynicism* (Prometheus Books, 2003); Joesph Raz, *Engaging Reason* (OUP, 1999); Michael S Moore, *Placing Blame* (OUP, 1997); John Rawls, *Political Liberalism* (Columbia University Press, 1993); Jeremy Waldron, *Liberal Rights: Collected Papers 1981–1991* (CUP, 1993); Stanley Cohen, *Against Criminology* (Transaction Books, 1988); Jules L Coleman, *Markets, Morals and the Law* (CUP, 1988); Harry G Frankfurt, *The Importance of What We Care About* (CUP, 1988); Charles Taylor, *Philosophy and the Human Sciences: Philosophical Papers 2* (CUP, 1985); Bernard Williams, *Moral Luck* (CUP, 1981); Thomas Nagel, *Mortal Questions* (CUP, 1979); H L A Hart, *Punishment and Responsibility* (OUP, 1968; 2nd edn, Gardner ed, 2008).

[30] Paul Roberts and Michael Stockdale (eds), *Forensic Science Evidence and Expert Witness Testimony: Reliability Through Reform?* (Edward Elgar, 2018); Jill Hunter, Paul Roberts, Simon N M Young and David Dixon (eds), *The Integrity of Criminal Process: From Theory into Practice* (Hart Publishing, 2016); Paul Roberts and Jill Hunter (eds), *Criminal Evidence and Human Rights: Reimagining Common Law Procedural Traditions* (Hart Publishing, 2012); Paul Roberts and Mike Redmayne (eds), *Innovations in Evidence and Proof: Integrating Theory, Research and Teaching* (Hart Publishing, 2007).

[31] This is all of a piece with a healthy dose of scepticism for totalising 'grand narratives', by no means the exclusive preserve of card-carrying postmodernists. Bernard Williams, for example, cautioned that '[t]heory looks characteristically for considerations that are very general and have as little distinctive

or orientation to the study of criminal law and penality rather than a comprehensive novel theory. Even if any such theory were imaginable, its comprehensive exposition would be a gargantuan undertaking. Analogous enterprises have been attempted before, never with encouraging results.[32]

Rather than producing a final integrative magnum opus, my method has been to develop a series of sketches, nibbling away at a succession of particular local problems, typically in conversation – or dispute – with other scholars. Contentious engagement has been the motor of this process. Maybe I am just by nature argumentative, as well as contrarian. But here is another (not mutually exclusive) salient possibility. Perhaps progress, especially in the humanities and social sciences, proceeds through dialectical opposition, converging on closer approximations to truth and wisdom through the modalities of thesis and antithesis, claim and counterclaim, conjectures and refutations,[33] adversarial argument and its cross-examination. The latter is, of course, very familiar to common lawyers,[34] but its general epistemic power across a range of institutional and social contexts should not be underestimated. For all its potential to go awry for a host of contingent reasons, adversarial argument may be truth-conducive.[35] In that case, social niceties such as deference to authority, cultural conformity, splitting the difference for the sake of harmonious interpersonal relationships and going out of one's way not to offend anybody may be corrosive of academic scholarship, blocking the way of inquiry.[36] Fidelity to professional ethics sometimes comes at the cost of friction with colleagues, university managers and friends. Those who appreciate the values of scholarship will understand the motivation for oppositional criticism and, I hope, forgive any minor trespasses into argumentative excess.

content as possible, because it is trying to systematize … Theory typically uses the assumption that we have too many … ideas, some of which may well turn out to be mere prejudices. Our major problem now is actually that we have not too many but too few, and we need to cherish as many as we can': Bernard Williams, *Ethics and the Limits of Philosophy* (Fontana, 1985) 116–17.

[32] Compare the impossible dream of producing A Big Book of All the Laws as a basis for comparative legal analysis: Ulrich Drobnig, 'The International Encyclopaedia of Comparative Law: Efforts Toward a Worldwide Comparison of Law' (1972) 5 *Cornell International Law Journal* 113. For theoretical diagnosis and suggestive remedies, see William Ewald, 'Comparative Jurisprudence (I): What Was it Like to Try a Rat?' (1995) 143 *University of Pennsylvania Law Review* 1898; Annelise Riles, 'Wigmore's Treasure Box: Comparative Law in the Era of Information' (1999) 40 *Harvard International Law Journal* 221.

[33] Karl R Popper, *Conjectures and Refutations: The Growth of Scientific Knowledge* (Routledge, 2002 [1963]).

[34] Stephan Landsman, 'The Rise of the Contentious Spirit: Adversary Procedure in Eighteenth Century England' (1990) 75 *Cornell Law Review* 497.

[35] Susan Haack, *Evidence Matters* (CUP, 2014).

[36] Susan Haack, 'Do Not Block the Way of Inquiry' (2014) 50 *Transactions of the Charles S Peirce Society* 319. Having long been an admirer of Susan Haack's work in the philosophy of science and legal epistemology, I have more recently become acquainted with the broader sweep of her writings (again, leaning heavily on convenient compilations of recycled essays): see Susan Haack, *Putting Philosophy to Work: Inquiry and Its Place in Culture* (Prometheus, 2013); Susan Haack, *Manifesto of a Passionate Moderate: Unfashionable Essays* (University of Chicago Press, 1998). Too late to be a formative influence, Haack is for me an unparalleled source of corroboration. I agree with pretty much everything she says.

Having renounced any aspiration to comprehensive restatement of previous critical engagements, there would be minimal value added to repackaging this material as a monograph. I will not have the luxury of another 20 years to write a fresh collection, and the pool of mentors whose formative influence I could draw upon is running dry. Admittedly, *Festschriften* essays have a spotty reputation. The lottery of author recruitment, the temptation to bask in the reflected glory of a celebrated 'big name', the impropriety of being too critical in a valedictory volume, the vagaries of peer review for edited collections, and the editorial embarrassment of rejecting any contribution once commissioned do not conduce to a uniformly high standard of scholarship. All I can say in mitigation is that I have always put my best work into these commissions, in the belief that the only genuine way to honour great lives in scholarship is not flattery or sycophantic emulation, but repayment in the same intellectual currency. Pupils must always try to outshine their masters to some degree or forever live in their shadow.

Although the essays in this volume are contiguous in subject matter and have been arranged in a logical narrative sequence, travelling from the general to the more particular and then out to the hinterlands, there is minimal repetition in content. The vision of criminal jurisprudence they present is a product of critical engagement with the extraordinary scholarship of the *festschriften* honorands for whom the essays were originally written, amongst many other formative influences, spanning the entire multi-disciplinary landscape of criminal justice. But if the inspiration for criminal jurisprudence is largely owed to them, the forms it takes in these pages is uniquely mine. The best proof of my having done a competent job will be that this volume inspires new generations of legal scholars (with more diverse characteristics and experience than were commonplace in my time)[37] to take up the cause of criminal jurisprudence and extend its principles and methods to new frontiers. I will now say a little more about what this enterprise would entail and how to go about it.

III. A Methodological Primer on 'Criminal Jurisprudence'

Criminal jurisprudence, as I have said, combines theorising about criminal law with intimate engagement with its institutional fabric and primary juridical sources. Criminal jurisprudence overlaps with the theoretical ambitions of philosophical approaches to criminal law and justice but equally encapsulates the

[37] You may notice (but had to be pointed out to me) that all the lives in scholarship featured in these pages are those of white men. But you should also know that one of them is Croatian-American, one Swiss-American, a third Israeli, and two more, proud Welshmen. Two have Jewish heritage, and three produced their main work as emigres. I consider myself Yorkshire before British, British before English, unquestionably European. Diversity is a diverse concept; identity is multifaceted; scholarship is international and instinctively, by aspiration, inclusive.

traditional research programmes of doctrinal legal scholarship. I regard all varieties of legal method as research tools rather than disciplinary identities; and it seems obvious to me that scholars' main ambition in formulating their inquiries should be to select the best methodological tools for the research job-in-hand, rather than being tied by habit or ideology to a subset of the available methods. Self-conscious reflection on the practical methods and methodological underpinnings of legal scholarship is integral to criminal jurisprudence.

Lawyers have not always distinguished themselves in their methodological facility or sophistication. This is odd in some ways, since legal education is essentially training in methods of legal research, reasoning and argumentation ('how to think like a lawyer').[38] But there is a world of difference between skilled performance in an activity (being good *at* lawyering) and the ability to offer coherent and compelling justifications of what one is doing whilst performing it (accounting *for* lawyering, or explaining lawyering to others). It is the difference between being an expert driver able to navigate all road layouts and weather conditions and being a qualified mechanic who can strip down and service the vehicle's engine and get it back purring on the road. Criminal jurisprudence aspires to proficiency at both levels of activity, doing *and* accounting for legal scholarship.

Comparative perspectives contribute additional layers of nuance and sophistication to criminal jurisprudence, as I understand it. One of the main attractions of the label for my chair was that common lawyers tend to associate 'jurisprudence' with legal theory, whereas in Continental European languages 'the jurisprudence' typically refers to case-law. *Both* associations are encompassed by 'criminal jurisprudence', to their mutual enrichment. I devised and started teaching postgraduate modules on comparative criminal justice in 1996, just as interest in comparative approaches to criminal procedure and process began to gather momentum and generate a specialist literature beyond the confines of generalist comparative law scholarship. Fascination with the exotic and an unwillingness to be penned in by orthodox disciplinary borders and categories soon extended into teaching and researching international criminal justice during the years in which that disciplinary specialism also, spectacularly, took flight.[39]

Criminal jurisprudence takes domestic law seriously but is cosmopolitan in its outlook and topical inclusivity, as befits the condition of modern legality. Theoretical questions that are prone to fall between disciplinary cracks, too institutional for legal philosophers but insufficiently practical for doctrinalists, are firmly on its jurisprudential agenda. These include questions about the sources and status of legal norms and the jurisdictional authority and competence of legal institutions in complex cosmopolitan configurations characteristic of multi-level governance and regulatory frameworks. Criminal law can no longer plausibly be conceptualised as a purely domestic, common-law subject. It intersects with

[38] Frederick Schauer, *Thinking Like a Lawyer* (Harvard University Press, 2009).

[39] Connections between teaching, programme design, scholarship and disciplinary constitution are explored in Chapter 8.

human rights law, constitutional law, European law and international law, amongst other varieties and subfields of legal regulation. Criminal jurisprudence interrogates these dynamic juridical formations, in theory and practice.

For one reason or another, criminal procedure has always been the poor relation in criminal law teaching and scholarship. The legislature, meanwhile, can barely leave criminal procedure alone, and the annual volume of judicial output is staggering and unrelenting. Criminal jurisprudence naturally encompasses substantive criminal law theorising and doctrinal analysis but also extends to criminal procedure and evidence. This is my particular area of research interest and expertise.[40] The essays in this volume devoted to theorising criminal procedure reflect the bias of my career, rather than implying anything significant about the scope, priorities or normative focus of criminal jurisprudence as disciplinary method. If this idiosyncratic selection produces an admittedly skewed impression of scholarly activity and publications in the general field, it can only serve to compensate for the relative neglect and marginalisation of procedure in the wider theoretical literature.

Criminal jurisprudence is concerned with process and institutions as well as doctrine and thus pays attention to the socio-legal contexts in which criminal laws are enforced and applied. The institutional contexts of criminal adjudication are prominent in international and comparative criminal justice scholarship ('adversarial' and 'inquisitorial' models, etc),[41] as are questions of purpose and effectiveness. Such inquiries dig deeper into normative foundations, probing the constitution of the rule of law, rationales for criminal censure and sanctioning, and the values of liberal democracy. Realistic appraisal of social justice concerns must figure in these inquiries, but criminal jurisprudence is not empirical sociology or social psychology. In order to remain coherent and tractable, criminal jurisprudence cannot attempt to say everything that could be said about criminal law and criminal justice in modern societies. This requires explicit reflection on disciplinary boundaries and methodological limits, even as criminal jurisprudence remains open to being informed by other sources of disciplinary knowledge and expertise. Recalling the autopoeticists' slogan,[42] criminal jurisprudence should remain 'cognitively open but normatively closed'. Let me explain.

The philosopher Richard Rorty once quipped that keeping an open mind should never be confused with letting your brains fall out.[43] The disciplinary analogue is that, at the methodological level, criminal jurisprudence should

[40] Paul Roberts, *Roberts and Zuckerman's Criminal Evidence*, 3rd edn (OUP, 2022); Paul Roberts (ed), *Theoretical Foundations of Criminal Trial Procedure* (Ashgate, 2014).

[41] See Chapter 4.

[42] See, eg, Richard Nobles and David Schiff, *Observing Law Through Systems Theory* (Hart Publishing, 2012).

[43] Richard Rorty, *Objectivity, Relativism, and Truth: Philosophical Papers vol 1* (CUP, 1991) 203. For conceptual elucidation, see Kasim Khorasanee, 'Being Open-Minded about Open-Mindedness' (2024) 99 *Philosophy* 191.

be epistemically open to relevant information but normatively impervious to obstruction, subversion or derailment. In its engagements with cognate disciplines such as Criminology, for example, criminal jurisprudence should absorb valuable insights without abandoning any of its constitutive commitment to 'censorial'[44] normative evaluation, argument and rational justification. Of course, criminal jurisprudence, in my conception, is 'critical', in the sense that every Enlightenment theorist since Kant has claimed for their theorising. By the same token, it rejects the decorative label 'critical' as a device of theoretical virtue-signalling or ideological legerdemain.

Methodological generalisations can only take us so far in communicating a sense of disciplinary specialisation and must now give way to concrete illustrations. This book adopts an essentially 'ostensive' approach to criminal jurisprudence, more show than tell. In short, the essays must speak for themselves.

IV. Ten Academic Lives in Nine *Festschriften*

The essays reproduced in this volume arose from multiple contingencies with no conscious planning or system. The first set of contingencies is that, with one exception, I happened to have encountered these nine legal scholars as teachers, collaborators, or both. The second set of contingencies is that, again with one (different) exception, I happened to be invited to contribute to edited collections celebrating their careers and scholarship. My work has been influenced or directly improved by all of them, but not in equal measure, and the roll call is far from complete. Some formative influences have yet to receive their *festschrift*; others had too many admirers and former students for me to make the cut for the invited author list. In view of the random fashion in which these essays came into being, over an extended period of time, one might wonder whether there could be any thematic coherence underpinning their sprawling subject-matter and original purposes and framing. And yet, despite the absence of any conscious masterplan, a consistent vision of criminal jurisprudence somehow emerges.

Rather than being an improbable stroke of immensely good fortune, this serendipitous result is more likely to represent the gradual coalescence and materialisation of implicit themes and methodological commitments that have become much clearer and more vivid over time. On each occasion when I have been invited to contribute to a *festschrift* volume, I have been drawn to the jurisprudential dimensions of a particular scholar's work. In each case, I was presented with an extraordinarily rich and influential corpus of scholarship on which to meditate: Andreas von Hirsch on penal theory; Bob Sullivan on criminal law; Mirjan Damaška on comparative criminal procedure; Andrew Ashworth on criminal

[44] Jeremy Bentham, 'Of the Limits of the Penal Branch of Jurisprudence', § 21, reproduced in J H Burns and H L A Hart (eds), *An Introduction to the Principles of Morals and Legislation* (OUP, 1996).

process and criminal justice; Adrian Zuckerman and Mike Redmayne on criminal evidence; Rob Cryer and Ralph Henham on international penal justice; and Colin Sumner on theoretical criminology. Each of these nine scholars had spent their professional lives developing, or at least in dialogue with, criminal jurisprudence, whether or not they would necessarily recognise or wish to advertise that disciplinary affiliation. It remained only for me to identify and embroider selected further implications for my own research agenda.

Nine academic careers celebrated in *festschriften*, combined with mine, making ten lives in scholarship. When I joined the Department of Law (as it then was) at Nottingham in 1993, a wise colleague remarked to me that being a law lecturer was more in the nature of a life-style choice than a job description. He was, I later realised, referring to the joys and demands of the life of the mind in legal scholarship. This life is at once immensely privileged, peculiarly exposed to personal criticism (and praise), and unremittingly hard work. The life of an academic is remarkable in many ways. They *pay you* to read books you would read anyway out of intrinsic subject-matter interest and desire for self-education? Playing around with words for days on end to compose more sonorous sentences *is work*? Who even knew that such jobs existed?[45] But you should also anticipate hard graft with no prospect of ever punching the clock and leaving your mental labours behind the factory gates. Whilst native talent confers some advantages, it cannot replace untold hours of strenuous labour on thinking and craft. Feminists in the 1970s proclaimed that one could 'have it all'. Like all iconic political slogans, this was true in one important sense and false in another. It is true that academic careers should be open to all types of people with the aptitude and motivation to contribute to scholarship and teaching, and this ideal is barely yet realised for too many shut out from fair opportunity to follow their dreams and realise their talents. But it is false to the extent that it implies that *a single individual* can 'have it all' without prioritising their ambitions and making some sacrifices along the way. Ask any celebrated artist or gold medal-winning Olympian: don't expect to achieve anything worthwhile without focus, resilience, temporary setbacks, and endless practice building up the muscle-memory of scholarly method.

This book brings the personal into the professional to a greater extent than is commonplace in academic publishing. There are sound reasons for this unconventional approach, reflected in aspects of the book's format and style. The following pages contain more conversational and didactic passages than are typical in academic legal publishing. Each essay opens with a short 'BioNote', briefly summarising honorands' contributions to legal, penal and criminological scholarship and explaining how I came to be part of their academic networks and subsequently invited to contribute to their *festschriften*. These BioNotes also share

[45] I recall a conversation with a hairdresser in the early days at Nottingham, chatting casually – as you do in the barber's chair – about what I was up to. Despite my convoluted explanations and protestations to the contrary, she remained convinced I must be a part-time lecturer, because I had only taught 10 hours that week and could sneak off at 3pm in the afternoon to get a haircut.

some reflections on how the intersections of personal and professional biographies influenced, and inspired, my intellectual formation and subsequent career. Aspiring scholars and colleagues in the earlier stages of their careers may be unfamiliar with the routines and rigmarole of academic networking. They may wonder how one gains admission to academic communities and builds a reputation as a potential contributor to high-quality[46] publications. The significance of collegiality in all its practical manifestations for the production of published legal scholarship is not self-evident to the uninitiated. There is consequently some value to posterity in memorialising how academic connections, project collaborations and lifelong friendships were formed. Three of the nine celebrated scholars were my university teachers. Two were academic contemporaries, who both died young.

It remains as true today as it was in the early 1990s when I joined the profession that – as one mid-level colleague recently complained to me – 'nobody tells you anything in this job'. That is to say, there is limited advice about the things that really matter in terms of career motivation, planning, disciplinary contributions and personal aspirations. Universities have attempted to formalise performance reviews and manage career development to a far greater extent than previously, but such – indubitably well-motivated, but also regulatory – efforts tend to be superficial and potentially self-defeating because it is not really possible to reduce sound career advice from knowledgeable mentors to bureaucratic administration. The most that can realistically be expected of institutional structures is that they facilitate, and do not stymie, the sorts of conversations that have always provided mentorship in healthy academic cultures. The (auto)biographical information supplied in these pages is intended to supplement such conversations.

I am sure that established communities of scholarship must sometimes appear distant, cliquey and even somewhat forbidding to many of those looking in from the outside. In my experience, the best scholars are the most receptive to fresh ideas and always looking to expand their networks. I suggest making the effort to make connections before you consider yourself excluded. Easy for me to say, from within the charmed circle? A typically complacent expression of privilege? In some respects, perhaps. However, both my parents left school aged 15 without a single qualification between them, and if you grew up in a house with internal sanitation and running hot water, your material circumstances were privileged compared to mine. An educational product of an imperfectly but genuinely meritocratic society, I studied law (twice) at Oxford and criminology at Cambridge on full state grants and didn't pay a penny in fees. Although I think I would have had the nous as an eighteen-year-old to recognise a university education as a sound career investment, I sincerely doubt whether I would now be writing a book on criminal jurisprudence if I had graduated today and needed to pay off eyewatering student loans.

[46] There is no mystery to publishing in predatory journals. You simply reply to the unsolicited email and pay the stipulated fee in US dollars.

A life in legal scholarship is not for everyone. A modicum of talent and a dollop of aptitude are essential. A vocation requiring regular production of 'internationally excellent' publications will be – and I have seen it – intolerably burdensome for somebody who cannot write fluently more or less on demand. The craft of legal writing is a professional performance requiring directed efforts and continual improvement. In legal scholarship, the means of communication is part of the message and should not be sold short as 'merely presentational'. As in many vocations, success comes slowly at first and then all at once. Practice and experience in scholarship build confidence and resilience to withstand temporary setbacks,[47] and breed their own success for those who stay the course. I have always been self-confident, but this is rooted not in delusions of genius,[48] but in the firm belief that I am trying my best and failure in scholarship is no shame and nothing to fear. As my father liked to say, 'the man who never made a mistake never made anything'. Part of the job of academic communities is to correct individual scholars' errors.

Having shared these snippets of autobiography for the sake of informed appraisal, I must signal an important caveat. I have confessed that the personal and the professional are inseparably interwoven in academic lives. It does not follow that 'the personal is political' to any appreciable degree[49] in criminal jurisprudence. Professionalism resides in disciplinary expertise. In this, I substantially agree with Stanley Fish.[50] If you want your opinions on criminal justice to carry any more weight than those of the average local councillor, taxi-driver, or social media influencer, you had better have some justifiable epistemic basis to warrant enhanced credibility. This can only come from discipline-specific knowledge, skills and professional judgement, irrespective of political preferences. Of course, biases attributable to personal experience and perspective are inescapable at some level, but we must insist on objectivity as a professional aspiration or concede that juristic science collapses into ideology. The world doesn't need any more ideologues or furious keyboard warriors. Scholars should accordingly cultivate an especially sceptical attitude towards arguments and conclusions congenial to their own political preferences and test them to the *n*th degree. No additional motivation is needed to put arguments advanced by ideological adversaries through the

[47] I will wager the weight of my still-growing pile of rejection letters and emails against yours, any day of the week. Experience in scholarship is not learning how never to fail, but rather how to cope with failure when it inevitably happens. Fail, fail again, fail better!

[48] To the contrary, I have spent the last 30 years telling students that genius is not a factor in legal studies. There are no Einsteins of the law. Regardless of how smart you think you are, if you haven't read it, you don't know it.

[49] Deliberately weasel words, because I do not deny that personal experience and even political preferences are *sometimes* relevant in scholarship. The pertinent questions are: when? why? And how often? My answers are: when personal biography supplies motivation or insight; because knowledge is sometimes experiential and/or perspectival; and, not as often as is sometimes claimed or assumed. For example, questions of analytical validity are *never* merely ideological projections. Interpretative judgements may be influenced by personal politics but are not merely their straightforward projections.

[50] Stanley Fish, *Save the World on Your Own Time* (OUP, 2008).

methodological wringer, but it is all too tempting to give political allies an intellectual free pass.

V. Chapter Synopsis and Major Themes

The following chapters explore models, theories, concepts, and jurisprudential principles and doctrines informing criminal law and the institutions of criminal justice. They also prominently address forms of argumentation and disciplinary taxonomies, suggesting adaptable tools and heuristics for use in scholarly inquiry. The tools themselves, moreover, are objects of critical appraisal at the metatheoretical level. Emphasising these methodological dimensions brings out the distinctive characteristics of criminal jurisprudence. Method is central to disciplinary formation and constitution.[51] The essays were written to be self-standing but can also be read (as I view them, in retrospect) as part of a larger programme. This section presents brief chapter overviews and synopses, drawing out structuring questions, recurrent themes, principal lines of inquiry and central arguments constitutive of criminal jurisprudence.

Inspired by the scholarship of Andreas von Hirsch, Chapter 2 is concerned with the relationship between criminal law and liberal political theory. It arose from my observation that, although many contemporary theorists of criminal law advocate or presuppose a liberal normative framework,[52] they seldom explore the liberal foundations of their theorising systematically or in any great depth. In what sense(s) is a theory of criminal law *liberal*? Two major disciplinary-theoretical obstacles stand in the way of clear thinking about this relationship. First, justificatory theories and practices of punishment are plainly *very* much older than liberalism, and many have theological origins which appear suspiciously illiberal. So, what could be distinctively 'liberal' about modern criminal law? Second, the major axis of contemporary penal theorising (mimicking central debates in Practical Ethics) pits 'utilitarian' or 'consequentialist' justifications for criminal punishment against 'retributive' or 'just deserts' (deontological) theories. This is puzzling viewed from the perspective of political theory and the historical evolution of liberal ideas, because Bentham[53] – the father of Utilitarianism – is no less a liberal thinker than Kant, the high priest of deontology. Liberal theory, it seems, cuts right across received penological wisdom. Clarity of thought is not assisted by a tendency in some quarters to invoke 'liberal' as a term of abuse. Long before Trumpian political discourse weaponised 'liberalism' as code for extreme left wokery, liberals were mocked as those individuals who are incapable of taking

[51] *Cf* Pier Giuseppe Monateri (ed), *Methods of Comparative Law* (Edward Elgar, 2012).
[52] A superior recent illustration is A P Simester, *Fundamentals of Criminal Law* (OUP, 2021).
[53] Likewise, with some theoretical complexities, Beccaria: see Antje du Bois-Pedain and Shachar Eldar (eds), *Re-Reading Beccaria: On the Contemporary Significance of a Penal Classic* (Hart Publishing, 2022).

their own side in an argument.[54] Without a serviceable, reasonably determinate and stable, normatively salient and historically plausible conception of 'liberalism', discussion cannot proceed beyond the Neanderthal level of mutual slanders.

Conceptual clarification is accordingly an essential preliminary task for Chapter 2.[55] Having identified the central kernel of liberal political morality in conceptions of (negative) liberty and personal autonomy and briefly neutralised some well-worn objections and criticisms, the chapter sketches a model, in miniature, of liberal criminal law. It is striking, I suggest, that so much of what we readily recognise as contemporary criminal jurisprudence can be derived quite directly from liberal axioms. Yet this elegant theoretical extrapolation soon runs up against persistent limitations. The chapter diagnoses two types of general problem, which I characterise as incompleteness and indeterminacy, offering examples of each. Here we encounter the limits of liberalism in criminal law theory.

Practical consequences flow from these theoretical limitations, as I illustrate through a real case example of a 'liberal dilemma'[56] in which a female Muslim criminal defendant wished to appear in court in a full-face burqa. In its unavoidably controversial ruling, the court insisted that face-coverings must be removed.[57] The dilemma for the liberal arises from the fact that advocates of personal autonomy would normally defend personal choice in clothing and other aspects of self-presentation, the more so when questions of identity also implicate freedom of religion. Working through this problem requires intellectual and practical resources that cannot be found solely within the liberal political tradition, but rather depend on detailed knowledge of jurisprudential principles, procedural traditions and local culture. This conclusion should not dismay liberals, because criminal jurisprudence, procedural tradition and local culture may be perfectly compatible with liberalism without being reducible to it. Moreover, the positive message for non-liberals is that principles of criminal jurisprudence may retain their normative purchase even for polities that reject liberal democracy as a suitable model of government (for them). This is an inference of vital importance for the architects and supporters of international human rights law and international criminal justice in a multipolar world in which liberal democracy has never been the only game in town and is arguably currently in retreat.

Chapter 3 narrows the focus somewhat from comprehensive theories of (liberal) criminal justice to more discrete institutional questions. It exemplifies

[54] See Andrew Koppelman, 'Unparadoxical Liberalism' (2017) 54 *San Diego Law Review* 257 (quoting Larry Alexander, who attributes the remark to Robert Frost).

[55] Generally, see Duncan Bell, 'What Is Liberalism?' (2014) 42 *Political Theory* 682; Steven Wall (ed), *The Cambridge Companion to Liberalism* (CUP, 2015); Edmund Fawcett, *Liberalism: The Life of an Idea* (Princeton University Press, 2014); Alan Ryan, *The Making of Modern Liberalism* (Princeton University Press, 2012); Domenico Losurdo, *Liberalism: A Counter-History*, trans Gregory Elliott (Verso, 2011); Will Kymlicka, *Contemporary Political Philosophy*, 2nd edn (OUP, 2002) ch 3.

[56] Doriane Lambelet Coleman, 'Individualizing Justice Through Multiculturalism: The Liberals' Dilemma' (1996) 96 *Columbia Law Review* 109.

[57] *R v D (R)*, Transcript of Ruling by H H J Peter Murphy at Blackfriars CC, 16 September 2013.

the methods and research programme of criminal jurisprudence by straddling substantive criminal law and criminal procedure, with a seasoning of European human rights law thickening the stew. The essay was provoked – exactly the right term in this instance – by a rather ingenious argument advanced by Bob Sullivan, hinted at in several places and then more fully expounded in a *festschrift* essay for Colin Warbrick.[58] Sullivan claimed that conduct and proof of conduct are two conjoined conceptual predicates of criminal conviction, such that a conviction in the absence of either would be a conceptual impossibility, inherently oxymoronic and not merely unjustified on normative grounds. If this argument were correct, it would have major implications for criminal litigation in England and Wales and human rights law across Europe. It would imply that the European Court of Human Rights has jurisdiction, under ECHR Art 6, to appraise states parties' domestic substantive criminal law for compliance with fair trial norms. That his argument contradicts subsisting English and European human rights law does not refute Sullivan's contention as a matter of critical jurisprudence. My essay sought to show that the argument failed, not merely as positive law but more fundamentally in its theoretical and jurisprudential suppositions. In this, I was partly reasserting a previously published analysis,[59] which Sullivan's account challenged.

We might think of this setup as a classic Whodunnit? Somebody, or something, was 'conceptually wrong'. But what, who and why? Answering this compound question was not straightforward with the intellectual and practical resources to hand. A central problem is the threshold difficulty of evaluating a claim about the conceptual requirements of criminal trial in the absence of an adequately articulated concept of criminal trial. Telling you that 'All swans are white' will not be very helpful if you have no means of distinguishing swans from blackbirds. Sullivan made no attempt to elucidate a conception of criminal trial, an omission reflecting the dominance of substantive criminal law over procedural issues in contemporary Criminal Law Theory. I have been banging this drum for some time,[60] to little appreciable effect.[61] Criminal law theorists are not *hostile* to the inclusion of criminal procedure in theoretical scholarship; they are just mostly interested in other things. Irrespective of motivation, the upshot is that Criminal Law and Criminal Procedure (in my jurisdiction, and perhaps elsewhere in the common law world) are too often like identical twins separated at birth and raised in very different environments. Superficially, there is obvious close family resemblance, but as soon

[58] G R Sullivan, 'Conduct and Proof of Conduct – Two Fundamental Conditions for the Imposition of Criminal Liability' in K H Kaikobad and M Bohlander (eds), *International Law and Power – Perspectives on Legal Order and Justice: Essays in Honour of Colin Warbrick* (Martinus Nijhoff, 2009) 235.

[59] Paul Roberts, 'The Presumption of Innocence Brought Home? *Kebilene* Deconstructed' (2002) 118 *Law Quarterly Review* 41.

[60] Paul Roberts, 'Groundwork for A Jurisprudence of Criminal Procedure' in R A Duff and Stuart Green (eds), *Philosophical Foundations of Criminal Law* (OUP, 2011).

[61] But not none, and besides, efforts to reorientate research programmes should be measured in generations rather than years. So here, as always, I am more realist than pessimist.

as they start talking, neither can recognise the other as kin or properly understand what is being said. Criminal jurisprudence could usefully perform some relationship counselling to restore familial harmony.

To be fair to criminal law theorists, it should be acknowledged that proceduralists have not given very much more thought or published attention to the *concept* of a criminal trial, either. In the absence of *prêt-à-porter* concepts, I set out to design my own. Chapter 3 sketches a conception of criminal trial with five definitional features. On my account, criminal trials are (1) institutionalised, formal, and legitimacy-claiming (2) conflict-resolution mechanisms conducted as (3) epistemically serious inquiries into (4) alleged criminal wrongdoing by (5) responsible agents entailing (6) verdict jeopardy. I explain what I mean by 'epistemically serious', 'verdict jeopardy' and other conceptual refinements, before testing the model against standard instances and deviant cases. I suggest ways in which this conception of criminal trial could be analytically useful, notably by reconsidering the notion of 'fair trial' in international human rights law and in differentiating between conceptual and normative considerations at the methodological limits of conceptual analysis. Sullivan inspired this effort to expound basic procedural concepts, without any direct invitation and – I am sure – completely unintentionally. This is how influence in scholarship works.[62]

Armed with this refurbished concept, Chapter 3 prosecutes a two-track argument. At the level of doctrinal criminal jurisprudence, it dissects Sullivan's contention that conduct attracting reasonable suspicion cannot be a conceptually fit and proper object of criminal liability. *Contra* Sullivan, a 'procedural' reading of Art 6(2)'s presumption of innocence is reasserted. At the meta-theoretical level, the chapter suggests that Sullivan's argument is (in my terms) conceptual*ist* rather than benignly conceptual. That is to say, it exhibits the vice of purporting to infer normative conclusions from strictly conceptual premisses. If I am right, we have bagged a valuable specimen of a commonplace reasoning fallacy, a pattern of argumentation that we should all strive to avoid; though that may be easier said than done since the fallacy appears in various guises and can often seem quite tempting. The chapter concludes with broad-brush reflections on the nature of theoretical work, the greater part of which is 'wrong' to a greater or lesser degree. This calls for a nuanced, pluralistic understanding of the virtues of theorising, and for epistemic modesty in advancing one's own theoretical conclusions, especially in interdisciplinary research.[63]

Chapter 4 introduces a comparative law dimension to the discussion. Comparative perspective and sensibility are vital ingredients of criminal

[62] Also see Paul Roberts, 'Philosophy, Feinberg, Codification and Consent: A Progress Report on English Experiences of Criminal Law Reform' (2001) 5 *Buffalo Criminal Law Review* 173.

[63] The argument for epistemic modesty is expounded (with greater modesty than I could honestly claim for myself) by Nathan Ballantyne, *Knowing Our Limits* (OUP, 2019). Ballantyne, at 249, confesses: 'I encounter disorder and chaos in most quarters of my intellectual world. Oftentimes, the best response I can muster is to confess that I don't know what on earth is going on out there.' This avowal may reflect an appropriate attitude for 'a doubtful epistemologist' (ibid 267), but from the pen of a judge would constitute a resignation statement.

jurisprudence, as I conceive it. It is not plausible to make claims about criminal justice *in general* if your only frame of reference is your own parochial legal system, procedural traditions and legal culture. Even more circumspect claims indexed to, for example, 'common law' or Anglophone or 'Anglo-American' (whatever that overused expression is taken to mean) criminal law are not robust if rooted in a single legal jurisdiction and are quite likely to be false or misleading beyond high-level generalisations. Chapter 4 is concerned, in particular, with comparative models of criminal procedure, starting with the unavoidable opposition between 'adversarial' and 'inquisitorial' systems and expanding the discussion into the style of institutional analysis pioneered by Croatian-US comparativist Marjan Damaška.

Whereas Chapter 2 takes its lead from the broad political morality backdrop to von Hirsch's penal theorising, and Chapter 3 zeros in on a particular argument advanced by Sullivan in a single (as it happens, relatively obscure and unrepresentative) publication, Chapter 4 adopts a blend of both critical strategies by reading Damaška's account of 'evidence law adrift'[64] somewhat in opposition to his earlier book on the structures of judicial authority and modes of political governance.[65]

The first half of Chapter 4 expounds and endorses Damaška's general methodological approach to comparative analysis of legal process. His skilful reworking of traditional comparative law models of 'adversarial' and 'inquisitorial' procedures stands as a powerful riposte to scholars tempted by the view that comparative modelling of criminal procedure systems is a fruitless enterprise. It demonstrates that comparative scholarship's evergreen adversarial/inquisitorial dichotomy remains a worthwhile, possibly even inescapable, frame of analysis, provided that it is employed with nuance and circumspection. The second half of the chapter takes a more critical turn. It queries Damaška's gloomy prognosis for common law evidence, which he based on the contention that three institutional pillars which have traditionally supported the common law's distinctive evidentiary character – adversarial structure, concentrated proceedings, and lay fact-finding – are all in decline. I argue in reply that this picture of 'crisis and impending doom'[66] did not accurately portray the status of criminal evidence law in England and Wales. Moreover, significant international developments are simultaneously spreading common law conceptions of procedure and evidence around the globe and extending their influence within supra-national institutional fora, lending new vitality to common law procedural traditions. The institutional dynamics of cosmopolitan criminal jurisprudence, I suggested *contra* Damaška's thesis, are exporting common law evidence further afield even as some of its traditional features may be losing support or being transformed in their ancestral heartlands.

[64] M R Damaška, *Evidence Law Adrift* (Yale University Press, 1997).
[65] M R Damaška, *The Faces of Justice and State Authority: A Comparative Approach to the Legal Process* (Yale University Press, 1986).
[66] Damaška (n 64) 142.

Prognostication is a dangerous game, but it cannot always be avoided in scholarship. Indeed, there is a muscular discipline in drawing out the logical implications of one's analysis in terms of future predictions, and making these concrete and public, inasmuch as events can then be taken as objective validation either corroborating or confounding the underlying analysis. Future prediction, in other words, is an experimental method for legal scholarship. Sound analysis should produce more correct predictions than falsified hypotheses. Part of the problem with Damaška's predictions for common law evidence is that there is no determinate timeframe and no clear criteria for measuring drift. Will anything resembling common law evidence still exist in a thousand years? The question seems preposterous, not just because it is impossible to know, but also because there is no tangible reason to care about the answer. The pace of technological and social change over the last several decades renders predictions beyond, say, a 30-year[67] horizon tendentiously speculative. We can be sure that criminal procedure will *change* over the next three decades, but distinguishing procedural evolution from decline is no easy matter. Institutional traditions are dynamic rather than static, responsive to changes in their social, cultural, political, economic, and technological circumstances.[68] Fossilised tradition is already dead.

It is worthwhile reflecting on why the relatively modest predictions I made in my essay have fared better than Damaška's more sweeping claims. It was a safe bet that new legislative provisions on hearsay and bad character evidence introduced by the Criminal Justice Act 2003[69] would run into conceptual difficulties and generate complex bodies of interpretative case law, because that is what virtually always happens when legislation attempts to redefine basic evidentiary concepts. Common lawyers have grappled with defining 'hearsay' and debated the legitimate uses of extraneous misconduct ('bad character' or 'similar fact') evidence for well over a century. Parliament was not going to resolve these deep conceptual and jurisprudential puzzles by definitional fiat, even supposing that legislative drafting was executed competently and successfully implemented through incremental reform. A second prediction concerned the durability of trial by jury in criminal proceedings. Experience suggests that once this type of 'efficiency' measure is on government agendas, it will keep revolving on the policy merry-go-round, waiting for a moment of perceived or real crisis to be given another outing. I noted that jury reform is often strenuously resisted, and almost two decades later we may be witnessing that scenario play out again.[70] Third, I noted that the 'principle of orality' closely associated with concentrated adversarial trials would not be seriously

[67] I said 50 years in the original essay. As you get older, time compresses.

[68] Generally, see Paul Roberts, *Roberts and Zuckerman's Criminal Evidence*, 3rd edn (OUP, 2022) chs 9 and 14.

[69] Discussed in Chapter 7.

[70] Sir Brian Leveson, *Independent Review of the Criminal Courts* (Ministry of Justice, 2025), www.gov.uk/government/publications/independent-review-of-the-criminal-courts-part-1; David Ormerod, 'Appreciating the Jury' [2020] *Criminal Law Review* 983; Hannah Quirk, 'Covid-19 and Jury-less Trials?' [2020] *Criminal Law Review* 569.

threatened by 'special measures' for vulnerable or intimidated witnesses provided that these modifications continued to be viewed as exceptions to the norm. Notice the conditionality of this prediction: I didn't say that it wouldn't happen, only that *if it did*, this would represent a decisive break with established procedural traditions. As a general rule of thumb, institutional practices and reforms susceptible to political controversy tend to be more unpredictable, because they could trigger public agitation or catch policymakers' eyes at any moment, whereas technical aspects of procedural law routinely fly under the radar of public opinion and remain issues of almost exclusively professional concern. At this juncture, English criminal trial procedure's historic attachment to orality seems attenuated but still intact.[71]

Zooming in from macroscopic models of criminal procedure systems, the next trio of essays addresses structural features of evidence law in England and Wales. Chapter 5 expounds the idea that criminal evidence should be regarded as a disciplinary specialism in its own right, distinct from civil procedure. This revisionist account represents a major departure from the traditional common law conception of the Law of Evidence as unified, trans-substantive, and rooted in predominantly epistemic considerations. The argument was originally proposed by Adrian Zuckerman[72] and subsequently developed through successive editions of our coauthored text.[73] As Chapter 5 endeavours to show, rethinking the foundational conceptual classifications of evidence law has major implications for both evidentiary theory and litigation practice. This essay highlights disciplinary taxonomies as significant objects of jurisprudential analysis.[74]

More specifically, the essay describes three conceptual shifts attributable to Zuckerman's pioneering procedural scholarship concerning: (1) the disciplinary domain; (2) institutional context(s); and (3) normative sources of evidence law. Each conceptual advance can be mapped onto corresponding dynamic transitions in disciplinary thinking: (1) from 'Law of Evidence' to 'Evidence and Proof'; (2) from transubstantivity to procedural differentiation; and (3) from evidentiary rules to principled discretion. The chapter engages critically with each of these strands in Zuckerman's thought, indicating some ways in which the project of rethinking evidence law remains incomplete. In suggesting directions for further normative development, I introduce the idea of criminal procedure law as an applied field of political morality; a description that could equally serve for the broader sweep of criminal jurisprudence.

Chapter 6 addresses exclusionary rules, one of the most characteristic features of common law evidence. However, the type of rule it explores is not paradigmatic of common law thinking, which traditionally posits epistemic rationales for

[71] For fuller consideration, see Paul Roberts, *Roberts and Zuckerman's Criminal Evidence*, 3rd edn (OUP, 2022) § 10.5.

[72] A A S Zuckerman, *The Principles of Criminal Evidence* (OUP, 1989).

[73] Paul Roberts and Adrian Zuckerman, *Criminal Evidence*, 1st edn (OUP, 2004).

[74] I first drew attention to internal and external disciplinary taxonomy as jurisprudential tasks in Paul Roberts, 'Rethinking the Law of Evidence: A Twenty-first Century Agenda for Teaching and Research' (2002) 55 *Current Legal Problems* 297.

excluding relevant information from the trial. The typical common law thought is that evidence should be excluded because it is unreliable, prone to misinterpretation or over-valuation, or is otherwise 'prejudicial' to accurate fact-finding. Chapter 6 is instead concerned with rules excluding evidence on grounds of *unfairness*, an explicitly normative – if vague – evidentiary standard not reducible to epistemic concerns. Why exclude relevant *and reliable* evidence from a criminal trial? In an enduringly influential article, Andrew Ashworth argued that the rationale was to be found in protecting rights.[75] Chapter 6 critically reconsiders 'Ashworth's protective principle' (as it became known in subsequent commentaries)[76] as a normative rationalisation for evidentiary exclusion. The ECHR-inspired evolution of procedural rights as human rights, coupled with increasing judicial receptivity to the idea that at least some procedural entitlements merit recognition as constitutional rights, burnish the allure of Ashworth's protective principle in contemporary jurisprudence.[77]

Despite these attractions, I argue that Ashworth's account is at best incomplete, essentially because procedural *rights* cannot accommodate the full range of normative considerations pertinent to criminal proceedings. Some values in criminal adjudication are not reducible to rights. I develop the argument employing an idea from complexity theory,[78] first introduced to me by Ron Allen[79] (and subsequently extended in Allen's more recent work).[80] This enterprise was partly inspired (provoked, really) by a tendency in recent Evidence scholarship to criticise fairness-based exclusionary doctrines as under-elaborated, indeterminate and inconsistently applied, but without suggesting tangible ways to improve them. My essay sought to show that the task is much more complex than can be appreciated without actually attempting to specify more particularistic exclusionary norms. I also thought that critics were underestimating the extent to which contextual adaptation to circumstances in particular cases warrants flexibility in application that could easily be construed, from a distance, as inconsistency and which, moreover, is inevitably somewhat unpredictable because, as wise judges have said, 'circumstances must alter cases'.[81]

This essay showcases many of the hallmarks of criminal jurisprudence. Its central topic is normative rationales for doctrinal rules of criminal evidence.

[75] A J Ashworth, 'Excluding Evidence as Protecting Rights' [1977] *Criminal Law Review* 723.

[76] See, eg, Tony Ward, 'Improperly Obtained Evidence and the Epistemic Conception of the Trial' (2017) 81 *Journal of Criminal Law* 328, 337; Laura Hoyano, 'What is Balanced on the Scales of Justice? In Search of the Essence of the Right to a Fair Trial' [2014] *Criminal Law Review* 4, 25 ('Ashworth's justly famous protective principle').

[77] Also see Andrew Ashworth, 'The Exclusion of Evidence Obtained by Violating a Fundamental Right: Pragmatism before Principle in the Strasbourg Jurisprudence' in Paul Roberts and Jill Hunter (eds), *Criminal Evidence and Human Rights* (Hart Publishing, 2012).

[78] Embracing the important notion of combinatorial explosion: see David A Schum, *The Evidential Foundations of Probabilistic Reasoning* (Northwestern University Press, 1994) 491–92; Gilbert Harman, *Change in View: Principles of Reasoning* (MIT Press, 1986) 25–27.

[79] Ronald J Allen, 'Rationality, Algorithms and Juridical Proof: A Preliminary Inquiry' (1997) 1 *International Journal of Evidence & Proof* 254.

[80] Ronald J Allen, 'Reflections on Complexity, Evidence, and Law' (2025) 38 *Ratio Juris* 72.

[81] *R* v *Brown* [1994] 1 AC 212, HL, 270 (Lord Mustill).

It leverages interdisciplinarity, not only in drawing on moral and political philosophy but also in borrowing from complexity theory, a combination of metaphysics, epistemology and information science. A subsidiary theme is normative innovation and plurality in the institutional sources of evidence law. Traditionally conceived as a judge-fashioned creature of common law precedent, modern criminal procedure in England and Wales is constituted by statutes, human rights law, and constitutional principles, amongst other sources of legal authority. Diffusion, diversification and expansion in sources of criminal law invite jurisprudential analysis and reflection. Finally, the essay underlines criminal jurisprudence's distance from more speculative philosophising through its concern for practical decision-making. Criticising judges for the quality of their reasoning is meat and drink for legal academics, and long may we feast with no prospect of famine. But legitimate criticism should be attuned to institutional objectives and realities. Chiding judges simply for being poor philosophers or law teachers, for example, is about as helpful as instructing academics to write better legal judgments.[82] Fairness-based exclusionary doctrines are not defective merely in virtue of being open-textured, indeterminate and flexibly applied. Without troubling to formulate tangible improvements to existing normative regulation, better adjusted to institutional objectives and realities, critics are reduced to reminding their audiences that criminal adjudication falls short of some notional ideal. That doesn't strike me as a very high bar for anybody who pays attention to news reports and is very unlikely to inform criminal practitioners who work in our beleaguered criminal justice process of anything they don't already know.

Chapter 7 reproduces a review article of Mike Redmayne's last book on *Character in the Criminal Trial*.[83] The circumstances of Redmayne's tragically foreshortened career qualify this piece as a de facto *festschrift* essay, with an unmistakable pedigree as criminal jurisprudence in both object and substance.[84] *Character in the Criminal Trial* is jurisprudential in its concern with normative philosophical foundations, reliance on multi-disciplinary literatures, and central problematic and framing. It pursues the issue of 'character' across conventional disciplinary boundaries demarcating criminal law, evidence law, sentencing law and practice, and penal theory. Redmayne's approach can be seen as a bridge between methodologically parallel developments in contemporary Criminal Law Theory and in Evidence and Proof scholarship which have largely proceeded in isolation from each other. Redmayne's book promotes their integration. Albeit somewhat nebulous and incomplete, a crystallising disciplinary specialism of

[82] Not to be confused with pretending to write legal judgments, which is a creative form of legal scholarship and pedagogy but not an exercise of judicial authority. A notable illustration is Rosemary Hunter, Clare McGlynn Erika Rackley (eds), *Feminist Judgments: From Theory to Practice* (Hart Publishing, 2010).

[83] Mike Redmayne, *Character in the Criminal Trial* (OUP, 2015).

[84] The original title was 'Redmayne's Character and Criminal Jurisprudence' (2016) 79 *Modern Law Review* 706.

Criminal Law Theory is recognisably the institutionalised counterpart of criminal jurisprudence as method.

A hallmark of Redmayne's scholarship was a healthy disregard for prevailing jurisprudential wisdom, reinforced by (well justified) impatience with immature theoretical argumentation and bad philosophy. Drawing on empirical data, Redmayne examined and found wanting most of the rationales traditionally advanced by legal commentators to justify exclusion of bad character evidence from criminal trials. Deftly navigating the obvious perils of interdisciplinary scholarship, he was an intelligently critical consumer of official statistics and experimental behavioural science data and drew appropriately cautious conclusions for legal practice and law reform. The challenge thrown down by Redmayne to orthodox common law evidentiary thinking merits a fuller answer than it has yet received.[85] To the extent that I part company with him in retaining more of the common law's sceptical attitude towards extraneous misconduct evidence, this may reflect my greater emphasis on pragmatic and contingent institutional factors. Specifically, I perceive that bad character evidence is open to institutional abuse even if its routine exclusion lacks cogent theoretical explanation. Regardless of any incidental doctrinal divergence between us, Redmayne exemplified the technique of subjecting doctrinal evidentiary law to systematic theoretical analysis, which is a leading characteristic of criminal jurisprudence.

The next pair of essays, comprising Chapters 8 and 9, extends the discussion from the domestic to the international legal setting. Hart (in)famously proposed that, by the light of his conceptualisation, international law could be regarded as constituting a legal system only by weak analogy.[86] We are no longer in the grip of such binary distinctions between national and international legal orders. Criminal jurisprudence in our time has taken a cosmopolitan turn, one important strand of which is constituted by historic innovation in international criminal law and process. International Criminal Justice (ICrimJ) supplies one remarkable case-study in rapid disciplinary formation, which could be observed in real time over a decade or so from the mid-1990s. Chapter 8 describes my collaboration with Nottingham colleagues in developing pioneering LLM (postgraduate) programmes in ICrimJ. It is concerned with the institutional contexts and material and intellectual infrastructure supporting scholarship through research-led teaching (a slogan that has now largely gone out of fashion,

[85] For some partial responses and critical engagements, see Federico Picinali, 'Generalisations, Causal Relationships and Moral Responsibility' (2016) 20 *International Journal of Evidence & Proof* 121; David Hamer, 'The Legal Structure of Propensity Evidence' (2016) 20 *International Journal of Evidence & Proof* 136; Jill Hunter, 'Character in the Criminal Trial' (2016) 20 *International Journal of Evidence & Proof* 162.

[86] 'Perhaps international law is at present in a stage of transition … If, and when, this transition is completed the formal analogies, which at present seem thin and even delusive, would acquire substance, and the sceptic's last doubts about the legal "quality" of international law may then be laid to rest. Till this stage is reached the analogies are surely those of function and content, not of form': H L A Hart, *The Concept of Law* (Clarendon, 1961) 231.

but to which I remain stubbornly attached). International criminal proceedings present new opportunities, as well as daunting challenges, for the application of jurisprudential principles largely fashioned in the context of domestic criminal law and process. The adequacy of 'domestic analogies' is consequently a central question of international criminal jurisprudence.[87] As a study in local institutional history, Chapter 8 underlines the importance of academic community and collegiality, the opportunities afforded by enlightened university administration, and the fragility of curriculum design and disciplinary empire-building when key personnel move on or the political wind changes direction and institutions trim their policy sails. These themes are revisited in Chapter 11's anxious reflections on the future of UK legal scholarship.

Chapter 9 reproduces a jurisprudential case-study on a more miniature scale. It takes one tiny evidential fragment of the landmark case of *Tadic* before the International Criminal Tribunal for the Former Yugoslavia (ICTY)[88] to illustrate the rich potential of international criminal proceedings for evidentiary analysis. In its context and framing, this chapter reinforces the methodological credentials and techniques of criminal jurisprudence. The chapter features excerpts from the testimony of a key witness at Tadic's trial and shows how this testimony was subsequently filtered by courts and commentators, producing striking discrepancies and misleading summaries of the evidential basis of Tadic's convictions. The discussion prompts further reflection on the epistemic implications of legal procedures for evaluating witness testimony, the evidential quality of legally sufficient proof, and the structural relationship between trials and appeals, particularly in light of the fact that trial transcripts are rarely available to researchers and commentators on domestic criminal trials. Although international criminal procedure is still in its doctrinal adolescence relative to municipal legal traditions cultivated over many centuries, international criminal adjudication's primary institutional materials are in some ways a richer and more accessible resource for jurisprudential scholarship.

This chapter also incidentally illustrates the contingency of academic research and publishing, which is sometimes a protracted enterprise requiring tenacity and long-range strategic thinking. I originally began researching this essay in 2006, giving workshop presentations at UNSW in Sydney (hosted by my long-term collaborator Jill Hunter)[89] and later in Dublin (organised by John Jackson and Yassin Brunger, whom John and I had both taught as a postgraduate).[90] I then

[87] See, eg, Carsten Stahn, 'Between "Faith" and "Facts": By What Standards Should We Assess International Criminal Justice?' (2012) 25 *Leiden Journal of International Law* 251; Larry May, 'Habeas Corpus and the Normative Jurisprudence of International Law' (2010) 23 *Leiden Journal of International Law* 291 (contending at 310 that 'it is very hard to think about international law at all except on the municipal or domestic law model'); Immi Tallgren, 'The Sensibility and Sense of International Criminal Law' (2002) 13 *European Journal of International Law* 561.

[88] *Prosecutor* v *Tadic*, IT-94-1 ('Prijedor'), Trial Chamber Judgement 7 May 1997.

[89] 'Mr Seferovic's Pigeons: A Brief Encounter with International Criminal Evidence', paper to Colloquium on *Evidence, Criminal Justice, and Adjudication*, UNSW School of Law, Sydney, April 2007.

[90] 'Mr Seferovic's Pigeons – A Brief Encounter with International Criminal Evidence', paper for conference on *Integrating a Socio-Legal Approach to Evidence in International Criminal Trials*, UCD School of Law, Dublin, November 2011.

became diverted by other projects and lost touch with international criminal justice, which I gave up teaching (as Chapter 8 describes). Participation in Ralph Henham's *festschrift* volume presented the perfect opportunity to reconnect with this project, and a – revised and updated – version was finally published in 2024, getting on for 20 years after the first drafts of the paper were written.

The final *festschrift* essay reproduced in Chapter 10 is concerned with disciplinary boundaries, intersections and overlaps. The chapter introduces a heuristic device, which I call 'the Eternal Triangle of Intellectual Inquiry' (ET), to facilitate meta-theoretical reflection on the institutional character, significance, and techniques of actively 'disciplining' Criminology as an academic discipline. This methodological framework is elucidated and put to work in interrogating the relationship between (what I characterise as) 'Criminal Justice' and 'Criminology'. These two disciplinary domains were constructed to emphasise a primary methodological distinction between normative and descriptive claims. In thereby reprising Hume's classic objection to 'naturalistic fallacies',[91] it is hardly a novel thought. Yet this schema encapsulates a point worth repeating, to the extent that there is a tendency in, especially, criminological writing merely to *assert* normative propositions that a philosopher would insist have to be *earnt* through argument. So I proposed (somewhat reductively, I confess) that Criminology is anchored in the discipline-defining question 'What is crime?' and its social scientific derivatives investigating causal processes (What causes crime?), whereas Criminal Justice is characteristically a philosophical and policy enterprise framed by the explicitly normative question 'What shall we do about crime?'. Criminal jurisprudence is, self-consciously and unapologetically, normative as well as analytical in its methods and aspirations.

The version of the argument presented in Chapter 10[92] develops in dialectical conversation with self-styled 'critical criminology', a variant of what I call 'adjectival criminologies'. 'Thinking through critical criminology' is, I suggest, a productive and insightful intellectual exercise. There is plenty to criticise in our existing faltering and misfiring penal practices and defective administrative machinery of criminal justice. Nonetheless, claiming the mantle of 'critical' for one's theoretical orientation is always a rhetorical gambit, since no disciplinary tradition ever nominates itself 'intellectually uncritical, conventional and conformist'. Inasmuch as 'critical criminology' rejects fundamental liberal values, I am against it. The

[91] In his *Treatise on Human Nature* (1740), Hume famously exclaimed 'of a sudden I am surpriz'd to find, that instead of the usual copulations of propositions, *is*, and *is not*, I meet with no proposition that is not connected with an *ought*, or an *ought not*. This change is imperceptible; but is, however, of the last consequence. For as this *ought*, or *ought not*, expresses some new relation or affirmation 'tis necessary that it shou'd be observ'd and explain'd; and at the same time that a reason should be given, for what seems altogether inconceivable, how this new relation can be a deduction from others, which are entirely different from it'.

[92] My first attempt to expound the argument was published as Paul Roberts, 'On the Preconditions and Possibilities of Criminal Law Theory' (1998) 11 *South African Journal of Criminal Justice* 285. I spent the (South African) Winter Semester 1998 as Visiting Lecturer at (what was then called) the University of Natal (Pietermaritzburg), where I was magnificently hosted by Jonathan Burchell and his family, and enjoyed many stimulating conversations with Jonathan, Mike Cowling, Mike Kidd, P J Swchikkard, Warren Freedman, John Milton, Douglas Farland and Ian Jennings.

idea of reshaping humanity to conform to some sectarian ideological blueprint (or else …) strikes me as just another religion with its improbable utopias, false prophets and unacceptable moral compromises. Whether I am right or wrong in these substantive (first-order) political convictions, the issues could only be settled through normative – including jurisprudential – argument.

VI. Inconclusive Work in Progress

Academic books conventionally end with a concluding chapter summarising the preceding narrative and drawing together the threads of its central thesis. This book sets out to identify, illustrate and promote criminal jurisprudence as a distinctive approach to criminal law scholarship. Beyond this methodological premiss, it doesn't have an elaborated central thesis, and so it doesn't have, or need, a conventional conclusion. Instead, the final chapter contains reflections on the current state of scholarship in UK university law schools. It was originally written during the first Covid lockdown in 2020, a grim time which might excuse its depressing tone. Unfortunately, although some of my initial anger has dissipated, I remain downbeat about the immediate prospects for legal scholarship, and criminal jurisprudence in particular, in my geographical location. But depression should not be confused with defeat or capitulation. UK universities are currently beleaguered and demoralised. It is vital to retain a sense of perspective when living in turbulent times: markets, as they say, can go down as well as up, and better times for the sector may be anticipated.

There is no denying the apparent incongruity of concluding a book professing inspiration for future scholarship with a chapter that could be read as an epitaph. Let me say two things by way of pre-emptive amelioration. First, any realistic programme for scholarship must attend to its institutional environment and material conditions, or stand condemned as utopian fantasy. To have any chance of flourishing, criminal jurisprudence as scholarly enterprise must be aware of institutional constraints and limitations and develop intelligent coping strategies to deal with them. Second, having reached the magical superannuation age of 55, I could have just thrown in the towel and retired on my pension – the pension that is half as good as the generation of scholars preceding me, and twice as generous as the next generation following will, if they are lucky, receive. The fact that I have bothered to work up this volume, buttressed by my intention to remain productive in criminal jurisprudence, should provide tangible reassurance of my undiminished commitment to disciplinary advancement. I still retain skin in the game.

When Tony Benn resigned as an MP in 2001, he said that he was leaving Parliament after 51 years to spend more time in politics. In semi-retiring from my university teaching post in 2023, 30 years since I joined the department, I feel much the same way about freeing up more time for research-led teaching and scholarship. If this sentiment implicitly indicts the pitiable state of contemporary university employment, it also underlines my fortunate career timing. I have been inspired by the most talented and dedicated scholars and have had the opportunity to forge my own path in inspiring others. Having learnt a few things worth knowing along the way, it is incumbent on me to share this experience before it evaporates into the ether; and simultaneously to bear witness to some uncomfortable home truths.

This volume represents a summative reflection on the cumulative product of over three decades' research and writing. I believe I have more to say and hope I can still find time to say it. But now seems like an opportune moment to offer signposts and charts for others to follow, should the intellectual journey appear sufficiently enticing to motivate new adventures. Clearing out my father's house over the last few months, I came across a small photo frame containing a made-up Roberts family crest, the sort of thing you can find in seaside tat shops amongst the inflatable dolphins and plastic buckets and spades. It bears the cod-Latin motto 'Dum spiro spero': where there's life there's hope. It struck me that this can be read in either of two ways, as eternal optimism for the future or a daunting reminder of looming finitude. Both are apposite. Academic lives don't last forever; some are cut far too short. You had better be inspired to advance your most important projects whilst you still can. *Carpe diem, tempus fugit.*

2

Criminal Law Theory and the Limits of Liberalism

BioNote: This essay first appeared in a volume marking Andreas von Hirsch's 80th birthday.[1] That book was actually von Hirsch's second *festschrift*, a sequel to the publication 16 years earlier of a collection of essays 'celebrat[ing] the influence of Andrew von Hirsch on contemporary sentencing theory'.[2] Born in Zurich in 1934, von Hirsch spent the earlier part of his academic career at Rutgers in the US and Cambridge in the UK, where he was known as and published under his Anglicised name 'Andrew'. He reverted to 'Andreas' when he relocated to Frankfurt in 2014, a physical move which simultaneously shifted the centre of gravity of his research networks and publications to German-language scholarship.

This biographical fragment already hints at significant dimensions of AvH's character, interests and professional achievements. Family history and personal experience forged in the cataclysm of mid-twentieth-century Europe equipped him with a lifelong passion to oppose injustice and official moral corruption. His earlier scholarship addressing sentencing and punishment theory was enormously influential not only in academic circles but also in driving penal reform most tangibly in the US, the UK and Sweden.[3] AvH frequently wrote with coauthors, especially Andrew Ashworth.[4] Later work, much of it in collaboration with Andrew Simester,[5] engaged with theories of criminalisation and the moral limits of the criminal law; always with an eye to practical policy impact.[6] Most recently,

[1] A P Simester, Antje du Bois-Pedain and Ulfrid Neumann (eds), *Liberal Criminal Law Theory: Essays for Andreas von Hirsch* (Hart Publishing, 2014).

[2] Andrew Ashworth and Martin Wasik (eds), *Fundamentals of Sentencing Theory: Essays in Honour of Andrew von Hirsch* (OUP, 1998) 1.

[3] For discussion and context, see Antje du Bois-Pedain and Anthony E Bottoms (eds), *Penal Censure: Engagements Within and Beyond Desert Theory* (Hart Publishing, 2019); Michael Tonry (ed), *Retributivism Has a Past: Has it a Future?* (OUP, 2011); Marie Manikis, 'The Principle of Proportionality in Sentencing: A Dynamic Evolution and Multiplication of Conceptions' (2022) 59 *Osgoode Hall Law Journal* 587, 604–5 (noting AvH's direct influence on the evolution of Canadian sentencing policy).

[4] Andrew von Hirsch and Andrew Ashworth, *Proportionate Sentencing: Exploring the Principles* (OUP, 2005); Andrew von Hirsch, Andrew Ashworth and Julian Roberts (eds), *Principled Sentencing: Readings on Theory and Policy*, 3rd edn (Hart Publishing, 2009). Also see ch 6.

[5] Notably A P Simester and Andreas von Hirsch, *Crimes, Harms and Wrongs: On the Principles of Criminalisation* (Hart Publishing, 2011).

[6] Andrew von Hirsch, Anthony E Bottoms, Elizabeth Burney and P-O Wikström, *Criminal Deterrence and Sentencing Severity: An Analysis of Recent Research* (Hart Publishing, 1999); Andrew von Hirsch, Andrew Ashworth, Martin Wasik, A T H Smith, Rod Morgan and John Gardner, 'Overtaking on the Right' (1995) 145 *New Law Journal* 1501.

AvH extended his comparative law interests into German penal theory[7] and even international criminal justice.[8] The rare distinction of inspiring multiple *festschriften* is reserved for scholars who build inclusive networks of collaborators and students and who combine the production of exemplary scholarship with intellectual openness in discussion and generosity in mentorship.

AvH visited Cambridge whilst I was an MPhil student at the Institute of Criminology in 1991, and I attended one of his trademark lectures on designing sentencing frameworks to implement just deserts principles. His general approach made sense to me,[9] and when a collection of his essays was strung together and published as a book[10] a few years later, I reviewed it favourably.[11] Some weeks after the review appeared in print, to my complete astonishment, AvH was on the 'phone saying that he had read my review and wanted to come up to Nottingham from Cambridge to discuss penal theory with me. Also, if there was any interest, he could give a lecture or seminar. Interest there emphatically was, and he did double-duty both delivering a lecture to my undergraduate Criminal Justice and the Penal System class (a pitch-perfect rendition, without notes, of his just deserts sentencing set-piece) and leading one of the inaugural year's Criminal Justice Discussion Group meetings,[12] with Sir John Smith in attendance.

Thereafter, I became one of AvH's Cambridge circle, participating in a dozen or more research projects and meetings[13] hosted by his Centre for Penal Theory and Penal Ethics on diverse topics traversing the philosophy of punishment and – as I would characterise it – criminal jurisprudence. Besides introducing me to the aristocracy of Anglophone criminal justice theorists – John Braithwaite, Kathy Daly, Antony Duff, David Garland, Barbara Hudson, Doug Husak, John Kleinig, Sandra Marshall, Julian Roberts, Paul Rock, Clifford Shearing,

[7] See Forschungsstelle für Strafrechtstheorie und Strafrechtsethik, Goethe Universität, Frankfurt am Main, www.jura.uni-frankfurt.de/42877287/Forschungsstelle_f%C3%BCr_Strafrechtstheorie_und_Strafrechtsethik (identifying principal collaborators as Ulfrid Neumann, Kurt Seelmann, Tatjana Hörnle, Frank Höpfel und Wolfgang Wohlers).

[8] Conference on *Philosophical Foundations of International Criminal Law*, Forschungsstelle für Strafrechtstheorie und Strafrechtsethik, Frankfurt, 24–25 March 2017; Andreas von Hirsch and Vivian C Schorscher, 'A System of International Criminal Justice for Human Rights Violations: What is the General Justification for its Existence?' in Lucia Zedner and Julian V Roberts (eds), *Principles and Values in Criminal Law and Criminal Justice: Essays in Honour of Andrew Ashworth* (OUP, 2012).

[9] As an MPhil student I was particularly impressed by von Hirsch's *Past or Future Crimes: Deservedness and Dangerousness in the Sentencing of Criminals* (Rutgers, 1986), which I studied in detail, probably in preparation for Nigel Walker's seminars on theories of punishment (having initially been introduced to these topics at Oxford by Niki Lacey and Andrew Rutherford).

[10] Andrew von Hirsch, *Censure and Sanctions* (OUP, 1993).

[11] [1994] *Criminal Law Review* 867–877.

[12] It was my initiative to set up the School of Law's CJDG in 1994. The CJDG was later subsumed into the activities of the Criminal Justice Research Centre and is still going strong. AvH presented an advanced version of the paper subsequently published as Andrew von Hirsch, 'Extending the Harm Principle: "Remote" Harms and Fair Imputation' in A P Simester and A T H Smith (eds), *Harm and Culpability* (OUP, 1996).

[13] Commencing with the project producing the inaugural volume in the *Studies in Penal Theory and Penal Ethics* series, Andrew von Hirsch, David Garland and Alison Wakefield (eds), *Ethical and Social Perspectives on Situational Criminal Prevention* (Hart Publishing, 2000).

Tony (ATH) Smith and Mike Tonry, amongst others – involvement in this Brains-Trust-cum-dining-club encouraged me to grapple with a range of topics and issues and to consume associated literatures with a dedication which I would not otherwise have devoted to them. Not infrequently when informed of the next research theme to be explored and dissected, I would think to myself, 'Well, I don't have much to say about that.' Invariably, when I learnt what other people had written and thought about the matter, it turned out that I had plenty to say after all – possibly too much![14] These were intensely educational and energising experiences, replicated only in supervising my best PhD students. My association with the Cambridge Centre, chiefly through AvH ably supported by Andrew Simester, Tony Bottoms and Antje du Bois-Pedain, has been amongst the most formative and productive of my academic career. And all originally attributable to a humble two-page book review. Proof positive, if any were needed, that there is more potential in academic writing than could ever be distilled into REF-friendly longform publications.

I. Questioning the Liberal Consensus in Contemporary Criminal Law Theory

Andreas von Hirsch is a pre-eminent exponent of liberal criminal law theory. His extensive and influential writings on sentencing, penal theory and criminalisation have been instrumental in establishing a distinctively liberal conception of deontological political morality as the broadly received orthodoxy amongst contemporary Anglophone criminal law theorists. Whereas for the theoretical pioneers of the 1960s and 1970s (prominently including the two transatlantic Herberts, Hart[15] and Packer[16]) some form of Bentham-inspired utilitarianism seemed like the natural default position for those in search of a justificatory theory of criminal law, variations on 'neo-Kantian' deontology rule the contemporary theoretical roost and avowed consequentialists have become an endangered species. Von Hirsch led the original charge against consequentialism in penal theory and sentencing practice from the mid-1970s onwards,[17] and in later collaborative work elucidated an increasingly nuanced and persuasive account of liberal criminal law.

This essay aims to provoke further critical reflection and debate concerning the specifically 'liberal' credentials of contemporary Anglo-American criminal law

[14] *Cf* Paul Roberts, 'Penal Offence in Question' in Andrew von Hirsch and A P Simester (eds), *Incivilities: Regulating Offensive Behaviour* (Hart Publishing, 2006).

[15] H L A Hart, *Punishment and Responsibility: Essays in the Philosophy of Law* (Clarendon Press, 1968); H L A Hart, *Law, Liberty and Morality* (OUP, 1962).

[16] H L Packer, *The Limits of the Criminal Sanction* (Stanford University Press, 1969).

[17] A von Hirsch, *Doing Justice* (Hill & Wang, 1976); A von Hirsch, 'Punishment Futures: The Desert-model Debate and the Importance of the Criminal Law Context' in Michael Tonry (ed), *Retributivism Has a Past: Has it a Future?* (OUP, 2011).

theory. Much contemporary theorising about criminal law is conducted against a backdrop of liberal ideals, values and assumptions which are seldom fully articulated, much less systematically explored. Liberal philosophical commitments often seem to operate, more or less unconsciously, as unexamined normative presuppositions. This is not necessarily problematic: there is nothing wrong in principle with a sensible division of theoretical labour between political philosophers and criminal law theorists. It should also be said that some contemporary theorists of the criminal law go out of their way to disown any association with liberalism, in either its theoretical or normative registers.[18] In my experience, however, those concerned to distance themselves from liberalism rarely work with sympathetic or well-articulated conceptions of liberal political morality. So even if we temporarily 'bracket' (ie, beg) questions about the substantive merits of liberalism as normative political philosophy, threshold (ontological or conceptual) issues of terminology and classification still remain unaddressed. Just what is it that makes a justificatory or normative theory of criminal law (as opposed, roughly speaking, to 'scientific' empirical description of positive law and existing institutions) distinctively *liberal*? Skating over debates *within* liberal theorising, this essay adopts an holistic, meta-disciplinary perspective. Given that there appears to be something like a loose liberal coalition uniting (most) contemporary criminal law theorists, what is the nature and character of that 'liberalism', and what role does it play in the best normative accounts of the criminal law?

The inquiry will be greatly facilitated if we can first clarify the nature of our questions and thereby cultivate a more refined notion of what should realistically be expected by way of answers. The enterprise of relating 'Criminal Law Theory' to 'liberalism' naturally begins with the meaning ascribed to these two key concepts, and I had therefore better be clear about my own field-defining conceptual presuppositions.[19] Conscious of the perils of trying to win any normative argument by definitional stipulation (ie, by cheating), and also of the inherently controversial nature of the exercise, I will adopt a paradigmatic or ideal-type approach. So far as Criminal Law Theory is concerned, I will simply point to that body of English language, predominantly Anglo-American scholarship on the theoretical and philosophical foundations of criminal law which has flourished over the last 30 years or so,[20] and to which Andreas von Hirsch has

[18] See, eg, Alan Norrie, *Crime, Reason and History: A Critical Introduction to Criminal Law*, 2nd edn (Butterworths, 2001) 31 ('we should put aside the continuing legal-liberal dream that [criminal law] is potentially rational'), 233 ('the practical necessity and the intellectual impossibility of the orthodox, liberal, positivist tradition in criminal law scholarship').

[19] For an entertaining (inadvertent) object lesson in the perils of definitional incontinence, see Jonah Goldberg, *Liberal Fascism* (Penguin, 2009). And *cf* Stanley Fish, 'Liberalism Doesn't Exist' [1987] *Duke Law Journal* 997.

[20] See, eg, R A Duff and Stuart P Green (eds), *Philosophical Foundations of Criminal Law* (OUP, 2011); Douglas Husak, *The Philosophy of Criminal Law* (OUP, 2010); Douglas Husak, *Overcriminalization: The Limits of the Criminal Law* (OUP, 2008); John Gardner, *Offences and Defences* (OUP, 2007); R A Duff, *Answering for Crime: Responsibility and Liability in the Criminal Law* (Hart Publishing, 2007); R A Duff, Lindsay Farmer, Sandra Marshall and Victor Tadros, *The Trial on Trial Vol 3: Towards a*

been a pioneering contributor. Elucidating a serviceable ideal-typical conception of liberalism as a distinctive political morality presents a more formidable challenge, which is taken up in section II of this essay. The aim will be to sketch, in miniature, an idealised model of liberal political theory which is tangible, comprehensible, recognisably attractive to liberals, adequately differentiated from theoretical rivals, and amenable to direct translation into institutionalised criminal law policies, principles, laws and practices.

Having mapped out the scope and nature of the inquiry and fixed basic concepts, the institutional or 'jurisprudential'[21] analysis developed in the remainder of the essay has two parts, the first predominantly expository and the second more theoretically substantive. Section III fleshes out a liberal conception of criminal law. The only purpose of this exceedingly broadbrush sketch is to show that a great deal of what is familiar in modern Anglo-American criminal law is plausibly explicable, and potentially also justifiable, in terms of the version of liberal political morality presented in section II. Theorists have already made significant progress in employing the tools of analytical philosophy to reconsider contemporary criminal law doctrine and trace its normative foundations into (aspects of) liberal political morality. Section IV will suggest, however, that a liberal conception of criminal law inevitably encounters two methodological stumbling blocks, which seem to curtail liberalism's capacity for theorising criminal law. I will call these twin obstacles to liberal theorising the problem of incompleteness and the problem of under-determination. Taken together, they suggest that comprehensive normative justifications of penal law must draw on theoretical and normative resources that could only be found (if they can be found at all) by venturing beyond the confines of liberal political philosophy.

What follows from a new appreciation, or more acute perception, of liberalism's limitations as a source of normative theorising about criminal law? Liberals might be disappointed by the deflationary implications for liberal theorising. It is important to stress, however, that liberalism's theoretical limitations do not imply that a comprehensive normative rationalisation of criminal law must therefore be in tension with, much less dissent from or contradict, liberal political morality. A normative theory of criminal law incorporating non-liberal (as opposed to illiberal) theoretical resources should still be counted an authentically *liberal* theory, from a normative point of view, if it fully coheres with liberal political

Normative Theory of the Criminal Trial (Hart Publishing, 2007); Victor Tadros, *Criminal Responsibility* (OUP, 2005); Stephen Shute and A P Simester (eds), *Criminal Law Theory: Doctrines of the General Part* (OUP, 2002); R A Duff, *Punishment, Communication and Community* (OUP, 2001); Andrew Ashworth and Martin Wasik (eds), *Fundamentals of Sentencing Theory* (OUP, 1998); George P Fletcher (ed), *New Voices in Criminal Theory* (1998) 1 *Buffalo Criminal Law Review* Special Issue; Michael Moore, *Placing Blame: A Theory of Criminal Law* (OUP, 1997); A P Simester and A T H Smith, *Harm and Culpability* (OUP, 1996); Michael Moore, *Act and Crime* (OUP, 1993); Stephen Shute, John Gardner and Jeremy Horder (eds), *Action and Value in Criminal Law* (OUP, 1993); R A Duff, *Intention, Agency and Criminal Liability* (Blackwell, 1990).

[21] By which I mean the discipline, process and methods of institutionalising political morality in concrete juridical formations, fusing, in practical reality, theory in law and law in theory.

morality. Nor do its theoretical limitations imply that liberalism lacks tangible critical purchase on contemporary criminal justice policy and practice, as this essay will show. Non-liberals, meanwhile, should properly regard liberalism's limitations in theorising criminal law as a strength rather than a weakness of normative theorising in general. If, as I suggest, much of what liberals typically find attractive in modern criminal law doctrine and theory is (merely) consistent with, rather than being derived from, liberal political morality, the path is cleared for forging theoretical alliances with non-liberals and building a broader, more inclusive and stable 'overlapping theoretical consensus' around criminal law's foundational normative requirements. I will venture, in this essay's concluding paragraphs, some brief ruminations on the implications of consensus-building in criminal law theory for sponsoring global penal justice in an era of international human rights law and cosmopolitan criminal jurisprudence.

II. Liberal Political Morality, in Miniature

Serious reflection on the notion of 'liberal criminal law' immediately encounters major conceptual and terminological difficulties. This essay has already implicitly counter-posed 'liberal' to 'utilitarian' criminal law. Yet Bentham, and even more so Mill, must surely count as 'liberals' on any historically respectable definition of liberalism. The movement in the history of philosophical ideas from Bentham to Kant, or in modern punishment theory from Hart to von Hirsch, is not well characterised as a shift *to* liberalism but rather as a realignment within it: from a utilitarian liberalism to contemporary deontological liberalisms. This does not show that the liberal foundations of modern criminal law are uninteresting or unproblematic, but it does underscore the methodological caveat that philosophical concepts and terminology derived from broader currents in the history of ideas may map onto exotic small islands in the stream, like criminal law theory, only imperfectly or obscurely, if at all.

Liberalism may be broad church, but there *is* a core liberal creed (to borrow Mill's revealing synecdoche) with articles of faith to which true believers must, and generally do, subscribe. Utilitarians like Bentham and Mill are inside the liberal big tent alongside Hobbes, Kant, Locke, Adam Smith, Rawls, Habermas, Rorty, Hart, Dworkin and their living secular co-religionists; just as assuredly Plato, Aristotle, Marcus Aurelius, Aquinas, Rousseau, Marx, Nietzsche, Heidegger, Roger Scruton, John Gray, and Alasdair MacIntyre – to say nothing of the likes of Carl Schmidt, Mao Tse Tung, or the Ayatollah Khommeini – represent those who would not be granted (and would never have requested) full admission. Lively debates about the liberal credentials of modern philosophers such as Charles Taylor, Michael Sandel and Joseph Raz indicate that the boundaries of liberalism may be blurry and productive of genuinely borderline cases. At least some contemporary theorists have thought it worthwhile to dispute the criteria for qualifying as a bona fide member of the liberal philosophical club. Such critical (self-) examinations hint at more than merely theoretical motivations for classifying philosophical theories as 'liberal' or otherwise – a possibility revisited in this essay's conclusion.

A *liberal* theory at its heart would have to be concerned with prioritising individuals' *liberty*.[22] Analytically, this means treating the individual as the primary unit of ethical concern. Liberalism is thereby immediately positioned as a secular philosophy. Political morality, on this view, is centrally concerned with the wellbeing and welfare of human beings rather than being orientated towards celebrating the glory of god(s), perfecting His Kingdom on Earth, or something of that order. This does not necessarily imply that liberal political morality is incompatible with or even mildly inhospitable towards religious conviction – of particular faiths or denominations, or in general – but it does mean that the problem of reconciling religious conviction with liberal political morality, assuming that such reconciliation may be possible and desirable (for particular religions, or at large), is already defined on this view as a problem for theology, not one for political philosophy. Religion is not a source of *theoretical* controversy for liberal theory, because liberalism is committed to rejecting all dogmatic arguments from religious faith or authority insofar as they purport to regulate the ordering of political relations in the public sphere. In this way, liberalism's thin militant secularism holds the ring for religious tolerance and pluralism. Freedom of religion, including the freedom to dissent or defect, is an important sphere of liberty with enormous historical resonances for liberals and – of course – undiminished contemporary significance for theists.[23] Those religions which conceive religious freedom primarily in terms of collective public worship, private conscience and everyday personal morality should not find liberal polities uncongenial or excessively burdensome, either spiritually or in practical life. Those religions which mandate theocracy, the uncompromising pursuit of one true path to enlightenment in all things, or preferential treatment in the public realm for believers over infidels and sinners, are, by contrast, set on a collision course with liberal political authority.

Liberal theory conceptualises individuals as the primary unit of ethical concern in the sense of Kant's fundamental injunction to treat every human being as an end in themselves and not merely as a means to somebody else's ends – a thing of merely instrumental value that can legitimately be bent to another's will, used, abused and discarded like denatured chewing gum or an old worn-out pair of boots. Rawls' famous critique of utilitarianism as 'no respecter of persons' is drawn from the same liberal wellspring.[24] Dworkin's more juridified rendering, in terms

[22] Isaiah Berlin, *Liberty*, Henry Hardy ed (OUP, 2002). And *per differentiam*, see Hannah Arendt, *The Origins of Totalitarianism* (Harcourt, 1976); Vasily Grossman, *Life and Fate* (Vintage, 2006); Jung Chang and Jon Halliday, *Mao: The Unknown Story* (Vintage, 2007).

[23] Michael J Perry, *The Political Morality of Liberal Democracy* (Cambridge University Press, 2010).

[24] John Rawls, *A Theory of Justice* (Oxford University Press, 1973) 29, 187 ('classical utilitarianism fails to take seriously the distinction between persons'). The 'no respecter' idiom is owed to H L A Hart, 'Natural Rights: Bentham and John Stuart Mill' in his *Essays on Bentham* (Oxford University Press, 1982) 99.

of every person's fundamental right to 'equal concern and respect',[25] articulates the equality norm underpinning modern liberal legal systems and which is invoked directly in non-discrimination suits. Individuals are seen as separate in having their own personal interests (eg, in continued survival, physical security, mental repose and stimulation, valuable opportunities, meaningful choices, etc), which could be advanced or harmed; *and* each individual's interests must be given equal consideration with everybody else's in public policy-making, legislation and law enforcement. The right is to equal *consideration*, not to formal equality of treatment or outcome – neither of which may be practically achievable given the diversity of individual needs, interests and desires, the tendency for interests to conflict in zero-sum configurations, finite resources and the brute unpredictability of happenstance. There are typically losers as well as winners in many, if not most, public policy choices, but at least everybody's interests are fairly (and in that sense *equally*) factored into the policy-making equation, irrespective of birth, colour, creed, class, gender, sexual orientation or other irrelevant personal characteristics.[26] That is the liberal polity's mutually constitutive promise to its citizens.

We should frankly concede that this line of argument has already narrowed the field of eligible theories to deontological variants of liberalism. So be it. In this instance, modest sacrifices of historical fidelity and theoretical inclusiveness are fair trade for the significant analytical and normative gains obtained by stiffening liberal theory's admissions criteria with some deontological fibre. For present purposes, we can safely set aside predominantly exegetical questions such as whether it is possible to reconcile Mill's liberal instincts with his official subscription to utilitarian dogma,[27] or how far Hart can square his avowedly utilitarian justification for punishment with his liberal preferences regarding the scope and detailed specification of substantive criminal laws.[28] Whether or not one is (also) persuaded by Bernard Williams' integrity-based objections to an unremittingly impartial utilitarian morality that denies any deep ethical significance to agent-relative reasons,[29] we should say, with Rawls,[30] that the utilitarian's professed egalitarianism is a sham equality in which all persons 'count' the same only because everybody ultimately counts for nothing under the tyranny of standard-issue

[25] Ronald Dworkin, *Justice for Hedgehogs* (Harvard University Press, 2011) Part 5; Ronald Dworkin, *Sovereign Virtue: The Theory and Practice of Equality* (Harvard University Press, 2002); Ronald Dworkin, A Matter of Principle (OUP, 1985) ch 9; Ronald Dworkin, *Taking Rights Seriously*, revsd edn (Duckworth, 1978).

[26] Birth, colour, creed etc are not *always* irrelevant characteristics for liberal public policy-makers, legislators or officials. I am speaking in broad terms.

[27] C L Ten (ed), *Mill's On Liberty: A Critical Guide* (CUP, 2010); Roger Crisp, *Mill on Utilitarianism* (Routledge, 1997); C L Ten, *Mill On Liberty* (OUP, 1980).

[28] *Cf* John Gardner, 'Introduction' to H L A Hart, *Punishment and Responsibility*, 2nd edn (OUP, 2008) xxviii–xxxi; Nicola Lacey, *State Punishment* (Routledge, 1986) 47–49, 187.

[29] Bernard Williams, 'A Critique of Utilitarianism' in J J C Smart and Bernard Williams (eds), *Utilitarianism: For and Against* (CUP, 1973); Bernard Williams, *Moral Luck* (CUP, 1981).

[30] John Rawls, *A Theory of Justice* (OUP, 1973) § 30.

monist consequentialisms. People are not merely experience machines whose value is exhausted by their utility as biological loci for welfare maximisation. Embodied individual *wellbeing*, rather than aggregated abstract welfare, should be government's ultimate ethical concern; reflecting liberal deontology's insistence that human beings are intrinsically valuable, Kantian ends-in-themselves. Or if this conception of liberal theory is too rich for some tastes, we should at least say, borrowing Dworkin's methodological apparatus,[31] that the utilitarian conception of individual wellbeing is so far removed from our current institutional practices and the ideals and values which we take to vindicate them that it does not qualify, even at the threshold pre-interpretative level, as a plausible account of criminal law in modern liberal polities. Nor have the utilitarians yet provided us with good reason to think that our public institutions for proscribing criminal wrongs and censuring and punishing criminal wrongdoers should be systematically rethought and reformed[32] along utilitarian lines.

The primacy of individuals, and by extension of their interests, in liberal theory has generated many widespread misconceptions about liberalism, by no means only amongst theorists. Political theory since the 1980s has been the battleground for an increasingly stylised series of theoretical hostilities between 'liberals' and a loose collection of generally left-leaning 'communitarian' critics.[33] These debates were illuminating in their heyday, but much of their intensity long seems to have dissipated. Several notable theorist-combatants have switched sides or claimed to have been closet liberals all along.[34] One canard associated with the first rash of communitarian critiques was that liberal theory is committed to an abstract, acontextual, dissociated, 'atomistic' conception of the self which is both completely unrealistic and ethically debased, in being estranged from its social environment

[31] Ronald Dworkin, *Justice for Hedgehogs* (Harvard University Press, 2011) Part 2; Ronald Dworkin, *Law's Empire* (Fontana, 1986) ch 2.

[32] Utilitarians are not necessarily committed to endorsing utility maximisation as the direct goal of individual action or official policy-making. Various models of 'two-level' thinking might be invoked to try to explain why acting for ostensibly non-utilitarian reasons at the first-order level of human decision-making can be squared with a second-order theoretical utilitarian justification. (Less frequently, utilitarians argue the converse, that conventional moral practice should be brought into conformity with utilitarian theoretical reason.) Despite their ingenuity, utilitarians of this persuasion always seem to me to end up relying on inherently undisprovable empirical predictions (an argumentative gambit I call the 'empirical dodge') or disappearing up their own axiology. This is all a very long way from what Bentham promised the world when urging us to substitute his supposedly empirically-vindicated utilitarian science of morals for all that metaphysical hocus pocus of philosophical tradition.

[33] Will Kymlicka, *Contemporary Political Philosophy: An Introduction*, 2nd edn (OUP, 2002); Stephen Mulhall and Adam Swift, *Liberals and Communitarians*, 2nd edn (Blackwell, 1996).

[34] Michael Sandel, for example, notes that '[t]he "liberal-communitarian" debate that has raged among political philosophers in recent years describes a range of issues', and confesses that 'I do not always find myself on the communitarian side': Michael J Sandel, *Liberalism and the Limits of Justice*, 2nd edn (CUP, 1998) ix. Also see Amitai Etzioni, 'A Liberal Communitarian Paradigm for Counterterrorism' (2013) 49 *Stanford Journal of International Law* 330; Richard Rorty, *Objectivity, Relativism and Truth: Philosophical Papers vol 1* (CUP, 1991); Charles Taylor, 'Cross Purposes: The Liberal-Communitarian Debate' in Nancy L Rosenblum (ed), *Liberalism and the Moral Life* (Harvard University Press, 1989); Philip Selznick, 'The Idea of A Communitarian Morality' (1987) 75 *California Law Review* 445.

and the fabric of interpersonal relations woven into and enriching real lives.[35] The primary target of these objections was Rawls' Original Position thought-experiment, in which disembodied pre-social 'selves' choose the basic constitution of society and its distribution of resources from behind a 'veil of ignorance'[36] – a supercharged, political theorists' reinterpretation of the prosaic wisdom that fair shares are best guaranteed if I cut the Mars Bar and you choose which 'half' you want. Yet the 'atomism' objection to liberal theory is baseless. In fact, liberalism as such does not need an articulated theory of the self, beyond the baseline proposition that there *are* individual selves and that these biologically embodied entities are of primary ethical concern. Liberals, that is to say, are entitled to adopt the best conception of individuated selves that can be reconstructed from critical introspection combined with cognitive science, social psychology, cultural anthropology, philosophy of mind or any cognate interdisciplinary inquiries – all of which, incidentally, are likely to be more instructive on the topic of 'selves' than conventional political theory. On any plausible conception, the liberal self would have to be embodied, socially situated, and framed within a network of projects and interpersonal relationships which in turn make liberty or 'personal autonomy' valuable; where that value is understood not in disembodied abstraction or as a goal of consequentialist maximising, but in terms of the constitutive role which liberty and personal autonomy play in enabling individual human beings to lead valuable and successful lives.[37]

Selfishness is another charge typically levelled at individualist philosophies, including liberalism. However, this familiar criticism confuses metaethical individualism with egotism. Liberals insist that individuals must be at liberty to prefer their own interests, preferences and projects over other people's competing interests, preferences and projects *sometimes* and *up to a point*. This is not just a question of preserving the freedom to be altruistic or, more generally, to *choose* to do good willingly and wholeheartedly rather than being forced into virtue.[38] The objection is far more basic and comprehensive. One's life would not be authentically one's own if one were under a pervasive general duty to assist the needy or to sacrifice one's projects to the general good. That kind of political morality would reduce us all to permanent public servitude. Liberal self-preference, then, is not a doctrine of egotistical greed or vain self-regard. It is a logical implication and necessary political precondition of personal freedom to follow your own path in life, to make your own choices about what to do and to strive within the limits of natural endowment and social opportunity to become the person you want to

[35] Charles Taylor, 'Atomism' reprinted in *Philosophy and the Human Sciences: Philosophical Papers 2* (CUP, 1985). *Cf* Douglas J Den Uyl and Douglas B Rasmussen, 'The Myth of Atomism' (2006) 59 *Review of Metaphysics* 841.

[36] John Rawls, *A Theory of Justice* (OUP, 1973) § 24.

[37] See further, Joseph Raz, *Value, Respect, and Attachment* (CUP, 2001).

[38] Assuming, *contra* Kant, that 'forced virtue' is not a conceptual oxymoron. There is no obvious abuse of language in saying that '*X* was forced to do the right thing', and sometimes it is enough that a person acted in accordance with the dictates of public morality, irrespective of her subjective motivation.

be with the life you want to have, to form, revise and pursue your own personal conception of the good,[39] as an autonomous (but necessarily, inescapably socially-situated) self-author of your own life and fate.

A related objection to liberal political morality is that it fails fully to acknowledge the demands of social or distributive justice. Unlike the first two theoretical objections we have canvassed, which turn out on closer inspection to melt away into indistinct shadows, social justice remains a genuine bone of contention between liberals and their communitarian, socialist or communist critics. Moreover, liberalism's historical association with laissez faire free market economics and Lockean theories of property makes it fair game for these offensives. Without purporting to resolve deep and enduring controversies in political theory, we should at least be clear that liberalism implies personal autonomy not merely in Kant's sense of having the intellectual faculties of the intelligent moral agent, but also in the practical sense emphasised by Raz[40] of having adequate social opportunities and material resources to make 'living your own life according to your own lights' a – normatively speaking – meaningful option. So long as what you want falls within the liberally acceptable parameters of pluralism and tolerance and is compatible with like freedom for all (the equality constraint previously noted), the liberal polity should prima facie respect your choices and even try to provide you with material assistance and the wherewithal to succeed in your ambitions. How far one person's efforts should be taxed in order to provide social welfare assistance to those more in need (whether as a result of their own choices or otherwise) is, needless to say, a pressing question for modern governments – and an ideological bellwether of the sort that used to differentiate mainstream political parties. For present purposes we need only note that questions of social justice are vigorously contested *within* liberalism, as well as between liberals and their critics. Rawls famously argued for a level of asset redistribution through tax-and-spend economic policies that many other liberals find implausible as a matter of *justice* rather than charity.[41] The idea of a 'social minimum' floor of welfare provision is more congenial to other liberal theorists.[42] All agree, however, that the 'liberty' to die on the street through starvation or in childbirth for want of basic medical provision, or to work ten-hour shifts down a coalmine until your lungs disintegrate and you drown in emphysema, is not what modern political liberalism stands for. Choosing the life you want for yourself implies both meaningful options *and* reasonably comfortable conditions of life and adequate material resources to have a fair chance of actually realising one's aspirations. Many governments, for reasons of internal

[39] Paraphrasing John Rawls, 'Kantian Constructivism in Moral Theory' (1980) 77 *Journal of Philosophy* 517, 525. Also see Ronald Dworkin, 'Liberalism' in his *A Matter of Principle* (OUP, 1985).

[40] Joseph Raz, *The Morality of Freedom* (OUP, 1986) Part V.

[41] John Rawls, *A Theory of Justice* (OUP, 1973) §§ 11–17 (outlining the Difference Principle).

[42] Jeremy Waldron, 'John Rawls and the Social Minimum' (1986) 3 *Journal of Applied Philosophy* 21. Further down the track, those at the libertarian end of liberalism argue for minimalist conceptions of the social minimum, eg, Robert Nozick, *Anarchy, State and Utopia* (Blackwell, 1974).

incapacity or external pressures, are apparently simply incapable of creating or sustaining the social conditions in which their citizens could lead truly autonomous lives. But where governments *can* bring about the conditions in which personal autonomy flourishes, and where this might be achieved in fair equality, governments should generally[43] strive to do so because, say liberals, (social) justice demands it.

This broad-brush sketch of liberal political morality would be seriously incomplete without mention of one additional characteristic. The ease with which the phrase 'liberal democracy' trips off the tongue is an important clue to the intimate association between the liberal's promotion of individual freedom and a distinctively democratic model of political association. True, liberty-lovers are not necessarily democrats. It is certainly possible to conceive, in theory, a liberal constitutional monarchy or benign dictatorship of liberally minded oligarchs in which equal liberty for all and the conditions of flourishing personal autonomy were maximally promoted and safeguarded, to the extent that prevailing social conditions might permit. Notwithstanding this theoretical possibility, modern liberals (and liberal institutions[44]) endorse democratic participation and accountability as another foundational article of faith. In a democracy, 'the people' make laws for themselves. In so doing, the *demos* ingeniously combines Hobbes' solution to the riddle of legitimate political authority (liberty, in a practical sense, is actually *increased* by coercive laws that guarantee security and make 'ordinary life' possible) with the salvageable elements of Rousseau's romantic dream of spontaneous collective self-government.

This is not the place to fret about the discontents of modern representative democracies and their evident institutional weaknesses and failings (worrying though they undoubtedly are).[45] More interesting for present purposes is the official accountability strand of liberal democracy. Liberals are weaned on the wisdom that the price of liberty is eternal vigilance. Public power in all its forms must be subject to the rule of law – because (paraphrasing Locke) where law ends, there tyranny begins. The British version of liberal constitutionalism makes an exception for the legislature: the Queen or King in the Mother of Parliaments wields unlimited legislative power, or so the constitutional fable goes. Other versions of liberal democracy do not concede even that, extending constitutional judicial

[43] In truly exigent circumstances, collective self-defence and public protection may sometimes legitimately take priority over the liberty of each individual rights-bearer (heeding Justice Robert Jackson's warning that if the logic of liberty is not tempered with 'a little practical wisdom, it will convert the constitutional Bill of Rights into a suicide pact': *Terminiello v City of Chicago*, 337 US 1, 37; 69 S Ct 894, 911 (1949)).

[44] The European Court of Human Rights, for example, has improvised its own basic constitutional theory according to which, '[h]uman rights form an integrated system for the protection of human dignity; in that connection, democracy and the rule of law have a key role to play. Democracy requires that the people should be given a role. … [T]he rule of law cannot be sustained over a long period if persons governed by the same laws do not have the last word on the subject of their content and implementation.' *Refah Partisi (Welfare Party) v Turkey* (2002) 35 EHRR 3, [43].

[45] A C Grayling, *Democracy and Its Crisis* (Oneworld Publications, 2017).

review to primary legislation.[46] The rule of law ideal implies a raft of further derivative principles of democratic accountability, including equality before the law for officials and private persons, unhindered access to law, natural justice in fair process, and even state assistance in making legal claims and, especially, in defending oneself against accusations of criminal wrongdoing. Individual liberty is protected by (positive) legal rights and (negative) legal proscriptions of others' potentially liberty-infringing conduct. Officials are supposed to respect and uphold these rights, but if they falter – possibly through corruption or incompetence – the citizen has direct access to the courts to force compliance and seek redress, sometimes from derelict officials as well as or instead of from primary wrongdoers. The virtuous circle of liberal self-government is thereby completed. The liberal citizen who takes her case to court is enforcing the laws that *qua* member of the *demos* she issued to herself, in service of the collective interest in preserving liberty and promoting autonomous lives, an interest in which she has her own, very personal and indivisible stake in leading a self-authored life in accordance with her own authentic preferences, projects, values and commitments.

III. Liberal Criminal Law Theory for Liberals

We have seen that liberalism is a secular political morality which, in its currently dominant deontological strains, takes individual human beings as the primary units of ethical concern and is fundamentally orientated towards safeguarding individuals' liberty and promoting their personal autonomy. This it does without denying the socially situated nature of the self, or neglecting (what it takes to be) the appropriate demands of distributive justice. As a public philosophy of government, liberalism is committed to equal liberty, non-discrimination, freedom of thought and conscience, toleration, pluralism, democratic accountability and the rule of law. The question now becomes: what, if anything, follows from this conception of liberal political morality for criminal law and criminal law theorising?

One is tempted to say a great many things potentially follow. A reasonably comprehensive understanding of liberal political morality's implications for criminal law would doubtless require exhaustive particularistic analyses extending, both in length and profundity, far beyond the scope of this essay. For example, there is likely to be a fairly direct connection between the liberal's scheme of fundamental values and the types of wrongs thought appropriate for ex ante restraint and ex post public condemnation by a liberal polity's criminal law. Being

[46] For a review of different theories and approaches, see Rivka Weill, 'The New Commonwealth Model of Constitutionalism Notwithstanding: On Judicial Review and Constitution-Making' (2014) 62 *American Journal of Comparative Law* 127. For theoretical critique of 'strong' judicial review, see Jeremy Waldron, 'The Core of the Case Against Judicial Review' (2006) 115 *Yale Law Journal* 1346.

founded on equal liberty, liberal criminal law should be expected to target wrongs which typically erode or destroy liberty (eg, homicide,[47] slavery, kidnapping, debilitating bodily injury, theft or criminal damage of major assets) or which tend to undermine personal security, freedom of movement, or an ontologically secure sense of self (eg, rape, burglary, threats and intimidation, stalking, unreasonable risk-taking), as well as wrongs that strike at the fundamental equality norm (eg, racially-motivated violence, misogynistic harassment or unfair discrimination). Conversely, the liberal's existential commitment to pluralism and tolerance in matters of faith, thought and conscience should generally preclude criminalisation of apostasy, blasphemy, unorthodox lifestyle choices, scientific inquiry, the free circulation of ideas (including through art and literature), and any essentially self-regarding forms of personal self-expression, such as choice of dress, hairstyle or the name to which one answers. Extended jurisprudential analysis, to elucidate well-defined criminal prohibitions with compelling all-things-considered justifications and to formulate generic liberal principles of criminalisation, cannot profitably be pursued here. But a bit more can be said about liberal criminal law in general terms, without slipping into vacuity.

An important thought for liberals is that whilst effective political authority may be necessary to preserve and indeed enhance everybody's effective sphere of liberty, political authority itself poses many direct and more indirect threats to liberty – not least through one of its most obviously coercive regulatory techniques, the criminal law. So the state and its laws are simultaneously both the guarantors of individual freedom and a constant source of – old and newly improvised – threats to liberty.[48] Applied to criminal law, this thought has inspired one of liberalism's greatest contributions to theories of legitimate government, Mill's Harm Principle:

> [T]he sole end for which mankind are warranted, individually or collectively, in interfering with the liberty of action of any one of their number is self-protection … [T]he only purpose for which power can be rightfully exercised over any member of a civilised community, against his will, is to prevent harm to others. His own good, either physical or moral, is not a sufficient warrant.[49]

Sustained critical attention by subsequent generations of scholars has identified some basic difficulties and many incidental complexities in Mill's 'one very simple principle'. One obvious difficulty is that 'interferences with liberty of action' are pervasive in the modern regulatory state, and they are justified (when they are) on

[47] Strictly speaking, one's interest in continuing to be alive is a precondition for liberty rather than part of its enjoyment. So to elucidate the point more fully, one should say that liberals will be likely to think that there are good prima facie reasons to criminalise both: (i) wrongs that strike at the preconditions for liberty; and (ii) wrongful infringements of liberty.

[48] *Cf* Judith Shklar, 'The Liberalism of Fear' in Nancy L Rosenblum (ed), *Liberalism and the Moral Life* (Harvard University Press, 1989). Shklar's stripped-down conception of liberalism's hard political core remains – justifiably – influential, though one might better ascribe a healthy suspicion of public power and its susceptibility to abuse (which is at least as old as Juvenal's timeless question, *quis custodiet ipsos custodes*?) to practical wisdom rather than fear.

[49] John S Mill, *On Liberty* (Penguin, 1985 [1859]) 68.

a variety of grounds, including the correction of historic injustices, the pursuit of social justice in contemporary society, and the promotion of efficient administration. 'Self-protection' is patently not the exclusive rationale for clipping freedom's wings in modern liberal democracies. A second problem is that paternalistic interventions in freedom of action are fairly commonplace and sometimes plausibly justifiable. Indeed, good faith paternalism, untainted by cynicism or hypocrisy (of the 'this is going to hurt me more than it hurts you' stripe), actually has much to recommend it.[50] Far from being seen as reasons to reject the harm principle entirely,[51] these and similar worries have only inspired contemporary liberals to attempt to improve upon Mill's original formulation. Suitably updated, the complementary principle that penal regulation should be a last resort[52] owing to its corrosive impact on liberty whilst, conversely, liberty-harming (or threatening) conduct is likely to present the best candidates for justified penal proscriptions, continue to inspire liberal conceptions of the moral limits of the criminal law. There is no contradiction in limiting liberty-taking conduct – now seen in its true colours as mere licence to victimise – for the sake of expanding liberty;[53] the liberty of all those (including most offenders, most of the time) who live law-abiding lives under the aegis of the rule of law.

Liberals, then, are penal minimalists – a conviction that consequentialists like Bentham shared and advocated no less fervently than modern deontological liberals.[54] A commitment to penal minimalism does not end with treating criminal law as a weapon of last resort in the government's regulatory armoury. Minimalism is, for liberals, a genuine golden thread binding together disparate chapters and departments of criminal law into a coherent normative vision.[55] Penal minimalism supplies a flexible, unified normative standard for appraising the liberal credentials of, inter alia, offence definitions in substantive criminal law; general principles of criminal liability ('the General Part', as Glanville

[50] Joel Feinberg, *The Moral Limits of the Criminal Law, Volume Three: Harm to Self* (OUP, 1986); Douglas Husak, 'Paternalism and Autonomy' (1981) 10 *Philosophy and Public Affairs* 27.

[51] *Cf* Bernard E Harcourt, 'The Collapse of the Harm Principle' (1999) 90 *Journal of Criminal Law and Criminology* 109, whose inflated expectations of the harm principle as a policy instrument are predictably disappointed.

[52] Panu Minkkinen, '"If Taken in Earnest": Criminal Law Doctrine and the Last Resort' (2006) 45 *Howard Journal of Criminal Justice* 521; cf Douglas Husak, 'The Criminal Law as Last Resort' (2004) 24 *Oxford Journal of Legal Studies* 207.

[53] Thus, Kant's doctrine of right in vindication of his 'universal law of freedom': 'if a certain use of freedom is itself a hindrance to freedom in accordance with universal laws (ie, wrong), coercion that is opposed to his (as a hindering of a hindrance to freedom) is consistent with freedom in accordance with universal laws, that is, it is right. Hence there is connected with right by the principle of contradiction an authorization to coerce someone who infringes upon it': Immanuel Kant, *The Metaphysics of Morals* Mary Gregor ed (CUP, 1996 [1797]) 25.

[54] Bentham favoured 'frugality' in punishment. See, eg, Hugo A Bedau, 'Bentham's Utilitarian Critique of the Death Penalty' (1983) 74 *Journal of Criminal Law and Criminology* 1033.

[55] As opposed to English law's more dubious reception of the 'one golden thread' extolled by Viscount Sankey in *Woolmington v DPP* [1935] AC 462, 481–82 (HL). See Pauk Roberts, *Roberts and Zuckerman's Criminal Evidence*, 3rd edn (OUP, 2022) 21–22 and ch 6.

Williams taught common lawyers to think of it[56]); the law of criminal procedure (including criminal evidence); the law and practice of sentencing and punishment; *and* the practical implementation of criminal law through policing, criminal investigations, prosecutions, trials and penal treatment, whether administered in closed custodial institutions or imposed under supervision in the community.

Legislating, interpreting, applying and enforcing criminal laws presents officials with myriad choices, some of which are – often irreducibly and quite properly – matters for the exercise of professional discretion. A liberal commitment to penal minimalism calls for restraint in the exercise of criminal law powers. Thus, investigative surveillance or other forms of 'proactive policing' should adopt the least intrusive, liberty-diminishing tactics consistent with operational effectiveness and the nature of the criminality being targeted. Police powers of stop, search, arrest and temporary custodial detention should not be invoked indiscriminately, but only on the basis of reasonable suspicion proportionate to the nature and extent of any given infringement on suspects' liberty. Momentary stops or fleeting street inspections of bags or pockets require less in the way of epistemically warranted suspicion than arrest and detention in a police station for several days, but liberals still insist that even minor interferences with liberty by state officials require *some* justification. It may be bad citizenship to refuse to help the police with their inquiries, but it should not be a crime.[57] Where criminal charges are warranted, prosecutors should pursue cases to trial only on the basis of solid evidence, and there should be procedural mechanisms for screening out evidentially weak cases before the accused is formally placed at peril of conviction. Nobody's liberty should be exposed on the precipice of criminal conviction unless the prosecutor has admissible evidence capable of making a jury sure of the accused's guilt.[58] Repeat prosecutions for the same, finally adjudicated, offence cannot be tolerated as routine policy.[59] Whilst allegations of criminal wrongdoing must be taken seriously, this does not mean pursuing suspected offenders until,

[56] Glanville Williams, *Criminal Law: The General Part*, 2nd edn (Stevens & Sons, 1961). And see John Gardner, 'On the General Part of the Criminal Law' in Antony Duff (ed), *Philosophy and the Criminal Law: Principle and Critique* (CUP, 1998).

[57] *Rice v Connolly* [1966] 2 QB 414, 419, DC, per Lord Parker CJ: 'though every citizen has a moral duty or, if you like, a social duty to assist the police, there is no legal duty to that effect … [T]he whole basis of the common law is the right of the individual to refuse to answer questions put to him by persons in authority …'.

[58] Hence, cases lacking sufficient evidence to constitute a material 'case to answer' are halted by judicial intervention, without ever reaching the jury: *R v Galbraith* [1981] 1 WLR 1039 (CA). Generally, see Andrew L-T Choo, *Abuse of Process and Judicial Stays of Criminal Proceedings*, 2nd edn (OUP, 2008); *Roberts and Zuckerman's Criminal Evidence*, § 2.5.

[59] Re-prosecution is *sometimes* warranted, as where the jury fails to agree a verdict or the accused tampers with the jury. Controversial exceptions to the common law double jeopardy prohibition were introduced in England and Wales by the Criminal Justice Act 2003, Part 10: see Ian Dennis, 'The Criminal Justice Act 2003: Prosecution Appeals and Retrial for Serious Offences' [2004] *Criminal Law Review* 619; David Hamer, 'The Expectation of Incorrect Acquittals and the "New and Compelling Evidence" Exception to Double Jeopardy' [2009] *Criminal Law Review* 63; *cf* Paul Roberts, 'Double Jeopardy Law Reform: A Criminal Justice Commentary' (2002) 65 *Modern Law Review* 393.

one way or another, a conviction is secured; on the model of Kafka's nightmares or Vyshinsky's stage-managed show trials, both powerful cautionary tales for liberals. In terms of meting out punishments to offenders, it is difficult to see how multiple prosecutions for the same offence could ever be justifiable, at least not within the same jurisdiction.[60] Whatever punishment is thought to be deserved, it should be imposed in a single proceeding. More generally, liberal penal minimalism implies that both the quantitative amount of punishment imposed and the particular forms and styles of hard treatment selected to implement it should infringe liberty as little as possible, consistent with prevailing theories of proportionality in sentencing and advertised penal aims.

It is worth underlining how the liberty-derived principle of penal minimalism has significant implications for each of these familiar divisions and phases of criminal law and the practical administration of criminal justice, not least because criminal law theorists have tended to lavish far more attention on substantive criminal law and theories of punishment than on questions of policing, enforcement, procedure or proof. In the heartlands of criminal law theorising, the priority of liberty is put to work across the spectrum of jurisprudential issues and puzzles comprising the General Part. Imposing criminal liability in circumstances where the accused could not realistically or reasonably avoid it will always seem suspect to liberals. This is one general objection to many forms of vicarious, accessorial or conspiracy-based criminal liability: the accused is rightly held accountable for her own conduct but cannot be expected to be her brother's keeper – or even her child's minder in relation to most forms of criminal liability. *Mens rea* standards satisfied by inadvertence are viewed as problematic on similar grounds. Even if negligence may sometimes be culpable enough to warrant penal censure,[61] creating extensive criminal law duties to take care would seriously burden liberty because citizens would have to be constantly 'looking over their shoulder' to ensure that they were not inadvertently committing criminal offences, distracting them from doing whatever it is that they would otherwise prefer to be concentrating on in leading their autonomous, (partly) self-authored lives. Where negligent wrongdoing would impose pronounced or obvious risks of very serious harm (as with those who carelessly throw broken electrical appliances off railway bridges or high-rise flats), or where additional duties of care are undertaken voluntarily (eg, by motorists or those who run safari parks), liberals may be content to criminalise for the sake of safeguarding potential victims' liberty. But these would be regarded as exceptional

[60] Note that the objection to repeat prosecutions by different 'sovereigns' rests on the injustice of being punished (allegedly) in excess of one's just deserts. The liberty-based objection is distinctively political, and operates only *within* polities, not – or at least not necessarily or straightforwardly – *between* different legal jurisdictions.

[61] A P Simester, 'Can Negligence be Culpable?' in Jeremy Horder (ed), *Oxford Essays in Jurisprudence*, 4th Series (OUP, 2000); Kyron Huigens, 'Virtue and Criminal Negligence' (1998) 1 *Buffalo Criminal Law Review* 431.

cases requiring clear justification. Strict liability offences[62] are a fortiori problematic for liberals if they imply potentially oppressive duties of advertence and compliance-monitoring in order to guard against liability – or, horror of horrors, impose criminal liability on accused who literally could not have avoided criminal censure, as may be the case with some (more often cited than sighted) 'status offences'.[63] And if criminal liability for omissions truly is 'special' from a liberal perspective,[64] it is only in the contingent sense that positive duties to act are typically more comprehensively liberty-eroding than the negative duties to forbear normally imposed by criminal prohibitions. 'Do this!' nearly always imposes a more substantial tax on personal autonomy than 'Do whatever you like, so long as you don't do that!' However, one should be wary of overgeneralising such contingencies. Contrary to prevailing common law assumptions, using the criminal law to impose a (near) costless duty of easy rescue of those in mortal danger would seem on its face to be consistent with a strong liberal preference for liberty. Moreover, the extent to which positive legal duties in fact impinge on personal autonomy always to some extent turns on the values, goals and projects that particular individuals have chosen to weave into their lives. It is possible, given conceivable schemes of personal values and prevailing social mores in particular political communities, that criminalising certain omissions would actually *promote* rather than burden personal autonomy, at least for the majority of citizens.

The liberty-premiss arguably has further implications for criminal law defences. Radical capacity deficits pre-empting legal responsibility should exculpate, on this view, since the infant, the automaton and the legally insane all (in their different ways) could not 'have done otherwise', rendering directives to them to respect others' liberties both pointless and unreasonable.[65] Affirmative defences like duress, as well as circumstances affording partial defences (diminished responsibility, provocation, etc), are explicable in terms of requiring citizens to tailor their choices and conduct to avoid harming other people's interests (including

[62] A P Simester (ed), *Appraising Strict Liability* (OUP, 2005); Jeremy Horder, 'Strict Liability, Statutory Construction, and the Spirit of Liberty' (2002) 118 *Law Quarterly Review* 458.

[63] The jurisprudential cause célèbre is *R v Larsonneur* (1933) 149 LT 542, discussed, eg, by A P Simester et al, *Simester and Sullivan's Criminal Law: Theory and Doctrine*, 5th edn (Hart Publishing, 2013) 79, 117–18.

[64] A P Simester, 'Why Omissions are Special' (1995) 1 *Legal Theory* 311; Andrew Ashworth, 'The Scope of Criminal Liability for Omissions' (1989) 105 *Law Quarterly Review* 424.

[65] K J M Smith and William Wilson, 'Impaired Voluntariness and Criminal Responsibility: Reworking Hart's Theory of Excuses – The English Judicial Response' (1993) 13 *Oxford Journal of Legal Studies* 69. (Note that this elaboration of the liberty-premiss into a capacity-based rationale for criminal law defences rivals more familiar, desert-based accounts of exculpation in criminal law, predicated on *blameworthiness*. 'Moral involuntariness' – whatever that might actually entail – ostensibly undercuts moral and legal responsibility in a more comprehensive fashion than exculpatory contextual excuses. See further, A P Simester, 'On Justifications and Excuses' in Lucia Zedner and Julian V Roberts (eds), *Principles and Values in Criminal Law and Criminal Justice: Essays in Honour of Andrew Ashworth* (OUP, 2012); John Gardner, 'The Gist of Excuses' (1998) 1 *Buffalo Criminal Law Review* 575.

victims' primary interests in liberty and personal autonomy) only to the extent that can reasonably be expected of ordinary human beings with their own lives to lead, as opposed to enforcing supererogatory self-sacrifice as the juridical norm – and punishing people for failing to live up to the standards of secular sainthood. Criminal law justifications as well as excuses can be seen to cohere with liberal political morality. Self-defence, in particular, answers to the compelling human imperative of self-preservation (recall Mill's specification of the Harm Principle) in exigent circumstances where formal guarantees of legal protection for one's vital interests offer too little, because their executive enforcement would come too late. Interventions to uphold the criminal law,[66] sometimes with fatal consequences, likewise find their justification in the desirability or, on more modest accounts, the permissibility of private citizens assuming the responsibilities of law enforcement – stepping into the shoes of a police officer, because there are no actual police officers around – in the agony of the moment or when fleeting opportunity adventitiously presents itself.

It should be evident, even from this cursory survey, that an impressive amount of contemporary criminal law doctrine can be spun out of the liberty-premiss. Substantial convergence between liberal political theory and orthodox criminal law can be viewed, in broad methodological terms, as mutual corroboration of both theory and practice. The criminal law of a liberal polity would, by hypothesis, exhibit a strong preference for liberty and personal autonomy, not only in its overarching penal minimalism but also in the institutional fabric of its principal liability doctrines, theories of attribution (as manifested, for example, in legal conceptions of causation and *novus actus interveniens*) and criminal law defences; and our data, in the form of Anglo-American criminal law theory extrapolating from common law penal traditions, broadly confirm the hypothesis. We are surely on the right track in supposing that liberal criminal law is centrally concerned with securing, enlarging and preserving individual liberty. Buoyed by this rather swift analytical success, it is tempting to imagine that parsimonious liberal premisses might be substantial enough to generate comprehensive explanatory accounts of penal law and penal institutions; that liberalism could explain *everything* about the normative foundations of criminal law needed to construct cogent justifications of what can, in fact, be justified in our existing penal practices, whilst exposing the remainder to more searching critical scrutiny and remedial attention. For example, one might follow Warren Quinn[67] in trying to argue that penal law is just an institutionalised collective form of self-defence. Or one might think that criminal law doctrine is an instrument – perhaps one amongst many – for maintaining social peace

[66] Criminal Law Act 1967, s 3. English law requires only genuine (not necessarily reasonable) belief in the need for reasonable force to prevent crime, and the defence extends to property crimes as well as to offences against the person: see, eg, *R v Morris* [2014] 1 WLR 16, [2013] EWCA Crim 436.

[67] Warren Quinn, 'The Right to Threaten and the Right to Punish' (1985) 14 *Philosophy & Public Affairs* 327.

under the rule of law[68] or for maximising aggregate liberty in society.[69] There are countless variations on this theme.

My view is that no such attempt to reduce criminal law theory and/or the philosophy of punishment to liberal political morality is, or can be, entirely successful. Some variants of the argument are consequentialist and hence fall prey to well-rehearsed objections to consequentialism in general; but my scepticism in this regard extends no less to deontological liberalisms. All reductive explanations of important social institutions should be approached with a healthy dose of scepticism, if only because it seems inherently unlikely that a set of social practices which are as historically embedded in institutionalised traditions, richly articulated in theory and practice, symbolically loaded, emotionally charged, and frequently controversial as criminal law will be satisfactorily explained by appealing to just one or two simple ideas or values. Of course, any useful theoretical model must necessarily be a lot simpler than the reality it represents. Simplification is inherent to *modelling*. However, good models or explanatory theories should emphasise key features and avoid distorting oversimplification. Liberal theory strikes me as suffering from two significant limitations in its efforts to rationalise criminal law. The first I call the problem of incompleteness; the second is the problem of indeterminacy.

IV. Two Theoretical Limitations: Incompleteness and Indeterminacy

Liberal theory, I suggest, is materially incomplete in its critical resources for understanding contemporary criminal law. Significant areas of theoretical incompleteness include the following three: liberal theory does not have its own distinctive or fully elucidated theory of moral agency; it offers no justificatory rationale for criminal prohibitions that are not concerned with protecting liberal values; and it cannot explain retributive justice as the ground of justified punishment for criminal wrongdoers.

Liberal theory is also materially indeterminate, in the sense that it seldom offers comprehensive or unequivocal guidance to policy-makers, legislators, judges, lawyers, or other criminal justice practitioners and officials who aspire to principled decision-making when confronted with difficult choices in their professional lives. Liberal political theory may address relevant practical issues (it is not *incomplete* in the first sense of theoretical omission) and supply a valuable intellectual framework for structuring normative reasoning, but its logic runs out, or

[68] Hyman Gross, *A Theory of Criminal Justice* (OUP, 1979).

[69] John Braithwaite and Philip Pettit, *Not Just Deserts: A Republican Theory of Criminal Justice* (OUP, 1990); Andrew Sanders, Richard Young and Mandy Burton, *Criminal Justice*, 4th edn (OUP, 2010) 47–56.

becomes tangled or equivocal, before determinate solutions to practical problems can be ascertained. Assuming that the exhaustion of liberal theory does not coincide with the limits of normative rationality,[70] policymakers and practitioners must then look beyond liberalism for practical normative guidance. The problem of indeterminacy is not supposed to represent a criticism of liberal theory *per se* but rather draws attention to its pronounced limitations *as a resource for theorising criminal law.*

These are large theoretical claims, which I cannot fully vindicate here. But the general tenor of each strand of argument can be drawn out far enough to indicate its potential significance for Criminal Law Theory and to provide some concrete illustrations of practical payoffs for criminal jurisprudence, policy-making and the practice of criminal law.

A. The Problem of Incompleteness

It is vital at the outset to distinguish between *liberal theories* of agency and theories of agency that may well be compatible with liberalism. The liberal agent, we have seen, is a concretely situated autonomous self-author of their own life; or (as Marx almost said) an individual who makes their own life but not in material circumstances of their own choosing (and *ceteris paribus*, people who live in liberal polities lead more autonomous lives than those who don't). Framed within the broader sweep of western thought, the model of the choosing self, endowed with free will and capable of making up its own mind about what to do and how to live, evidently predates liberalism by millennia. Liberalism is distinctive in propounding a normative conception of autonomy (one which would have been bewildering to the ancients), but this is projected onto a much older conception of human agency; a conception which (to my knowledge) has been shared by most non-liberals throughout history, and continues to represent the 'common sense view' embraced by modern criminal justice systems around the world.[71] Thus, a theocratic polity might pass emphatically illiberal laws – eg, making apostasy or adultery crimes punishable by death – but this does not necessarily imply a different conception of moral agency to that presupposed by liberals. The criminal law of this theoretic polity might well excuse infants and the insane from criminal liability on grounds of lack of capacity, prefer advertent standards of culpability to criminalising negligence, eschew strict liability, permit proportionate self-defence and exigent private law enforcement, and so forth, in much the same way *and for much the same reasons* as liberal states. The theocratic state passes illiberal

[70] Being the point where normative reasons run out entirely and decision-makers are entitled to indulge their own subjective preferences untrammelled by any institutional constraint. I surmise that criminal justice officials never have such complete discretion, or that it applies only to matters of complete normative indifference, like the prosecutor's favourite perfume or the judge's choice of socks.

[71] Larry Siedentop, *Inventing the Individual: The Origins of Western Liberalism* (Allen Lane, 2014).

criminal laws because it rejects the liberal's secular premiss: state criminal law must conform to its god's will, and crimes against god cannot be tempered by secular mercy – lest the souls of god's obedient servants in government should be damned alongside the abandoned souls of criminals. There is certainly a disagreement with liberalism here – but it is located exactly where one should expect to find it, in liberal *political theory* (or in *theology*, from the opposite perspective), rather than in rival conceptions of moral agency. Theories of agency, extending into theorising about criteria of attribution in criminal law, are pre-eminently topics for metaphysics and practical ethics. Most, if not all, of the analytical and normative work has already been done before we get to political theory in the strict sense. Given that the prevailing conception of moral agency in modern criminal law is not merely consistent with liberal political premisses, but in fact coheres with them perfectly (which still does not make it *a liberal theory* of moral agency), this traditional division of philosophical labour and its (implicit) translation into criminal jurisprudence should not disconcert liberals.

A second strand of incompleteness relates to ascertaining the justified moral limits of the criminal law. We have seen that the Millian move from liberty to the Harm Principle is both slick – almost frictionless in its intellectual progress – and impressively fecund in accounting for a significant chunk of modern criminal law. It can hardly be doubted that a great many criminal law prohibitions, in liberal and non-liberal polities alike, target actual or threatened harms *qua* setbacks to individuals' interests, including their primary interests in liberty and personal autonomy. Other familiar kinds of criminal prohibitions, including corrupting public officials and offences against the administration of justice, can be justified by extension as necessary safeguards for the integrity of public institutions, which are themselves necessary to protect individuals' primary interests. Theorists who have embarked upon systematic inquiries into the moral limits of the criminal law have discovered, however, that sooner or later the Harm Principle's bountiful theoretical well runs dry.[72] Particular prohibitions either defy rationalisation in distinctively liberal terms, or the intellectual contortions required to achieve theoretical reconciliation seem both extravagant and anyway ultimately fail to capture the essence of the prohibition under examination; not so much a successful explanation of puzzling phenomena as a pyrrhic victory for changing the subject. You can say, for example, that the reason for criminalising cruelty to animals is that animal abusers have a habit of graduating to hurting humans; or that criminalising grave desecration retrospectively harms the deceased, or inflicts psychological harm on the living, or is really anyway a property crime harming the owner of the land. But a better explanation is probably that these actions are morally wrongful, and the wrong supplies a prima

[72] Recall that Joel Feinberg's epic quadrilogy exploring *The Moral Limits of the Criminal Law* contains just one book on the Harm Principle (*Volume One: Harm to Others* (OUP, 1984)), and three more exploring other candidate principles of criminalisation: *Volume Two: Offence to Others* (OUP, 1985); *Volume Three: Harm to Self* (OUP, 1986); and *Volume Four: Harmless Wrongdoing* (OUP, 1988).

facie reason for criminalisation irrespective of any more or less tendentious connection to a living person's liberty interest.[73]

A variant of this argument, which overlaps with criminal law theorists' discussions of 'fair labelling',[74] extends to legislative strategies for individuating offences in positive criminal law. Why distinguish 'rape' from 'sexual assault', or 'grievous bodily harm' from 'actual bodily harm', or 'murder' from 'manslaughter', etc? Why not have a single offence of, say, 'physical assault' and mark gradations of seriousness and culpability through differential sentencing? Why not collapse the distinction between sexual and non-sexual assaults into a single category of unconsented bodily intrusion? This kind of proposal has recommended itself to those who insist that rape and other sexual assaults are more about violence than sex,[75] and consequently that the criminal law should reflect and clearly signal that reality. Purely institutional reasons can be advanced to try to explain criminal law's traditional taxonomies of offences. For example, it might be said that different gradations of offence seriousness are needed to allocate proceedings to the appropriate level of trial venue – a particularly important consideration in common law jurisdictions, where the hallowed, but comparatively expensive, trial by jury is reserved for the most serious, 'indictable' offences. But again, the ingenuity of these rationalisations either runs out or fails, ultimately, to provide satisfactory explanations for institutionally embedded practices. It proves to be very difficult to dispense with the thought that a primary goal of criminal prohibitions is to track moral wrongs, or sometimes to create them.[76] Yet liberalism cannot claim any monopoly of wisdom across the panoramic vista of moral wrongdoing. Such light as can be shed on the problem of evil must be found in the entire canon of western philosophy, theology and literature, increasingly now in dialogue with

[73] The argument here, I should stress, is simply that a plausible rationale for criminalising wanton cruelty to animals cannot be derived from the liberal's liberty-premiss. The fact that there are special welfarist and humanitarian reasons for protecting non-human sentient life forms, which do not apply to inanimate objects or cultural artefacts, is beside the point. Many people – including many non-liberals, and some non-deontological liberals, such as Peter Singer, *Animal Liberation*, 2nd edn (Pimlico, 1995) – share the strong intuitions that animals should not suffer needlessly, and that deliberately harming animals for no good reason is evil. However, nobody – to my knowledge – argues that non-human animals can and should lead autonomous lives in the Razian sense, nor that *this* supplies the justification for criminalising harm to animals. In short, the evil of wanton cruelty to animals is not explained by liberal political theory.

[74] James Chalmers and Fiona Leverick, 'Fair Labelling in Criminal Law' (2008) 71 *Modern Law Review* 217; Glanville Williams, 'Convictions and Fair Labelling' (1983) 42 *Cambridge Law Journal* 85; A J Ashworth, 'The Elasticity of Mens Rea' in C F H Tapper (ed), *Crime, Proof and Punishment: Essays in Memory of Sir Rupert Cross* (Butterworths, 1981).

[75] On the politics of competing legislative programmes, see Aya Gruber, 'Rape, Feminism and the War on Crime' (2009) 84 *Washington Law Review* 581; Samuel H Pillsbury, 'Crimes Against the Heart: Recognizing the Wrongs of Forced Sex' (2002) 35 *Loyola of Los Angeles Law Review* 845. And see John Gardner and Stephen Shute, 'The Wrongness of Rape' in Jeremy Horder (ed), *Oxford Essays in Jurisprudence: 4th Series* (OUP, 2000); Nicola Lacey, 'Unspeakable Subjects, Impossible Rights: Sexuality, Integrity and Criminal Law' (1998) 11 *Canadian Journal of Law & Jurisprudence* 47.

[76] Positive criminal law creates new, more particularistic moral wrongs by concretising general moral prohibitions. Thus, driving on the right-hand side of the road is not immoral unless and until state law decrees that everybody must drive on the left.

global philosophical traditions. Liberals will naturally have their own distinctive 'take' on these intellectual resources; and the solace of philosophical modesty can be grasped with no obvious political strings attached. Granted that (some) wrongs supply *prima facie* reasons for criminalisation, liberals will not accept all-things-considered arguments without running candidate prohibitions through liberal political filters, starting with the strong liberal commitment to penal minimalism and the presumption that criminal law should be the last resort. All that being said, liberal political morality contains no comprehensive institutional or principled objection to any and every conceivable criminal prohibition deriving from normative principles not reducible to liberal equality. If, plausibly, torturing animals for fun is evil and there is no good reason to do it; and if, again plausibly, there are no comprehensive institutional objections to criminalising (serious, intentional) harm to animals for sadistic pleasure, then liberal states a fortiori plausibly should criminalise sadistic cruelty to animals. Liberalism cannot authorise this conclusion without theoretical and normative reinforcements, which it is able to muster precisely because liberals' ethical theories of the good are richer, broader and, in some sense,[77] anterior to liberalism's theories of good government and legitimate political authority.

A third area of theoretical incompleteness concerns liberal conceptions of punishment; a problem located in 'penal theory' or the philosophy of punishment, whether conceived as a specialist department of Penology or Criminal Law Theory or possibly as a distinct, though obviously still very closely related, sub-specialism. To complain that liberalism lacks a convincing account of retributive justice will admittedly not cut any ice with theorists who regard retributivism as an antediluvian moral error or those who think that the long-running (and now rather stylised) dispute in penal theory between 'utilitarians' and 'retributivists' is either hopelessly stalemated or can be made to disappear with a bit of fancy philosophical prestidigitation.[78] My own view is that no theory of punishment can fully succeed, either as sociologically accurate description or as philosophically cogent normative justification, unless it engages with the ethics of retribution at the level of practical detail and psycho-social complexity that we find, for example, in Michael Moore's illuminating studies.[79]

[77] I am not propounding an excessively rigid, and consequently fallacious, distinction between personal ethics and collective morality. The two are patently merged or integrated in mature theories of political morality, including theories of liberal democracy. This does not imply that the entire sphere of personal ethics collapses into political morality – a normative proposition that liberals, in particular, emphatically deny.

[78] See, eg, Mitchell N Berman, 'Two Kinds of Retributivism' in R A Duff and Stuart P Green, *Philosophical Foundations of Criminal Law* (OUP, 2011); Paul H Robinson, 'The Ongoing Revolution in Punishment Theory: Doing Justice as Controlling Crime' (2011) 42 *Arizona State Law Journal* 1089; Guyora Binder, 'Punishment Theory: Moral or Political?' (2002) 5 *Buffalo Criminal Law Review* 321.

[79] Michael S Moore, 'The Moral Worth of Retribution' in F Schoeman (ed), *Responsibility, Character and the Emotions* (CUP, 1987). Also see, eg, William I Miller, *Eye for an Eye* (CUP, 2006); Jeffrie G Murphy, *Getting Even: Forgiveness and its Limits* (OUP, 2003); Jeffrie G Murphy and Jean Hampton, *Forgiveness and Mercy* (CUP, 1988); K D Rutledge, 'Giving the Devil his Due: The Pursuit and Capture of Nazi War Criminals – A Call for Retributive Justice in International Criminal Law' (2005) 3 *Regent Journal of International Law* 27.

Retribution, needless to say, is a much older idea than liberalism. It is shot through with theological resonance and associated, historically, with barbaric and inhumane forms of penal sanction, some of which make 'an eye for an eye' look positively genteel.[80] Many liberals instinctively and understandably want to dissociate themselves from this historical and theological legacy. It does not follow that objections to barbaric punishments are distinctively liberal. Enlightened despots as much as liberal democrats might strive to rid their criminal laws of wanton cruelty and inhumanity. English law dispensed with amputation, branding and disembowelment as punishments long before most people were democratically enfranchised. So – reprising a pattern of argumentation utilised before – the fact that liberals are committed to respecting human dignity should not be confused with the misapprehension that respect for human dignity is peculiar to liberal political morality. Most modern political philosophies claim to respect human dignity;[81] issue is then joined over how exactly human dignity should be respected and with what further institutional implications in the arenas of political theory and policy debate. Liberals naturally put a liberal spin on protecting human dignity, prioritising individual liberty in ways and to an extent that non-liberals often find problematic. But those who in good faith advocate criminal prohibitions on, say, paternalistic grounds are not, generally speaking, fairly characterised as disparaging human dignity. The criminal law paternalist is more aptly described as somebody with a different, competing conception of human dignity, or a different understanding of the implications of human dignity for legitimate criminalisation.

Puncturing liberals' proprietorial pretensions regarding humane punishments is barely half the theoretical story. The central plotlines must attempt to reconcile retributivism with liberal political morality – a philosophical tale which, I recognise, may require the suspension of widespread disbelief. This narrative is not entirely unknown to penal theory,[82] but concerted examination of the relationship between liberalism and retributivism has been isolated and infrequent relative to the oceans of ink devoted to theorising about punishment, and I do not think that anybody has yet made very substantial progress in producing a fully integrated theory of liberal retribution. If and when such a theory appears, it will be heavily indebted to a much older philosophical tradition that, for many centuries before and after the emergence of liberalism in modern western political thought, has been trying to explain when, why, and how much punishment is deserved. The indispensability of these theoretical supplements highlights the methodological limitations of liberal political theory for theorising penal law.

[80] Michel Foucault, *Discipline and Punish: The Birth of the Prison*, Alan Sheridan trans (Penguin, 1991) Part I. And see www.torturamuseum.com/index.html (accessed 17 December 2025).

[81] George Kateb, *Human Dignity* (Harvard University Press, 2011).

[82] Paul Butler, 'Retribution, For Liberals' (1999) 46 *UCLA Law Review* 1873; Jean Hampton, 'Retribution and the Liberal State' [1994] *Journal of Contemporary Legal Issues* 117.

B. The Problem of Indeterminacy

The previous section identified areas of criminal law theory and the philosophy of punishment that liberal political theory does not reach. The problem of indeterminacy, to which we now turn, arises in relation to questions that liberal political theory *does* address but does not fully answer, in the sense of providing comprehensive normative guidance to policymakers and practitioners. Liberal theory, in other words, *under-determines* criminal justice policy and practice. Indeterminacy of this kind is a general feature of the relationship between political theorising and practical action, and not something that should be regarded as a peculiar defect of liberalism. A parallel methodological stricture would constrain adherents of any other, non-liberal or illiberal political philosophy.

One kind of indeterminacy was hinted at previously, when it was noted that liberals' love of individual liberty goes hand-in-hand with tolerant pluralism in matters of freedom of thought, conscience and religion. Suppose, however, that a planned religious rally is expected to erupt into violence at the cost of many lives. Should the liberal state ban the rally to preserve the lives and liberties of potential victims, freedom of religion notwithstanding? Or should the lives that will be lost be regarded as regrettable but unavoidable collateral damage incidental to discharging the state's more pressing duty to vindicate a fundamental liberal right of religious expression? Such practical tensions within the liberal scheme of fundamental values permeate down to the root of Hobbes' ingenious solution to the paradox of legitimate liberal government.[83] Leviathan enhances individual liberty by guaranteeing collective security. But if individual liberty for all but the most brutish and nasty would be exceedingly impoverished and short-lived once ever deprived of the state's security blanket, wouldn't just about any less-than-debilitating or more or less temporary sacrifice of liberty seem justified in order to keep that security blanket in place? Isn't the problem with pinning our hopes for liberty on security just that security always wins out in a crisis; and that Leviathan could actually start behaving like a despot, even whilst wearing the mask of majoritarian democracy and adhering to its institutional forms and graces?

In rehearsing these deep theoretical tensions in political liberalism, I do not mean to imply that its critical resources are completely impotent in criminal justice policy-making or in political debate more generally. On the contrary: liberal political theory has considerable normative purchase and rhetorical force in polities like the UK, which publicly subscribes to liberal political orthodoxies and likes to regard itself as a haven of liberal freedom and tolerance, but frequently appears to forget its official philosophical allegiances when it comes to legislating new criminal laws, developing penal policies, extending police powers of surveillance and investigation, or reforming criminal procedure to make it easier

[83] Alice Ristroph, 'Hobbes on "Diffidence" and the Criminal Law' in Markus D Dubber (ed), *Foundational Texts in Modern Criminal Law* (OUP, 2014).

to convict more villains.[84] In the area of counter-terrorism, for example, 'security' has been trotted out as the all-purpose rationale for authorising extended periods of police custody and introducing post-charge questioning,[85] reliance on secret evidence in contested legal proceedings,[86] detention without trial, intrusive forms of surveillance and restrictions on liberty for terrorist suspects who have not been convicted of any offence,[87] and legislating new prophylactic criminal offences of extraordinary breadth and highly attenuated connections to anticipated harms.[88] None of this, however, reflects any deep tension in liberal political ideals, because the kind of terrorism at which these measures are aimed does not truly present any existential threat to collective security or 'the life of the nation'.[89] It is only the prosaic case of governments, running scared before the twin-scourges of a volatile electorate and the Murdoch press, choosing to sacrifice the liberty of a few for an illusion of security for the many. The political calculation is all the easier when the few who bear the brunt are foreigners (like the Belmarsh detainees) or numerically small minority groups (predominantly non-white muslims) – even though discriminating against minorities in this way, albeit more careless than intentional, betrays fundamental liberal values.

[84] See, eg, Ministry of Justice, *Swift and Sure Justice: The Government's Plans for Reform of the Criminal Justice System*, Cm 8388 (The Stationery Office, 2012); Home Office, *Rebalancing the Criminal Justice System in Favour of the Law-Abiding Majority* (Home Office, 2006); Home Office, *Respect and Responsibility – Taking a Stand Against Anti-Social Behaviour*, Cm 5778 (The Stationery Office, 2003); CJS, *Justice for All*, Cm 5563 (The Stationery Office, 2002). For critical (and overtly pessimistic) discussion, see Michael Tonry, *Punishment and Politics* (Willan Publishing, 2004); Phillip Pettit, 'Is Criminal Justice Politically Feasible?' (2002) 5 *Buffalo Criminal Law Review* 427; David Garland, *The Culture of Control* (OUP, 2001); Andrew Ashworth, 'Is The Criminal Law A Lost Cause?' (2000) 116 *Law Quarterly Review* 225.

[85] Counter-Terrorism Act 2008, s 22; Clive Walker, 'Post-Charge Questioning of Suspects' [2008] *Criminal Law Review* 509.

[86] Justice and Security Act 2013, Part 2; *Tariq v Home Office* [2012] 1 AC 452, [2011] UKSC 35; *Al Rawi v Security Service* [2012] 1 AC 531, [2011] UKSC 34; *R (Roberts) v Parole Board* [2005] 2 AC 738, [2005] UKHL 45 (the applicant's position in *Roberts* being described by Lord Steyn, dissenting at [95]–[96], as 'Kafkaesque').

[87] Terrorism Prevention and Investigation Measures Act 2011 ('TPIMs'), superseding the Prevention of Terrorism Act 2005 (control orders), which in turn replaced the Anti-Terrorism, Crime and Security Act 2001, Part 4 (indefinite detention without trial). For discussion, see D Dyzenhaus, 'Preventive Justice and the Rule-of-Law Project' in Andrew Ashworth, Lucia Zedner and Patrick Tomlin (eds), *Prevention and the Limits of the Criminal Law* (OUP, 2013); Lucia Zedner, 'Preventive Justice or Pre-Punishment? The Case of Control Orders' (2007) 60 *Current Legal Problems* 174.

[88] G R Sullivan and Ian Dennis (eds), *Seeking Security: Pre-empting the Commission of Criminal Harms* (Hart Publishing, 2012); Andrew Ashworth and Lucia Zedner, 'Just Prevention: Preventive Rationales and the Limits of the Criminal Law' in R A Duff and Stuart P Green (eds), *Philosophical Foundations of Criminal Law* (OUP, 2011); J Hodgson and Victor Tadros, 'How to Make a Terrorist Out of Nothing' (2009) 72 *Modern Law Review* 984.

[89] Although a majority of their Lordships in *A v Home Secretary* [2005] 2 AC 68, [2004] UKHL 56 refused to second-guess the minister's judgement in this matter, Lord Hoffmann was surely right when he insisted, dissenting at [96], that '[w]hether we would survive Hitler hung in the balance, but there is no doubt that we shall survive Al-Qaeda .... Terrorist violence, serious as it is, does not threaten our institutions of government or our existence as a civil community.' For general discussion of the liberty/security nexus see Jeremy Waldron, *Torture, Terror and Trade-offs: Philosophy for the White House* (OUP, 2010).

Similarly pointed liberal critiques could be levelled against recent legislation and operational policy in relation to the routine administration of criminal justice, including such dubious policing practices as indiscriminate public surveillance[90] and an over-extended National DNA Database,[91] not to mention concerted efforts to rebrand criminality as 'anti-social behaviour' so that it can be regulated more effectively (along with troublesome behaviour that is not actually criminal) without having to comply with liberal principles of criminalisation or traditional due process guarantees.[92] Projected against this policy backcloth, reassertion of orthodox liberal principles and criticism of government's illiberal tendencies might appear almost radical.

The indeterminacy of liberal political theory is exposed, not in cases of policymakers' ignorance, miscalculation or bad faith (involving institutional failings or betrayals of liberal principles), but in practical situations where liberal commitments provide seemingly conflicted guidance or at least fail to indicate an unequivocally desirable course of action. Examples are legion: almost any randomly chosen volume of the *Criminal Appeal Reports* would supply pertinent illustrations. Consider this question of trial procedure which recently confronted the English Crown Court:[93] should a defendant be permitted to wear the *niqab*, covering her head and face except for her eyes, whilst standing trial for a criminal offence? Muslim women are instructed by the Koran to dress modestly,[94] and some – by no means all – versions of Islam interpret this injunction as requiring women to appear veiled in public. To the extent that wearing a veil is treated as a requirement of religious observance, the liberal's foundational commitment to pluralism and tolerance, most especially in matters of religious freedom, speaks strongly in favour of allowing the *niqab* to be worn in legal proceedings. Moreover, muslim women often say that wearing the veil and dressing 'modestly' makes them feel safer and more secure in their person, enhancing their liberty and personal autonomy. This consideration takes on an

[90] Beatrice von Silva-Tarouca Larsen, *Setting the Watch: Privacy and the Ethics of CCTV Surveillance* (Hart Publishing, 2011); Andrew von Hirsch, 'The Ethics of Public Television Surveillance' in Andrew von Hirsch, David Garland and Alison Wakefield (eds), *Ethical and Social Perspectives on Situational Crime Prevention* (Hart Publishing, 2000).

[91] Liz Campbell, 'A Rights-based Analysis of DNA Retention: "Non-conviction" Databases and the Liberal State' [2010] *Criminal Law Review* 889.

[92] Andrew von Hirsch and A P Simester (eds), *Incivilities: Regulating Offensive Behaviour* (Hart Publishing, 2006); Andrew Ashworth, 'Social Control and "Anti-Social Behaviour": The Subversion of Human Rights' (2004) 120 *Law Quarterly Review* 263.

[93] *R v D (R)*, Transcript of Ruling by HHJ Peter Murphy at Blackfriars CC, 16 September 2013 (*Judgement of HHJ Peter Murphy in Relation to Wearing of Niqaab by Defendant During Proceedings in Crown Court.*) The Canadian Supreme Court in *R v NS* [2012] 3 SCR 726 had recently addressed the related, but distinct, question of whether *witnesses* should be allowed to testify veiled in criminal trials. Judge Murphy treated the question as a matter of first impression, with 'no authority directly on point in our domestic law' (at [9]).

[94] The *hijab* (concealing, covering up), as per Koran 24:31 (trans Yusuf Ali) ('[a]nd say to the believing women that they should lower their gaze and guard their modesty; that they should not display their beauty and ornaments except what (must ordinarily) appear thereof; that they should draw their veils over their bosoms and not display their beauty except to their husbands ....').

important additional dimension in the context of defending a criminal charge, since requiring the accused to remove the *niqab* in court might conceivably inhibit her ability to mount an effective defence. She might, for example, be too embarrassed or intimidated to testify properly in her own defence, or to testify at all. Finally, liberals supposedly celebrate personal choice and self-expression, especially in relation to those choices that have a significant bearing on personal identity and 'the presentation of self in everyday life',[95] at least so long as these choices do not interfere with anybody else's rights. If a defendant wants to wear the *niqab* in court, or anywhere else in public, why should she be denied her right to present her authentic self to the world as she sees fit?

One response is that we do not, in fact, have an unqualified right to present ourselves to the world as we see fit. Dangerous or offensive clothing may in general be proscribed and a fortiori wearing such items in a courtroom. The defendant who turns up to court in a tee-shirt bearing an offensive slogan will be told to take it off; the naturist who finds clothing inhibiting and prefers to appear au naturel will nonetheless be instructed to cover up in the dock. Forms of (un)dress conventionally regarded as offensive or disturbing are not tolerated, partly because of their reciprocal adverse effects on unwilling[96] viewers' personal autonomy, partly because they do not comport with the solemnity of the occasion. But does the *niqab* offend? Plainly, it does offend some people, but not, I think, on grounds that should trouble conscientious liberals. Some people are offended because they confuse Islamic dress with anti-western feeling, threats to traditional western institutions or ways of life, unwanted immigration or even terrorism. Since these associations are tenuous, contingent and – often – merely imagined, creatures of ignorance and suspicion, they pose no serious philosophical challenge to liberal tolerance and pluralism. It might be said that overt displays of religious affiliation implying 'foreign' allegiances, especially those which are highly visible because they depart from locally prevailing conventions of suitable habiliment, have no place in the public life of a secular democracy. It is for something like this reason that the French have 'banned the *burqa*'.[97] Notice, however, that the French ban arises from a republican sense of unity in social solidarity, and as such reflects – if not strictly an illiberal impulse – then at least a corporatist strain inflecting the French conception of liberalism. Neither inflection nor ban are themselves products of liberalism, which should be expected to prioritise pluralistic religious freedom – at least up to the point at which religious dissent poses an existential threat to the preservation of social peace or the life of the nation. But nobody is

[95] *Cf* Erving Goffman, *The Presentation of Self in Everyday Life* (Penguin, 1990 [1959]).

[96] Recall that witnesses and jurors appear in court under compulsion, whilst judges and lawyers are only doing their job and can reasonably expect safe and wholesome working conditions.

[97] Angelique Chrisafis, 'French Veil Ban: First Woman Fined for Wearing Niqab', *The Guardian* 12 April 2011; *R (B) v Home Secretary* [2013] EWHC 2281 (Admin). *Cf* the position in Turkey, where restrictions on wearing religious dress in public have been regarded as logical outgrowths of the founding principles of Kemalist secular nationhood. Fear of foreigners does not come into it. Also see *Şahin v Turkey* (2007) 44 EHRR 5, ECtHR (GC).

arguing that allowing female muslims to wear the *niqab* in court might bring the British state to its knees or precipitate bloody revolution.

Another reason for objecting to the *niqab* might be that it is a visible symbol of patriarchy which celebrates women's oppression and demeans their subjectivity, thereby striking at the root of the liberal equality norm. Permitting defendants to appear so attired in a key, highly visible public institution like the criminal trial, it might be argued, amounts to state collusion in women's oppression, just as if the accused were permitted to come to court sporting a tee-shirt bearing an offensive misogynist slogan. Liberals would have no difficulty denouncing and intervening to prevent *coerced* religious dress. However, the Koran specifically prohibits forced compliance with any aspect of *hijab*,[98] and the vast majority of muslim women who take the veil (including western converts) insist that doing so is their own voluntary choice. This inconvenient empirical truth lands liberals on the horns of a dilemma. The first horn is labelled 'false consciousness': muslim women may *say* they freely choose the veil, but this only goes to demonstrate the comprehensiveness of their disempowerment and oppression. These women have so completely internalised the oppressor's values that they now speak in the self-negating voice of patriarchy! The problem with all false-consciousness arguments is that they invariably prove far too much. In philosophical debate, 'false consciousness' tends to degenerate into 'anything I do not agree with'; in political practice, false consciousness leads to places liberals should never want to go. So it is tempting to veer towards the second horn of the dilemma, labelled *pour décourager les autres*. Granted now that *niqab* wearers really do freely choose the veil, won't the image of females appearing in court covered up in black from head to toe send out very bad messages about women's bondage and inferiority to other citizens, including non-muslims and those far less sophisticated in their interpretation of curial imagery than the *niqab* wearers themselves? Isn't regulation demure clothing, leaving only the wearer's eyes visible to the world, all of a piece with the litany of historical and contemporary ways in which women and girls have been silenced, effaced, deformed and oppressed, denied full citizenship and excluded from political power – the relatively mild end of all-too-familiar practices extending to domestic violence, foot-binding, genital mutilation, suttee and all the rest?[99] Perhaps it will; perhaps it is. The problem for liberals is that many similar personal choices plausibly carry analogous risks. If we are to be prevented from exercising our choices in predominantly self-regarding matters of personal taste and preference, not because of any harm

[98] 'Let there be no compulsion in religion' (Koran 2: 256). The Muslim Council of Britain interprets this injunction to imply that 'although *Hijab* is certainly an integral part of the overall Islamic dress code, it is not for anyone to force it upon another human being' (as quoted in *R v D (R)*, [19]).

[99] Natasha Walter, *Living Dolls: The Return of Sexism* (Virago, 2010); Marianne Hester, Liz Kelly and Jill Radford (eds), *Women, Violence and Male Power* (Open University Press, 1996); Jill Radford and Diana E H Russell, *Femicide: The Politics of Woman Killing* (Open University Press, 1992); Naomi Wolf, *The Beauty Myth* (Vintage, 1991); Catharine A MacKinnon, *Feminism Unmodified: Discourses on Life and Law* (Harvard University Press, 1988).

or risk that we ourselves pose but simply because careless observers might get the wrong idea, then individual liberty would always be hostage to the censure of – possibly ignorant or bigoted – public opinion. This is not a road that liberals have been inclined to travel, since Mill clearly signalled its propensity to become a liberty-eroding slippery slope.[100]

To this point, liberal political theory has seemingly generated rich and powerful critical resources for addressing the problem of the *niqab*-wearing defendant. Potential arguments for demanding that criminals accused appear in court unveiled were smartly refuted by authentically liberal rejoinders. Even if certain objections plausibly gain more traction in liberal political morality (eg, modest variants of the 'false consciousness' or 'bad example' arguments might fly if they could be adequately constrained by competing principles), it is difficult to see how such considerations could be sufficiently weighty to trump the liberal's foundational commitment to religious tolerance and pluralism. That liberal principles have taken us this far confirms that the *niqab*-wearing defendant does not present a problem of theoretical incompleteness of the kind identified in the previous section. Rather, we have reached the point of theoretical exhaustion where the indeterminacy of liberal theory is revealed in practice.

Suppose that a defendant wanted to wear a full-face crash helmet in court, which, with the visor up, would leave exactly the same strip of face and eyes visible to the observer as the *niqab*. The helmet itself is completely plain black and inoffensive (like the *niqab*), the defendant has a sincere and strong desire to wear it in court (she is not faking or playing for time),[101] and the motivation for her desire is not per se institutionally problematic in the sense of being incompatible with the nature and solemnity of the proceedings, eg, she is not wearing the crash helmet in order to express her rejection of the court's authority or as an ironic commentary on the state's – metaphorical or literal – predilection for bashing people over the head. Let us also assume that the accused's identity can be verified in a mutually acceptable fashion.[102] Of course, a trial court would not hesitate: this defendant would simply be ordered to remove the crash helmet without a moment's concern for her liberal freedom to choose what to wear; and this even though she would be perfectly at liberty to appear in court (albeit doubtless against defence counsel's advice) with green hair, or a nose ring, or in the costume of a Jedi knight (having surrendered her lightsabre to security). The discriminating factor is that *we expect to see people's faces in court*. More specifically, it is the firm expectation of our legal trial process that the faces of all of the courtroom participants – judge, jurors, lawyers and witnesses, as well as the

[100] For a modern restatement, see Andrew von Hirsch, 'Extending the Harm Principle: "Remote" Harms and Fair Imputation' in A P Simester and A T H Smith (eds), *Harm and Culpability* (OUP, 1996).

[101] Perhaps the accused is suffering from some kind of delusion or phobia (which would have to be consistent with legal fitness to plead for any trial to proceed).

[102] This was achieved in *R v D (R)* by having a female police officer confirm the accused's identity in private during a short adjournment.

accused – will be visible, both to the court (including the fact-finder) and to the public.

If we inquire further why it is that our inherited trial procedures invest such institutional capital in face-to-face encounters, we would doubtless find that the story is long, complicated and, in several chapters, obscure and contested. We would certainly discover that it cannot be told only within the confines of and restricted to the intellectual resources of liberal political theory. Some of the reasons why 'face' is so important in criminal trials relate to broader social conventions and cultural styles supplying readymade 'scripts' for meaningful human interaction. Not for nothing do we unselfconsciously refer to 'saving face' or 'losing face', extol the virtues of dealing face-to-face, summon the courage to face our demons, or rail at faceless bureaucrats. These commonplace expressions are symptomatic of deeply held convictions about how we should assess the character and behaviour of other people, how we should present ourselves to the world so that favourable impressions of us may be formed, and how social bonds of mutual trust can be cultivated as a basis for on-going cooperation in myriad spheres, dealings and relationships across all walks of life. Human (self-) recognition in the 'face' of the Other has been characterised as the generative precondition of all ethical conduct.[103] If that seems extravagant as a metaethical claim, few in the West would deny the importance of 'showing your face' if you want your interests to count, or of showing *by* your face that you mean business and should be taken seriously. Face up, and face facts: the human face, in our culture, is a loquacious site of personal expression and social communication (and those who are incapable of reading faces consequently incur the penalties of being socially maladroit).

Overlaid on these deeply embedded psycho-social conventions are additional institutional investments peculiar to criminal proceedings. An intriguing feature of these supervening institutional practices and expectations is that they tend to be quite specific and even idiosyncratic to particular legal cultures and procedural traditions. Over time, working legal systems have improvised their own distinctive variations on the shared western cultural investment in facial recognition. Moreover, these concretised institutional forms typically become freighted and infused with further layers of meaning, so that they end up standing for more – possibly, a great deal more – than their instrumental function or formal institutional history might suggest to the uninitiated. Consider Magna Carta's impact on the development of English criminal adjudication. One cannot begin to grasp its contemporary significance either from the (arcane) wording of the document itself or even from detailed historical knowledge of its political origins or formal

[103] A thought attributed to Emmanuel Lévinas by Zygmunt Bauman, *Postmodern Ethics* (Blackwell, 1993) 73–75, who elucidates: '[c]onfronting the Other not as a person (*persona*: the mask worn to signify the role played …), but as the *face*, is already the act of transcendence …. Responsibility conjures up the Face I face, but it also creates me as moral self … the only foundation morality can have.'

juridical status.[104] Invocations of 'Magna Carta' today operate as legal-cultural shorthand for a richly articulated common law narrative. This ramified juridical tradition encodes a set of institutional values that are grasped by insiders at a pre-theoretical, semi-conscious, partly affective level which often seems to pre-empt any need for further (self)explanation, let alone elaborated normative rationalisations. The institutional work performed by such legal-cultural signifiers might be characterised as chiefly 'symbolic' or the deployment of 'legal fictions', though neither term really does justice to the complexity, subtlety or importance of their contribution to the practical administration of criminal justice. Their significance is all the greater because the circulation of legal-cultural signifiers is not confined within professional legal circles. Many of these cultural narratives also exert powerful holds on the popular imagination and thereby come to play a pivotal role in maintaining social trust and popular respect for law, which are in turn vital sociological ingredients in the practical efficacy of law and law enforcement and the sheet-anchor of their normative legitimacy.

Magna Carta is anything but a garden-variety piece of English legal history, but the methodological lesson is, I suggest, broadly generalisable. English criminal procedure law encompasses a host of these legal-cultural signifiers, and some of them have been enormously influential in generating and sustaining our procedural traditions. More elaborated 'thick description' of criminal adjudication is postponed to Chapter 3. In brief, the significance of observing a defendant's face during a criminal trial is likely to be informed by some or all of the following ten institutional variables (over and above the broader considerations of political morality that have already been discussed): (i) local conceptions of 'public trial' and its implications for public 'accessibility' (of various kinds) to the accused's person, image and identity; (ii) the extent to which[105] demeanour in general, and facial expression in particular, is regarded as indicative of reliability and/or veracity, both by legal professionals and by the community at large; (iii) the extent to which oral evidence at trial is regarded as a primary evidential source, or merely as an incidental supplement to documentary proofs of one kind or another; (iv) the extent to which the accused is regarded as an eligible (and important) source of relevant evidential information, and the terms

[104] Also see Lord Irvine of Lairg, 'The Spirit of Magna Carta Continues to Resonate in Modern Law' (2003) 119 *Law Quarterly Review* 227. Strictly speaking, most provisions of Magna Carta have been repealed: see *City of London Corporation v Samede* [2012] EWCA Civ 160, [30]. It is nonetheless regularly invoked in legal judgments as a source of fundamental legal principle, traditional institutional values and judicial cultural authority. Recently, see, eg, *R (Lumba) v Home Secretary* [2012] 1 AC 245, [2011] UKSC 12, [219], per Lord Collins JSC (quoting 'no free man shall be seized, or imprisoned … except … by the law of the land'); *R (AA) v Home Secretary* [2012] EWCA Civ 1383, [21] ('[t]he importance attributed to personal freedom can be traced back at least to *Magna Carta*'); *R (McAuley) v Crown Court at Coventry* [2012] 1 WLR 2766, [2012] EWHC 860 (Admin), [25] ('a principle of the common law as old as Magna Carta that justice delayed is justice denied'); *Frank Cook v Telegraph Media Group* [2011] EWHC 763 (QB), [98] (quoting Blackstone's invocation of Magna Carta as the basis for jury trial).

[105] Here and following, 'if at all' should be taken as read.

on which the accused is permitted – or required[106] – to furnish information, in the form of sworn testimony or otherwise, at trial; (v) the extent to which the accused's reactions and demeanour throughout the trial process are regarded as a legitimate (and important) source of evidential information to which fact-finders should have access (in most cases); (vi) the extent to which effective cross-examination may be hampered if the accused's face cannot be seen, coupled with prevailing institutional understandings of the significance of cross-examination in a criminal trial; (vii) the relationship of party cross-examination to other institutional means of verifying or testing evidential information in criminal trial proceedings, which in turn is partly a function of (viii), the extent to which a trial, or criminal prosecutions viewed in their entirety, are 'adversarial' rather than 'inquisitorial'; (ix) the composition of the fact-finder – individual or collegiate? lay, professional or mixed panel? – coupled with prevailing institutional beliefs about the chosen fact-finder's abilities and limitations in accessing or processing particular kinds of evidential information; and (x) local conceptions of procedural fairness, and the relationship between procedural fairness and accurate fact-finding in comprehensive normative (more or less fully jurisprudentially articulated and legally institutionalised) conceptions of legitimate criminal adjudication.

This roster of considerations bearing on the institutional significance of 'face' in criminal trials may not be exhaustive. In fact, it would probably prove impossible to produce any definitive list of such factors for many prominent features of legal institutional practices precisely because choices about what to include on the list, as well as their classification and relative priority, themselves reflect distinctive aspects of procedural tradition on which modern legal systems diverge, sometimes radically, and not merely in incidental matters of local colour and custom such as judicial costume or architectural preferences in courthouse construction. I hope, nonetheless, to have said enough to vindicate the methodological conclusion that urgent and highly consequential choices in the design and operation of criminal trial proceedings cannot be settled merely by appealing to 'liberal political morality'. This argument does not imply any failure of liberal theorising on its own terms. Whilst liberal states should certainly strive to ensure that key public institutions such as criminal adjudication function in a manner consistent with fundamental liberal principles, aspects of criminal law's institutional architecture and practical implementation can be fully understood, and some difficult operational questions satisfactorily answered, only in the light

[106] Of course, the accused is not literally compelled to testify in modern legal proceedings. However, even legal systems which proclaim full adherence to the privilege against self-incrimination may place considerable social and moral pressure on the accused to speak (as continental legal systems are said to do), or alternatively treat silence as a partial admission by conduct in some situations (as English law does, pursuant to the Criminal Justice and Public Order Act 1994, ss 34–38). See Andrew L-T Choo, *The Privilege Against Self-Incrimination and Criminal Justice* (Hart Publishing, 2013); *Roberts and Zuckerman's Criminal Evidence*, ch 13.

of detailed knowledge of local procedural history and its contemporary reception and status in modern legal cultures. Liberal states might well give different answers to important procedural questions without necessarily jeopardising their liberal credentials, and for reasons that liberal political morality, unsupplemented, cannot supply.

V. From Liberal Criminal Law Theory to Cosmopolitan Criminal Jurisprudence

This essay set out to encourage more sustained reflection and provoke further debate on the liberal presuppositions of contemporary Anglo-American Criminal Law Theory. Liberal theorists, prominently including Andreas von Hirsch, have conceptualised and elucidated criminal law doctrine in ways which, avowedly or implicitly, closely cohere with liberal political morality. Section III of this essay endeavoured to show how great swathes of contemporary Anglo-American criminal law (including legislative principles of criminalisation, taxonomies of criminal offences and defences, principles of attribution, and theories of culpability) might be reconstructed as institutional derivations of a plausible conception of liberal political morality, such as the model of liberalism expounded in miniaturised bonsai form in section II. But coherence is not isomorphic with normative justification. Section IV went on to suggest that liberal political theory does not explain or justify as much of modern criminal law as might commonly be supposed. Two kinds of methodological limitation were identified: *incompleteness*, where liberal theorising does not reach foundational questions of (for example) agency, criminal wrongdoing or retributive justice; and *indeterminacy*, where intensely practical issues, such as whether female muslim defendants should be permitted to appear veiled in court, are addressed but ultimately left unresolved by appeals to liberal political morality. When they find themselves in these uncharted or dimly lit theoretical waters, criminal law theorists – and criminal justice policymakers and practitioners no less – must seek further and better illumination from normative supplements to liberal political theory.

Liberals, I have been at pains to stress, should not be demoralised by the deflationary implications of this argument for liberal political theory. The need for liberal criminal law theorists to draw on non-liberal intellectual resources hardly commits them to *illiberal* laws, policies or practices. Nor is liberal theory neutered as a source of critical commentary on contemporary criminal justice policy, especially when senior officials and policymakers often betray an uneven commitment to (or tenuous grasp of) liberal traditions in criminal law.

The implications of the argument for non-liberals seem especially significant, however, since the condition of legality in our time is increasingly cosmopolitan. Modern law is simultaneously international, supra-national and transnational, as well as regional, domestic and local. It travels around the globe and pings across the internet, freely crossing national borders and bestriding traditional jurisdictional boundaries.[107] It is moulded into novel juridical institutions, normative configurations, regimes of governance and styles of regulation. Cosmopolitan law is a creature of multi-layered comparative jurisprudence and many-sided transnational judicial conversations.[108] Its penal dimensions have been fostered by a phalanx of interlocking institutional innovations, notably including the post-1945 framework of international human rights (prominently featuring the right to a fair trial), the burgeoning field of International Criminal Law, an emergent EU criminal law and policy, and the historic creation of a permanent International Criminal Court.[109] Although law has always to some extent crossed jurisdictional boundaries and produced institutional hybrids, contemporary cosmopolitan criminal jurisprudence is distinguished by the frequency, pace, intensity, complexity and global reach of its activities, ambitions and effects. Mirroring the broader processes of globalisation of which it forms an integral part, the novelty of legal cosmopolitanism lies in our distinctively twenty-first-century experiences of it.

To characterise a law or policy as 'liberal' is not necessarily to recommend it to the global constituency of state and non-state actors today engaged in the co-construction of cosmopolitan criminal jurisprudence. Whilst liberals are primed to find liberal criminal laws and policies congenial, there are many other significant elements within the international community, including numerous non-democratic and some theocratic polities, for whom liberalism is associated (fairly or not) with western bias and aggression, capitalist greed, social injustice, neo-colonialism, racism, militant Christianity, Islamophobia or moral degeneracy. Liberal criminal law would be a 'hard sell' to these hardboiled sceptics, some of whom (the BRICs, Turkey, Egypt, Israel, Pakistan, Nigeria, Indonesia, Iran, the Arab League …) are, or could be, important strategic partners in the cosmopolitan development of criminal law. Of course, merely trying to conceal or sugar-coat the liberal foundations of criminal law as an exercise in salesmanship or propaganda would be self-defeating from a normative point of view (even on the unlikely supposition that sceptical audiences could actually be fooled). If the argument advanced in this essay is broadly correct, however, there is no need for bad faith or self-deception. The criminal laws endorsed by liberals are not necessarily *liberal criminal laws*, in the sense of finding their direct or exclusive normative grounding

[107] Neil Boister, *An Introduction to Transnational Criminal Law* (OUP, 2012); William Twining, *Globalisation and Legal Scholarship* (Wolf Legal Publishers, 2011); Andrew Halpin and Volker Roeben (eds), *Theorising the Global Legal Order* (Hart Publishing, 2009).

[108] Anne-Marie Slaughter, 'A Global Community of Courts' (2003) 44 *Harvard International Law Journal* 191; Christopher McCrudden, 'A Common Law of Human Rights? Transnational Judicial Conversations on Constitutional Rights' (2000) 20 *Oxford Journal of Legal Studies* 499; Paul Roberts, 'Normative Evolution in Evidentiary Exclusion: Coercion, Deception and the Right to a Fair Trial' in Paul Roberts and Jill Hunter (eds), *Criminal Evidence and Human Rights* (Hart Publishing, 2012).

[109] Antonio Cassese, Paola Gaeta et al, *Cassese's International Criminal Law*, 3rd edn (OUP, 2013); Robert Cryer, Hakan Friman, Darryl Robinson and Elizabeth Wilmshurst, *An Introduction to International Criminal Law and Procedure*, 2nd edn (CUP, 2010).

in liberal political morality. Comprehensive justificatory theories of criminal law are obliged to fill in the gaps in (liberal, or any other) political theory by drawing on supplementary normative resources and incorporating significant features of local institutional architecture, legal culture and procedural tradition.

The benefits of reorganising ideas and correctly classifying arguments are not merely theoretical. There are also instrumental payoffs. Clarifying the philosophical pedigree of penal law and practice might spur the development of a robust and ethically substantial[110] overlapping consensus fixing the core requirements of cosmopolitan criminal law. It should also reinforce the normative and epistemological basis for recognising[111] criminal injustices wherever they occur in the world and whomever might be responsible. These are amongst the urgent tasks for an emerging cosmopolitan criminal jurisprudence whose rich intellectual resources assuredly encompass, but are not confined or exhausted by, liberal criminal law theory.

[110] Implying substantively thicker moral agreement than the merely political (albeit principled) overlapping consensus envisaged by Rawls as applying to global justice generally: John Rawls, *The Law of Peoples*, revsd edn (Harvard University Press, 2001); John Rawls, *Political Liberalism* (New York, Columbia University Press, 1993), Lecture IV. Whereas Rawls' account of global political justice is a *general* normative theory of international relations, ethically substantive overlapping consensus in criminal law could be particularistic, piecemeal and (partly) motivated by pragmatism.

[111] Recognition being a necessary precursor to criticism or remedial intervention. Whether in any given scenario the one should lead to either of the others is, of course, a complicated and contentious matter.

3

Conceptually Wrong!

BioNote: This essay was written as a contribution to a *festschrift* for G R (Bob) Sullivan,[1] following retirement from his UCL chair and transition to emeritus professor. It is reproduced here under its original title, which is entirely apt but also susceptible to uncharitable interpretations that were neither intended nor appropriate for the occasion. Sullivan's renown was cemented by his textbook (coauthored with Andrew Simester) on *Criminal Law: Theory and Doctrine*, originally published in 2000[2] and now in its eighth edition under the stewardship of a refreshed editorial team.[3] Fraud, corporate law and dishonesty offences comprise one longstanding cluster of topical expertise. However, Bob Sullivan is much more than a technical expert on the substantive criminal law. He is also a practical philosopher, an original member of the new wave of UK-based criminal law theorists active from the early 1990s,[4] and an exemplary exponent of what I call criminal jurisprudence. Sullivan set out to interrogate 'the enormous gap between the normative aspirations of a large part of [liberal] criminal law scholarship and the reality of criminal law and punishment'.[5]

When I was taking my first baby steps as a law lecturer, Bob Sullivan was already a towering presence in British legal scholarship. I well remember meeting him at an SPTL[6] conference in the mid-1990s and was both amazed and flushed with pride by his praise for a book review I had recently published (not the von Hirsch review mentioned in the previous chapter).[7] Typically, Bob took an interest and was generous in his encouragement. I had originally taken up book reviewing as a way of obtaining expensive academic titles that, as a student, I couldn't afford to buy. These instrumental fringe benefits for academic networking were an unanticipated bonus. Only some time later did I come to appreciate the art of

[1] 'What Does a Conceptual Argument Prove? Sullivan's Presumptive Conduct on Criminal Trial' in A P Simester (ed), *Modern Criminal Law: Essays in Honour of GR Sullivan* (Hart Publishing, 2024).

[2] A P Simester and G R Sullivan, *Criminal Law: Theory and Doctrine* (Hart Publishing, 2000).

[3] John J Child, A P Simester, John R Spencer, Findlay Stark and Graham J Virgo, *Simester and Sullivan's Criminal Law: Theory and Doctrine*, 8th edn (Hart Publishing, 2022).

[4] G R Sullivan, 'Making Excuses' in A P Simester and A T H Smith (eds), *Harm and Culpability* (OUP, 1996).

[5] G R Sullivan and Ian Dennis, 'Seeking Security: An Introduction' in G R Sullivan and Ian Dennis (eds), *Seeking Security: Pre-empting the Commission of Criminal Harms* (Hart Publishing, 2012) 2.

[6] Society of the Public Teachers of Law, since rebranded as the Society of Legal Scholars.

[7] [1994] *Criminal Law Review* 393–394, reviewing Michael Moore, *Act and Crime: The Philosophy of Action and its Implications for Criminal Law* (OUP, 1993).

reviewing, and academic criticism more generally, as a distinctive literary genre with its own techniques and qualities. Book reviewing is never going to be the apogee of legal scholarship, but it does claim a distinctive place in the landscape of academic legal literature, a diverse and multi-faceted publishing ecosystem that would be impoverished were the art of good criticism to wither on the vine.

Bob Sullivan's publications are wide-ranging and originally conceived, addressing topics beyond the standard criminal law canon[8] and posing jurisprudential questions that would never have occurred to most thinkers.[9] Bob later told me that he often just wrote about what he found fascinating: an excellent piece of advice for any aspiring academic, and a model of curiosity-driven scholarship all the more inspiring and relevant today in institutions increasingly incapable of allowing proper time for it (though still styling themselves 'universities'). Impertinent questions concerning institutional capacity to support work in criminal jurisprudence and legal scholarship generally will be taken up in this book's concluding chapter. Resisting the temptation to digress, let us return to our principal theme of inspiring criminal jurisprudence.

I. Bob Sullivan's Jurisprudential Problem

One intriguing problem imaginatively addressed by Bob Sullivan is located on the cusp of substantive criminal law and criminal procedure. This is exactly the kind of jurisprudential problem calculated to capture my attention. In a series of overlapping articles and essays, Sullivan develops an avowedly 'conceptual' argument designed to show that criminal trials are (conceptually) bound to satisfy certain prescriptive criteria. Absent particular constitutive features, institutional arrangements purporting to be criminal trials lack authenticity. They are only faking, simulacra, going through the motions, pale imitations of the real thing. To call these deficient institutional arrangements 'criminal trials' (as they claim for themselves) is a 'category error'. The type of argument advanced by Sullivan is emphatically *conceptual*, not normative or (merely) semantic. Definitional stipulation, notoriously,[10] does not settle any controversy concerning the nature of the world or human affairs: you can call a cat a fish if that floats your boat, but it still won't swim underwater. Conceptual arguments succeed for our purposes only if they carry robust theoretical or practical implications – and Sullivan wants both for his account of criminal trials.

As a general methodological predicate, I am wary of conceptual arguments. They often take a dogmatically 'conceptualist' turn, by which I mean that they

[8] See, eg, G R Sullivan, 'Ministering Death' (1997) 17 *Oxford Journal of Legal Studies* 123.

[9] One memorable illustration is G R Sullivan and C J Warbrick, 'Territoriality, Theft and *Atakpu*' [1994] *Criminal Law Review* 650.

[10] Ian Hacking, *The Social Construction of What?* (Harvard University Press, 1999); Susan Haack, *Manifesto of A Passionate Moderate* (University of Chicago Press, 1998).

illegitimately purport to derive normative (political morality) conclusions by logical derivation from (merely) conceptual analysis. 'Conceptualist argument' is my term designating (conceptually) invalid arguments, a species of fallacious reasoning. Normative (political morality) conclusions can generally be derived only through normative (political morality) argument and reasoning. Conceptual analysis, by contrast, is a tool for *analytical* inquiry and argumentation. Analytical results may be interesting and important. They contribute to the development and clarification of concepts. *Conceptualist* reasoning, however, involves a fundamental (not necessarily *obvious*) methodological error, the fallacy of purporting to derive normative conclusions from conceptual analysis. Rather than settling normative disputes, conceptual analysis typically only repackages them. The fallacy lies in thinking or claiming that a perfectly sound analytical tool is capable of performing a normative job for which it is unsuitable, like trying to drive nails with a saw or cut planks with a hammer.

Does Sullivan's account demonstrate, as he contends, that certain forms of criminal adjudication are, simply, categorically, *conceptually* wrong? Or is Sullivan's position redolent of a more general form of fallacious *conceptualist* argumentation? Section II of this essay first summarises Sullivan's core thesis, which extrapolates claims about criminal procedure from a novel conception of the conceptual limits of substantive criminal law specifically indexed to 'conduct'. This recapitulation identifies significant gaps and pressure points in Sullivan's argument, motivating Section III's excursion into the conceptual heartlands and definitional extremities of 'criminal trial'. With the benefit of back-to-basics conceptual refurbishment, Section IV draws out some practical implications of conceptual argumentation. It examines the constraints on legitimately criminalisable conduct asserted by Sullivan and reassesses their suggested implications for English law's presumption of innocence. The essay concludes by burnishing the wisdom of an old philosophical truism about seeking answers to difficult questions: the pilgrimage is often more enlightening than any ultimate revelation.

II. A Conceptual(ist) Argument

Sullivan presents the most fully elucidated version of his conceptual argument in an essay titled 'Conduct and Proof of Conduct'[11] proposing 'two fundamental conditions … prerequisite for any criminal conviction'.[12] Without conduct and proof of conduct, Sullivan insists, there can be no legitimate attribution of

[11] G R Sullivan, 'Conduct and Proof of Conduct – Two Fundamental Conditions for the Imposition of Criminal Liability' in Kaiyan H Kaikobad and Michael Bohlander (eds), *International Law and Power – Perspectives on Legal Order and Justice: Essays in Honour of Colin Warbrick* (Martinus Nijhoff, 2009) 235.

[12] ibid.

responsibility for criminal wrongs; and absent responsibility, criminal liability is 'conceptually untenable'.[13] Tempted by the prospect of cheap and easy fixes for difficult social problems, politicians and policymakers too readily invoke criminal law for tasks that would be better discharged by other, less coercive and condemnatory regulatory techniques or through positive incentives, public information campaigns and moral suasion. There is consequently a modern 'crisis of over-criminalisation',[14] extending criminal prescriptions and punishments into areas of life where they have no business to be at all or with such intensity. Legislative mission-creep in proliferating criminal prohibitions is not the only culprit. Penal excess is also the inevitable implication, as Sullivan has prominently argued,[15] of interpreting general doctrines of criminal liability to restrict or water down *mens rea* requirements, multiply forms of inchoate liability, and expand liability for accomplices, accessories and conspirators.

Sullivan depicts what is 'essential if the criminal law is to constitute a distinctive domain distinguishable from other forms of coercion that a state may deploy against its citizens'.[16] He is at pains to stress that his two conditions are merely threshold criteria for the legitimacy of criminal conviction: they do not furnish a comprehensive account of normative adequacy or justification. Thus, 'compliance with these two conditions is compatible with a harsh and human rights insensitive criminal law'[17] susceptible to normative criticism on those or other grounds. What the conceptual argument lacks in normative extension, however, is more than compensated by its methodological primacy and purchase. Criminal convictions violating either of the two conditions perpetrate a fundamental 'category error'.[18] They involve an abuse of conceptual language: 'A criminal trial properly so called requires some issue relating to responsibility to be resolved, otherwise the very language and process of the trial rings false'.[19] Criminal convictions obtained in disregard of the two complementary responsibility conditions are not merely problematic or unjustified in terms of institutional political morality. We are invited to regard them as penal abominations, categorically illegitimate, conceptually wrong. These are powerful claims with intuitive plausibility. Sullivan is building on the compelling thought, elucidated by many contemporary jurists and philosophers,[20] that penal censure is a distinctive form of

[13] ibid.

[14] J Chalmers and Fiona Leverick, 'Tracking the Creation of Criminal Offences' [2013] *Criminal Law Review* 543, 560. Also see, eg, Douglas Husak, *Overcriminalization: The Limits of the Criminal Law* (OUP, 2008); Andrew Ashworth, 'Is the Criminal Law A Lost Cause?' (2000) 116 *Law Quarterly Review* 225.

[15] G R Sullivan, 'Wrongs and Responsibility for Wrongs in Crime and Tort' in Matthew Dyson (ed), *Unravelling Tort and Crime* (CUP, 2014); G R Sullivan and Ian Dennis (eds), *Seeking Security: Pre-Empting the Commission of Criminal Harms* (Hart Publishing, 2012).

[16] Sullivan (n 11) 235.

[17] ibid.

[18] ibid 249.

[19] ibid 242.

[20] Prominently including Andrew von Hirsch, *Censure and Sanctions* (OUP, 1993); R A Duff, *Punishment, Communication, and Community* (OUP, 2001); A P Simester and Andrew von Hirsch, *Crimes, Harms and Wrongs* (Hart Publishing, 2011).

regulation and that this modality implies certain normative and practical constraints on its appropriate uses. Sledgehammers should not be employed to crack nuts – or heads.[21] From this point of convergence, penal theorists divide on the contentious issues of what, exactly, those constraints are, and what – if any – consequences should flow from failing to observe them in any institutional context or on any particular occasion.

Sullivan's first constraint addresses substantive criteria of criminal liability. His conduct condition embraces both acts and omissions and, with a little bit of further stretching, can be made to accommodate many status offences. Sullivan's second, procedural constraint is concerned with *proving* conduct of the required sort in a (contested) criminal trial. Crucially, Sullivan regards these two constraints as intimately related. Substantively, the imposition of criminal censure and punishment must respect 'the "no liability without responsibility" condition'.[22] The proof condition is the procedural counterpart of the substantive condition. From the foundational premiss that 'imposition of criminal liability in the absence of anything done or omitted by D defies the most basic assumptions of the criminal law',[23] Sullivan infers the secondary condition that legitimate criminal convictions demand proof of whatever conduct is proscribed:[24]

> What is necessary is that a finding based at least on the balance of probabilities be made against D in respect of the conduct requirement. If such a finding is not a prerequisite for a conviction, in substance any conduct requirement will be negated. A legislature cannot coherently enact an offence requiring conduct yet waive any need for proof of that conduct.

And for the avoidance of any residual doubt about the methodological status and ambitions of the argument, Sullivan reiterates that 'the condition is conceptual. The state cannot logically set down the actus reus of an offence whilst waiving the need for proof that D's conduct had brought about the actus reus.'[25]

In the first part of 'Conduct and Proof of Conduct', Sullivan expounds his conduct condition and diagnoses its dilution in offences of strict liability. This leads into a discussion of the presumption of innocence and its doctrinal status under Article 6(2) of the ECHR. Sullivan is disappointed that English courts have resisted the argument that Article 6(2) should bite on substantive criteria

[21] '[A]s regulatory tools go, the criminal law is a sledgehammer … and its judgments of the accused have a symbolic significance that civil judgments lack. They condemn not merely the defendant's ϕing, but *the defendant for ϕing*': A P Simester, *Fundamentals of Criminal Law* (OUP, 2021) 6.

[22] G R Sullivan, 'Parents and their Truanting Children: An English Lesson in Liability without Responsibility' (2010) 12 *Otago Law Review* 285, 298.

[23] Sullivan (n 11) 238.

[24] ibid. Note that proof 'at least on the balance of probabilities' (correctly) tracks the minimal epistemic threshold for rational belief, and (appropriately) states only an institutional threshold, not an ideal.

[25] ibid. Further underlined ibid, 245: 'we are making a conceptual argument not an argument based on justice'.

of criminal liability. He suggests that 'engagement with the concept of innocence should raise a query whether the issue of guilt and innocence is in any real sense implicated if liability for a state of affairs can be imposed in the absence of proof of any act or omission falling within the control of the defendant'.[26] The doctrinal implication is that '[g]uilt imposed without responsibility should have been castigated as a breach of Article 6(2)':[27]

> [I]f the process of proof makes no connection with anything done or not done by D within the competence of his agency, he is in a very real sense uninvolved, a spectator to his own fate. We are confronted with the simulacrum of a trial, not the real thing. Such a fact finding process, by whatever name called, should be ruled incompatible with Article 6(1), if used to determine criminal guilt.

The second part of 'Conduct and Proof of Conduct' extends the argument, on the procedural side, to reverse onus clauses imposing probative burdens on the accused. The vital nexus between conduct and proof of conduct is reflected in 'a baseline where the presumption of innocence and the minimum conditions for the imposition of criminal liability meet'.[28] Sullivan argues that post-HRA 1998 jurisprudence[29] on the presumption of innocence has fallen into conceptual incoherence because courts have failed to appreciate the significance of his two conditions and their fateful combination:[30]

> [T]hese are formal constraints with no normative bite on the content of the prohibitory norms of the criminal law. An eccentric, despotic ruler could create a criminal offence consisting of stepping on the cracks between paving stones. What he could not do, faithful with a system of criminal law, is stipulate that anyone found walking the pavements falls under a reasonable suspicion of stepping on the cracks and will be convicted of the offence unless he can prove that he has not transgressed.

Sullivan concludes that English law has sinned in failing to 'insist on conduct as a predicate for criminal liability', but remains hopeful of some redemption

[26] ibid 243.

[27] ibid 243–44. This passage notably invokes Art 6(1), the general right to a fair trial. Within the Strasbourg system, '[t]he presumption of innocence is one of the elements of a fair criminal trial required by Article 6(1)': *Euro Wines Ltd v HM Revenue and Customs* [2018] EWCA Civ 46, [14]. Combining Art 6(1) and 6(2) indicates that Sullivan's central argument is directed to the concept of a (fair) trial. Any residual disagreement between us (explored in section IV, below) cannot (wholly) be attributable to competing conceptions of the presumption of innocence.

[28] Sullivan (n 11) 250.

[29] For critical surveys, see Paul Roberts, 'Criminal Procedure, the Presumption of Innocence and Judicial Reasoning under the Human Rights Act' in Helen Fenwick, Gavin Phillipson and Roger Masterman (eds), *Judicial Reasoning under the UK Human Rights Act* (CUP, 2007); David Hamer, 'The Presumption of Innocence and Reverse Burdens: A Balancing Act' (2007) 66 *Cambridge Law Journal* 143; Ian Dennis, 'Reverse Onuses and the Presumption of Innocence: In Search of Principle' [2005] *Criminal Law Review* 901; Andrew Stumer, *The Presumption of Innocence: Evidential and Human Rights Perspectives* (Hart Publishing, 2010).

[30] Sullivan (n 11) 250.

courtesy of the jurisprudential latitude afforded to UK judges by the Human Rights Act:[31]

> If the potential of Article 6 of the European Convention – fair trial and the presumption of innocence – were to be fully realised by the judiciary, all offences would be construed as requiring a conduct element and proof of the conduct element by the prosecution. This would improve the conceptual and to some extent the normative condition of English criminal law.

Surveying the potential impact of the ECHR on English criminal law more generally, Sullivan had previously argued that 'Article 6(2) should be interpreted to protect against the imposition of what may be regarded as the ultimate form of strict liability, a liability that may be imposed without proof of anything, either *actus reus* or *mens rea*.'[32] More particularly, 'mere proof that the defendant may be reasonably suspected of such [proscribed] conduct will not satisfy the presumption of innocence guaranteed by Article 6(2)'.[33]

Article 6(2) of the ECHR, in my view, gains no traction on the substantive criminal law. The Conventional presumption of innocence, I have consistently argued,[34] is procedural rather than substantive. This is a *jurisprudential* rather than a philosophical – much less conceptual – claim.[35] Of course, theorists may give the presumption of innocence a substantive spin, and many do.[36] All that is required, conceptually speaking, is to interpret 'innocence' as *moral* innocence, and then it is possible to say that any morally unjustified criminal law violates the presumption of innocence. Even if it is proved to the criminal standard that the accused committed the proscribed conduct with the requisite *mens rea*, if the offence itself is morally decrepit, the accused, though legally guilty, is morally innocent. Hence, conviction of an illegitimate criminal law breaches the presumption of innocence. More nuanced versions of the argument attempt to show that only a subset of encroachments on moral innocence infringes

[31] ibid 253. Does tacking on 'to some extent the normative' anticipate this essay's methodological critique? *Cf* Sullivan's clarifications that '[t]he responsibility condition is best understood as a conceptual/logical requirement but not without normative implications'; and 'when liability requires nothing in the way of positive conduct on the part of D, this formal requirement can only be satisfied by reading in a normative element': Sullivan (n 22) 299, 301.

[32] G R Sullivan, 'Strict Liability for Criminal Offences in England and Wales Following Incorporation into English Law of the European Convention on Human Rights' in A P Simester (ed), *Appraising Strict Liability* (OUP, 2005) 211.

[33] ibid 213.

[34] Paul Roberts, 'The Presumption of Innocence Brought Home? *Kebilene* Deconstructed' (2002) 118 *Law Quarterly Review* 41; Paul Roberts, 'Drug-Dealing and the Presumption of Innocence: The Human Rights Act (Almost) Bites' (2002) 6 *International Journal of Evidence & Proof* 17.

[35] Paul Roberts, 'Presumptuous or Pluralistic Presumptions of Innocence? Methodological Diagnosis towards Conceptual Reinvigoration' (2021) 198 *Synthese* 8901.

[36] See, eg, Patrick Tomlin, 'Extending the Golden Thread? Criminalisation and the Presumption of Innocence' (2013) 21 *Journal of Political Philosophy* 44; Victor Tadros and Stephen Tierney, 'The Presumption of Innocence and the Human Rights Act' (2004) 67 *Modern Law Review* 402.

the juridical presumption.[37] Sullivan's argument is distinctive, inasmuch as he rejects roving appeals to moral innocence,[38] and agrees with me that 'Article 6(2) has no bearing on the elements of offences or on the provision or denial of defences.'[39] Yet he also insists that '[i]f something short of proof of a fact such as establishing a "reasonable suspicion" suffices for criminal liability then, effectively, the prosecution is relieved of the burden of proof'[40] and Article 6(2) is thereby engaged.

It is important to appreciate how Sullivan's moderated thesis still endows Article 6(2) with jurisdiction over substantive criminal law doctrines, albeit on a narrower doctrinal ('conceptual') footing. An explicit reverse onus provision is properly classified as procedural and *might* breach Article 6(2),[41] but an offence element that (merely) 'effectively' relieves the prosecution of the burden of proof is a creature of substantive law, and the same objection could theoretically be posed to *any* aspect of 'strict liability' in substantive offence definitions or even in the specification of criminal law defences.[42] So Article 6(2) would still purport to arbitrate the scope of states parties' substantive criminal laws, ostensibly as a guardian of trial fairness, even on Sullivan's relatively moderate thesis. Once already on this substantive slope, it may be too late to discover just how slippery it could become under adverse environmental conditions. According to my *jurisprudential* analysis, it is necessary to take relevant institutional facts more seriously, prominently including the following four: (1) criminal courts in England and Wales, the House of Lords[43] and – subsequently – the UK Supreme Court[44] have never materially deviated from the proposition that Article 6(2) ECHR is limited to procedural effects; (2) the European Court of Human Rights consistently endorses this view;[45] (3) there is nothing

[37] A notably more cautious restatement is advanced by Victor Tadros, 'The Ideal of the Presumption of Innocence' (2014) 8 *Criminal Law and Philosophy* 449.

[38] Thus, Sullivan rejects the argument advanced by Tadros and Tierney: Sullivan (n 32) 211.

[39] ibid 217.

[40] ibid.

[41] Establishing that Art 6(2) is engaged is only the first analytical step: *Salabiaku v France* (1991) 13 EHRR 379, [28]; *Sheldrake* v *DPP; Attorney General's Reference (No 4 of 2002)* [2005] 1 AC 264, [2004] UKHL 43.

[42] One implication would appear to be that English law's refusal to extend the defence of duress to murder breaches Art 6(2). For extended elucidation and critique of this 'functionalist' manoeuvre, see Paul Roberts, 'Strict Liability and the Presumption of Innocence: An Exposé of Functionalist Assumptions' in A P Simester (ed), *Appraising Strict Liability* (OUP, 2005).

[43] *R v G* [2009] 1 AC 92, [2008] UKHL 37.

[44] *R (Hallam) v Secretary of State for Justice* [2020] AC 279, [2019] UKSC 2; *Serious Organised Crime Agency v Gale* [2011] 1 WLR 2760, [2011] UKSC 49.

[45] See, eg, *Kangers* v *Latvia* (2020) 70 EHRR 5, [50]: 'Article 6(2) safeguards the right to be presumed innocent until proved guilty according to law. Viewed as a procedural guarantee in the context of a criminal trial itself, the presumption of innocence imposes requirements in respect of, inter alia, the burden of proof; legal presumptions of fact and law; the privilege against self-incrimination; pre-trial publicity; and premature expressions, by the trial court or by other public officials, of a defendant's guilt'; *G v United Kingdom* (2011) 53 EHRR SE25, [26]–[27]: 'It is not the Court's role under art.6(1) or (2) to dictate the content of domestic criminal law, including whether or not a blameworthy state of mind should be one of the elements of the offence or whether there should be any particular defence available to the accused'.

in the *traveaux preparatoire*,[46] the structure of the Convention, or the 'evolutive' teleology of Article 6(2) jurisprudence to suggest a broader jurisdiction; and (4) the ECtHR has no institutional capacity, competence, or desire to shoulder the burden of reviewing the entirety of states parties' substantive criminal laws for compliance with Article 6(2).

For the time being at least, the scope of Article 6(2)'s presumption of innocence appears fairly well-settled in Strasbourg jurisprudence and in English law on reverse onus clauses.[47] Theoretical debates meanwhile rumble on without much tangible resolution.[48] Sullivan's imaginative resort to *conceptual* argument, expounding 'two fundamental conditions for the imposition of criminal liability', tantalises with the dual promise of theoretical progress and practical implications for fair trials jurisprudence. If the argument is, in my terms, conceptual*ist*, it will ultimately fail. But final judgement should be reserved pending more methodical appraisal. Focusing principally on Sullivan's second, procedural, 'proof of conduct' condition, it would be helpful to have a clearer picture of what a 'concept of the criminal trial' actually is, and what it does (and doesn't do), before attempting to assess any institutional extrapolations or practical consequences. To say that any given instance of institutional performance fails at a threshold conceptual level implies measurement against some cognisable criterion (or criteria) of success. What are the necessary and sufficient (constituent) conditions qualifying a trial *as* a trial? The next section accordingly takes up Sullivan's implicit challenge to develop a more fully theorised and articulated conceptual understanding of the criminal trial.

III. What's in a Concept of the Criminal Trial?

Conceptual comprehension, analysis and arguments relate to *concepts*. A concept is, roughly, an idea, notion or mental scaffolding for expanding, organising and sharpening thinking, reasoning or perception. As on building sites, so in philosophical and jurisprudential theorising, robust scaffolding can support more elaborate and impressive constructions. To be a *useful* idea to think with

[46] G Marston, 'The United Kingdom's Part in the Preparation of the European Convention on Human Rights, 1950' (1993) 42 *International & Comparative Law Quarterly* 796.

[47] Paul Roberts, *Roberts and Zuckerman's Criminal Evidence*, 3rd edn (OUP, 2022) ch 6. Article 6(2) has broader procedural applications generating their own controversies: see Liz Campbell, 'Criminal Labels, the European Convention on Human Rights and the Presumption of Innocence' (2013) 75 *Modern Law Review* 681.

[48] Generally, see Paul Roberts, 'Presumptuous or Pluralistic Presumptions of Innocence? A Methodological Diagnosis towards Conceptual Reinvigoration' (2021) 198 *Synthese* 8901; Federico Picinali, 'The Presumption of Innocence: A Deflationary Account' (2021) 84 *Modern Law Review* 708; Jackson Allen, 'Rethinking the Relationship between Reverse Burdens and the Presumption of Innocence' (2021) 25 *International Journal of Evidence & Proof* 115; Pamela R Ferguson, 'The Presumption of Innocence and its Role in the Criminal Process' (2016) 27 *Criminal Law Forum* 131; Richard L Lippke, *Taming the Presumption of Innocence* (OUP, 2016); R A Duff, 'Who Must Presume Whom to be Innocent of What?' (2013) 42 *Netherlands Journal of Legal Philosophy* 170.

or through, a concept should be functionally well-calibrated to the particular purpose or purposes it is designed or adapted to serve.[49] There are no 'innocent' concepts, devoid of purpose, just as there are no tools without intent.[50] A flint is just a rock until somebody employs it as a scraper. Idle musings or spontaneous mental activity are not concepts until the thinker fashions inchoate thoughts into tools for rational introspection, reflection, analysis, criticism, discourse and argumentation. Given their functional character, concepts cannot be appraised acontextually. Scraping tools are great for scraping but lousy writing implements and positively dangerous hair combs. It is therefore an elementary methodological error to rate concepts 'good' or 'bad' *tout court*. The inescapably evaluative character of concepts, indexed to their purpose(s), appears to extend even to the most basic concepts invoked by criminal law theorists (and philosophers generally), including agency and rationality.[51]

The goodness of concepts depends on their intended use. Does this constitutive intentionality imply that concepts cannot be objective or – worse – that concepts must be irremediably subjective and 'relativistic' in a pejorative sense? Not at all. Like all linguistic phenomena, concepts could not function in thought or communication unless they were objective, in the sense of having shared conventional meaning and reference. If you are tempted to think that the intentionality of concepts implies some kind of recursive subjectivity verging on solipsism, you are probably in the grip of the wrong concept of objectivity.[52] Contested concepts frequently require definitional clarification, but largely idiosyncratic definitions butter no parsnips in the philosophical kitchen. Unless we have a core agreed understanding of what a criminal trial is, for example, we will not be having any *discussion* about anything. Conceptual incontinence is a recipe for talking at cross-purposes. You say 'trial', I say 'schmile': let's call the whole thing froth.

What kind of concept of 'criminal trial' will serve the present inquiry (as a particular instance of criminal law theorising more generally)? Refined conceptual analysis builds on ordinary life experience and linguistic competence and can legitimately make theoretical assumptions, 'bracketing' issues that are either beside the present point or agreed[53] by participants in the discussion. Criminal trials are plainly organised social institutions of significant complexity, but they are not football matches, or general elections, or university lectures on

[49] Answers to the 'What?', 'Why?' and 'How?' of a concept constitute its 'Eternal Triangle': see Paul Roberts, 'Interdisciplinarity in Legal Research' in Mike McConville and Wing Hong Cui (eds), *Research Methods for Law*, 3rd edn (Edinburgh University Press, 2024). See further, Chapter 10.

[50] On the 'intentional stance' enabling us, for example, to make sense of the idea of non-human animals or even robots 'using tools', see Daniel C Dennett, *Intuition Pumps and Other Tools for Thinking* (Penguin, 2014).

[51] See, eg, Ralf Wedgwood, *The Value of Rationality* (OUP, 2017).

[52] For helpful conceptual clarifications, see Guy Axtell, *Objectivity* (Polity Press, 2016).

[53] Agreement could be *arguendo*, or from conviction. Either way, the methodological objective is to cut the contentious issue down to size and promote more focused investigation and debate.

criminal procedure. Criminal trials are a special kind of complex social institution. On a conventional understanding, crimes are public wrongs which disturb social peace, violate protected interests and offend public morality. Criminality consequently calls for appropriate official responses. With this very generalised thought,[54] richly embroidered by rival penal theories down the centuries, we begin to get a grip on the conceptual issue. Social conflict resolution must be integral to the concept of a criminal trial, inasmuch as trials are the contentious remedial mechanism of legal regulation more generally.[55] This is one reason why trial systems (as opposed to individual trials in every case[56]) prize finality so highly. The aim is to *resolve* conflicts, not merely to defer or displace them. Moreover, pacific dispute resolution claims for itself not merely instrumental efficacy but normative *legitimacy*. Social conflicts must be resolved *in the right way*, not any which way that arguably 'works'. Modern democratic governments assume the normative burden of answering for the legitimacy claims of their penal institutions. The manner in which criminal trials are themselves conducted is part – but only part – of the institutional machinery through which governments discharge this burden of public justification.

It is important not to confuse the concept of a criminal *trial* with the related, more capacious and pliable concept of criminal law. The animating purpose(s) and values of criminal law should be continuous with and, to some extent, reflected in criminal adjudication, minimally to avoid self-defeating institutional paralysis or normative incoherence. However, criminal law and criminal trials have distinctive normative structures, neither reducible to the other. If everybody always and reliably admitted their guilt,[57] the purpose(s) of criminal law (whatever they are thought to be) might conceivably be implemented without resorting to trials. Indeed, this is essentially the reality of the greater part of modern municipal criminal law, which achieves its aims (to the extent that it does) through a combination of ex ante prescription and *ex post facto*

[54] Although my way of putting it has an undeniably deontological flavour, utilitarians, welfare economists, and other consequentialists are accommodated, because theorists can define 'public wrong' according to their own normative preferences, in terms of 'harmful conduct', 'disutility', 'inefficiency', or whatever. Likewise, to the extent that nonliberal or authoritarian polities employ criminal adjudication as a distinct mode of social ordering, rather than as ideological camouflage for naked coercion etc., they do so to maintain social peace and in the name of legitimate government (as they see and claim it).

[55] For institutional and jurisprudential elaborations, see, eg, Neil MacCormick, *Institutions of Law: An Essay in Legal Theory* (OUP, 2007); Charles Nesson, 'The Evidence or the Event? On Judicial Proof and the Acceptability of Verdicts' (1985) 98 *Harvard Law Review* 1357; Lon L Fuller, 'The Forms and Limits of Adjudication' (1978) 92 *Harvard Law Review* 353 ('adjudication should be viewed as a form of social ordering, as a way in which the relations of men to one another are governed and regulated').

[56] *Cf* John D Jackson, 'Managing Uncertainty and Finality: The Function of the Criminal Trial in Legal Inquiry' in R A Duff, Lindsay Farmer, Sandra Marshall and Victor Tadros (eds), *The Trial on Trial Volume One: Truth and Due Process* (Hart Publishing, 2004).

[57] I am simplifying. There are actually multiple preconditions, including: the absence of official impropriety or error in the conduct of criminal investigations and prosecutions; adequate opportunities for victim participation; and social trust in authoritative pronouncements of guilt, untainted by coercion or improper influence.

managed guilty pleas.[58] Contested trials, when they occur, are *inherently* disputatious in some threshold sense. In the absence of any issue to be tried, there could not be any 'trial of the issue'. Although trials generally focus on factual disputes concerning who did what to whom on designated occasions, criminal trials also sometimes adjudicate social disputes and uncertainties about norms and their contextual applications. At the retail end of the administration of criminal justice, trials play a supplementary role in determining the scope of criminal wrongs and their relative gravity.

Two further conceptual refinements are largely self-evident: not all mechanisms of social conflict resolution are trials, and not all trials are criminal trials. The second contrast engages the familiar jurisprudential task of demarcating criminal law from other regulatory subsystems, including private law and non-criminal public law. Most legal scholars (including Sullivan) insist or assume that it is possible to differentiate criminal law and criminal trials[59] from other kinds of law and their associated trials (or other adjudicative mechanisms) in one or more ways that are both conceptually robust and normatively coherent. It is telling that expositors traditionally demarcated criminal law by ostensive reference to the laws applied by criminal courts, ie, they began with the tangible institutions of trials and court structures and worked back to the abstractions of substantive criminal law.[60] But I will say no more here about the historical priority of procedure over substance. The condemnatory character of criminal law is a quintessential characteristic on which contemporary theoretical constructions converge. The first, more macroscopic conceptual refinement merits closer examination. Further reflection on differentiating (criminal) trials from other forms of social dispute resolution will put us on the right track to identifying a core concept of criminal trial.

A. The Conceptual Core

In the general conceptual neighbourhood of criminal trials, we encounter a variety of conflict-resolution mechanisms that are not conventionally regarded as trials. Pertinent institutional arrangements include public inquiries, disciplinary tribunals, coronial inquests, and truth and reconciliation commissions. Such institutional mechanisms generally adopt an 'inquisitorial' method and style, but it cannot be their inquisitorialism (in the comparative lawyer's sense)[61] that places these mechanisms outside the trial concept.

[58] For context and critical appraisal, see Máximo Langer, Mike McConville and Luke Marsh (eds), *Research Handbook on Plea Bargaining and Criminal Justice* (Edward Elgar, 2024).

[59] See further, Roberts (n 47) §1.2.

[60] See, eg, Glanville Williams, 'The Definition of Crime' (1955) 8 *Current Legal Problems* 107; J C Smith and Brian Hogan, *Criminal Law*, 1st edn (Butterworths, 1965) ch 2.

[61] Models of 'adversarial' and 'inquisitorial' procedure are ideal-types with explanatory and cultural power but should not be taken *too* seriously. See further, Máximo Langer, 'The Long Shadow of the Adversarial and Inquisitorial Categories' in Markus D Dubber and Tatjana Hörnle (eds), *The Oxford Handbook of Criminal Law* (OUP, 2014); Paul Roberts, 'Comparative Criminal Justice Goes Global' (2008) 28 *Oxford Journal of Legal Studies* 369.

A conception of trials restricted to institutions adopting 'adversarial' procedures would push us in the direction of saying that criminal trials have existed only in the common law Anglosphere and its contemporary geopolitical extensions, which is implausibly exclusive. Even the most ardent Anglophiles should accept that criminal trials *exist* within the civilian juristic orbit, albeit (by their lights) in debased currency relative to the common law gold standard. Public inquiries, disciplinary tribunals, and the like are focused on fact-finding – discovering the truth about events of concern – and they adopt an essentially inquisitorial methodology because that is how rational inquiry proceeds, through the identification, organisation, analysis, testing and evaluation of evidence as a basis for inferential reasoning and conclusions.[62] But if these institutional arrangements are calibrated for fact-finding, does this undercut their presumptive classification as dispute-resolution mechanisms? Not at all. For one thing, criminal trials are also centrally concerned with fact-finding, and that epistemic ambition (obviously) does not prevent them from being criminal trials. We will return to this. More significantly for present purposes, institutional fact-finding is largely *in the service of* social conflict management and pacific dispute resolution, sensitive to legal entitlements and more comprehensive (substantive) schemes of justice.[63]

Public inquiries, tribunal hearings and coronial inquests are frequently followed by related criminal proceedings. But even when there is no criminal law sequel, inquiries, hearings and inquests are all, in part, prophylactic social measures that aim to interdict brewing or anticipated troubles and engineer remediation before they escalate into something (much) worse. Consider, for example, how the family of a deceased relative might react if there were no official inquiry into an, even minimally, suspicious death. Or imagine that the survivors of the Grenfell Tower fire[64] or the Manchester Arena bombing[65] (not to mention Bloody Sunday[66]) had been met with an official shrug of the shoulders and sincere wishes for better luck in the future. We don't need imagination to anticipate how people might react if lethal police force went unquestioned[67] or the criminality of particular officers threatened catastrophic loss of trust in the policing response:[68] we need

[62] Peter Tillers and David Schum, 'A Theory of Preliminary Fact Investigation' (1991) 24 *UC Davis Law Review* 931; D A Schum, 'Marshaling Thoughts and Evidence During Fact Investigation' (1999) 40 *South Texas Law Review* 401.

[63] To spell this out, pacific dispute resolution does not legitimately shore up social peace irrespective of the (in)justice of background social arrangements. That would be compatible with stable despotism and exploitation. Rather, the point is that any defensible scheme of justice will require pacific dispute resolution for its maintenance and prospective viability.

[64] Grenfell Tower Inquiry, www.grenfelltowerinquiry.org.uk/ (accessed 17 December 2025).

[65] Manchester Arena Inquiry, manchesterarenainquiry.org.uk/ (accessed 17 December 2025).

[66] The Bloody Sunday Inquiry, webarchive.nationalarchives.gov.uk/ukgwa/20101017060831/http://report.bloody-sunday-inquiry.org/index.html.

[67] D B Taylor, 'George Floyd Protests: A Timeline', *New York Times*, 5 November 2021 (noting that '[s]ince the death of Mr. Floyd, protests have erupted in at least 140 cities across the United States, and the National Guard has been activated in at least 21 states').

[68] E Graham-Harrison, 'Police Clash with Mourners at Sarah Everard Vigil in London', *The Observer*, 14 March 2021; H Siddique, 'Sarah Everard Vigil Report further Damages Trust in Met Chief, Say Activists' *The Guardian*, 1 July 2021.

only switch on the news. Less dramatically but far more routinely, non-criminal tribunals resolve disputes between neighbours, in the workplace, on family break-up, when commercial transactions turn sour, when consumers are dissatisfied, when interactions with professionals or public officials become contentious, and so on. The translation of human suffering, frustration and anger into social disruption is surely predictable (and understandable) unless mechanisms are put in place to communicate official recognition and concern, defuse immediate tensions and temptations to self-help, establish a reliable factual record of events (including refuting pernicious falsehoods), and – ideally – provide recompense or social security to victims (consistent with some defensible conception of justice). Jurisdictionally speaking, criminal adjudication is the ultimate non-negotiable[69] mechanism of social conflict resolution in peacetime,[70] but it is only (conceptually) the last in a phalanx of institutional arrangements deployed by modern democracies for maintaining civility and *ordre public*, safeguarding rights, and dispensing justice.

This discussion hints at another important role for concepts of 'trial' in modern jurisprudential and penal discourse. Critics of traditional or orthodox criminal trial practice frequently propose alternative dispute resolution mechanisms, explicitly *not* styled *trials*. Forms of conciliation, mediation, negotiation, reparation and restorative justice, for example, may be characterised as 'diversion' from trial or formal process.[71] Are all of these diversionary processes and mechanisms self-evidently not trials? There is surely room for debate. It seems pretty obvious that, say, restorative cautioning[72] and family mediation[73] are not trials. At the other end of the institutional spectrum, however, a victim-offender mediation or a sentencing circle[74] might easily be regarded as an adjunct to trial, or possibly even as a novel additional component of trials on the conventional model. A trial does not automatically cease to be a trial in consequence of any non-trivial[75] procedural innovation. The related concept of criminal adjudication may be useful here.

[69] Disposals in particular cases may be 'negotiated', by plea bargain or otherwise: see, eg, Nicholas Cowdery, 'Negotiating Justice with Integrity in New South Wales' in Jill Hunter et al (eds), *The Integrity of Criminal Process* (OUP, 2016). But this is a forced choice between limited alternatives, none of which might be especially palatable to defendants. Opting out entirely is never an option.

[70] Thus, prison represents the final terminus for 'clients' of social intervention, who cannot be refused entry or involuntarily referred on to other agencies not prepared to accept them.

[71] Gavin Dingwall and Christopher Harding, *Diversion in the Criminal Process* (Sweet & Maxwell, 1998).

[72] R Young and B Goold, 'Restorative Cautioning in Aylesbury – From Degrading to Reintegrative Shaming Ceremonies?' [1999] *Criminal Law Review* 126.

[73] Joe Hudson, Allison Morris, Gabrielle Maxwell and Burt Galaway, *Family Group Conferences: Perspectives on Policy and Practice* (Federation Press, 1996).

[74] Toby S Goldbach, 'Instrumentalizing the Expressive: Transplanting Sentencing Circles into the Canadian Criminal Trial' (2015) 25 *Transnational Law and Contemporary Problems* 61.

[75] Some procedural refinements are obviously de minimis. Trials would not cease to be trials if barristers and judges abandoned horsehair wigs. More interesting conceptual questions are posed by major or significant procedural reform. A tailless Manx cat is still a cat. What else would it need to lose or gain over evolutionary time to qualify as a new species?

Adjudication encompasses non-trial case disposals (ie, dispute resolution), including guilty pleas, as well as trial verdicts. Any criminal process resulting in a formal determination can plausibly be termed an adjudication, including non-judicial final outcomes such as formal cautions administered by police officers.[76] It makes more sense to me to describe criminal proceedings, from (say) charge to final disposal, as an adjudicative process rather than a 'criminal trial process'. Common lawyers tend to regard 'the trial' as a discrete event and hence can intelligibly refer to 'pre-trial process', 'pre-trial disclosure', 'pre-trial hearings' etc, as antecedent procedural phases or events. Civilians generally conceptualise 'trials' less dichotomously in formal procedural terms,[77] though perhaps share with common lawyers a narrower understanding of 'the trial' as the public courtroom stage of criminal adjudication. On one influential interpretation of the civilian principle of 'immediacy' (or 'orality'),[78] criminal convictions must be based only on evidence presented in a procedurally differentiated public trial. Still, I would not go so far as to say that somebody describing the entirety of criminal proceedings as 'criminal trial process' has made a conceptual error or lapsed into incoherence. To the extent that such usage is non-standard, it would be wise to press this interlocutor on what, exactly, they understand by 'criminal trial process' and why they are deploying that term in preference to any alternative. Is it really *trials* they are interested in, after all? Would a different concept (adjudication, process, proceedings …) not encapsulate their intent with greater perspicacity and precision? It is always advisable to check and coordinate conceptual definitions in any event. Sooner or later the point will be reached where a concept in play, in fair and transparent discussion, may fairly accommodate thicker (more inclusive) or thinner (more parsimonious) usage. Clarity of purpose, effective communication of one's intentions, and mutual understanding are then required to keep the conversation alive and productive, rather than appealing to the limits of conventional terminology in an effort to rule certain applications conceptually off-side and definitively out of bounds.[79]

We have proceeded on the basis that criminal trials comprise a subset of modern society's institutional machinery for pacific dispute resolution. One mark of progress in human civilisation is that conflict resolution through violence is no longer regarded as the default setting.[80] Let us add, as a second conceptual

[76] And, in Scotland, 'fiscal fines': P Duff, 'The Prosecutor Fine and Social Control: The Introduction of the Fiscal Fine to Scotland' (1993) 33 *British Journal of Criminology* 481.

[77] The European Court of Human Rights encountered no theoretical or conceptual difficulty in extending 'fair trial' rights to the entirety of criminal process: see, eg, *Teixeira de Castro v Portugal* (1998) 28 EHRR 101; *Salduz v Turkey* (2009) 49 EHRR 19 (GC). The text of Art 6 enumerates rights 'to be informed promptly, in a language which [the accused] understands and in detail, of the nature and cause of the accusation' and to 'adequate time and facilities for the preparation of his defence'.

[78] John D Jackson and Thomas Weigend, 'Witness Evidence in Pre-Trial and Trial Procedure' in Kai Ambos et al (eds), *Core Concepts in Criminal Law and Criminal Justice – Volume 2* (CUP, 2022) 260.

[79] The 'definitional stop' famously denounced by H L A Hart, *Punishment and Responsibility* (Clarendon Press, 1968) 5–6.

[80] *Cf* Emile Durkheim, 'Two Laws of Penal Evolution' (1973) 2 *Economy and Society* 285 (translating the French original published in 1900).

ingredient in the mix, that criminal trials must be epistemically[81] *serious*, that is, they must affirm and enact a threshold commitment to rationalism, evidence-based proof and the logic of inferential reasoning. Epistemological seriousness is not strictly mandated by the concept of a (criminal) trial. As we know from the common law's (pre)history, it is possible to have trial by battle, ordeal or ducking stool.[82] These procedures were designed as *tests* of some kind, and thus share a recognisable etymological root with modern-day criminal trials,[83] but their modus operandi is so far removed from our current understanding of criminal adjudication that it would be a misuse of language, and not merely a controversial extension, to describe them as 'trials' without further (historical) contextual explanation. Imagine that prosecuting and defence counsel turned up to court to be presented with duelling pistols or fencing foils. Or if the presiding judge were to unveil a roulette wheel or deal out cards for a round of poker. How about a penalty shootout? Although pretty much any game or contest of skill or chance could, in a sense, settle litigated issues by producing a 'result', sports and games are, precisely, not criminal trials; and this is so, irrespective of venue or participants' attire. Although social conventions change over time and are not necessarily determinative of linguistic reference, a post-Enlightenment conception of the criminal trial must be epistemically serious, or it is not a serious invocation or application of the concept.

This much is trite. Procedural scholars routinely invoke accurate fact-finding (or 'truth-seeking') as a pre-eminent concern and objective of criminal adjudication.[84] Even though the epistemic credentials of 'the rationalist tradition of evidence scholarship'[85] are sometimes probed and questioned,[86] nobody to my knowledge – certainly not Sullivan – is arguing for a reversion to

[81] A synonymous shortening of 'epistemologically' now widely employed in Anglophone Evidence scholarship.

[82] James B Thayer, *A Preliminary Treatise on Evidence at the Common Law* (Little, Brown & Co, 1898) ch 1; Malcolm Gaskill, 'Witchcraft and Evidence in Early Modern England' (2008) 198 *Past and Present* 33; Mirjan Damaška, 'Rational and Irrational Proof Revisited' (1997) 5 *Cardozo Journal of International and Comparative Law* 25.

[83] *OED* definitions of trial include: 'The action of testing or putting to the proof the fitness, truth, strength, or other quality of anything …'; 'A testing of qualifications, attainments, or progress; examination'; 'That which puts one to the test, esp. a painful test of one's endurance, patience, or faith; hence, affliction, trouble, misfortune'; 'A contest in which horses, dogs etc., are put through various tests and assessed on their performance'.

[84] See, eg, Thomas Weigend, 'Should We Search for the Truth, And Who Should Do It?' (2011) 36 *North Carolina Journal of International Law and Commercial Regulation* 389; Hock Lai Ho, *A Philosophy of Evidence Law – Justice in the Search for Truth* (OUP, 2008); Mirjan R Damaška, *The Faces of Justice and State Authority* (Yale University Press, 1986). The point may appear self-evident to non-lawyers: *cf* Larry Laudan, *Truth, Error, and Criminal Law: An Essay in Legal Epistemology* (CUP, 2006).

[85] William Twining, 'The Rationalist Tradition of Evidence Scholarship', reprinted in Twining *Rethinking Evidence*, 2nd edn (CUP, 2006) ch 3; William Twining, *Theories of Evidence: Bentham & Wigmore* (Weidenfeld and Nicolson, 1985) ch 1.

[86] Donald Nicolson, 'Taking Epistemology Seriously: "Truth, Reason and Justice" Revisited' (2013) 17 *International Journal of Evidence & Proof* 1; K W Graham Jr, '"There'll Always be an England": The Instrumental Ideology of Evidence' (1987) 85 *Michigan Law Review* 1204.

pre-Enlightenment irrationalism. If the issue were genuinely open to debate, it would be necessary to deploy *normative* arguments to establish the moral superiority of epistemologically serious forms of trial over their non-serious rivals. Such arguments would show that law's rights, duties and instrumental effectiveness are essentially meaningless in the absence of a strong institutional commitment to factual rectitude.[87] Given the broadly-based and enduring consensus on the indispensability of rationalist epistemology, however, it is legitimate to treat epistemic seriousness as a constitutive element and necessary condition of our concept of criminal trial. Somebody who argues, deliberately or otherwise, that criminal trials can or should dispense with epistemic seriousness either doesn't know what a criminal trial is or is actually – possibly unwittingly – talking about something else. Conceptual parameters operate to rule out of court (so to speak) particular arguments, deployed on particular occasions, for particular reasons. This is not, ultimately, a question of linguistic meaning or conceptual *possibility* (short of Humpty Dumpty's solipsism). Arguments that are legitimately conceptual in one context might be, or need to be, normative in different circumstances. Somebody who rejects epistemic seriousness in criminal trials is not (necessarily) spouting gibberish, but even when such arguments are intelligible, they remain, for all practical purposes, (conceptually) beyond the pale. An analogue in the field of ethics would be an argument that challenged the foundational normative ideal that all human beings are equal in dignity and should be treated with ethical concern and respect. That premiss is logically deniable, and has been denied repeatedly throughout human history,[88] but the argument (as opposed to the people making it) is not jurisprudentially serious. Human equality is a conceptual premiss of post-1945 global political morality.

Criminal trials, we can now say, are epistemically serious mechanisms for the pacific resolution of disputes concerning (alleged) violations of the (jurisdictionally competent) criminal law. One significant implication is that criminal trials involve inquiries into past events: their temporal orientation is fundamentally historical rather than future-predictive. This characteristic differentiates judicial trials from tests of current ability (eg, trials of strength; endurance trials; motocross trials) or of prospective suitability (eg, trials for sports teams; 'trial runs'; trial periods). Although criminal law assuredly has future-orientated objectives, notably guiding lawful behaviour and deterring criminality, a criminal *trial* is quintessentially backward-looking. To be tried today for what you will[89] do tomorrow or in five years' time is not merely illegitimate; it is a conceptual impossibility – according

[87] Paul Roberts, 'The Priority of Procedure and the Neglect of Evidence and Proof: Facing Facts in International Criminal Law' (2015) 13 *Journal of International Criminal Justice* 479; Ronald J Allen, 'Laudan, Stein, and the Limits of Theorizing about Juridical Proof' (2010) 29 *Law & Philosophy* 195.

[88] Jonathan Glover, *Humanity: A Moral History of the Twentieth Century* (Pimlico, 2001); Eric Hobsbawm, *The Age of Extremes* (Abacus, 1995).

[89] Or *might* do? I am unapologetically skating over interminable problems of Determinism: see Daniel C Dennett and Gregg D Caruso, *Just Deserts: Debating Free Will* (Wiley, 2021).

to our[90] prevailing conceptual understanding. Stated more fully, then, the second constitutive feature of our concept of criminal trial is that it must be an epistemically serious inquiry into (allegations of) past events of a particular kind, namely (alleged) criminal wrongdoing.

A third, independent, conceptual ingredient I now propose is that criminal trials must involve *jeopardy*. The notion of jeopardy most familiar to discussions of criminal adjudication is (thanks to Blackstone[91]) encapsulated in the common law prohibition on *double jeopardy*. The double jeopardy prohibition throws up many conceptual puzzles (and policy controversies) of its own,[92] but for present purposes the essential idea is that criminal trials are, ideally, one-shot affairs with no repeat performances. The state cannot keep retrying the accused for the same offence until the 'right result' – presumptively a conviction[93] – is achieved. What I want to highlight is that a related, but more comprehensive and fundamental, sense of jeopardy attaches to the *first* trial, as well. The accused is always in jeopardy of criminal conviction and punishment. There is also jeopardy for complainants and prosecutors in the prospect of a guilty accused securing an unmerited, or possibly even an unwarranted, acquittal. Fact-finders, too, are exposed to the jeopardy of fateful public decision-making in which they are conscripted participants (willingly or otherwise).[94] Trials, in short, are inherently *risky* events which can misfire in various ways. The specifically *epistemic* dimension of criminal trial jeopardy flows from the inherent uncertainty of contested facts and the pervasive possibility of adjudicative error which trial procedure is designed to mitigate and manage. By conceptual extrapolation, the outcome of a criminal trial can never be, literally, a foregone conclusion.

To be sure, where incriminating evidence is strong and uncontradicted by any innocent explanation, a conviction may be highly likely and eminently predictable. The prosecutor might be convinced of the accused's guilt. Victims of crime sometimes know that the accused is guilty; though this is far less common than might be imagined, because much acquisitive crime is perpetrated by

[90] Anglophones conceive of 'trial and sentencing' as two distinct phases of criminal adjudication. In legal cultures in which the court deliberates on and pronounces guilt and sentence as an integrated package, the retrospective orientation of criminal trials may be less pronounced. But even sentencing is partly backward-looking. The punishment must 'fit' the crime, and this is an exclusively future-orientated criterion only for monomaniacal consequentialists.

[91] Sir William Blackstone, *Commentaries on the Laws of England* (1765-69), Book IV, ch 26, 329–30 ('no man is to be brought into jeopardy of his life, more than once, for the same offence … no man ought to be twice brought in danger of his life for one and the same crime').

[92] Ian Dennis, 'Quashing Acquittals: Applying the "New and Compelling Evidence" Exception to Double Jeopardy' [2014] *Criminal Law Review* 247; Paul Roberts, 'Double Jeopardy Law Reform: A Criminal Justice Commentary' (2002) 65 *Modern Law Review* 393.

[93] Nothing sinister implied. Prosecutors in England and Wales cannot lawfully initiate or continue a prosecution unless they assess that a conviction is more likely than not on the evidence. Prosecutors are thus ex ante professionally committed to endorsing a conviction at trial as the (probable) right result (which is not to say that they should *express* such a view or be hostile to changing their minds in light of new information).

[94] James Q Whitman, *The Origins of Reasonable Doubt: Theological Roots of the Criminal Trial* (Yale University Press, 2008).

individuals unknown to the victim, and perpetrators' identities are frequently plausibly contested even in relation to offences of interpersonal violence and sexual exploitation. Irrespective of what the victim, police, prosecutor or anybody else might believe (or even know), however, the inherent jeopardy of a criminal trial is that the verdict could always, in principle, go either way. A contested trial is a unique event, and its performance cannot be minutely scripted or foretold. Cases on paper sometimes materialise differently in the flesh. Witnesses fail to show up, or do not 'come up to proof' in the witness box. Scientific evidence that seemed watertight in an expert's analytical report turns out under cross-examination to be full of questionable assumptions and conjectures.[95] The accused suddenly presents an unanticipated line of defence. Previously undisclosed material contradicts the complainant's narrative.[96] The accused elects to testify in his own defence but proceeds to perform as the prosecution's best witness. There are innumerable contingencies, with compound effects. Moreover, the way in which the case is argued and presented to the fact-finder in the courtroom is a profoundly human interaction of such dynamism, complexity and emotional intensity that even a full retrial on the same facts and evidence (eg, where the jury fails to return a verdict) could only be an approximate surrogate, never a completely faithful replica. It is reasonable to surmise that these performance dimensions of the criminal trial are accentuated in cases involving lay jurors or magistrates, but they are not eliminated even in bench trials before professional judges. Truly open-and-shut cases exist only in police procedural fiction.[97] Loss of control over trial outcomes is one reason why many lawyers prefer to negotiate pleas, achieving more or less predictable case disposals, rather than 'roll the dice' in a contested trial.[98] Once a trial is underway, no particular verdict is assured.

What if criminal verdicts in contested proceedings[99] *were* literally foregone conclusions, eliminating all (epistemic) jeopardy from criminal trial adjudication?

[95] Scientific evidence is both highly probative *and* susceptible to a raft of infirmities, errors and misapplications: Paul Roberts, 'Making Sense of Forensic Science Evidence' in Paul Roberts and Michael Stockdale (eds), *Forensic Science Evidence and Expert Witness Testimony: Reliability Through Reform?* (Edward Elgar, 2018) 27.

[96] Dramatically illustrated by Tom Smith, 'The "Near Miss" of Liam Allan: Critical Problems in Police Disclosure, Investigation Culture and the Resourcing of Criminal Justice' [2018] *Criminal Law Review* 711.

[97] '[T]he path of the law is strewn with examples of open and shut cases which, somehow, were not; of unanswerable charges which, in the event, were completely answered; of inexplicable conduct which was fully explained; of fixed and unalterable determinations that, by discussion, suffered a change': *John v Rees* [1970] Ch 345, 402 (Megarry J).

[98] Invoking the language of lotteries might be interpreted as an implicit confession of institutional weakness. '[E]ven those who work in the system – lawyers and judges – don't respect it .... But if the outcome of a trial is simply, as those in the system often put it, "a crapshoot", who can blame them for not wanting to gamble when very important issues are at stake?': William T Pizzi, *Trials Without Truth* (New York University Press, 1999) 88. It seems to me, however, that uncertainty is an inherent – conceptual – feature of adjudication, and lawyers (and judges) inevitably cede some of their power to influence trial outcomes once the case is put to the jury.

[99] Caution mandates confining the conceptual necessity of jeopardy to *contested* trials. Even with routine guilty pleas, however, the deal is not sealed until the accused actually pleads guilty, and that plea

That would be a show trial, a purely symbolic performance that was neither epistemically serious nor orientated to fact-finding (as opposed to announcing, broadcasting or performatively reenacting preordained facts).[100] Linguistic usage is not friendly to conceptual clarity in this instance. When we say 'show trial', we mean 'not a real trial', rather than a trial that was (merely) deficient in its excessive showiness. If a trial is materially flawed, for example because the court lacked jurisdiction or on account of a significant violation of due process, an appellate court might quash the conviction, but it would not say that the accused didn't have a trial. Indeed, fair trial jurisprudence in general is predicated on the assumption that trials may be marred by unfairness, not that unfairness deprives criminal trials of their conceptual identity. An unfair trial is *still a trial*, though flawed. But a show trial is not a flawed trial in any parallel sense. A show trial is not any genuine kind of trial. It would not be enough, I think, to say that a show trial was a legal nullity. Trials found and held to be legal nullities, ex post, never had any legal effect (we now know) but were conceived as valid trials at the time, at least by key participants.[101] Show trials are nullities ex ante. Key participants *knew* all along (not merely guessed or predicted) what the final conclusion would be. Observers were intentionally fooled, or their cynicism was disregarded. The proceedings were devoid of all verdict jeopardy, all epistemic seriousness, and all fact-finding aspirations. It hardly suffices to characterise such arrangements as flawed trials or trials vulnerable to being declared nullities. Show trials are bad-faith parodies of the authentic adjudicative procedure. And just as a Hollywood moon landing is not a moon landing and deepfake photography is not merely poor likeness, show trials are not trials, conceptually and constitutively speaking.

The jeopardy in a criminal verdict is not only a question of epistemic uncertainty, but also, from the accused's point of view,[102] a matter of highly consequential personal risk. Liberty, amenity, prosperity and reputation are routinely on the line in criminal proceedings. A criminal verdict of guilty may seriously set back the accused's life, or – in some places – even end it. This is bad enough if the accused is actually guilty and deserves conviction and punishment, simply excruciating for those who are innocent (or genuinely believe themselves to be so). Given that the focal point of criminal adjudication is

is accepted by the court: see, eg, *R v NJ* [2022] EWCA Crim 790. For as long as the accused retains the right to a contested trial, some element of verdict jeopardy remains.

[100] Jeremy Peterson, 'Unpacking Show Trials: Situating the Trial of Saddam Hussein' (2007) 48 *Harvard International Law Journal* 257; Gerry Simpson, 'Objective Responsibility: Show Trials and War Crimes Trials' (2006) 4(1) *International Commentary on Evidence*, Article 2.

[101] Conversely, acquittals procured through chicanery do not attract the protection of the double jeopardy prohibition, because there was no real jeopardy in the first place: *cf* Criminal Procedure and Investigations Act 1996, s 57 ('tainted acquittals'). Proceedings were fixed. These are defence-orchestrated 'show trials'.

[102] As mentioned, there is also jeopardy for complainants, for legal professionals, and for other trial participants, including witnesses and jurors. The verdict jeopardy to which the accused is exposed takes a unique form – the accused is *literally* on trial – but the risks borne by others should not be underestimated.

public censure and sanction of the guilty (but only of them, and only of the right charge and in the right way, with epistemic warrant and procedural due process), it seems to be a precondition of criminal trials that there must be an identifiable defendant to hold responsible for proven criminal wrongdoing. Thus, verdicts pronounce 'guilty' or 'not guilty' in relation to one or more named accused.[103] They do not make declarations about past events without attributing those events to some responsible agency. Verdict jeopardy infuses allocations of responsibility in criminal adjudication. Holding to account[104] is the paradigmatic instrumentality of the criminal trial. This poses further questions of criminal capacity, that is, who (or what) qualifies as the type of moral agent who (or which) can be answerable for criminal wrongdoing *and* is 'fit to plead' (ie, stand trial) on criminal charges. Conceptions of criminal capacity vary across time and place. On the theory of criminal capacity embraced by modern legal systems, a criminal defendant cannot be a non-human animal,[105] a child below the age of criminal responsibility at the material time, or a person suffering from a mental condition incompatible with moral agency. Conversely, corporations, states and some other non-natural persons do possess the right kind of agency to be defendants in criminal trials.

What if the suspected perpetrator has already died? It is conceivable that a trial could still be conducted, with a variety of possible objectives: to vindicate victims, to pursue remedies against the offender's estate, to set the historical record straight, to defuse social tensions, and so forth. It seems to me, however, that the existence (as opposed to physical presence)[106] of a living accused who could be held responsible for public wrongs is an essential component of the jeopardy we expect from our criminal trials, in the English common law tradition. If it is possible symbolically to execute a corpse – as the Restoration Stuarts did with Cromwell – it is possible symbolically to try a corpse; yet we never do. This seldom remarked procedural axiom was revisited in *Turk*,[107] where the accused stood his trial for historic child sexual abuse offences until after the jury's retirement but committed suicide before a verdict could be returned. The jury was deadlocked on certain counts. Not unreasonably, the trial judge thought that public investment

[103] An imposter will not do: *R (Bahbahani) v Ealing Magistrates' Court* [2020] QB 478, [2019] EWHC 1385 (Admin).

[104] More precisely, I think, than 'calling to account'. *Cf* R A Duff, *Answering for Crime* (Hart Publishing, 2007).

[105] Animal trials were commonplace in medieval Europe, vividly demonstrating the historical relativity of concepts of agency and responsibility: William Ewald, 'Comparative Jurisprudence (I): What Was it Like to Try a Rat?' (1995) 143 *University of Pennsylvania Law Review* 1898; E P Evans, *The Criminal Prosecution and Capital Punishment of Animals: The Lost History of Europe's Animal Trials* (Faber & Faber, 1987 [1906]).

[106] Physical availability to stand trial is a normal expectation but not a conceptual precondition. Criminal trials *in absentia* may be vulnerable to principled objections, but their status *as trials* producing valid judgments is settled law. See, eg, *R v Jones (Anthony)* [2003] 1 AC 1, [2002] UKHL 1; *Sejdovic v Italy*, App no 56581/00, Grand Chamber Judgment, 1 March 2006.

[107] *R v Turk* [2017] 1 WLR 2919, [2017] EWCA Crim 391.

in the proceedings and the victims' expectations and desire for closure militated in favour of hearing the jury's verdicts in relation to those counts on which agreement had already been reached. Verdicts of guilty on ten counts (and acquittals of six others) were duly returned. The Court of Appeal quashed the convictions and reiterated the orthodox common law position:[108]

> [I]n order to preserve the bright line that criminal prosecutions are not pursued against those who have died, there is no discretion as to the course of action then to be taken. As soon as a judge learns that a defendant has died, it is his duty to take no further step in the case against that defendant save for receiving proof of death whereupon the indictment as far as it concerns that defendant must be declared of no effect … We appreciate that, in relation to many of the allegations pursued at trial, complainants may well consider that they had been vindicated and that, by this decision, there was important recognition of their position; so far as the record is concerned, that would be lost. We recognise that entirely understandable view but we repeat that it is critical to maintain an approach to criminal justice that is consistent and even-handed, maintaining a definitive position that the death of a defendant brings any criminal prosecution of that defendant to an end.

Death of the accused automatically concludes trial proceedings against them. This is not a self-evident proposition from an ethical perspective, but it is both normatively defensible and settled English criminal jurisprudence. These institutional facts support the conclusion that a living accused in jeopardy is a conceptual prerequisite of a criminal trial, at least in England and Wales. Inquiries or hearings concerned with the deeds of the dead are not criminal trials,[109] conceptually speaking, because in our procedural tradition[110] verdict jeopardy is confined by mortality. Unless and until we invest our concept of the criminal trial with revised metaphysical assumptions, the class of potentially responsible defendants excludes souls or ghosts impervious to secular justice.

B. Conceptual Boundary Work

Discussion to this point has built up a core conception of the criminal trial as an epistemically serious institutional mechanism for pacific dispute resolution

[108] ibid [22], [25].

[109] Criminal *appeals* may be pursued on behalf of deceased appellants by virtue of s 44A of the Criminal Appeal Act 1968. The stigma and pain of wrongful conviction survive the accused's death. The Criminal Cases Review Commission has referred high-profile cases involving deceased (indeed, executed) accused back to the Court of Appeal, notably *R v Derek Bentley (Deceased)* [2001] 1 Cr App R 307, CA (conviction quashed); and *R v Hanratty (Deceased)* [2002] EWCA Crim 1141; [2002] 2 Cr App R 419 (conviction upheld).

[110] And in others: *cf Nölkenbockhoff v Germany* (1988) 10 EHRR 163. Besides, juridical concepts are always more or less particularistic according to their intended field(s) of application, making trade-offs between generality and usefulness unavoidable in jurisprudential analysis: William Twining, 'Have Concepts, Will Travel: Analytical Jurisprudence in a Global Context' (2005) 1 *International Journal of Law in Context* 5.

with verdict jeopardy (both epistemic and personal), not least for a living accused. We can further elucidate and test this conception of the concept and simultaneously develop a deeper understanding of its usefulness and limitations, by probing its conceptual boundaries. Existing institutional practices will almost certainly combine constitutive with contingent features. In fact, when institutional practices are delineated in sufficiently granular detail, this will necessarily be so. The colour of judicial robes or the architectural style of courthouses cannot plausibly be conceptual prerequisites of criminal trials. Inverting our perspective, it is illuminating to consider which features of contemporary criminal trial practice are *not* conceptually constitutive. There are plainly many contingent features of criminal adjudication that could be altered, subtracted, augmented or supplemented without stripping a criminal trial of its conceptual identity. Contingency extends to features of criminal adjudication that are widely regarded as very important, notwithstanding their dispensability in a strictly conceptual sense.

We have already peremptorily ruled out the notion that a criminal trial must necessarily adopt a party-driven adversarial procedure. Inquisitorialism can be epistemologically serious; indeed it is arguably intuitively more congruent with rational fact-finding than an adversarial contest model of trial.[111] It follows that justifications of adversarial procedure cannot succeed merely on the basis of (conceptualist) appeals to the concept of a criminal trial. Geographical inclusivity and tolerance of jurisdictional variation are methodological strengths of this conceptual analysis. A test of pedigree would not be much use if it failed to recognise and claim uncontroversial tokens of the pertinent type. A viable concept of criminal trial cannot afford to take sides in debates between adversarial and inquisitorial models of adjudication, because it is self-evident that criminal trials are not confined to common law jurisdictions (or jurisdictions importing common law thinking). Adversarial and inquisitorial procedures can alike, in principle, accommodate epistemically serious pacific dispute resolution with verdict jeopardy, three primary conceptual hallmarks of authentic criminal trials.

A parallel analysis disqualifies juries and lay fact-finding more generally as conceptual predicates of criminal trial. Juries are, of course, core features of the common law tradition of criminal adjudication. Whilst some think their importance exaggerated,[112] others (including me) believe that trial by jury has constitutional significance in England and Wales.[113] Either way, the justification

[111] 'The continental system would tend to embrace a paradigm closer to that of scientific investigation': Mirjan Damaška, 'Presentation of Evidence and Factfinding Precision' (1975) 123 *University of Pennsylvania Law Review* 1083, 1104–5; Mirjan Damaška, *Evaluation of Evidence: Pre-Modern and Modern Approaches* (CUP, 2019). Adversarial procedure undeniably has numerous epistemic pressure points as well as practical strengths: *cf* Gordon van Kessel, 'Adversary Excesses in the American Criminal Trial' (1992) 67 *Notre Dame Law Review* 403.

[112] Lord Justice Auld, *Review of the Criminal Courts of England and Wales* (TSO, 2001) ch 5; Penny Darbyshire, 'The Lamp That Shows that Freedom Lives: Is it Worth the Candle?' [1991] *Criminal Law Review* 740.

[113] 'In this country trial by jury is a hallowed principle of the administration of criminal justice. It is properly identified as a right, available to be exercised by a defendant unless and until the right is amended or circumscribed by express legislation': *R v Twomey* [2009] 2 Cr App R 25, [10] (Judge CJ).

for fact-finding by lay jury cannot rest on conceptualist appeals to the concept of a criminal trial. That would imply that only trials on indictment in the Crown Court are actually trials, whereas instances of adjudication in magistrates' courts – statistically, the vast majority of criminal case disposals – would be … well, I am not sure what we would call them. 'Summary justice'? 'Magisterial adjudications'? The professional discourse of 'summary trial' is not merely a linguistic habit or an implicit admission of lack of terminological imagination. Summary trials are distinctive because they employ summary procedure, not because they fail at being trials. A conceptualist approach cannot be saved by relaxing 'juries' to 'lay participation in fact-finding', because although this would accommodate trials by magistrates in England and Wales and trials involving mixed panels in Continental Europe and further afield, it would still fail to recognise bench trials in common law jurisdictions[114] and criminal adjudication in procedural systems with no lay involvement whatsoever. If your concept of criminal trial implies that there are no criminal trials in the Netherlands[115] or Singapore or entails that the Diplock system in Northern Ireland involved detention without trial,[116] then your concept is maladapted for service in current controversies and debates. There may be reasons to oppose the introduction in England and Wales of judge-only trials on indictment,[117] and legitimate concerns may be expressed about the quality of justice routinely dispensed by District Judges in magistrates' courts,[118] but critics do not suggest that these proceedings are not trials. If such a conceptualist argument were ever mounted or encountered, the most likely reaction to it would be bemusement rather than opposition or assent. It makes sense to claim that such trials are deficient, either categorically in design or contingently in practice, and normative arguments might then be marshalled and assessed on both sides of the issue. To insist that such procedures are *not trials*, however, is merely a counter-intuitive assertion that begs all the significant normative and policy questions.

[114] S Doran, J D Jackson and M L Seigel, 'Rethinking Adversariness in Nonjury Criminal Trials' (1995) 23 *American Journal of Criminal Law* 1; Paul Roberts, 'Reasonable Doubts? Rationalising Appellate Review of Witness Credibility in Criminal Trials' (2025) 28 *Canadian Criminal Law Review* 21.

[115] The Netherlands stands out as having the most professionalised criminal process in western Europe: Christina Peristeridou and André Klip (eds), *Comparative Perspectives of Criminal Procedure* (Intersentia, 2024), 44 (observing that '[t]he Netherlands is one of the few states that has never had a jury. Lay participation is regarded as endangering the quality of the process'). Generally, see Peter J P Tak, *The Dutch Criminal Justice System*, 3rd edn (Wolf Legal Publishers, 2008); Phil Fennell, Christopher Harding, Nico Jörg and Bert Swart (eds), *Criminal Justice in Europe: A Comparative Study* (OUP, 1995). The ECtHR Grand Chamber in *Taxquet v Belgium* (2012) 54 EHRR 26, [14], identified 14 Council of Europe states with no lay involvement in criminal adjudication.

[116] The ECtHR affirmed that 'Diplock courts and the procedures which have evolved in a system where the trial judge is both tribunal of fact and tribunal of law' were ECHR Art 6 compliant: *McKeown v United Kingdom* (2012) 54 EHRR 7, [48]. The system of 'Diplock courts' for 'scheduled' (terrorist) offences was abolished by the Justice and Security (Northern Ireland) Act 2007. Generally, see John Jackson and Sean Doran, *Judge Without Jury: Diplock Trials in the Adversary System* (OUP, 1995).

[117] Criminal Justice Act 2003, s 44 introduced a power to order judge only trial to forestall 'a real and present danger that jury tampering would take place'.

[118] *Cf* The Secret Barrister, *Stories of the Law and How It's Broken* (Picador, 2019) ch 2 (characterising magistrates' courts as 'The Wild West').

If major architectural features of criminal adjudication, such as adversarial structure and lay participation in fact-finding, are not conceptually constitutive of criminal trials, it must follow (a fortiori, as only lawyers ever say) that more granular details of local criminal procedure are not conceptually decisive, either. For example, whether or not a particular jurisdiction operates an exclusionary rule of evidence attaching to improperly obtained 'fruit of the poisoned tree'[119] or interposes a 'rape shield' against the admission of previous sexual history evidence[120] will not shift conceptual understanding of the criminal trial; still less will idiosyncratic choices of procedural doctrine or institutional design trouble the core concept. Arguments about the underlying rationale for excluding improperly obtained evidence,[121] for example, appeal directly to normative ideals (eg, moral integrity), instrumental objectives (eg, safeguarding rights) and institutional incentives (eg, 'disciplining the police'), rather than trading rival concepts. These patterns of argumentation are both mundane and entirely appropriate. Any non-parochial concept of criminal trial must be capable of handling the diverse traditions and major contemporary configurations of cosmopolitan criminal jurisprudence, accommodating stupendous institutional variability at the microscopic level. Nor should procedural evolution and variation over time within a single trial system warrant arbitrary conceptual disqualification.

These strictures do not preclude further conceptual refinements. Consider the normative injunction that fair trials must be 'conducted by an independent and impartial tribunal established by law'.[122] Allowing that a criminal trial is an institutional mechanism governed by the rule of law,[123] this formula's legality requirement seems unproblematic. Criminal trials in liberal democracies must satisfy minimum preconditions for legitimate exercises of public power. A mafia interrogation preliminary to a punishment beating, or murder, is not a criminal trial; even though it may be (somewhat) epistemologically serious, it might resolve a (mafia) dispute and could well entail (mortal) jeopardy for those at the sticky end of Don Corleone's suspicions. At the limit, a drumhead court martial can be a trial (only) to the extent that the commanding officer exercises lawful authority

[119] England and Wales never endorsed such a doctrine: Police and Criminal Evidence Act 1984, s 76(4); *R v Twigg* [2019] 1 WLR 6533, [2019] EWCA Crim 1553; *R v Warwickshall* (1783) 1 Leach 263.

[120] Youth Justice and Criminal Evidence Act 1999, s 41.

[121] Roberts (n 47) ch 5; Dominik Brodowski, Brenner Fissell and Paul Roberts, 'Pretext, Deception and Entrapment in Criminal Investigations' in Kai Ambos et al (eds), *Core Concepts in Criminal Law and Criminal Justice: Volume III* (CUP, 2024).

[122] ECHR Art 6(1); ICCPR Art 14. See UN Basic Principles on the Independence of the Judiciary, GA Res 40/32 (29 November 1985) and GA Res 40/146 (13 December 1985), www.ohchr.org/EN/ProfessionalInterest/Pages/IndependenceJudiciary.aspx.

[123] Not necessarily embracing every aspect of the liberal conception: *cf*, Joseph Raz, 'The Rule of Law and its Virtue' (1977) 93 *Law Quarterly Review* 195; Lord Bingham, 'The Rule of Law' (2007) 66 *Cambridge Law Journal* 67. For example, bills of attainder contradict the generality requirement of legality, but it is at least a theoretical possibility that, say, Thomas More or Mary Queen of Scots could have received fair *trials*, so long as proceedings against them were epistemically serious and guilty verdicts were not a foregone conclusion. (In reality, bills of attainder might also breach the non-retroactivity norm, but that is a different objection, engaging Sullivan's primary conduct condition.)

to conduct it. Rule of law procedures are not incompatible with official discretion, nor do they necessarily require elaborate rules of procedure for the conduct of hearings, but properly constituted legal authority is conceptually indispensable. Any procedure outside the law, and irrespective of its substantive merits, is not within our modern concept of criminal trial, which seems to presuppose non-delegable public duties.[124]

Turning to the twin criteria of independence and impartiality, a more nuanced analysis is required. Some defects would plausibly be conceptually fatal; others might not be. If we envisage complete abnegation of independence, akin to the old Soviet 'telephone law' tradition of judges calling up prosecutors to ask what their verdicts should be,[125] or complete lack of impartiality – as where the judge is driven by personal animosity to nobble a despised litigant – then I think it would be appropriate to place such procedures beyond the conceptual pale. The process is not epistemologically serious, and there is minimal, if any, true verdict jeopardy. To the extent that the result is preordained, by complete lack of independence or extreme partiality, we encounter a sham – a show trial/non-trial – rather than the genuine forensic article. By the same token, tribunals can fail to be independent owing to improper influence or lack of (perceived) impartiality falling far short of these extreme (and, one would hope, unusual) scenarios. For example, a judge might be a director of an NGO charity which is also an intervener in the case.[126] Or the judge might have received submissions from a prosecutor, in the guise of amicus curiae or advocate general, to which defence counsel has not been able to respond on equal terms, thus creating a *perception* of bias even where there is no lack of impartiality in fact.[127] In these and similar instances, it seems more natural to say that a flawed, unfair trial occurred rather than invoking the more extravagant categorical claim that there was never any trial. Inasmuch as the independence and impartiality of the tribunal are constitutive of a fair trial, we might properly categorise such constitutively defective trials as legal nullities. Still, it seems to me that we are here describing the absence of a *fair* trial, rather than the absence of any trial *tout court*. If this impression is correct, then an authentic jurisprudential concept of criminal trial cuts across the institutional (human rights) concept of a fair (criminal) trial – which is an interesting analytical insight, to which I hope to return and explore more systematically in future work.

[124] Hence, adjudicative processes conducted by employers, associations or institutions such as universities are not criminal trials, even when they concern alleged criminal conduct.

[125] Kathryn Hendley, '"Telephone Law" and the "Rule of Law": The Russian Case' (2009) 1 *Hague Journal on the Rule of Law* 241; Peter H Solomon, Jr, *Soviet Criminal Justice Under Stalin* (CUP, 1996) ch 7.

[126] 'If the absolute impartiality of the judiciary is to be maintained, there must be a rule which automatically disqualifies a judge who is involved, whether personally or as a director of a company, in promoting the same causes in the same organisation as is a party to the suit. There is no room for fine distinctions': *R v Bow Street Metropolitan Stipendiary Magistrate ex parte Pinochet Ugarte (No 2)* [2000] 1 AC 119, 135, HL (Lord Browne-Wilkinson).

[127] *Borgers v Belgium* (1993) 15 EHRR 92; *Reinhardt and Slimane-Kaïd v France* (1998) 28 EHRR 59; echoing the common law principle that justice must also be 'seen to be done': *R v Breslin* (1985) 80 Cr App R 226, 230, CA; *R v Sussex Justices, ex p McCarthy* [1924] 1 KB 256, 259.

Having now admitted institutional criteria, namely compliance with the rule of law, into the conceptual definition of criminal trials, one might wonder at the extent of this normative bridgehead. Might it be argued, for example, that a trial process lacking in procedural integrity or marred by some serious failure of due process forfeits its conceptual identity as a criminal trial? Only, I must insist, at the extremities of normative tolerance. A sound concept of criminal trial will not purport to resolve live controversies through conceptual fiat. Concepts collapse in on themselves when ill-advisedly over-extended. Well-designed conceptual scaffolding should help to frame normative controversies and thereby assist in clarifying the nature and significance of normative disagreement. It is methodologically inept (or rhetorical legerdemain) to try to circumvent or conceal ethical controversies by gerrymandering concepts. It may be tempting, for example, to try to argue that a trial process that fails to uphold standards of procedural propriety or which affords too little weight to procedural safeguards such as the privilege against self-incrimination[128] is a conceptual impossibility, a self-refuting contradiction that cannot logically exist.[129] That style of argument is reminiscent of Kant's attempts to derive ethical duties from a substantive account of rationality,[130] and it is methodologically problematic for much the same reasons that neo-Kantian rationalism seems question-begging or obscure to non-Kantians. To demonstrate that evil deeds are not merely wrong, but irrational requires the same, or similar, normative resources as moral arguments to establish directly why evil deeds should not be done. You can bundle these arguments up in a capacious conception of rationality if that is your theoretical preference, but this conceptualist manoeuvre does not automatically vindicate any normative claim. It simply repackages and restates the question.[131] Likewise, in the criminal procedure context, notions of procedural impropriety and complex jurisprudential doctrines are shot through with normative controversy, extending from the primary threads of ethical principle right down into the dense institutional fabric of legal definitions

[128] *Cf* Boštjan M Zupančič, 'The Privilege Against Self-Incrimination' [1981] *Arizona State Law Journal* 1, 25: 'If the privilege against self-incrimination is a logical concomitant of adversary adjudication and if, furthermore, the privilege against self-incrimination cannot exist without the exclusion of evidence obtained in violation of that privilege, then the exclusionary rule itself can be deduced from the postulate of impartial adversary adjudication.'

[129] '[I]n criminal procedure, too, the violation of certain basic rules should affect the substantive outcome of the case. … To put it bluntly, if the constable does blunder, the criminal should go free …. [Violation of the privilege against self-incrimination] covers the pristine Kafkaesque absurd in which the State uses the fraudulent semblance of the legal process to conceal law's precise opposite – the instant regression to anti-law': Boštjan M Zupančič, 'The Crown and the Criminal: The Privilege Against Self-Incrimination – Towards General Principles of Criminal Procedure' (1996) 5 *Nottingham Law Journal* 32, 45, 50.

[130] Onora O'Neill, 'Kant' in Alfred R Mele and Piers Rawling (eds), *The Oxford Handbook of Rationality* (OUP, 2004); Joseph Raz, *Engaging Reason* (OUP, 1999). *Cf* John Gardner and Timothy Macklem, 'Reasons' in Jules L Coleman, Kenneth E Himma and Scott J Shapiro (eds), *The Oxford Handbook of Jurisprudence and Philosophy of Law* (OUP, 2002) 440.

[131] For example, 'Why should I not do evil?', via 'Because evil is irrational', becomes 'Why would it be irrational for me to do evil?'. *Cf* Peter Unger, *Empty Ideas: A Critique of Analytic Philosophy* (OUP, 2014) (mercilessly eviscerating conceptual logic-chopping in the realm of metaphysics).

and doctrinal constructs. Even where the rules themselves are clear and settled, criminal adjudication constantly throws up hard cases where detailed facts and circumstances muddy the waters of general principles and pull in the direction of allowing exceptions (finding reasons to distinguish the precedent, in the common lawyer's lexicon). Thus, cultivation of ethical practice in the administration of criminal justice is not exhausted by conscientious rule-following; it also requires sound judgement in context. It will not do to side-step these controversies simply by proclaiming that anybody who does not (apparently) share your normative preferences is making an elementary conceptual error. Practical reasoning is not axiomatic. Inasmuch as conceptual redefinition announces normatively salient conclusions without putting in the normative hard yards or showing its working, conceptualist arguments never truly resolve jurisprudential issues of any moral significance.

We should not foreclose the possibility that some extreme instances of procedural impropriety or failures of due process could be so corrosively delegitimising that proceedings are cast beyond the conceptual pale of a criminal trial. Such dereliction would imply radical loss of legitimacy in social dispute resolution and forfeiture of normative standing to adjudicate. Most likely, conceptual limits would be reached or breached where the impropriety in question effectively reneges on one or more of the core conceptual commitments previously identified. For example, a criminal trial that was so racist or sectarian that any defendant from a particular pariah group would always be convicted is not epistemically serious and lacks threshold verdict jeopardy. Likewise, if criminal justice officials were systematically[132] corrupt or derelict in their professional duties, it is difficult to see how criminal adjudication would be taking evidence, proof or fact-finding sufficiently seriously. Other components of the standard specification of fair trial in international human rights law could be warped and stretched to such an extent that procedures officially labelled 'trials' would no longer be trials. For example, the accused could be held on pre-trial remand for such protracted periods that the prospect of reaching a final verdict becomes implausibly remote. Suppose that the majority of suspects die in the squalor of remand gaols, or from disease or old age, before their cases are finally resolved by a court. In these circumstances, it seems inadequate to complain that excessive delay renders trial proceedings unfair. The reality is a system of executive justice (or liquidation of social enemies) masquerading as criminal adjudication. These proceedings are not show trials, but no-show trials. The promise of trial is, for the majority, only for show. Either extreme form of institutional bad faith would be sufficient to dissolve the conceptual integrity of a criminal trial.

[132] The (fuzzy) thought here is that sporadic or geographically delimited corruption is 'only' a normative problem, not a conceptual existential threat. Trial systems can exist with bad apples, and even tolerate some corrupted barrels, but if the entire orchard is worm-eaten, the harvest is lost – or the business is different to that advertised (producing poison rather than wine, oppression rather than justice).

IV. From Conceptual Analysis to Conceptualist Argument? Implicating the Presumption of Innocence

Let us recap progress thus far. Inspired by Sullivan's intriguing – if sketchy – 'conceptual' claims proposing proof of conduct as an essential precondition of criminal liability, the foregoing discussion proceeded in two steps. First, I established some general methodological preconditions and expectations for a virtuous concept of criminal trial. Concepts are appropriately formulated, and – by extension – should be judged, relative to context and purpose. There could be different, equally valid, concepts of criminal trial, calibrated to different theoretical or practical tasks (just as chainsaws and hacksaws are both saws, but are far from interchangeable in use – if you want to keep all your fingers). Secondly, I took up the challenge, implicit in Sullivan's exposition, to elucidate a serviceable concept of 'criminal trial'. As threshold criteria of methodological validity, this concept must plausibly cohere with prevailing jurisprudence, contemporary institutional practices and evolved procedural traditions.

Conceptual analysis precedes or is presupposed by normative evaluation: before we can say whether a criminal trial was 'fair' or achieved justice, for example, we have to be able to identify what a criminal trial is. Distilling the essence of the previous section's analysis, criminal trials may now be conceptualised as (1) institutionalised, formal, and legitimacy-claiming (2) conflict-resolution mechanisms conducted as (3) epistemically serious inquiries into (4) alleged criminal wrongdoing by (5) responsible agents entailing (6) verdict jeopardy. The preceding discussion mostly concentrated on items (2), (3) and (6), with incidental observations on the other three components. The terminology of 'epistemic seriousness' and 'verdict jeopardy', though superficially novel, mainly serves to encapsulate and organise familiar trial-related values and objectives, including rational fact-finding, reliable evidence, proof of guilt, legitimate verdicts, judgement under uncertainty, holding offenders to account, and public censure of criminal wrongdoing. One important set of functions for concepts is diagnostic and remedial. A robust concept of criminal trial should help us identify instances of radical institutional failure, where official shortcomings or misconduct fatally compromise constitutive features of this distinctively penal conflict resolution mechanism. Where perversions of trial process exceed the limits of conceptual tolerance we should say, with Sullivan, that imposing criminal liability in such circumstances would be incoherent and illogical, not 'merely' unfair or unjust.

Conceptual objections claim a certain methodological priority. Contentious normative issues are not even reached where conceptual default pre-empts any further discussion or analysis. With such awesome methodological power comes commensurately great discursive responsibility. Conceptual arguments should be deployed only to close down propositions that are not legitimately arguable. If overextended to debatable controversies, conceptual argument becomes conceptual*ist* – an illegitimate definitional stop. This general methodological principle extrapolates to institutional contexts where, for example, conceptualist claims may be deployed in attempts to choke off doctrinal or jurisprudential propositions meriting further critical examination and considered normative appraisal. The 'presumption of innocence' is, I think, particularly susceptible to such conceptualist assumptions and arguments. Longstanding theoretical and jurisprudential puzzles clouding the presumption's conceptual parameters have been exacerbated in recent decades by a rebarbative[133] post-HRA 1998 jurisprudence on reverse onus clauses. Article 6(2)'s right to be presumed innocent in criminal proceedings is conceptualised as part of the ECHR's more comprehensive Article 6(1) right to a fair trial. Alleged violations of Article 6(2) consequently afford a doctrinal toehold for testing the conceptual limits of (fair) trials.

Sullivan affords few clues to the details of *his* conception of the criminal trial, save that it must – on pain of conceptual incoherence – establish proof of proscribed conduct. On a minimalist reading, Sullivan's thesis might be confined to an argument about substantive criminal law, entirely consistent with the conceptual reconstruction of criminal adjudication presented in this essay. That cramped interpretation would, however, trivialise the second of Sullivan's 'two fundamental conditions' for imposing criminal liability. One would be hard-pressed to name any post-Enlightenment jurist, judge or lawyer in the common law tradition[134] who would disagree with the elementary principle that the prosecution must prove the material facts establishing each prescribed element of a criminal offence. Indeed, it is difficult to see how Sullivan could derive conclusions regarding '[a] criminal trial properly so called'[135] or 'the simulacrum of a trial'[136] if the second proof condition were merely an idle wheel in the argumentative works. On a fair reading, Sullivan appears to be committed to two more substantial propositions. First, his concept of 'conduct' imposes material constraints on the legitimate scope of criminal prohibitions. Second, and cumulatively, Sullivan's own illustrations and commentary imply that Article 6(2) ECHR is somehow implicated in satisfying (or not) his 'proof of conduct' precondition. Thus, Sullivan characterises 'proof of conduct as an entailment of the presumption of innocence'.[137] *Entailment* can here mean only logical entailment, consistent with Sullivan's methodological conceptualism and his repeated reassurances that convictions secured by unjust means may still be *conceptually* sound even when normatively illegitimate.[138]

[133] A *mot juste* I owe to Bob Sullivan.

[134] Indeed, the proposition should be uncontroversial in any 'accusatorial' system separating the prosecutorial from the judicial function, encompassing a pan-European procedural heritage: Sarah J Summers, *Fair Trials: The European Criminal Procedural Tradition and the European Court of Human Rights* (Hart Publishing, 2007).

[135] Sullivan (n 11) 248.

[136] ibid 244.

[137] ibid 248.

[138] ibid 245.

To this extent, and as previously noted in Section II, Sullivan aligns himself with those theorists and legal commentators who want to invest ECHR Article 6(2) with some measure of jurisdiction over state parties' substantive criminal law. This manoeuvre would achieve something of a jurisprudential coup, if it could be executed successfully, since it would open up to collateral attack, via an 'unfair trial' objection, substantive offence definitions that would be doctrinally unimpeachable on ordinary canons of statutory interpretation, presupposing the primacy of literal construction and an orthodox constitutional theory of the separation of powers. This argument, moreover, would be available in domestic criminal proceedings, irrespective of whether the question ever reached Strasbourg. Essential to this manoeuvre is the fusing of substantive and procedural elements of criminal liability, represented, in Sullivan's account, by his 'two fundamental conditions': conduct, and proof of conduct. Without this merging, or conflation, a purely conceptual argument addressed only to the conduct element of criminal offences could not achieve the institutional traction claimed for it. More specifically, the argument would not engage Article 6(2) ECHR if framed in purely substantive law terms. We can try to reconstruct the general argument's somewhat elusive logic through the particular doctrinal and hypothetical examples that Sullivan deploys to vindicate his central conceptual claims.

The offence of possessing otherwise innocent articles for (apparently) terrorist purposes proscribed by section 57 of the Terrorism Act 2000 is the direct statutory descendant of the offence litigated in *Kebilene*,[139] an early authority on the application of Article 6(2) to criminal proceedings in England and Wales. 'This offence', says Sullivan, 'has been defended as a conceptually defensible criminal offence on the basis that the actus reus is possession which gives rise to the reasonable suspicion' of terrorist intent:[140]

> Apparently, all is well, at least in conceptual terms, provided the prosecution has the burden of proving the possession and the presence of reasonable suspicion. It is submitted that this is a flawed analysis if we insist that minimum standards of responsibility must be satisfied in respect of criminal liability. Conduct giving rise to mere suspicion cannot be characterised as the wrong with which the offence is engaged.

The section 57 offence, so construed, offends Sullivan's concept of legitimately criminalisable conduct. How so? Sullivan apparently thinks that epistemic standards short of belief are incapable of constituting authentic elements of a criminal offence. Yet that proposition is far from self-evident and is not grounded in direct doctrinal or broader jurisprudential authority, so far as I can tell. According to Sullivan:[141]

> [A] full reading of *Kebilene* and subsequent authority, together with consideration of the jurisprudence of Article 6(2), establishes that offences which purport to convict

[139] *R v DPP, ex p. Kebilene* [2000] 2 AC 326, DC and HL.
[140] Sullivan (n 11) 246.
[141] ibid 247.

on the basis of a reasonable suspicion must be read so as to require proof of the wrong underlying the offence.

Section 57-type offences fall into conceptual dereliction, in other words, when they disregard 'a basic and unyielding principle that conduct which constitutes the underlying wrong must be proved'.[142] After the Human Rights Act, however, ECHR Article 6(2) supposedly empowers judges to restore conceptual rectitude.

For all its theoretical ingenuity and potential strategic utility in criminal litigation, I cannot see how this argument succeeds without presupposing a *normatively* controversial conception of criminal responsibility. Plainly, an epistemic standard *qua* offence element – eg, a circumstantial element of an offence *actus reus* stipulating 'reasonable suspicion' of legislatively particularised conduct – must not be confused with the standard of proof required to establish that element. In *purely* conceptual terms, there is no difficulty in stipulating that reasonable suspicion, say, must be proved to the criminal standard, requiring the fact-finder to be 'sure' that said conduct *was* reasonably suspected. If this were all that conceptual defensibility entailed, section 57 would not violate the 'basic and unyielding principle' stipulating that 'conduct which constitutes the underlying wrong must be proved'. More emphatically, Sullivan is adamant that '[c]onduct giving rise to mere suspicion cannot be characterised as the wrong with which the offence is engaged.' I agree that there must be *some* conceptual limitations on what can count as a crime, broadly corresponding to legally defined wrongs for which a moral agent can plausibly be held criminally responsible. For example, one cannot be criminally responsible for events that occurred before one was born, and one cannot – as we have seen – be tried for future deeds or events occurring after one's death (even though one may be said to 'commit a crime' whilst alive that eventuates in a completed criminal wrong only after one's death).[143] The *nullum crimen* principle imposes further conceptual limitations on the scope of criminal liability, inasmuch as ex post facto criminalisation of past conduct forestalls any possibility of compliance and would reduce the accused to a hapless 'spectator to his own fate' in exactly the way Sullivan laments.[144] Of course, as Sullivan

[142] ibid.

[143] I am alive to the conceptual awkwardness in saying that 'D commits crime C at T_1', when C is not fully consummated until T_3 (eg, when V dies), D having died at T_2. There is no conceptual or linguistic problem in saying that there is nobody to hold criminally responsible at T_3. But when was the crime committed? If the alternatives are T_1 (when D acted), T_3 (when D is already dead), or 'a crime occurred but nobody committed it', T_1 seems to me the best default option. And in fact, I think this is what people generally would say: 'D murdered V, but died himself before he could be brought to justice', etc.

[144] The *nullum crimen* principle is a constraint on criminal legislation, rather than a fair trial norm. Thus, it relates to Sullivan's first fundamental condition (conduct), rather than the second (proof of conduct) – unless the second is a trivial derivation of the first.

says, imposing criminal liability for the state of the weather would be absurd;[145] more precisely, because the state of the weather is not something that human agents (absent superhero powers or evil genius technology) can be responsible for orchestrating. Weather events are, in my terms, beyond the cognisable scope of legitimate trial jeopardy.

By virtue of requiring *reasonable* suspicion, however, the section 57 offence isn't conceptually absurd in any equivalent sense. It *would be* absurd if the normative requirement of reasonableness were dropped, so that a person could be convicted on the strength of any far-fetched, crazy or prejudiced suspicion that some random onlooker happened to entertain. In that nightmare world, all our lives would be hostage to vicissitudes as unfathomable and uncontrollable as the weather. Back in our world, if the correct doctrinal interpretation of the offence is that (objective) reasonable suspicion ousts (subjectively) innocent intent – because, on the correct reading, that's what Parliament did in enacting the offence – then that legally authentic interpretation fixes 'the wrong', in positive law, which the offence proscribes. Article 6(2)'s presumption of innocence cannot render practical assistance to revise or countermand that conclusion, any more than direct appeals to authentic moral wrongs or blameless moral innocence (the legal positivist's caricature of natural law) can step in to save the day. These normative arguments are not institutionally cognisable. Those who wish to avoid conviction of the section 57 offence will need to conduct themselves accordingly. They should not hoard large quantities of sodium hydroxide in their cellars, drive across town centres with caches of fertiliser secreted in domestic vehicles, or download copies of the Al-Qaeda Manual or white supremacist literature on how to start a race riot.[146] Failing that, they had better have some credible exculpatory explanation for their conduct by way of affirmative defence. Those who choose to skate on thin ice are held, at law, *volenti* to the risk of calamity.

On my account, the decisive considerations are jurisprudential and institutional, not conceptual. There is undeniably a problem of inconsistency if a court first identifies some component of a criminal wrong as part of the offence definition and then says, without further rationale or authority, that the prosecutor doesn't have to prove it. In England and Wales, *Woolmington*[147] emphatically dictates otherwise. Post-HRA 1998 reverse onus jurisprudence is admittedly sometimes unhelpfully obscure or self-contradictory, not least in its reliance on the slippery concept of

[145] 'Any attempt to decouple liability for a criminal wrong from any degree of involvement in the wrong will entail straying from the path of the criminal law. Indeed if such a decoupling were made a general principle, the sky would be the limit. One could be made liable for anything and everything, such as the state of the weather': Sullivan (n 22) 296.

[146] *Cf R v Dunleavy* [2021] EWCA Crim 39, [16].

[147] *Woolmington v DPP* 1935] AC 462, HL.

'gravamen'.[148] Scything through the doctrinal thicket,[149] the question always comes down to this: *what is the pertinent criminal wrong encapsulated in the offence definition*? The answer to that question follows from jurisprudential analysis of relevant institutional materials (statutes, case law precedents, hard-working soft law, canons of statutory interpretation, broader jurisprudential principles, etc) supplemented by institutionally cognisable normative sources (including comparative law influences and political morality) and general intellectual resources (eg, logic, reasoning by analogy, rational inference, common sense relevancy). Most of the offences perplexing courts and debated by commentators in relation to Article 6(2) are statutory. Whilst models of statutory interpretation too closely aligned to parliamentary intent are typically reductive and institutionally unrealistic, the literal wording and structural organisation of penal statutes must always command judicial respect and are often decisive. This is the nub of (liberal) law's normative formalism. The question is not what Parliament said, or even what Parliament intended, but what Parliament *did* in enacting a particular offence. What Parliament did is located in the relational institutional space between Parliament's deeds and their authentic interpretation in authoritative rulings by appellate courts.

Excessively broad criminal offences may well be illegitimate as a matter of legislative policy.[150] If sentencing practice enables more individualised culpability assessments to mitigate the harshness of extravagant liability doctrines,[151] this is welcome. Moreover, English criminal jurisprudence contains well-established principles of statutory interpretation designed to curb legislative overarching. Penal statutes should be interpreted strictly in favour of the accused.[152] In cases of doubt, courts should lean towards reading advertent

[148] Sullivan (n 32) 213 suggests, by interpolation, that '[f]or Roberts … the gravamen of the [*Kebilene*] offence was proof of possessing an article giving rise to a reasonable suspicion of such connection or use and there was, therefore, no contravention of Article 6(2)'. On my reading, judicial appeals to the 'gravamen' of an offence in reverse onus clause jurisprudence (see, eg, *R v DPP, ex p Kebilene* [2000] 2 AC 326, 344, DC (Lord Bingham); *R v S* [2003] 1 Cr App R 35, [2002] EWCA Crim 2558 (Davis J)) are seldom helpful, sometimes obfuscating and generally best avoided. 'Gravamen' can be invoked intelligibly to characterise the core wrong targeted by the prohibition. But this is at most a stepping-stone towards the decisive doctrinal issue, ie, defining the offence at law. If the *offence*, properly interpreted, criminalises conduct inciting reasonable suspicion, then that's the definition of the offence. Neither 'gravamen' nor Art 6(2) has obvious (let alone decisive) interpretational significance.

[149] To be clear, I don't seek to defend every court decision or passage of judicial analysis addressing reverse onus clauses. When primary materials are not logically reconcilable, the jurist's task is principled reconstruction. Superior judgments include: *R v Williams (Orette)* [2013] 1 WLR 1200; [2012] EWCA Crim 2162; *R v Wilcocks* [2017] 4 WLR 39, [2016] EWCA Crim 2043; *R v K(M)*; *R v Gega* [2019] QB 86, [2018] EWCA Crim 667; *R v Webster* [2011] 1 Cr App R 16, [2010] EWCA Crim 2819.

[150] *Cf* Roberts, 'The Presumption of Innocence Brought Home?' (n 34) 67, 66 (castigating the *Kebilene* offence as 'procedurally sound, but substantively bad … a thoroughly bad piece of over-criminalisation … mak[ing] unnecessary in-roads into individuals' personal autonomy').

[151] For creative thinking along these lines, see Sullivan (n 32) 214.

[152] *Tuck & Sons v Priester* (1887) 19 QBD 629. But this (weak?) presumption is overridden by clear parliamentary intent expressed in literal meaning, as Lord Reid elaborated in *R v Ottewell* [1970] AC 642, 649, HL: 'I would never seek to diminish in any way the importance of that principle within its proper sphere. But it only applies where after full inquiry and consideration one is left in real doubt'. Also see, eg, *Isle of Wight Council v Platt* [2017] 1 WLR 1441, [2017] UKSC 28, [45].

mens rea into offence definitions.[153] Reverse onus clauses can be imposed by implication, but there is a strong presumption against it.[154] Where reverse onuses have been imposed, courts should 'read down' the burden to a mere burden of production if a fully probative onus would be incompatible with Article 6(2).[155] But these jurisprudential and broader normative considerations are ancillary to Sullivan's meticulously 'non-normative'[156] central thesis. Violation of Sullivan's responsibility condition is supposedly 'not merely unduly harsh, it is incoherent'.[157] As demonstrated in relation to the section 57 offence, the argument – on pain of circularity – seemingly trades on an undeclared (and therefore undefended) normative stipulation, to the effect that (objectively) suspicious behaviour should never be enough to constitute criminal liability, even when proved to the criminal standard. Even if this normative stipulation were vindicated by explicit doctrinal authority in English criminal law, I cannot see how any jurisprudentially credible interpretation of Article 6(2) can be used to shore it up. Purely conceptual analysis, either of 'conduct' or of 'proof of conduct' (or of both combined), furnishes neither the substantive destination nor a doctrinal vehicle capable of reaching it.

V. Conclusion

Compared with the gallons of ink (nowadays, pixels) devoted to jurisprudential reconstruction and doctrinal criticism of criminal procedure law, relatively little has been written on the concept of criminal trial.[158] This essay accepted the challenge implicit in Bob Sullivan's influential writings to develop a more fully articulated conception, at least in preliminary outline. According to Sullivan, 'proof of conduct' is a necessary attribute of a criminal trial properly so-called. But what, exactly, does 'proof of conduct' entail in either theoretical or practical jurisprudence? It seems entirely plausible that there could be distinctive hallmarks or distinguishing features of criminal trials, some of which may be conceptually essential. Yet Sullivan offers only a few emblematic illustrations and never attempts more systematic analysis. In taking up these suggestive threads, one methodological aim was to demonstrate

[153] *Pwr v DPP* [2022] 1 WLR 789, [2022] UKSC 2; *Attorney General's Reference (No 1 of 2020)* [2021] QB 441, [2020] EWCA Crim 1665; *DPP v Jagnauth* [2019] UKPC 8; *B v DPP* [2000] 2 AC 428, HL; *Sweet v Parsley* [1970] AC 132, HL.

[154] *R v Hunt* [1987] AC 352, HL; *R v K(M)*; *R v Gega* [2019] QB 86, [2018] EWCA Crim 667.

[155] *Sheldrake v DPP* [2005] 1 AC 264, [2004] UKHL 43; *R v Lambert* [2002] 2 AC 545, HL; *DPP v Wright (Anthony)* [2009] 3 All ER 726, [2009] EWHC 105 (Admin).

[156] Sullivan (n 22) 293 (advancing 'a non-normative line of attack' underpinned by 'non-normative critique').

[157] ibid.

[158] *Cf* Anthony Duff, Lindsay Farmer, Sandra Marshall and Victor Tadros, *The Trial on Trial Volume Three: Towards a Normative Theory of the Criminal Trial* (Hart Publishing, 2007) (avowedly *normative* ambitions).

(with no pretension to definitive or comprehensive treatment[159]) the viability and analytical value of a general conceptual analysis.

Concepts should be judged contextually and relative to their uses. In the context of criminal jurisprudence, a useful concept of the trial must be sufficiently capacious to accommodate a variety of paradigm instances but without becoming conceptually incontinent or vacuously uninformative. On the account developed here, trials are, roughly, epistemically serious institutional mechanisms for (legitimate) pacific dispute resolution with outcome jeopardy. Criminal trials are, by derivation, epistemically serious institutional mechanisms for the legitimate resolution of disputed allegations of criminal wrongdoing by responsible agents, with verdict jeopardy.[160] This conception of the concept of (criminal) trial underscores the importance of rational inquiry and evidential warrant in adjudicative outcomes claiming legitimacy, where pacific dispute resolution demands that criminal verdicts be *demonstrably* justifiable – not merely supported by good reasons. In functional terms, our conceptual reconstruction established criteria for distinguishing constitutive from merely contingent features of trial practice (which do *not* map neatly onto the most emblematic or celebrated aspects of procedural traditions), clarified why show trials are not trials, and yielded some non-obvious analytical results, including identifying an intriguing (and still largely unexplored) intersection between the theoretical concept of a criminal trial and the human rights law concept of a fair trial. The concept of a trial, we saw, also partly incorporates rule of law values. However, this normative component must be strictly policed to avoid pre-empting legitimate arguments or foreclosing live controversies in criminal law theory, policy or practice. 'Criminal trial', then, is a Goldilocks concept: it must be calibrated at just the right level of generality, neither too broad nor too narrow, to serve its intended purposes.

Sullivan and I are substantially in agreement about the basic tenets of liberal criminal law, as expounded in Chapter 1. We both think that criminal liability should be reserved for responsible agents who deserve condemnation for (serious) wrongdoing. We agree that 'wrongdoing' of the relevant kind must be confined to forms of conduct for which an agent can properly be held (criminally) responsible, and this stipulation rules out liability for many things (including involuntary behaviour, future conduct, and the weather). On the procedural side, we agree that criminal liability should not be imposed without proof of each element of the offence. Diagnosis of lingering disagreement converged on three issues: (1) the rigour of the 'conduct' requirement in its application to particular offences;

[159] One respect in which the foregoing account is somewhat vague and non-committal concerns the distinction between the constitutive elements of a concept of criminal trial, and its necessary preconditions or assumptions. I hope to clarify this in future work.

[160] More precisely, I proposed that criminal trials are (1) institutionalised, formal, and legitimacy-claiming (2) conflict-resolution mechanisms conducted as (3) epistemically serious inquiries into (4) alleged criminal wrongdoing by (5) responsible agents entailing (6) verdict jeopardy. Note, however, that greater precision increases complexity, and does not necessarily enhance intelligibility of core claims.

(2) the competent jurisdiction of ECHR Article 6(2)'s presumption of innocence; and (3) the scope, in English law or otherwise, for invoking purely conceptual objections to excessively broad criminal liability. Proceeding chiefly along the third, methodological dimension, this essay directly engaged with Sullivan's central thesis proposing 'conduct' and 'proof of conduct' as two conceptual preconditions of legitimate criminal convictions and authentic criminal trials.

Conceptual analysis is an essential tool in the jurist's toolkit and a staple of legal doctrinal method. Just about any notable concept can benefit from conceptual elucidation.[161] Sullivan's attempt to leverage conceptual analysis into an argument about the scope of the substantive criminal law and the institutional purchase of the presumption of innocence is a typically bold and imaginative methodological gambit. Compared with Sullivan's apparently muscular contrivance, however, my concept of the trial is relatively thin, abstract and ill-equipped for doctrinal heavy lifting. It could not bear the weight of the jurisprudential and institutional conclusions that Sullivan wants to claim for his conceptual preferences. Though it is possible to envisage very extreme scenarios in which violations of the presumption of innocence would undercut the status of a criminal trial (eg, because they would destroy epistemic seriousness and/or verdict jeopardy), such thought experiments are very far removed from the real-life litigated cases thrown up by post-HRA 1998 jurisprudence. When it moves from abstract theoretical speculation to concrete illustrations, Sullivan's conceptual argument becomes, in my terms, *conceptualist*: a form of argumentation trading on the false promise to deliver through peremptory conceptual analysis what can only be obtained by more extended normative (political morality) argument and institutional (jurisprudential and doctrinal) reasoning.

In reflective register, Sullivan muses that 'conceptual critique [may] have as little effect on legislators and policy makers as the more familiar normative critiques'.[162] My hunch, for what it is worth, inverts this rhetorical priority: if the argument for liberal criminal law fails to carry the day through direct appeal to political morality and jurisprudential tradition,[163] informing policymakers that their opposition is incoherent, illogical or a categorical impossibility is unlikely to shift opinion. Likewise, if judges cannot be persuaded to utilise the familiar interpretative tools at their disposal in order to tether criminal offence definitions to cohere with – or at least better approximate – judgements of moral culpability for conduct, I cannot see how appealing to a conception of 'conduct' with minimal doctrinal recognition is going to exert any additional institutional pressure. Right and wrong can be debated as questions of legal validity or moral propriety; conceptual incoherence is a conversational guillotine inviting forensic stalemate.

[161] For the ultimate proof, see Harry G Frankfurt, *The Importance of What We Care About: Philosophical Essays* (CUP, 1988) ch 10 ('On Bullshit').

[162] Sullivan (n 22) 303.

[163] Sullivan (n 32) 213 succinctly encapsulates several of the best arguments: 'It would be a flagrant breach of the harm principle to penalize persons merely suspected of being associated with an immediate or more remote harm. … It is an essential safeguard of liberal democracy that persons merely under suspicion should not be obliged, on pain of conviction and punishment, to clear their name.'

Being wrong is an occupational hazard of theoretical work. On a clear-eyed view, most of the philosophical giants of the Enlightenment made major theoretical errors. Kant: wrong about the rigour of deontological ethics; Hume: wrong about the limits of reason; Bentham: promiscuously wrong on diverse subjects, at inordinate length, in spidery handwriting. In contrast to legal doctrinal analysis, where being right is at a premium (few clients or judges award style points for wrong advice or faulty legal submissions), the best theoretical work may be valued for its imagination, innovation, pioneering exploration, provocation to engagement, potential for development, fecundity in spawning research programmes, productive error, or glorious failure. Is it better to be right or interesting in theorising criminal law, if you can't be both? That could be an intriguing topic for another round of conceptual analysis, but the issue could be settled only by normative argument.

4

Damaška's Comparative Method and the Future of Common Law Evidence

BioNote: Mirjan Damaška is the pre-eminent comparative criminal justice scholar of his generation and one of the all-time greats of academic law, a recipient of the Ruder Bošković Award for Legal Science in Croatia and an elected Fellow of the American Academy of Arts and Sciences.[1] Like von Hirsch, an émigré from central Europe, Damaška found a secure intellectual berth at Yale Law School, where he remained for the balance of his career. His principal publications span judicial institutions, models of adjudication, criminal procedure and criminal evidence, always in comparative[2] (sometimes explicitly international)[3] context and with a refined historical sensibility.[4]

Damaška's first[5] *festschrift*[6] was the only one featured in this collection to which I was invited to contribute without already knowing the honorand personally, albeit I was very well-acquainted with his work, which I employed extensively in teaching postgraduate options on Comparative Criminal Justice. My inclusion in this project was a long-range consequence of attending academic conferences. The story begins with meeting John Jackson at the 1996 Law & Society Association

[1] Harold Hongju Koh, 'Mirjan Damaška: A Bridge Between Legal Cultures' in John Jackson, Máximo Langer and Peter Tillers (eds), *Crime, Procedure and Evidence in a Comparative and International Context: Essays in Honour of Professor Mirjan Damaška* (Hart Publishing, 2008) 29.

[2] Notably, the evergreen classic Mirjan Damaška, 'Evidentiary Barriers to Conviction and Two Models of Criminal Procedure: A Comparative Study' (1973) 121 *University of Pennsylvania Law Review* 506.

[3] Mirjan Damaška, 'The International Criminal Court Between Aspiration and Achievement' (2009) 14 *UCLA Journal of International Law and Foreign Affairs* 19; Mirjan Damaška, 'What is the Point of International Criminal Justice?' (2008) 83 *Chicago-Kent Law Review* 329. Also see Bert Swart, 'Damaška and the Faces of International Criminal Justice' (2008) 6 *Journal of International Criminal Justice* 87.

[4] Mirjan Damaška, *Evaluation of Evidence: Pre-Modern and Modern Approaches* (CUP, 2018); Mirjan Damaška, 'The Quest for Due Process in the Age of Inquisition' (2012) 60 *American Journal of Comparative Law* 919; Mirjan Damaška, 'The Death of Legal Torture' (1978) 87 *Yale Law Journal* 860.

[5] A second celebratory volume in the German series *Beiträge zum Internationalen und Europäischen Strafrecht* came later: Bruce Ackerman, Kai Ambos and Hrvoje Sikirić (eds), *Visions of Justice: Liber Amicorum Mirjan Damaška* (Duncker & Humblot, 2016).

[6] Jackon, Langer and Tillers (n 1).

Annual Conference hosted by Strathclyde University in Glasgow. Having met up with John again in planning meetings for the launch of the *International Journal of Evidence & Proof* (E&P) – the brainchild of Mike McConville and Roger Leng at Warwick – I was invited to participate in a major international conference on 'The Judicial Role in Criminal Proceedings' hosted by John and his QUB colleague Sean Doran in Belfast in 1998.[7] As well as getting to know John and Sean on this occasion, I also met for the first time keynote speakers Ron Allen, Alex Stein and Andrew Ligertwood – all of whom would become friends, collaborators and sparring partners in Evidence law teaching, research and publications. Von Hirsch was also an attendee. After a frustrating session trying to persuade sceptical penologists of the ethical limitations of consequentialism, we shared an unforgettable impromptu tour of Belfast's atrocity sites narrated by a knowledgeable and well-connected taxi driver.[8] Thus are academic friendships formed and deepened through ongoing conversations at successive meetings in far-flung locations. Graduating to the stage of international procedural scholarship, if only as a minor bit player, secured me the invitation to Damaška's celebratory party.

The actual launch party for Damaška's festschrift was a lavish affair at Yale. A two-day workshop featuring academic luminaries such as George Fletcher and Antonio Cassese culminated in a steak dinner at the New England-swanky Quinnipiac Club; an occasion slightly spoilt for me by ongoing root canal work and an angry temporary filling. This is the only time I can recall being almost – not quite! – starstruck by the elevated academic company. I gravitated towards the US Evidence and Criminal Procedure crowd, chatting with Michele Taruffo, Michael Risinger, Peter Tillers, Jennifer Mnookin and Máximo Langer. I also had a long discussion with John Jackson about whether a move to Nottingham might be feasible, as so in short order it proved – inaugurating a decade-long active collaboration in teaching, co-supervising PhD students, sharing research ideas and discussing and commenting on work in progress. John and I have published just one coauthored essay,[9] but this is only the most visible product of a long and fruitful working relationship as professorial colleagues in the same institution.

[7] Sean Doran and John D Jackson (eds), *The Judicial Role in Criminal Proceedings* (Hart Publishing, 2000).

[8] Returning to my hotel, The Europa (with its proud reputation as 'the most bombed hotel in Europe'), I couldn't figure out why the lobby was so crowded and had to elbow my way through a jostling horde to get to the lifts to my floor. Back in my room and turning on the tv news, the image on the screen was …. the lobby of the Europa hotel; where Northern Ireland's soon-to-be First Minister David Trimble (a former law lecturer at QUB) was announcing the conclusion of the Belfast/Good Friday Agreement. This is one of only two occasions when I can credibly claim to have been an eyewitness to unfolding world history (the other was in Kyiv in 2003, when – sat alongside an approving US Ambassador – I watched the Ukrainian Foreign Minister announcing that Ukraine would join the US-led 'coalition of the willing' to replace Saddam Hussain by invading Iraq).

[9] John Jackson and Paul Roberts, 'Beyond Common Law Evidence: Reimagining, and Reinvigorating, Evidence Law as Forensic Science' in Darryl K Brown, Jenia Iontcheva Turner and Bettina Weisser (eds), *The Oxford Handbook of Criminal Process* (OUP, 2019).

'Networking' at academic meetings has the ring of a rather instrumentalist exercise in entrepreneurial self-promotion, and perhaps that is sometimes all it is. For me, participating in academic conferences and workshops, often – to be sure, and with increasing regularity – by personal invitation, has been my point of entry to an expanding international academic community and opened more doors to opportunity than I could ever have imagined. Admission to Damaška's festschrift is a shining illustration. They say that you should never meet your heroes, but I have rarely been disappointed when encountering in real life scholars whose work I have read and admired. (Damaška in person was urbane, gracious and utterly charming). Besides, the best discussions often occur outside the formal conference programme, sometimes with liquid lubrication for those who enjoy it. For all the miracles of modern internet communications and the convenience (and economy) of teleconferencing, virtual attendance in academic meetings is no true substitute for actually being there.

I. Introduction: From *Faces of Justice* to *Evidence Law Adrift*

Over many decades, Mirjan Damaška has been one of the most inventive, incisive, and influential voices in the comparative study of legal process, procedure, and evidence. His two major works, published 11 years apart, are sweeping, state-of-the-art reflections on legal procedure at key moments in the evolution of the discipline. In *The Faces of Justice and State Authority* (hereinafter FoJ),[10] published in 1986, Damaška brilliantly demonstrated the explanatory force of modelling legal processes in terms of their affinity with distinctive styles of government and structures of judicial authority. This compelling exposition made a major contribution to comparative legal studies and can be credited with helping to inspire contemporary comparative scholars' keen interest in connections between law and (political) culture.[11] FoJ concluded in a tone of serene authorial satisfaction:

> [T]he task set in this volume is largely complete: a framework has been created within which to examine the legal process as it is rooted in attitudes toward state authority and influenced by the changing role of government .... If my scheme contributes to the storehouse of concepts with which the variation of procedural form can be identified and analyzed, and if it suggests new and fruitful lines of inquiry, we can live with the scheme's imperfections.[12]

Published some 11 years later in 1997, *Evidence Law Adrift* (hereinafter ELA)[13] shared its predecessor's preoccupation with models of adversary and inquisitorial

[10] Mirjan Damaška, *The Faces of Justice and State Authority: A Comparative Approach to the Legal Process* (Yale University Press, 1986).
[11] See, eg, David Nelken (ed), *Comparing Legal Cultures* (Dartmouth, 1997).
[12] FoJ, 240, 242.
[13] Mirjan Damaška, *Evidence Law Adrift* (Yale University Press, 1997).

procedure, this time concentrated more specifically on the structure and doctrinal details of the law of evidence. But having lulled the reader with these reassuringly familiar themes, the narrative takes a disturbing turn and concludes with this almost apocalyptic prediction:

> [T]he institutional environment appears to have decayed that supplied distinctive features of common law evidence with a strong argumentative rationale .... In its absence, shorn of adequate justification, they face the danger of becoming antiquated period pieces, intellectual curiosa confined to an oubliette in the castle of justice.[14]

It is tempting to characterise this sequential brace of publications as marking a shift from the confident modernism of FoJ to the 'postmodern' anxiety of ELA. Postmodern doubt, uncertainty and scepticism, imported from the humanities and social theory, became two of the *leitmotifs* of legal scholarship in the 1990s, finding expression in various forms and places.[15] These sceptical tendencies have spilled over into the present century, not least regarding the use of models of 'adversarial' and 'inquisitorial' legal procedure as explanatory heuristics, which is now regarded as distinctly passé in certain quarters.[16] Swimming against this sceptical tide, the first sections of this essay reconsider the methodological foundations of FoJ 20 years after its publication, and defend the essentials of Damaška's methodology of comparative modelling against recent critics of orthodox procedural conceptualisations. In the second half of the essay, however, I turn critic myself by arguing, *pace* ELA, that common law evidence is no more 'adrift' than the still securely grounded methodology of comparative modelling pioneered by Damaška in his earlier work.

II. The Methodology of Comparative Modelling

Generally speaking, lawyers spend less time reflecting on their basic methodological tools and techniques in comparison to scholars in other disciplines. In consequence, legal method is often not stated as explicitly or understood as widely or profoundly as it ideally ought to be. Method is explicitly addressed to the 'How?' dimension of scholarly inquiry, but it is always also implicitly determined

[14] ELA, 142.

[15] Specifically in relation to procedure, evidence and proof see, eg, Carrie Menkel-Meadow, 'The Trouble with the Adversary System in a Postmodern, Multicultural World' (1996) 38 *William and Mary Law Review* 5; Donald Nicolson, 'Truth, Reason and Justice: Epistemology and Politics in Evidence Discourse' (1994) 57 *Modern Law Review* 726. *Cf* William Twining, 'Some Scepticisms about Some Scepticisms' (1984) 11 *Journal of Law and Society* 137 & 285 (reprinted in William Twining, *Rethinking Evidence*, 2nd edn (CUP, 2006) ch 4).

[16] See, eg, Sarah Summers, *Fair Trials: The European Criminal Procedural Tradition and the European Court of Human Rights* (Hart Publishing, 2007) ch 1; John D Jackson, 'The Effect of Human Rights on Criminal Evidentiary Processes: Towards Convergence, Divergence or Realignment?' (2005) 68 *Modern Law Review* 737, 747, suggesting that 'the adversarial/inquisitorial dichotomy has obscured the truly transformative nature of the [European Court of Human Rights'] jurisprudence'.

by mutually conditioning 'What?' and 'Why?' considerations.[17] In order to select a suitable methodology, it is necessary to define the parameters of one's inquiry and to clarify the reasons for undertaking it. Subject matter is determined by motivation, which in turn pre-selects method; but choice of subject matter is also influenced by available methods (research is the art of the possible), which in turn provide motivation (ought implies can).

Exemplifying these methodological truisms, Damaška simultaneously introduced both his subject matter and the motivation for his study in FoJ's very first sentence:

> An immense and bewildering subject opens up before one who contemplates the diversity of arrangements and institutions through which justice is variously administered in modern states.[18]

Such pronounced variety in the legal processes encountered across national jurisdictions constitutes a standing provocation to the legal scholar. In matters of such patent social, political and moral significance as legal procedure, adjudication and law enforcement, why have otherwise quite similar western industrialised nations evolved such distinctive forms of justice? Law and justice are not trifling ornaments, like ceremonial national dress or English judges' horsehair wigs, which can be indulged as (mostly) harmless quaint anachronisms. Nor yet are they so obviously features of cultural heritage in which diversity should be positively celebrated, such as national language and cuisine. One senses that there is something strange, if not faintly sinister, in the notion that twenty-first-century justice looks quite different in France, Germany and England (to mention only three close European neighbours). Can 'justice by geography' be anything other than an international postcode lottery, with ever-declining legitimacy in an increasingly globalised world? There is clearly something here that stands in need of explanation, and – in view of the vital interests at stake – *should* be explained. As Damaška framed the issue:

> Can this stupendous diversity be made intelligible, or reduced to a manageable set of patterns? At a minimum, can a conceptual framework be developed to assist us in tracing similarities and differences in component parts?[19]

Damaška's project in FoJ was therefore characterised from the outset as an exercise in promoting *understanding*, in search of 'new meaning for the previously incomprehensible'.[20] Since 'to know things is to watch them from the outside',[21]

[17] Expressed somewhat more formally, Questions of Method form one point on an Eternal Triangle of intellectual inquiry, with Questions of Subject-Matter (entailing conceptual taxonomy and definition) and Questions of Motivation completing the timeless geometric triad: see further, Paul Roberts, 'Interdisciplinarity in Legal Research' in Mike McConville and Wing Hong Eric Chui (eds), *Research Methods for Law*, 3rd edn (Edinburgh University Press, 2024).

[18] FoJ, 1.

[19] FoJ, 3.

[20] FoJ, 14.

[21] FoJ, 44.

comparative methodology was naturally selected for its unrivalled powers of illumination, notwithstanding existential costs for the researcher:

> [T]he illumination provided here will be at best like winter sun: emitting light but little warmth .... [T]he reader should be aware of the unavoidable costs of looking at things from the outside: it is hard to be at once comfortable everywhere and at home anywhere.[22]

Like comparative legal scholars before and since, Damaška found himself in dialogue with an established comparative literature emphasising contrasts between 'adversarial' and 'inquisitorial' legal process. Damaška traced this 'well-trodden path' to a juridical distinction already evident in twelfth-century legal thought.[23] However, for reasons that have since become commonplace (partly owing to Damaška's influential writings), the adversarial-inquisitorial dichotomy came to be viewed as an unsatisfactory conceptual prism through which to scrutinise modern legal process in comparative perspective. This conventional dichotomy's principal methodological flaw is traceable to its tendency to confuse normative and descriptive analysis of procedural systems, so that it becomes unclear whether 'adversarial' and 'inquisitorial' characteristics are being defined by the historical evolution of extant, institutionalised legal procedures, or whether existing procedural systems are to be interpreted and evaluated by reference to idealised models of 'adversarial' and 'inquisitorial' process. For example, trial by lay jury has certainly been an historical concomitant of adversarial process in common law jurisdictions, but does this imply that trial by lay jury is a definitive characteristic of 'adversarial' trial? An historical interpretation might suggest that it is, whereas a conceptual approach could maintain that the core adversary notion of party-contest does not logically entail trial by jury, or indeed any other particular institutional model of fact-finding. Such ambiguity blunts analytical precision and risks the onset of a vicious circularity: might the adversarial-inquisitorial dichotomy be to historical and contemporary procedural systems as the chicken is to the egg? Basic conceptual confusions are then compounded by florid terminological inconsistency, such that concepts such as 'accusatorial' are routinely claimed for *both* common law *and* modern Continental process.[24] However, exposing the limitations of the adversarial-inquisitorial dichotomy as an analytical device should not automatically be equated with advocating its complete abandonment. Indeed, Damaška worked with and augmented the conceptual models of legal process already to hand, rather than starting from an analytical Year Zero.

[22] FoJ, 15.
[23] FoJ, 3.
[24] If 'accusatorial' refers to the institutional division between prosecution and adjudication, Continental criminal procedure systems became accusatorial when they dispensed with the omni-competent medieval inquisitor by splitting the magistracy into two separate branches – prosecutors and judges – with clearly defined, albeit complementary, roles. See JR Spencer, 'Introduction' in Mireille Delmas-Marty and J R Spencer (eds), *European Criminal Procedures* (CUP, 2002).

The key to Damaška's reconstruction of the traditional adversarial-inquisitorial dichotomy lies in his realisation that models of legal procedure are intimately related to structures of political authority; a basic insight Damaška freely concedes to Marx.[25] As Damaška himself memorably put it, '[t]o consider forms of justice in monadic isolation from their social and economic context is – for many purposes – like playing *Hamlet* without the Prince'.[26] What Damaška perceived more clearly than his predecessors, however, was that political theorists dealt only in rather sweeping generalities about the law – Marx, indeed, is a case in point[27] – and stopped well short of elaborating any detailed conceptions of legal process and adjudication in terms of their underlying political values, executive ideologies and institutional structures. Recognising that 'most questions relevant to the study of procedural diversity lie beyond the opposition of capitalism, socialism and similar vague socioeconomic concepts',[28] Damaška had discerned the contours of a jurisprudential niche which he proceeded to occupy, furnish and make his own.

The procedural models Damaška elaborated in FoJ were unambiguously ideal-types devised for analytical purposes. Such models were perfectly suited to Damaška's ambition to understand the complexities of existing procedural practices in terms of their underlying patterns, logics and values, rather than compiling detailed sociological descriptions of contemporary legal proceedings or scrupulously documented historical exegesis:

> [C]haracteristics of the two archetypes should not be understood as repositories of essential facets of *existing* procedures in civil- and common-law countries. They are meant to be used in seeking to understand the complex mixtures of arrangements, as means to analyze them in terms of their components, as one would study compounds in analytical chemistry.[29]

To the challenge that model-building is an unwelcome distraction from the urgent task of becoming better acquainted with the world around us, Damaška counterposed Weber's powerful retort that it is not possible to understand the real world without constructing abstract analytical models through which to organise and interpret the empirical data which bombard our senses.[30] Meaning

[25] FoJ, 6.

[26] FoJ, 7.

[27] Marx's scattered jurisprudential pensées barely constitute a mature theory of law: see Maureen Cain and Alan Hunt, *Marx and Engels on Law* (Academic Press, 1979).

[28] FoJ, 8.

[29] FoJ, 12.

[30] 'I believe it is to Weber that we owe the paradoxical dictum to the effect that in order to grasp the real context we have to construct an unreal one': Mirjan Damaška, 'Evidentiary Barriers to Conviction and Two Models of Criminal Procedure: A Comparative Study' (1973) 121 *University of Pennsylvania Law Review* 506, 577. See, eg, Charles Ragin and David Zaret, 'Theory and Method in Comparative Research: Two Strategies' (1983) 61 *Social Forces* 731, 732, noting 'Weber's conviction that social reality is sufficiently complex as to be unknowable in the absence of theoretical interests that guide construction of one-sided type concepts [ie ideal types]'. Also see Mirjan Damaška, 'Structures of Authority and Comparative Criminal Procedure' (1975) 84 *Yale Law Journal* 480, 482: 'I concede that there are levels of analysis at which procedural models are generally misleading stereotypes or lifeless clichés. They are

is an achievement of 'artificial' (non-empirical) categories of human thought and perception, and generalisation is an inescapable requirement of this human capacity (and existential necessity) to make sense of our physical and social environment and to orientate ourselves within it. In this fundamental sense, utilising models of legal procedure is not so much a legitimate methodological preference as a threshold requirement for undertaking legal analysis of any description:

> [W]ithout a suitable typology, comparative studies of procedural form cannot even begin .... [E]xplorations of individuality become possible only after one has first obtained conceptual instruments with which to see and discuss individuality in terms of generic notions.[31]

Damaška was nonetheless at pains to emphasise that his abstracted models should not be taken literally, as faithful depictions of existing legal phenomena. The models were conceived as collections of family resemblances, or artistic genres:

> [a]ctual Anglo-American and Continental procedures will be seen to belong to one or another mode, as buildings can be said to belong to one or another architectural style .... Of course, one should not expect more from this type of analysis than it can deliver: that a building may be classified as an exemplar of a particular style ... tells us very little about the individuality of the building.[32]

Damaška's procedural models were constructed along two intersecting axes. The first axis characterises the structure of procedural authority in legal institutions, running from 'hierarchical' officialdom at one pole to 'coordinate' adjudication at the other. The second axis measures modern styles of government, running from the 'activist' policy-implementation of the social engineers to the 'reactive' laissez-faire of the *nachtwächterstaat*. Since, at least in theory (and Damaška argued, in practice as well), these characteristics can be found in any combination, there are four ideal types to which any actual legal process might most closely correspond: hierarchical-activist, hierarchical-reactive, co-ordinate-activist, and co-ordinate-reactive. The way in which FoJ mapped these analytical categories onto real legal systems traced patterns which are often familiar and predictable, but there were also some unexpected associations and surprising conclusions.

Perhaps the line between idealised models and empirical reality is always blurred so that the danger of their confusion is, practically speaking, ineradicable. It is, furthermore, *always* a mistake to think that any single conceptualisation can encapsulate *everything* of potential interest about empirical phenomena. To emphasise particular contrasts and continuities, one must always ignore others that might conceivably have been prioritised. But for all the well-known risks of wishful thinking and over-generalisation, in law as in life, it seems that Damaška's

also simplifications; but this is precisely their default de qualité, indeed their virtue. They are used to liberate us from the tyranny of details, so that we can discern the overall distinguishing attributes of complex phenomena.'

[31] FoJ, 241, 242.

[32] FoJ, 10, 242.

use of idealised procedural models was, in principle, methodologically impeccable, as well as exceptionally illuminating.[33]

III. Four Methodological Strengths

Damaška's comparative modelling of legal process boasted several notable strengths which, in my opinion, convincingly demonstrate the enduring heuristic value of differentiating between 'adversarial' and 'inquisitorial' procedures, at least as a point of departure for more refined analysis. This section highlights four particular attributes of Damaška's methodology. First, the bridge to political theory constructed by Damaška provides an escape route from the viciously circular logics of 'adversarial' and 'inquisitorial' conceptual models. Second, Damaška's intersecting axes are better able to encapsulate the complexities of real legal processes (albeit still in the relatively abstract conceptualisations of an idealised model) than one-dimensional versions of the adversarial-inquisitorial dichotomy. Third, the modular structure of Damaška's basic conceptual building blocks facilitates modelling of relatively unusual combinations of features, which brings to light aspects of legal process which tend to be overlooked because they defy the normative expectations of orthodox procedural models. Fourth, when set in comparative perspective, Damaška's models of legal process demonstrate the perspectival nature of all conceptualisations of legal procedure, which are shown to be relative to the standpoint of the observer. This is a novel inflection of the too-little-respected methodological truism that concepts are always ideologically loaded; or, in the language I introduced earlier, subject-matter is partly defined by motivation. This section elaborates on each of these four strengths in turn.

On reflection, it should always have been patently obvious that the primitive concepts of 'contest' and 'inquest' can only convey a limited amount of information about the workings and values of modern legal systems. If common law trials can plausibly be described as a contest between opposed parties and their advocate-champions, Roman gladiatorial combat, Olympic shotput and the world chess championships are likewise no less properly characterised as 'contests'. Again, it is true to say, broadly speaking, that modern Continental legal procedure is structured around the notion of systematic factual inquiry ('inquest'), but the same could be said for investigative journalism, archival research by professional

[33] This was also, broadly speaking, the conclusion of Inga Markovits, 'Playing the Opposites Game: On Mirjan Damaška's *The Faces of Justice and State Authority*' (1989) 41 *Stanford Law Review* 1313, 1341, who noted that 'by steering our thoughts along one specific path only, we exclude others. But we can always retrace our steps, start anew, try out the road not taken. If the concepts we use impoverish our view by crowding out alternative perspectives, the concepts we did not use, in their different ways, would have done the same. How could we ever chart the globe without a grid, any grid, of meridians? … Dichotomies create order, not meaning. But do not underrate order as a prerequisite to finding meaning. Like an archeologist's grid of trenches, Damaška's conceptual system has prepared the ground for less formal investigations.'

historians and the intelligence-gathering activities of the CIA.[34] As Damaška himself observed elsewhere,[35] Continental legal process in this respect conforms to the precepts for *any* type of rational inquiry into empirical states of affairs.

We can learn much more about the distinctive character of *legal* process, Damaška showed, by situating adjudication within broader styles of government and political authority. A liberal polity wedded to rugged individualism and unencumbered free markets will tend to regard legal process as a mechanism for dispute resolution and the maintenance of social peace, especially if – as in the United States – these ideological preferences are ramified by a political culture suffused with deep suspicion of an overweening, centralised (federal) government credited with expansionist ambitions:

> [T]he reactive state is first and foremost an adjudicative body. All other state activities are an extension of and subordinated to dispute resolution. Far from being the least dangerous branch of government, the judiciary is – with little exaggeration – indeed the only branch of government .... The verdict in the conflict-solving mode is not so much a pronouncement on the true state of the world as it is a decision resolving the debate between the parties, like a peace treaty putting an end to combat.[36]

A more paternalistic or communitarian polity, by contrast, will easily regard legal process as an extension of official state bureaucracy with an overarching mandate to implement desirable social policies. From this elevated vantage point, the logic of adversary process in common law jurisdictions is seen to be inspired by a political preference for 'light-touch' conflict resolution; whilst the logic of inquisitorial legal process in the jurisdictions of Continental Europe (and their (post)colonial satellites) can be explained in terms of a political preference for relatively interventionist policy-implementation through prescriptive legal regulation and a distinctively bureaucratic mode of adjudication:

> In contrast to law in the reactive state, whose stress is on defining forms in which freely chosen goals may be pursued, activist law is directive, sometimes even hectoring: it tells citizens what to do and how to behave .... [A]nimated by its perception of the objective of administering justice, an activist state must seriously consider designing its legal process as an inquiry controlled by state officials. In lieu of privately controlled contest, the idea of officially controlled *inquest* epitomizes the procedural style.[37]

This outline sketch of the affiliations between legal process and alternative conceptions of the point and remit of government acquired greater light and shade from

[34] See, further, Terence Anderson, David Schum and William Twining, *Analysis of Evidence*, 2nd edn (CUP, 2005); William Twining and Ian Hampsher-Monk, *Evidence and Inference in History and Law: Interdisciplinary Dialogues* (Northwestern University Press, 2003); David A Schum, *The Evidential Foundations of Probabilistic Reasoning* (Northwestern University Press, 2001).

[35] 'The officially controlled fact-finding method of Continental procedure – inasmuch as it accords a larger role in the development of evidence to disinterested third parties – comes closer [than adversary process] to the demands of dispassionate, rational inquiry': ELA, 101–102.

[36] FoJ, 75, 123.

[37] FoJ, 82, 87.

Damaška's intersecting analysis of contrasting structures of legal authority and institutionalised divisions of juridical labour. The attributes of legal officials, the nature of the relationships between them, and the characteristics of their decision-making are the key variables on this second interpretational axis.[38] In legal systems corresponding to the 'hierarchical ideal of officialdom', a premium is placed upon bureaucratic audit, consistency and predictability in decision-making, and deference to superiors in the vertically ordered institutional hierarchy. Legal decision-making is professionalised and depersonalised in a way which 'promotes institutional thinking',[39] whilst 'official discretion is anathema'.[40] Legal reasoning tends to be relatively formalistic. It is characterised by abstraction from concrete factual particulars, a penchant for normative generalisation and logical dogmatism in jurisprudential thought.

Essentially the mirror image of its polar opposite, Damaška's 'coordinate ideal' of legal officialdom embraces lay involvement in legal decision-making whilst eschewing rigid pyramids of formal legal authority in favour of roughly co-equal decision-makers capable of dominating their own spheres of influence. This combination goes hand-in-hand with an affinity for substantive justice on the particularised facts of the case, and correspondingly less interest in the systematic application of generalised norms. These ideological preferences and institutional functions and competences tend to be mutually reinforcing over time: thus, a preference for substantively just outcomes over formally correct procedures is predictably reinforced by the practical inability of part-time amateur decision-makers (eg, lay jurors) to comprehend technically sophisticated normative standards and to apply them consistently across a variety of factual contexts. The resulting unpredictability and lack of consistency in adjudication, contemplated with horror as elementary and intolerable deficiencies by an hierarchically ordered legal process, are borne lightly by a legal system in which the coordinate ideal of officialdom is embraced:

> [T]he regulation that appeals to logical legalists is alien to laymen. It displays insensitivity to the singularity of human drama, and its capacity to assure principled decision making leaves laymen unimpressed. They are likely to prefer warm confusion to cool consistency .... And in this vision of authority, vague standards of substantive justice combine with the absence of hierarchical supervision to ensure that the theme of official discretion becomes the essential accompaniment of coordinate judicial organization.[41]

There are, then, evident affinities between styles of government and structures of legal authority, as well as between Damaška's reconstituted procedural models and the historical evolution and contemporary characteristics of real legal systems.

[38] FoJ, 16.
[39] FoJ, 19.
[40] FoJ, 20.
[41] FoJ, 28.

Reactive government, with its focus on dispute resolution, is naturally attracted to the substantively orientated, broadly participative coordinate ideal of officialdom; activist states, meanwhile, will naturally try to establish or co-opt hierarchically organised judicial bureaucracies into their policy-implementing agendas. Historical and contemporary real-world manifestations of these models are, of course, perfectly familiar. The common law jury trial represents a close approximation to the coordinate ideal; the Roman-canon medieval inquisition and its reformed Napoleonic offspring, which colonised the legal procedures of most of Continental Europe during the early decades of the nineteenth century and remain more or less dominant to this day, exemplify many of the core characteristics of the hierarchical ideal of officialdom.

With these basic contrasts and connections established, it now becomes possible to glimpse the interpretative power of Damaška's comparative modelling over more conventional analyses utilising a one-dimensional adversarial-inquisitorial dichotomy. For example, lay participation in fact-finding favours temporally compressed proceedings and finality in adjudication, whereas bureaucratic fact-finding is more likely to be episodic (so that the sources of information can be thoroughly checked and triangulated against other evidentiary sources) and subject to review and reconsideration by judicial superiors, who are presumptively more skilled and knowledgeable, or at any rate more authoritative, than front-line decision-makers. Episodic, professionalised factual inquiries thrive on extensive record-keeping, which encourages a preference for information presented in documentary form, whereas lay involvement in temporally concentrated, 'main event' trials will tend to favour oral testimony. Once a unique adjudicative event has been staged, moreover, it cannot easily be replicated, and there is no official record of how the verdict was reached for any hierarchically superior judicial authority to reassess – which goes a long way towards explaining why appeals were so late to develop in common law jurisdictions.[42] Even today, appellate proceedings create tensions in the Anglophone legal world,[43] especially in cases originally tried by juries,[44] which are not experienced by Continental legal systems. None of these distinctive characteristics of modern legal process, nor many more besides, could be deduced from conceptual

[42] On the historical evolution of criminal appeals in common law jurisdictions, see Benjamin L Berger, 'Criminal Appeals as Jury Control: An Anglo-Canadian Historical Perspective on the Rise of Criminal Appeals' (2005) 10 *Canadian Criminal Law Review* 1; Rosemary Pattenden, *English Criminal Appeals 1844–1994* (OUP, 1996); Lester B Orfield, 'History of Criminal Appeal in England' (1936) 1 *Missouri Law Review* 326. For comparative perspective, see Peter D Marshall, 'A Comparative Analysis of the Right to Appeal' (2011) 22 *Duke Journal of Comparative & International Law* 1.

[43] Richard Nobles and David Schiff, 'The Right to Appeal and Workable Systems of Justice' (2002) 65 *Modern Law Review* 676.

[44] *Cf R v Pendleton* [2002] 1 Cr App R 441, HL, [6] per Lord Bingham: 'The role of an appellate court reviewing a conviction by a jury can never be the same as that of a court reviewing the reasoned decision of a judge.' Also see John D Jackson, 'Making Juries Accountable' (2002) 50 *American Journal of Comparative Law* 477; J C Smith, 'Is Ignorance Bliss? Could Jury Trial Survive Investigation?' (1998) 38 *Medicine, Science and the Law* 98.

analysis of adversarial or inquisitorial procedural forms. It was Damaška's pioneering attention to contrasting structures of legal officialdom and their corresponding styles of legal decision-making which supplied 'a key to [unlock] several bizarre comparative law paradoxes'.[45]

It must be stressed, however, that Damaška set out to describe broad tendencies and loose associations, not cast-iron laws of political structure and legal form (and he was thus careful to distance himself from Marx's overly deterministic historicism on this account[46]). In this way, Damaška engineered a political theory escape route from the arid conceptualism of orthodox adversarial-inquisitorial dichotomies. His reformulated procedural ideals function as heuristic devices in the study of legal process, purged of any dirigiste preconceptions about the characteristics which legal systems conventionally regarded as 'adversarial' or 'inquisitorial' are supposed to exhibit.[47] The modular flexibility of Damaška's models was a major strength, because real legal systems do not evolve precisely in accordance with the exquisitely drawn blueprints of procedural ideals. In the empirical world, legal institutions continue to adapt themselves to modern conditions without fully self-conscious or all-encompassing allegiance to procedural heritage. What we observe, in reality, are 'pastiches of procedural form'.[48] Nor is this only a manifestation of predictable variation between the real and the ideal. In certain respects, tensions are already built into what might be regarded, on casual acquaintance, as ideal conjunctions between political morality and structures of legal authority. For example, whereas coordinate authority favours substantive justice on the merits, laissez-faire reactive government will tend to sponsor formal conceptions of due process – fairness rather than justice – in order to insulate adjudication from substantive political controversies and thus preserve its independence.[49] Activist government, for its part, needs to temper its instrumentalisation of law as a technique of political administration with appropriate regard for legal certainty, predictability in adjudication, and a reasonable measure of confidence in the stability of legal entitlements. In conditions of legal and social anarchy, few policies can be implemented successfully or cultivated over time.

Damaška's comparative modelling is arguably at its most illuminating when applied to criminal proceedings. English Crown Court jury trials (and their American and Commonwealth transplants) represent the acme of adversary

[45] FoJ, 56.

[46] FoJ, 6–8.

[47] It was in order to cast off the blinkers of preconception that Damaška, 'reluctantly', substituted his two neologisms, 'conflict-resolving process' and 'policy-implementing process', for the conventional terminology of 'adversarial' and 'inquisitorial' procedural models: FoJ, 80, 88.

[48] FoJ, 93.

[49] '[T]he reactive state does not hesitate to place impartiality of process above accuracy of result. If one equates accuracy of outcomes with the attainment of justice, and equal treatment with fairness, one must conclude that the reactive state – and thus the conflict-solving process as well – values fairness above justice': FoJ, 136.

process, in popular conceptions of British criminal justice no less than in scholarly exegesis. And yet one would have to delve into the annals of history at least as far back as the Tudor reforms of governmental administration in the sixteenth century[50] to find a time when large tracts of criminality were truly regarded as a private matter between the offender and his victim (and their respective families, clans and supporters). Ever since crime has been apprehended as a threat to public order – an assault on the monarch's peace – the administration of criminal justice has been an increasing preoccupation of government: in Damaška's typology, an arena of policy implementation. Twenty-first century governments have come to perceive crime control and the formation and implementation of criminal justice policy as amongst their most pressing (and challenging) responsibilities,[51] and at the level of macro-political analysis there is no real difference in this regard between common law and civilian jurisdictions. For example, whilst there are still important structural differences between the organisation of policing in England and in France,[52] there is no doubt that – as in every other modern (post)industrial democracy – English and French policing functions are alike discharged by hierarchical, policy-implementing, governmental bureaucracies.[53] In England, criminal investigations have shed many of their informal, 'privatised' trappings and become highly professionalised and extensively regulated by law,[54] whilst the Crown Prosecution Service is gradually acquiring the formal legal powers and de facto policy leadership of a continental-style procuracy.[55] English criminal process, in other words, has come to resemble an instrument of policy implementation, just as its intimate connection with the maintenance of public order would lead one to expect. However, viewing these developments through the lens of Damaška's procedural models cultivates a considerably more nuanced understanding of this complex – and somewhat conflicted – procedural hybrid.

[50] See Sir John Baker, *The Oxford History of the Laws of England: Volume VI, 1483–1558* (OUP, 2003), esp. 514–16; Sir William Holdsworth, *A History of English Law*, 3rd edn (Sweet & Maxwell, 1945) 492–532. The story is one of progressive development over several centuries from private tort to state crime, in both substantive and procedural law: see Holdsworth, ibid vol viii, ch 5; John H Baker, *An Introduction to English Legal History*, 4th edn (Butterworths, 2002) 501–7. The survival of private prosecution in modern English law might be said to demonstrate that the final chapter of this story remains unwritten.

[51] David Garland, *The Culture of Control: Crime and Social Order in Contemporary Society* (OUP, 2001).

[52] British policing still retains its county-based structure, although this is increasingly being eroded and supplemented by national policing agencies; French policing is characterised by a more militaristic style: see Jacqueline Hodgson, *French Criminal Justice* (Hart Publishing, 2005) 86–93.

[53] In relation to England and Wales, see Rob C Mawby and Alan Wright, 'The Police Organisation' and T Jones, 'The Governance and Accountability of Policing' both in Tim Newburn (ed), *Handbook of Policing* (Willan Publishing, 2003).

[54] See, further, Paul Roberts, 'Law and Criminal Investigation' in Tim Newburn, Tom Williamson and Alan Wright (eds), *Handbook of Criminal Investigation* (Willan Publishing, 2007).

[55] *Cf* the illuminating comparative analysis of Julia Fionda, *Public Prosecutors and Discretion: A Comparative Study* (OUP, 1995) which, however, now requires substantial updating in relation to the CPS in England and Wales.

An enduring allegiance to conflict resolution has left its indelible mark on criminal proceedings in England and Wales. Thus, English criminal process continues to allow the accused (in effect) to 'privatise' the implementation of criminal policy through guilty pleas,[56] factual stipulations,[57] and strategic choices (not) to adduce particular sources of information or to develop particular lines of argument (including potentially eligible defences subject to a burden of production).[58] All of these characteristics of Anglo-American law scandalise Continental criminal procedure[59] with its more purist ideological commitment to policy implementation, conceived as a quintessentially *public* function which cannot be delegated to private litigants under any circumstances. Conversely, by treating the accused who chooses to testify more or less as an ordinary witness, who gives evidence on oath and could at least theoretically be prosecuted for perjury, Anglo-American criminal procedure can be said to tolerate a greater departure from 'pure conflict-solving forms' than Continental process, in which the needs of the accused as a litigant-party are prioritised over his forensic usefulness as a testimonial source of information.[60] In short, whilst 'Anglo-American criminal procedure remains, in the last analysis, a policy-implementing process', Damaška's models illuminate, contextualise and in certain respects qualify 'the comparatively striking fact that more contest forms can be identified in Anglo-American criminal prosecution than in any other contemporary system of criminal justice'.[61]

At least something of the flavour has now been suggested of FoJ's attributes in terms of establishing a bridge to political theory, the sophistication of its modelling utilising intersecting axes, and the versatility and dynamism of its components' modular structure. The fourth strength of Damaška's comparative methodology, to which I alluded at the start of this section, is perhaps its most valuable, if somewhat elusive, quality. Damaška demonstrated the perspectival nature of comparative legal studies in two distinct but closely related senses. First, Damaška established that the basic categories of analysis through which legal processes are interpreted, taxonomised and evaluated *are already* laced with idiosyncratic local meanings and significance. For example, the concept of 'adjudication', which in common law countries is treated as synonymous with judicial (lay or professional)

[56] Formalised by the Court of Appeal in *R v Goodyear* [2005] 2 Cr App R 20, CA.

[57] Criminal Justice Act 1967, s 10.

[58] See, eg, *R v Greenwood* [2005] 1 Cr App R 7, CA.

[59] *Cf* FoJ, 113, 119 (footnote omitted): 'That a private individual should decide whether criminal law should use a crude or a refined measure of liability is clearly an idea from the ideological storehouse of laissez-faire government: individuals can themselves decide whether to go to prison or not .... It is thought totally unacceptable, even absurd, in Continental systems to let the prosecution and the defense control the choice or the dosage of the criminal sanction. To let the defendant negotiate with state officials on this score seems to compromise the sovereign prerogative of the government to dispense criminal justice.'

[60] FoJ, 130. This particular example is complicated by the thought that an accused with the option of testifying on oath might conceivably be more effective as a party to the proceedings (having been presented with additional strategic options) than an accused who is prohibited from assuming the testimonial status of a non-party witness.

[61] FoJ, 222.

decision-making at a decisive 'main event' trial, typically extends over a much broader forensic landscape in jurisdictions with an inquisitorial pedigree. This subtle shift in meaning is nicely encapsulated in the English translation of Kafka's *Der Prozess* as 'The Trial'.[62] Moreover, the different concepts of 'adjudication' which are brought into focus under the microscope of comparative analysis are indicative of fundamentally divergent conceptions of the relationship between legal process and bureaucratic administration – competing conceptions of judicial independence and the separation of powers, as Anglophones would say. They also hint at the relative priority of dispute resolution and policy implementation on the activity roster of good government, as that ideal is comprehended in particular jurisdictions. Theories of law and political administration are in this way reflected in, and reinforced by, juridical taxonomies, terminology and basic concepts, interpreted 'naturalistically' in their local settings:

> Whereas all activities of a radically laissez-faire state, including administration, acquire a flavour of adjudication, all activities of a fully activist state, including adjudication acquire a flavour of administration. But it would be parochial to assume that this narrow concept of adjudication covers activities that are perceived as instances of 'judging' or even activities that are thought to be quintessentially judicial, in all legal cultures of the world .... This is still the prevailing view on the Continent: the idea that to adjudicate need not necessarily imply resolution of contested matters continues to appear natural to lawyer and layman alike .... [I]f in his wanderings from culture to culture, a comparativist were to use the narrow analytical concept of adjudication, many activities widely perceived as instances of adjudication would elude him.[63]

Damaška further illustrated the inherently perspectival nature of conceptions of legal process by expanding his field of vision beyond the routine contrasts between 'common law' (mostly English and American) and 'Continental' (typically French or German) legal systems, which tend to dominate comparative legal studies, to include Soviet law (as it then was)[64] and Chinese conceptions of legality.[65] In this expanded frame, modern Continental process might appear 'inquisitorial' in comparison to common law procedure, yet markedly adversarial and legalistic when set against the inquisitorial jurisdiction of the Soviet *prokuratura*, to say nothing of Mao's China, where '[c]riminal justice and administration merged [and] dealing with offenders became part of the broader effort to manage and transform society'.[66] One of the most telling observations to emerge from this analysis is the ease with which defamatory comparisons with the medieval Inquisition – which incidentally libel all parties, including the medieval inquisitors! – can almost effortlessly be recycled and deflected down the legal evolutionary pecking

[62] FoJ, 48.

[63] FoJ, 89, 90 (footnote omitted).

[64] Peter H Solomon, Jr., *Soviet Criminal Justice Under Stalin* (CUP, 1996).

[65] Now see Liling Yue, *Principles of Chinese Criminal Procedure* (Hart Publishing, 2021); reviewed in Paul Roberts, 'Discovering Chinese Criminal Procedure' (2023) 63 *British Journal of Criminology* 803.

[66] FoJ, 199. Also see Richard Vogler, *A World View of Criminal Justice* (Ashgate, 2005).

order. Though Continental jurists might indignantly reject common lawyers' characterisations of modern Continental legal procedure as 'inquisitorial', this did not necessarily prevent Civilians from criticising Soviet law in terms of their own notions of legal form and function. And Soviet lawyers, in their turn, would probably have looked askance at the 'primitive' character of Maoist legal ordering, judged by their own jurisprudential lights:

> In their totality, the features of the Soviet system … appear to Western European lawyers as a partial throwback to Continental inquisitorial procedure after the abolition of judicial torture but before liberals began to leaven it with elements of the contest style. Observe the subtle irony, however: such assessments reproduce almost exactly the impressions which common lawyers regularly express about the conventional Continental amalgam – impressions dismissed as caricatures by classical Continental lawyers, much as the similar impressions just registered are dismissed by officials in the Soviet judicial apparatus …. At least to the modern Soviet eye, the blatancy with which the Chinese Communist party interfered in pending cases or justice officials consulted with the party would be repugnant. In short, Soviet lawyers would likely express the same criticisms that are directed against their own criminal procedure by Continental lawyers, accustomed to the conventional pastiche of contest and inquest forms. On the other hand, as seen from Mao's Beijing, Soviet criminal process would reveal a family resemblance with conventional Continental systems …[67]

In these jarring contrasts and disorientating shifts of standpoint, we are forced to confront the enormity of the theoretical and practical challenges facing those 'groping toward a legal language common to mankind in the [twenty-first] century'.[68] The perspectival nature of legal analysis, which seeps deep into the basic categories of jurisprudential thought, implies not merely that 'lawyers socialized in different settings of authority can look at the same object and see different things',[69] but that their perceptions of reality almost certainly *will* diverge, perhaps radically.

This fundamental epistemological challenge must not be ducked. Measured and unsentimental recognition of the inescapable influence of cultural conditioning is an essential first step to overcoming the formidable, but not necessarily insurmountable, obstacles to meaningful communication and mutual understanding across legal institutions, systems and cultures.[70] In FoJ, Damaška supplied powerful and versatile conceptual tools for comparative legal analysis. His self-consciously reflexive modelling methodology thereafter served comparative legal scholarship as an exemplary riposte to 'the dogmatism of the untravelled'.[71]

[67] FoJ, 195, 199 (footnote omitted).

[68] FoJ, 199.

[69] FoJ, 66.

[70] See further, David Nelken (ed), *Contrasting Criminal Justice: Getting from Here to There* (Ashgate, 2000); Paul Roberts, 'On Method: The Ascent of Comparative Criminal Justice' (2002) 22 *Oxford Journal of Legal Studies* 539.

[71] FoJ, 66. I do have further incidental reservations about the methodology of FoJ, in particular regarding its use of normative moral and political theory, but I set them aside for present purposes.

IV. W(h)ither Common Law Evidence?

Published a decade later, ELA largely adopted the conceptual framework and modelling methodology pioneered in FoJ, but in this book Damaška focused much more systematically than before on the procedural structure and doctrinal peculiarities of common law evidence and fact-finding. To explain why, on Damaška's account, the common law's complex evidentiary superstructure had by the late twentieth century found itself 'adrift', it was first necessary for ELA to identify the features of Anglo-American legal process which had hitherto provided common law evidence with secure institutional moorings.

This exercise called for some preliminary conceptual clarification and a note of methodological explanation. Damaška emphasised that, as in FoJ, his approach would be 'predominantly analytical and interpretive',[72] rather than historical: that is, he set out to explain the meaning and significance of contemporary common law evidence rather than investigating the causal factors responsible for its historical evolution. Frequent recourse to 'the comparative looking glass' to examine features of Anglo-American evidence and proof so basic to our 'procedural architecture that we live by them – and, by the same token, rarely notice them',[73] would be another methodological trade mark. Comparative analysis was immediately put to work in qualifying the 'gross exaggeration'[74] that exclusionary rules of evidence are unique to common law procedural systems. In fact, the exclusion of information procured through breaches of rights or other procedural impropriety – those exclusionary standards characterised by Wigmore as 'rules of extrinsic policy'[75] – is commonplace in Continental jurisprudence,[76] which also concedes broad testimonial privileges to potential witnesses.[77] But if analysis is pursued with greater subtlety and sophistication, truly distinctive features of common law evidence and proof do emerge when viewed in comparative perspective:

> To an outsider looking in, three broad tendencies of Anglo-American evidence law appear to express its most distinctive properties. First is the complexity of evidentiary

[72] ELA, 3.
[73] ELA, 5.
[74] ELA, 12.
[75] John H Wigmore, *A Treatise on the Anglo-American System of Evidence in Trials at Common Law*, 3rd edn (Little, Brown & Co, 1940; revised by JT McNaughton 1961), vol 8.
[76] See, eg, Stephen C Thaman and Dominik Brodowski, 'Exclusion or Non-Use of Illegally Gathered Evidence in the Criminal Process: Focus on Common Law and German Approaches' in Kai Ambos et al (eds), *Core Concepts in Criminal Law and Criminal Justice – Volume I* (CUP, 2020); Dimitrios Giannoulopoulos, *Improperly Obtained Evidence in Anglo-American and Continental Law* (Hart Publishing, 2019); Jacqueline Hodgson, 'EU Criminal Justice: The Challenge of Due Process Rights within a Framework of Mutual Recognition' (2011) 37 *North Carolina Journal of International Law and Commercial Regulation* 308; Edward A Tomlinson, 'The Saga of Wiretapping in France: What it Tells Us About the French Criminal Justice System' (1993) 53 *Louisiana Law Review* 1091; Walter Pakter, 'Exclusionary Rules in France, Germany and Italy' (1985) 9 *Hastings International and Comparative Law Review* 1; Craig M Bradley, 'The Exclusionary Rule in Germany' (1983) 96 *Harvard Law Review* 1032.
[77] ELA, 12–14.

> regulation, especially its departure from methods of inquiry that prevail in general social practice. Second is the great sensitivity of the law to the possible misuse of evidence – a sensitivity most prominently manifested in the rejection of probative material on the theory that it might be overvalued or might exert a biasing effect on the decision maker. The last is the pronounced aspiration of Anglo-American law to structure the fact-finders' analysis of evidence.[78]

These, then, are the features which were said to lend common law evidence its distinctive character and whose institutional logic and alleged recent vulnerability stood in need of explanation.

Thayer popularised the notion that common law evidence is the 'child of the jury system'.[79] Damaška, however, lined up with those contemporary theorists who regard this as, at best, only a very partial explanation.[80] For Damaška, the truly salient feature of trial by jury for the logic of common law evidence was not so much the infusion of lay standards of decision-making into legal adjudication, but rather the functional bifurcation of the trial court into two separate components. Where legal norms are applied by professional judges but fact-finding is entrusted to lay jurors, the opportunity is created for meaningful exclusion of evidence obtained in breach of evidentiary norms. If, say, an improperly obtained admission or inadmissible hearsay statement is proffered in evidence, the judge can exclude it in *voir dire* proceedings without the jury ever becoming aware of its existence. Tainted or otherwise suspect information is thereby categorically and effectively quarantined and prevented from infecting the jury's ultimate verdict. Setting aside for present purposes the durability of rationales for particular exclusionary doctrines, this institutional separation will tend to support the proliferation of technical legal standards of admissibility to an extent that a unified fact-finding and law-applying tribunal cannot plausibly sustain. Once a fact-finding tribunal has already heard (sticking with the same examples) an unlawfully obtained confession or hearsay statements of dubious provenance, it makes little sense to talk about such information being 'inadmissible', though the tribunal will probably still want to insist that tainted information has exerted little or no influence on its decision-making in the instant case. In a unified trial court, such as one finds in Continental European jurisdictions utilising collegiate benches of professional magistrates or 'mixed panels' of judges and lay jurors, technical standards of admissibility should

[78] ELA, 24.

[79] James Bradley Thayer, *A Preliminary Treatise on Evidence at the Common Law* (Little, Brown & Co, 1898) 180–81 and 508–9.

[80] For elaboration, see Paul Roberts, *Roberts and Zuckerman's Criminal Evidence*, 3rd edn (OUP, 2022), ch 2 (observing at 105 that '[o]ne can insist that rules and principles of criminal evidence have been moulded by their institutional context without falling into the trap of thinking that common law evidence is merely outgrowth of the jury'); William Twining, *Theories of Evidence: Bentham & Wigmore* (Weidenfeld & Nicolson, 1985). For historical discussion emphasising mutually reinforcing procedural factors, see John H Langbein, 'Historical Foundations of the Law of Evidence: A View from the Ryder Sources' (1996) 96 *Columbia Law Review* 1168; Stephan Landsman, 'From Gilbert to Bentham: The Reconceptualization of Evidence Theory' (1990) 36 *Wayne Law Review* 1149.

be expected to give way to 'naturalistic' precepts of rational inference, proof and fact-finding.

Damaška characterised the bifurcated trial court as the first of three 'pillars' of common law evidence. His second pillar was the concentrated, 'main event' trial which, as we previously learnt in FoJ, is a concomitant of a relatively 'privatised' form of justice with substantial lay input. Owing to the comparative lack of preparation of evidence and testimony prior to trial, and in particular to the absence of any neutral evidence-gathering and fact-checking official inquiry on the Continental model, Anglo-American legal process came to adopt a pronounced sceptical attitude towards proffers of evidence by the litigant parties.[81] Unless information purporting to bear on the matters in dispute could be authenticated, paradigmatically by the oath of a percipient witness,[82] it was liable to be excluded from the common law trial altogether:

> Procedural concentration is thus the strongest rationale for the characteristic demand by common law procedural systems that a secure foundation be laid under the rules for the development of evidence. So long as causes come before the adjudicator without extensive prior investigation, these preludes to proof-taking have strong credentials indeed: they provide an important guaranty of decisional rectitude.[83]

The third pillar of common law evidence identified by Damaška in ELA was adversary process itself, an artefact of reactive government and its preference for legal process orientated towards dispute resolution, as FoJ had already painstakingly explained. Competitive proof-taking breeds a contentious spirit[84] in which the parties each insist on strict application of the rules against their opponent. And robust procedural rules are urgently required to keep the parties' self-serving evidence-gathering activities and litigation strategies within reasonable bounds, lest a forensic free-for-all should sever any plausible connection with truth-finding in adjudication,[85] which in turn would undermine the predictability and security of legal entitlements and the finality of court verdicts – a vision of Armageddon for the reactive state. In a party-driven legal process 'it is vitally important that each party have an immediate opportunity to challenge sources of information presented by the opponent',[86] since partisan proof is inherently biased and state officials are not equipped, or even allowed,[87] to test its evidential basis thoroughly. Each of these adversarial tendencies is exacerbated when professional advocates

[81] *Cf* Edward J Imwinkelried, 'The Worst Evidence Principle: The Best Hypothesis as to the Logical Structure of Evidence Law' (1992) 46 *University of Miami Law Review* 1069.

[82] Hence, 'the principle of orality': see Roberts (n 80) 60–64 and chs 7–10.

[83] ELA, 64.

[84] Stephan Landsman, 'The Rise of the Contentious Spirit: Adversary Procedure in Eighteenth Century England' (1990) 75 *Cornell Law Review* 497.

[85] *Cf* Charles Nesson, 'The Evidence or the Event? On Judicial Proof and the Acceptability of Verdicts' (1985) 98 *Harvard Law Review* 1357.

[86] ELA, 79.

[87] Marvin E Frankel, 'The Search for the Truth: An Umpireal View' (1975) 123 *University of Pennsylvania Law Review* 1031.

come on the scene, in England from the later eighteenth century onwards, from which point the quantity and complexity of evidentiary norms appear to have increased exponentially.[88] Partisan proof, characterised by the forensic clash of two competing 'cases' unknown to Continental jurisprudence,[89] predictably encourages the development of a normative framework to regulate highly stylised forms of witness examination and cross-examination, which in many respects depart from what would normally be regarded as cognitively optimal fact-finding conditions. 'Attempts to elicit facts in the cross fire of partisan proof-taking', Damaška observed, 'can produce in this confrontational context more heat than light'.[90] Notably, in the context of this discussion, the pervasive influence of adversary process on normative development in the common law tradition encourages the Law of Evidence to be conceptualised as a unified whole, transcending the jurisprudential taxonomies and institutional balkanisation which have parcelled out substantive laws into discrete fields of practice and analysis. Somewhat idiosyncratically, 'the law of evidence appears as a subject suitable to be treated as a unified field of regulation and study'.[91]

The main contours of Damaška's argument in ELA can now be discerned. Common law evidence, it was argued, rests on the 'three pillars' of bifurcated trial court, concentrated proceedings and adversary process. The continued vitality of 'the Anglo-American distinctiveness in matters of evidence'[92] would therefore seem to depend upon the support it derives from these architectural features of common law adjudication; and if the pillars should weaken or crumble, the whole elaborate superstructure of common law evidentiary norms might be in danger of tumbling down:

> Erode any of these three pillars, and the rationale for the most characteristic admissibility rule of Anglo-American evidence [i.e. the hearsay prohibition] is seriously weakened. Erosion of these three pillars has been, however, the central tendency of the twentieth century. If the process advances much further, it could threaten the stability of the whole normative edifice.[93]

There is no shortage of readily available empirical data to support Damaška's thesis of erosion. Trial by jury rapidly declined across the common law world in the latter part of the twentieth century,[94] even in the United States, where jury

[88] John H Langbein, *The Origins of Adversary Criminal Trial* (OUP, 2003).

[89] ELA, 91–93: 'This highly artificial and formalized mode of supplying the fact finder with information is alien to the Continental procedural tradition, according to which the division of proof-taking into two evidentiary versions of the case is unknown: proof-taking is always structured as a single integrated inquiry presided over by the bench.'

[90] ELA, 100 (footnote omitted).

[91] ELA, 109. See Chapter 4 for systematic elucidation.

[92] ELA, 142.

[93] ELA, 126.

[94] Sally Lloyd-Bostock and Cheryl Thomas, 'The Continuing Decline of the English Jury' in N Vidmar (ed) *World Jury Systems* (OUP, 2000).

trial is a constitutional right in *civil* as well as criminal proceedings.[95] The bifurcated trial court has consequently lost ground to institutional variations on the unified law-applying and fact-finding tribunal, such as US bench trials[96] and the 'Diplock' courts in Northern Ireland,[97] not forgetting that most criminal cases in England and Wales are tried by lay magistrates advised by a legally qualified clerk – a procedural configuration capable of replicating the bifurcated trial court's exclusionary solution to inadmissible evidence only very imperfectly.[98] The palpable decline of trial by jury appeared to Damaška to presage common law evidence's demise:

> As the tribunal whose peculiar organization supported classical evidentiary arrangements is thus marginalized, many rules of evidence are now applied in settings where their original raison d'être is no longer certain .... Arrangements and modes of argument that are imbued with pragmatic meaning in jury trials survive in multiplying nonjury contexts mainly by force of habit, dwindled in stature to mere formalities perpetuated by the inertia of the members of the legal profession .... Having ceased to carry most of the structural weight, the oldest prop of common law evidence seems currently in most procedural contexts more ornamental than functional.[99]

The temporal parameters of concentrated trial proceedings have meanwhile been extended through increasingly interventionist judicial trial management (principally motivated by the desire for greater efficiency in litigation)[100] and more demanding pre-trial disclosure obligations.[101] Enhanced opportunities for pre-trial preparation and a more 'episodic' approach to fact-finding go hand-in-hand with declining lay involvement in adjudication.[102] Even party-control of adversary

[95] The Seventh Amendment to the US Constitution provides that in 'Suits at common law, where the value in controversy shall exceed twenty dollars, the right of trial by jury shall be preserved ….' The Sixth Amendment guarantees that '[i]n all criminal prosecutions, the accused shall enjoy the right to a speedy and public trial, by an impartial jury ….'

[96] Sean Doran, John D Jackson and Michael L Seigel, 'Rethinking Adversariness in Nonjury Criminal Trials' (1995) 23 *American Journal of Criminal Law* 1.

[97] John D Jackson and Sean Doran, *Judge Without Jury: Diplock Trials in the Adversary System* (OUP, 1995).

[98] *Cf* Penny Darbyshire, 'Previous Misconduct and Magistrates' Courts – Some Tales from the Real World' [1997] *Criminal Law Review* 105; M Wasik, 'Magistrates: Knowledge of Previous Convictions' [1996] *Criminal Law Review* 851.

[99] ELA, 127, 129.

[100] Jenny McEwan, 'Co-operative Justice and the Adversarial Criminal Trial: Lessons from the Woolf Report' in Sean Doran and John D Jackson (eds), *The Judicial Role in Criminal Proceedings* (Hart Publishing, 2000).

[101] Peter Duff, 'Disclosure in Scottish Criminal Procedure: Another Step in an Inquisitorial Direction?' (2007) 11 *International Journal of Evidence & Proof* 153; Mike Redmayne, 'Disclosure and its Discontents' [2004] *Criminal Law Review* 441; Roger Leng, 'The Exchange of Information and Disclosure' in Mike McConville and Geoffrey Wilson (eds), *The Handbook of the Criminal Justice Process* (OUP, 2002).

[102] *Cf* FoJ, 52–53: '[U]nless concentrated trials are imposed on judicial bureaucracies, they are likely to adopt the piecemeal style .... Officials argue that observations made at trial must be checked against information methodically assembled over time and preserved in the written record. To decide independently from the file, solely on first impressions, is to decide with inadequate preparation, on flimsy and uncertain grounds.'

process – the ultimate talisman of Anglo-American legality – is being eroded by the expanding role of trial and appellate judges with a newly-acquired appetite for demanding factually accurate verdicts,[103] particularly in criminal proceedings where the fundamental orientation of adjudication towards policy-implementation (foretold in FoJ) is gradually becoming more evident and influential: 'The greater judicial involvement in fact-finding, even if it falls well short of leading to independent investigations, alters the adversary climate of the trial .... [T]he court's influence on proof-taking grows and dilutes the adversary flavor of evidentiary arrangements.'[104] With its first supporting pillar greatly diminished in stature and the second leaning heavily on the third,[105] which itself betrayed signs of serious structural stress, Damaška's prognosis for common law evidence concluded on a note of 'crisis and impending doom'. The bleak *denouement* advertised in this essay's introduction can now be quoted in full:

> With jury trials marginalized, procedural concentration abandoned, and the adversary system somewhat weakened, the institutional environment appears to have decayed that supplied distinctive features of common law evidence with a strong argumentative rationale. As a result, doctrines and practices widely associated with Anglo-American fact-finding style are now often deprived of a convincing theoretical basis. In its absence, shorn of adequate justification, they face the danger of becoming antiquated period pieces, intellectual curiosa confined to an oubliette in the castle of justice.[106]

Then as now, this was an arresting, and doubtless for some alarming, thesis, developed within a magisterial frame of reference and punctuated by Damaška's inimitable stylistic flourishes and pyrotechnic fusillades. But for all its power of shock-and-awe, did the argument presented in ELA really establish that common law evidence was perilously 'adrift' from its institutional moorings? With the benefit of a decade's hindsight, I suggest it did not. There are, moreover, methodological as well as political, moral and pragmatic reasons for challenging the cogency of Damaška's portentous thesis.

The first thing to notice is that Damaška's own analysis was in some ways at odds with his more alarmist conclusions. Indeed, he was careful to qualify his thesis at various key junctures, conceding that '[a]ctivist impulses have so far only sporadically contributed to the relaxation of the litigants' grip on the

[103] Reinforced in England and Wales by the reformed test of 'safety' applied in determining criminal appeals: see *R v Pendleton* [2002] 1 Cr App R 441, HL; *R v Togher, Doran and Parsons* [2001] 1 Cr App R 457, CA; Nick Taylor and David Ormerod, 'Mind the Gaps: Safety, Fairness and Moral Legitimacy' [2004] *Criminal Law Review* 266; J C Smith, 'Appeals Against Conviction' [1995] *Criminal Law Review* 920.

[104] ELA, 135, 138.

[105] ELA, 134: 'Once procedural concentration has been abandoned, this pillar no longer carries the weight of the original evidentiary edifice. What prevents it from disintegrating and crumbling in changed circumstances is only the peculiar mode of trial preparation entrusted to partisan lawyers. But since this mode of preparation is an aspect of the contemporary adversary process, the second pillar of the common law evidence rationale has become dependent upon the third.'

[106] ELA, 142.

legal process'[107] such that the crucial 'third [adversarial] pillar is far from collapsing. In addition to forces of habit and tradition, it is bolstered now by the pressing needs of court systems clogged by swelling caseloads'.[108] Furthermore, on Damaška's own account, adversarial culture had made gains as well as suffering setbacks in recent decades, sometimes as a direct consequence of the erosion of the other two pillars. Less concentrated trial proceedings have extended adversarial litigation styles and strategies into the pre-trial process, for example; and in this connection, Damaška's observations regarding the significance of plea-bargaining and negotiated settlements[109] could be compounded by invoking contemporaneous developments in English criminal proceedings affecting custodial interrogation,[110] charging practice,[111] pre-trial disclosure,[112] and witness preparation.[113] Once it is conceded that the recent fortunes of adversary culture are marked by gains as well as losses on the balance sheet, we cannot arrive at any final accounting without constructing some appropriate metric for making comparative judgements of aggregate 'adversariness' at different points in time. But this ambitious enterprise was not even attempted by Damaška in ELA.

Perhaps the attempt was never made, moreover, because such an exercise would be insufferably complex, methodologically intractable and, quite possibly, ultimately futile. What would it mean to say that a whole legal culture or system was 'more' or 'less' adversarial than it was at some point in the past? There is an immediate suspicion that making such aggregative judgements would require incommensurable factors to be weighed in the same balance,[114] or at least that crucial distinctions would be submerged in sweeping generalisations. A more fine-grained, empirically grounded analysis might conclude, for example, that whilst civil proceedings (or some subset of civil process, eg, 'administrative law claims against government bureaucracies') became markedly less adversarial in

[107] ELA, 138.
[108] ELA, 141.
[109] ELA, 134.
[110] John D Jackson, 'Silence and Proof: Extending the Boundaries of Criminal Proceedings in the United Kingdom' (2001) 5 *International Journal of Evidence & Proof* 145.
[111] See Ian D Brownlee, 'The Statutory Charging Scheme in England and Wales: Towards a Unified Prosecution System?' [2004] *Criminal Law Review* 896.
[112] See above, n 101.
[113] Paul Roberts, 'Prosecutors Interviewing Witnesses: A Question of Integrity' in Hunter, Roberts, Young and Dixon (eds), *The Integrity of Criminal Process* (Hart Publishing, 2016); Paul Roberts and Candida Saunders, 'Introducing Pre-Trial Witness Interviews – A Flexible New Fixture in the Crown Prosecutor's Toolkit' [2008] *Criminal Law Review* 831; Office of the Attorney-General, *Pre-Trial Witness Interviews by Prosecutors – Report* (December 2004); Laura McGowan, 'Prosecution Interviews of Witnesses: What More will be Sacrificed to "Narrow the Justice Gap"?' (2006) 70 *Journal of Criminal Law* 351; Louise Ellison, 'Witness Preparation and the Prosecution of Rape' (2007) 27 *Legal Studies* 171.
[114] Incommensurability is a sprawling topic which we cannot get to grips with here, but the basic thought is this: if the meaning and value of adversariness are distinctive to particular types of legal proceedings and their related goals and ideals, then trying to measure a gain in adversariness in, say, small claims personal injury actions against a loss of adversariness in, say, criminal litigation may be, not just difficult, but essentially incoherent.

the closing decades of the twentieth century, Anglo-American criminal litigation remained, in many respects, as trenchantly adversarial as it ever was. To be sure, Damaška was well aware of this deviating subplot in his story:

> As arrangements tailored to jury trials are dethroned from their exalted position, common law evidence as we now know it is likely to be *confined to a narrower sphere, perhaps serious criminal cases*, or even completely discarded.[115]

Suppose for the sake of argument that this assessment is broadly correct in relation to national legal process, taken in the round. One might nonetheless still insist that the real story – at least for certain audiences – is the continued vitality of party-dominated process and adversarial culture in (serious) criminal cases. It may be a highly significant feature of recent Anglo-American jurisprudential thought that a sharper differentiation between civil and criminal procedure, so long associated with Continental legal theory,[116] is emerging as a serious rival to the traditional common law orthodoxy of a unified Law of Evidence[117] – and this without challenging the essentially adversarial cast of Anglo-American criminal litigation. Indeed, sharper conceptual differentiation might be regarded as partially insulating criminal process from the declining party dominance and expanding judicial case management which today characterise Anglo-American civil proceedings.[118]

This example shows why conceding the continued vitality of pockets of adversarial culture unavoidably complicates and problematises an aggregated bird's-eye view of legal process. In order to draw empirically well-grounded conclusions about the character of a particular legal system, it would be necessary to try to assess the relative contributions of different types of legal proceedings to the prevailing national scene, particularly bearing in mind that 'serious criminal cases' tend to exert a disproportionate influence on the character and temper of a nation's legal culture. After all, high-profile criminal trials – Louise Woodward; OJ Simpson; Enron[119] – loom much larger in the public imagination, even though

[115] ELA, 149 (emphasis supplied).

[116] *Cf* ELA, 110: 'Where mainstream Anglo-American thought embraced the idea of a single, overarching purpose of legal proceedings, Continental thought was in the habit of sharply separating the purposes of civil and criminal justice. The contrast in thinking about the aims of adjudication still affects evidence.'

[117] The argument is developed in Chapter 5. Also see Roberts (n 80) ch 1; but *cf* John Jackson, 'Taking Comparative Evidence Seriously' in Paul Roberts and Mike Redmayne (eds), *Innovations in Evidence and Proof* (Hart Publishing, 2007).

[118] Adrian Zuckerman, *Zuckerman on Civil Procedure: Principles of Practice*, 4th edn (Sweet & Maxwell, 2021).

[119] Media *cause célèbres* burn brightly in contemporary public consciousness but soon fizzle out, sometimes fading from popular memory without a trace. For the benefit of readers who weren't there at the time: *Louise Woodard* is the 'British Nanny Case', briefly discussed under the rubric of 'informal evidence' in Roberts (n 80) 133–35. OJ Simpson was a famous American Football star, who probably murdered his wife and her lover but was acquitted in his criminal trial which was marred by investigative malpractice and police racism: see Christopher B Mueller, 'Introduction: OJ Simpson and the Criminal Justice System on Trial' (1996) 67(4) *University of Colorado Law Review* 727. *Enron* involved a

they constitute only the very tip of the litigation iceberg, than the dark mass of civil and administrative actions which swells, unobtrusively, below the media-filtered waterline of public consciousness. Damaška did not enter these methodologically turbulent waters, preferring instead to rest his erosion thesis on rough holistic impressions of quantitative legal change.

There is a further methodological difficulty in evaluating Damaška's erosion thesis, relating to the choice of baseline for measuring a legal system's 'standard' or prototypical degree of adversariness. On what non-arbitrary basis could two discrete points in time be selected for the purposes of making a comparison between a legal system's adversariness 'now' and 'then'? When was adversarial legal culture at its zenith in Anglo-American law? Or at its lowest ebb? Is the high point, or the mean average, the appropriate baseline for making global comparisons? I do not know how one would even begin to go about answering such questions. Legal change is an inherent feature of legal culture. The law is a living instrument, and when it stops changing to meet the exigencies of the day, it tends to atrophy and enter terminal decline. The common law tradition arose in the first place partly because the energies of Roman law were finally dissipated in the cloisters of scholasticism. ELA concludes with this rather enigmatic prediction:

> The new Anglo-American method of establishing facts in adjudication will thus most likely be the product of slow adaptation of traditional institutions to the changing environment. And the cracking pillars of common law evidence examined in the pages of this book will most likely be repaired – or replaced – by domestic masons and by indigenous building material. What lineaments the new construction will assume is of course unforeseeable …[120]

Damaška presumably regarded these remarks as a suitably open-ended coda to his book's central theme, but it is tempting to read this passage as a moment of revelation tantamount to comprehensively deconstructive auto-critique. If common law evidence is changing through gradual, evolutionary adaptation to prevailing circumstances, as it always has and presumably always will, in what sense is 'the distinctive character of the common law fact-finding process'[121] an artefact of 'decaying institutions'[122] facing 'crisis and impending doom'?[123] Why is common law evidence 'adrift', and not merely adjusting its course in response to the fluctuating demands of political, social and technological influences on modern litigation? Whilst Damaška's diagnosis of procedural change is insightful and, in

major Wall Street accounting fraud leading to corporate bankruptcy and shareholder losses of over $6 billion. See Doreen McBarnet, 'After Enron will "Whiter than White Collar Crime" Still Wash?' (2006) 46 *British Journal of Criminology* 1091; James W Williams, 'The Lessons of 'Enron': Media Accounts, Corporate Crimes, and Financial Markets' (2008) 12 *Theoretical Criminology* 471.

[120] ELA, 152.

[121] ELA, 3.

[122] ELA, 150.

[123] ELA, 142.

many respects, compelling, the pessimism of his prognosis seems to leap beyond any clearly visible signs of pathology.

Damaška did not indicate any temporal limits on the predicted demise of common law evidence, an omission calling to mind Keynes' bromide that, in the long run, we are all dead. Historical experience teaches that procedural law will change dramatically over the course of a century;[124] a prognosis covering half that duration would be more than sufficiently ambitious. What might English criminal litigation look like in 50 years' time? At the turn of the twenty-first century English law underwent the most extensive reform of criminal hearsay and character evidence for at least a century; and some of the provisions of the Criminal Justice Act 2003, the reforming statute in question, are in keeping with Damaška's erosion thesis. There is in general greater receptivity to both hearsay and evidence of the accused's extraneous misconduct,[125] and the common law's studiously cultivated conceptual dichotomy between (i) facts in issue and (ii) evidence and questions on collateral issues has been substantially denatured.[126] On the other hand, there is no indication of reduced technical complexity[127] – quite the reverse, in several respects – and the determination of admissibility remains a focal point of criminal trials. Even if hearsay or character evidence turns out, on closer inspection, to be admissible, it is still necessary for advocates and judges to conceptualise information correctly as hearsay or non-hearsay, 'bad character' evidence or otherwise, as a prelude to debating its suitability for presentation to the jury. Controversial changes to the privilege against self-incrimination introduced by the Criminal Justice and Public Order Act 1994 paint a similarly contradictory picture. In permitting greater evidential use of testimonial and pre-trial silence, the 1994 Act arguably[128] conforms with a policy-implementing (crime control) agenda.[129] But this has been accompanied by a raft of expanding jury directions of almost mind-boggling complexity – the type of forensic reasoning rules which Damaška characterised as uniquely idiomatic to common law evidence.[130] Recent

[124] In 1900, for example, England did not have a criminal appeal court (let alone a Criminal Cases Review Commission), jury service was limited to property-holders, it was unclear whether the Crown bore the burden of proof on self-defence, duress and other denials of constitutive elements of the offence, police impropriety never resulted in the exclusion of evidence, and the accused had only just become generally competent as a witness in his own defence.

[125] See Roberts (n 80) chs 11–12.

[126] CJA 2003, ss 119–20.

[127] *Cf* ELA, 12 (footnote omitted): 'Markedly less technical in both [civil and criminal] branches of adjudication, Continental fact-finding presents a stark contrast to the common law. The technical character of evidentiary regulation … is indeed one of the leitmotifs of the present volume ….'

[128] Providing that drawing inferences from silence actually does improve the factual accuracy of verdicts in criminal adjudication, at least in the aggregate. This, however, is contested: see Mike Redmayne, 'Analysing Evidence Case Law' in Paul Roberts and Mike Redmayne (eds), *Innovations in Evidence and Proof* (Hart Publishing, 2007); Roger Leng, 'Silence Pre-trial, Reasonable Expectations, and the Normative Distortion of Fact-finding' (2001) 5 *International Journal of Evidence & Proof* 240.

[129] Hannah Quirk, *The Rise and Fall of the Right of Silence* (Routledge, 2017).

[130] ELA, 18–24: 'the Anglo-American repertoire of devices telling the fact finder how to process evidence strikes Continental observers as too rich and even inappropriate'.

modifications to the ways in which certain witnesses testify in English criminal trials, utilising modern video and digital technologies, do represent something of a revolution in common law adjudication, and their implementation could well continue to expand in the coming years and decades.[131] By sanctioning the admissibility of what is technically hearsay, and extending proof-taking deep into the pre-trial process, these 'special measures' undoubtedly depart from common law orthodoxy. On the other hand, they have also introduced greater technical complexity into procedural law, without necessarily diminishing the essentially adversarial structure of common law proof. For as long as 'special measures' are self-consciously reserved for particularly vulnerable categories of witness, and live *viva voce* cross-examination is a normative expectation in all cases,[132] the party-dominated orality of criminal adjudication seems assured, even if proceedings are allowed to become somewhat less concentrated. Perhaps advocates will in future be required to abide by a more stringent code of ethics, emphasising the humane and decent treatment of witnesses alongside traditions of vigorous defence,[133] but this welcome development would be perfectly compatible with the basic structures of adversary process, just as purging criminal adjudication of some of its traditional sexism[134] barely augurs procedural apostasy. Further restricting access to jury trial has been a more or less constant objective of UK government policy – both Tory and Labour – since the major reclassification of indictable offences undertaken in the 1970s entrusted a slew of offences to the exclusive jurisdiction of the magistrates' courts.[135] However, further legislative initiatives in this vein have lately been strenuously resisted both inside and outside Parliament,[136] and

[131] See Paul Roberts, Debbie Cooper and Sheelagh Judge, 'Monitoring Success, Accounting for Failure: The Outcome of Prosecutors' Applications for Special Measures under the Youth Justice and Criminal Evidence Act 1999' (2005) 9 *International Journal of Evidence & Proof* 269.

[132] It is notable in this regard that the most radical provision, dispensing entirely with live cross-examination at trial in relation to certain witnesses, was the most difficult to implement and long-resisted: Debbie Cooper, 'Pigot Unfulfilled: Video-recorded Cross-Examination under Section 28 of the Youth Justice and Criminal Evidence Act 1999' [2005] *Criminal Law Review* 456. Now see *R v White* [2025] EWCA Crim 426; J R Spencer, 'Section 28 YJCEA 1999 and Pre-trial Cross-examination: Where We've Got to Now and How We Got There' [2019] 4 *Archbold Review* 4; Joyce Plotnikoff and Richard Woolfson, 'Worth Waiting For: The Benefits of Section 28 Pre-Trial Cross-Examination' [2016] 8 *Archbold Review* 6.

[133] On the state's 'duty of humane treatment' in criminal proceedings, see Paul Roberts, 'Theorising Procedural Tradition: Subjects, Objects and Values in Criminal Adjudication' in Anthony Duff, Lindsay Farmer, Sandra Marshall and Victor Tadros (eds), *The Trial on Trial Volume 2: Judgment and Calling to Account* (Hart Publishing, 2006).

[134] For example, by reforming the law of corroboration: see Law Com No 202, *Criminal Law: Corroboration of Evidence in Criminal Trials* (HMSO, 1991), implemented by the Criminal Justice and Public Order Act 1994, ss 32–33.

[135] See Michael Zander, *Cases and Materials on the English Legal System*, 9th edn (Butterworths, 2003) 37–46.

[136] See, eg, Sean Enright, 'A Graceful Withdrawal?' (2000) 150 *New Law Journal* 1560 (27 October); Jack Straw, 'Changes to Mode of Trial' (2000) 150 *New Law Journal* 670 (12 May); Michael Zander, 'Why Jack Straw's Jury Reform Has Lost the Plot' (2000) 150 *New Law Journal* 366 (10 March); Lee Bridges, 'Welcome Conversion' (Letter) (2000) 150 *New Law Journal* 380 (17 March).

even Tony Blair, with his sizeable parliamentary majority, was repeatedly forced to back down or compromise with the jury's defenders.[137] Finally, it is worth mentioning that features of criminal litigation which Americans tend to regard as recent departures from adversarialism, such as extensive pre-trial disclosure by the prosecution[138] and judicial summing-up on the facts,[139] have been routine and, in principle, uncontroversial procedural requirements in England and Wales for decades. All in all, certainly in its application to English criminal litigation,[140] I would wager that Damaška's analysis of 'evidence law adrift' will be about as accurate in 2047 as it was in 1997.

Damaška's final gambit in ELA was to invoke 'the creeping scientization of factual inquiry'.[141] He predicted that the burgeoning impact of science and technology on all aspects of modern life would be a further nail in the coffin of traditional proof-taking procedures in Anglo-American jurisdictions:

> [T]he Anglo-American procedural environment is poorly adapted to the use of scientific information. If scientific methods continue to creep into the legal process, this feature, presently tolerable, could turn into a major irritant .... [B]ecause the law follows the dominant epistemological temper of the historical period – albeit with some time lag – the scientization of proof is likely to exacerbate the presently minor frictions within traditional procedural arrangements. Their further deterioration should be considered likely on this ground alone.[142]

There can be no question about the vital importance of science and technology in modern life, nor that scientific and other forms of expert testimony present stern challenges, as well as hitherto unimaginable opportunities, for fact-finding in contemporary legal process. But how the march of science buttresses Damaška's erosion thesis is not so easy to discern. Given the vital importance of securing moral and political legitimacy for criminal verdicts, and the intensifying differentiation

[137] Richard Taylor, Martin Wasik and Roger Leng, *Blackstone's Guide to the Criminal Justice Act 2003* (OUP, 2004) ch 4. Covid-exacerbated case backlogs subsequently put restriction of jury trial back on the policy agenda: Sir Brian Leveson, *Independent Review of the Criminal Courts* (Ministry of Justice, 2025), www.gov.uk/government/publications/independent-review-of-the-criminal-courts-part-1 (accessed 17 December 2025); David Ormerod, 'Appreciating the Jury' [2020] *Criminal Law Review* 983; Hannah Quirk, 'Covid-19 and Jury-less Trials?' [2020] *Criminal Law Review* 569.

[138] For the common law position prior to the enactment of the Criminal Procedure and Investigations Act 1996, see *R v Ward* (1993) 96 Cr App R 1, CA; *Practice Note (Criminal Evidence: Unused Material)* [1982] 1 All ER 734; (1982) 74 Cr App R 302.

[139] *R v Derek William Bentley (Deceased)* [2001] 1 Cr App R 307, CA; *R v Cohen and Bateman* (1909) 2 Cr App R 197, CCA. For comparative discussion, see Paul Marcus, 'Judges Talking to Jurors in Criminal Cases: Why US Judges Do It So Differently from Just About Everyone Else' (2013) 30 *Arizona Journal of International and Comparative Law* 1.

[140] American scholars have made similar arguments in relation to US law: see, eg, Ronald J Allen and Georgia N Alexakis, 'Utility and Truth in the Scholarship of Mirijan Damaška' in John Jackson, Máximo Langer, Peter Tillers (eds), *Crime, Procedure and Evidence in a Comparative and International Context* (Hart Publishing, 2008); Samuel R Gross, 'Law in the Backwaters: A Comment on Mirjan Damaška's *Evidence Law Adrift*' (1998) 49 *Hastings Law Journal* 369.

[141] ELA, 143.

[142] ELA, 147.

of procedural forms (which Damaška himself announced[143]), the fact that 'the law follows the dominant epistemological temper of the historical period' might be invoked as a significant *constraint* on institutional erosion or evidentiary drift. Society's attitudes towards science and technology are deeply ambivalent, if not self-contradictory, much in the way that nuclear fission might solve the world's energy crisis or just as easily blow us all to Kingdom Come. Within my suggested 50-year temporal horizon, I do not envisage men and women in white coats replacing the criminal jury's verdict to any appreciable extent, though scientific evidence may well proliferate in criminal trials. And if it does, adversarial defence challenges and 'battles of experts' will proliferate as well.[144] English criminal courts currently show no signs of adopting excessively deferential attitudes towards scientific and other expert testimony.[145]

It seems fatuous to speculate about the future shape of common law evidence beyond the next half-century, precisely because the pace and magnitude of technological development have become so staggering in our time. For all I know, by 2050 the problems of proof-taking which common law evidence evolved to address may have been solved, conclusively, by androids with the ability to read brainwaves or the discovery of powers of precognition rendering criminal adjudication entirely obsolete.[146] More firmly anchored in the here-and-now, modern law's increasingly cosmopolitan character is another significant factor telling against Damaška's pessimistic prognosis for common law evidence. I will elaborate a little further on this observation by way of conclusion, having first summarised the main lines of argument presented in this chapter.

V. Conclusion: Comparative Legal Method and Cosmopolitan Law

This essay has contended that the innovative modelling methodology pioneered by Mirjan Damaška in FoJ remains a powerful tool for comparative analysis of legal process. Notwithstanding the inherent limitations of any generalising method, interpreting legal procedures by reference to their overarching political ideals and distinctive structures of legal authority affords a unique vantage point for comparative scholarship which is capable of generating genuinely

[143] ELA, 148: 'The coming differentiation of procedural forms is likely to occur in all dimensions of the institutional environment … In the sphere of court organization, one should anticipate the emergence of a greater variety of both unitary and bifurcated tribunals.'

[144] To cite one, admittedly extreme, recent example: in *R v Harris* [2006] 1 Cr App R 5, CA, which involved four conjoined appeals all featuring evidence of 'shaken baby syndrome', the court heard testimony from 11 expert medical witnesses instructed by the prosecution and 10 defence experts in reply.

[145] Paul Roberts, 'The Science of Proof: Forensic Science Evidence in English Criminal Trials' in James Fraser and Robin Williams (eds), *Handbook of Forensic Science* (Willan Publishing, 2008).

[146] Setting aside strong philosophical reasons for doubting even the possibility of any such eventuality, the present point is simple: who can really say what the future holds two generations down the line?

novel insights. Damaška skilfully demonstrated how procedural form tends to reflect either the policy-implementing agendas of activist government or the conflict-solving orientation of reactive polities, as well as being moulded by hierarchical, vertically-ordered professional legal bureaucracies on the one hand, or co-ordinate, horizontally-ordered judiciaries equipped with extensive discretionary powers and substantial lay involvement in adjudication on the other. Damaška's models breathed new life into the staid dichotomy between 'inquisitorial' and 'adversarial' legal processes. They constitute a persuasive riposte to those commentators who would too lightly dispense with the modelling methodology in general, or with the concepts of 'adversarial' and 'inquisitorial' process in particular; provided that it is clearly understood that constructing ideal-typical models should be a starting point, rather than the ultimate destination, of comparative legal analysis.

Published a decade later, ELA applied FoJ's conceptual framework to the more narrowly circumscribed topic of evidence and proof, to produce an illuminating commentary on the affinities between particular institutional structures and their characteristic forms and styles of evidentiary regulation. The distinctive characteristics of common law evidence, shorn of some confounding myths, were shown to be related to the bifurcated trial court, temporally concentrated proceedings, and party-dominated adversarial culture which are today recognised the world over as the hallmarks of Anglo-American legal process. However, where Damaška inferred that noticeable weakening of these 'three pillars' spelled doomed for common law evidence, I suggested that visible symptoms of decline are matched by countervailing indications of continued vitality, at least if we confine our gaze to English criminal adjudication within a realistic 50-year temporal horizon.

I will conclude by drawing attention to a contemporary jurisprudential development of enormous significance which, I believe, lends further support to my more ambivalent reading of empirical trends against Damaška's apocalyptic vision. Ten years on, a striking absence from the analysis presented in ELA, and one crucial determinant of common law evidence's future which Damaška evidently failed to predict, is the increasingly pervasive influence of supra-national norms and decisions by international courts on domestic law and legal process. Law's growing 'cosmopolitanism' is exemplified by the conjunction of an increasingly robust international human rights law implemented by supra-national judicial institutions such as the Strasbourg-based European Court of Human Rights, with the rapid evolution of transnational criminal justice policy-making. Such policies are co-ordinated through the overlapping initiatives of the United Nations and regional organisations such as the Council of Europe and the EU, utilising normal diplomatic channels, and implemented through international judicial co-operation and mutual assistance at the operational level. (The global 'war on terror' is, of course, a major pretext and motivation for transnational penal policy-making and law enforcement.) Further institutional manifestations of cosmopolitanism in penal law can be seen in the UN's ad hoc criminal tribunals for the former Yugoslavia and Rwanda,[147] in proliferating examples of hybrid 'internationalised' tribunals from Sierra Leone to Iraq,[148] and – above all – in the International Criminal Court, now fully operational and running trials at its seat in The Hague.[149] An intriguing feature of such developments, for present purposes, is that the model of criminal adjudication to which all of these international courts more or less subscribe has pronounced adversarial features, in large measure because these characteristics were written into Article 6 of the European Convention on Human Rights (ECHR) (and therefore by extension into Article 14 of the International Covenant on Civil and Political Rights) by their British draftsmen.[150] To the extent that characteristically adversarial procedural guarantees, such as access to effective legal advice and representation and the right to cross-examine opposing witnesses,[151] are being incorporated into a prescriptive international standard of fair trial,[152] the scope for national jurisdictions to depart from adversary norms becomes increasingly restricted, at least for those states wishing to remain part of the law-abiding family of nations welcomed into the 'international community'.

Damaška's analysis in ELA remained cosseted within the statal paradigm of classical comparative law, typified by the over-wrought idiom of 'transplants' between one national legal system and another.[153] Despite frequently drawing unavoidably transnational contrasts between 'Anglo-American' and 'Continental' laws, institutions and procedures, ELA's implicit unit of analysis for judging the ebbing fortunes of common law evidence was the territorial national state. Thus, in a revealing footnote, Damaška mused:

> It is unlikely that the movement toward new institutional arrangements will proceed evenly or along the same path in all common law jurisdictions. There are many indications that the pace of change may be faster in England than in the United States. For one thing, England has been drawn into the vortex of European integration without a textually fixed constitution. In contrast to the United States, there is no entrenched

[147] See Chapters 8 and 9.

[148] See Cesare P R Romano, André Nollkaemper and Jann K Kleffner (eds), *Internationalized Criminal Courts: Sierra Leone, East Timor, Kosovo, and Cambodia* (OUP, 2004).

[149] www.icc-cpi.int/. See Antonio Cassese, Paola Gaeta and John R W D Jones (eds), *The Rome Statute of the International Criminal Court: A Commentary* (OUP, 2002).

[150] Geoffrey Marston, 'The United Kingdom's Part in the Preparation of the European Convention on Human Rights, 1950' (1993) 42 *International and Comparative Law Quarterly* 796, 811. The influential UK draft is reproduced in Council of Europe, *Collected Edition of the 'Travaux Préparatoires' of the European Convention on Human Rights* (Martinus Nijhoff, 1976), vol III, 280–88.

[151] ECHR Art 6(3)(c) and (d); ICCPR Art 14(3)(d) and (e); ICC Statute Art 67(d) and (e).

[152] Stefan Trechsel with Sarah J Summers, *Human Rights in Criminal Proceedings* (OUP, 2005); Christoph J M Safferling, *Towards an International Criminal Procedure* (OUP, 2001); Craig M Bradley, 'The Emerging International Consensus as to Criminal Procedure Rules' (1993) 14 *Michigan Journal of International Law* 171.

[153] *Cf* Mirjan Damaška, 'The Uncertain Fate of Evidentiary Transplants: Anglo-American and Continental Experiments' (1997) 45 *American Journal of Comparative Law* 839. For further discussion, see Máximo Langer, 'From Legal Transplants to Legal Translations: The Globalization of Plea Bargaining and the Americanization Thesis in Criminal Procedure' (2004) 45 *Harvard International Law Journal* 1; David Nelken and Johannes Feest (eds), *Adapting Legal Cultures* (Hart Publishing, 2001).

document in England that can impose serious limits on open departures from existing institutional arrangements.[154]

I have already indicated my reasons for thinking that traditional features of common law evidence will find a secure home in English criminal litigation for at least the foreseeable future. Now viewed in cosmopolitan perspective, it can be seen that the UK's entanglement in 'the vortex of European integration' – reinforced by broader developments in international penal law – is quite likely to produce the opposite effects to those foretold by Damaška. To be sure, the point should not be overstated: for example, neither the ECHR nor the UK's own Human Rights Act 1998 guarantees trial by jury in criminal trials, unlike the US Bill of Rights. But, by the same token, Damaška seems to me to have overrated the significance of a national written constitution for the defence of procedural tradition,[155] whilst simultaneously underrating both the distinctive ideals of criminal justice as an inspiration for procedural design and the tenacity of English legal culture in a time of cosmopolitan law.

Globalisation theorists assure us that international pressures towards homogeneity (inspiring the 'McDonaldization' of global culture and similar dystopian visions[156]) are virtually always, in practical experience, subverted by local resistance and adaptive variation,[157] so that globalisation generates as much diversity as sameness in the bazaars of the global village. Likewise, cosmopolitan law – itself conceived as an artefact of globalisation – is caught between an homogenising idealistic or market-driven internationalism and the quotidian demands of local conditions 'on the ground', where the ingenuity of human problem-solving in practical contexts (which are always, ultimately, 'local' to the problem-solvers[158]) tends to reinforce the durability of municipal expectations and traditions. These factors together perpetuate, and indeed reinvigorate and extend, the diversity and distinctiveness of national legal cultures.[159] English law, for example, can draw upon deeply-rooted institutional and cultural resources in defence of its procedural traditions. Moreover, these indigenous resources have lately been fortified

[154] ELA, 147.

[155] In his implicit reverence for the US Constitution, Damaška reveals himself more of an acculturated insider to local jurisprudential thought than his self-image as the wandering comparativist would strictly warrant. But what else should one expect? Even the master is occasionally seduced by the normative assumptions of his (adopted) home.

[156] George Ritzer, *The McDonaldization of Society* (Pine Forge Press, revised New Century Edition 2004).

[157] Eg, Anthony McGrew, 'Globalization and Global Politics' in John Baylis, Steve Smith and Patricia Owens (eds), *The Globalization of World Politics: An Introduction to International Relations*, 4th edn (OUP, 2008); U Beck, *What is Globalization?* (Polity, 2000); William Twining, *Globalisation and Legal Theory* (Butterworths, 2000).

[158] Generally, see David Nelken, 'The Globalization of Crime and Criminal Justice' (1997) 50 *Current Legal Problems* 251; and see Angelina S Godoy, 'When "Justice" is Criminal: Lynchings in Contemporary Latin America' (2004) 33 *Theory and Society* 621 for a particularly extreme version of 'local resistance'.

[159] For cogent demonstration of this thesis in relation to US-style plea-bargaining, see Langer, above n 153.

by a supra-national legal framework prescribing elements of adversary process as part of the international community's normative conception of a fair trial. Of course, to the extent that this normative ideal is implemented also in Continental legal jurisdictions, it will be true to say that Anglo-American legal procedure, and even some aspects of common law evidence, will become less *distinctive* around the world. However, this prospect of global normative transmission, migration and transplantation is more naturally associated with latter-day voyages of discovery and colonisation – sharper critics might call it a new or re-intensified era of Anglophone legal imperialism[160] – rather than Damaška's despairing image of a declining common law evidence precariously adrift from its institutional moorings.

[160] *Cf* the critiques of critical comparativists such as Ugo Mattei, 'A Theory of Imperial Law: A Study on US Hegemony and the Latin Resistance' (2003) 10 *Indiana Journal of Global Legal Studies* 383; Günter Frankenberg, 'Stranger Than Paradise: Identity and Politics in Comparative Law' [1997] *Utah Law Review* 259.

5

Zuckerman's New Evidence Scholarship

BioNote: I first encountered Adrian Zuckerman as a BCL student at Oxford, where I attended his lectures on theories of evidence and factfinding. Adrian was not my tutor in the Law of Evidence. If he had been, I might not have acquired the skills and reverence for rigorous doctrinal analysis that were instilled in me during weekly tutorials (each requiring *two* essays) by Colin Tapper.[1] Adrian is not a slave to the law reports, which he has been known to deride as 'the jurisprudence of gossip' (an AZ-ism I first heard, appropriately enough, by hearsay from my then Nottingham colleague David Ormerod). As a student learning Evidence law for the first time, Adrian and Colin were each other's perfect antidote. I should also mention the positive influence of Peter Mirfield, who gave an excellent set of lectures on bad character evidence that year, and – as book review editor of the LQR – was a generous source of expensive hardback books for me to review.

My next meeting with Adrian arose from his stint as the JC Smith Senior Visiting Fellow at Nottingham, arranged by Di Birch (who, it turns out, had been external examiner for my BCL cohort, and had set a paper with no character evidence points in it – a topic on which, unbeknownst to her, a dozen or more lectures had been delivered!).[2] Adrian came to see me after his week in residence, I assumed to say farewell and hoping to cross paths at some future date. In fact, he had more instrumental business in mind. He wanted to pick my brain as to who might be a good person to update his well-regarded Clarendon Law series title on *The Principles of Criminal Evidence*.[3] I suggested a few names; Adrian didn't look too enthusiastic. Could I think of *anyone else*? I am not very good at taking hints. If you want something from me, you are probably going to have to spell it out. This must have dawned on Adrian, who now adopted a more direct approach. Would *I* write the second edition of his book? No; I was flattered to be asked, but already had too much on my plate to accept another big project. That this protestation was perfectly true is corroborated by the fact that I have still not

[1] By then, also the author of *Cross on Evidence*, 7th edn (Butterworths, 1990). Being taught by the scholar who wrote the book is the epitome of research-led university teaching.

[2] In addition to Peter Mirfield's self-standing lectures on similar facts, Colin Tapper gave 16 lectures on The Course of the Trial, much of them taken up with cross-examination on credibility and bad character, good character at common law, and the application of the Criminal Evidence Act 1898.

[3] A A S Zuckerman, *The Principles of Criminal Evidence* (OUP, 1989).

completed the textbook on Criminal Justice that I was supposed to be writing at the time. Fortunately, Adrian doesn't easily take no for an answer. He persuaded me to have another conversation about it in Oxford, which led to a plan, which – eventually, after six years' hard work – produced a new, much bigger book than either of us had originally intended.[4] Thus was forged the most consequential writing partnership of my academic career.

Adrian was effectively the PhD supervisor I never had. Or rather, he was a surrogate for the final year of a PhD I never did.[5] The year I spent at Bristol as a Research Officer on a project on forensic science evidence led by Chris Willmore[6] was the equivalent experience of the first two or three years of a PhD, telescoped in time but with the advantage of four de facto supervisors: Rod Morgan, Gwynn Davis, David Feldman and Chris herself. I am indebted, in particular, to Gwynn Davis, Professor of Socio-Legal Studies but also an English graduate who cared about the quality of writing, got me to care about it, and showed me how to do it better, essentially through (his) trial and (my) error. Adrian completed[7] this education through a style of co-authorship which was neither precious nor hierarchical regarding his own contributions, whilst judiciously balancing encouragement, probing questions and constructive edits on my drafts. Over the course of a dozen or more meetings (effectively, graduate supervisions) in his University College rooms, high table dinners and walks across Christ Church Meadow and along the Isis to the boathouses, the first edition of our *Criminal Evidence* took shape. It has been a privilege to collaborate over successive editions with a scholar of his calibre and creativity, from whom I continue to learn, even whilst increasingly taking the labouring oar and steering my own course. I doubt I would ever have written a text on criminal evidence if Adrian hadn't supplied me with the one he had written earlier, and I know that any book I could have produced as sole author would not have been as good as the one we originally wrote together. The following essay opens with some further remarks on Adrian's landmark contributions to procedural scholarship.

I. A Tale of Two Zuckermans

It is barely contentious to say that Adrian Zuckerman has exerted a profound and lasting influence on the procedural law and scholarship of his adopted jurisdiction,

[4] Paul Roberts and Adrian Zuckerman, *Criminal Evidence*, 1st edn (OUP, 2004).

[5] I was offered a PhD place at Cambridge on the strength of my performance in the MPhil in Criminology, but had no aspiration to a career in scholarship at that time. During the final months of the BCL, I interviewed for a funded PhD place at Leicester, where Andrew Choo would have been my supervisor, but pulled out when I was offered a permanent lectureship at Nottingham.

[6] Paul Roberts and Chris Willmore, *The Role of Forensic Science Evidence in Criminal Proceedings*, Royal Commission on Criminal Justice Research Study No.11 (HMSO, 1993); Paul Roberts, 'Science in the Criminal Process' (1994) 14 *Oxford Journal of Legal Studies* 469.

[7] In the sense of acquiring the essential tools, rather than achieving perfection, which is always demanding more.

England and Wales. Searching Westlaw UK by full name produces 183 hits, including 18 judicial citations. Impressive enough, you might think – and they are all him (Google, incidentally, is not so discriminating). But refine the search to 'Zuckerman on', and you will need to sift through 3,465 hits, including 3,376 case-related mentions, mostly in commentaries. In terms of direct citation, Zuckerman's arguments and analysis have been recognised as authoritative by the UK Supreme Court,[8] the House of Lords (the UKSC's judicial predecessor),[9] the Court of Appeal (Civil Division),[10] and the English High Court.[11] Counsel have leveraged their submissions with citations to what Cranston J, in the Commercial Court, hailed as 'Professor Adrian Zuckerman's well-recognised book.'[12] In one judgment the Court of Appeal scrutinised 'a bold passage in Chapter 4 of his book [where] Mr Zuckerman suggests that Denning LJ got things wrong',[13] but on that occasion Denning trumped Zuckerman.[14] Brooke LJ concluded, albeit without the benefit of full submissions, that 'the point is without substance' and could not 'see anything in the new [Civil Procedure Rules] which contravenes Article 6 of the European Convention on Human Rights in the way which Mr Zuckerman suggests.'[15] Nobody can win them all. Zuckerman may be quoted at length as the only relevant commentator on a contested issue before the court.[16] The Court of Appeal has commended his 'valuable discussion of the principles'

[8] *Financial Services Authority v Sinaloa Gold Plc* [2013] 2 AC 28, [2013] UKSC 11, [18] (Lord Mance JSC, Lord Neuberger, Baroness Hale, Lord Clarke and Lord Sumption concurring).

[9] *Somerville v Scottish Ministers (No 2)* [2007] UKHL 44, 2008 SC (HL) 45, [205] (Lord Mance); *Three Rivers DC v Bank of England (No 6)* [2005] 1 AC 610, [2004] UKHL 48, [34] (Lord Scott observing that Zuckerman 'refers to the rationale underlying legal advice privilege as "the rule of law rationale"… I, for my part, subscribe to this idea. It justifies, in my opinion, the retention of legal advice privilege in our law, notwithstanding that as a result cases may sometimes have to be decided in ignorance of relevant probative material').

[10] *Collier v Williams* [2006] 1 WLR 1945, [2006] EWCA Civ 20, [19]; *Hashtroodi v Hancock* [2004] 1 WLR 3206, [2004] EWCA Civ 652, [10]; *C Plc v P* [2008] Ch 1, [36] (Longmore LJ finding that 'there is no privilege in the offending material itself, which is material which existed independently of the order. This is essentially the position maintained by Professor Adrian Zuckerman').

[11] *Winterthur Swiss Insurance Co v AG (Manchester) Ltd (In Liquidation)* [2006] EWHC 839 (Comm), [69], n 31.

[12] *Hutchison 3G UK Ltd v EE Ltd*, High Court of Justice Commercial Court, 6 October 2017; 2017 WL 04477790, [24]. Also see *Bidgood v Barclays Bank Plc* [2017] EWHC 2942 (QB), [35]; *Harley Street Capital Ltd v Tchigirinsky (No 2)* [2005] EWHC 1897 (Ch), [71].

[13] *Akram v Adam* [2005] 1 WLR 2762, [2004] EWCA Civ 1601, [37].

[14] Contrary to form, one might think, on points of procedure, where Denning was characteristically unorthodox. According to Denning LJ in *Bater v Bater* [1951] P 35, 36–37 (CA), whilst '[i]t is of course true that by our law a higher standard of proof is required in criminal cases than in civil cases … this is subject to the qualification that there is no absolute standard in either case. In criminal cases the charge must be proved beyond reasonable doubt, but there may be degrees of proof within that standard.' Also see *Hornal v Neuberger Products Ltd* [1957] 1 QB 247 (CA), 258 ('[T]he standard of proof depends on the nature of the issue. The more serious the allegation the higher the degree of probability that is required'). Denning's 'floating standard' heresy (albeit an historically plausible interpretation of a common law maxim) was authoritatively rejected by the House of Lords in *In re D* [2008] 1 WLR 1499, [2008] UKHL 33, [23]–[28].

[15] ibid [38]–[41] (Jonathan Parker and Keene LJJ agreeing).

[16] *Cape Distribution Ltd v Cape Intermediate Holdings* [2016] EWHC 1786 (QB), [169].

pertaining to striking out misbehaving claimants[17] and acknowledged 'the very interesting discussion by Professor Zuckerman' on judicial sanctions for non-disclosure of witness statements.[18] It is thought to count against the authority of a putative precedent, even where 'the Civil Appeals Office has been accustomed to act on the faith of it', that Zuckerman no longer cites it.[19] Even a Zuckerman footnote may attract judicial attention and adversarial argument.[20] Zuckerman's influence further extends geographically, north of the border to Scottish civil litigation,[21] and all the way to Strasbourg.[22]

Attentive readers will have noticed that all of these judicial sightings and notices relate to points of civil procedure, and 'the well-recognised' book in question is, of course, *Zuckerman on Civil Procedure: Principles of Practice* (as the fourth edition is titled).[23] This is the harvest of what we might describe as Zuckerman's second career in procedural scholarship and teaching. In this chapter, however, I want to celebrate an earlier phase of Zuckerman's intellectual journey, in which his central – albeit never exclusive[24] – focus was criminal rather than civil procedure. And my principal claim will be that Zuckerman's influence on British evidentiary scholarship would still have been profound and lasting even if he had never had that remarkable second incarnation as a guru of civil litigation practice and had never written a single word on civil procedure.

The influence I have in mind is not measurable by court citations (with no apology to metrics mongers),[25] and its lasting significance might only be fully appreciated in generational terms over the span of decades (bad luck, then, if you think that the REF cycle marks the horizon of scholarly endeavour). My topic relates to how we think about the disciplinary contours and methodologies, intellectual foundations, and normative value of procedural scholarship. I will suggest, in this essay, that in the earlier phase of his work, Zuckerman made three particularly significant conceptual advances which together reconfigure the terrain of common law evidentiary scholarship and pedagogy. These conceptual advances concern the (1) disciplinary domain; (2) institutional context(s); and (3) normative sources of evidence law. This essay elucidates and evaluates each of these three conceptual innovations, which can be summarised in terms of three corresponding

[17] *Masood v Zahoor* [2010] 1 WLR 746, [2009] EWCA Civ 650, [71] (Mummery LJ).

[18] *Chartwell Estate Agents Ltd v Fergies Properties SA* [2014] EWCA Civ 506, [31] (Davis LJ).

[19] *Handley v Lake Jackson Solicitors* [2016] 1 WLR 3138, [42].

[20] *New Century Media Ltd v Makhlay* [2013] EWHC 3556 (QB), [42].

[21] *Prospect Healthcare (Hairmyres) Ltd v Kier Build Ltd* 2018 SLT 815, [27].

[22] *MGN Ltd v United Kingdom* [2011] 1 Costs LO 84 (ECtHR), [113] (quoting the Jackson Costs Review's reference to Zuckerman's 'forceful' submissions).

[23] Adrian Zuckerman, *Zuckerman on Civil Procedure: Principles of Practice*, 4th edn (Sweet & Maxwell, 2021). The first edition, which appeared in 2003, was simply titled *Civil Procedure*. Generally, see Rabeea Assy and Andrew Higgins (eds), *Principles, Procedure, and Justice: Essays in Honour of Adrian Zuckerman* (OUP, 2020).

[24] Privilege has been for Zuckerman an abiding specialist subject. A notable early essay is Adrian Zuckerman, 'Privilege and Public Interest' in C F H Tapper (ed), *Crime, Proof and Punishment: Essays in Memory of Sir Rupert Cross* (Butterworths, 1981).

[25] *Cf* Rob van Gestel, 'Ranking, Peer Review, Bibliometrics and Alternative Ways to Improve the Quality of Doctrinal Legal Scholarship' in Rob van Gestel, Hans-W Micklitz and Edward L Rubin (eds), *Rethinking Legal Scholarship: A Transatlantic Dialogue* (CUP, 2017).

dynamic transitions: (1) from 'Law of Evidence' to 'Evidence and Proof'; (2) from transubstantivity to procedural differentiation; and (3) from evidentiary rules to principled discretion. Although this triad comes as an integrated package and should, ultimately, be evaluated holistically, there are interesting and important things to be said about each of its individual components, as we shall see.

II. Disciplinary Domain: From 'Law of Evidence' to 'Evidence and Proof'

Zuckerman's first claim to be regarded as a pivotal figure in evidentiary scholarship is that he was one of the very few UK-based academic lawyers to participate in 'the New Evidence Scholarship', a convenient if not entirely transparent umbrella for theoretical developments in (predominantly US) evidence law stretching back to the 1970s. On a narrow reading, the New Evidence Scholarship is associated with a specifically American interest in the study of the science of proof, in which formal logic, mathematics, probability, and decision theory feature prominently.[26] Viewed more expansively, New Evidence Scholarship could be stretched to embrace all of the diverse strands of multi-disciplinary interest in the topic of evidence and proof which, aside from doctrinal analysis, might encompass procedural scholarship, sociological or socio-legal studies of legal institutions and processes, the logic of inference, intelligence analysis and 'information science', discourse analysis (including structuralism, deconstruction, semiotics, rhetoric, narrative and phenomenological approaches), psychological research, scientific and technical developments including forensic science, computer applications and expert systems, and historical inquiries relating to all of the foregoing.[27] The New Evidence Scholars were the shock troops in a campaign to reconfigure the disciplinary parameters and methodologies of Evidence law, with potentially far-reaching implications for scholarship, pedagogy, and institutional practice. 'This profusion of theoretical approaches', enthused one of its leading exponents 30 years ago, 'evinces tremendous intellectual ferment. A profound transformation in human thinking about inference and probability is under way.'[28] Zuckerman

[26] See Richard O Lempert, 'The New Evidence Scholarship: Analyzing the Process of Proof' (1986) 66 *Boston University Law Review* 439; Roger C Park, 'Evidence Scholarship, Old and New' (1991) 75 *Minnesota Law Review* 849; John D Jackson, 'Analysing the New Evidence Scholarship: Towards a New Conception of the Law of Evidence' (1996) 16 *Oxford Journal of Legal Studies* 309.

[27] For accessible entry points into a large and diverse literature, see Paul Roberts, 'Theorising Evidence Law' (2023) 43 *Oxford Journal of Legal Studies* 629; Paul Roberts (ed), *Theoretical Foundations of Criminal Trial Procedure* (Ashgate, 2014); Philip Dawid, William Twining and Mimi Vasilaki (eds), *Evidence, Inference and Enquiry* (OUP, 2011); William Twining, *Rethinking Evidence*, 2nd edn (CUP, 2006); Roger C Park and Michael J Saks, 'Evidence Scholarship Reconsidered: Results of the Interdisciplinary Turn' (2006) 47 *Boston College Law Review* 1; Paul Roberts and Mike Redmayne (eds), *Innovations in Evidence and Proof* (Hart Publishing, 2007).

[28] Peter Tillers, 'Introduction' (1986) 66 *Boston University Law Review* 381, 383.

was a torchbearer and catalyst for British participation and engagement with this ambitious project.

To appreciate what is 'new', and significant, about the New Evidence Scholarship one must view it in contrast with prevailing disciplinary orthodoxy. Since Thayer[29] and then Cross,[30] the widely accepted model of Evidence law envisages a collection of more or less discrete exclusionary exceptions to a threshold relevancy standard. Plainly, only relevant evidence is admissible at trial. This is a principle of logic which any system of adjudication aspiring to rationality must accept. The Law of Evidence, then, comprises a set of 'rules of exclusion' further regulating admissibility. It is an elegant and, in some ways, beguiling model. When the rules – and the exceptions to the rules; and the exceptions to the exceptions to the rules – become complex and wondrously refined through judicial dialectics and sedimentary accretion, common law jurisprudence produces an impressive doctrinal corpus capable of bulking out fearsomely erudite tomes with which to torture law students and keep professors endlessly preoccupied.

The New Evidence Scholarship brought intellectual excitement and theoretical renewal to this bastion of doctrinalism.[31] It rediscovered questions of epistemology, argumentation, inferential reasoning and proof that had fascinated pioneers such as Bentham, Thayer and Wigmore,[32] but had somehow been mislaid after so much effort had been diverted into collecting, organising, analysing and synthesising case law precedents into new doctrinal rules. The New Evidence Scholarship built up enthusiasm and resources for pressing the Law of Evidence *qua* rules of admissibility in the direction of interdisciplinary studies of Evidence and Proof. This might be viewed as a major staging post on the road towards a more fully realised Forensic Science of inquiry, evidence, inference and proof in criminal adjudication.[33]

Zuckerman contributed an essay titled 'Law, Fact or Justice?'[34] to a symposium on 'Probability and Inference in the Law of Evidence' published in the *Boston University Law Review* in 1986,[35] a landmark event now lionised in the history

[29] James Bradley Thayer, *A Preliminary Treatise on Evidence at the Common Law* (Little, Brown & Co, 1898). See Eleanor Swift, 'One Hundred Years of Evidence Law Reform: Thayer's Triumph' (2000) 88 *California Law Review* 2437; Jay Hook, 'A Brief Life of James Bradley Thayer' (1993) 88 *Northwestern University Law Review* 1.

[30] Page 1 of *Cross on Evidence* begins by addressing 'the law of evidence', and in the very next breath is talking about 'the modern rules of evidence'. This telling elision has been repeated by successive editors and coauthors, appearing unchanged in the latest edition: Roderick Munday, *Cross and Tapper on Evidence*, 13th edn (OUP, 2018).

[31] Also see Paul Roberts, 'Groundwork for A Jurisprudence of Criminal Procedure' in R A Duff and Stuart Green (eds), *Philosophical Foundations of Criminal Law* (OUP, 2011).

[32] William Twining, *Theories of Evidence: Bentham and Wigmore* (Weidenfeld & Nicolson, 1985).

[33] See further, John Jackson and Paul Roberts, 'Beyond Common Law Evidence: Reimagining, and Reinvigorating, Evidence Law as Forensic Science' in Darryl K Brown, Jenia Iontcheva Turner and Bettina Weisser (eds), *The Oxford Handbook of Criminal Process* (OUP, 2019); Paul Roberts, 'The New Interdisciplinary Forensic Science' (2016) 43 *Journal of Law and Society* 647.

[34] Adrian A S Zuckerman, 'Law, Fact or Justice?' (1986) 66 *Boston University Law Review* 487.

[35] Eric D Green, 'Boston University Law Review Symposium: Foreword' (1986) 66 *Boston University Law Review* 377. The Symposium occupied two entire issues of volume 66 of the journal, spanning some 580 pages.

of the New Evidence Scholarship and an important catalyst for its further development and propagation. The architect and principal dynamo of the project was Peter Tillers, then Visiting Professor at Cardozo School of Law in New York. He was supported, notably, by 'Adrian Zuckerman, William Twining, and David Schum, who, together with Peter Tillers, saw the need for the symposium and contributed to its organization.'[36] The symposium was said to have 'brought together virtually all the leading scholars concerned with issues of probabilistic and mathematical proof in court',[37] and the roll-call is undeniably impressive. Yet most of the recognisable names it contains – Ron Allen, Craig Callen, Richard Friedman, David Kaye, Rick Lempert, Dale Nance, Charles Nesson, David Schum, Peter Tillers – are American.[38] British representation was limited to Twining, Zuckerman and the Oxford philosopher L Jonathan Cohen.[39]

It is immediately apparent from the first introductory sentences of Eric Green's Foreword that the methodology of inquiry shared by Symposium participants departed radically from the orthodox Thayerite model of evidence law as a system of exclusionary rules:

> The central question in evidence is, 'What does it mean to prove something so that a court will either order a person imprisoned or order a transfer of money or property?' Related issues include the extent to which proof in courts is concerned with finding 'truth' in the abstract (as opposed to some acceptable operational surrogate); the procedural structure of the fact-finding process; the allocation of responsibilities among judge, jury, and advocates and witnesses; the application of rules of evidence to achieve the objectives of the fact-finding system; and the kinds of reasoning to be employed in adjudication .... Because most tried cases involve circumstantial evidence, questions about the nature of proof invariably raise questions about theories of inference and the proper use of mathematical and statistical evidence and probability arguments in courts.[40]

The New Evidence Scholarship was still at that time labouring under the long shadow of the remarkable judgment in *People v Collins*,[41] and many of the contributions to the symposium did indeed concern themselves with questions of probability, Bayes Theorem and statistics. But the New Evidence Scholarship was never circumscribed or delimited by its fascination with probability theory and the undeniably engrossing 'thought experiments' that go with it (Blue and

[36] ibid 380.

[37] ibid 379.

[38] They are also all male, with the exception of Lea Brilmayer, 'Second-Order Evidence and Bayesian Logic' (1986) 66 *Boston University Law Review* 673; and one of her commentators, Anne W Martin, 'Comment' (1986) 66 *Boston University Law Review* 709. This pronounced gender imbalance was presumably, in part, generational. Now see Mary Childs and Louise Ellison (eds), *Feminist Perspectives on Evidence* (Cavendish, 2000).

[39] L Jonathan Cohen, 'The Role of Evidential Weight in Criminal Proof' (1986) 66 *Boston University Law Review* 635.

[40] Green (n 35) 377.

[41] *People v Collins*, 68 Cal 2d 319 (1968). See Laurence H Tribe, 'Trial by Mathematics: Precision and Ritual in the Legal Process' (1971) 84 *Harvard Law Review* 1329.

Green Buses; The Rodeo/Gatecrasher Paradox; Prison Yard, etc).[42] Once the question becomes, not 'What are the doctrinal rules?' but 'What does it mean to prove something …?' the entire vista of epistemology, rational inference and forensic argumentation, together with the procedural architecture, intellectual frameworks, pedagogy and practical tools to support effective litigation and sound adjudication, are opened up to the Evidence and Proof research agenda.

Zuckerman's contribution to the Boston symposium set out to reconsider three basic concepts of the Law of Evidence – 'law', 'fact' and 'justice' – and to explore their interrelationship. On the face of it, the meaning of these concepts appears reasonably well-defined and their roles discrete. The law allocates legal entitlements and duties, and, in trials, issues of law are determined by the judge. Facts relate to 'what happened', the disputed issues in contested litigation, and fact-finding is entrusted to the common law jury or lay magistrates in criminal trials.[43] Legal reasoning, then, is normative, whereas forensic fact-finding concerns empirical matters and is performed through ordinary processes of inferential reasoning for which lay jurors and magistrates are well-equipped by their accumulated 'common sense' rooted in ordinary, everyday experience. Justice requires faithful application of legal rules to the true facts of the case, ascertained through a rational process of evidence gathering, testing and proof. Zuckerman's aim was to complicate this overly simplistic picture of conceptual demarcation, and thereby to challenge the assumption that forms of reasoning applicable in other areas of life – including probabilistic and statistical reasoning – could be extrapolated to the forensic context without any major adjustment or contextualisation. This misapprehension, Zuckerman argued, rested on a fallacious 'assumption of objectivity; the assumption that the sole function of the judicial process is to search for the objective truth that lies beyond, and is independent of, the law'.[44] Yet this assumption could not survive better and closer acquaintance with the institutional facts: 'present procedural practices denote the existence of a meeting ground between fact-finding and law application, where normative values shape the facts as well as the law …. [L]aw application and fact-finding converge in adjudication'.[45]

[42] As Green (n 35) 378, quipped of *Collins*' direct legacy: 'In the ensuing debate, numerous blue buses have run untold numbers of near-sighted elderly ladies off the road, hundreds of alleged gatecrashers have been collared, dozens of murderous prisoners have been brought to justice, and countless articles, books, and opinions have been written on the subject' (footnotes omitted). Generally, see Mike Redmayne, 'Exploring the Proof Paradoxes' (2008) 14 *Legal Theory* 281; Stephen E Fienberg, 'Gatecrashers, Blue Buses, and the Bayesian Representation of Legal Evidence' (1986) 66 *Boston University Law Review* 693; David H Kaye, 'The Paradox of the Gate-Crasher and Other Stories' [1979] *Arizona State Law Journal* 101.

[43] See, eg, *Daniel v State of Trinidad and Tobago* [2014] AC 1290, [2014] UKPC 3, [48] ('The general rule for the conduct of a criminal trial is that questions of law are for the judge and questions of fact are for the jury'). But also note *R v Fanning* [2016] 1 WLR 4175, [2016] EWCA Crim 550, [2] (referring to 'the constitutional position of the jury in a criminal trial …. [T]rial by jury developed in a way that, although questions of fact were for the jury and questions of law were for the judge, rules were established which delineated the jury's function to determine issues of fact').

[44] Zuckerman (n 34) 488.

[45] ibid 489.

Legal disputes are framed by distinctively *legal* conceptions of materiality indexed to the applicable substantive law. This implies not only that the law stipulates 'the issues in the case', which define the subject matter of any contested trial, and by extension supply (legal) criteria of evidential relevancy; more fundamentally, it is not even possible to describe 'the facts of the case' without reference to legal concepts and categories. For example, the question of whether the accused 'occasioned' a particular level of injury ('actual bodily harm', 'grievous bodily harm', 'wounding', etc) implicates legal tests of 'occasioning'[46] and classifications of injury as much as it concerns the metaphysics of action or the physical state of bodies: the 'brute facts',[47] so to speak, of 'what the accused did'. Interestingly, though, these juridical questions of legal classification are often in practice left to juries to determine. Is this conceptual seepage some kind of oversight or deficiency in legal process? Zuckerman argued, to the contrary, that the policy was calculated and deliberate: 'The assimilation, for the purpose of adjudication, of fact-finding and law application is vital for the role that we expect adjudication to fulfil.'[48] This blending flows from the twin imperatives of securing social approval for verdicts and maintaining public confidence in the administration of justice, especially in criminal adjudication, which in turn presupposes and leverages the *normative* (moral) quality of forensic fact-finding. Juries are prized precisely because, not in spite of, their ability to inject prevailing social morality into criminal verdicts. A procedural system orientated towards moral legitimacy will predictably invest considerable institutional capital in individualised justice on the merits, through which empirical truths are subjected to moral appraisal. This rationale, suggested Zuckerman, goes a long way towards explaining the law's traditional hostility to (overt) probabilistic reasoning and illuminates the intuition that 'naked statistical evidence' should never be sufficient to establish proof to the criminal standard. In the end, however, we face an unresolved tension which takes us to the limit of the human epistemic condition:

> The debate about the introduction of probabilistic assessment into the judicial process reflects much of th[e] age old conflict between our deeply rooted attitudes concerning fact-finding. On the one hand, the doubts that we entertain regarding our ability to arrive at the truth would seem to argue for the adoption of mathematical methods which would at least maximize the number of correct decisions in the long run. On the other hand, such a step would involve us in giving up, to a considerable extent, the hope of seeing justice supervene in individual trials.[49]

Having been energised by first wave New Evidence Scholarship, debates about the role of probability and statistical information in legal proceedings have raged on unabated.[50] They have lately been infused with even greater theoretical significance

[46] Section 47 of the Offences Against the Person Act 1861 (still in force and routine use in England and Wales) proscribes 'assault occasioning actual bodily harm'.

[47] Zuckerman was here following G E M Anscombe, 'On Brute Facts' (1958) 18 *Analysis* 69.

[48] Zuckerman (n 34) 494.

[49] ibid 508.

[50] See, eg, Colin Aitken, 'An Introduction to a Debate' (2012) 11 *Law, Probability & Risk* 255; Mike Redmayne, Paul Roberts, Colin Aitken and Graham Jackson, 'Forensic Science Evidence

and practical urgency by the dawning realisation that all scientific evidence is probabilistic and, in principle, probatively quantifiable.[51] DNA profiling has inaugurated a new era of statistically-based forensics, generating quantified measures of (estimated)[52] probative value.[53] Zuckerman's qualified scepticism about forensic probability, and his unqualified insistence that criminal adjudication ultimately subordinates fact-finding and conceptual formalisms such as the theoretical fact-law distinction to individualised justice on the merits, remain forceful and highly salient counterweights to the juggernaut of contemporary scientific logic. Besides, the significance for British jurisprudence of Zuckerman's engagement and participation in the New Evidence Scholarship extends beyond discrete contributions to particular debates.

Zuckerman is not the most influential UK-based contributor to the New Evidence Scholarship. That accolade undoubtedly belongs to William Twining, whose historical excavations of Evidence theory, decades-long campaign to promote 'taking facts seriously' in legal pedagogy, and central involvement in disinterring and reinventing the Wigmorean graphical method of evidence analysis

in Question' [2011] *Criminal Law Review* 347; Bernard Robertson, G A Vignaux and Charles E H Berger, 'Extending the Confusion about Bayes' (2011) 74 *Modern Law Review* 444; Colin Aitken, Paul Roberts and Graham Jackson, *Fundamentals of Probability and Statistical Evidence in Criminal Proceedings* (Royal Statistical Society, 2010); Ronald J Allen and Michael S Pardo, 'The Problematic Value of Mathematical Models of Evidence' (2007) 36 *Journal of Legal Studies* 107; Mike Redmayne, *Expert Evidence and Criminal Justice* (OUP, 2001); Mike Redmayne and Ron Allen (eds), *Bayesianism and Juridical Proof* (1997) 1(5) *International Journal of Evidence and Proof* 253; Bernard Robertson and G A Vignaux, 'Probability – The Logic of the Law' (1993) 13 *Oxford Journal of Legal Studies* 457; Craig R Callen, 'Notes on a Grand Illusion: Some Limits on the Use of Bayesian Theory in Evidence Law' (1982) 57 *Indiana Law Journal* 1.

[51] Michael J Saks and Jonathan J Koehler, 'The Coming Paradigm Shift in Forensic Identification Science' (2005) 309 *Science* 892; Ian Evett, 'The Logical Foundations of Forensic Science: Towards Reliable Knowledge' (2015) 370 *Philosophical Transactions B* Article 20140263; Graham Jackson, Colin Aitken and Paul Roberts, *Case Assessment and Interpretation of Expert Evidence* (Royal Statistical Society, 2014).

[52] An important qualification, because forensic scientists invariably work with factual assumptions over which the jury has the final decisive authority to accept or reject: *cf* Charles E H Berger and Klaas Slooten, 'The LR Does Not Exist' (2016) 56 *Science and Justice* 388.

[53] See *ENFSI Guideline for Evaluative Reporting in Forensic Science*, v.3.0 (8 March 2015), enfsi.eu/wp-content/uploads/2016/09/m1_guideline.pdf (accessed 17 December 2025); PCAST, *Report to the President: Forensic Science in Criminal Courts – Ensuring Scientific Validity of Feature-Comparison Methods* (Washington DC, Executive Office of the President, 2016), www.justice.gov/d9/2023-07/07.13.23.%20-%20PCAST%20-%20Interim.pdf (accessed 17 December 2025); Michael Lynch, Simon A Cole, Ruth McNally and Kathleen Jordan, *Truth Machine: The Contentious History of DNA Fingerprinting* (Chicago University Press, 2008). For more broadly contextualising discussion, see Gary Edmond, 'Re-assessing Reliability' in Paul Roberts and Michael Stockdale (eds), *Forensic Science Evidence and Expert Witness Testimony* (Edward Elgar, 2018); Geoffrey Stewart Morrison and William C Thompson, 'Assessing the Admissibility of a New Generation of Forensic Voice Comparison Testimony' (2017) 18 *Columbia Science & Technology Law Review* 326; Paul Roberts, 'Paradigms of Forensic Science and Legal Process' (2015) 370 *Philosophical Transactions B* Article 3 (20140256); Simon A Cole, 'Forensics without Uniqueness, Conclusions without Individualization: The New Epistemology of Forensic Identification' (2009) 8 *Law, Probability and Risk* 233; Michael J Saks, 'Forensic Identification: From a Faith-based "Science" to a Scientific Science' (2010) 201 *Forensic Science International* 14; Michael J Saks and Jonathan J Koehler, 'The Individualization Fallacy in Forensic Science Evidence' (2008) 61 *Vanderbilt Law Review* 199.

and argumentation rank as peerless, trans-jurisdictional contributions to Evidence and Proof scholarship.[54] Zuckerman probably wasn't even the most influential New Evidence scholar on Oxford's High Street[55] (if we follow orthodox conceptions of New Evidence Scholarship as being primarily focused on epistemology, probability, information science, argumentation and forensic logic).[56] Embroidering on his highly original, widely read and hotly debated book *The Probable and the Provable*,[57] Jonathan Cohen produced a clutch of important papers on cognition, belief and forensic process, including his Boston symposium essay.[58] It is telling, however, that neither Twining nor Cohen could be described as Law of Evidence specialists in the sense of being intimately acquainted with doctrinal sources and institutional materials and practices. This is precisely where Zuckerman led the way. Being knowledgeable in evidence law *and* theory, Zuckerman was able to combine both together to their mutual enrichment. This methodological premium can be seen, for example, in Zuckerman's distinctive approach to the right of silence, which combines attention to the logic of factual inference (gleaned, one might speculate, from Bentham[59] and Cross[60]) with an astute eye to the institutional dynamics of criminal investigations and the pragmatic requirements of effective procedural regulation.[61] Whilst his reformist strategy, dubbed 'exchange

[54] See in particular Terrence Anderson, David Schum and William Twining, *Analysis of Evidence*, 2nd edn (CUP, 2005); William Twining, 'Hot Air in the Redwoods, A Sequel to the Wind in the Willows' (1988) 86 *Michigan Law Review* 1523; William Twining, 'Taking Facts Seriously' in Neil Gold (ed), *Essays on Legal Education* (Butterworths, 1982); William Twining, 'Taking Facts Seriously – Again' in Paul Roberts and Mike Redmayne (eds), *Innovations in Evidence and Proof* (Hart Publishing, 2007); William Twining, 'The Boston Symposium: A Comment' (1986) 66 *Boston University Law Review* 391. Also see Paul Roberts, 'Rethinking the Law of Evidence: A Twenty-first Century Agenda for Teaching and Research' (2002) 55 *Current Legal Problems* 297.

[55] L Jonathan Cohen was a fellow of Queen's College, Oxford, which is right across the High Street from Zuckerman's academic home, University College, and can be seen from the window of Zuckerman's old college rooms.

[56] Vacuous as they are, any such ranking would be influenced by whether one regards attention to procedural context (undoubtedly a great strength of Zuckerman's approach, discussed below) as a trademark methodology of New Evidence Scholarship. I am doubtful: but *cf* Bernard Robertson, 'Principles of Criminal Evidence' (1990) 106 *Law Quarterly Review* 510 (praising Zuckerman for 'breaking down the traditional distinction between evidence and procedure drawn by Cross' and linking his general approach to 'the "New Evidence" thinking').

[57] (OUP, 1977). Cohen's Preface acknowledges 'details I discussed again and again with Dr A Zuckerman, and I owe very much to the patience and generosity with which he let me use his time'.

[58] Cohen (n 39). Also see L Jonathan Cohen, 'Should A Jury Say What it Believes or What it Accepts?' (1991) 13 *Cardozo Law Review* 465; L Jonathan Cohen, 'Freedom of Proof' in William Twining (ed), *Facts in Law* (Franz Steiner, 1983).

[59] See Michael A Menlowe, 'Bentham, Self-incrimination and the Law of Evidence' (1988) 104 *Law Quarterly Review* 286.

[60] Rupert Cross, 'A Very Wicked Animal Defends the 11th Report of the Criminal Law Revision Committee' [1973] *Criminal Law Review* 329; Rupert Cross, 'The Right to Silence and the Presumption of Innocence – Sacred Cows or Safeguards of Liberty?' (1970) 11 *Journal of the Society of Public Teachers of Law* 66.

[61] Adrian Zuckerman, 'Trial by Unfair Means' [1989] *Criminal Law Review* 855; Adrian Zuckerman, 'The Right Against Self-Incrimination: An Obstacle to the Supervision of Interrogation' (1986) 102 *Law Quarterly Review* 43.

abolitionism' by critics,[62] may have perturbed criminal justice scholars with strong pro-defendant sympathies,[63] Zuckerman's general jurisprudential method clearly influenced the next generation of theoretically-inclined Evidence scholars including Andrew Choo,[64] Mike Redmayne,[65] Hock Lai Ho[66] and David Hamer,[67] amongst many others.

The value of sustained attention to institutional context, exhibited in Zuckerman's Boston symposium paper and in several subsequent articles, leads directly to the second conceptual innovation that I want to highlight in this essay. As evidentiary discussion increasingly centres on jury verdicts, the right of silence, police interrogation and confessions,[68] unlawfully obtained evidence[69] and miscarriages of justice,[70] it becomes hard to ignore the indisputable fact that we are now chiefly concerned with evidence in *criminal* proceedings. Curiosity, if nothing else, should prompt reconsideration of what this topical refocusing might imply for the adequacy of a generic common law model of the Law of Evidence.

III. Institutional Context: From Transubstantivity to Procedural Differentiation

According to the standard common law model, the Law of Evidence is generic and unified or, as some US scholars put it, 'trans-substantive'.[71] That is to say, a single

[62] Steven Greer, 'The Right to Silence: A Review of the Current Debate' (1990) 53 *Modern Law Review* 709; Steven Greer and Rod Morgan (eds), *The Right to Silence Debate* (Bristol and Bath Centre for Criminal Justice, 1990). Generally, see Roger Leng, 'Silence Pre-trial, Reasonable Expectations, and the Normative Distortion of Fact-finding' (2001) 5 *International Journal of Evidence & Proof* 240; John D Jackson, 'Silence and Proof: Extending the Boundaries of Criminal Proceedings in the United Kingdom' (2001) 5 *International Journal of Evidence & Proof* 145; David Morgan and Geoffrey Stephenson, *Suspicion and Silence: The Right to Silence in Criminal Investigations* (Blackstone, 1994).

[63] More recently, see Hannah Quirk, 'Twenty Years On, The Right of Silence and Legal Advice: The Spiralling Costs of Unfair Exchange' (2013) 64 *Northern Ireland Legal Quarterly* 465.

[64] Andrew Choo's Oxford DPhil thesis, supervised by Zuckerman, was published as Andrew L-T Choo, *Abuse of Process and Judicial Stays of Criminal Proceedings* (OUP, 1993; 2nd edn 2008).

[65] See in particular, Mike Redmayne, 'English Warnings' (2008) 30 *Cardozo Law Review* 1047; Mike Redmayne, 'Rethinking the Privilege Against Self-Incrimination' (2007) 27 *Oxford Journal of Legal Studies* 209.

[66] Hock Lai Ho, *A Philosophy of Evidence Law: Justice in the Search for Truth* (OUP, 2008).

[67] David Hamer, 'The Structure and Strength of the Propensity Inference: Singularity, Linkage and the Other Evidence' (2003) 29 *Monash University Law Review* 137; David Hamer, 'Probabilistic Standards of Proof, Their Complements and the Errors that are Expected to Flow from Them' (2004) 1 *University of New England Law Journal* 71.

[68] Adrian A S Zuckerman, 'Procedural Fairness During Police Interrogation and the Right of Silence' (1990) 54 *Journal of Criminal Law* 499.

[69] See above, n 61; Adrian A S Zuckerman 'Illegally-Obtained Evidence – Discretion as a Guardian of Legitimacy' (1987) 40 *Current Legal Problems* 55.

[70] Adrian A S Zuckerman, 'The Protection of the Accused from Miscarriages of Justice' (1997) 31 *Israel Law Review* 590; Adrian A S Zuckerman, 'Miscarriage of Justice – A Root Treatment' [1992] *Criminal Law Review* 323; Adrian A S Zuckerman, 'Miscarriage of Justice and Judicial Responsibility' [1991] *Criminal Law Review* 492.

[71] See, eg, David Marcus, 'Trans-substantivity and the Processes of American Law' [2013] *Brigham Young University Law Review* 1191; Stephan Landsman, 'Are the Federal Rules of Evidence Dynamite?'

Law of Evidence regulates proof-taking and fact-finding across all types of litigation, including criminal prosecutions, private law civil actions, family matters and public law judicial review of administrative action. It is recognised that adaptations may be required to accommodate particular aspects of special procedural regimes, but these are regarded as exceptions to the common shared core of legal doctrines and principles. For example, criminal and civil cases have traditionally operated with different standards of proof, but this is not regarded as a serious threat to the transubstantive model. Marginal exceptions excepted, a generic and unified Law of Evidence is embraced as the default setting for evidentiary regulation in all types of legal proceedings.

The publication in 1989 of *The Principles of Criminal Evidence*, Adrian Zuckerman's landmark contribution to the well-regarded Clarendon Law Series published by Oxford University Press, issued a direct challenge to orthodox transubstantivity in the Law of Evidence. Having acknowledged a convergent epistemological investment in accurate fact-finding and a common adversarial heritage, Zuckerman nonetheless insisted on procedural differentiation:

> The law of evidence, as it is traditionally conceived, does not deal with every single legal procedure; it is confined to criminal and civil proceedings in the superior courts of the law and in magistrates' courts. However, even those procedures that the traditional law of evidence encompasses are so diverse as to make it impossible to observe any general underlying principles that might give coherence to this body of law. There are at least two distinct procedures, the criminal and the civil, which are not only governed by different rules but also reflect entirely different concerns.[72]

Procedural differentiation is logical and pragmatic, Zuckerman insisted, because different rules of evidence apply to criminal and civil proceedings, respectively, and even when generic rules nominally apply, they 'often undergo special modification when employed in criminal cases'.[73] Civil litigation is increasingly preoccupied with contested discovery, merging rules of evidence and procedure in a manner foreign to criminal process; and what is more, 'the parties' to criminal litigation are in reality the state and the accused, not the disputants of 'symmetrically competing claims'[74] as is typical of civil litigation. Recognising the special role of the state in criminal prosecutions calls to mind a range of additional considerations reinforcing procedural differentiation. State officials involved in criminal investigations and prosecutions are entrusted with intrusive and coercive powers of surveillance, search, evidence-gathering (today including swabbing for DNA profiling),[75] detention and interrogation, necessitating the provision of countervailing safeguards,

(2015) 33 *Boston University International Law Journal* 343, 351–52. Zuckerman employed the term to describe nineteenth century unification of civil procedure under the Judicature Acts: see Adrian Zuckerman, 'The Jackson Final Report on Costs: Plastering the Cracks to Shore Up a Dysfunctional System' (2010) 29 *Civil Justice Quarterly* 263, 276.

[72] Zuckerman (n 3) 2–3.

[73] ibid 4.

[74] ibid.

[75] PACE 1984, ss 63–63U (as amended).

such as the privilege against self-incrimination, to insulate the accused against abuse or oppression. Coupled with the primary objective of criminal adjudication, which is to censure and sanction criminal wrongdoers,[76] it becomes apparent that '[a] legal system which respects the rights of the individual has to devise a criminal procedure that affords due protection from punishment to the innocent citizen and the law of criminal evidence includes several measures for achieving this end'.[77]

Viewed in broader social and political context, criminal adjudication and the censure and punishment of offenders would not even be viable, at least in a democracy, without being able to generate some measure of normative legitimacy and social acceptance. 'Verdicts', in short, 'have to command public approval'.[78] There are many strands to this endeavour. For example, trial by lay jury is clearly an important factor in securing the public acceptability of verdicts, inasmuch as 'the people' themselves are called upon to decide whether the accused should be found guilty (a judgement with normative as well as epistemological credentials, as we have seen). The form of trial process is also significant in ensuring the credibility of verdicts. As a general proposition, one may have greater confidence in the rectitude of outcomes if the process producing them is demonstrably fair, rational and rigorous in its assessment of evidence, arguments and claims. This is all the more significant in criminal adjudication, given the absence of any systematic or socially credible external metric by which to assess the correctness of verdicts.[79] The upshot of these reflections (mostly rehearsing what everybody already knows), is that the more one contemplates the special public character, penal objectives and social significance of criminal adjudication, the more sharply pronounced the contrast with routine civil litigation is drawn, not merely in incidental features, but also and especially in core values and basic procedural architecture. When systematically reviewed and squarely confronted, '[s]uch extensive differences between the law governing criminal and civil cases could hardly be accidental'.[80]

After a crisp three or four pages of argument throwing down the gauntlet to orthodox common law thinking, Zuckerman drew the logical conclusion:

> [A]s a result of numerous reforms, starting in the middle of the nineteenth century, criminal proceedings have been set on a separate course. This divergence reflects the special functions of our system of criminal justice. Consequently, whatever might have been the case half a century ago, it would be idle to pretend that today there is only one law of evidence subject merely to variations in criminal and civil proceedings. The law

[76] See Chapters 2 and 3.
[77] Zuckerman (n 3) 5.
[78] ibid 5.
[79] 'There is … no external test for judging whether a criminal verdict reflects the truth. The past cannot, as it were, be revived for the purpose of checking conformity between the facts as they really happened and as they have been reflected in the verdict of the court': ibid.
[80] ibid 4.

> of criminal evidence has an independence of purpose and a cohesion of principle such that it requires a discrete treatment.[81]

The significance of this fundamental disciplinary re-conceptualisation cannot be overstated, in my estimation, although the elegance, concision and apparent simplicity of Zuckerman's original exposition may have contributed to its widespread under-appreciation and muted short-term impact. Disciplinary rethinking has immediately tangible and transparent pay-offs. Switching to an exclusive focus on Criminal Evidence makes room to accommodate new evidentiary topics and facilitates the rearrangement of old material now seen in new light. The orthodox Law of Evidence, as crystallised in – one might almost say *defined by* – Rupert Cross's authoritative textbook, does not devote entire chapters, as *The Principles of Criminal Evidence* did, to 'Proof Beyond Reasonable Doubt: The Law's Commitment to the Innocent', 'The Privilege Against Self-Incrimination' or 'Improperly Obtained Evidence', partly because these topical foci elude, and implicitly refute, transubstantivity. On the normative plane, procedural differentiation points the way towards systematic reconceptualisation of criminal evidence as an applied branch of political morality, characterised by principled asymmetry (rather than presumptive equality in the application of procedural norms) and animated by normative (rather than epistemic) coherence. Subsequent developments in the law of criminal evidence and procedure, briefly summarised below, have amply confirmed the merits – arguably, the *necessity* – of this intellectual shift. To appreciate its radical creativity, however, we should first pause to consider how deeply transubstantivity is embedded within the common law evidentiary tradition.

There have been other texts, published before and after *The Principles of Criminal Evidence*, which have taken a procedurally differentiated approach to criminal evidence and procedure.[82] But the overwhelming weight of common law jurisprudential tradition, reflected in the array of contemporary textbooks on English evidence law,[83] lends immense ballast to the trans-substantive flagship. The conventional notion of a unified and generic Law of Evidence has been an article of faith for common lawyers since at least the mid-nineteenth century. Already by 1820, Best J was able to declare in *R v Burdett*:[84]

[81] ibid 6.

[82] See, eg, J A Andrews and Michael Hirst, *Andrews and Hirst on Criminal Evidence*, 4th edn (Jordans, 2001); Richard May, *Criminal Evidence*, 4th edn (Sweet & Maxwell, 1999); J C Smith, *Criminal Evidence* (Sweet & Maxwell, 1995).

[83] Leading works include Roderick Munday, *Cross & Tapper on Evidence*, 13th edn (OUP, 2018); Ian Dennis, *The Law of Evidence*, 8th edn (Sweet & Maxwell, 2024); Andrew Choo, *Evidence*, 6th edn (OUP, 2021); Richard Glover, *Murphy on Evidence*, 15th edn (OUP, 2017); Adrian Kean and Paul McKeown, *The Modern Law of Evidence*, 15th edn (OUP, 2024); Roderick Munday, *Evidence*, 11th edn (OUP, 2022); Hodge M Malek (ed), *Phipson on Evidence*, 20th edn (Sweet & Maxwell, 2024). At least one book has travelled in reverse: Jonathan Doak, Claire McGourlay and Mark Thomas, *Evidence: Law and Context*, 5th edn (Routledge, 2018) was originally titled *Criminal Evidence in Context* (Sage, 2005).

[84] *R v Burdett* (1820) 4 B & Ald 95, 122.

> It has been solemnly decided that there is no difference between the rules of evidence in civil and criminal cases. If the rules of evidence prescribe the best course to get at truth, they must be and are the same in all cases, and in all civilised countries. There is scarcely a criminal case, from the highest down to the lowest, in which courts of evidence do not act upon this principle.

Wigmore was emphatic in propagating this orthodoxy, insisting that '[t]here are … by no means two systems of rules, distinct in history and in method … There is but one system of rules for criminal and for civil trials'.[85] On the Wigmorean account (which subsequently dominated American common law jurisprudence, in particular), transsubstantivity was both theoretically and pragmatically sound: '[n]ot only in practice, but in principle and in spirit, there is no occasion for a distinction'.[86] In fact, Wigmore regarded any attempt to disaggregate the Law of Evidence into discrete institutional variants as itself an impertinent and wrong-headed fallacy ripe for refutation:

> [T]he occasional appearance, in works on the law, of the title 'Criminal Evidence' has tended to foster the fallacy that there is some separate group of rules or some large number of modifications. On the contrary, much is lost in utility in attempting a separate treatment; for most of the large principles of evidence are equally illustrated in both kinds of trials, and cannot be adequately followed, either in theory or in authority, if the precedents in either class of cases are ignored. The fallacy, however, is an inveterate one, and has had repeatedly to be repudiated …[87]

Wigmore's zealotry on the question of disciplinary unity may be compared, I think unfavourably, with the more nuanced position expressed 20 years earlier by Stephen, who noted that 'some of the more detailed rules of evidence … apply exclusively, and others most frequently to criminal cases, and … give much of its special character to an English criminal trial'.[88]

In this, as in so many other matters of jurisprudential controversy, comparative law affords welcome perspective. Conceptualising the Law of Evidence as a unified field of legal scholarship and practice is a peculiarity of the common law imagination. Thayer marvelled, 'no other country has it; we alone have generated and evolved this large, elaborate, and difficult doctrine'.[89] Discovering that other major legal traditions lack any equivalent disciplinary taxonomy has even led some commentators to the preposterous conclusion that *rules of evidence* exist only in the common law world.[90] This is akin to saying that because the

[85] *Wigmore on Evidence*, (Little, Brown & Co, 1904) vol 1, §4.

[86] ibid.

[87] ibid.

[88] Sir James Fitzjames Stephen, *A History of the Criminal Law of England* (Routledge, 1996 [1883]) vol 1, 437.

[89] James Bradley Thayer, *A Preliminary Treatise on Evidence at the Common Law* (Little, Brown & Co, 1898) 7.

[90] See, eg, James W Jeans, Sr, 'A Modest Proposal: Scrap the Rules of Evidence' (2007) 2 *Liberty University Law Review* 1, 8 ('When the fact-finder is a jurist or a tribunal of jurists, as in most European countries, there are no rules of evidence'). As William T Pizzi, 'Soccer, Football and Trial Systems'

French don't drive on the left, they don't have any cars. The orthodox common law conception of the Law of Evidence, in my view, suffers from multiple intellectual and practical deficiencies. These serious shortcomings ought to prompt scholars and practitioners alike to reconsider its continuing fitness for purpose and give serious consideration to differentiating criminal evidence and procedure from civil procedure – as Zuckerman contended, and as civilian jurists have always done.

The institutional reality of procedural differentiation is perforce more marked today than it was in 1989 when Zuckerman's *Principles* impertinently demanded foundational conceptual rethinking. At that time, PACE 1984 had only recently entered into force, and its evidentiary implications, which have since proven extensive and voluminous,[91] were barely being explored. Since that time, major legislative reform and an avalanche of new case-law have accumulated relentlessly. Even if generic transubstantive rules of evidence were commonplace in the century approximately bookended by Stephen's Indian Evidence Act and the last edition of *Cross on Evidence* written by Cross himself,[92] the traditional common law model is no longer even proximately faithful to the reality of contemporary procedural law and practice in England and Wales.

During the classical Stephen/Cross era there was an intuitive plausibility to treating significant chapters of evidentiary doctrine as common to all types of litigation. The rule against hearsay (and its common law exceptions), the law of presumptions and burdens[93] of proof, witness competency and credibility, privilege, collateral finality and the rule against narrative, the rules regulating expert opinion testimony, and so forth constituted a solid and substantial core of generic evidentiary law. But this convergence represented a phase in the historical evolution of common law evidence doctrine which has now passed. One way of understanding this transition is to say that a subject which was fashioned, historically, by common law judges responding on a more or less ad hoc basis to the practical challenges of litigation, has since been radically restructured through legislation. Parliament has relaxed or abolished evidentiary doctrines on the civil side,[94] whilst energetically introducing successive waves of new procedural and evidentiary rules applicable only to criminal proceedings. There

(1995) 1 *Columbia Journal of European Law* 369, 370, wisely cautions, '[m]any of the generalizations that are frequently offered to describe continental trial systems – that they have no rules of evidence, that they are not adversarial, that they have no presumption of innocence, etc – are either inaccurate or misleading'.

[91] By my reckoning, there are over 1,000 cases invoking (or at least mentioning) a single provision, PACE 1984, s 78 (judicial discretion to exclude prosecution evidence obtained unfairly).

[92] *Cross on Evidence*, 5th edn (Butterworths, 1979).

[93] As opposed to *standards* of proof, which are deviantly pluralistic on the orthodox view, as we have noted.

[94] Notably abrogating the common law hearsay prohibition: Civil Evidence Act 1995, s 1; facilitating the admissibility of expert (opinion) evidence: Civil Evidence Act 1972; and limiting the privilege against self-incrimination: Civil Evidence Act 1968.

has been statutory reform of police investigative procedures,[95] radical innovation in the area of 'special measures' for vulnerable and intimidated witnesses,[96] and systematic overhaul of hearsay and bad character evidence.[97] Case-law remains important, to be sure; and thanks to the indefatigable industry of the Court of Appeal (Criminal Division) and other appellate tribunals, it is never in short supply. However, this burgeoning corpus of precedents and judicial guidelines is increasingly preoccupied with points of statutory interpretation confined to criminal litigation, rather than elucidating generic common law evidentiary doctrines.

De facto disaggregation of Evidence law has been in full swing for 30 years or more. Zuckerman was the first UK-based scholar to really grasp its implications. Two further institutional developments, which have significantly affected the law of England and Wales only since the turn of the twenty-first century, have made the divergence of criminal procedure and evidence from civil procedure more decisive and, to all intents and purposes, irrevocable. The first development is the 'human rights revolution' in English criminal procedure law precipitated by the entry into force of the Human Rights Act 1998 in October 2000.[98] From that decisive moment, traditional evidentiary doctrines and new statutory provisions have come under the scrutiny of the European Court of Human Rights (ECtHR) and have been obliged to comply with the Strasbourg Court's extensive 'fair trial' jurisprudence. Although Article 6(1) of the ECHR stipulates criteria of fairness applicable to all types of adjudication (including the threshold requirements of an 'independent and impartial tribunal constituted by law'), Article 6(2) and – especially – Article 6(3) specify detailed additional procedural requirements for fair *criminal* trials. The institutional wedge between criminal and civil proceedings is thus hammered home at the supra-national level. A second significant development of relatively recent vintage is the introduction of a set of Criminal Procedure Rules (CrimPR) in 2005. Subsequently updated at regular intervals, the CrimPR are an exemplar of what I call 'hard-working soft law': their enormous impact on the day-to-day conduct of criminal litigation is belied by their lowly formal status as delegated legislation or mere rules of court.[99] Revealingly, for our

[95] See, eg, Investigatory Powers Act 2016; Protection of Freedoms Act 2012; Regulation of Investigatory Powers Act 2000; Criminal Procedure and Investigations Act 1996; Police and Criminal Evidence Act 1984; and their related, ever-expanding Codes of Practice.

[96] Youth Justice and Criminal Evidence Act 1999; Coroners and Justice Act 2009.

[97] Criminal Justice Act 2003, ss 98–139.

[98] Paul Roberts and Jill Hunter, 'Introduction – The Human Rights Revolution in Criminal Evidence and Procedure' in Paul Roberts and Jill Hunter (eds), *Criminal Evidence and Human Rights: Reimagining Common Law Procedural Traditions* (Hart Publishing, 2012).

[99] The desirability and detailed implications of this impact are hotly contested, but its scale is beyond dispute. For contrasting evaluations, see Mike McConville and Luke Marsh, 'Adversarialism Goes West: Case Management in Criminal Courts' (2015) 19 *International Journal of Evidence & Proof* 172; Lord Thomas of Cwmgiedd, 'The Criminal Procedure Rules: 10 Years On' [2015] *Criminal Law Review* 395; Jenny McEwan, 'From Adversarialism to Managerialism: Criminal Justice in Transition' (2011) 31 *Legal Studies* 519.

purposes, the Civil Procedure Rules (CPR) were introduced separately seven years earlier, following Lord Woolf's root-and-branch review of civil proceedings,[100] as a discrete legislative exercise divorced from criminal procedure. In content, the two sets of rules are overlapping but substantially divergent and even prescribe different 'overriding objectives'.[101]

The advent of the CrimPR might be regarded, in retrospect, as supplying the missing half of the procedural equation. At the operational level of real trials, Criminal Procedure and Civil Procedure are now formalistically, as well as institutionally, disaggregated. Meanwhile, Law of Evidence textbooks continue to propound a mythical conception of evidentiary law that exists only in commentators' imaginations; or else, they trip over themselves repeating the solecism that criminal evidence represents an 'exception' to supposedly generic evidentiary doctrines. The fact is that the doctrinal law of criminal evidence has lately evolved into an almost entirely separate branch of procedural law, with precious little in common with its civil counterpart below the level of macroscopic normative and epistemic generalities. In England and Wales at least,[102] the traditional common law model has been transformed by events into a spectral anachronism. The argument was, to my mind, quite persuasive when Zuckerman first made it. Subsequent events make it compelling.

IV. Normative Sources: From Evidentiary Rules to Principled Discretion

A third major conceptual innovation in Zuckerman's thinking about evidence law in general, and criminal evidence in particular, concerns the sources and nature of evidentiary norms and their role in legal and judicial reasoning. It is important to stress that these ideas come as a package and need careful unpacking. There is nothing particularly distinctive about wanting to rid evidence law of excessive

[100] Lord Woolf, *Access to Justice: Final Report to the Lord Chancellor on the Civil Justice System in England and Wales* (HMSO, 1996). Now see www.justice.gov.uk/courts/procedure-rules/civil/rules (accessed 17 December 2025).

[101] For criminal procedure, the prescribed 'overriding objective' is 'that criminal cases be dealt with justly': CrimPR, r 1. The corresponding provision in the CPR specifies 'enabling the court to deal with cases justly and at proportionate cost' as the 'overriding objective' of civil procedure. For further discussions, see Paul Roberts, *Roberts and Zuckerman's Criminal Evidence*, 3rd edn (OUP, 2022) 19–26, 41–44; Adrian Zuckerman, *Zuckerman on Civil Procedure: Principles of Practice*, 4th edn (Sweet & Maxwell, 2021) ch 1.

[102] For a rare concurring US voice, see Margaret A Berger, 'Does the Search for Truth in Our Scholarship Continue in Our Classrooms?' (1998) 49 *Hastings Law Journal* 1179: '[A]n enormous split exists between our scholarship and pedagogy … In our classrooms, evidence is treated as a set of trans-substantive rules that apply across the board to all cases, except for a few carefully noted instances. The trial at which these rules apply is viewed as an isolated, disconnected moment in time. The consequence is the cutting-edge issues that most intrigue us as scholars often cannot be handled meaningfully in our classrooms.'

technicality, spurious distinctions, make-weight arguments or doctrinally embedded irrationality. Cross, the author of the leading textbook on the English Law of Evidence, was barely less enthusiastic about modernist reform, rationalisation and simplification of procedural law than Bentham.[103] In fact, these rationalist objectives might plausibly be ascribed to just about any orthodox Evidence scholar or legal commentator in the analytical common law tradition. What is distinctive about Zuckerman's argument lies in the combination of what he wanted to subtract *and* add to the existing disciplinary corpus. His general preference for judicial discretion over inflexible evidentiary rules should not be equated with Benthamite antinomianism,[104] because Zuckerman insisted that exercises of judicial discretion should be rooted in a foundation of evidentiary *principle*. Inasmuch as criminal adjudication implements distinctively *penal* values and objectives (as opposed to the corrective, restitutionary or social justice normative frameworks structuring other types of adjudicative process), a principled approach to evidentiary regulation will necessarily reinforce procedural differentiation. In short, '[a] critical exposition of the law of criminal evidence has to be conducted by reference to *its* general principles'.[105]

Zuckerman originally proposed three core principles of the law of criminal evidence: truth discovery, protecting the innocent from conviction, and the maintenance of standards of propriety in criminal process. In *Principles*' successor, we subsequently worked this trio up into a revised 'five foundational principles of criminal evidence', adding in considerations of minimum state intervention and humane treatment and clarifying that all five principles serve the more basic objective of penal justice, ie, censure and punishment of criminal wrongdoing.[106] Zuckerman advanced two main objections to the orthodox conception of evidentiary regulation as a set of exclusionary rules: firstly, he said, it presents a misleading picture of the institutional realities of law and legal practice; secondly, it is counterproductive in safeguarding foundational principles. The conventional picture is distorted because the rules, when examined more closely, are often subject to exceptions or overriding judicial discretions, falsifying any expectation of their rigid and predictable application in the instant case. The rules might *appear* fixed and determinate when rehearsed in Evidence textbooks, but such appearances are deceptive:

> What is the difference between a fixed rule that may be side-stepped by the exercise of discretion when justice so requires and a declaration that the matter is governed by

[103] According to William Twining, *Rethinking Evidence*, 2nd edn (CUP, 2006) 1, Cross once interjected into 'a heated debate about proposed reforms of Criminal Evidence' that he was working for the day when his subject would be abolished. The reforms in question were contained in the – to posterity, notorious – Eleventh Report of the Criminal Law Revision Committee on *Evidence: General*: see Colin Tapper, 'Evidence (General): Eleventh Report of the Criminal Law Revision Committee' (1972) 35 *Modern Law Review* 621.

[104] On Bentham's 'anti-nomian thesis … an attack on the idea that adjudicative decisions on questions of fact are susceptible to regulation by binding rules', see William Twining, *Theories of Evidence: Bentham and Wigmore* (Weidenfeld & Nicolson, 1985) 66–75.

[105] Zuckerman (n 3) 6 (emphasis supplied).

[106] Roberts (n 101) § 1.3.

> discretion to see that justice is done? …. [I]n many contexts an explanation of the existing law in terms of such discretion is much more accurate than an exposition based on strict definitions of permissible and impermissible practices.[107]

The model of rules ill-serves institutional values in two conceptually divergent but, in their result, mutually aggravating ways. Strict application of evidentiary rules is problematic when the doctrinal law has, through judicial over-interpretation and embedded institutional wrong turnings, become detached from its underlying rationales. This occurs, for example, when perfectly reliable evidence is rejected simply because it falls into the technical definition of 'hearsay'.[108] Conversely, preoccupation with exclusionary rules crowds out other salient considerations. Foundational principles, in particular, do not figure as prominently in judicial thinking or feature as explicitly in courts' decision-making as they should do. More open and honest engagement with the discretionary reality of evidentiary practices, Zuckerman contended, would contribute to the continuous refinement of principled standards, 'bring into the open the full range of the considerations that affect judicial decisions',[109] and promote 'the development of the judicial instinct'[110] in their application. In this way, '[t]he development of guidelines for the exercise of discretion, far from weakening the protection of the innocent or undermining standards of propriety … will promote better awareness of these important principles'.[111]

Zuckerman's conceptual innovation lay not in his *discovery* of judicial discretion in the application of evidentiary standards, but in his insistence that principled discretion should feature centrally in expository accounts of legal doctrine and in judicial reasoning. It has always been patently obvious that pockets of evidentiary doctrine involve a fair amount of judicial creativity and fact-specific determinations. Perhaps the most extreme illustration is the *res gestae* exception to the hearsay prohibition, a doctrine so amorphous and nubile that it is not even clear what the (conveniently Latin) words mean.[112] Having laboured to invest it with some sort of conceptual continence, Cross candidly wrote of *res gestae* that, 'owing to the fact that the cases in which it is employed are often ones in which the judge has a wide discretion, it is not a subject on which extreme precision is either possible or desirable'.[113] By the time that *The Principles of Criminal Evidence* appeared, it was already widely appreciated that judicial discretion is an important dimension

[107] Zuckerman (n 3) 11.
[108] Also see A A S Zuckerman, 'The Futility of Hearsay' [1996] *Criminal Law Review* 4.
[109] Zuckerman (n 3) 12.
[110] ibid 13.
[111] ibid.
[112] Or as Lord Wilberforce once more decorously put it, '[t]he expression "res gestae", like many Latin phrases, is often used to cover situations insufficiently analysed in clear English terms': *Ratten v R* [1972] AC 378 (PC) 388. For discussion, see David Ormerod, 'Redundant Res Gestae?' [1998] *Criminal Law Review* 301; Andrew L-T Choo, *Hearsay and Confrontation in Criminal Trials* (OUP, 1996) ch 5.
[113] *Cross on Evidence*, 2nd edn (Butterworths, 1963) 480.

of criminal litigation,[114] Hart's general model of law as a system of rules had been challenged by Dworkin's advocacy of jurisprudential principle,[115] and the idea of 'discretion' had benefitted from extended critical exegesis.[116] Nonetheless, the tendency amongst Law of Evidence specialists to marginalise discretionary decision-making as a mere afterthought or largely inconsequential supplement to the main business of stating and applying rules was obdurate. Early editions of *Cross on Evidence* flagged 'an increasing recognition of a wide field of judicial discretion with regard both to the inclusion and exclusion of evidence', but the topic merited only a half-page discussion, and concluded abruptly with the underwhelming observation that '[i]t remains to be seen whether the existence of a wide sphere of judicial discretion will be recognised in yet other branches of the English law of evidence'.[117] It is ingrained habit in the common law tradition to think and talk of rules, not only in characterising major doctrinal subdivisions ('the rule against hearsay', 'the opinion evidence rule', 'the similar fact evidence rule', 'the rule against narrative', 'the rule against third party admissions', etc), but even in describing quite technical, fine-grained procedural practices and standards ('the rule in *Turnbull*',[118] 'the rule in *Browne v Dunn*',[119] 'the rule in *Hollington v Hewthorn*',[120] etc) Zuckerman turned the tables on the traditional disciplinary model, insisting that faithful exposition should *begin with* evidentiary principles and keep them firmly in mind in the discretionary application and flexible development of the law of criminal evidence.

Three decades on, Zuckerman's argument has largely been vindicated by subsequent institutional developments, though there are some caveats and qualifications that need to be applied to the original – compactly stated – thesis, in my opinion. Five major jurisprudential innovations, none of them very predictable in the mid-1980s, are particularly pertinent in the context of criminal adjudication in England and Wales. First, the previously-mentioned Human Rights Act 1998 and ensuing 'human rights revolution' in English criminal procedure and evidence law[121] supplied English courts with new normative resources for

[114] Rosemary Pattenden, *The Judge, Discretion and the Criminal Law* (OUP, 1982); *Judicial Discretion and Criminal Litigation*, 2nd edn (OUP, 1990).

[115] Ronald Dworkin, *Taking Rights Seriously* (Duckworth, 1977); Ronald Dworkin, *A Matter of Principle* (OUP, 1985).

[116] D J Galligan, *Discretionary Powers: A Legal Study of Official Discretion* (OUP, 1986).

[117] *Cross on Evidence*, 22–23. By the fifth edition (1979), Cross was (still) acknowledging 'increasing recognition of a wide field of judicial discretion in relation to the admissibility of evidence': above n 86, 29. Coverage had expanded to eight pages and, notably, was divided up into 'Improperly Obtained Evidence in Criminal Cases' (7 pages) and 'Civil Cases' (half a page).

[118] See, eg, *R v Yates* [2003] EWCA Crim 629, [25] (holding that the judicial direction challenged on appeal 'was adequate to cover the rule in *Turnbull*').

[119] *Browne v Dunn* (1894) 6 R 67 (HL); *R v M & N* [2011] EWCA Crim 1458, [48].

[120] *Hollington v F Hewthorn & Co Ltd* [1943] KB 587, CA; abolished in English civil proceedings by Civil Evidence 1968, s 11; and superseded in criminal proceedings by PACE 1984, s 74. But *cf R v Hayter* [2005] 1 WLR 605, [2005] UKHL 6 (for a fleeting recent cameo).

[121] Roberts and Hunter (n 98).

principled argumentation,[122] and also contributed more generally to an intellectual climate in which direct appeals to principle are more commonplace, and potentially gain more judicial traction, than was evident in the pre-HRA era. Second, numerous statutory provisions have been enacted, conferring 'structured discretions' on judicial decision makers.[123] These legislative provisions typically specify a general admissibility standard and then identify a set of potentially relevant criteria to be applied contextually to the demands of the instant case. These structured statutory discretions are, in effect, Parliament's implementation of Zuckerman's preferred technique of evidentiary regulation. Third, the Court of Appeal (Criminal Division) has become a lot less rule-focused or hidebound by precedent than it used to be in matters of procedural law. This is partly in pragmatic recognition of the truism (which courts ignore at their peril) that the application of evidentiary standards often involves inherently vague and open-ended conceptual classifications that necessarily turn on the facts of the instant case.[124] The Court of Appeal could never provide definitive rulings on the meaning of terms such as 'misconduct', 'unreliable', 'probative value', 'unfairly prejudicial' or 'adverse effect on the fairness of the proceedings' (or for that matter, 'relevant', 'evidence' or 'contrary to the interests of justice') even if it did not already have a massive caseload and stretched capacity. Fourth, the proliferation of hard-working soft law as a bourgeoning source of evidentiary practice has upgraded the de facto jurisprudential status of a large miscellany of norms that are often framed in terms of general principles, competing criteria and non-binding exhortations. The 'overriding objective' specified by the CrimPR is emblematic in this respect.[125] Finally, fifth, it bears repeating that since *Principles*

[122] See, eg, Paul Roberts, 'Normative Evolution in Evidentiary Exclusion: Coercion, Deception and the Right to a Fair Trial' in Roberts and Hunter (eds), *Criminal Evidence and Human Rights* (Hart Publishing, 2012); Paul Roberts, 'Criminal Procedure, the Presumption of Innocence and Judicial Reasoning under the Human Rights Act' in Helen Fenwick, Gavin Phillipson and Roger Masterman (eds), *Judicial Reasoning under the UK Human Rights Act* (CUP, 2007). Generally, see John Jackson and Sarah Summers, *The Internationalisation of Criminal Evidence* (CUP, 2012); Ian Dennis, 'The Human Rights Act and the Law of Criminal Evidence: Ten Years On' (2011) 33 *Sydney Law Review* 333; Andrew L-T Choo and Susan Nash, 'Evidence Law in England and Wales: The Impact of the Human Rights Act 1998' (2003) 7 *International Journal of Evidence & Proof* 31.

[123] See, eg, Criminal Justice Act 2003, ss 114(2), 116(2) and 117(7); Coroners and Justice Act 2009, s 89.

[124] See especially *R v Renda* [2006] 1 WLR 2948, [2005] EWCA Crim 2826, [3], where Lord Judge admonished counsel that 'the trial judge's "feel" for the case is usually the critical ingredient of the decision at first instance which this court lacks. Context therefore is vital. The creation and subsequent citation from a vast body of so-called "authority", in reality representing no more than observations on a fact-specific decision of the judge in the Crown Court, is unnecessary and may well be counter-productive'.

[125] Rule 1.1 of the CrimPR provides that '[t]he overriding objective of this procedural code is that criminal cases be dealt with justly', and then further specifies that: 'Dealing with a criminal case justly includes— (a) acquitting the innocent and convicting the guilty; (b) treating all participants with politeness and respect; (c) dealing with the prosecution and the defence fairly; (d) recognising the rights of a defendant, particularly those under Article 6 of the European Convention on Human Rights; (e) respecting the interests of witnesses, victims and jurors and keeping them informed of the progress of the case; (f) dealing with the case efficiently and expeditiously; (g) ensuring that appropriate

was published, the jurisprudence of section 78 of PACE 1984, latterly super-charged by Article 6 of the ECHR, has mushroomed beyond all anticipation into its own major chapter of evidentiary scholarship and practice.[126] Zuckerman wrote that, 'so far there has been little inclination to elucidate the principles which should govern the exercise of this discretion'.[127] We now have over 1,000 cases, scores of which make a decent stab at elucidating a principled approach to issues such as police 'entrapment',[128] deceptive custodial interrogation,[129] fair disclosure,[130] and the moral integrity of criminal procedure.[131]

Marching in step with the trajectory of recent institutional history does not necessarily put one on the right side of procedural law's *longue durée*. To the extent that excessive conceptual rigidity, doctrinal obsolescence and bad faith rationalisations of the normatively indefensible[132] have been consigned to history's trashcan by a more principled approach to evidentiary regulation, nobody will mourn their passing. Yet that is not quite the whole of the story. Zuckerman anticipated the sceptical response that principled discretion could not achieve predictability and stability in the law or adequately safeguard procedural rights. His rejoinder denied the premiss: the *existing*, ostensibly rule-based law was far from certain or predictable, since '[m]ost of the rules of evidence do not in fact provide fixed definitions of acceptable or unacceptable practices but rather lay down guidelines for decisions'[133] and what is more, 'the courts refuse to observe strict definitions when they consider the results of observance unsatisfactory'.[134] This is not entirely convincing; and Zuckerman was surely over-reaching in

information is available to the court when bail and sentence are considered; and (h) dealing with the case in ways that take into account (i) the gravity of the offence alleged, (ii) the complexity of what is in issue, (iii) the severity of the consequences for the defendant and others affected, and (iv) the needs of other cases.'

[126] See Roberts (n 101) ch 5. On the – initially unpromising – legislative history, see Sybil Sharpe, *Judicial Discretion and Criminal Investigation* (Sweet & Maxwell, 1998), 81–85; David Ormerod and Di Birch, 'The Evolution of the Discretionary Exclusion of Evidence' [2004] *Criminal Law Review* 767.

[127] Zuckerman (n 3) 352.

[128] *R v Looseley; Attorney-General's Reference (No 3 of 2000)* [2001] 1 WLR 2060, [2001] UKHL 53; *R v Palmer* [2014] EWCA Crim 1681; *R v Redmond* [2009] 1 Cr App R 25, [2006] EWCA Crim 1744; *R v Jones (Ian)* [2008] QB 460, [2007] EWCA Crim 1118.

[129] *R v Mason* [1988] 1 WLR 139, CA: *cf R v Plunkett and Plunkett* [2013] 2 Cr App R 2, [2013] EWCA Crim 261; *R v Bailey and Smith* (1993) 97 Cr App R 365, CA.

[130] *R v Boardman* [2015] 1 Cr App R 33, [2015] EWCA Crim 175; *R v Bard (and 28 others)* [2014] EWCA Crim 463.

[131] *R v S(D) and S(T)* [2015] 2 Cr App R 27, [2015] EWCA Crim 662; *R v Newell* [2012] 2 Cr App R 10, [2012] EWCA Crim 650.

[132] Zuckerman contemplated that 'the existence of strict definitions can be said to have undermined the protection of the innocent from conviction and the maintenance of standards of propriety in the criminal process. Definitions often provide the courts with an excuse for concealing the real reasons for their decisions by enabling them to take refuge in refined technical distinctions': Zuckerman (n 3) 11–12. Judicial resistance to a more principled approach could be attributed to 'a legal methodology, fast becoming the exclusive preserve of the English profession, according to which major problems of principle receive the kind of treatment that is more appropriate to the interpretation of technical tax provisions': ibid 352–53.

[133] ibid 10.

[134] ibid 11.

arguing that when admissibility decisions 'have to be justified on a case-by-case basis … [this] will ensure that, instead of finding a convenient and often spurious exception for the purpose of admitting evidence, the trial judge has to consider the interest of the individual accused in a more open and reviewable manner'.[135] Really? The simplicity of this depiction of judicial psychology, innocent of the institutional realities of criminal litigation and the malleability of doctrinal rationalisations, appears almost *faux naïf*; albeit that we are now admittedly opening up complex and methodologically fraught issues, that can receive only superficial treatment in the balance of this chapter.

To begin with the transparency claim, one may doubt that a principled approach to evidentiary regulation will necessarily enhance public scrutiny of judicial reasoning or render its exercise more tractable to appellate supervision. Although express articulation of pertinent criteria is certainly a valuable feature of judicial deliberation, merely listing factors to be taken into account does not provide much insight into the actual processes of arriving at a decision or really explain the trade-offs made in ubiquitous judicial 'balancing'. In many ways, the more factors that are fastidiously enumerated, the more opaque the motivating or decisive considerations may become. Complexity is exacerbated by the realisation, not widely reflected in 1980s evidence law scholarship, that the interests of complainants and witnesses should also be taken into account in assessing procedural fairness[136] alongside 'the interest of the individual accused'. When the range of cognisable interests and considerations expands in this manner, trial judges are often left with a variety of plausible options and a correspondingly capacious normative repertoire for rationalising their ultimate choices, wherever the chips may fall in individual cases. So it is difficult to see how a methodological shift from rule to principle *in itself* makes judicial decision-making more transparent or less susceptible to bad faith rationalisations. This does not, however, contradict the plausible contention that more self-consciously principled decision-making is superior on its own intrinsic merits to formalistic rule-following irrespective of transparency or reviewability.

The role that 'principles' do, or should, play in theoretical explanation or practical reasoning is controversial in modern normative philosophy.[137] Steadfast adherence to principles can be derided as priggishness or moral fanaticism, as where the Kantian categorical imperative against lying is 'logically' extrapolated to

[135] ibid 12.

[136] The standard position in English law now holds that 'fairness to the defence is of prime importance but fairness to the prosecution must also be taken into account': *R v Hayward* [2001] QB 862, [2001] EWCA Crim 168, [22]. As a basic conceptual matter, '[t]he concept of a fair trial involves fairness to the prosecution and to the public, as well as fairness to the defendant': *DPP v Meakin* [2006] EWJC 1067 (Admin), [23]. In assessing procedural fairness in the round, English courts have regard to 'the familiar triangulation of interests of the accused, the victim and society': *R v A (No 2)* [2002] 1 AC 45, [2001] UKHL 25, [38] (Lord Steyn).

[137] See Jonathan Dancy, *Ethics Without Principles* (OUP, 2004); John Gardner, 'Ashworth on Principles' in Lucia Zedner and Julian V Roberts (eds), *Principles and Values in Criminal Law and Criminal Justice* (OUP, 2012).

demand truthful betrayal of Jewish refugees' hiding place to the murderous Nazi Stormtrooper.[138] Principles, it might be said, are no less capable of misuse and normative perversity than rigid rules with 'strict definitions'. Sensibly[139] restricting ourselves to the specific institutional context of criminal adjudication in England and Wales, it is clear that contemporary procedural law routinely employs both general principles and well-specified, formalistic rules as regulative mechanisms. Many of the bright-line rules, moreover, are widely endorsed, and some of them – such as the rule that the accused is never compellable in his or her own trial, even by a co-accused[140] – are about as specific, determinable and uncontested as any legal rule could be. Other norms are agreed in principle – trials must be fair; the accused enjoys the presumption of innocence; coerced confessions are inadmissible; witnesses must not be exposed to gratuitous vilification or anguish – but controversial in their more detailed elucidation and applications. It then becomes an interesting question of institutional design to explore when the law does, and should, adopt one kind of regulative mechanism over another. Why, for example, is procedural integrity a question of general principle, whereas legal professional privilege is an absolute rule?[141] This design vector is bisected by another dimension of procedural architecture, which was not very evident when *Principles* was published but has since become a major question in evidence law reform: to what extent can evidentiary rules of exclusion adequately be replaced by judicial warnings against misuses of information presented to the jury? Zuckerman presciently argued that the policies underlying some of the traditional exclusionary categories might be implemented more effectively by allowing the jury access to more (presumptively relevant) information with a careful judicial explanation clarifying why 'the principles of criminal justice, which require resisting prejudice, reflect their own perceptions of justice'.[142] This revised approach, propounding renewed efforts to develop *effective* judicial directions[143] (under the rubric of what we later

[138] *Cf* Michael Cholbi, 'The Murderer at the Door: What Kant Should Have Said' (2009) 79 *Philosophy and Phenomenological Research* 17.

[139] Because normative ethics is a vast sprawling field, and normative propositions are bedevilled by over-generalisation and extrapolation to new contexts they have no business colonising.

[140] Youth Justice and Criminal Evidence Act 1999, s 53(4); PACE 1984, s 80(4); Criminal Evidence Act 1898, s 1(1).

[141] *R v Derby Magistrates' Court ex p. B* [1996] 1 AC 487, HL; reversing, or possibly correcting, the position asserted in *R v Ataou* [1988] QB 798, CA, and reported in Zuckerman (n 3) 300, according to which 'the privilege is overridden where the information is required by an accused person to prove his innocence'. Zuckerman doubted the wisdom of the 'absolutist' stance adopted in *Derby Magistrates*, since '[i]n reality … there is no escaping the need for balancing interests', and speculated that 'the absolutist approach to legal professional privilege may well turn out to be short-lived': A A S Zuckerman, 'Legal Professional Privilege: The Cost of Absolutism' (1996) 112 *Law Quarterly Review* 535, 538, 539. In the event, English courts have steadfastly held the line (at least as regards the *admissibility* of privileged communications): *Three Rivers District Council v Bank of England (No 6)* [2005] 1 AC 610, [2004] UKHL 48; *McE v Prison Service of Northern Ireland* [2009] 1 AC 908, [2009] UKHL 15.

[142] Zuckerman (n 3) 245.

[143] Linking this point with the first conceptual innovation discussed earlier, Zuckerman complained that 'the effectiveness of judicial directions has been somewhat undermined by insufficient appreciation of the overall function of the jury …. [W]ithin the law of evidence there is a dogged reluctance to accept the role of the jury as more than fact-finder': ibid 42–43.

called 'forensic reasoning rules'),[144] would – Zuckerman anticipated – facilitate a shift in regulatory policy, which subsequent events have in large measure enacted:

> The availability of more effective means of persuading a jury to abide by the principles of criminal justice will make the question of admissibility less important because the tools will be in place for counteracting prejudice.[145]

For all its bold reinvention of common law tradition and impressive prognostication of future landscapes, there remains a missing dimension to this discussion, and in this respect Zuckerman might be regarded as channelling a general methodological limitation of orthodox evidentiary scholarship. Bluntly, there is too much focus on appellate decisions and not enough sociological realism about the conduct of criminal trial proceedings. Even in Crown Court practice,[146] it seems likely (as the fragmentary empirical record tends to confirm)[147] that counsel and trial judges operate according to general precepts of fair process and reasonable litigation practice, local courtroom conventions and a shared institutional ethos expecting, and rewarding, 'adversarial' behaviour only in certain contexts and within defined limits, rather than by the strict letter of procedural law.[148] This is not to deny any real-world significance to legal doctrine as appellate courts and law professors know and state it: rather, it is to call attention to the sociological fact that formal law, whether styled 'rules' or 'principles' (or something else), is always mediated by a set of more informal institutional understandings and behaviours, and we also need to think about *that relationship* between juridical and informal norms when we consider the propriety and effectiveness of evidentiary regulation. Whether discretionary standards of admissibility will sustain enough predictability and stability in litigation practice, for example, is not itself primarily a doctrinal question, but rather turns on how, if at all, reconceptualising the theoretical basis of admissibility determinations will impact on subsisting courtroom routines and legal professionals' habitual working practices and expectations. Likewise, traditional common law approaches to, say, hearsay exceptions only really threaten the rule of law[149] as a practical achievement if institutional routines are incapable of making up for the absence of conceptual clarity and determinative normative guidance by improvising a reasonably stable and consistent judicial practice in borderline hearsay

[144] Roberts (n 101) ch 15.

[145] Zuckerman (n 3) 246.

[146] It is barely controversial to say that magistrates' court trials present a rather different picture of (non)compliance with formal evidentiary doctrine. Not for nothing are these characterised as 'summary' proceedings.

[147] Consider, for example, Quirk's empirical findings describing the mediated (non)impact on litigation practice of ss 34–38 of the Criminal Justice and Public Order Act 1994, regulating judicial directions on drawing inferences from silence: Hannah Quirk, *The Rise and Fall of the Right of Silence* (Routledge, 2017) 145–54.

[148] Matt Thomason, 'Admitting Evidence by Agreement: Recalibrating Managerialism and Adversarialism in Crown Court Criminal Trials' [2021] *Criminal Law Review* 727.

[149] *Cf* Colin Tapper, 'The Law of Evidence and the Rule of Law' (2009) 68 *Cambridge Law Journal* 67.

'hard cases'.[150] From the perspective of institutional sociology, then, repackaging rules as principled discretion *might* just be rearranging the disciplinary deckchairs. Only through other types of inquiry, including empirical studies of first instance proceedings, can it be discerned with any confidence whether we are sailing to our salvation in Noah's Ark or going under with the RMS *Titanic*.

The recent prominence of informal 'hard-working soft law' norms in English criminal evidence and procedure becomes salient again at this point in the discussion. Some of these provisions are formulated in sweeping terms, such that their application could easily be overextended if read out of context. This is not merely an hypothetical speculation: in one notable appeal, for example, the High Court had to remind a first instance judge that the CrimPR are not competent to erode settled common law rules of legal professional privilege.[151] Other norms are formulated as judicial 'guidance',[152] and in a perfectly laudable effort to maximise their helpfulness to practitioners, they tend to be presented in relatively loose, discursive treatments. Still other secondary norms overlap with statutory and common law evidentiary standards,[153] posing questions of selectivity, authenticity and fidelity to the primary doctrinal corpus. It goes without saying that secondary sources have inferior constitutional pedigree, and in some instances no formal legal pedigree at all.[154] Much of their institutional value resides in the comparative ease and speed with which delegated legislation and soft law guidance can be improvised, developed and adapted to meet unfolding contingencies, but their prosaic implementation – leveraging the de facto professional authority of judicial

[150] The perennial question of 'implied assertions' provides the best demonstration of this diagnosis. If the logic of the majority's reasoning in *R v Kearley* [1992] AC 228, HL, had been taken seriously it should have created havoc in criminal litigation, but it did not do so because, as a practical matter, the ruling was treated as being confined to particular factual scenarios, chiefly those involving anonymous telephone calls. Conversely, s 115 of the CJA 2003, as masterfully elucidated in *R v Twist* [2011] 2 Cr App R 17, [2011] EWCA Crim 1143, should have solved the implied assertion problem in English law, but has not done so because (some) criminal practitioners and judges are still operating primarily on instinct: see, eg, *R v Midmore* [2017] 2 Cr App R 8, [2017] EWCA Crim 533; *R v KN* [2006] EWCA Crim 3309. For conceptually astute discussion, see Diane Birch and Michael Hirst, 'Interpreting the New Concept of Hearsay' (2010) 69 *Cambridge Law Journal* 72; Craig Callen, 'Interdisciplinary and Comparative Perspectives on Hearsay and Confrontation' in Paul Roberts and Mike Redmayne (eds), *Innovations in Evidence and Proof* (Hart Publishing, 2007); Christopher B Mueller, 'Incoming Drug Calls and Performative Words: They're Not Just Talking About It, Baron Parke!' (1995) 16 *Mississippi College Law Review* 117; Rosemary Pattenden, 'Conceptual versus Pragmatic Approaches to Hearsay' (1993) 56 *Modern Law Review* 138.

[151] *R (Kelly) v Warley Magistrates' Court* [2008] 1 WLR 2001, [2007] EWHC 1836 (Admin).

[152] See especially the *Crown Court Compendium Part 1: Jury and Trial Management and Summing Up* (Judicial College, October 2025), www.judiciary.uk/guidance-and-resources/crown-court-compendium-october-2025/ (accessed 17 December 2025).

[153] Notably, the *Criminal Procedure Rules 2025 and Criminal Practice Directions 2023*, www.gov.uk/guidance/rules-and-practice-directions-2020 (accessed 17 December 2025).

[154] See, eg, the guidance and materials provided to criminal advocates through The Advocate's Gateway, www.theadvocatesgateway.org/, which have judicial backing and are 'mandated as best practice by Criminal Practice Direction 3D.7': *R v Grant-Murray* [2017] EWCA Crim 1228, [113].

training delivered by the Judicial College[155] – occurs largely under the radar of routine democratic scrutiny.

English law is experiencing unprecedented fluidity and uncertainty in the jurisprudential constitution of modern criminal procedure. Some commentators worry that traditional principles of adversarial criminal litigation are being eroded piecemeal and almost by default, as individual judges and courts grapple with the practical exigencies of austerity policies, and in the absence of any wider public debate.[156] Zuckerman's argument for articulating and developing fundamental principles to structure and guide the exercise of judicial discretion in evidentiary regulation has lost none of its original currency, cogency and vigour in this new institutional environment. In a world of fewer hard-and-fast rules, however, the project of formulating and propagating the right set of principles for criminal procedure and evidence acquires heightened, possibly existential, significance for the legitimacy of criminal adjudication.

V. Conclusion

This chapter celebrates Adrian Zuckerman's profound and lasting influence on the procedural law and scholarship of England and Wales. Having acknowledged the importance of Zuckerman's 'second career' as an expert on English civil procedure, I then ignored it to concentrate on earlier, 'phase one' work addressing more foundational jurisprudential themes (or at any rate, themes more important and interesting to me). Specifically, I identified and elaborated on three conceptual innovations concerning: (1) the disciplinary domain; (2) institutional context(s); and (3) normative sources of evidence law, which I take to be especially important contributions to disciplinary thinking in evidentiary scholarship and practice. These conceptual advances may be encapsulated in terms of three correlative dynamic transitions: (1) from 'Law of Evidence' to 'Evidence and Proof'; (2) from transubstantivity to procedural differentiation; and (3) from evidentiary rules to principled discretion.

In relation to (1), I suggested that Zuckerman played a supporting but still pivotal role in the transmission of the New Evidence Scholarship to British shores, through his distinctively *jurisprudential* combination of new interdisciplinary studies of evidence and proof with more traditional doctrinal questions and materials. This first conceptual contribution, however, is something in the nature of a prelude to two further, more consequential innovations. Emphatic rejection of common law Evidence's orthodox transubstantivity in favour of procedural

[155] Courts and Tribunals Judiciary – Judicial College: www.judiciary.uk/about-the-judiciary/training-support/judicial-college/ (accessed 17 December 2025).

[156] Mike McConville and Luke Marsh, 'Adversarialism Goes West: Case Management in Criminal Courts' (2015) 19 *International Journal of Evidence & Proof* 172; Jenny McEwan, 'From Adversarialism to Managerialism: Criminal Justice in Transition' (2011) 31 *Legal Studies* 519.

differentiation, focusing exclusively on the law of *criminal* evidence (2), and an inversion of the standard jurisprudential hierarchy to downgrade evidentiary rules to the servants of principled discretion (3), are unmistakably proprietary Zuckermanism. Subsequent developments in English criminal procedure law reform and practice over the last three decades have followed the trajectory of Zuckerman's disciplinary blueprint with almost uncanny resemblance. Is there any scholar better qualified as modern Evidence law's Nostradamus? Regardless, Zuckerman's reputation and esteem in our field rest on nothing so precarious or transient as fairground futurology.

In his 'first career' work on the principles of criminal evidence, Zuckerman challenged us to rethink the disciplinary contours, normative foundations and jurisprudential methodologies of common law evidence. Against the prevailing common law orthodoxy of a Thayerite model of generic exclusionary rules, Zuckerman insisted that criminal evidence should be reconceptualised as the practical wisdom of principled discretion rooted in the normative values and objectives of penal justice. That general argument, to my mind, remains entirely persuasive, eclipsing any incidental objections that some of the finer details of its original exposition have, almost inevitably, better withstood the test of time than others. If criminal adjudication and evidentiary scholarship both face new environmental stresses and agitations and an uncertain future in the coming decades (as I have intimated), litigation and legal theory are alike better equipped to cope, adapt and survive as beneficiaries of Zuckerman's extraordinarily productive conceptual innovation.

6

Excluding Evidence as Protecting Constitutional or Human Rights?

BioNote: Andrew Ashworth is a criminal justice polymath who produced ground-breaking student texts on sentencing law and penal policy,[1] substantive criminal law,[2] criminal process,[3] and penal theory,[4] in addition to an extensive library of influential articles and books.[5] Ashworth was also active in penal administration and reform, serving on – and ultimately chairing – the Sentencing Advisory Panel, a precursor of the current Sentencing Council for England and Wales.[6] As Editor of the *Criminal Law Review* (1975–1999) and Series Editor of OUP's flagship *Monographs on Criminal Law and Justice*, he facilitated and nurtured the publications of countless other scholars and researchers (sometimes 'co-authoring' published articles that, to my eye, look like editorial salvage operations).

It was my great good fortune to be assigned Andrew Ashworth as my first-year Criminal Law tutor; indeed, my very first Oxford tutorial was in Andrew's Worcester College office. Neither my tutorial partner nor I had made it far enough through the reading list to know anything about strict liability offences, but Andrew graciously accepted our mumbling apologies with no hint of irritation. To say that Andrew carried his status as a Criminal Law titan lightly would be a glaring understatement. He seemed like a friendly uncle imparting gentle advice and encouragement. Andrew's stock as a tutor amongst Oxford undergraduates was barely less buoyant than his – then, still growing – international reputation as a scholar. I was informed by second years in my college that Ashworth's criminal law lectures were the only

[1] Andrew Ashworth, *Sentencing and Penal Policy* (Weidenfeld & Nicolson, 1983); which evolved into Andrew Ashworth, *Sentencing and Criminal Justice* (Weidenfeld & Nicolson, 1992). Now see Andrew Ashworth and Rory Kelly, *Sentencing and Criminal Justice*, 7th edn (Hart Publishing, 2021).

[2] Andrew Ashworth, *Principles of Criminal Law* (OUP, 1991); now Jeremy Horder, *Ashworth's Principles of Criminal Law*, 10th edn (OUP, 2022).

[3] Andrew Ashworth, *The Criminal Process: An Evaluative Study* (OUP, 1994); now Liz Campbell, Andrew Ashworth and Mike Redmayne, *The Criminal Process*, 5th edn (OUP, 2019).

[4] Andrew von Hirsch and Andrew Ashworth, *Principled Sentencing* (Northeastern UP, 1992); now Andrew Ashworth, Andreas von Hrisch and Julian Roberts (eds), *Principled Sentencing: Readings on Theory and Policy*, 3rd edn (Hart Publishing, 2009).

[5] Including Andrew Ashworth and Lucia Zedner, *Preventive Justice* (OUP, 2014); Andrew Ashworth, *Positive Obligations in Criminal Law* (Hart Publishing, 2015); Andrew von Hirsch and Andrew Ashworth, *Proportionate Sentencing: Exploring the Principles* (OUP, 2005); Andrew Ashworth, *Serious Crime, Human Rights and Criminal Procedure* (Sweet & Maxwell, 2002). Also see Lucia Zedner and Julian V Roberts (eds), *Principles and Values in Criminal Law and Criminal Justice: Essays in Honour of Andrew Ashworth* (OUP, 2012).

[6] sentencingcouncil.org.uk/ (accessed 17 December 2025).

first-year lectures worth attending: a critical judgement that was at least half-right on the positive side of its recommendation, if possibly harshly reductive in its rejection of the rest. These lectures were compulsory instruction and would later form the backbone of Andrew's text on substantive criminal law.

One consequence for Andrew of our meeting in that tutorial in 1987 is that he has spent the following thirty years writing academic references on my behalf for fellowships and research grants, a lifetime's unpaid labour all the more heroic for the fact of my dismal rate of success. I often joke that including me on a grant proposal is a surefire way to hex it. In reality, I am not sure that my failure rate – well over 90 per cent – is very much worse than par for the course. I am confident that my applications are strong, objectively speaking, not only on account of my academic record, but also because I frequently evaluate grant proposals, and sometimes chair awards committees, not only for all the major UK funders but also for governmental organisations and charities in continental Europe and the Asia Pacific region. In every instance, funding calls have attracted more deserving proposals than fixed budgets could accommodate. The pressure for legal scholars to obtain external grant-funding has greatly intensified over the last several decades (and is increasingly a precondition of academic promotions and career progression in higher education), yet awards ring-fenced for Law are few and far between. Legal scholars must take their chances in open competitions with social scientists and humanities scholars, effectively diluting static, or in real terms declining, research budgets and sometimes being required to compete on methodologically unfamiliar terrain or otherwise unequal terms. This funding landscape has potentially deleterious implications for legal scholarship, a topic taken up in earnest in this book's concluding chapter.

There is no direct way to repay our own teachers and academic mentors, or to recompense the charity of the anonymous army of journal editors and manuscript referees who labour in the background (often on their own time) to improve authors' published work, other than in kind: by actively participating in our collective scholarly enterprise and paying it forward to the next generation. True, a *festschrift* essay critically dissecting and debating one of the honorand's early articles might seem a dubious expression of gratitude for three decades of career mentorship and support. But that's how it goes in scholarship; and those in the know recognise genuine admiration when they see it.

I. Introduction: Rewind to 1977

In an article published in the *Criminal Law Review* in 1977, Andrew Ashworth advanced his 'protective principle' as a novel rationale for excluding improperly obtained evidence from criminal trials.[7] 'Excluding Evidence as Protecting Rights'

[7] A J Ashworth, 'Excluding Evidence as Protecting Rights' [1977] *Criminal Law Review* 723.

(EEPR) became an instant classic. Profusely cited ever since, 'the protective principle' soon passed into the terminological canon of criminal procedure scholarship. EEPR anticipates many of the hallmarks of Ashworth's voluminous and enormously influential contributions to the study of criminal law, criminal process, sentencing and punishment: in emphasising 'principle and policy';[8] in its appeal to underlying moral values like human dignity;[9] and through its integration of normative theoretical inquiries and detailed doctrinal analysis. Moreover, Ashworth has never wavered from EEPR's substantive thesis. The argument that rights violations should sometimes trigger evidentiary exclusion is reiterated in several subsequent essays.[10]

In the meantime, the law of criminal procedure in England and Wales has evolved almost beyond recognition from the pre-PACE 1984 patchwork of case law, Judges' Rules, and disparate statutory provisions confronting the legal analyst in the 1970s. After three decades of extensive statutory reform[11] culminating in the Criminal Procedure Rules[12] and the transformation of criminal evidence and procedure into 'a human rights subject',[13] the exclusion of improperly obtained evidence might today be rationalised in terms of protecting *human* or *constitutional* rights. Yet these reinvigorated protective principles themselves pose new questions of conceptual definition and normative analysis. What is a 'human right' in the context of criminal adjudication? How does one identify a 'constitutional right' in the absence of a comprehensive written Constitution? And why should these juridical classifications have any bearing on the admissibility of material evidence in criminal trials?

II. Ashworth's Original Argument for the Protective Principle

EEPR begins by observing that '[t]he justifications for excluding involuntary confessions and other improperly obtained evidence have been much debated'.[14]

[8] EEPR, 723.

[9] ibid 726.

[10] See, eg, Andrew Ashworth, 'The Exclusion of Evidence Obtained by Violating a Fundamental Right: Pragmatism Before Principle in the Strasbourg Jurisprudence' in Paul Roberts and Jill Hunter (eds), *Criminal Evidence and Human Rights* (Hart Publishing, 2012); Andrew Ashworth, 'Exploring the Integrity Principle in Evidence and Procedure' in Peter Mirfield and Roger Smith (eds), *Essays for Colin Tapper* (OUP, 2003).

[11] Notably including PACE 1984 and its expanding Codes of Practice; Prosecution of Offences Act 1985; Criminal Justice Act 1988; Criminal Justice and Public Order Act 1994; Criminal Procedure and Investigations Act 1996; Youth Justice and Criminal Evidence Act 1999; Regulation of Investigatory Powers Act 2000; Criminal Justice Act 2003; and Coroners and Justice Act 2009.

[12] First promulgated in 2005. Now see CrimPR 2025, www.gov.uk/guidance/rules-and-practice-directions-2020 (accessed 17 December 2025).

[13] See Ben Emmerson, Andrew Ashworth, and Alison Macdonald, *Human Rights and Criminal Justice*, 3rd edn (Sweet & Maxwell 2012); Andrew L-T Choo and Susan Nash, 'Evidence Law in England and Wales: The Impact of the Human Rights Act 1998' (2003) 7 *International Journal of Evidence & Proof* 31.

[14] EEPR, 723. The textbooks cite cases going back to the eighteenth century, eg, *R v Warwickshall* (1783) 1 Leach 263.

Much debated by scholars, perhaps, but not by English courts. Confessions regarded as 'involuntary' were inadmissible at common law, but voluntariness was largely a practical question of factual classification with minimal jurisprudential interest. As for non-confessional or 'real' (physical) evidence, English courts were strongly influenced by what Ashworth dubbed 'the reliability principle'. This was not so much a genuine 'principle' as a hard-headed pragmatic preference for receiving relevant information bearing on the issues in the trial, almost irrespective of its provenance.[15] '[T]he court is not concerned with how the evidence was obtained', stated Lord Goddard CJ matter-of-factly in a mid-twentieth-century Privy Council case.[16] According to Ashworth, 'Even in answer to the question "should evidence obtained by torture be admitted?", advocates of the reliability principle stand their ground.'[17] For reliabilists, impropriety in criminal investigations (no matter how serious) is one thing and the admissibility of reliable evidence at trial quite another.

Lined up against the reliability principle, explained Ashworth, is the 'disciplinary principle'. Disciplinarians believe that evidence should be excluded 'even when its reliability is in no doubt, since the court should use its position to discourage improper practices in the investigation of crime'.[18] EEPR's iteration of the disciplinary principle covered two related ideas, neither of which Ashworth himself endorsed. First, that evidentiary exclusion will deter illegality and other investigative impropriety in future proceedings. Second, that exclusion would 'punish an errant law enforcement officer'[19] in the instant case. The second rationale for the disciplinary principle is patently dubious. Police officers are 'punished' by excluding improperly obtained evidence only in a highly attenuated sense. Investigators can usually count on a guilty plea to conceal minor procedural irregularities from scrutiny in open court, whilst truly corrupt officers would presumably ensure that cases involving serious police wrongdoing would be prosecuted, if at all, only once their tracks were safely covered.

The deterrence theory of evidentiary exclusion is popular with some courts and commentators in the US but vociferously contested by others.[20] The debate rumbles on, inconclusively. English courts have never been much impressed with the disciplinary rationale; though the point might have seemed more arguable in 1977 than

[15] The principle standing behind this pragmatic preference is Bentham's injunction that if 'you exclude evidence, you exclude justice': *Rationale of Judicial Evidence* (1827), quoted by Terrence Anderson, David Schum and William Twining, *Analysis of Evidence*, 2nd edn (CUP, 2005), 1.

[16] *Kuruma v R* [1955] AC 197, 203, PC. Also see Crompton J's notorious remark a century earlier, in *R v Leatham* (1861) 8 Cox CC 498, 501, that '[i]t matters not how you get [relevant evidence]; if you steal it even, it would be admissible'.

[17] EEPR, 724.

[18] EEPR, 723.

[19] ibid fn 2.

[20] See, eg, Robert M Bloom and David H Fentin, '"A More Majestic Conception": The Importance of Judicial Integrity in Preserving the Exclusionary Rule' (2010) 13 *University of Pennsylvania Journal of Constitutional Law* 47; Donald Dripps, 'The Case for the Contingent Exclusionary Rule' (2001) 38 *American Criminal Law Review* 1.

hindsight would suggest.[21] Judge Buzzard's first instance ruling in the well-known case of *Sang* encapsulated contemporary orthodoxy: '[T]he object of the rules of evidence and the rules regulating the exercise of discretion is to achieve justice in the instant case, not, for example, to discipline the police or anyone else'.[22] The Court of Appeal has reiterated many times since that 'it is not in general the function of criminal courts to discipline the police'[23] (though the Court's motivation in ruling evidence inadmissible occasionally appears tinged by disciplinary sentiments).[24]

Breaking the deadlock between reliabilists and disciplinarians, EEPR argued that 'a third, "protective" principle provides both a stronger justification for the exclusion of improperly obtained evidence and a plausible explanation of some relevant judicial decisions'.[25] Later in the article Ashworth endorsed the following 'qualified protective principle':

> [E]vidence obtained by means of a departure from a declared standard or procedure should be liable to exclusion, unless the court is satisfied that the accused in fact suffered no disadvantage as a result of the breach.[26]

The protective principle was not to be equated with 'the view that *all* improperly obtained evidence should be peremptorily excluded'.[27] Mindful that 'the prima facie justification for exclusion … may occasionally be outweighed by other considerations',[28] Ashworth envisaged his protective principle being applied through judicial discretion. Crucially, however, discretionary exclusion must be structured by a framework of principle, lest 'the unique facts of the case' should become an all-purpose alibi for excessive judicial passivity or lazy reasoning. '[T]he dangers of a wide and unstructured discretion to exclude evidence on grounds of unfairness', Ashworth warned, 'are manifest in the haphazard approach of English courts to improperly obtained evidence'.[29]

The normative rationale for the protective principle was elucidated in the following key passage:

> If a legal system declares certain standards for the conduct of criminal investigation … then it can be argued that citizens have corresponding rights to be accorded certain facilities and not to be treated in certain ways. If the legal system is to

[21] There is one reported case in which the Court of Appeal mused that 'there may be cases where the exclusion of evidence for disciplinary purposes may be justified': *R v Trump* (1980) 70 Cr App R 300, 304. Eveleigh LJ self-cited this passage in *R v Birtwhistle* [1980] RTR 342, 348, CA, but no other English court to my knowledge has ever endorsed the disciplinary principle before or since.

[22] *R v Sang and Mangan* (1979) 68 Cr App R 240, 244, CCC.

[23] *R v Grant* [2006] QB 60, [2005] EWCA Crim 1089, [55]. Also see, eg, *R v Bailey and Smith* [1993] 97 Cr App R 365, 370, CA; *R v F*, CA Trans no 199906023/W4, 2000 WL 1720357, [48]; *R v Oliphant* [1992] Crim LR 40, CA; *Fox* v *Chief Constable of Gwent* [1986] 1 AC 281, 292, HL (Lord Fraser).

[24] *Cf R* v *Mason* [1988] 1 WLR 139, 144, CA.

[25] EEPR, 723.

[26] ibid 729.

[27] ibid 725 (original emphasis).

[28] ibid 725–2.6.

[29] ibid 734.

> respect those rights, then it is arguable that a suspect whose rights have been infringed should not thereby be placed at any disadvantage … [i.e.] evidence obtained by the investigators as a result of the infringement should not be used against the suspect. And the appropriate way of ensuring that the suspect does not suffer this disadvantage is for the court of trial to have the power to exclude evidence obtained by improper methods.[30]

Ultimately, for Ashworth, the question was one of recognising and protecting suspects' rights without hypocrisy:

> [T]he primary question remains whether we are willing to recognise rights in suspects and to protect them; recognition without any protection would be a pretence.[31]

Modern legal discourse is saturated with rights-talk, and criminal procedure is exemplary in this regard, not least because 'the right to a fair trial' has been in the vanguard of the broader human rights revolution in contemporary jurisprudence.[32] It is easy to forget just how recent these profound tectonic shifts in the legal landscape really are. With his visionary argument for 'protecting rights', Ashworth was taking rights seriously[33] before most British judges and lawyers had read their Dworkin.[34] To assess whether the protective principle is more than just a catchy – and highly successful – slogan, we need to consider what role, exactly, rights do or should play in arguments about the exclusion of improperly obtained evidence in English criminal trials.

III. Elucidating (and Complicating) the Protective Principle

The deceptive simplicity of the 'protective principle' is belied by the variety of ways in which the principle can be cashed out in theory and practice. Here is the simplest iteration:

> PP#1: it is a reason for excluding evidence in criminal trials that the evidence was obtained in violation of the accused's legal rights.

The 'is a reason' formulation preserves the possibility of weighty countervailing reasons which, on balance, demand admissibility in the instant case. This tracks Ashworth's concession that 'the protective principle may occasionally be

[30] ibid 725.
[31] ibid 735.
[32] David Harris, Michael O'Boyle, Ed Bates and Carla M Buckley, *Harris, O'Boyle and Warbrick: Law of the European Convention on Human Rights*, 5th edn (OUP, 2023) ch 9; Stefan Trechsel with Sarah J Summers, *Human Rights in Criminal Proceedings* (OUP, 2005).
[33] Literally: *cf* EEPR, 731, fn 42.
[34] Ronald Dworkin, *Taking Rights Seriously*, revsd edn (Duckworth, 1978).

outweighed by other considerations'.[35] Being tied to legal rights, PP#1 excludes (arguable) moral rights which have not been recognised and enshrined in positive law. This is faithful to Ashworth's stated conditional premiss for the protective principle: '*If* a legal system declares certain standards for the conduct of criminal investigation …'[36]

The following trio specifies textually defensible alternative interpretations of EEPR's protective principle:

> PP#2: it is a reason for excluding evidence in criminal trials that the evidence was obtained in violation of one of the accused's substantive legal rights.
>
> PP#3: it is a reason for excluding evidence in criminal trials that the evidence was obtained in violation of one of the accused's criminal process rights.
>
> PP#4: it is a reason for excluding evidence in criminal trials that the evidence was obtained in such a way that the accused has a right that it be excluded, and *that* right would be violated if the evidence were admitted.

An example falling under PP#2 would be evidence procured through violations of the accused's rights to bodily integrity, property, or privacy which exist independently of any criminal investigation or prosecution. These are rights which criminal investigators must work around if they are to conduct lawful investigations. An example falling within the scope of PP#3 would be evidence obtained in violation of criminal process guarantees such as the rights not to be held incommunicado,[37] to receive custodial legal advice,[38] to know the substance of the charge,[39] to be shielded from forced self-incrimination,[40] and to question or 'confront' incriminating evidence and witnesses adduced by the prosecution.[41] These rights would not exist independently of their distinctive institutional context. They are constitutive features of a system of criminal trial and punishment which makes certain claims to legitimacy.

Ashworth's own discussion of the protective principle is largely confined to the types of rights violations encompassed by PP#3, deriving from 'certain standards for the conduct of criminal investigations – whether they are enshrined in a constitution, detailed in a comprehensive code or scattered in various statutes and judicial precedents'.[42] However, it is evident that the protective principle was also intended to cover evidence falling within the jurisdiction of PP#2.

[35] EEPR, 726.

[36] ibid 725 (emphasis supplied). The legal positivist assumptions of the argument are underlined a few pages later, where Ashworth observes: 'What is essential … is that if … a right is not protected it should not be proclaimed, and if it is proclaimed it ought to be protected': ibid 728.

[37] PACE 1984, s 56.

[38] PACE 1984, s 58; ECHR Art 6(3)(c); *Salduz v Turkey* (2009) 49 EHRR 19.

[39] PACE Code of Practice C, para 16.3; ECHR Art 6(3)(a).

[40] *R v S(F)* [2009] 1 WLR 1489, [2008] EWCA Crim 2177; *Saunders v UK* (1996) 23 EHRR 313.

[41] *R v Davis* [2008] 1 AC 1128, [2008] UKHL 36; *R v Horncastle* [2010] 2 AC 373, [2009] UKSC 14; ECHR Art 6(3)(d); *Al-Khawaja and Tahery v UK* (2009) 49 EHRR 1.

[42] EEPR, 725.

Even without retrospective reliance on Ashworth's later writings, this inference is confirmed by brief references to torture[43] and arrest powers[44] in EEPR itself. Torture is criminalised in the first instance through the general criminal law of offences against the person,[45] quite apart from whether it is also proscribed by more context-specific constraints on criminal investigations. Arrest powers are obviously part of the law of policing, and their exercise *may* – though in fact it usually does not – lead to criminal charges, prosecution and trial. However, the law of arrest is not aptly conceptualised as an aspect of the criminal process rights envisaged by PP#3. Arrest powers, properly conceived, constitute an important exception to the right to liberty,[46] which is a general (non-criminal process) right within the bailiwick of PP#2.

PP#4 presents greater analytical difficulties, starting with its apparent circularity: the evidence is to be excluded *because* the accused has a right that it be excluded. However, PP#4 is not tautologous. On any conception of a right which allows for the possibility of conflicting rights (as all the best conceptions do),[47] the accused might have a right to exclusion which is overridden or – in Dworkinian idiom – out-trumped[48] by a competing right, perhaps the right of a deceased murder victim to have their dying accusation read out in court[49] or the right of an abused child to have the state make serious efforts to bring their abuser to justice.[50] So long as the accused's right to evidentiary exclusion is merely defeasible in particular circumstances and not routinely trumped or traduced, there is no deep conceptual paradox or normative mystery in recognising such a right.

Another distinctive feature of PP#4 is that a rights violation is not required to trigger it. The evidence must have been obtained '*in such a way* that the accused has a right that it be excluded', but the improper methods in question may or may not have included the infringement of one of the accused's rights. PP#4 stretches Ashworth's original conception of 'corresponding rights' so that the relevant 'standard for the conduct of criminal investigation' just *is* the right to have evidence excluded in certain designated circumstances. I will later explain why this feature of PP#4 is a conceptual and normative strength, richly justifying an element of purposive textual construal.

[43] 'Even in answer to the question "should evidence obtained by torture be admitted?", advocates of the reliability principle stand their ground': ibid 724.

[44] Characterising *Scott v Baker* [1969] 1 QB 659, DC, as an excessively 'rigid application of the protective principle' which 'only tends to bring the law into disrepute': EEPR, 728.

[45] Offences Against the Person Act 1861, ss 18, 20 and 47; Criminal Justice Act 1988, s 134.

[46] Thus, within the framework of the European Convention on Human Rights, arrest powers are subject to Art 5's right to liberty, not to the right to a fair trial under Art 6.

[47] See, eg, Jeremy Waldron, *Liberal Rights* (CUP, 1993) chs 3 & 9.

[48] Ronald Dworkin, 'Rights As Trumps' in Jeremy Waldron (ed), *Theories of Rights* (OUP, 1984).

[49] *R v Al-Khawaja* [2005] EWCA Crim 2697; *Nembhard v R* (1982) 74 Cr App R 144, PC.

[50] *Judge v United Kingdom* (2011) 52 EHRR SE17; Jonathan Doak, *Victims' Rights, Human Rights and Criminal Justice* (Hart Publishing, 2008) ch 2; Alastair Mowbray, *The Development of Positive Obligations under the European Convention on Human Rights by the European Court of Human Rights* (Hart Publishing, 2004) 127–30.

The next step for conceptual elucidation is to perm our first four interpretations to produce new, composite iterations of the protective principle. Combining PP#1 and PP#4 produces:

> PP#5: it is a reason for excluding evidence in criminal trials that (i) the evidence was obtained in violation of the accused's legal rights, such that (ii) the accused has a right that it be excluded, and *that* right would also be violated if the evidence were admitted.

PP#5 states a more stringent protective principle with a presumptively narrower field of application. There are now *two* necessary and sufficient preconditions for establishing a reason to exclude evidence. Not only must the accused's rights have been violated, as envisaged by PP#1, but in addition that rights violation should be regarded as triggering a right to exclusion in accordance with PP#4. We could relax the causal relationship between the two triggering factors slightly, to produce:

> PP#6: it is a reason for excluding evidence in criminal trials that (i) the evidence was obtained in violation of the accused's legal rights, such that – taking that rights violation in combination with other relevant circumstances – (ii) the accused has a right that it be excluded, and *that* right would also be violated if the evidence were admitted.

On the face of it, interposing a further condition between the initial rights violation and the right to exclusion might be thought to reduce the stringency of PP#6 relative to PP#5. For example, if bad faith on the part of police investigators is regarded as a salient consideration,[51] a rights violation which (let us assume) would not be sufficient in gravity to satisfy the second limb of PP#5 might nonetheless trigger PP#6 if the right were violated deliberately in bad faith. In other words, bad faith would be a 'relevant circumstance' which, in combination with the initial rights violation, satisfied PP#6. Alternatively, 'other relevant circumstances' could conceivably make PP#6 *more* stringent than PP#5. For example, a breach of a suspect's right, say, to prompt custodial legal advice might be thought sufficient to satisfy PP#5, but might *also* require a showing of bad faith to satisfy PP#6.[52] In that event, police misconduct establishing a reason for excluding evidence under PP#5 would not provide a reason for exclusion under PP#6. In short, the relative stringency of PP#5 and PP#6 pivots on the detailed specification of 'in combination with other relevant circumstances'.

We can be more precise about the meaning of 'the accused's legal rights' in composite, dual-criterion interpretations of the protective principle, just as we were before when considering single-criterion interpretations. Combining PP#4 with PP#2 and PP#3 generates, respectively:

> PP#7: it is a reason for excluding evidence in criminal trials that (i) the evidence was obtained in violation of one of the accused's substantive legal rights, such that (ii) the

[51] Having noted the obvious salience of police bad faith for the disciplinary principle, Ashworth asserts: '[b]ut on a protective principle this factor is irrelevant': EEPR, 731. PP#6 demonstrates why Ashworth's argument does not substantiate his assertion.

[52] *Cf R v Alladice* (1988) 87 Cr App R 380, 386, CA; *R v Fulling* [1987] QB 426, 432, CA.

> accused has a right that it be excluded, and *that* right would also be violated if the evidence were admitted.
>
> PP#8: it is a reason for excluding evidence in criminal trials that (i) the evidence was obtained in violation of one of the accused's criminal process rights, such that (ii) the accused has a right that it be excluded, and *that* right would also be violated if the evidence were admitted.

Alternatively, PP#2 and PP#3 could in turn combine with PP#6 to produce:

> PP#9: it is a reason for excluding evidence in criminal trials that (i) the evidence was obtained in violation of one of the accused's substantive legal rights, such that – taking that rights violation in combination with other relevant circumstances – (ii) the accused has a right that it be excluded, and *that* right would also be violated if the evidence were admitted.
>
> PP#10: it is a reason for excluding evidence in criminal trials that (i) the evidence was obtained in violation of one of the accused's criminal process rights, such that – taking that rights violation in combination with other relevant circumstances – (ii) the accused has a right that it be excluded, and *that* right would also be violated if the evidence were admitted.

In view of the intended scope of Ashworth's original protective principle, PP#5 and PP#6 are probably more interesting and potentially useful interpretations than any of the more particularised variations, PP#7–PP#10. But all of them are certainly logically possible elucidations of the core principle, with divergent implications for the scope of evidentiary exclusion.

Our inventory of alternative specifications has run into double figures without yet broaching a vital further question. This concerns the *moral ground* or justificatory rationale of a relevant right, as opposed to its scope, content, strength or doctrinal legal basis. EEPR advanced several, not entirely consistent, claims bearing on this question. This is Ashworth's most explicit statement of the moral ground of the rights generated by the protective principle:

> A legal system must reach a decision on an acceptable demarcation between permissible and impermissible methods [in the enforcement of criminal law] …. [O]nce agreement has been reached the rights which flow from it should be respected and protected. An essential part of taking such an agreement seriously is *to protect suspects and accused persons from any disadvantage which results from an infringement of the rights declared or implied*. The relevance of this theory to the law of evidence is that where a legal system lays down certain standards or procedures for criminal investigation, *it is both appropriate and desirable to protect defendants from any disadvantage resulting from the breach of a declared standard or procedure* by excluding evidence obtained as a result of that breach.[53]

Concern with forensic disadvantage suggests an instrumental or consequentialist[54] justification of evidentiary exclusion: unless the evidential fruits of a rights

[53] EEPR, 733 (emphasis supplied).

[54] Though Ashworth is plainly not a consequentialist through-and-through: *cf* Andrew Ashworth, 'Crime, Community and Creeping Consequentialism' [1996] *Criminal Law Review* 220; Andrew Ashworth and Mike Redmayne, *The Criminal Process*, 4th edn (OUP, 2010) 45–7.

violation are excluded from the trial, the accused will have suffered unfair disadvantage from the violation of his rights; and this is what the protective principle prohibits (albeit defeasibly). Finessing PP#1 with this justificatory rationale leads to:

> PP#11: it is a reason for excluding evidence in criminal trials that (i) the evidence was obtained in violation of the accused's legal rights, *and* (ii) exclusion is necessary to prevent the accused from suffering consequential forensic disadvantage.

It would be possible to tack the 'forensic disadvantage' rationale onto each of the variations PP#2–PP#10, which would give us PP#12–PP#20. We can skip their exhaustive elaboration on grounds of economy and tedium.

Ashworth comes closest to propounding a consequentialist conception of the forensic disadvantage rationale in his discussion of the admissibility of confessions at common law.[55] '[B]y concentrating on the *effect on the accused* of the words or conduct of his questioner', Ashworth suggests, 'the courts are in fact recognising the rights of suspects not to be subjected to certain forms of inducement and oppression, and protecting suspects from the disadvantage which might result if evidence obtained through a violation of those rights were admitted at his trial'.[56] The 'effect on the accused' might connote the *actual* effect (if any) on *this* accused in the instant case; or the anticipated effects on the majority of similarly-situated defendants in the general run of cases. Applying our now familiar method, this conceptual refinement would contribute PP#21–PP#30 and PP#31–PP#40, respectively, to our burgeoning roster of protective principles.

Significantly, only the first set of these latest interpretations is susceptible to case-specific 'harmless error' analysis. Under PP#21–PP#30, if violation of the accused's rights had no material bearing on the conduct or outcome of the proceedings – say, because the accused is a hardened professional criminal who (supposedly) does not need custodial legal advice[57] – evidentiary exclusion will not be triggered by any interpretation of the protective principle rooted in forensic disadvantage. In relation to a search warrant specifying the wrong address, for example, Ashworth explains that 'advocates of the disciplinary principle would look to the source of error, whereas the protective principle might ask whether in fact the accused was misled by the error'.[58] The implication seems to be that the protective principle might not authorise evidentiary exclusion in the absence of tangible forensic disadvantage, either because a relevant right has not been infringed; or because the kind of rights violation involved does not rise to the level of grounding a (defeasible) right of exclusion; or possibly both (these being the dual criteria specified by PP#11 and its more particularised derivatives).

When discussing other examples, however, EEPR intimates a different tack, more in keeping with the second group of forensic disadvantage rationales,

[55] *DPP v Ping Lin* [1976] AC 574, 606, HL.
[56] EEPR, 727 (original emphasis).
[57] *R v Alladice* (1988) 87 Cr App R 380, CA.
[58] EEPR, 731.

PP#31–PP#40. In the following passage, Ashworth explains how the protective principle would differ from the reliability principle in responding to the argument that investigative impropriety was too trivial to warrant inadmissibility:

> The triviality or seriousness of the breach is measured according to its consequences for the accused, and the reason behind the particular procedure must be examined. If the procedure was intended not to safeguard individual liberty but rather to ensure the accuracy of the evidence collected, the protective principle does not require the exclusion of evidence obtained in contravention of the procedure: its admissibility should depend purely on its reliability. If on the other hand it appears that the procedure was intended as a safeguard for liberty, the court must go on to consider whether the breach actually had the effect of prejudicing that liberty. If it did, the evidence ought to be excluded.[59]

Where the admissibility of evidence would not, in practice, fall to be determined unless the accused necessarily *had been* disadvantaged by violation of his rights (eg, a speculative DNA match where the accused's profile was retained illegally),[60] this position would equate to a (defeasible) justification for automatic evidentiary exclusion. As Ashworth adds in a footnote, '[i]f rights are to be taken seriously then any infringement which actually disadvantages the accused would justify the exclusion of evidence gained thereby'.[61] To similar effect but more systematically, PP#31–PP#40 rationalise presumptive exclusion on the basis of generalised predictions of forensic disadvantage in particular scenarios, eg, where interrogators employed tactics known to produce false confessions (irrespective of the truth of the accused's admissions in the instant case).

Yet there is something vitally important missing from the argument here. In the absence of further normative grounding, Ashworth's contention *is* tautologous. Why should evidence be excluded under the protective principle? Because it was obtained by violating the accused's rights. But why should rights violations trigger an exclusionary remedy, rather than providing the accused with direct redress through tort liability, human rights legislation or criminal prosecutions, or by subjecting individual miscreants to disciplinary sanctions? We have ended up restating the very conundrum which every attempted rationalisation of the exclusion of improperly obtained evidence, before and after EEPR, has sought to resolve. In order to break out of this vicious circularity, we need to extend and deepen our inquiry into the nature of rights.

IV. What's in a Right?

Ashworth's hypothetical introduces a new variable into the discussion – procedures, presumably including procedural rights, 'intended as a safeguard for liberty'.

[59] ibid 731 (footnotes omitted).
[60] *Attorney General's Reference (No 3 of 1999)* [2001] 2 AC 91, HL.
[61] EEPR, 731, fn 42.

It is unclear how liberty-safeguarding procedural rights are supposed to relate to the protective principle's threshold criterion of forensic disadvantage. Breach of a right designed 'to ensure the accuracy of the evidence', which Ashworth excludes from his principle's protective mantle, could certainly leave the accused at a serious forensic disadvantage, as where the accused's conviction rests on untested hearsay or irrelevant bad character which the Court of Appeal rules improperly admitted at trial but without, on balance, affecting the 'safety' of the accused's conviction.[62] Reliability-based exclusionary doctrines easily lend themselves to harmless error analysis, where the court reasons that, after all, the accused was found guilty on ample evidence and has not suffered any material disadvantage from 'technical' violations of his procedural rights. Indeed, this is exactly the sort of suspiciously convenient rationalisation that Ashworth's protective principle was supposed to pre-empt:

> If standards for the conduct of criminal investigation are to be taken seriously, then the reliability principle cannot be an adequate criterion for the admissibility of improperly obtained evidence. It fails to provide any protection for the accused against the disadvantageous consequences of a breach, and therefore subverts the values which the standards and procedures for investigation promote.[63]

Now, 'standards and procedures for investigation' can be regarded as 'promoting' many and diverse values. If we stick with Ashworth's own example of procedures 'intended to safeguard individual liberty', this might suggest:

> PP#41: it is a reason for excluding evidence in criminal trials that (i) the evidence was obtained in violation of one of the accused's legal rights; (ii) the right in question was designed to safeguard individual liberty; *and* (iii) exclusion is necessary to ensure that the accused does not suffer any forensic disadvantage from the violation of his rights.

PP#41 reconciles two prominent strands of Ashworth's argument, accommodating both the moral ground of the right (here, liberty) and forensic disadvantage as (part of) the rationale for evidentiary exclusion. Since the liberty ground – part (ii) of PP#41 – could be incorporated as a further condition into any of the interpretations of the protective principle previously canvassed, this generates another raft of possible interpretations, PP#41–PP#80. However, it is evident that EEPR invoked liberty-protecting 'standards and procedures' only by way of illustration and not to define the scope of the protective principle. We can easily think of other important values that procedures and standards in criminal investigations might serve. Non-discrimination on objectionable grounds of nationality, race, gender, sexual orientation, disability, etc, is one obvious candidate, which – on the now well-established formula – could give us PP#81–PP#120. Standards in criminal investigations also protect bodily integrity and physical

[62] See, eg, *R v Adams (Ishmael)* [2008] 1 Cr App R 35, [2007] EWCA Crim 3025; *R v Edwards and Rowlands* [2006] 2 Cr App R 4, [2005] EWCA Crim 3244.

[63] EEPR, 729.

security, suggesting PP#121–PP#160. Ensuring humane treatment is another major institutional concern, producing PP#161–PP#200, and we certainly must not overlook the special criminal procedure right identified by Dworkin and others[64] not to be exposed to an unreasonable risk of wrongful conviction: PP#201–PP#240. And so on.

The abiding lesson is that one must pay careful attention to the moral grounding of any salient right. This is usually a significant factor in deciding whether evidentiary exclusion might be an appropriate (defeasible) remedy for rights violations, as PP#41–PP#240 bring to the fore. Moral and legal rights vary enormously in their importance, depending on the nature of the interests they protect and serve – the ground of the right. Likewise, the strength of the (defeasible) argument for evidentiary exclusion will usually reflect the nature and importance of any right that was breached in order to obtain the evidence. The case for evidentiary exclusion, in other words, is sensitive to the moral ground of the violated right and the importance of the interest(s) that right protects. This supports the assumption, more or less consistently adopted by English courts, that the very fact that a right (any old right) has been violated in the process of obtaining evidence does not, in and of itself, provide a reason for excluding the evidence.[65] Of course, this leaves open the possibility that breaches of *specific* rights might warrant – or even mandate – exclusion, depending inter alia on the nature and importance of the moral grounding of the right and the interest(s) it serves.

Refocusing the inquiry on the moral grounds of rights rather than their scope, structure or formal pedigree can be pressed still further to produce a second preliminary conclusion, in which rights drop out of the analysis altogether. There may, in short, be important values in criminal investigations that do not ground any rights, or at any rate no rights of the accused. So if evidentiary exclusion supposedly operates as a procedural mechanism for vindicating 'standards for the conduct of criminal investigation', it presumably should not rest content with 'protecting rights', as EEPR's title and analysis strongly implied.

Consider the House of Lords' ruling in *A v Home Secretary*[66] that evidence probably procured by torture of a third-party non-British national overseas by foreign security agents is never admissible in English courts. The accused in criminal proceedings does not have a right that a third-party non-British national should not be tortured overseas by foreign security agents (although, of course, the torture victim himself has a moral right and a legal right under international law not to be tortured).[67] The House of Lords stated unequivocally that, '[t]orture is

[64] Ronald Dworkin, 'Principle, Policy, Procedure' in C F H Tapper (ed), *Crime, Proof and Punishment* (Butterworths, 1981); Paul Roberts, *Roberts and Zuckerman's Criminal Evidence*, 3rd edn (OUP, 2022) § 6.3.

[65] Perhaps courts always have a rule-of-law reason to vindicate legal rights. Even so, this will not necessarily establish – even a defeasible – reason for excluding probative evidence in criminal trials. For example, rights violations may be clearly justifiable (permitted) or excused in particular circumstances.

[66] *A v Secretary of State for the Home Department (No 2)* [2006] 2 AC 221, [2005] UKHL 71.

[67] Antonio Cassese, *International Criminal Law*, 2nd edn (OUP, 2008) ch 7.

not acceptable. This is a bedrock moral principle in this country'.[68] The inherently abominable nature of torture makes its informational fruits inadmissible, irrespective of whether the accused's – or anybody else's – rights under English law have been violated. Whilst torture is an extreme example, the same principle supports a multitude of more prosaic instantiations. Thus, breaches of the PACE Codes of Practice may be sufficiently 'significant and substantial'[69] to warrant exclusion of improperly obtained evidence even if the provisions in question do not confer legal rights on the accused.[70]

We can now see why the absence of any reference to rights violations in PP#4 should be regarded as a conceptual and normative strength rather than a weakness. Legal and ethical standards in criminal investigations, in all their normative complexity, cannot be comprehensively vindicated by an exclusionary rule delimited by substantive legal rights, still less by an evidentiary remedy restricted to violations of the rights of the accused (*cf* PP#2 and PP#3).

V. Constitutional Rights

With relentless tenacity but relatively little imagination, the previous two sections managed to accumulate some 240 different interpretations of Ashworth's protective principle. It would be a simple matter to generate many more conceptual possibilities, by identifying other relevant values and grounds of rights, adding in further circumstantial factors, and recombining all these elements in a spiralling inventory of novel permutations. My intention was to demonstrate the range and variety of considerations bearing on the question of whether rights violations should sometimes (always/often/occasionally/never) precipitate evidentiary exclusion. If, as most commentators insist,[71] judicial rulings on the admissibility of improperly obtained evidence are frequently inadequately reasoned, part of the explanation might be found in the geometric complexity and finely nuanced moral discriminations characterising contextual exercises of judicial discretion. The inherent practical difficulty of the judicial task is compounded by the (largely unexplored) conceptual fecundity of general rationales for evidentiary exclusion, which – as we have seen – can be magnificently protean and malleable.

A promising strategy for alleviating the burdens of judicial decision-making in this context would be to designate a special class of rights which, in view of their moral ground or for some other important reason, should occupy an elevated role

[68] [2006] 2 AC 221, [64] (Lord Nicholls).

[69] *R v Keenan* [1990] 2 QB 54, 69–70, CA.

[70] *Cf* PACE 1984, s 67(10): 'A failure on the part … of a police officer to comply with any provision of such a code … shall not of itself render him liable to any criminal or civil proceedings'.

[71] See, eg, David Ormerod and Di Birch, 'The Evolution of the Discretionary Exclusion of Evidence' [2004] *Criminal Law Review* 767; Andrew L-T Choo and Susan Nash, 'What's the Matter with Section 78?' [1999] *Criminal Law Review* 929.

in the analysis. Specifically, for our purposes, one might designate a sub-class of rights which always have material implications for the admissibility of evidence obtained through their violation. Though still deliberately vague at the point of application, at least one could now confidently say that violation of *these* particular designated rights, if not others, presumptively provides a reason for triggering evidentiary exclusion in appropriate cases. One way of demarcating this special sub-class of rights, employing terminology which clearly announces their elevated normative status, is to categorise them as 'constitutional' rights.

In a legal system with a comprehensive written Constitution, 'constitutional rights' are those rights which are declared in the text of the Constitution or elaborated or implied into it through judicial interpretation. Inferring or improvising constitutional rights from a common law Constitution is a far more difficult and precarious business.[72] Nonetheless, significant developments in English criminal procedure law during the last 40 years bear out Ashworth's insistence that the common law contains important procedural standards whose vindication should not be left at the mercy of the reliability principle.[73] Reference has already been made to the judgment of the House of Lords in *A v Home Secretary (No 2)*, categorically rejecting evidence probably obtained through torture of a third-party witness overseas.[74] Notably, Lord Bingham announced that, '[i]t trivialises the issue before the House to treat it as an argument about the law of evidence. The issue is one of constitutional principle'.[75] Nor was this the first English sighting of self-consciously constitutionalised procedural standards. As long ago as 1979, the House of Lords declared compulsory process, secured through the compellability of witness testimony, a constitutional principle.[76] Subsequently, the absolute nature of legal professional privilege[77] was explicitly singled out for its constitutional pedigree.

It is plausible to suppose that breaches of exceptionally weighty procedural norms might give rise to a defeasible right to evidentiary exclusion, in accordance with:

> PP#241: it is a reason for excluding evidence in criminal trials that the evidence was obtained in violation of a constitutional right.

The constitutional right in question could be the accused's right, as it is in relation to compulsory process. But it need not be. In *Derby Magistrates ex p B*,[78] the constitutional right of legal professional privilege was invoked to prevent *the accused* from

[72] *Cf* T R S Allan, *Constitutional Justice: A Liberal Theory of the Rule of Law* (OUP, 2001).

[73] '[T]he absence of such declarations from English law no more means that there are no standards of conduct than does the absence of a written constitution or bill of rights mean that Englishmen have no rights or civil liberties': EEPR, 726.

[74] *A v Secretary of State for the Home Department (No 2)* [2006] 2 AC 221.

[75] ibid [51].

[76] *Hoskyn v MPC* [1979] AC 474, 484, HL (Lord Wilberforce).

[77] *R v Derby Magistrates' Court ex p. B* [1996] 1 AC 487, HL.

[78] ibid.

obtaining information that he claimed would help prove his innocence. And in *A v Home Secretary (No 2)*, third-party foreign torture evidence was to be excluded not in virtue of any right of the torture victim himself, but in order to uphold the moral integrity of English law. This example suggests an interesting variation on PP#4:

> PP#242: it is a reason for excluding evidence in criminal trials that the evidence was obtained in such a way that the accused has a *constitutional right* that it be excluded, and *that* right would be violated if the evidence were admitted.

This interpretation of the protective principle exploits an important, but little noticed, feature of rights.[79] Whilst the ground of a right is typically some feature of the right holder's interest sufficient to warrant rights-based protection, the ground of a right may be some other individual's interest (as where parents are afforded rights designed to protect their children's interests) or a collective interest in which the accused herself may or may not have a stake. In *A v Home Secretary (No 2)*, the weighty interest worthy of constitutional protection was safeguarding the moral integrity of British legal proceedings from being corrupted by association with torture,[80] a collective interest in which the applicants shared just in so far as the quality of British justice formed part of their (moral) interests – which, given that the applicants in question were not British nationals, may have been a highly attenuated or possibly non-existent interest.[81] The important idea that the accused might be afforded procedural rights to safeguard interests that are not merely, or at all, personal to him is reflected in the concept of 'private attorneys-general'[82] which has surfaced in US debates surrounding the Fourth Amendment exclusionary rule.

Some version of PP#242 might well be a viable basis for excluding improperly obtained evidence in criminal trials in England and Wales.[83] Indeed, a nascent PP#242 may already be implicit in the precedents just mentioned. Its applications and further development would need to be evaluated contextually, taking account

[79] But see Joseph Raz, *Ethics in the Public Domain* (OUP, 1994) ch 2.

[80] 'The use of torture is dishonourable. It corrupts and degrades the state which uses it and the legal system which accepts it': *A v Secretary of State for the Home Department (No 2)* [2006] 2 AC 221, [82] (Lord Hoffmann).

[81] The applicants clearly had an instrumental interest in having the evidence excluded if it – rightly or wrongly – was going to incriminate them, but *this*, narrowly instrumental interest is not the (moral) ground of the constitutional right to exclusion recognised by English law. Do foreign nationals have *any* interest in the moral integrity of foreign (English) law? If justice is a truly global concern, then we *all* have an interest, no matter how attenuated, in the quality of justice dispensed by *any* legal system anywhere in the world. But that is plainly a controversial, and some will think highly tendentious, proposition that I cannot explore further here.

[82] Daniel J Meltzer, 'Deterring Constitutional Violations by Law Enforcement Officials: Plaintiffs and Defendants as Private Attorneys General' (1988) 88 *Columbia Law Review* 247.

[83] There are international and comparative exemplars, eg, *People (AG) v O'Brien* [1965] IR 142; Statute of the International Criminal Court, Art 69(7); Dimitrios Giannoulopoulos, 'The Exclusion of Improperly Obtained Evidence in Greece: Putting Constitutional Rights First' (2007) 11 *International Journal of Evidence & Proof* 181.

of the generic features and limitations of rights analysis identified in the previous two sections and – especially if the technique is much further expanded – of more general challenges to the legitimacy of common law constitutionalism.[84]

VI. Human Rights

EEPR makes fleeting reference to the possibility of 'a constitutional Bill of Rights in England',[85] but never mentions 'human rights' as such. Few, if any, common lawyers at that time could have envisaged the extent of human rights law's subsequent influence on criminal proceedings in England and Wales. The advent of the Human Rights Act 1998 launched a whole new raft of interpretations of the protective principle, starting with the following elementary variant:

> PP#243: it is a reason for excluding evidence in criminal trials that the evidence was obtained in violation of a human right.

PP#243 has one tangible advantage over the constitutional rights-based interpretations of the protective principle canvassed in the previous section. International human rights has undergone a prolonged period of institutionalisation and progressive refinement, in particular through the text of the European Convention on Human Rights (translated into English law by Schedule 1 to the HRA) and the interpretational jurisprudence of the European Court of Human Rights,[86] to which English courts must have regard pursuant to section 2 of the HRA. Compared with trying to divine from first principles which common law standards, if any, have attained the Olympian heights of constitutional imperative, it is far easier in practice to identify the existence and scope of a 'human right' whose breach might potentially trigger the exclusionary remedy contemplated by PP#243 and its (multifarious) derivatives.

However, the apparent institutional advantage of 'human rights' over 'constitutional rights' is short-lived, for at least two significant reasons. First, the substantive rights specified by the ECHR are not necessarily all of equal importance, and more particularly in the present context, their relation to the exclusionary remedy is far from uniform or self-evident. Second, the status of the ECHR as an international treaty and the institutional role and competence of the Strasbourg Court, as a collegiate multinational bench reviewing states parties' compliance with the Convention, introduce further complications with major ramifications for our topic.

The structure of the ECHR itself implies that the rights it safeguards are not all of equal importance.[87] Notably, Article 3 is not open to derogation even in

[84] See, eg, Thomas Poole, 'Questioning Common Law Constitutionalism' (2005) 25 *Legal Studies* 142.
[85] EEPR, 735.
[86] Harris et al (n 32).
[87] Also see Ashworth (n 10).

times of emergency threatening the life of the nation, whereas Articles 8–11 are subject to a range of broadly worded exceptions specified in the text of the Convention. This reflects the point stressed in section 4 that the importance of rights can vary enormously depending on the nature of the interest(s) the right is supposed to protect. Even (human) rights with identical grounds may differ greatly in their relative importance. There are material differences of degree and kind differentiating, say, the right to life and the right to respect for one's private life; or the right not to be subject to arbitrary detention without trial and the right to test the evidence for the prosecution in criminal proceedings. There is even scope for debating whether different aspects of the same substantive legal right are of equal importance. For example, is the right not to be tortured of greater importance than the right not to be exposed to 'inhuman and degrading treatment'? What about 'inhuman and degrading' *punishment*? All of these abuses are proscribed by ECHR Article 3, but is any breach of any part of the provision equally reprehensible? And, crucially for us, should the remedial consequences be identical in every case?

To clarify the potential scope of a human rights-based protective principle, we also need to link different Convention rights, or particular strands of them, to arguments for the exclusionary remedy. Some of the rights protected by the ECHR, such as the right not to be reduced into slavery,[88] do not have much obvious salience for the exclusion of evidence. Other enumerated rights have more bearing on the substantive criminal law than its enforcement.[89] Issues pertaining to the exclusion of evidence in legal proceedings have predictably revolved around Article 6's fair trial guarantee, and methods of evidence-gathering potentially breaching Article 3 or Article 8. Although the ECtHR was bold enough to extend the concept of 'fair trial' to cover (pre-trial) investigative techniques where 'from the outset, the applicant was definitively deprived of a fair trial',[90] it is revealing that the Strasbourg Court has baulked at pronouncing any comprehensive per se exclusionary remedy covering all the evidential fruits of breaches of ECHR rights, even in relation to Article 3. In *Khan v UK*[91] the Strasbourg Court was not prepared to hold that evidence procured in breach of Article 8 is automatically inadmissible under Article 6. More strikingly still, in *Gäfgen*,[92] the Grand Chamber of the European Court of Human Rights concluded that Article 6 had not been breached by the admission of evidence procured through inhuman or degrading treatment, in violation of Article 3, because '[t]he additional evidence admitted at the trial was not used by the domestic court against the applicant to

[88] ECHR Art 4. It is always possible to imagine more or less fanciful hypotheticals, eg, the admissibility of a statement made by person subjected to forced labour which subsequently becomes material to another person's criminal trial.

[89] Eg, Art 7's explicit ban on retroactive penal legislation.

[90] *Teixeira de Castro v Portugal* (1998) 28 EHRR 101, [39].

[91] *Khan v UK* (2001) 31 EHRR 45.

[92] *Gäfgen v Germany* (2011) 52 EHRR 1.

prove his guilt, but only to test the veracity of his confession.'[93] Consequently, the 'impugned real evidence was not necessary, and was not used to prove him guilty or to determine his sentence .... [T]here was a break in the causal chain leading from the prohibited methods of investigation to the applicant's conviction and sentence in respect of the impugned real evidence.'[94]

Khan, and still more so *Gäfgen*, were serious disappointments to human rights advocates, and dissenting judicial voices on the Court itself are increasingly being heard.[95] Irrespective of their substantive merits and the quality of the Court's reasoning (which has often been pretty sparse and unpersuasive on any view), these decisions – and others like them – exemplify the inherent moral complexity and associated practical difficulties attending the application of any version of PP#243 to concrete cases. Even a Court whose raison d'etre is to apply and develop a pan-European legal framework of fundamental human rights has struggled to trace the logic of protecting the array of diverse interests grounding particular human rights, through to evidentiary exclusion as a presumptive – let alone mandatory – remedy for human rights violations.

These observations hint at a second major obstacle inhibiting the protective principle from hitching an easier ride in the ECHR caravan. The Strasbourg Court is a supra-national tribunal reviewing states parties' compliance with their treaty obligations under the Convention. It has neither the jurisdictional authority nor the jurisprudential competence to interfere directly in the conduct of national criminal proceedings. This is why the Strasbourg Court repeatedly disavows being a 'fourth instance' court of appeal, and frequently (if somewhat misleadingly) asserts that 'Article 6 of the Convention ... does not lay down any rules on the admissibility of evidence as such, which is therefore primarily a matter for regulation under national law.'[96] As the Strasbourg Court itself is well aware, its pivotal jurisprudential challenge is to concede to individual states parties an appropriate 'margin of appreciation' in designing their own criminal justice processes in accordance with local procedural traditions whilst still ensuring respect for a floor of minimum human rights in criminal adjudication across the Council of Europe. But even as it clearly recognises this challenge in abstract terms, Strasbourg jurisprudence interpreting Article 6 has evolved to such a degree of refinement that the Strasbourg Court now not infrequently finds itself embroiled in the technicalities of national law, with predictably uneven and sometimes perplexing results.[97] After

[93] ibid [179].

[94] ibid [180].

[95] Also see *Bykov v Russia*, App No 4378/02, ECtHR Grand Chamber Judgment, 10 March 2009.

[96] *Schenk v Switzerland*, (A/140) (1991) 13 EHRR 242, [46]. Also see: *Teixeira de Castro v Portugal* (1998) 28 EHRR 101, [34].

[97] Well-illustrated by the twists and turns of 'the Al-Khawaja saga': *Al-Khawaja and Tahery v United Kingdom* (2012) 54 EHRR 23 (GC); *R v Horncastle* [2010] 2 AC 373, [2009] UKSC 14; *Al-Khawaja and Tahery v UK* (2009) 49 EHRR 1. For commentary, see Roberts (n 64) 402–7; John Jackson and Sarah Summers, 'Confrontation With Strasbourg: UK and Swiss Approaches to Criminal Evidence' [2013] *Criminal Law Review* 114; Mike Redmayne, 'Hearsay and Human Rights: *Al-Khawaja* in the Grand Chamber' (2012) 75 *Modern Law Review* 865.

all, it is inherently unlikely that an international court comprising 46[98] national judges working in multiple languages and across different legal and procedural traditions, and approaching the issues from an oblique (human rights, rather than criminal justice) angle, is going to make much headway in prescribing solutions to some of criminal jurisprudence's trickiest and most enduring puzzles. So the promise of fully articulated procedural standards capable of guiding admissibility determinations without needing to reason from first principles, which appeared to be international human rights law's greatest asset in the design and practical implementation of a robust protective principle, turns out to be mostly wishful thinking.

Technical challenges of cosmopolitan adjudication are exacerbated by deeper controversies of political morality. Adducing the statement of a deceased complainant in a criminal trial, for example, might reflect a deeply held conviction that such accusations ought to be given a public hearing, as it were, from beyond the grave.[99] Again, protecting a witness from the risk of violent reprisals engages the witness's rights, and the state's corresponding duties, under Article 8 and even, regarding mortal threats, under Article 2 of the ECHR. Of course, no defensible system of criminal justice is going to say that these interests should be promoted to the point at which a criminal trial becomes unfair for the accused. However, these countervailing interests might lead one to reappraise just what a fair trial must entail: and this is where the views of the Strasbourg judges and the traditions of domestic legal systems may collide. In addition to the difficulties already highlighted, the possibility of human rights norms impinging on cherished values embedded in national legal traditions (some of which may have been elevated to constitutional status) is another reason for doubting whether the protective principle can legitimately be invoked to extend the exclusionary remedy to all violations of human rights, even as a defeasible presumption.

VII. Conclusion: Fast-Forward Back to the Future

This chapter's retrospective re-reading of EEPR, more than 30 years after its original publication, celebrates in microcosm the virtues of Andrew Ashworth's peerless scholarship and its extraordinary influence across our discipline. It should be evident that EEPR was a remarkably prescient contribution which anticipated some of the most acute controversies today confronting English criminal procedure law and practice. Its enduring significance and undiminished popularity are

[98] Russia was expelled from the Council of Europe on 16 March 2022, in response to its illegal invasion of Ukraine. Fooling nobody, Russia had signalled its intention to denounce the ECHR on the previous day.

[99] See, eg, *Nembhard v R* (1982) 74 Cr App R 144, 146, PC: '[I]t is important in the interests of justice that a person implicated in a killing should be obliged to meet in court the dying accusation of the victim …'.

attributable to what EEPR can still teach us about contemporary criminal litigation and its possible futures, through critical engagement with its themes and arguments.

The protective principle's rights-based rationale for excluding improperly obtained evidence is perfectly attuned to the language and judicial culture of the post-Human Rights Act era. Recent decades have simultaneously witnessed growing judicial awareness of the self-consciously constitutional dimensions of criminal procedure and evidence. Constitutional rights and European human rights law both present promising opportunities for developing a rejuvenated and super-charged protective principle, albeit with complementary shortcomings. Common law constitutionalism is securely rooted in indigenous procedural traditions, but its doctrinal shape and jurisprudential status are embryonic, contested and uncertain. Conversely, European human rights law has undergone rapid doctrinal development thanks to the Strasbourg Court's impressive industry, but these fair trial norms are necessarily pitched at the generic pan-European level and may be somewhat deficient in local suitability, political legitimacy or professional credibility. These institutional challenges compound deeper conceptual and normative puzzles about the nature and scope of rights and their moral grounds. In the absence of a tolerably clear, coherent and normatively defensible conception of rights, it will surely be impossible to specify appropriate legal remedies for their violation.

We have seen how alternative conceptions of the protective principle quickly multiply when this methodological injunction is taken seriously. If the admissibility of improperly obtained evidence is always a function of concatenated and irreducible moral and legal complexity (debatable facts, open-ended norms *and* contested evidentiary rationales), commentators who hanker after a bright-line exclusionary rule or even any elaborate doctrinal framework articulated beyond the level of flexible general principles seem destined to be forever disappointed. That this chapter has presented little more than a preliminary structural survey of this rich seam of theorising further underlines the enduring salience and adaptability of Ashworth's original argument for excluding evidence as protecting rights.

7

Redmayne's Character

BioNote: I first met Mike Redmayne at the annual Socio-Legal Studies Association conference hosted by Nottingham in 1994. We were both working on expert evidence, Mike completing a PhD at Birmingham,[1] me on a temporary research contract at Bristol undertaking a project devised by Chris Willmore on forensic science and miscarriages of justice funded by the Royal Commission on Criminal Justice. We had plenty to discuss and immediately recognised kindred spirits. Our life-long friendship was cemented by membership of the inaugural E & P Editorial Board (in the days when we used to attend regular Editorial Board meetings in person) and collaborations in numerous projects,[2] including a co-edited book.[3]

Politely declining serial attempts to persuade him to come to Nottingham, Mike was set on a London base, and in due course secured his ideal job at the LSE, where he combined his exemplary scholarship with great popularity as a law teacher. Mike was also a famously diligent member of the *Modern Law Review*'s Editorial Committee, providing very detailed editorial feedback to rescue marginal papers otherwise headed for the rejection pile. This is a tradition I have tried to maintain in succeeding Mike as the MLR's resident evidence law specialist.

Mike conceptualised evidence law within the broader jurisprudential framework of criminal procedure, a contextual approach to law and legal process I had learnt at Oxford from Andrew Ashworth, Nicola Lacey and Andrew Rutherford. Birmingham's law department was a trailblazer in socio-legal studies, spearheaded in the 1970s by John Baldwin and Mike McConville (who, having moved to Warwick Law School, later served as Mike's PhD external examiner). Cutting one's teeth in research on forensic science evidence is a fine education in interdisciplinarity. Mike is well-known for his collaboration with Andrew Ashworth on later editions of Ashworth's *Criminal Process* book.[4] But this was in fact Mike's *second*

[1] Substantially reworked and published as Mike Redmayne, *Expert Evidence and Criminal Justice* (OUP, 2001).

[2] Mike Redmayne, Paul Roberts, Colin Aitken and Graham Jackson, 'Forensic Science Evidence in Question' [2011] *Criminal Law Review* 347; Mike Redmayne, 'Confronting Confrontation' in Paul Roberts and Jill Hunter (eds), *Criminal Evidence and Human Rights* (Hart Publishing, 2012).

[3] Paul Roberts and Mike Redmayne (eds), *Innovations in Evidence and Proof* (Hart Publishing, 2007).

[4] Andrew Ashworth and Mike Redmayne, *The Criminal Process* 3rd edn (OUP, 2005; 4th edn 2010).

textbook on criminal process. His first was a now largely forgotten, and I think unjustly overlooked, collaboration with Manchester colleagues Martin Wasik and Tom Gibbons.[5]

Mike's untimely death in 2015, aged only 47, was a professional as well as personal tragedy.[6] It takes expertise and experience to produce mature works of criminal jurisprudence with lasting disciplinary impact. There is much to learn through long years of study and many wrong turnings to be taken before the dawn of intellectual enlightenment finally strikes. Mike's last monograph on *Character in the Criminal Trial* demonstrates that he was then at the peak of his powers. I am convinced that he would have written further major works of equal, or even greater, scholarly accomplishment, originality and influence if he had been granted the time to produce them.

I. Jurisprudential Context

With the publication of his final book on *Character in the Criminal Trial* (CitCT),[7] Mike Redmayne cemented his reputation as one of the foremost criminal justice scholars of his generation. CitCT is an eminently worthy addition to the *Oxford Monographs on Criminal Law and Justice* series, edited by Andrew Ashworth, which over the last quarter century has showcased some of the best contemporary criminal law scholarship in the English language. It is a mature work, written in a crisp, disarmingly accessible, matter-of-fact style which, at first blush, might belie both the book's erudition and the provocative unorthodoxy of some of its central contentions.

The Preface promises 'an in-depth analysis of particular uses of character evidence in relation to defendants: good character and bad character evidence, used as evidence of propensity to commit crime and as evidence of credibility' (p.ix). Readers anticipating a pedestrian perambulation through the evidentiary landscape, however, should take a hint from the (aptly chosen) cover design, featuring Blake at his most Old Testament. CitCT adopts an interdisciplinary methodology, combining doctrinal analysis with broader socio-legal, criminological, psychological and forensic science literature, and underpinned by firm foundations in penal theory. In its broad vision and determination to pursue its topic across conventional disciplinary taxonomies, CitCT represents a major contribution both to

[5] Martin Wasik, Thomas Gibbons and Mike Redmayne, *Criminal Justice: Text and Materials* (Longman, 1999). I have always wondered whether this book suffered from an unfortunate choice of publisher.

[6] 'Obituary: Mike Redmayne' (2015) 78 *Modern Law Review* 727; Paul Roberts, 'Mike Redmayne 1967-2015' (2015) 19 *International Journal of Evidence & Proof* 207; N Duxbury, 'Mike Redmayne Obituary', *The Guardian* 23 June 2015; Paul Roberts and Jonathan Doak (eds), *Special Memorial Issue for Mike Redmayne (1967-2015)* (2016) 20(2) *International Journal of Evidence and Proof* 89–174.

[7] Mike Redmayne, *Character in the Criminal Trial* (OUP, 2015).

Evidence and Proof scholarship and to criminal jurisprudence (being the theoretical part of Criminal Law, holistically and inclusively conceived).

The first section of this chapter amplifies these – admittedly delphic – claims by summarising methodological developments in the Law of Evidence and noting the emergence of Criminal Law Theory as a distinct (inter)disciplinary specialism. Criminal Law Theory is perhaps the more institutionalised disciplinary counterpart to criminal jurisprudence as scholarly method, or at least substantially overlaps with it. This minor detour into disciplinary constitution and taxonomy leads naturally into a fuller discussion of CitCT's central themes.

II. Disciplinary Transformations

Although perceptions are changing, the Law of Evidence is still widely regarded as a practitioner-oriented practical discipline, dominated by a stifling weight of case-law precedents, and with minimal theoretical interest for serious legal scholarship. Many textbooks seemingly pander to this uninspiring disciplinary model. Moreover, the majority of Law graduates in England and Wales (though not, intriguingly, in Northern Ireland, where the Law of Evidence is a compulsory subject)[8] leave university with at best a rudimentary understanding of criminal evidence and procedure, and even less knowledge of civil litigation. These gaps are filled, of course, by later practical instruction at 'the vocational stage' of legal education for graduates intending to enter the legal professions,[9] but this institutionalised division of pedagogic labour only tends to reinforce problematic tendencies and assumptions. In my – assuredly partisan – opinion, the model of Evidence law dominated by doctrinal technicality and narrowly devoted to practical utility always betrayed a very partial grasp of what evidentiary scholarship and teaching have to offer. Today, it represents a travesty of a subject that, over the last several decades, has been evolving towards thoroughly interdisciplinary studies of evidence and proof,[10] which are concerned as much with the uses and evaluation of evidence in institutional settings as with its legal admissibility and which aspire to

[8] I knew about the situation in Northern Ireland partly from my stint as External Examiner at QUB from 2008 to 2012. Findlay Stark subsequently pointed out to me that the same position prevails in Scotland. So it seems that England and Wales is the outlier UK jurisdiction in not treating Evidence law as a compulsory undergraduate subject.

[9] Proposals tabled by the Solicitors Regulation Authority, *Training for Tomorrow: Assessing Competence* (SRA, 7 December 2015) announced a new framework for qualifying as a solicitor in England and Wales with significant implications for legal education. The Solicitors Qualifying Examination (SQE) was introduced in 2021 and is open to non-graduates.

[10] Paul Roberts, 'Theorising Evidence Law' (2023) 43 *Oxford Journal of Legal Studies* 629; Christian Dahlman, Alex Stein and Giovanni Tuzet (eds), *Philosophical Foundations of Evidence Law* (OUP, 2021); William Twining, 'Evidence as a Multi-disciplinary Subject' (2003) 2 *Law, Probability and Risk* 91; Philip Dawid, William Twining, and Mimi Vasilaki (eds), *Evidence, Inference and Enquiry* (OUP, 2011); Paul Roberts and Mike Redmayne (eds), *Innovations in Evidence and Proof* (Hart Publishing, 2007).

epistemological sophistication.[11] Contemporary Evidence and Proof scholarship is interdisciplinary both in its theoretical commitments and in its programmatic, practical and policy interventions, notably in the area of forensic science.[12] It also prominently incorporates formal models of inferential reasoning, drawing on logic, statistics, probability theory, computer science and other heuristic models of factual inference.[13] Another important strand of this scholarship emphasises narrative, storytelling, rhetoric, hermeneutics and interpretational approaches to judicial evidence and proof.[14]

Exemplifying the interdisciplinarity of contemporary Evidence and Proof scholarship, Chapter 2 of CitCT extensively draws on criminological and behavioural science research to establish the logical relevance of previous conduct in assessing the truth of allegations of subsequent criminality. The thrust of the argument is to rehabilitate the common-sense notion that 'nothing predicts behaviour like behaviour'. I am personally sceptical about the robustness of crime statistics in predicting recidivism, given their notorious fallibilities and manipulability;[15] some methodological issues are highlighted in CitCT, others are breezily glossed over. However, Redmayne is studiously cautious in his reliance on these data, and it is difficult to take issue with his modest and heavily qualified conclusions:

> [T]he argument is simply that those with recent previous convictions are significantly more likely to offend than those without. To the extent that the largest group of offenders comprises those who only offend once, we should be cautious about reading much into a single previous conviction, at least unless it is for a serious offence. When the defendant has serious, or multiple, convictions, it is important to bear in mind the age-crime curve [indicating rapid desistance with aging – young offenders 'grow up and out of crime'] and the significance of the increasing number of previous convictions ....

[11] See, eg, Paul Roberts (ed), *Theoretical Foundations of Criminal Trial Procedure* (Ashgate, 2014) Part III; Susan Haack, *Evidence Matters: Science, Proof, and Truth in the Law* (CUP, 2014); Hock Lai Ho, *A Philosophy of Evidence Law – Justice in the Search for Truth* (OUP, 2008).

[12] Paul Roberts (ed), *Expert Evidence and Scientific Proof in Criminal Trials* (Ashgate, 2014); Graham Jackson, Colin Aitken and Paul Roberts, *Case Assessment and Interpretation of Expert Evidence*, RSS Practitioner Guide No 4 (Royal Statistical Society, 2014), www.rss.org.uk/news-publication/publications/law-guides/ (accessed 17 December 2025); Erica Beecher-Monas, *Evaluating Scientific Evidence: An Interdisciplinary Framework for Intellectual Due Process* (CUP, 2007).

[13] Paul Roberts and Colin Aitken, *The Logic of Forensic Proof: Inferential Reasoning in Criminal Evidence and Forensic Science*, RSS Practitioner Guide No 3 (Royal Statistical Society, 2014), www.rss.org.uk/news-publication/publications/law-guides/ (accessed 17 December 2025); Henry Prakken, 'Analysing Reasoning about Evidence with Formal Models of Argumentation' (2004) 3 *Law, Probability and Risk* 33; David Schum and Peter Tillers, 'Marshalling Evidence for Adversary Litigation' (1991) 13 *Cardozo Law Review* 657; Terence Anderson, David Schum and William Twining, *Analysis of Evidence*, 2nd edn (CUP, 2005).

[14] Lisa K Griffin, 'Narrative, Truth, and Trial' (2013) 101 *Georgetown Law Journal* 281; Floris J Bex, *Arguments, Stories and Criminal Evidence* (Springer, 2011); Robert P Burns, *A Theory of the Trial* (Princeton University Press, 1999); Nancy Pennington and Reid Hastie, 'A Cognitive Theory of Juror Decision Making: The Story Model' (1991) 13 *Cardozo Law Review* 519; Louise Ellison and Vanessa E Munro, '"Telling Tales": Exploring Narratives of Life and Law within the (Mock) Jury Room' (2015) 35 *Legal Studies* 201.

[15] Mike Maguire, 'Crime Statistics and the Construction of Crime' in Mike Maguire, Rod Morgan and Robert Reiner (eds), *The Oxford Handbook of Criminology*, 5th edn (OUP, 2012).

A single previous conviction for an offence of modest seriousness says little about future risk. (pp.29, 32)

In paying close attention to the micro-dynamics of inferential reasoning linking past and future behaviour, CitCT extends a rich vein of evidentiary theorising about the nature of 'relevance' which was prospected over a century ago by the American jurist, Thayer,[16] but has since remained under-exploited; until relatively recently, when Twining's patient advocacy for 'taking facts seriously' has stimulated wider interest.[17] It might seem paradoxical that common-sense reasoning should require formal modelling. Shouldn't 'common sense' fact-finding be, well, a matter of common sense? In fact, the ways in which human beings routinely acquire, process and act on information in their everyday lives are extraordinarily complex and still highly conjectural topics of scientific inquiry. This is why problems of artificial intelligence have proven so obdurate.[18] Even a 'simple' legal case with relatively few material facts and pieces of evidence is capable of generating intricate webs of interweaving inferential linkages far surpassing most people's capacity to hold them steadily and reliably in the mind's eye.[19] Formal modelling, including the use of graphical representations of inferential structures, can therefore be very helpful in subjecting legal (aka 'forensic') evidence and argumentation to systematic rational scrutiny and evaluation.[20] It also potentially unlocks the vast computational power of modern microcomputers and harnesses it to evidential analysis. Redmayne makes effective use of simple graphical figures in his efforts to deconstruct and model 'the propensity inference' in Chapter 6. In these sections (pp.112–116, 122–126), CitCT demonstrates the power and versatility of graphical modelling techniques in illuminating the inferential structure of recurrent

[16] James Bradley Thayer, *A Preliminary Treatise on Evidence at the Common Law* (Little, Brown & Co, 1898).

[17] William Twining, 'Taking Facts Seriously' in Neil Gold (ed), *Essays on Legal Education* (Toronto, Butterworths, 1982); William Twining, 'Taking Facts Seriously – Again' in Roberts and Redmayne, above n 3; Paul Roberts, 'Rethinking the Law of Evidence: A Twenty-first Century Agenda for Teaching and Research' (2002) 55 *Current Legal Problems* 297.

[18] Ten years, since this chapter was first published as a review article, is a long time in AI development. But notice that the essential point about the limits of sheer computation remains valid. Insofar as Large Language Models are solving problems of generative AI, they are doing so through the development of heuristics that mimic human reasoning and through novel quantum computing technology.

[19] This is one practical instance of a general problem in information science known as the 'combinatorial explosion', here expounded by David Schum, *The Evidential Foundations of Probabilistic Reasoning* (Northwestern UP, 1994) 491–92: 'We need to find connections among our data; they are there, all we need to do is to find them. This is where the real trouble starts .... For *n* data there are 2*n* – (n + 1) possible combinations of two or more data taken together. Suppose that you have just fifty items of data on record at this point. You would then have $1.1259(10)^{15}$ possible combinations of data to search through; for 100 items the number of possible combinations is 1.2677(10).'[30] The term is owed to Gilbert Harman, *Change in View: Principles of Reasoning* (MIT Press, 1986) 25–27. Also see Hilary Kornblith, 'The Laws of Thought' (1992) 52 *Philosophy and Phenomenological Research* 895.

[20] Practical illustrations are elucidated in the sources cited at n 6, above. Also see Yvonne McDermott and John D Jackson (eds), 'Symposium: Proof in International Criminal Trials' (2015) 13(3) *Journal of International Criminal Justice* 475; Peter Tillers (ed), 'Special Issue: Graphic and Visual Representations of Evidence and Inference in Legal Settings' (2007) 6 *Law, Probability & Risk* 1.

factual scenarios and clarifying persistent confusions in legal reasoning. This, though, barely scratches the surface of the vast untapped potential for applying formal heuristics to problems of character evidence and in evidentiary scholarship generally.

Thirty years ago, one could barely speak of Criminal Law Theory as a distinct disciplinary sub-specialism.[21] In the ensuing decades, there has been a veritable explosion in self-consciously theoretical work in criminal law, accompanied by all the institutional trappings of disciplinary formation: conferences, journals, courses and textbooks.[22] Criminal Law Theory brings together theoretical work on the foundations of substantive criminal law with somewhat more established research programmes in penal theory and the philosophy of punishment.[23] There has hitherto been a topical bias towards standards of responsibility, culpability and liability and other doctrines of the General Part.[24] Procedural issues have never been completely excluded from Criminal Law Theory's ambit, not least because divisions between 'substantive' and 'procedural' law are themselves institutional artefacts, and different common law systems (to say nothing of more ambitiously comparative contrasts) draw the line between substance and procedure in somewhat different places. Topics such as the presumption of innocence have attracted the criminal law theorist's critical attention,[25] partly because they transcend, and tend to subvert, neat taxonomical pigeonholing.[26] However, there have been noticeably fewer attempts to extend the intellectual resources and methods of criminal law theorising to truly *evidentiary* topics and questions.[27] Put another way,

[21] Notwithstanding Anglo-American criminal law scholarship's impeccable theoretical ambitions and pedigree, including H L A Hart, *Punishment and Responsibility* (OUP, 1968; 2nd edn, Gardner ed 2008); and Herbert L Packer, *The Limits of the Criminal Sanction* (Stanford University Press, 1969).

[22] See, eg, R A Duff and Stuart P Green (eds), *Philosophical Foundations of Criminal Law* (OUP, 2011); Douglas Husak, *The Philosophy of Criminal Law* (OUP, 2010); R A Duff, Claire Grant, Douglas Husak, Ronnie Lippens and Matt Matravers, 'Editorial' (2007) 1 *Criminal Law and Philosophy* 1; George P Fletcher (ed), *New Voices in Criminal Theory* (1998) 1 *Buffalo Criminal Law Review* Special Issue.

[23] A P Simester and Andreas von Hirsch, *Crimes, Harms and Wrongs: On the Principles of Criminalisation* (Hart Publishing, 2011); Victor Tadros, *The Ends of Harm: The Moral Foundations of Criminal Law* (OUP, 2011); R A Duff, *Answering for Crime: Responsibility and Liability in the Criminal Law* (Hart Publishing, 2007); Michael Moore, *Placing Blame: A Theory of Criminal Law* (OUP, 1997).

[24] Trailblazers included A P Simester and A T H Smith (eds), *Harm and Culpability* (OUP, 1996); Stephen Shute, John Gardner and Jeremy Horder (eds), *Action and Value in Criminal Law* (OUP, 1993); and R A Duff, *Intention, Agency and Criminal Liability* (Blackwell, 1990). In addition to building on the pioneering contributions of Hart and Packer, inspiration was evidently taken from Glanville Williams, *Criminal Law: The General Part*, 2nd edn (Stevens & Sons, 1961); and George P Fletcher, *Rethinking Criminal Law* (Little, Brown, 1978).

[25] See, eg, Patrick Tomlin, 'Extending the Golden Thread? Criminalisation and the Presumption of Innocence' (2013) 21 *Journal of Political Philosophy* 44; R A Duff, 'Presuming Innocence' in Lucia Zedner and Julian V Roberts (eds), *Principles and Values in Criminal Law and Criminal Justice* (OUP, 2012).

[26] See further, Paul Roberts, 'Loss of Innocence in Common Law Presumptions' (2014) 8 *Criminal Law and Philosophy* 317; Liz Campbell, 'Criminal Labels, the European Convention on Human Rights and the Presumption of Innocence' (2013) 76 *Modern Law Review* 681.

[27] Major exceptions to this generalisation include R A Duff, Lindsay Farmer, Sandra Marshall and Victor Tadros, *The Trial on Trial Volume Three: Towards a Normative Theory of the Criminal Trial* (Hart Publishing, 2007), elucidating themes first suggested by R A Duff, *Trials and Punishments* (CUP, 1986).

methodologically parallel developments in Criminal Law Theory and Evidence and Proof scholarship have proceeded largely in isolation from each other. CitCT promotes their integration.[28]

CitCT is a direct contribution to Criminal Law Theory in at least two significant respects. Firstly, in taking 'character' as its inquiry-defining object of analysis, CitCT deliberately disregards conventional (sub)disciplinary taxonomies differentiating substantive criminal law, criminal procedure, and sentencing and the penal system. If questions concerning character arise in each of these institutional spheres, as Redmayne instructively demonstrates, why should theorising be constrained by disciplinary taxonomies owing more to convenience and force of habit than reflective theoretical justification? Thus, in Chapter 11 Redmayne revisits the philosophical merits of character as a legitimate ground of punishment, and this leads him into well-worn debates between criminal law theorists pitting 'character' against 'choice' as a basis of criminal liability,[29] and onwards into the theoretical literature on sentencing rationales and their application to recidivist offenders.[30] Redmayne is open to the possibility of character playing a role at sentencing, but also evinces strong liberal scruples against punishing personalities rather than choices (no neo-Aristotelian criminal law theorist he[31]) or allowing sentencing to become a prying moral audit of an offender's entire life. Von Hirsch's theory of progressive loss of mitigation[32] coupled with penological data indicating the questionable efficacy of deterrence through marginal increases in sentencing severity,[33] especially in terms of imprisonment with its well-documented criminogenic side-effects, suggests the basis for a liberal approach placing robust legal limitations on the uses of previous convictions as aggravating factors in sentencing whilst still retaining humanising elements of penal reductionism, for example,

[28] Also see Paul Roberts, 'Groundwork for a Jurisprudence of Criminal Procedure' in R A Duff and Stuart P Green (eds), *Philosophical Foundations of Criminal Law* (OUP, 2011).

[29] See, eg, Samuel H Pillsbury, 'The Meaning of Deserved Punishment: An Essay on Choice, Character, and Responsibility' (1992) 67 *Indiana Law Journal* 719; John Gardner, 'The Gist of Excuses' (1998) 1 *Buffalo Criminal Law Review* 575; R A Duff, *Criminal Attempts* (OUP, 1996) chs 6–7; Jeremy Horder, 'Criminal Culpability: The Possibility of A General Theory' (1993) 12 *Law and Philosophy* 193; Michael Moore, 'Choice, Character, and Excuse' (1990) 7 *Social Philosophy and Policy* 29; Nicola Lacey, *State Punishment* (Routledge, 1988) ch 3; Michael D Bayles, 'Character, Purpose, and Criminal Responsibility' (1982) 1 *Law and Philosophy* 5.

[30] Julian V Roberts and Andrew von Hirsch (eds), *Previous Convictions at Sentencing: Theoretical and Applied Perspectives* (Hart Publishing, 2010).

[31] Character-based conceptions of criminal liability often appeal to Aristotle's writings on virtue: see, eg, Kyron Huigens, 'Virtue and Inculpation' (1995) 108 *Harvard Law Review* 1423. For criticism, see R A Duff, 'Virtue, Vice, and Criminal Liability: Do We Want an Aristotelian Criminal Law?' (2002) 6 *Buffalo Criminal Law Review* 147.

[32] Andrew von Hirsch and Andrew Ashworth, *Proportionate Sentencing: Exploring the Principles* (OUP, 2005); Andrew von Hirsch, *Past or Future Crimes: Deservedness and Dangerousness in the Sentencing of Criminals* (Manchester University Press, 1986).

[33] Andrew von Hirsch, Anthony E Bottoms, Elizabeth Burney and P-O Wikström, *Criminal Deterrence and Sentencing Severity* (Hart Publishing, 1999); Deryck Beyleveld, 'Deterrence Research as a Basis for Deterrence Policies' (1979) 18 *Howard Journal of Criminal Justice* 135; Michael Tonry, 'Learning from the Limitations of Deterrence Research' (2008) 37 *Crime & Justice* 279.

in giving some credit for (formal) 'good character' inferred from an absence of previous convictions. This view integrates backward-looking and forward-looking considerations, in deference to the fact that '[a] crime committed in the past may be the necessary basis for punishment, but it is an offender, with an ongoing life, who is punished' (p.248). Sentencing can be calibrated to reflect *degrees* of blameworthiness that are not fully registered at the point of conviction, and assessments of the offender's character might legitimately inform judicial recognition of mitigating or aggravating factors when imposing punishment. One does not need to profess much faith in the epistemic credentials of such judicial character assessments in order to appreciate their potential institutional significance. Redmayne is 'fairly sceptical about the value of … good character evidence in telling us much about what offenders are really like' (p.242), but is receptive to the various ways in which appeals to character might represent useful 'moral fictions', for example, in enhancing the legitimacy of trial proceedings and encouraging desistance from future offending. There is a critical edge to this exposition. Whilst current sentencing law and practice in England and Wales reflect some of these underlying principles and policies, 'convictions almost certainly play a greater aggravating role than is justified' with the troubling consequence that 'proportionality … is threatened' (p.246).

Discussion of recent developments in English sentencing law and practice and critical evaluation of their compatibility with underlying theoretical rationales is extended into Chapter 12's consideration of 'dangerous characters'. Redmayne questions contemporary policies of risk-orientated incapacitative sentencing justified by official predictions of 'dangerousness'. Some of the arguments advanced by criminal lawyers, he shows, would benefit from better acquaintance with Evidence scholarship.[34] A notable virtue of this discussion is that it emphasises technical challenges, logical gaps and practical failures of implementation in extrapolating from risk assessment protocols to sentencing policies, rather than simply rehearsing ideological objections, which typically exhaust themselves in normative stalemate. '[A]sking character to predict reoffending with sufficient certainty to justify incapacitation of large numbers of offenders' is simply, warns Redmayne, 'to ask too much of it' (p.273). Moreover, intellectual honesty and transparency in justificatory rationales are not merely virtues for theorists:

> If we are to continue to go down the incapacitative path, as no doubt we will, policymakers and judges should at least use [actuarial and other predictive cost-benefit] measures to explain who they think should be incapacitated and what they expect to gain from it. (p.273)

[34] See, eg, Redmayne's telling observations on the well-known 'reference class problem' (pp.256–58). See further, Ronald J Allen and Michael S Pardo, 'The Problematic Value of Mathematical Models of Evidence' (2007) 36 *Journal of Legal Studies* 107; Ronald J Allen and Paul Roberts (eds), *Special Issue on the Reference Class Problem* (2007) 11(4) *International Journal of Evidence and Proof* 243.

As well as contributing to substantive debates in penal theory, policy and practice, this pair of chapters presents an implicit challenge to criminal law theorists and Evidence scholars to keep their conventional disciplinary taxonomies under critical review. One major strand of such reflexivity, developed elsewhere,[35] questions the logic of the orthodox common law conception of the Law of Evidence as a unified disciplinary field. Redmayne's exclusive focus on character in *criminal* trial proceedings demonstrates the value of disaggregating criminal procedure and evidence from civil litigation in order to elucidate the theoretical foundations and deeper normative coherence of, specifically, criminal adjudication, procedure and proof.[36] Redmayne's willingness to extend his analysis of character beyond the point of conviction and into the penalty phase of criminal trials is equally thought-provoking. I doubt whether many common lawyers would regard sentencing as part of substantive criminal law. If one were forced to choose, sentencing would presumably have greater affinity with criminal procedure, yet books on the Law of Evidence nearly always stop abruptly at the point of verdict – even though sentencing law and practice plainly encompass matters of information management and sentencing cases sometimes raise contested points of fact, especially following a guilty plea where material facts were never ventilated at trial.[37] CitCT leverages the methodological purchase of rethinking conventional taxonomies, an approach that could equally be extended to pre-trial proceedings, for example, by considering the role of character evidence in police evidence-gathering and detection or prosecutors' decisions to charge or discontinue and in case-building. Why should studies of evidence, proof and procedure be exclusively trial-centric?

The second major way in which CitCT contributes directly to Criminal Law Theory is through its engagement with the substantive moral and political values animating criminal adjudication. The chapters on penal theory and sentencing rationales contain concise summaries of existing learning and offer insightful extrapolation to the issues under discussion. Chapter 4 on 'the ethics of character evidence' is, however, the more substantial theoretical contribution in my opinion.[38] Generations of Evidence scholars have argued, and many more common lawyers have long assumed, that inferring guilt from bad character is incompatible with a fair and legitimate trial process. It is still the prevailing assumption in the common law world that bad character evidence requires special pleading

[35] See Chapter 5 of the present volume.

[36] Civil litigation constitutes its own subdisciplinary field, with scope for illuminating comparative studies cutting across the institutionalised criminal-civil divide, especially in terms of shared epistemic – as opposed to normative moral and political – theoretical foundations.

[37] 'Newton hearings' may be conducted to establish the factual basis for imposing sentence: see, eg, *R v Boguslawska* [2015] EWCA Crim 497 (B pleading guilty to opportunistic theft, whilst denying aggravating factors of premeditation and preying on vulnerable victims); *R v Bendriss* [2014] EWCA Crim 1326 (emphasising 'the importance of dealing, both from the point of view of judge and counsel, with bases of plea in a way which cannot later give rise to hostages to fortune': ibid [9]).

[38] The material previously published as Mike Redmayne, 'The Ethics of Character Evidence' (2008) 61 *Current Legal Problems* 371 is now contextualised within the book's more comprehensive narrative.

to be admissible for the prosecution in a criminal trial[39] (though, as we will see in a moment, the ideological compass in England and Wales has been reset by statute). Redmayne systematically reconsiders and, one by one, rejects principled moral and political objections to the use of bad character evidence in criminal trials. His global evaluation is that 'arguments which have been put forward for a "moralized" exclusionary rule are unconvincing' (p.90), compelling the unorthodox conclusion that, after all, 'the increased use of bad character evidence in the guilt-determination stage of the trial is defensible' (p.283). But he immediately, and wisely, cautions: '[t]his does not mean that the ethical issues analysed … give no cause for concern' (p.90).

Redmayne's theoretical arguments are considered cogent and invigorating. A hallmark of his scholarship was a healthy disregard for prevailing jurisprudential wisdom, reinforced by (well justified) impatience with immature theoretical argumentation and pseudo-philosophical flummery. Objections to reliance on bad character as prosecution evidence in criminal trials variously invoke primary liberal values such as autonomy, dignity and privacy, or question its compatibility with more-or-less axiomatic criminal procedure doctrines, for example by suggesting that bad character evidence contravenes the presumption of innocence, or that it amounts to double jeopardy, or that it undercuts penal rationales predicated on offender rehabilitation or reform. Liberals should not be in the business of 'giving a dog a bad name and hanging him for it', any more than they should countenance trusting the state with wide-ranging powers to investigate and judge a citizen's life choices every time he or she happens to transgress the criminal law, perhaps in venial matters or where the authority of the criminal law to regulate is itself contested through forms of conscientious objection and the like. Redmayne does not dissent from any of the foundational values constituting liberal legality in criminal adjudication. Instead his strategy is, firstly, not to be fazed by the mere invocation of attractive values, and to demand a fuller explanation of why reliance on bad character in criminal trials is supposedly at odds with them;[40] and secondly, to demonstrate through patient analysis why arguments defending common law orthodoxy are typically overstated and/or under-informed concerning the nuances of legal doctrine or the practical realities of its implementation. This is one respect in which Evidence scholars immersed in doctrinal

[39] See, eg, *R v Hart* [2014] 2 SCR 544, 2014 SCC 52, [76] (referring to 'the well-established presumption that bad character evidence is inadmissible'); *R v HML* (2008) 235 CLR 334, [2008] HCA 16 (Gleeson CJ reciting at [12] that if 'the prosecution adduces the evidence for the purpose of leading to the conclusion that the accused is a person likely from his criminal conduct or character to have committed the offence for which he is being tried, then the law excludes such evidence as a matter of fundamental principle'); Rule 404(b)(1) of the US Federal Rules of Evidence (FRE) provides that: 'Evidence of a crime, wrong, or other act is not admissible to prove a person's character in order to show that on a particular occasion the person acted in accordance with the character.' But evidence of prior acts may be adduced for the other purposes, 'such as proving motive, opportunity, intent, preparation, plan, knowledge, identity, absence of mistake, or lack of accident': FRE Rule 4043(b)(2).

[40] The two most characteristically Redmaynean sentences in the entire book are: 'Beyond the rhetoric lurk difficult questions' (p.232); and: 'These arguments need some unpacking' (p.253).

analysis might actually enjoy a methodological advantage over criminal law theorists who construct normative rationalisations at some distance from the institutional facts.[41] Case law includes very compelling illustrations of highly probative bad character, predicating the almost inescapable need for exceptions to any blanket exclusionary rule.[42] Criminal courts and practitioners, being well-acquainted with these realities, would need more than vague appeals to political morality to jettison highly probative character evidence. Moreover, Redmayne argues, theorists have overplayed their hand by, for example, insisting that reliance on bad character implies a deterministic conception of criminal offending which fails to respect individual autonomy and undercuts penal objectives, encouraging apology, repentance and reform. In reality, the logic of inferential reasoning from past behaviour is perfectly consistent with autonomous conduct. For example, I very predictably drink coffee rather than tea[43] every day, but that's still my voluntary choice of hot beverage on each occasion; to bring me a coffee on the assumption that I will behave in character does not demean my dignity or deny my personal autonomy.[44] The institutional communication of penal censure, in harmony with sound epistemological principles, is more nuanced than one-dimensional theorising allows.

Redmayne's theoretical jujitsu inflicts telling blows on his opponents. His criticism is always studiously balanced and fair-minded, and careful to disentangle penal theorising from its contingent associations with particular political programmes. Redmayne rightly insists on being 'wary of viewing negatively all law reforms which have been influenced by the often toxic criminal justice politics of the last 20 years' (p.282). For all that, I am not entirely sold on Chapter 4's normative argument, which I think remains incomplete in significant respects. For one thing, Redmayne does not investigate the normative implications or pragmatic semiotics of re-orientating the law's *existing* theoretical commitments in relation to bad character evidence. Law reform does not come out of nowhere or begin with a blank slate from Year Zero. Change involves an intervention in the fabric of subsisting institutional arrangements and practices, the intentional or implicit message of which may be that we no longer believe in the ideals and values we once did or no longer believe in them in quite the same way. Does the admission of

[41] To similar effect, see Mike Redmayne, 'Theorizing the Criminal Trial' (2009) 12 *New Criminal Law Review* 287.

[42] This was achieved at common law under the (not very transparent) rubric of 'similar fact evidence'. A powerful illustration is the notorious 'brides in the bath' murder case of *R v George Joseph Smith* (1916) 11 Cr App R 229 (CCA), discussed in Mike Redmayne, 'A Likely Story!' (1999) 19 *Oxford Journal of Legal Studies* 659. For more recent illustrations, see *R v Nicholson* [2012] 2 Cr App R 31, [2012] EWCA Crim 1568; *R v Chopra* [2007] 1 Cr App R 16, [2006] EWCA Crim 2133.

[43] Interestingly, if all you knew about me is my Yorkshire heritage, you might infer a cultural predisposition towards tea-drinking! On the fertile topic of generalisations in inferential reasoning, see William Twining, 'Narrative and Generalizations in Argumentation about Questions of Fact' (1999) 40 *South Texas Law Review* 351.

[44] For parallel arguments in relation to proving non-consent in sexual offences, see Helen Reece, 'Rape Myths: Is Elite Opinion Right and Popular Opinion Wrong?' (2013) 33 *Oxford Journal of Legal Studies* 445.

more bad character evidence in criminal trials signal greater willingness to convict the accused on their past records? Such reflections should prompt further worries about ripple effects and unintended consequences, such as the possible impact of relaxed admissibility regimes on criminal investigations and prosecutorial decision-making. One risk of relying heavily on confessions in criminal adjudication, for example, is that the police will concentrate their investigative resources on securing admissions from suspects rather than looking for possibly more reliable sources of proof or corroboration, such as physical and scientific evidence.[45] Might a relaxed admissibility regime for bad character evidence, which has hitherto been widely regarded – at least in the absence of compelling 'similar facts' – as the last desperate throw of the dice by prosecutors with evidentially dubious cases, exert a similarly disinhibiting effect on cultures of investigation and prosecution, ratcheting up oppressive plea-bargaining[46] and diluting epistemic standards of proof in contested criminal trials? Will factfinders allow records of previous offending to put otherwise reasonable doubts out of their minds in rushing to judgement? Will they fail to make appropriate adjustments in drawing inferences from bad character to accommodate investigative practices, such as 'rounding up the usual suspects', which may skew uninformed expectations of defendants' previous records? Does it not affect the legitimacy of criminal adjudication, at some level, simply to know that criminal juries *could* now be making these inferential errors (given that they have heard misconduct evidence that previously would have been excluded from the trial), even if, in fact, their deliberations and verdicts remain unaffected?

Questions such as these open up substantial further research agendas. Suffice it here to say that, although I am persuaded by Redmayne's theoretical critiques, I am more cautious than him in extrapolating law reform implications and see a greater role for procedural traditions and institutional sociology in normative theorising. There is more to the justificatory rationales underpinning procedural and evidentiary practices than the internal logic of normative argument.

III. Character Evidence and Prejudice

Common lawyers sometimes say that bad character evidence is 'irrelevant', either by way of habituated *façon de parler* or because they are labouring under

[45] See further, Rosemary Pattenden, 'Should Confessions be Corroborated?' (1991) 107 *Law Quarterly Review* 317.

[46] Whilst the ethics and merits of negotiated case outcomes may be debatable in principle (see Richard L Lippke, *The Ethics of Plea Bargaining* (OUP, 2011); N Vamos, 'Please Don't Call it "Plea Bargaining"' [2009] *Criminal Law Review* 617), some empirical practice seems indefensible on any account: see Mike McConville and Luke Marsh, *Criminal Judges: Legitimacy, Courts and State-Induced Guilty Pleas in Britain* (Edward Elgar, 2014); Daniel Newman, *Legal Aid Lawyers and the Quest for Justice* (Hart Publishing, 2013); Mike McConville and C Mirsky, 'Guilty Plea Courts: A Social Disciplinary Model of Criminal Justice' (1995) 42 *Social Problems* 216. Generally, see Máximo Langer, Mike McConville and Luke Marsh (eds), *Research Handbook on Plea Bargaining and Criminal Justice* (Edward Elgar, 2024).

a conceptual confusion propagated by, amongst others, Stephen's influential nineteenth-century writings on the law of evidence.[47] Conceptual classification has important practical implications for the admissibility of evidence. Irrelevant evidence is categorically inadmissible, period. So if bad character is irrelevant, it is categorically inadmissible. Common lawyers and judges have often thought and argued in this way.

Yet as Redmayne convincingly demonstrates in Chapter 2 of CitCT, it is simply false that character is irrelevant in assessing conduct. To the contrary, in ordinary life we routinely rely on judgements of character to predict future behaviour and judge the past in small things – like whether I would welcome you bringing me coffee or tea this morning – and great, such as whether we can rely on our family and friends in times of crisis or whether we should steer clear of enemies who have attacked us in the past. English law is committed to a conception of relevancy predicated on ordinary, everyday, 'common sense' inferential reasoning.[48] So if character is relevant to conduct in daily experience, character evidence should in principle be legally relevant whenever – as a matter of ordinary common-sense reasoning – it bears on material facts in the trial. Now, 'common sense' is a notoriously slippery, contested and in many ways problematic concept,[49] and it might be countered that prevailing popular wisdom is badly misinformed about the salience of character in judging conduct. Most fundamentally, what if 'character' is merely a socially constructed 'presentation of self'[50] or vapid self-delusion, when in reality people generally react to their circumstances, and there is no telling how one might respond to adversity or temptation until one is actually tested by events?[51] This worry – not unknown to Evidence scholars[52] – reignites enduring controversies between 'situationism' and 'personism' in the psychology of personality, which are briefly reviewed in Chapter 2. Redmayne is able to slice through some of the theoretical tangles and thickets encountered in this research tradition, owing to

[47] See Paul Roberts, *Roberts and Zuckerman's Criminal Evidence*, 3rd edn (OUP, 2022) 110–11, 116–117 (criticising the conceptual taxonomy presented by James F Stephen, *Digest of the Law of Evidence* (Macmillan, 1874); and reprinted in successive editions until 1948).

[48] *R v A* [2002] 1 AC 45, [2001] UKHL 25, [31] (Lord Steyn): 'to be relevant the evidence need merely have some tendency in logic and common sense to advance the proposition in issue'.

[49] See further, Ronald J Allen, 'Common Sense, Rationality, and the Legal Process' (2001) 22 *Cardozo Law Review* 1417; Marilyn MacCrimmon, 'What is "Common" About Common Sense?: Cautionary Tales for Travelers Crossing Disciplinary Boundaries' (2001) 22 *Cardozo Law Review* 1433; H Baillot, Sharon Cowan and V E Munro, '"Hearing the Right Gaps": Enabling and Responding to Disclosures of Sexual Violence with the UK Asylum Process' (2012) 21 *Social & Legal Studies* 269; Emma Cunliffe, *Murder, Medicine and Motherhood* (Hart Publishing, 2011).

[50] Erving Goffman, *The Presentation of Self in Everyday Life* (Penguin, 1990 [1959]).

[51] *Cf* the chilling thesis that 'ordinary Germans' became 'Hitler's willing executioners' during the Nazi period: Daniel J Goldhagen, *Hitler's Willing Executioners: Ordinary Germans and the Holocaust* (Alfred A Knopf, 1996); Christopher R Browning, *Ordinary Men: Reserve Police Battalion 101 and the Final Solution in Poland* (Penguin, 2001); Zygmunt Bauman, *Modernity and the Holocaust* (Polity, 1989). For a philosophical riposte, see Erik J Wielenberg, 'Saving Character' (2006) 9 *Ethical Theory and Moral Practice* 461.

[52] See, eg, Roderick Munday, 'The Paradox of Cross-Examination to Credit – Simply Too Close for Comfort' (1994) 53 *Cambridge Law Journal* 303.

the well-defined, institutionally circumscribed purposes for which inferences are drawn from character in criminal trials. As a general proposition, '[t]he rather predictable consensus is that both persons and situations are important factors in explaining behaviour ("interactionism")' (p.12). In the specific context of criminal adjudication, 'information about past behaviour can be powerful evidence in a comparative exercise' (p.15). All we need to be able to say to meet the law's minimal relevancy threshold is that people who have behaved badly in the past (given reasonably robust and relevant criteria of 'bad behaviour') are *more likely than* people with spotless records to have committed the offence(s) charged. This is an essentially *comparative* judgement, indexed to a baseline of factfinders' prevailing assumptions about the (notional) 'average defendant' in a criminal trial before acquiring individualising information about any particular accused. Redmayne reviews crime statistics purporting to establish that violent offenders are '98 times more likely to commit an offence of violence than a member of the general population' (p.22), but being well aware of the methodological shakiness of this kind of extrapolation, emphasises that very rough-and-ready associations are perfectly adequate, at law, to establish the required inferential connection:

> [P]revious convictions work in a similar way to motive evidence. Previous convictions are probative because people with previous convictions are more likely to commit crime than those without previous convictions .... [E]ven if the figures are all reduced by a factor of ten, they still represent significant differences. If a person with previous convictions is only twice as likely to offend as someone without, that is still significant in terms of probative value. (pp.17, 25)

Legal commentators and practitioners today mostly accept the basic proposition that bad character evidence can be relevant, and sometimes highly probative, as a basis for inferring offending conduct. But relevancy only establishes a prima facie case for legal admissibility. Relevant evidence is excluded from criminal trials, on elementary common law principles, when its 'prejudicial effect' outweighs its 'probative value'; PE > PV in (my) notational shorthand. Both sides of this cost-benefit analysis invoke complex operative concepts. Probative value is highly contextual, and turns on the strategic conduct of criminal litigation, as well as substantive law definitions of offence categories, liability standards and eligible defences which fix evidential 'materiality' for the instant case. Prejudicial effect is even more intangible, partly because the adversarial parties and courts are making speculative – often counterfactual – assessments of how a jury *might* use information were it permitted access to it. These are judgements, in other words, of *potential* prejudicial effect. Evidence scholars and law reformers have identified different kinds of (potential) prejudice that might result from the jury's exposure to bad character evidence. The primary distinction is between 'moral prejudice' (aka 'bad man prejudice'), whereby the jury decides, self-consciously or otherwise and in defiance of its oath, that the accused deserves punishment *whether or not he is actually guilty of the instant charge*; and prejudicial reasoning (aka 'reasoning prejudice'), whereby the jury affords excessive probative value to extraneous bad character evidence and too easily draws an inference of guilt, albeit in a conscientious effort to assess the prosecution's case in proving the offence(s) for which the accused is on trial. Prejudice may also, in a third conceptual variation, arise from confusion, owing to the multiplication of charges or the proliferation of collateral issues and evidence associated with uncharged 'extraneous' misconduct.[53] Different varieties of prejudice may be cumulative and mutually aggravating.

Problems of prejudice are canvassed in Chapter 3 of CitCT, which draws liberally on behavioural science research and also introduces a Bayesian framework for the logical evaluation of evidence,[54] featuring the Likelihood Ratio as an objective measure of (conditional) probative value, which structures the discussion in later chapters. Redmayne points out that the jury's use of bad character evidence is, in principle, researchable empirically (p.34), even if there may be practical and legal obstacles to comprehensive investigation; and he is anxious that '[s]peculation about [common sense] default assumptions and jury reasoning is not a very satisfactory basis for an exclusionary rule' (p.38). In another valuable interdisciplinary conspectus and critical dissection of scholarly literature, Chapter 3 works its way through theoretical arguments and behavioural science and socio-legal empirical data bearing on the jury prejudice conjecture. There is, in fact, a sizeable research base, but the external validity of many studies is dubious (the complex dynamics of real-life criminal trials are not easily replicated in experimental research) and their findings must be interpreted with circumspection, especially if some researchers and commentators are not as careful in extrapolating reform implications as they ought to be. An equivocal, somewhat confusing picture emerges from the data, research reports and practical experiences surveyed, and Redmayne's headline conclusion, if typically cautious and fully reasoned, might also seem frustratingly non-committal:

> Is bad character evidence prejudicial? No one can answer that question with complete confidence. (p.60)

Redmayne is nonetheless willing to venture some granular conclusions. He does not think research findings 'support anything like a strict exclusionary rule for bad character evidence' (p.60). Even though automatic admissibility 'is not unthinkable' (p.62), however, he does not on balance favour complete reversal of common law orthodoxy, either. Redmayne's solution is moderately reformist and pragmatic:

> It is likely that criminal trials are awash with character inferences whether we like it or not. The best policy is surely not to ignore this by not mentioning character – and

[53] A good illustration is *R v O'Dowd* [2009] 2 Cr App R 16, [2009] EWCA Crim 905.

[54] For accessible explanations, see Mike Redmayne, 'Bayesianism and Proof' in Michael Freeman and Helen Reece (eds), *Science in Court* (Ashgate, 1998); Richard O Lempert, 'Analyzing Relevance' (1977) 75 *Michigan Law Review* 1021. For applications in forensic science, see Jackson, Aitken and Roberts, above n 12; Roberto Puch-Solis, Paul Roberts, Susan Pope and Colin Aitken, *Assessing the Probative Value of DNA Evidence* (Royal Statistical Society, 2012); Charles E H Berger, John Buckleton, Christophe Champod, Ian W Evett and Graham Jackson, 'Evidence Evaluation: A Response to the Court of Appeal Judgment in *R v T*' (2011) 51 *Science and Justice* 43.

> therefore letting whatever inferences fact-finders draw do their work uncorrected – but to let fact-finders know about a defendant's previous convictions, at least when they are relevant to guilt .... [T]he current English position is not as unattractive as it might first look. (pp.61, 62)

Much empirical research suggests that juries often simply ignore bad character evidence, or at least it has no discernible impact on their pre-existing assumptions about the defendants they observe in the dock. Only convictions of especially abhorrent crimes, such as child abuse, buck these experimental trends.[55] If offenders are typically generalists, as some criminological research posits, even previous convictions of offences wholly unrelated to the current charge may have some probative value in supporting the prosecution's case. It should be stressed that common sense reasoning is not unremittingly bad news for defendants. Empirical research lends credence to the idea that juries will punish prosecutors who try to make unfair use of tenuously relevant extraneous bad character. In one respect, however, Redmayne countenances a harder line than even common law orthodoxy tolerates: 'limiting instructions telling juries to use criminal record as a gauge of credibility but not of propensity do not work. The empirical evidence provides a strong case for dropping credibility uses of bad character evidence' (p.63). This concrete policy conclusion is taken forward into the doctrinal criticism developed in succeeding chapters.

IV. Doctrinal Jurisprudence

The admissibility and forensic uses of bad character evidence in criminal trials in England and Wales were systematically reformed by sections 98–113 of the Criminal Justice Act 2003 (CJA 2003). Section 99 promptly weighs in with the rather startling (if commendably concise) pronouncement that '[t]he common law rules governing the admissibility of evidence of bad character in criminal proceedings are abolished'. The CJA 2003's character evidence provisions substantially enacted the legislative scheme recommended by the Law Commission,[56] the estimable virtues of which, unfortunately, do not extend either to simplicity

[55] S Lloyd-Bostock, 'The Effects on Juries of Hearing About the Defendant's Previous Criminal Record: A Simulation Study' [2000] *Criminal Law Review* 734.

[56] Law Com No 273, *Evidence of Bad Character in Criminal Proceedings* Cm 5257 (TSO, 2001). One notable *conceptual* difference between the Law Commission's recommendations and the provisions as enacted was that the Commission proposed retaining the common law's rule of presumptive inadmissibility, stipulating an 'enhanced relevance' test as a precondition of admissibility for bad character evidence. The contrast is between an exclusionary rule with inclusionary exceptions (as the Law Commission favoured) and presumptive admissibility of relevant information with additional exclusionary criteria applicable to certain kinds of bad character evidence, the model adopted by the CJA 2003. Where both sets of criteria are similar in substance, the practical difference, if any, between the two styles of regulatory framework is not a function of legal doctrine, but rather of judicial culture, adversarial argument and factual reasoning.

or comprehensiveness. The law of *good* character evidence remains a recalcitrant creature of common law,[57] whilst the principal statutory provisions themselves are strongly informed by pre-existing common law thinking. The statute also inherited genetic weaknesses from unresolved policy agendas. The New Labour administration of the day aimed to sweep away 'technical' legal objections to admitting bad character evidence as proof of guilt,[58] but also wanted to protect complainants and other witnesses from unwarranted attacks on their credibility by reference to (allegations of) extraneous misconduct. So there was to be both more, and less, bad character evidence in English criminal trials. In character evidence law reform, sauce for the goose is not invariably basting for the gander.

Although the CJA 2003's character evidence provisions represent evolution rather than revolution in common law evidentiary doctrines, the enactment precipitated a veritable avalanche of case law, as each freshly minted statutory test, concept and phraseology was re-litigated to ascertain whether the pre-existing common law had survived intact or been transformed. Even the threshold concept of 'bad character' produced doctrinal perturbation.[59] The Court of Appeal, whilst willing to provide interpretative guidance in general terms, was soon warning criminal advocates against dressing up case-specific arguments or inflating fact-sensitive admissibility rulings into (appealable) fixed rules and general principles of law.[60] Judicial approaches to character evidence have always turned on fine-grained factual analysis, even if this has not always been clearly signalled in the leading precedents. Indeed, in US Evidence law teaching (contrasting with British legal education), the topic of character evidence is often taught as a contextual exemplification of relevancy doctrines,[61] mirroring its placement in the structure and classification of evidentiary topics popularised by the Federal Rules of Evidence.[62]

CitCT gets to grips with developments in English law in Chapters 5–10, comprising the doctrinal (hard)core of the exposition, some 130 pages or about half the book's substantive content. This balance of sustained doctrinal analysis

[57] See, eg, *R v Ahmed (Aneela)* [2015] 1 Cr App R 21, [2014] EWCA Crim 2466; *R v Junior* [2013] EWCA Crim 987.

[58] CJS, *Justice for All* Cm 5563 (TSO, 2002), paras 4.52–4.57; Home Office, *Criminal Justice: The Way Ahead* Cm 5074 (2001), paras 3.50–3.52.

[59] See Roderick Munday, 'What Constitutes "Other Reprehensible Behaviour" under the Bad Character Provisions of the Criminal Justice Act 2003?' [2005] *Criminal Law Review* 24; James Goudkamp, 'Bad Character Evidence and Reprehensible Behaviour' (2008) 12 *International Journal of Evidence & Proof* 116.

[60] In *R v Renda* [2006] 1 WLR 2948, [2005] EWCA Crim 2826, [3], for example, Sir Igor Judge P (as he then was) digressed, with almost palpable irritation: 'The creation and subsequent citation from a vast body of so-called "authority", in reality representing no more than observations on a fact-specific decision of the judge in the Crown Court, is unnecessary and may well be counter-productive .... The principles have been considered by this court on a number of occasions. The responsibility for their application is not for this court but for trial judges.'

[61] See, eg, Ronald J Allen, Richard B Kuhns, Eleanor Swift, David S Schwartz and Michael S Pardo, *Evidence: Text, Problems, and Cases*, 5th edn (Aspen, 2011) ch 5.

[62] The character evidence rules, including Rule 404 (above n 39), appear in Art IV FRE under the heading 'Relevance and its Limits'.

and criticism with equally extended theoretical reflection, and incorporating pertinent empirical data and other interdisciplinary perspectives, exemplifies what I call 'criminal jurisprudence', meaning 'jurisprudence' in both its Anglophone common law ('theory') and continental civilian ('case law', 'judicial practice') senses. Criminal jurisprudence, on my account,[63] takes both doctrinal analysis and normative theorising equally seriously. CitCT does not purport to offer a comprehensive treatise on character evidence in English law.[64] Important topics, such as character battles between co-accused and bad character evidence pertaining to non-defendants (plausibly encompassing the fissile material of complainants' previous sexual history evidence[65]), barely receive passing mention. Comprehensiveness is deliberately eschewed in order to subject selected core questions and problems to sustained jurisprudential analysis. At the heart of this exposition is critical reconsideration of the 'propensity inference'.

The propensity inference, in fact,[66] typically involves at least *two* successive, concatenated inferences: (1) a first inference from evidence of previous misconduct (including previous convictions, but in principle extending to any other evidence of past bad behaviour) to the intermediate inferential conclusion that the accused actually has a particular propensity, eg, to offend in a particular way or to commit certain kinds of crime, such as violent offences, or to commit crimes generally; and (2) a second inference from the existence of that propensity to the ultimate inferential conclusion that the accused is guilty of the offence(s) charged in the instant proceedings. Further inferences will almost always be required, factoring in all the other evidence in the case and drawing together the intermediate inferential conclusions derived from that body of evidence, to arrive at a final, integrated verdict. Propensity rarely[67] singlehandedly proves guilt of crime.

[63] See Chapter 1 of the present volume.

[64] See Roberts (n 47) ch 14; Ian H Dennis, *The Law of Evidence*, 8th edn (Sweet & Maxwell, 2024) chs 18–19; J R Spencer, *Evidence of Bad Character*, 2nd edn (Hart Publishing, 2009).

[65] But see Mike Redmayne, 'Myths, Relationships and Coincidences: The New Problems of Sexual History' (2003) 7 *International Journal of Evidence and Proof* 75.

[66] This is, I think, the most transparent way to conceptualise the relevant inferential process in general terms, though there are admittedly different – indeed, infinitely many – ways of individuating the logic of inference. Discussion of 'the propensity inference' suffers from idiomatic dissonance (eg, can you really have a *propensity* to walk to work every morning or to brush your teeth every night?), and often jumbles up ordinary conventional language with doctrinal concepts. Howsoever characterised, one first needs to establish previous misconduct (whether or not styled 'bad character', at law or elsewhere) by inference form evidence of that misconduct, before undertaking the further inferential step of using proven extraneous misconduct (intermediate inferential conclusion) to prove guilt of the instant charge (ultimate probandum). Redmayne sometimes writes as though 'the propensity inference' refers only to the second step in this intellectual process (eg, pp.112–16), but at other times he implicitly acknowledges both inferential steps, eg: 'The fact that previous convictions – or a single conviction – establish propensity does not mean that they establish a propensity to commit the currently charged offence' (pp.156–57).

[67] Or *never*, if one factors in inferential conclusions from 'missing evidence' (eg, the absence of a plausible alibi or justification) which tend to be overlooked in formal or doctrinal accounts of 'the evidence in the case'. See further, Dale A Nance, 'Missing Evidence' (1991) 13 *Cardozo Law Review* 831; Douglas Walton, 'Nonfallacious Arguments From Ignorance' (1992) 29 *American Philosophical Quarterly* 381.

But the propensity inference may lend additional probative force to other direct and circumstantial evidence of guilt and, when placed within the context of the totality of incriminating evidence in the case, play a possibly vital role in enabling the prosecution to satisfy the criminal standard of proof and secure a conviction. According to one version of common law orthodoxy, propensity inferences are forbidden in criminal trials.[68] However, as Chapter 5's historical retrospective on character evidence in English law prior to the CJA 2003 demonstrates, judicial practice – as reflected in reported appeals – belied doctrinal formalisms: 'the history shows a tendency for high admissibility standards to be proclaimed but then abandoned in practice' (p.109); 'creative judges had so much choice between similarity, probative value, categories, forbidden reasoning, and other criteria that almost any decision could be justified' (p.108); and 'the forbidden reasoning test frankly invited abuse' (p.99), producing an 'admissibility lottery' (p.104). My own view is that the supposed ban on propensity reasoning was never an authentic reading of English jurisprudence.[69]

The CJA 2003 rendered this particular doctrinal debate moot, because the Act goes out of its way to specify that propensity reasoning is permitted, both to guilt and to credit (ie, a propensity to lie, including perjurious lying on oath), so long as propensity is *relevant* to a material issue and logically supports the stated inferential conclusion.[70] Over the course of the previous century, English law had assimilated some highly dubious notions about the relevance and legal status of bad character evidence.[71] One of the more conspicuous successes of the 2003 Act, abetted by sensible judicial interpretation, has been to sweep away these cobwebs and restore assessments of relevance to the pristine logic of inferential reasoning.[72] Chapter 6 expounds this logic by isolating four recurrent patterns of reasoning from propensity. Redmayne cleverly shows that 'propensity reasoning' is implicated in many routine inferential conclusions in and beyond legal process, although it often remains submerged within conventional linguistic categories such as 'coincidence' and 'corroboration' or their noteworthy absence, which cloak the implicit logic of the propensity inference. Once the pervasiveness of propensity reasoning is recognised, and its logical role in supporting types of inferences that we intuitively grasp as epistemically well warranted is appreciated, the spell of supposedly 'forbidden reasoning' is broken. Freed from

[68] This is the idea incorporated into Rule 404 of the FRE (above n 39). Its best support in English law derives from *DPP v Boardman* [1975] AC 421 (HL) and *Makin v AG for New South Wales* [1894] AC 57 (PC).

[69] Cases that seem irreconcilable with the supposed ban on propensity reasoning include *R v Ball* [1911] AC 47 (HL), *Thompson v R* [1918] AC 221 (HL) and – ultimately the leading authority at common law – *R v P* [1991] 2 AC 447 (HL).

[70] CJA 2003, s 103.

[71] Including the dogma that all previous convictions went to credit, (almost) no matter how venial or stale: *R v Sweet-Escott* (1971) 55 Cr App R 316 (Derby Assizes); and the fiction that 'character is indivisible': *R v Winfield* [1939] 4 All ER 164 (CCA).

[72] Redmayne concurs: 'After the Act, judges see the relevance of previous behaviour differently' (p.149).

their ideological conditioning, common lawyers may revisit the logical plausibility of particular types of propensity inference and assess the probative value of any propensity-based inferential conclusion on its own, contextual merits. Applying this theoretical framework to common law approaches, Redmayne observes that many reported cases partially track the intuitive logic of character-based reasoning. Yet lacking a clear apprehension and focus on comparative propensity, judicial reasoning is often obscure and misleading, and admissibility tests sometimes result in the exclusion of probative information – an undeserved forensic windfall to defendants. Common law judicial categories did not articulate the primary variables that should logically determine admissibility, in terms of comparative propensity, strength of linkage between propensity and conduct, and the relationship between propensity reasoning and other evidence in the case. Consequently, concludes Redmayne, 'the lessons to be drawn from the pre-2003 case law are largely negative':

> [T]his is not the way to do things. Ultimately, none of the approaches taken by the courts worked well in all scenarios .... [C]ourts end up picking and choosing from a multitude of tests. There are even few words of wisdom to take from the case law, because judicial pronouncements on propensity evidence were so often muddled. (p.144)

Does the admissibility framework introduced by the CJA 2003, with its seven admissibility 'gateways' and their burgeoning interpretive jurisprudence, fare any better when tested against the logical structure of propensity inferences elucidated in Chapter 6? Although the report card tallied through Chapters 7–10 is not unblemished, Redmayne finds much to praise in the reformed law – starting with the elementary improvement that 'the CJA states clearly that evidence of misconduct is admissible to show propensity' (p.149). Beyond that, the leading case of *Hanson*[73] 'does a decent job of outlining key features of the concept of comparative propensity [and] ... made a promising start to placing the law on a more rational footing' (p.151); and the Court of Appeal's decisive ruling in *Campbell*[74] restricting the scope for propensity reasoning to credit 'gets it more or less right' (p.203) by effectively 'kill[ing] off the credibility limb of gateway (d)' (p.199). Courts have rejected the misguided notion that propensity cannot be relied upon to establish a case to answer (pp.163–64); the logical position on previous acquitted misconduct evidence carved out by the House of Lords in *R v Z*[75] has rightly been retained (pp.188–89); '[t]he good character direction is taken very seriously by the Court of Appeal' (p.217), and this is, on balance, a defensible approach. Given the practical exigencies of contested criminal trials, 'such evidence can

[73] *R v Hanson, Gilmore and Pickstone* [2005] 1 WLR 316, [2005] EWCA Crim 824.

[74] *R v Campbell (Kenneth)* [2007] 1 WLR 2798, [2007] EWCA Crim 1472. Also see Peter Mirfield, 'Character and Credibility' [2009] *Criminal Law Review* 135.

[75] *R v Z* [2000] 2 AC 483 (HL), critically analysed in Paul Roberts, 'Acquitted Misconduct Evidence and Double Jeopardy Principles, From *Sambasivam* to *Z*' [2000] *Criminal Law Review* 952.

play an important role in rebutting the jury's assumptions about defendants' (p.220). Overall:

> In the vast majority of cases, judges are now happy to embrace the idea of propensity. This sea change could not have been predicted with confidence: denial and doublethink might have continued, but by and large they have not. In terms of intellectual honesty, this can only be a good thing. (p.194)

On the negative side of the balance sheet, however, 'courts do not always give the relevance questions the attention they deserve' (p.162); and 'there is something to the complaint that the Court of Appeal has gone too far in leaving trial judges to their own devices' (p.172). More fundamentally, '[t]he reasoning underlying the use of propensity evidence continues to be misunderstood' (p.172), and whilst 'sometimes the confusion is harmless, at other times it can be prejudicial … because it may mean that the evidence does not get the scrutiny it deserves' (ibid) or creates tangible risks of unfair 'double-counting' to the detriment of the accused (p.194). 'Especially troublesome in the case law has been the distinction between propensity and coincidence reasoning' (p.172). 'Defendants are treated unfairly when lawyers fail to understand how to reason with bad character evidence' (p.194). But the most blatant defect of the existing admissibility framework must be laid at the door of the legislature rather than the judges, inasmuch as 'gateway (g)' of section 101 CJA 2003, explicitly authorises tit-for-tat retaliation lacking any rational foundation in the logic of inferential reasoning from propensity or otherwise:

> The continued use of tit for tat under gateway (g) is indefensible. This provision attaches a price to legitimate defence, a price which sometimes involves the revelation of stale convictions. Juries are asked to make fine distinctions between credibility and propensity, distinctions which we have little reason to believe they will make. The justifications for tit for tat are for the most part risible. We would be far better off without gateway (g). (p.215)

Amen to that.[76] As we wrote in *Roberts and Zuckerman*, 'sometimes the interests of justice may need to be rescued from the clutches of political opportunism',[77] notwithstanding Parliament's evidently contrary (or conflicted) intentions.

Chapters 7–10 constitute a substantial and enduring contribution to critical commentary on the CJA 2003. There is plenty to engage the aficionado – many of the cases Redmayne discusses are unreported, and few readers will be familiar with them all – whilst strong central themes and brisk narrative progression, without getting bogged down in doctrinalism, should ensure accessibility for the more generalist reader and captivate wider interest. Of course, Redmayne's

[76] To similar effect, see Paul Roberts, 'All the Usual Suspects: A Critical Appraisal of Law Commission Consultation Paper No.141' [1997] *Criminal Law Review* 75; Peter Mirfield 'The Argument from Consistency for Overruling *Selvey*' (1991) 50 *Cambridge Law Journal* 490.

[77] Roberts (n 47) 651.

analysis is selective, and the flow of new cases is unrelenting.[78] Featured decisions should be taken as emblematic of recurrent doctrinal arguments and broader patterns of judicial reasoning. In this respect Redmayne's timing was propitious because, after over a decade's experience with the new statutory framework, the Court of Appeal had more or less got its main doctrinal stories straight – which is not to deny the existence of unresolved controversies and elements of judicial backsliding.[79] Given its firm theoretical foundations, Redmayne's analysis will remain current notwithstanding predictable churn in the case law. Some of the admissibility rulings[80] and passages of judicial reasoning[81] discussed in CitCT are highly fact-specific; or, perhaps, best treated as if they were. One can always quibble with doctrinal trifles.[82] But if Redmayne's evaluations of this evolving jurisprudential corpus are equivocal or flirt with contradiction in places, this is chiefly a mark of the commentator's fidelity to prevailing institutional realities, reflecting persistent reasoning errors and enduring doctrinal defects.

[78] Now also see, eg, *R v Green* [2025] EWCA Crim 923; *R v BEF* [2023] EWCA Crim 1362; *R v Pierini* [2024] 1 Cr App R 15, [2023] EWCA Crim 1189; *R v Virdee* [2023] EWCA Crim 786; *R v Dixon-Kenton* [2021] EWCA Crim 6773; *R v Gabbana* [2020] 4 WLR 160, [2020] EWCA Crim 1473; *R v Mitchell* [2017] AC 571, [2016] UKSC 55; *R v Platt* [2016] EWCA Crim 4; *R v Khan and Rahman* [2015] EWCA Crim 1755; *R v Hodgkinson* [2015] EWCA Crim 1509; *R v Fitzpatrick* [2015] EWCA Crim 1286; *R v Hunter* [2015] 1 WLR 5367, [2015] EWCA Crim 631.

[79] See further, Gareth Branston, 'A Reprehensible Use of Cautions as Bad Character Evidence?' [2015] *Criminal Law Review* 594; J R Spencer, 'Cautions as Character Evidence: A Reply to Judge Branston' [2015] *Criminal Law Review* 611; Phil Huxley, 'Mental Gymnastics and Intellectual Acrobatics: The Meanings of Statutory and Common Law "Bad Character"' (2011) 75 *Journal of Criminal Law* 132; Roderick Munday, 'Single-Act Propensity' (2010) 74 *Journal of Criminal Law* 127; Colin Tapper, 'The Law of Evidence and the Rule of Law' (2009) 68 *Cambridge Law Journal* 67.

[80] For example, *R v Lamaletie* [2008] EWCA Crim 314 and *R v Lafayette* [2008] EWCA Crim 3238 are castigated for encouraging 'one of the most embarrassing aspects of the old law [to] linger[] on' (p.206), namely the direction to juries that extraneous bad character may be used to assess the accused's credibility as a witness but not as direct proof of guilt. Such directions have been the source of much judicial logic-chopping and animadversions on implausible 'mental gymnastics': see, eg, *R v Koc* [2008] EWCA Crim 77; *R v McLeod* [1995] 1 Cr App R 591 (CA); *R v Powell* (1986) 82 Cr App R 165 (CA); *R v Watts* (1983) 77 Cr App R 126 (CA).

[81] Of a line of sexual assault cases traceable to *R v Sully* [2007] EWCA Crim 3512, Redmayne laconically remarks: 'It is probably not helpful to label certain offenders as abnormal' (p.155).

[82] Redmayne suggests a quibble with me (fnn 77 and 100, ch 8), but the point seems to be semantic. When I wrote that 'evidence of a sequence of strikingly similar [events] is different from, and greater than, the sum of its individual parts' and that the evidential value of previously acquitted misconduct 'changes in the light of new discoveries and with the benefit of hindsight' (Roberts n 75, 958), I meant only that its probative significance for the original or any subsequent trials is relative to the entirety of relevant information at any given moment in time. In cases involving incriminating patterns of behaviour, '[i]t is *the sequence* of events in its totality which constitutes cogent proof' (ibid) rather than discrete events viewed in isolation or with missing links. I am not sure if Redmayne is really saying anything different by insisting that 'the evidence in the original trial is worth exactly what it always was, we simply have more evidence' (p.188, fn 77). Perhaps the point is only that probative value is indexed to temporally fixed epistemic situations, and *that* is not altered by hindsight, except counterfactually ('what we would have believed had we known …'). Orthodox (subjective) Bayesianism propounds a *conditional*, and thus contingently relativistic, conception of evidential weight.

V. Character and the Book of Life

Even a lengthy review must flatten out some of the nuances, digressions and incidental insights of a major, extensively researched and meticulously reasoned monograph. But I trust that enough has been said to communicate CitCT's central arguments and methodological virtues, whilst persuading specialist Evidence scholars and criminal law theorists of the absolute necessity of engaging directly with this rich text and forming their own critical judgements. Redmayne early on informs his readers that '[t]he focus of much of the book … is on the law of evidence' (p.8), but – unless this review has been a miserable failure – any lingering suspicions of narrowly evidentiary preoccupations should hopefully have been dispelled.

Redmayne confesses in the book's Preface to grander ambitions, including an unfulfilled wish to incorporate more comparative material. Comparative analysis,[83] encompassing an emergent international criminal procedure[84] and the broader cosmopolitan context of contemporary evidentiary norms and scholarship,[85] would certainly be a profitable direction for further research on character evidence in criminal trials, or on just about any imaginable topic in criminal evidence and procedure. But I am not sure that it would have materially improved the coherence of this monograph or enhanced its jurisprudential significance. More is not necessarily more. Besides, it is idle to speculate on what might have been. Mike Redmayne was an industrious and exceptionally talented legal scholar, an original thinker, a master of counterintuitive legal argument and the clipped *coup de grâce*. His writing was a model of clarity in both thought and expression. CitCT hones these qualities to the pinnacle of accomplishment. It is a fine bequest to legal scholarship, and a fitting tribute to its author's character.

[83] Stewart Field, 'State, Citizen, and Character in French Criminal Process' (2006) 33 *Journal of Law and Society* 522; Roderick Munday, 'Comparative Law and English Law's Character Evidence Rules' (1993) 13 *Oxford Journal of Legal Studies* 589; Mirjan R Damaška, 'Propensity Evidence in Continental Legal Systems' (1994) 70 *Chicago-Kent Law Review* 55.

[84] See, eg, John D Jackson and Yassin M Brunger, 'Fragmentation and Harmonization in the Development of Evidentiary Practices in International Criminal Tribunals' in Elies van Sliedregt and Sergey Vasiliev (eds), *Pluralism in International Criminal Law* (OUP, 2014); Paul Roberts 'The Priority of Procedure and the Neglect of Evidence and Proof: Facing Facts in International Criminal Law' (2015) 13 *Journal of International Criminal Justice* 479; Nancy A Combs, *Fact-Finding without Facts* (CUP, 2010).

[85] For elucidation, see Paul Roberts, 'Normative Evolution in Evidentiary Exclusion: Coercion, Deception and the Right to a Fair Trial' in Paul Roberts and Jill Hunter (eds), *Criminal Evidence and Human Rights* (Hart Publishing, 2012); Dimitrios Giannoulopoulos, 'Custodial Legal Assistance and Notification of the Right to Silence in France: Legal Cosmopolitanism and Local Resistance' (2013) 24 *Criminal Law Forum* 291; John D Jackson and Sarah J Summers, *The Internationalisation of Criminal Evidence* (CUP, 2012).

8

Envisioning International Criminal Justice

BioNote: Rob Cryer joined the Department of Law (as it then was) at Nottingham as an LLM student a few years after I was hired to a lectureship. Having excelled on the LLM in International Law and Armed Conflict, he stayed on at Nottingham to write his PhD, supervised by Nigel White and Dino Kritsiotis. I came to know Rob well through participation in staff seminars and countless informal conversations about law, music and football. As recounted in the following pages, Rob's influence was prominent in my initial thinking about setting up and populating a dedicated LLM in International Criminal Justice, in collaboration with Nigel and Dino. Rob Cryer would go on to become one of the UK's leading scholars and pioneering disciplinary architects of International Criminal Law. This chapter contains further biographical information indicating the scale of Rob's professional achievements and scholarly contribution.[1]

To say that Rob lived his life in scholarship is not to imply that he never did anything else. Early doors, he occasionally kept goal for the law department staff five-a-side football team (though lacking Nigel's height advantage or Andrew Simester's agility). He travelled, went to gigs, collected guitars, binge-watched *Buffy the Vampire Slayer* and ate a lot of late-night curries. In later life, with the security of a professorial income, he acquired many collectable first editions. But invariably, whatever else he was doing at the time, the conversation would veer back to some knotty problem in legal theory or international law. Those who are fully immersed in the life of the mind are never truly off the clock.

I was briefly Rob's personal tutor, but he was more like a colleague than a student long before he was appointed to the staff. At one of many convivial evenings at his house, a group of us watched England fail (again) at the Euros, and he house-sat for me whilst I was in South Africa during my first period of study leave. After Rob left Nottingham to take up his chair at Birmingham Law School, our contact became less frequent, but it was always a real pleasure to see him back in the common room on one of his return visits to contribute to short courses on armed conflict law for Services personnel run by Nigel, Dino,

[1] Emma J Breeze, Mark Drumbl, Gerry Simpson and Marianne Wade (eds), *The Character of International Law: A Festschrift for Rob Cryer* (Hart Publishing, 2025).

and – after his return to Nottingham from Liverpool – Dominic McGoldrick. The last time I saw Rob was on one of these occasions, when we were able to tour some of our old Beeston haunts, middle-aged moderation now preserving us from the morning hangovers which would have been the inevitable consequence of these outings in our youth.

It was a terrible shock to learn of Rob's death in the midst of Covid-lockdown in early January 2021, and just a few weeks after my mother had died in hospital in very difficult circumstances. I hadn't realised that Rob was so gravely ill. He was just 46 years old, six years my junior. In the final days of leading on the School of Law's REF submission, lingering grief was a luxury that my schedule could not indulge, but I do remember the combined loss feeling like a physical body-blow. I am not sure where I found the strength to write back-to-back eulogies, inadequate though they both must have been. Rob was a larger-than-life character, a humanitarian who threw himself into research, teaching and scholarship with passion and verve. He enriched the lives of his international collaborators, colleagues, students and friends, and made an indelible mark on his discipline. No half measures with Rob: an inspirational life in scholarship if ever there were one.[2]

I. Daydream Believers

International criminal justice is first and foremost a work of visionary idealism. For most of the twentieth century, the primacy of ideals was self-evident: in the absence of live international criminal prosecutions or other concrete institutional embodiments, on either side of the sui generis post-WWII tribunals, coherent conceptions of international criminal justice lived only in the fertile imaginations of law reformers, planners and dreamers.[3] Frenetic institutional innovation and rapid normative development during the 1990s[4] transformed international criminal law into a living, breathing, censuring and sanctioning system of international penal justice. Thirty years on, it is easy to lose sight of just how recently all this impressive juridical architecture existed, for the most part,[5] only in the minds of prophets and visionaries.

[2] Nigel D White and Eric Myjer, 'In Memory of Professor Rob Cryer' (2021) 26 *Journal of Conflict and Security Law* 1; Neil Boister, Darryl Robinson, Sergey Vasiliev, Martins Paparinskis, Meagan Wong and Ioannis Kalpouzos 'In Memoriam: Robert Cryer, b. 2 August 1974 – d. 3 January 2021' (2021) 19 *Journal of International Criminal Justice* 235.

[3] Timothy L H McCormack, 'From Sun Tzu to the Sixth Committee: The Evolution of an International Criminal Law Regime' in Timothy L H McCormack and Gerry J Simpson (eds), *The Law of War Crimes: National and International Approaches* (Kluwer, 1997); Georg Schwarzenberger, 'The Problem of an International Criminal Law' (1950) 3 *Current Legal Problems* 263.

[4] For an engaging tour de horizon, see Gary Jonathan Bass, Sta*y the Hand of Vengeance: The Politics of War Crimes Tribunals* (Princeton University Press, 2000).

[5] The doctrinal corpus of international criminal law, such as it was, had to be reconstructed from miscellaneous suppression conventions and fragmentary municipal legal practice. See Lyal S Sunga, *The Emerging System of International Criminal Law* (Kluwer, 1997).

This chapter is concerned with the genesis of international criminal justice as a distinct disciplinary field, chiefly in response to global events and responsive institution-building in the 1990s and 2000s. The discussion is anchored in one fragment of local institutional history: the launch and development of the LLM in International Criminal Justice and Armed Conflict at the University of Nottingham. Rob Cryer was intimately involved in this pioneering venture and, especially in subsequent years when he also taught on the programme, actively shaped its content. In light of the novelty of the subject-matter and its fresh conceptualisations and innovative modes of delivery (described below), this formative influence could not fail to animate Rob's teaching philosophy and spur the discipline-generative body of scholarship he had already begun to produce.[6]

David Sugarman suggests that legal (auto)biography 'not only appeals to a universal human interest in gossip, but answers a need within us to understand each other better'.[7] Mitigating undeniable risks of narcissism and sentimentality, I aim to synthesise more general lessons from this personal memoir. The progressive, organic and programmatic 'disciplining' of international criminal justice is a case-study in the evolution of specialist legal sub-fields. It exposes the institutional preconditions for successful disciplinary formation and resilience and showcases, in particular, the value to scholarship of research-led teaching. The following account draws on contemporary documentation (my filing cabinets), digital archives (my computer files) and first-hand testimony (personal memories), in the manner of law school oral history.[8] Rob Cryer lived the intellectual history of international criminal justice in its modern disciplinary incarnation, and I was fortunate to be one of his earliest travelling companions on the metaphorical road 'from Nuremberg to Rome'. This essay tells the tale of how this somewhat unexpected journey began and unfolded and what, with the benefit of hindsight, it taught me about pedagogy, collegiality, scholarship and jurisprudence.

II. Dream, Dream, Dream: Inventing International Criminal Justice

Curriculum formation and development in university-based legal education retain an enigmatic quality. Aside from box-ticking review exercises and

[6] Robert Cryer, 'A Commentary on the Rome Statute for an International Criminal Court: A Cadenza for the Song of Those Who Died in Vain?' (1998) 3 *Journal of Armed Conflict Law* 271; Robert Cryer, 'The Boundaries of Liability in International Criminal Law, or "Selectivity by Stealth"' (2001) 6 *Journal of Conflict and Security Law* 3; Robert Cryer, 'A "Special Court" for Sierra Leone?' (2001) 50 *International and Comparative Law Quarterly* 435.

[7] David Sugarman, 'From Legal Biography to Legal Life Writing: Broadening Conceptions of Legal History and Socio-Legal Scholarship' (2015) 42 *Journal of Law and Society* 7, 8.

[8] *Cf* Lesley Dingle, 'Legal Oral Histories in the Cambridge ESA: Some Examples of Researching Personal, Institutional and Social Developments' (2019) 19 *Legal Information Management* 192; Gwynedd Parry, 'Is Legal Biography Really Legal Scholarship?' (2010) 30 *Legal Studies* 208; Fiona Cownie, *Legal Academics: Culture and Identities* (Hart Publishing, 2004).

endless redrafting of pro forma module 'specifications' and 'learning outcomes' (recited in *nomenklatura* Dalek), it is rarely discussed with much intellectual seriousness. Undergraduates studying Law in the UK might easily presume that orthodox taxonomies of legal material neatly packaged into discrete 'subjects' have existed, more or less in their currently recognisable form, for many decades if not centuries. Academic law tends to live in the now, with pervasive disciplinary amnesia.[9]

The standard Law School curricular subdivisions betray few hints of their deliberate creation through the modern 'textbook tradition'.[10] These texts were written by scholar-teachers seeking to cater for rapidly expanding university-based legal education, a project which gathered momentum in the wake of the influential Robbins Report in 1963[11] and was further catalysed by the creation of another cohort of 'new' universities after 1992.[12] The sprawling, undisciplined realities of law in practice had to be reduced, reordered and repackaged to meet the pragmatic demands and pedagogical objectives of law teachers and their students. And so the familiar law school diet of 'Criminal Law', 'Law of Contract', 'Torts', etc came into being, selectively sampling primary materials and only faintly echoing the day-to-day realities of legal practice.

The value and importance of placing law in context,[13] and of associated pedagogical developments such as clinical legal education,[14] are nowadays taken as read in UK law schools. In this atmospheric sense at least, 'we are all socio-legal now'.[15] Yet no reductive criticism of traditional law teaching is implied. To the contrary, the vision, skill and industry of these textbook-writing disciplinary architects should be recognised and celebrated. If law school were merely professional 'trade' education, designed and delivered as training for legal practice, it would barely deserve its place in the modern university.

[9] Peter Goodrich, 'R.I.A. to R.A.E.: Aporia and Amour Propre in the Legal Academy' (2006) 15 *Social & Legal Studies* 129.

[10] David Sugarman, 'Legal Theory, the Common Law Mind and the Making of the Textbook Tradition' in William Twining (ed), *Legal Theory and Common Law* (Basil Blackwell, 1986).

[11] Committee on Higher Education, *Report*, Cmnd 2154 (HMSO, 1963) (describing the immediate need for expansion in university places as 'an emergency of the same importance as the emergency produced by demobilisation after the last war and demanding the same type of extraordinary measures to meet it').

[12] Further and Higher Education Act 1992, s 77. The term 'new' university was recycled throughout the course of the twentieth century to apply to successive phases of development in British higher education. The University of Nottingham, formally founded in 1948, is arguably the oldest 'new' British university, closer in time to the 1960s plate glass and concrete campuses than to the nineteenth-century civic 'red bricks'.

[13] Roscoe Pound, 'Law in Books and Law in Action' (1910) 44 *American Law Review* 12; Karl N Llewellyn, 'Law and the Social Sciences – Especially Sociology' (1949) 62 *Harvard Law Review* 1286.

[14] Ross Cranston, 'Law and Society: A Different Approach to Legal Education' (1978) 5 *Monash University Law Review* 54.

[15] Fiona Cownie and Anthony Bradney, 'Socio-Legal Studies: A Challenge to the Doctrinal Approach' in Dawn Watkins and Mandy Burton (eds), *Research Methods in Law*, 2nd edn (Routledge, 2017); *cf* Richard Collier, '"We're All Socio-Legal Now?" Legal Education, Scholarship and the "Global Knowledge Economy" – Reflections on the UK Experience' (2004) 26 *Sydney Law Review* 503.

My point is simply that the disciplinary contours of contemporary legal education are more recent and selective than most law students ever appreciate, and few law teachers typically pause to acknowledge. After all, the entire system of university legal education, at least in the common law world,[16] was constructed essentially from scratch from the late nineteenth century onwards.[17]

Curriculum development has, in reality, always been a routine and continuous part of law teaching. New law school 'subjects' have been added to augment the curricular core on a rolling basis, responsive to the changing complexion of law in politics, society and culture. Family Law, Employment Law, European Law, Environmental Law, Public International Law and Human Rights Law readily spring to mind as significant additions to UK law schools' disciplinary offer during the post-Robbins period. An emergent specialism in International Criminal Justice would later follow a similar institutional dynamic and trajectory.

When I first encountered Rob Cryer at the University of Nottingham in the mid-1990s, there was no International Criminal Court, the jurisdictional competence of UN Security Council ad hoc tribunals remained highly contentious,[18] and the ICTY had yet to conclude a single trial. Having graduated from the LLM in International Law and Armed Conflict in 1996, Rob had begun his PhD research on international criminal prosecutions,[19] which he would eventually work up into his first published monograph.[20] In those days, any mention of international criminal law would typically be met with blank expressions from all but a handful of specialists. When trying to explain his research topic in casual conversation, Rob sometimes mentioned the post-WWII Nuremberg and Tokyo international military tribunals.[21] This popular reference might garner some flicker of recognition,

[16] David Sugerman, 'Making Respected Gentlemen out of Law Professors. A Commentary on Albert Venn Dicey, Can English Law Be Taught at the Universities?' in Isabella Löhr, Matthias Middell and Hannes Siegrist (eds), *Kultur und Beruf in Europa* (Franz Steiner Verlag, 2012); R C van Caenegem, *Judges, Legislators and Professors: Chapters in European Legal History* (CUP, 1987).

[17] William Twining, *Blackstone's Tower: The English Law School* (Sweet & Maxwell, 1994) (observing that 'the modern English law school is in most important respects a post Second World War creation', with the caveat that '[a]s late as 1900 most of the academic subjects we know today had either barely been accepted in the university or had not been invented'); Steve Sheppard, 'Casebooks, Commentaries, and Curmudgeons: An Introductory History of Law in the Lecture Hall' (1997) 82 *Iowa Law Review* 547.

[18] Colin Warbrick and Peter Rowe, 'The International Criminal Tribunal for Yugoslavia: The Decision of the Appeals Chamber on the Interlocutory Appeal on Jurisdiction in the *Tadic* Case' (1996) 45 *International and Comparative Law Quarterly* 691 (observing that '[t]he significance of the decision of the Appeals Chamber cannot be underestimated', and asking rhetorically: 'What if it had reached the opposite conclusion? Would the lights have been turned out and the microphones switched off?'); Hazel Fox, 'The Objections to Transfer of Criminal Jurisdiction to the UN Tribunal' (1997) 46 *International and Comparative Law Quarterly* 434.

[19] Completed as Cryer, *Towards an Integrated Regime for the Prosecution of International Crimes* (2000), eprints.nottingham.ac.uk/11305/ (accessed 17 December 2025).

[20] Robert Cryer, *Prosecuting International Crimes: Selectivity and the International Criminal Law Regime* (CUP, 2005).

[21] This proved to be an enduring research interest: Neil Boister and Robert Cryer, *The Tokyo International Military Tribunal – A Reappraisal* (OUP, 2008).

but only at the risk of being mistaken for a legal historian. Beyond the realms of public international law, certainly, 'Nuremberg'[22] was regarded as an arcane topic of merely antiquarian interest. I was insulated from this widespread misconception only through accidental proximity with Nottingham's well-established tradition in teaching and research on the international law of armed conflict. I had it directly from Hilaire McCoubrey[23] that individual criminal responsibility for war crimes was a topic of contemporary legal salience, if only in the jurisdictionally discrete and – as a law school subject – marginal context of military justice.

Disciplinary specialisms may arise from law teachers' imaginative responses to events in the world, but they develop, thrive and endure only through institutionalisation. Concrete expressions of institutionalisation are manifold and, for the most part, mutually reinforcing. They include specialist modules, degree programmes, journals, societies and associations, research centres and, of course, textbooks and other dedicated resources to support teaching and its dissemination across the sector. All of this pedagogic and discipline-forming activity will ideally be underpinned by high-quality research and innovative scholarship, but there is no guarantee that scholarship will translate into curriculum development or that law teaching will be research-led. Harnessing synergies between research and teaching requires self-conscious choices and directed efforts. It presupposes an inclusive conception of scholarly activity in which postgraduate students, and preferably undergraduates too, are regarded as an integral part of the university research environment and valued contributors to the wider research ecosystem and culture.

For a masterclass in how to institutionalise a new disciplinary specialism, one need look no further than the development of human rights law at Nottingham, led by David Harris.[24] When I joined the law department, Harris and colleagues were in the process of setting up what became Nottingham's flagship Human Rights Law Centre (HRLC).[25] This was closely linked to the teaching of bespoke

[22] Joseph E Persico, *Nuremberg: Infamy on Trial* (Penguin, 1994); Telford Taylor, *The Anatomy of the Nuremberg Trial* (Little, Brown & Co, 1993). The historical 'Nuremberg' encompassed much more than the famous trial of high-ranking Nazis and political and military leadership: see Matthew Lippman, 'The Other Nuremberg: American Prosecutions of Nazi War Criminals in Occupied Germany' (1992) 2 *Indiana International and Comparative Law Review* 1.

[23] McCoubrey left Nottingham for Hull in 1995 to assume a professorship and found the Centre that now bears his name. His death was, like Rob's, tragically premature: see Nigel White and Eric Myjer, 'Editorial' (2000) 5 *Journal of Conflict and Security Law* 131; Richard Burchill, Nigel D White and Justin Morris (eds), *International Conflict and Security Law: Essays in Memory of Hilaire McCoubrey* (CUP, 2005).

[24] Behind which stretches a much longer departmental history establishing Nottingham's reputation as a 'legal textbook factory'. Landmark contributions to student-orientated publications include: Harry Street, *The Law of Torts* (Butterworths, 1955); J C Smith and J A C Thomas, *A Casebook on Contract* (Sweet & Maxwell, 1957); J C Smith and Brian Hogan, *Criminal Law* (Butterworths, 1965); David J Harris, *Cases and Materials on International Law* (Sweet & Maxwell, 1973); Stephen H Bailey, David J Harris and B L Jones, *Civil Liberties: Cases and Materials* (Butterworths, 1980); Peter F Smith and Stephen H Bailey, *The Modern English Legal System* (Sweet & Maxwell, 1984). Prominent additions to this roster since the early 1990s are too numerous to list.

[25] www.nottingham.ac.uk/hrlc/ (accessed 17 December 2025).

LLM modules and a new degree pathway. Although this postgraduate provision built directly on the success of Nottingham's existing LLM in International Law, a conscious decision was taken to badge both Centre and LLM as 'human rights law' rather than 'international human rights law', to ensure that 'human rights' would not be interpreted narrowly as a sub-specialism within PIL. The prescience of this decision would be emphatically vindicated within five years by the advent of the Human Rights Act 1998, by which time nobody could seriously think that 'human rights' was a topic of interest only to international lawyers.[26] Its deliberately expansive conceptualisation and inclusive agenda attracted me to participate in the HRLC's inaugural planning meetings, despite having no PIL background whatsoever. The expanding research portfolio of the Centre and the instant success of the LLM degree programme were soon reinforced by a pioneering textbook[27] and a dedicated *Human Rights Law Review*,[28] originally published in-house by Nottingham University Press and subsequently adopted by OUP.[29] LLM programmes are excellent breeding grounds for talented and inspired PhD students, who in time replenish and expand the ranks of legal scholars and law teachers, replicating the best features of their own student experience and enriching the disciplinary corpus with new ideas, courses and publications. A sole law teacher's module is, at best, a cult of personality with a temporal horizon delimited by one individual's academic career. Once institutionalised and disseminated through degree programmes, textbooks, journals, and centres, however, disciplinary specialisms become endowed with stabilising characteristics of mass, vitality, and endurance somewhat reminiscent of evangelical religions.

In this intellectually stimulating and creative environment, it soon occurred to me that there could, and should, be more to criminal law teaching in the department beyond the conventional parameters of the undergraduate core module[30] and the more penology-orientated undergraduate elective on Criminal Justice and the Penal System.[31] The LLM in Human Rights Law afforded an accommodating

[26] *Cf* the range of topics surveyed in Helen Fenwick, Roger Masterman and Gavin Phillipson (eds), *Judicial Reasoning Under the UK Human Rights Act* (CUP, 2007); Alastair Mowbray, *Cases, Materials, and Commentary on the European Convention on Human Rights*, 3rd edn (OUP, 2012).

[27] David J Harris, Michael O'Boyle and C Warbrick, *Law of the European Convention on Human Rights* (OUP, 1995). Now see David J Harris, Michael O'Boyle, Ed Bates and Carla M Buckley, *Harris, O'Boyle, and Warbrick: Law of the European Convention on Human Rights*, 5th edn (OUP, 2023).

[28] Launched in 2001: see www.nottingham.ac.uk/hrlc/publications/humanrightslawreview.aspx (accessed 17 December 2025).

[29] academic.oup.com/hrlr (accessed 17 December 2025). Now in its 24th volume, the current Editor-in-Chief is Dominic McGoldrick and scholars with a Nottingham connection remain very well-represented on the Editorial Board.

[30] Also see Peter Alldridge 'What's Wrong with the Traditional Criminal Law Course?' (1990) 10 *Legal Studies* 38; Nicola Lacey, Celia Wells and Dirk Meure, *Reconstructing Criminal Law: Text and Materials* (Weidenfeld, 1990); Colin Sumner (ed), *Censure, Politics and Criminal Justice* (Open University Press, 1990).

[31] Michael Cavadino and James Dignan, *The Penal System: An Introduction*, 2nd edn (Sage, 1997); Andrew von Hirsch and Andrew Ashworth (eds), *Principled Sentencing: Readings on Theory and Policy*, 2nd edn (Hart Publishing, 1998).

structure for injecting elements of criminal justice into masters-level teaching. As originally conceived and first offered in 1996, my 'Comparative Criminal Justice' module was a (benign) Trojan horse for smuggling material on penal theory and domestic criminal process into an overarching degree programme still at that point styled the 'LLM in International Law'. With the benefit of classroom experience and in response to jurisprudential developments in the wider world, the module offerings progressively became more relevant, focused and conceptually coherent. I split off the theoretical material into a dedicated module on the Philosophical Foundations of Human Rights and Criminal Justice.[32] The criminal process content forked in two directions. A module on Fair Trials, Human Rights and Criminal Justice took criminal adjudication as a locus for productive engagement between overlapping, but still largely siloed and estranged, 'criminal justice' and 'human rights' literatures.[33] A second module on Comparative Criminal Justice limped on for a while with small but enthusiastic cohorts before being rebranded, refreshed and relaunched in 2009 as 'Globalisation and Criminal Justice'.

Co-taught with Dirk van Zyl Smit, and in consequence now tilted more towards transnational criminal justice, penal systems and policy transfers, the Globalisation module ran for six years.[34] It was, from my perspective, highly successful both as a vehicle for expanding disciplinary horizons and in recruiting healthy numbers of students. An average of 5–10 annual enrolments for Comparative Criminal Justice instantly became 25–30 for Globalisation. The power of effective (including intramural) advertising in postgraduate legal education should not be underestimated, because no matter how engaging and relevant a module's content, coverage and approach might be, students will never reap the educational rewards unless they are first enticed to walk through the classroom door. Leveraging events in the news is one surefire way of generating student interest: our module specification name-checked Julian Assange and the Wikileaks scandal, a prominent evolving story in contemporary media headlines.[35] Whilst a globalisation-orientated syllabus promised to 'investigate issues that cut across national borders and territorial boundaries and shed new light on the fundamental questions of contemporary criminal justice, in theory, policy

[32] In fact, it was originally just 'Philosophical Foundations of Criminal Justice', but after several years I realised that (western) moral and political philosophy could provide a shared foundation for human rights more broadly conceived, without necessarily filtering the arguments and analysis through a narrower penal lens. The rebranded module was more inclusive and expanded student choice (and in a sense, repaid some of my debt to the broad conception of 'human rights' that had opened the door to criminal justice teaching on the LLM in the first place).

[33] The same methodological premiss inspired Paul Roberts and Jill Hunter (eds), *Criminal Evidence and Human Rights: Reimagining Common Law Procedural Traditions* (Hart Publishing, 2012).

[34] It was cut short at the height of its popularity when Dirk moved on to become Head of School.

[35] See, eg, Andrew Ward, 'Swedish Prosecutors Seek to Interview WikiLeaks Founder', *Financial Times*, 26 August 2010; Catherine Philp, 'New Spying Claim Against Assange: WikiLeaks Founder could be Extradited to US', *The Times*, 24 December 2011. Plus ça change in 2024: Jill Lawless, 'WikiLeaks Founder Assange Starts Final UK Legal Battle to Avoid Extradition to US on Spy Charges', *The Independent*, 20 February 2024.

and practice', the module retained substantial comparative elements carried over from legacy teaching. This design feature will not surprise readers already convinced that comparative perspectives and methodology must be integral to robust transnational, international and global analytical frameworks. My own experience during these first two decades of masters-level teaching was that I never had any difficulty in encouraging student engagement with comparative topics and literature, *provided that the label itself was downplayed or, preferably, avoided altogether.*[36] Which does, alas, tend to corroborate comparative legal scholars' frequent complaint that ill-informed preconceptions of their subject drive students (and other scholars) away.[37] At any rate, 'globalisation' as an organising concept appears to have captivated parts of the postgraduate student market that 'comparative criminal justice' evidently could not reach.

The final seminar of the Comparative Criminal Justice module in its original format was interrogatively titled 'International Criminal Justice?' At this embryonic stage, my thinking on the subject had barely progressed beyond formulating that question. I had noticed a recent uptick in literature putting the prospect of systematising international criminal justice on the agenda for discussion. By now fully immersed in his doctoral research, Rob was a receptive sounding board and expert informant, sharing his already voluminous knowledge of the history of international criminal proceedings and pointing me in the direction of additional reading material.[38] I was also curious about the place of European law in this novel configuration, since it was obvious that neither EU law[39] nor European human rights law[40] could be considered parts of domestic criminal law as conventionally conceived. Institutionalisation of disciplinary innovation is always a team game, and at Nottingham I was fortunate to be surrounded by colleagues with expertise in just about every aspect of international law. In particular, Nigel White had written

[36] One student memorably told me at the end of the term that they had been amazed by how interesting and relevant comparative criminal justice turned out to be, having chosen the module only because 'it was the only option timetabled on Friday afternoons when I needed to be on campus anyway'.

[37] *Cf* Vernon Valentine Palmer, 'Insularity and Leadership in American Comparative Law: The Past One Hundred Years' (2001) 75 *Tulane Law Review* 1093; Basil Markesinis, 'Comparative Law – A Subject in Search of an Audience' (1990) 53 *Modern Law Review* 1; Günter Frankenberg, 'Critical Comparisons: Re-thinking Comparative Law' (1985) 26 *Harvard International Law Journal* 411.

[38] Prescribed reading for the seminar included Rupa Bhattacharyya, 'Establishing a Rule-of-Law International Criminal Justice System' (1996) 31 *Texas International Law Journal* 57; Timothy L H McCormick and Gerry J Simpson, 'A New International Criminal Law Regime?' (1995) 42 *Netherlands International Law Review* 177. Also see Colin Warbrick, 'International Criminal Law' (1995) 44 *International and Comparative Law Quarterly* 466; Payam Akhavan, 'Punishing War Crimes in the Former Yugoslavia: A Critical Juncture for the New World Order' (1993) 15 *Human Rights Quarterly* 262.

[39] Rene Guldenmund, Christopher Harding and Ann Sherlock, 'The European Community and Criminal Law' in Phil Fennell, Christopher Harding, Nico Jorg and Bert Swart (eds), *Criminal Justice in Europe: A Comparative Study* (OUP, 1995). Now see Kai Ambos, *European Criminal Law* (CUP, 2018).

[40] Bert Swart and James Young, 'The European Convention on Human Rights and Criminal Justice in the Netherlands and the United Kingdom' in Phil Fennell, Christopher Harding, Nico Jorg and Bert Swart (eds), *Criminal Justice in Europe: A Comparative Study* (OUP, 1995).

his PhD under David Harris' supervision[41] and was already an established authority on UN institutions and collective security law;[42] and my contemporary Dino Kritsiotis specialised in international humanitarian law (IHL). When I broached with Dino and Nigel the possibility of launching an LLM in International Criminal Justice, both wanted to hear more. The proposal was intellectually coherent, inasmuch as 'penal justice', 'policing', 'criminalisation', 'criminal responsibility' and so on, could serve as unifying themes and analytical heuristics comfortably encompassing both domestic and international criminal proceedings. However, to avoid confusing and wasteful duplication, the new programme would inevitably supersede the established degree specialism in International Law and Armed Conflict. In other words, Dino and Nigel had vested interests in existing LLM teaching, whereas I had nothing to lose and everything to gain from major structural redesign. Some effort would naturally be required to persuade colleagues to share my vision and to turn theoretical hunches into an elaborated plan for a deliverable programme.

A charm offensive was launched, and, with a few minor hiccups and temporary setbacks along the way, the campaign was won. As memorialised in a report to the departmental (general) meeting in October 1997, '[a]fter lengthy and wide-ranging discussion, a meeting of relevant teachers … concluded that the proposal to relaunch the LLM in International Law and Armed Conflict as an LLM in International Criminal Justice and Armed Conflict was supported on intellectual, educational and pragmatic grounds'.[43] With the support of the Head of Department,[44] the proposal was duly approved in full committee, and authorised to be advertised for commencement in Autumn 1998. It would comprise six modules split evenly between 'criminal justice options'[45] and 'armed conflict options',[46] and would require candidates to choose at least one option from either side of the disciplinary conjunctive '[i]n order to retain the intellectual integrity and coherence of the new degree'. Mirroring the incipient institutional evolution of the fledgling international criminal tribunals themselves, we were up and running.

[41] Nigel D White, *The United Nations and the Maintenance of International Peace and Security* (Manchester University Press, 1990; 2nd edn 1997).

[42] Hilaire McCoubrey and Nigel D White, *International Law and Armed Conflict* (Ashgate, 1992); Nigel D White, *The Law of International Organisations* (Manchester University Press, 1996); Hilaire McCoubrey and Nigel D White, *The Blue Helmets: The Legal Regulation of UN Military Operations* (Dartmouth, 1996).

[43] *Proposal to Modify an Existing Specialist LLM: LLM in International Criminal Justice and Armed Conflict*, University of Nottingham, Department of Law, 30 October 1997.

[44] Geoffrey Morse, a company and tax lawyer with no particular interest in international criminal justice, but a keen sense that if junior faculty were not encouraged and supported in their aspirations, they could easily take them somewhere else. I would almost certainly have left Nottingham within five years without the opportunities afforded by LLM teaching.

[45] International Criminal Justice; Comparative Criminal Justice; Philosophical Foundations of Criminal Justice.

[46] International Humanitarian Law; International Law of the Use of Force; Collective Security Law.

III. Implementation: How Ya Gonna have a Dream Come True?

The start of the 1998–99 academic year was especially keenly anticipated. The Statute for the International Criminal Court (ICC) had been successfully concluded at the Rome Conference in July 1998. Rob Cryer had been in Rome for the duration, as an observer attached to the UK delegation, and returned from summer vacation brimming with enthusiasm and armed with cloak-and-dagger tales of last-minute negotiations on textual amendments between national delegations huddled in hotel rooms. By all accounts, the final acts of the Rome Conference were chaotic[47] and ultimate success in producing a Treaty was by no means guaranteed.[48] Events in the Balkans, meanwhile, were unfolding rapidly and regularly featured on evening news bulletins.[49] The ICTY had concluded its first contested trial in 1997,[50] but the appeal proceedings in *Tadic* were still ongoing, and the trial chamber's verdict and sentence would not be finally confirmed until 1999.[51] In September 1998, Rwandan local politician Jean-Paul Akayesu was convicted of genocide after a contested trial lasting 20 months.[52] This was the first trial verdict to be handed down by the ICTR based in Arusha, Tanzania, and a landmark in international criminal jurisprudence.[53] The following month, Chile's former dictator General Pinochet was arrested in London in response to an international warrant alleging systematic state torture, precipitating the most high-profile extradition proceedings for many years.[54] On and off campus, there was a palpable buzz surrounding anything related to international criminal justice. Addressing the incoming cohort of LLM students

[47] Immi Tallgren, 'We Did It? The Vertigo of Law and Everyday Life at the Diplomatic Conference on the Establishment of an International Criminal Court' (1999) 12 *Leiden Journal of International Law* 683; M Cherif Bassiouni, 'Negotiating the Treaty of Rome on the Establishment of an International Criminal Court' (1999) 32 *Cornell International Law Journal* 443.

[48] David J Harris, 'Progress and Problems in Creating an International Criminal Court' (1998) 3 *Journal of Armed Conflict Law* 1.

[49] See, eg, Tim Judah, 'Serb Mayor's Suicide Ends Key War Trial – UN Shamed as Man Charged with Deaths of 260 Hospital Patients in Croatia Hangs Himself after Alibi was Destroyed', *Independent*, 30 June 1998; Tom Walker, 'Peace in Jeopardy after Radicals Gain Ground in Bosnia', *The Times*, 17 September 1998; 'NATO Intervention is A Necessity, Not an Option', *Independent*, 12 October 1998; Martin Woollacott, 'Noose Tightens for the Architects of Evil', *Guardian*, 13 December 1998; Rupert Cornwell, 'NATO Delivers Final Warning to Milosevic', *Independent*, 19 January 1999.

[50] *Prosecutor v Tadic*, IT-94-1 ('Prijedor'), Trial Chamber Judgement 7 May 1997.

[51] *Prosecutor v Tadic*, IT-94-1-A (Appeals Chamber), 15 July 1999; (2002) 9 IHRR 1051. See Chapter 9 for further discussion.

[52] *Prosecutor v Jean-Paul Akayesu*, ICTR-96-4-T, 2 September 1998; (2002) 9 IHRR 608.

[53] Particularly in relation to rape and sexual violence: Alexandra Adams, 'The Legacy of the International Criminal Tribunals for the Former Yugoslavia and Rwanda and their Contribution to the Crime of Rape' (2018) 29 *European Journal of International Law* 749.

[54] *R v Bow Street Metropolitan Stipendiary Magistrates, ex parte Pinochet Ugarte (No 3)* [2000] 1 AC 147, HL; Neil Boister and Richard Burchill, 'The *Pinochet* Precedent: Don't Leave Home Without It' (1999) 10 *Criminal Law Forum* 405.

during Induction Week in September 1998, Dino quipped that, whereas Nottingham's postgraduate programmes always aspired to be cutting-edge, with the launch of the LLM in International Criminal Justice and Armed Conflict we had anticipated the cut!

To the best of my knowledge, this was the first LLM degree in International Criminal Justice (ICrimJ) to be offered in the UK, and possibly anywhere in the world. Certainly, we were not aware of any models to emulate. Our course design and module content were innovated from the ground up. The first iterations of module seminars posed foundational questions of disciplinary constitution, normative purposes, and juridical basis. What were ICrimJ's motivating ideas and ideals?[55] What is an international crime?[56] How can the (putative) existence of universal criminal jurisdiction be squared with traditional conceptions of state sovereignty?[57] What had been the UN's contribution to the project thus far?[58] What had international criminal tribunals achieved to-date, and how might they develop in future?[59] Where did (international) human rights law fit into this blurry picture?[60] What about the potential contribution of supranational legal entities such as the EU?[61] Or the status of domestic criminal processes applying international norms or claiming international authority?[62] Naturally, we had many more

[55] Steven R Ratner, 'The Schizophrenias of International Criminal Law' (1998) 33 *Texas International Law Journal* 237; George P Fletcher, 'The Law of War and its Pathologies' (2007) 38 *Columbia Human Rights Law Review* 517; Stanley Cohen, 'Crime and Politics: Spot the Difference' (1996) 47 *British Journal of Sociology* 1.

[56] Georges Abi-Saab, 'The Concept of "International Crimes" and Its Place in Contemporary International Law' in J H H Weiler, Antonio Cassese and Maria Spinedi (eds), *International Crimes of States: A Critical Analysis of the ILC's Draft Article 19 on State Responsibility* (EUI/de Gruyter, 1989); Alain Pellet, 'Can A State Commit A Crime? Definitely, Yes!' (1999) 10 *European Journal of International Law* 425; Nina HB Jørgensen, *The Responsibility of States for International Crimes* (OUP, 2000).

[57] Willard B Cowles, 'Universality of Jurisdiction over War Crimes' (1945) 33 *California Law Review* 177; Jordan Paust, 'Universality and the Responsibility to Enforce International Criminal Law' (1989) 11 *Houston Journal of International Law* 337.

[58] Gabriel H Oosthuizen, 'Some Preliminary Remarks on the Relationship Between the Envisaged International Criminal Court and the UN Security Council' (1999) 46 *Netherlands International Law Review* 313; Todd Howland and William Calathes, 'The UN's International Criminal Tribunal: Is it Justice or Jingoism for Rwanda? A Call for Transformation' (1998) 39 *Virginia Journal of International Law* 135; Oliver Schuett, 'The International War Crimes Tribunal for the Former Yugoslavia and the Dayton Peace Agreement: Peace Versus Justice?' (1997) 4 *International Peacekeeping* 91.

[59] Jose E Alvarez, 'Rush to Closure: Lessons of the *Tadic* Judgment' (1998) 96 *Michigan Law Review* 2031; Payam Akhavan, 'Justice and Reconciliation in the Great Lakes Region of Africa: The Contribution of the International Criminal Tribunal For Rwanda' (1997) 7 *Duke Journal of Comparative and International Law* 325.

[60] M Cherif Bassiouni, 'Human Rights in the Context of Criminal Justice: Identifying International Procedural Protections and Equivalent Protections in National Constitutions' (1993) 3 *Duke Journal of Comparative and International Law* 235.

[61] George A Bermann, 'Taking Subsidiarity Seriously: Federalism in the European Community and the United States' (1994) 94 *Columbia Law Review* 331; Christopher Harding, 'The Identity of European Law: Mapping Out the European Legal Space' (2000) 6 *European Law Journal* 128; Estella Baker, 'Taking European Criminal Law Seriously' [1998] *Criminal Law Review* 361.

[62] Timothy L H McCormack and Gerry J Simpson (eds), *The Law of War Crimes: National and International Approaches* (Kluwer, 1997); Hannah Arendt, *Eichmann in Jerusalem: A Report on the Banality of Evil* (Penguin, 1994 [1963]).

questions than answers. But formulating the right questions with focus and precision is generally, in intellectual labour, more than half the battle.

Forty-one students formally enrolled on the ICrimJ module. LLM seminar classes were notionally capped at 30 students (most attracting fewer than 20 enrolments), but excluding enthusiastic subscribers above an arbitrary quota would have been excessively formalistic, and largely self-defeating, in this evangelical phase of module recruitment and foundation. For the inaugural seminar, scheduled in a draughty set of crumbling prefab classrooms lyrically nominated 'Cherry Tree Buildings',[63] it was literally standing room only. Curious PhD students, miscellaneous Law department researchers, and window-shopping masters students yet to finalise their options swelled the attendees to well over 50. The crackling electric atmosphere in the room exceeded anything I have ever experienced in teaching, before or since. It had always been our intention for seminars in this module to be 'triple-headed' by Dino, Nigel and me. For this inaugural occasion, we were joined on the tables at the head of the classroom by two doctoral student 'special guests'. The first was Neil Boister, then in the final weeks of submitting his PhD on *The Suppression of Illicit Drugs through International Law*,[64] supervised by David Harris. The second was Rob Cryer, supervised by Dino and Nigel.

Team teaching in seminars was a vital part of the module design. On the premiss that international criminal justice itself represented an unprecedented amalgam of international law and criminal law, the idea was that our own classroom conversations would mimic and enact evolutionary interdisciplinary encounters between previously disparate literatures, jurisprudence and theoretical frameworks. Roughly speaking, Nigel would represent the perspective of a UN institutional lawyer; Dino would advance the agenda of international humanitarian law; and I would speak for criminal law and criminal justice. This 'tournament of ideas' format, notwithstanding some pedagogical risks, served marvellously well as a vehicle for orchestrating lively discussion and wide-ranging debate worthy of our contentious subject matter. Less comfortable than me with philosophical argumentation, Dino might tut-tut at my 'pulpit' moralising in advancing normative claims about penal justice. I would respond in kind, by swatting away his (deliberately[65]) provocative remark that 'international law owns the intellectual property to international criminal justice' as tendentious disciplinary imperialism. Anxious claims to proprietorship were rife at the time.[66] Beneath the veneer of

[63] Aka 'the cowsheds', Cherry Tree Buildings were demolished in 2004 as part of a comprehensive programme of campus modernisation, though some of the eponymous cherry trees were saved and can still be viewed in blossom to this day, if you know where and when to look.

[64] eprints.nottingham.ac.uk/11121/ (accessed 17 December 2025); Neil Boister, *Penal Aspects of the UN Drug Conventions* (Brill, 2001).

[65] Dino assures me.

[66] 'For many decades, the study of international criminal tribunals was the jealous preserve, the mascot almost, of international lawyers … who kept the discipline of international criminal law alive, when the more worldly inclined would have dismissed it as a quaint irrelevance': Frédéric Mégret, 'The Politics of International Criminal Justice' (2002) 13 *European Journal of International Law* 1261. This is part of a larger story about the disciplinary identity of Public International Law, which was then

theatre, these exchanges were profoundly educational, not least for the teachers. Over the course of a term, I graduated from a position of near-total ignorance to a plausible *flâneur* of international law. Team-teaching this module was also, incidentally, enormous fun.

The danger, of course, was that we might spend two hours jousting with each other, while a bemused student audience never got a look in. There may be *some* pedagogic value to spectating clashes between disciplinary perspectives thrown together in unfamiliar configurations, but active engagement is undoubtedly preferable. My recollection is that there was always at least a solid core of any given year's cohort with the diligence in preparation and confidence in self-expression to ask questions and get involved in seminar discussions. Dead air was unknown; the two-hour slot generally flew by. The calibre of students taking this module should be stressed: many have since gone on to distinguished careers in international legal practice or academia, including several who now teach their own versions of international criminal law and justice modules.[67]

The unusual dialogic format did not suit every student who was exposed to it over the seven years in which multi-headed teaching was retained. One disgruntled class member wrote in a course evaluation that the teachers seemed to lack basic lecturing skills and should 'write out the main points on the whiteboard'! Some students were perplexed by my standard disclaimer that 'I am not an international lawyer'. Surely, this implied that I was unqualified to teach the module? On balance, my impression is that the majority of students did take away the primary messages (which we continually underlined in the classroom), that the entire field was under construction, its parameters and content were hotly contested, and nobody was yet a bona fide expert in the interdisciplinary scholarship its mature evolution would entail. Triple-heading or even double-heading seminars is resource-intensive. To its eternal credit in my eyes, the Law Department underwrote a significant chunk of this investment, and the remainder the teachers volunteered, as fair quid pro quo for the fringe benefits we derived in professional development and stimulus to further research. Double-heading seminars was retained, with rotating personnel, until the academic year 2005–06. Limited staff availability was the immediate driver for its abandonment, but with the module now into its eighth year and boasting an evolved syllabus and course

experiencing existential anxiety about the prospect of 'fragmentation' into discrete regimes and consequent loss of normative and disciplinary coherence: see Report of the Study Group of the International Law Commission, *Fragmentation of International Law: Difficulties Arising from the Diversification and Expansion of International Law*, A/CN.4/L.682 (13 April 2006).

[67] Notably, Annika Jones at Exeter Law School: law.exeter.ac.uk/people/profile/index.php?web_id=annika_jones#research; Hemi Mistry at Nottingham: www.nottingham.ac.uk/law/people/hemi.mistry; Roisin Mulgrew at the Irish Centre for Human Rights, University of Galway: www.universityofgalway.ie/our-research/people/law/roisinmulgrew/; Yassin Brunger at Queens University Belfast: pure.qub.ac.uk/en/persons/yassin-brunger (all accessed 17 December 2025).

materials, team-teaching in seminars had mostly served its intended purpose in any event.

For its third iteration in the academic year 2000–01, the LLM's international criminal justice offering underwent a major structural upgrade. The material comprising the original module was reorganised and expanded into two new modules, (roughly) functionally differentiated into Foundations of International Criminal Justice, taught in the first term, and Principles of International Criminal Justice, running in the second. As well as expanding to accommodate the now rapidly accumulating primary sources and secondary literature, this framework afforded more seminar time for closer examination of doctrinal, substantive and procedural international criminal law, alongside the conceptual questions (What is 'international criminal justice'? Can a state commit a crime? What is international criminal jurisdiction?), institutional history ('From Nuremberg to the Hague') and international politics (Are the Security Council's powers appropriate and legitimate? Should the US join the ICC?) towards which our initial focus had gravitated. The twin Foundations and Principles modules became the compulsory backbone of the LLM degree, obviating the need to insist on students studying IHL or collective security options in order to retain the overall coherence of the programme.

When Nigel White's teaching hours significantly reduced on becoming Head of School, Rob Cryer was his obvious replacement in the international criminal justice triumvirate. Rob co-taught Foundations of International Criminal Justice with Dino and me in the academic years 2001–02 and 2002–03, and with Olympia Bekou and me in the following 2003–04 session. The companion Principles of International Criminal Justice module was designed and originally taught by Olympia, me and Dirk van Zyl Smit, but it existed in this format only for two years. The module content was inherited by Olympia and Rob and rebranded as International Criminal Law, which continues to be taught, with a predominantly juridical focus, on the contemporary LLM. Rob and Olympia concomitantly developed a new undergraduate optional module on International Criminal Law, which proved an instant hit and continues to thrive, with large student enrolments in some years topping three figures. As well as introducing hundreds of Nottingham undergraduates to the specialist field of international criminal law, the experience of collaborating with Olympia in crafting and delivering this module undoubtedly influenced Rob's future teaching and scholarship and represents a major strand of Rob's enduring institutional legacy at Nottingham.

On the LLM meanwhile, I persevered in teaching Foundations of International Criminal Justice, soon single-handedly, until the academic year 2010–11. With Olympia (and later Sandy Sivakumaran)[68] minding the doctrinal side of the shop, I reimagined the Foundations module as an interdisciplinary exercise in

[68] Sandesh Sivakumaran, *The Law of Non-International Armed Conflict* (OUP, 2012).

conceptualising and researching international criminal justice. This final iteration of the module considered international criminal justice from the overlapping perspectives of global politics and international relations, jurisprudence, penal philosophy, historiography and criminology. It culminated in reflections on genocide as a liminal theme, melding together jurisprudence[69] and legal process,[70] historical[71] and criminological[72] context, survivor testimonies,[73] representations in art, literature[74] and popular culture,[75] and concluding with tentative thoughts on constitutive (inter)disciplinary questions of taxonomy,[76] scope,[77] focus[78] and ethics.[79] The module was rewarding to teach and reliably attracted 20-plus students, but I gave it up in the end, partly to concentrate on other things but also because I sensed that I was becoming too far estranged from the institutional fabric and burgeoning jurisprudence of international criminal law and process. In the 12 years since we had launched the LLM, international criminal justice had blossomed into a fully-fledged disciplinary specialism, with its own courses,

[69] David Fraser, *Law After Auschwitz: Towards a Jurisprudence of the Holocaust* (Carolina Academic Press, 2005); José E Alvarez, 'Crimes of States/Crimes of Hate: Lessons from Rwanda' (1999) 24 *Yale Journal of International Law* 365.

[70] Mark A Drumbl, *Atrocity, Punishment and International Law* (CUP, 2007); Lawrence Douglas, *The Memory of Judgment: Making Law and History in the Trials of the Holocaust* (Yale University Press, 2001); Hannah Arendt, *Eichmann in Jerusalem: A Report on the Banality of Evil* (Penguin, 1994 [1963]).

[71] Omer Bartov, 'Defining Enemies, Making Victims: Germans, Jews and the Holocaust' (1998) 103 *American Historical Review* 771; Daniel Jonah Goldhagen, *Hitler's Willing Executioners: Ordinary Germans and the Holocaust* (Alfred A Knopf, 1996); Richard J Evans, *Telling Lies about Hitler: The Holocaust, History and the David Irving Trial* (Verso, 2002).

[72] Wayne Morrison, Criminology, Civilisation and the New World Order (Cavendish, 2006); Lt.-Gen. Roméo Dallaire, *Shake Hands with the Devil: The Failure of Humanity in Rwanda* (Arrow Books, 2004).

[73] Yad Vashem, 'Survivor Testimonies', www.yadvashem.org/collections/testimonies.html (accessed 17 December 2025); Christopher W Mullins, '"He Would Kill Me with his Penis": Genocidal Rape in Rwanda as a State Crime' (2009) 17 *Critical Criminology* 15.

[74] Tadeusz Borowski, *This Way for the Gas, Ladies and Gentlemen* (Penguin, 1992); Primo Levi, *The Drowned and the Saved* (Abacus, 1991).

[75] Art Spiegelman, *The Complete Maus* (Penguin, 2003); Primo Levi (Belpolti, ed), *The Black Hole of Auschwitz* (Polity Press, 2005); Wayne Morrison, '"Reflections with Memories": Everyday Photography Capturing Genocide' (2004) 8 *Theoretical Criminology* 341.

[76] George S Yacoubian Jr, 'The (In)significance of Genocidal Behavior to the Discipline of Criminology' (2000) 34 *Crime, Law & Social Change* 7.

[77] Misha Glenny, *McMafia: Crime Without Frontiers* (Bodley Head, 2008); James Sheptycki and Ali Wardak (eds), *Transnational and Comparative Criminology* (Glasshouse Press, 2005); Vincenzo Ruggiero, Nigel South and Ian Taylor (eds), *The New European Criminology: Crime and Social Order in Europe* (Routledge, 1998).

[78] David O Friedrichs, 'The Crime of the Century? The Case for the Holocaust' (2000) 34 *Crime, Law & Social Change* 21; Kjersti Ericsson, 'Rape, Love and War – Personal or Political?' (2011) 15 *Theoretical Criminology* 67.

[79] Karl Jaspers, *The Question of German Guilt* (Fordham University Press, 2001 [1947]); Raul Hilberg, *Perpetrators, Victims, Bystanders* (Harper Collins, 1992); Alan Norrie, 'Albert Speer, Guilt, and "The Space Between"' in Matt Matravers (ed), *Punishment and Political Theory* (Hart Publishing, 1999); Zygmunt Bauman, *Modernity and the Holocaust* (Polity, 2000).

textbooks,[80] journals,[81] treatises,[82] institutional structures and frontline practitioners industriously generating ever more voluminous material for scholars to consume, editorialise and critique. This was no longer a safe space for *flâneurs* and dilettante theorising. Jurisprudential muscle is built up and maintained only by putting in the doctrinal hard yards.

Beyond satisfying native curiosity in a set of juridical puzzles, my engagement with international criminal justice had been motivated by three primary considerations. First, I was determined that it should be conceptualised as a genuinely interdisciplinary – or at least multi-disciplinary – enterprise, rather than as a subfield of PIL. My modest contributions to the early literature stressed the salience of penal theory[83] and criminological perspectives.[84] This argument initially encountered some resistance and miscomprehension,[85] but seems to be widely acknowledged nowadays, at least by perceptive observers.[86] Second, it occurred to me that, whereas in its design phase international criminal justice was largely the preserve of diplomats and international lawyers, once real-life criminal trials were underway, expertise in the practical conduct of criminal litigation would be at a premium. This hunch quickly became received wisdom amongst those with direct

[80] By the time that a secondary wave of 'companions' and 'handbooks' starts to appear, the disciplinary deal is sealed: see, eg, Antonio Cassese, *The Oxford Companion to International Criminal Justice* (OUP, 2009); Bartram S Brown (ed), *Research Handbook on International Criminal Law* (Edward Elgar, 2011); William A Schabas and Nadia Bernaz (eds), *Routledge Handbook of International Criminal Law* (Routledge, 2012); Kevin Heller, Frederic Megret, Sarah Nouwen, Jens Ohlin, and Darryl Robinson (eds), *The Oxford Handbook of International Criminal Law* (OUP, 2020).

[81] Brill's *International Criminal Law Review* first appeared in 2001, edited by Michael Bohlander and dedicated to 'the exciting task of establishing a forum for the exchange of ideas and opinions in the growing discipline of international criminal law': 'Editorial' (2011) 1 *International Criminal Law Review* 1, 3. OUP's *Journal of International Criminal Justice*, led by Antonio Cassese as Editor-in-Chief, was launched two years later with ambitiously theoretical and interdisciplinary aspirations. '[I]nternational criminal justice cannot be allowed to become a ghetto of public international law: indeed, the issues it raises are also of great interest to human rights experts and criminal lawyers, comparativists, proceduralists, penal philosophers, and criminologists': 'Editorial' (2003) 1 *Journal of International Criminal Justice* 1.

[82] Antonio Cassese, Paola Gaeta and John R W D Jones (eds), *The Rome Statute of the International Criminal Court: A Commentary* (OUP, 2002); Kai Ambos, *Treatise on International Criminal Law* (OUP, 2013; 2nd edn 2021).

[83] Paul Roberts, 'Restoration and Retribution in International Criminal Justice: An Exploratory Analysis' in Andrew von Hirsch et al (eds), *Restorative Justice and Criminal Justice* (Hart Publishing, 2003).

[84] Paul Roberts and Nesam McMillan, 'For Criminology in International Criminal Justice' (2003) 1 *Journal of International Criminal Justice* 315.

[85] Despite professing allegiance to interdisciplinarity (and, in all probability, borrowing from me its warning against propagating intellectual ghettos) in its founding Editorial, the *Journal of International Criminal Justice* still managed to publish our 'For Criminology' article (with no prior notification) under the performatively othering subtitle of 'The Contribution of Other Disciplines to International Criminal Law'! Disciplinary preconceptions and assumptions operate at the level of 'unconscious bias'. They are formative, pervasive, and difficult to shake.

[86] Mark A Drumbl, 'Toward a Criminology of International Crime' (2003) 19 *Ohio State Journal on Dispute Resolution* 263; Ruth Jamieson (ed), *The Criminology of War* (Ashgate, 2014).

experience of international criminal trials.[87] Third, I thought it important to stress that interdisciplinary learning is a two-way street. International criminal justice should benefit from the accumulated wisdom of more established legal disciplines and scholarship at the domestic level,[88] but just as surely might repay the compliment by enriching traditional strands of jurisprudence and legal theorising.[89] The injection of international perspectives should encourage legal scholarship and teaching to cast off their statist blinkers and become more cosmopolitan in outlook.[90]

A fourth preoccupation, initially unanticipated, became to devise an original conceptualisation of 'international criminal justice' capable of accommodating the disparate planetarium of norms, processes and jurisdictions with a plausible claim to inclusion in its disciplinary universe. For this mapping task, I proposed 'seven concentric circles of international criminal justice'.[91] Questions of disciplinary taxonomy and organisation naturally occupy teachers of novel subjects with no textbooks or conventional syllabi to guide them. As disciplinary specialisms become institutionalised over time, such questions may be regarded as transitional and increasingly superseded. My longstanding view is that periodic reflection on constitutive disciplinary taxonomies is essential for the continued salience and intellectual vitality of the disciplines.[92] For example, I think it would be

[87] Patricia M Wald, 'Running the Trial of the Century: The Nuremberg Legacy' (2006) 27 *Cardozo Law Review* 1559; Peter Murphy, 'No Free Lunch, No Free Proof: The Indiscriminate Admission of Evidence is a Serious Flaw in International Criminal Trials' (2010) 8 *Journal of International Criminal Justice* 539; Richard May, David Tolbert, John Hocking, Ken Roberts, Bing Bing Jia, Daryl Mundis and Gabriël Oosthuizen (eds), *Essays on ICTY Procedure and Evidence in Honour of Gabrielle Kirk McDonald* (Kluwer, 2001).

[88] Eg, Paul Roberts, 'The Priority of Procedure and the Neglect of Evidence and Proof: Facing Facts in International Criminal Law' (2015) 13 *Journal of International Criminal Justice* 479.

[89] See Chapter 9 for a worked illustration; and generally, Paul Roberts, 'Why International Criminal Evidence?' in Paul Roberts and Mike Redmayne (eds), *Innovations in Evidence and Proof: Integrating Theory, Research and Teaching* (Hart Publishing, 2007).

[90] Paul Roberts, 'Confronting the Challenges of Cosmopolitan Criminal Jurisprudence', Inaugural Lecture, University of Nottingham, 10 September 2010; Patrick Glenn, 'Cosmopolitan Legal Orders' in Andrew Halpin and Volker Roeben (eds), *Theorising the Global Legal Order* (Hart Publishing, 2009). For worked illustrations, see Dimitrios Giannoulopoulos, *Improperly Obtained Evidence in Anglo-American and Continental Law* (Hart Publishing, 2019); Jacqueline Hodgson, 'EU Criminal Justice: The Challenge of Due Process Rights within a Framework of Mutual Recognition' (2011) 37 *North Carolina Journal of International Law and Commercial Regulation* 308; John D Jackson and Sarah J Summers (eds), *Obstacles to Fairness in Criminal Proceedings* (Hart Publishing, 2018); Paul Roberts, 'Normative Evolution in Evidentiary Exclusion: Coercion, Deception and the Right to a Fair Trial' in Paul Roberts and Jill Hunter (eds), *Criminal Evidence and Human Rights* (Hart Publishing, 2012); Kai Ambos, 'The Transnational Use of Torture Evidence' (2009) 42 *Israel Law Review* 362; Máximo Langer, 'From Legal Transplants to Legal Translations: The Globalization of Plea Bargaining and the Americanization Thesis in Criminal Procedure' (2004) 45 *Harvard International Law Journal* 1.

[91] Paul Roberts, 'Comparative Law for International Criminal Justice' in Esin Örücü and David Nelken (eds), *Comparative Law – A Handbook* (Hart Publishing, 2007).

[92] Also see Chapter 5; Paul Roberts, 'Rethinking the Law of Evidence: A Twenty-first Century Agenda for Teaching and Research' (2002) 55 *Current Legal Problems* 297; John Jackson and Paul Roberts, 'Beyond Common Law Evidence: Reimagining, and Reinvigorating, Evidence Law as Forensic Science' in Darryl K Brown, Jenia Iontcheva Turner and Bettina Weisser (eds), *The Oxford Handbook of Criminal Process* (OUP, 2019).

regrettable if broad interdisciplinary conceptions of International Criminal Justice were allowed to degenerate into narrow(er), doctrinally dominated, exclusionary conceptions of International Criminal Law. But I agree that preoccupations with taxonomy can become compulsive and an unhealthy distraction from more substantive work, and that a sensible division of academic labour will entrust theorists to take the labouring oar on theoretical tasks and inquiries.[93]

The advent of the first widely employed textbook is a pivotal moment in the formation of a new disciplinary specialism. A textbook is always, by implication if not design, an attempt to define the parameters, subject-matter, central debates, research methods, and animating values and objectives of any juridical field. Textbook writers are the legislators of law curricula and the poets of the classroom. Antonio Cassese's *International Criminal Law*, first published in 2003,[94] scooped that accolade in supplying the first course book to supplement our LLM handouts and reading lists. However, the work produced by Rob Cryer and co-authors four years later is a weightier, more considered contribution to research-led pedagogy, in my estimation. *An Introduction to International Criminal Law and Procedure*[95] is structured and written in an accessible style more obviously tailored to an upper-level student readership. Although the book concentrates on international criminal *law*, the opening chapters provide contextual scaffolding by ventilating questions of disciplinary taxonomy, normative jurisprudence and penal theory. The book's attention to highlighting procedural topics alongside substantive doctrinal analysis is another commendable feature, and might hopefully serve to inoculate international criminal jurisprudence from the unfortunate aversion to procedural (including evidentiary) considerations which too often infects domestic criminal law scholarship and teaching.[96] Above all, whereas Cassese was essentially a dyed-in-the-wool international lawyer to his core,[97] Cryer and colleagues made strenuous efforts to afford appropriate billing to the criminal law

[93] See, eg, Paul Roberts, 'Theorising Evidence Law' (2023) 43 *Oxford Journal of Legal Studies* 629.

[94] Antonio Cassese, *International Criminal Law*, 1st edn (OUP, 2003). Now see Antonio Cassese and Paola Gaeta, *Cassese's International Criminal Law*, 3rd edn (OUP, 2013).

[95] Robert Cryer, Håkan Friman, Darryl Robinson and Elizabeth Wilmshurst, *An Introduction to International Criminal Law and Procedure*, 1st edn (CUP, 2007). Now see Robert Cryer, Darryl Robinson and Sergey Vasiliev, *An Introduction to International Criminal Law and Procedure*, 4th edn (CUP, 2019).

[96] A recurring overture with which I bent Rob's ear on more than one occasion. Also see Robert Cryer, 'A Message from Elsewhere: Witnesses before International Criminal Tribunals' in Paul Roberts and Mike Redmayne (eds), *Innovations in Evidence and Proof: Integrating Theory, Research and Teaching* (Hart Publishing, 2007). But *cf* Patricia M Wald, 'Rules of Evidence in the Yugoslav War Tribunal' (2003) 21 *Quinnipiac Law Review* 761, 763 ('scholars and commentators on the Tribunals appear to pay much more attention to substantive law developments than to procedure and process').

[97] As he would have it, '[i]nternational criminal law is a branch of *public international law*': Cassese (n 94) 16. See further, '*In Memoriam*: Antonio Cassese (1937–2011)' (2011) 93 *International Review of the Red Cross* 1265; Lal Chand Vohrah, Fausto Pocar, Yvonne Featherstone, Olivier Fourmy, Michael F Graham, John Hocking and Nicholas Robson (eds), *Man's Inhumanity to Man: Essays on International Law in Honour of Antonio Cassese* (Brill, 2003).

dimensions of their subject-matter. They insisted that '[i]nternational criminal law is double-structured, comprising both international law and criminal law. It should be appraised from the standpoints of both bodies of law'.[98] Rob rated this formative methodological commitment so significant that he enshrined it in the title of his personal chair at Birmingham, where he was 'Professor of International *and* Criminal Law' (his conjunction, my emphasis).

IV. Conclusion: Any Dream Won't Do

Rob Cryer's life and professional career were cruelly truncated, but this misfortune will not be readily apparent to future generations of scholars and students, who will make the entirely reasonable assumption that his extensive library of influential publications could have been produced only by an author who was active long into retirement. Though cheated in duration, Rob's timing was charmed. From *Tadic* and the signing of the Rome Statute, via the completion strategies of the ad hoc UN Tribunals, to the institutionalised casework of a permanent International Criminal Court (and the sense of deflation that almost inevitably attends the practical frustrations of routine criminal proceedings),[99] the progression of Rob's academic career uncannily mirrored the arc of international criminal justice itself in the decades either side of the new Millennium. As the field crystallised, Rob was on hand to populate it with his prodigious production of articles, notes and reviews. Subsequently, as the lead author of a market-leading textbook, Rob exerted a major influence on the shape and content of the disciplinary field of International Criminal Law as we know it today.

Whilst Rob's professorial stage was Birmingham Law School, his formative years were spent at Nottingham (with a brief loan spell in Manchester).[100] Besides the enduring influence of his masters year and doctoral apprenticeship, a positive experience of committed expert supervision common – one would hope – to all PhD graduates, Rob's involvement in co-teaching and developing the LLM in International Criminal Justice and Armed Conflict evidently continued to infuse his pedagogical practice and maturing scholarship throughout his blossoming

[98] Cryer et al (2007) (n 95) 12.

[99] David Luban, 'After the Honeymoon: Reflections on the Current State of International Criminal Justice' (2013) 11 *Journal of International Criminal Justice* 505; Ernst Hirsch Ballin, 'The Value of International Criminal Justice: How Much International Criminal Justice Can the World Afford?' (2019) 19 *International Criminal Law Review* 201 (sounding 'a wake-up call for younger generations to avoid a situation in which growing cynicism about the international rule of law and international human rights, and diminishing support for multilateralism, undermine the project of international criminal justice').

[100] Tempting though it is to dismiss this interlude as more about music and football than scholarship, historical candour compels me to record Rob's avowed lifelong debt to Neil Duxbury, John Murphy and other Manchester colleagues for generous mentorship during his first lecturing post.

career. As the old Jesuit motto proclaims,[101] character and commitment are forged in the educationally formative years. But Rob would not have wanted this reflection to be maudlin or self-indulgently solipsistic: we have real ale and Joy Division for those moods. The creation story recounted in this memoir will have been worth retelling if it serves, incidentally, to inspire and inform reinvigorated cycles of creativity, ambition, social responsiveness and global vision in legal education. And there is a cautionary coda to this tale.[102]

Ideas supply the vital creative spark driving innovation, but material conditions – as Marx taught – are equally important and often fatefully decisive. Effective vision must be *embodied*; and for disciplinary formation and development, this implies anchoring in nurturing, collegial, institutional environments. In a curious twist of fate, this chapter may now also serve as an epitaph to the specialist LLM, which – I discovered at an advanced stage of writing – was to be offered for the last time in the academic year 2024–25. It is inevitable and appropriate that degree programmes will come and go, in tune with current staff interests and the rhythm of world events. The euphoria surrounding international criminal justice in 1998 is long dissipated; the excitement of cutting-edge innovation in legal education now belongs to AI and the Law, climate change and culture wars.

Meanwhile, actual wars rage in Ukraine and Palestine,[103] a resurgence of authoritarian populism stalks European and North American politics, and an epidemic of weak, corrupt governance and failing (or frankly speaking, failed) states, especially in the global South, poses tangible risks of systematic human rights violations (including torture and gender-based violence), war crimes, crimes against humanity, and even genocide. It is barely credible that international criminal justice is any less relevant in today's fragile world than it was in the 1990s, when it was possible to believe that the fall of the Berlin Wall and the dissolution of the USSR heralded universal assent to liberal democracy at 'the end of history'.[104] In fact, the arguments I have heard for cancelling the LLM in International Criminal Justice and Armed Conflict seem either muddled or spurious. A cursory internet trawl will confirm that more than a dozen UK universities currently offer

[101] Though Loyola, apparently, never said 'give me the boy at seven …', which has been described as 'a bromide which has been fathered on us': Paul Andrews SJ, 'The Jesuits and Education' (1991) 80 *Studies: An Irish Quarterly Review* 22, 28.

[102] One additional, slightly facetious observation: if you have the good fortune to collaborate in teaching with talented and able colleagues, be sure to have a Plan B ready for when they jump ship to become Head of School!

[103] As well as in other places with less media attention: *cf* Dame Rosalind Marsden, 'Sudan's Forgotten War: A New Diplomatic Push is Needed', Chatham House, 14 March 2024, www.chathamhouse.org/2024/03/sudans-forgotten-war-new-diplomatic-push-needed (accessed 17 December 2025); Samer Al-Atrush, Richard Spencer and Gabrielle Weiniger, 'Saudis back West in Strikes against Red Sea Rebels', *The Times*, 9 January 2024; Richard Assheton, 'The World's Forgotten War: A Rare Journey Beyond Boko Haram Lines', *Sunday Times*, 31 December 2023.

[104] Francis Fukuyama, *The End of History and the Last Man* (Free Press, 1992).

comparable or related programmes,[105] and there are many more similarly focused masters degrees taught in English overseas,[106] refuting any impression of market exhaustion. The popularity of international criminal justice may have receded from its spectacular zenith, but it remains a prominent specialism in masters-level legal education in the UK and farther afield.

Twenty-seven years is a decent innings for any degree programme, and the legacy of Nottingham's LLM in International Criminal Justice and Armed Conflict is assured, not least through Rob Cryer's direct missionary work in conveying its material and intellectual DNA from the East to the West Midlands. In addition to the scores of LLM graduates with this qualification on their CVs in perpetuity, there will be ten times as many students who participated in some of the individual modules comprising the degree. As well as the LLM graduates who went on to teach international criminal justice in their own academic careers,[107] there are countless PhD students who attended occasional seminars or were otherwise indirectly influenced by the programme (if only through their supervisors), including many who would become prominent and productive scholars in the field: Neil

[105] Bangor (LLM in International Criminal Law and International Human Rights Law); Birmingham (LLM in International Criminal Law and Justice); BPP (LLM in Transnational Criminal Justice); Cardiff (MSc in International Criminology and Criminal Justice); Essex (LLM in International Criminal Law); Huddersfield (LLM in International Criminal Law); Hull (LLM in International Law: Conflict, Security and Human Rights); Kent (LLM in International Criminal Justice); London (LLM in International Criminal Justice); Northampton (LLM in International Criminal Law and Security); Northumbria (LLM in International Criminal Law and Practice); Portsmouth (MSc in International Criminal Justice and Intelligence); Sheffield (LLM in International Law and Global Justice); University of Law (LLM in International Criminal Law).

[106] Including: UVA Amsterdam Law School in partnership with Columbia Law School (LLM in International Criminal Law); UVA Amsterdam Law School (LLM in International and Transnational Criminal Law); Case Western Reserve University (LLM in International Criminal Law); Galway (LLM in international Criminal Law); Groningen (LLM in Global Criminal Law); Limerick (LLM in Law, Human Rights and Criminal Justice); University of New Hampshire Franklin Pierce School of Law (LLM in International Criminal Law and Justice); University of the Western Cape (LLM in Transnational Criminal Justice); Utrecht (LLM in European Criminal Justice in a Global Context).

[107] See above (n 67). Published work includes: Annika Jones, 'Measuring Performance and Shaping Identity: Performance Indicators and the International Criminal Court' (2021) 18 *Journal of International Criminal Justice* 825; Yassin Brunger, *Investigations and Prosecutions of Sexual and Gender-based Violence by the International Criminal Court* (Institute for Justice and Reconciliation, 2017); Hemi Mistry, 'The Significance of Institutional Culture in Enhancing the Validity of International Criminal Tribunals' (2017) 17 *International Criminal Law Review* 703; Hemi Mistry, 'The Paradox of Dissent: Judicial Dissent and the Projects of International Criminal Justice' (2015) 13 *Journal of International Criminal Justice* 449; John D Jackson and Yassin M Brunger, 'Fragmentation and Harmonisation in the Development of Evidentiary Practices in International Criminal Tribunals' in Elies van Sliedregt and Sergey Vasiliev (eds), *Pluralism in International Criminal Law* (OUP, 2014); Roisin Mulgrew, *Towards the Development of the International Penal System* (CUP, 2013); John Jackson and Yassin M'Boge, 'Integrating A Socio-Legal Approach to Evidence in the International Criminal Tribunals' (2013) 26 *Leiden Journal of International Law* 933 & (2014) 27 *Leiden Journal of International Law* 189; Morten Bergsmo, Olympia Bekou and Annika Jones, 'New Technologies in Criminal Justice for Core International Crimes: The ICC Legal Tools Project' (2010) 10 *Human Rights Law Review* 715.

Boister,[108] Olympia Bekou,[109] Tom Obokata,[110] Ademola Abass,[111] Mashood Baderin,[112] Christy Shucksmith-Wesley,[113] Giovanna Frisso,[114] to name-drop only those I can vividly recall. Most of the individual option choices currently comprising the degree, including its International Criminal Law centrepiece and those modules on humanitarian law and collective security which actually predate the specialist LLM, will continue to be offered under the umbrella of an LLM in International Law. What will be lost, however, is the specialist focus, which has both outward-facing and internal structural dimensions. For external audiences, we will no longer advertise International Criminal Justice as a dedicated masters-level specialism, and this omission is likely to harm student recruitment and narrow the career pipeline supplying talented doctoral researchers and early-career scholars.[115] More tangibly and immediately, loss of an explicitly interdisciplinary degree pathway will make it more difficult to offer new modules blending topics in international criminal law, human rights law, criminal justice, criminology and penology, an opportunity for research-led teaching that dozens of Nottingham colleagues, past and present, have exploited in developing their own bespoke additions to the degree programme since 1998. In curriculum design and structure, as in much else, innovation begets innovation. Conversely, when the entire programme was presented and organised as the 'LLM in International Law', it was difficult to get a hearing for anything relating to criminal justice, and some students were even resistant to domestic (as opposed to *international*) human rights law. Relocating a doctrinally fashioned International Criminal Law within International Law's conceptual framework risks reinstating the pedagogic

[108] Neil Boister, '"Transnational Criminal Law"?' (2003) 14 *European Journal of International Law* 953; Neil Boister and Robert J Currie (eds), *Routledge Handbook of Transnational Criminal Law* (Routledge, 2015); Neil Boister, *An Introduction to Transnational Criminal Law*, 2nd edn (OUP, 2018); Neil Boister, Sabine Gless, and Florian Jeßberger (eds), *Histories of Transnational Criminal Law* (OUP, 2021).

[109] Olympia Bekou and Rob Cryer (eds), *The International Criminal Court* (Ashgate, 2004); Olympia Bekou and Daley Birkett (eds), *Cooperation and the International Criminal Court: Perspectives from Theory and Practice* (Brill, 2016); Andraž Zidar and Olympia Bekou (eds), *Contemporary Challenges for the International Criminal Court* (BIICL, 2022).

[110] Tomoya Obokata, *Transnational Organised Crime in International Law* (Hart Publishing, 2010); Tomoya Obokata, *Transnational Organised Crime: A Comparative Analysis* (Routledge, 2016).

[111] Ademola Abass (ed), *Protecting Human Security in Africa* (OUP, 2010); Ademola Abass, 'Prosecuting International Crimes in Africa: Rationale, Prospects and Challenges' (2013) 24 *European Journal of International Law* 933.

[112] Mashood Baderin, *International Human Rights and Islamic Law* (OUP, 2003).

[113] Christy Shucksmith-Wesley, *The International Committee of the Red Cross and its Mandate to Protect and Assist: Law and Practice* (Hart Publishing, 2017).

[114] Giovanna M Frisso, 'The Winding Down of the ICTY: The Impact of the Completion Strategy and the Residual Mechanism on Victims' (2011) 3 *Goettingen Journal of International Law* 1093.

[115] In 2023–24 enrolment for the International Criminal Law module stood at 61, making it easily, by some distance, the most popular option on the entire LLM programme, with more takers than even commercial and business law options. Time will tell how much of this popularity is the legacy of a dedicated LLM in International Criminal Justice and Armed Conflict and its halo effect for the reputation of the institution, and how much of it can be sustained within the framework of a generalist LLM in International Law. I predict numbers will plummet by half.

and intellectual silos that the LLM in International Criminal Justice and Armed Conflict was designed to escape.

Although arguably more an exercise in rebranding than substantive curriculum overhaul, therefore, it remains a shame in my eyes to see the specialist degree culled and butchered on the altar of bureaucratic centralisation and administrative convenience,[116] with all the impeccable logic of the man who decapitated himself to cure a toothache.[117] Under this *dirigiste* model of university management,[118] the LLM in International Criminal Justice and Armed Conflict would hardly have been viable and most likely would never have existed. The idea would have arrived stillborn, and innumerable academic careers, together with the education of hundreds of postgraduate[119] students and a chunk of disciplinary literature, would have been impoverished. All this comes too late to ask Rob for his assessment of the specialist LLM's demise, but I can venture an educated guess. Knowing him as a passionate believer in pedagogical ideals and one of our foremost imagineers of international criminal justice, he would not have been favourably impressed.

[116] Nowadays embedded into the technological infrastructure. International Criminal Justice? Computer says No! www.youtube.com/watch?v=x0YGZPycMEU (accessed 17 December 2025).

[117] I don't deny the reality of prevailing exigencies (*cf* Richard Adams, 'Three in Four England Universities Expected to be in the Red Next Year', *The Guardian*, 15 November 2024; Alisha Rahaman Sarkar, 'Universities Consider Firing Staff and Cutting Courses as Foreign Student Enrolments Plummet', *The Independent*, 16 March 2024), but question the intelligence and agility of institutional responses.

[118] Pervasive across the sector and driven in part by government policies and commercial pressures for which universities themselves are not responsible but are forced to navigate in order to stay afloat. Chapter 11 revisits this theme. For constructive critique, see Stefan Collini, *What Are Universities For?* (Penguin, 2012); Susan Haack, 'Out of Step: Academic Ethics in A Preposterous Environment' in Susan Haack, *Putting Philosophy to Work* (Prometheus Books, 2013); Susan Haack, 'Universities' Research Imperative: Paying the Price for Perverse Incentives' (2022), www.againstprof-phil.org/wp-content/uploads/haack_universities_research_imperative_APP_SH_version_sept22.pdf (accessed 17 December 2025). At the more doom-laden end of the market, see Peter Fleming, *Dark Academia: How Universities Die* (Pluto Press, 2021).

[119] In addition to paving the way for Rob and Olympia's undergraduate International Criminal Law option (above, p 228) Dino reminds me that the thinking we put into devising the LLM degree also percolated into the first-year undergraduate curriculum, not least by injecting 'a good dose of the Pinochet saga' into the introductory Understanding Law module.

9

Mr Seferovic's Pigeons

BioNote: When I joined UoN in 1993, institutional relations with NTU were somewhat frosty, owing to a difference of opinion regarding whether 'Nottingham Law School' was a confusingly misleading name for a new venture in professional legal education. Such matters were – and still are – way above my pay grade, though I do know that several of my visitors have ended up lost on Chaucer Street over the years, and to this day some of my mail still gets routed via NTU. I suppose it didn't help that my Department of Law was located in the Trent Building, nor did changing our name to the School of Law presumably mitigate any confusion. Happily, none of this institutional friction chilled relations between individual members of staff working in the fields of criminal law and criminal justice, which in my experience have been unfailingly warm, collegial and collaborative.

Ralph Henham was a central figure in this informal Nottingham network, and we would soon become firm friends as well as academic colleagues. Particularly in the early years after my arrival in the leafy Beeston suburbs, I would regularly find myself driving the few miles along Derby Road and down into the city centre to attend lectures and seminars at NTU, including, in due course, Ralph's own inaugural professorial lecture. Frequent return visits were made in the opposite direction. Ralph was a stalwart of our termly Criminal Justice Discussion Group meetings, a tireless reader of material in draft, and an astute sparring partner for knocking unformed ideas into shape.

Two features of Ralph's own research and extensive publications stand out, to me, as particularly admirable. First, whether exploring plea bargaining, sentencing, victimology, or general penal policy, Ralph's writing is informed by a strong sociological sensibility, inherited from Durkheim via Roger Cotterrell. This strand of thought constitutes a significant, and sometimes challenging, corrective for those of us inclined to more austerely normative perspectives, analyses and argumentation. Interdisciplinarity, and the close attention to methodological questions to which it almost inevitably leads, are a second notable feature of Ralph's scholarship. Shifting focus from (primarily) domestic to international criminal justice might appear, in retrospect, an obvious extrapolation from existing penal theorising, but this is an illusion cast by the speed with which new disciplinary genres – when timely and successful – coalesce, solidify and institutionalise. When Ralph originally saw the potential connections, in the days before International Criminal Law was a recognised subject, his publications (many in collaboration with Mark Findlay) mapped out bold and original new directions for criminal justice research and international penal policy. Ralph Henham was in the first cohort of disciplinary scouts and outriders mapping a penologically-informed approach to international criminal justice.[1]

Personal relationships between scholars are perhaps, after all, not so different from relations between institutional neighbours. If we sometimes disagree, explicitly and in public, this is only the logical consequence of a shared commitment to deeper intellectual projects and values. The creative tensions of academic debate, when conducted in the generous spirit exemplified by Ralph Henham throughout his long and distinguished career, cement enduring friendships and keep the conversation alive.

I. Institutional and Disciplinary Context

Ralph Henham has throughout his career consistently advocated 'contextual modelling', insisting on '[t]he evaluation of legal process in its socio-political and historical context'.[2] This research agenda calls for 'the development of a comparative contextual model to facilitate this task'.[3] Contextualisation is the midwife of methodological reflection,[4] encouraging exploration of the various *methods* through which legal institutions (amongst other things) may be placed in context. This orientation tends to produce a healthy disregard for conventional disciplinary boundaries coupled with a pragmatic preference for methodological pluralism: follow the research problem wherever it leads, using whatever intellectual tools and methodological protocols may be best suited to the task! Interdisciplinarity is an almost obligatory implication of this way of thinking;[5] a rejection, not of doctrinal scholarship, but of doctrinalism: the false idea that close textual analysis of primary legal authorities is the only valid or worthwhile form of jurisprudence.[6]

[1] See, in particular, Ralph Henham, 'Theorising Law and Legitimacy in International Criminal Justice' (2007) 3 *International Journal of Law in Context* 257 (engaging with me on issues of the intrinsic or instrumental value of criminal adjudication that I am still chewing over!); Ralph Henham, 'The Philosophical Foundations of International Sentencing' (2003) 1 *Journal of International Criminal Justice* 64. Generally, see Paul Behrens (ed), *Contemporary Challenges to Criminal Justice: Liber Amicorum for Ralph Henham* (Hart, 2023).

[2] See, eg, Ralph Henham, *Sentencing and the Legitimacy of Trial Justice* (Routledge, 2012); Ralph Henham, 'Theory and Contextual Analysis in Sentencing' (2001) 29 *International Journal of the Sociology of Law* 253.

[3] Ralph Henham, 'Theorizing the Penality of Sentencing in International Criminal Trials' (2004) 8 *Theoretical Criminology* 429, 435.

[4] *Cf* Mark Findlay and Ralph Henham, 'Integrating Theory and Method in the Comparative Contextual Analysis of Trial Process' in Mike McConville and Wing Hong Chui (eds), *Research Methods for Law*, 2nd edn (Edinburgh University Press, 2017).

[5] Also see Chapter 11. For theoretical elucidation and practical applications, see Paul Roberts, 'Interdisciplinarity in Legal Research' in Mike McConville and Wing H Chui (eds), *Research Methods for Law*, 3rd edn (Edinburgh University Press, 2024); Paul Roberts, 'Renegotiating Forensic Cultures: Between Law, Science and Criminal Justice' (2013) 44 *Studies in the History and Philosophy of Biological and Biomedical Sciences* 47; Paul Roberts, 'Penal Offence in Question: Some Reference Points for Interdisciplinary Conversation' in A P Simester and Andrew von Hirsch (eds), *Incivilities: Regulating Offensive Behaviour* (Hart Publishing, 2006).

[6] For a powerful antidote, see William Twining, *General Jurisprudence* (CUP, 2012).

Contextualisation, sophisticated methodological pluralism, and intelligent interdisciplinarity together constitute a powerful compound lens through which to examine novel institutional developments and disciplinary formations, such as the unprecedented expansion and reconfiguration of international criminal law which took flight in the final decade of the twentieth century. Dreamers have always dreamed,[7] and there were significant if disparate historical precedents,[8] but a living, breathing, censuring and sanctioning system of international criminal trials and punishments was something entirely new and – for many seasoned observers – somewhat unexpected.[9] This was intellectually energising, if head-scratchingly unfamiliar and potentially disorientating, terrain for those of us schooled primarily in domestic criminal law and penality[10] but equipped with the methodological nous to pay attention and ponder wider theoretical, institutional and disciplinary implications.[11]

The previous chapter reflected on the disciplinary constitution of International Criminal Law. This chapter combines more granular evidentiary inquiries with broader themes in international criminal trial procedure. It employs a detailed case-study as a vehicle for advancing a general proposition: that scholars of evidence, proof and procedure could learn a great deal from experiences of international

[7] For a sense of enduring idealism, see, eg, Richard J Goldstone, *For Humanity: Reflections of a War Crimes Investigator* (Yale University Press, 2000); Kofi Annan, 'Advocating for an International Criminal Court' (1997) 21 *Fordham International Law Journal* 363; Henry T King, Jr, 'The Meaning of Nuremberg' (1998) 30 *Case Western Reserve Journal of International Law* 143; M Cherif Bassiouni, 'Searching for Peace and Achieving Justice: The Need for Accountability' (1996) 59 *Law and Contemporary Problems* 9.

[8] Robert Cryer, *Prosecuting International Crimes: Selectivity and the International Criminal Law Regime* (CUP, 2005); Gary J Bass, *Stay the Hand of Vengeance: The Politics of War Crimes Tribunals* (Princeton University Press, 2002); Tim L H McCormack, 'From Sun Tzu to the Sixth Committee: The Evolution of an International Criminal Law Regime' in Timothy L H McCormack and Gerry Simpson (eds), *The Law of War Crimes: National and International Approaches* (Kluwer, 1997); Telford Taylor, *The Anatomy of the Nuremberg Trial* (Little, Brown & Co 1993); Matthew Lippman, 'The Other Nuremberg: American Prosecutions of Nazi War Criminals in Occupied Germany' (1992) 3 *Indiana International and Comparative Law Review* 1.

[9] Creating a trial court empowered to adjudicate individual criminal responsibility was an unprecedented application of the UN Security Council's Chapter VII enforcement powers, and the successful outcome of the Rome Conference to establish a permanent International Criminal Court was by no means assured: see J Hooper and I Black, 'Self-Interest Brings Court into Contempt', *The Guardian*, 15 July 1998; D J Harris, 'Progress and Problems in Creating an International Criminal Court' (1998) 3 *Journal of Armed Conflict Law* 1; Immi Tallgren, 'We Did It? The Vertigo of Law and Everyday Life at the Diplomatic Conference on the Establishment of an International Criminal Court' (1999) 12 *Leiden Journal of International Law* 683.

[10] David Garland's handy neologism encapsulating 'the whole of the penal complex, including its laws, sanctions, institutions, and practices and its discourses, symbols, rituals, and performances': David Garland, 'Penality and the Penal State' (2013) 51 *Criminology* 475.

[11] For embryonic thoughts, see Paul Roberts, 'Comparative Law for International Criminal Justice' in Esin Örücü and David Nelken (eds), *Comparative Law – A Handbook* (Hart Publishing, 2007); Paul Roberts and Nesam McMillan, 'For Criminology in International Criminal Justice' (2003) 1 *Journal of International Criminal Justice* 315 and reprinted in Ruth Jamieson (ed), *The Criminology of War* (Ashgate, 2014); Paul Roberts, 'Restoration and Retribution in International Criminal Justice: An Exploratory Analysis' in Andrew von Hirsch et al (eds), *Restorative Justice and Criminal Justice* (Hart Publishing, 2003).

criminal adjudication accumulated over the last three decades. This endeavour forms part of a programmatic agenda to supplement and contextualise primarily expository studies of the Law of Evidence[12] by 'taking facts seriously',[13] exploiting interdisciplinary resources,[14] and reimagining disciplinary frameworks in terms of Evidence and Proof or 'forensic science' in the literal, juristic sense.[15] The following discussion examines just one fragment of a single case, the trial of Dusko Tadic for war crimes and crimes against humanity before the UN's International Criminal Tribunal for the Former Yugoslavia (ICTY), which was conducted in The Hague in 1996–97.

Tadic was, in fact, the first decision handed down by the ICTY.[16] In pronouncing the first truly international criminal conviction since the post-WWII military tribunals held in Nuremberg and Tokyo in 1945–48, this new contender for 'trial of the century'[17] predictably, and quite properly, attracted international media coverage[18] and extensive academic analysis.[19] Most of this commentary was, however, initially skewed towards examining the status of the ICTY in international law, the extent of its legal jurisdiction, broader political questions about the Tribunal's legitimacy, and the likely impact and consequences of its on-going work – including the Tribunal's major contributions to the normative development of international humanitarian law, as a precursor to what would become, within another decade or so, the evolved jurisdiction of a permanent International Criminal Court (ICC).[20] The judgment in *Tadic* was, in short, primarily of interest to international lawyers, who understandably viewed it through Public

[12] Also see Chapters 5 and 7.

[13] William Twining, 'Taking Facts Seriously' in Neil Gold (ed), *Essays on Legal Education* (Toronto, Butterworths, 1982); Paul Roberts, 'Rethinking the Law of Evidence: A Twenty-First Century Agenda for Teaching and Research' (2002) 55 *Current Legal Problems* 297; William Twining, 'Taking Facts Seriously – Again' in Paul Roberts and Mike Redmayne (eds), *Innovations in Evidence and Proof* (Hart Publishing, 2007).

[14] William Twining, 'Evidence as a Multi-disciplinary Subject' (2003) 2 *Law, Probability and Risk* 91; Paul Roberts, 'Groundwork for A Jurisprudence of Criminal Procedure' in R A Duff and Stuart Green (eds), *Philosophical Foundations of Criminal Law* (OUP, 2011).

[15] John Jackson and Paul Roberts, 'Beyond Common Law Evidence: Reimagining, and Reinvigorating, Evidence Law as Forensic Science' in Darryl K Brown, Jenia Iontcheva Turner and Bettina Weisser (eds), *The Oxford Handbook of Criminal Process* (OUP, 2019); David Schum, 'Classifying Forms and Combinations of Evidence: Necessary in a Science of Evidence' in Philip Dawid, William Twining and Mimi Vasilaki (eds), *Evidence, Inference and Enquiry* (OUP, 2011).

[16] *Prosecutor v Tadic*, IT-94-1 ('Prijedor'), Trial Chamber Judgement 7 May 1997.

[17] M S Zaid, 'Trial of the Century? Assessing the Case of Dusko Tadic before the International Criminal Tribunal for the Former Yugoslavia' (1997) 2 *ILSA Journal of International and Comparative Law* 589. *Cf* Patricia M Wald, 'Running the Trial of the Century: The Nuremberg Legacy' (2006) 27 *Cardozo Law Review* 1559.

[18] Eg, C Bellamy, 'Bosnian Serb Found Guilty of War Crimes', *The Guardian*, 8 May 1997; Reuters, 'A Bosnian Serb Gets 20 Years for War Crimes', *New York Times*, 15 July 1997.

[19] A vast literature rapidly accumulated. For nuanced analysis, see Jose E Alvarez, 'Rush to Closure: Lessons of the *Tadic* Judgment' (1998) 96 *Michigan Law Review* 2031.

[20] Antonio Cassese, Paola Gaeta and John R W D Jones (eds), *The Rome Statute of the International Criminal Court: A Commentary* (OUP, 2002); Dominic McGoldrick, 'A Permanent International Criminal Court: An End to a Culture of Impunity' [1999] *Criminal Law Review* 627.

International Law (PIL) – and subsequently, International Criminal Law – lenses. As an American judge at the ICTY observed, one implication of this spontaneous division of disciplinary curation or colonisation was that 'scholars and commentators on the Tribunals appear to pay much more attention to substantive law developments than to procedure and process'.[21]

In discussing some of *Tadic*'s evidentiary dimensions, and more generally in bringing international criminal adjudication to the attention of predominantly domestically orientated Evidence law scholars and teachers, this chapter provides a modest corrective to these lopsided tendencies in the scholarly literature on international criminal adjudication. As a contribution to a nascent scholarship developing international criminal procedure,[22] it might even encourage proceduralists to venture into the theoretical and policy debates surrounding, and to some extent still shaping, international criminal proceedings.

II. Witness to Cold-blooded Murder

In civilian life, Dusko – aka 'Dule' – Tadic was a café owner and part-time policeman. During the vicious civil wars which tore through the Balkan region in the early 1990s, he served as a mid-ranking commander of a Serb paramilitary unit. Tadic was subsequently indicted by the ICTY for various war crimes and crimes against humanity, including torture and murder of civilians, forced expulsions of non-Serb populations from the Prijedor region of Bosnia ('ethnic cleansing') and appalling mistreatment of prisoners of war. Amongst this grisly catalogue of indicted offences featured the cold-blooded murder of two Bosnian Muslim police officers, Edin Besic and Osman Didovic, who were allegedly pulled out of a line-up of surrendered prisoners standing with their hands behind their heads and stabbed to death by the accused. Although this was far from being the worst of Tadic's behaviour in these dark days of civil war and sectarian occupation, these particular murders were significant because the prosecution could produce an apparently impressive eyewitness claiming to have seen the victims die at Tadic's own hand, rather than as part of a common enterprise (potentially diluting

[21] P M Wald, 'Rules of Evidence in the Yugoslav War Tribunal' (2003) 21 *Quinnipiac Law Review* 761, 763.

[22] Early contributions include John R W D Jones, *The Practice of the International Criminal Tribunals for the Former Yugoslavia and Rwanda* (Transnational Publishers, 1998); P M Wald, 'Rules of Evidence in the Yugoslav War Tribunal' (2003) 21 *Quinnipiac Law Review* 761; Michael P Scharf, 'Trial and Error: An Assessment of the First Judgment of the Yugoslavia War Crimes Tribunal' (1997–98) 30 *New York University Journal of International Law and Politics* 167; P L Robinson, 'Ensuring Fair and Expeditious Trials at the International Criminal Tribunal for the Former Yugoslavia' (2000) 11 *European Journal of International Law* 569; Kellye L Fabian, 'Proof and Consequences: an Analysis of the *Tadic* & *Akayesu* Trials' (2000) 49 *DePaul Law Review* 981. For pioneering theorisation, see Ralph Henham, *Punishment and Process in International Criminal Trials* (Ashgate, 2005).

criminal responsibility amongst several co-accused) or un-witnessed murders of the 'disappeared'.

Nihad Seferovic had been at school with Dusko Tadic. Indeed, their families lived within ten houses of each other on the same street where Tadic and Seferovic both grew up in a town called Kozarac in the Prijedor region of the former Yugoslavia. However, Seferovic was a Muslim, not a Serb like Tadic, and when the order came for Bosnian Muslims to report to Serb army collection points, Seferovic fled to the hills, periodically thereafter venturing back down into the town on various errands. It was on one of these sorties that, whilst hiding in tall grass and concealed by overhanging plum trees, Seferovic caught sight of Tadic standing in a group of 15 or so Serb paramilitaries in front of the Serb Orthodox Church. The Serbs were apparently harassing a line of Muslim prisoners. Hiding less than 30 metres away, Seferovic was adamant that he recognised Tadic and saw him murder the two defenceless, already-detained policemen.

III. Trial and Appeal before the ICTY

The judgment of the ICTY Trial Chamber briefly rehearsed the testimony of witness Seferovic:

> Nihad Seferovic testified that on the afternoon of 26 May 1992, on his way back home from the hills in Besici, he stopped at the orchard of a house across from the Serbian Orthodox church. In front of the church he saw approximately six Muslim policemen from Kozarac, including Edin Besic, Ekrem Besic, Emir Karabasic and one Osman with their hands behind their necks standing in line. In front of them were the accused, Goran Borovnica, 'Dule' and about 15 other Serb paramilitaries who had weapons pointed at the Muslim policemen. He saw the accused pull two of the policemen, Osman and Edin Besic, out of the line and kill them by slitting their throats and stabbing each one several times.[23]

It was also recalled that '[t]he Defence challenged the witness's ability to view clearly the events occurring in the churchyard'.[24] Nonetheless, basing itself almost entirely on Seferovic's testimony, the Trial Chamber found 'beyond reasonable doubt that the accused … killed two policemen, Osman [Didovic] and Edin Besic, in front of the Serbian Orthodox church in Kozarac'.[25] Tadic was accordingly convicted of murdering Besic and Didovic, amongst other atrocities, and sentenced to a term of 25 years' imprisonment.

On appeal, the defence took exception to Seferovic's evidence on several grounds, including the possibility that Seferovic was a Bosnian government 'plant'

[23] *Prosecutor v Tadic*, IT-94-1 ('Prijedor'), Trial Chamber Judgment 7 May 1997, [393].
[24] ibid.
[25] ibid [397].

who had lied to the ICTY in order to exact revenge on Serbs.[26] Another argument, of particular interest to Evidence scholars, was that Seferovic's account was inherently implausible, for the reason later summarised by the ICTY Appeals Chamber:

> The Defence argues that the Trial Chamber erred in relying on the evidence of Mr Seferovic because it is implausible. Mr Seferovic, a Muslim who lived in an area under bombardment by Serbian paramilitary forces, fled to the mountains for safety. He testified at trial that he was so concerned about the welfare of his pet pigeons that he returned to town to feed them while the Serbian paramilitaries were still there. On his return to town, he saw Mr Tadic kill two policemen. Defence counsel contended at trial that the witness was never in town at the time of the killings ...[27]

Indeed, this contention was advanced with some force in defence counsel's submissions to the ICTY Appeals Chamber. Appellate counsel called into question the Trial Chamber's willingness to conclude, beyond reasonable doubt, that Tadic had murdered Besic and Didovic solely in reliance on one eyewitness's testimony:

> That decision depended solely on the evidence of one witness, Nihad Seferovic. In our submission, the evidence of that witness was implausible when analysed .... The background to his evidence is that he was a Muslim living in the area that had been under attack by Serb paramilitary forces. There had been a bombardment of the town where he lived, and he had fled to some nearby hills or mountains for safety. The cornerstone of his evidence was that before the bombardment, he had kept tame pigeons, and he was so concerned about their welfare that when the Serb paramilitaries were still in the town, he decided to return to the town in order to feed his pet birds. As a rational decision, that is, on any view, curious, because he was placing himself in the gravest of jeopardy in order to do no more than feed some pet birds who would have been most unlikely to have survived the bombardment of the town in any event; but that was the only explanation for him being in the town at the moment that these two men were killed, the evidence that he gave being that he approached the killing in an orchard to the distance of some 30 metres and, at that distance, was able to identify the defendant as the man who took two men out of a line of five and killed them in the area immediately in front of the Orthodox church. The evidence was identified in the judgement of the Trial Chamber at paragraph 393, and it merely recounts there the evidence that the witness gave ... It was not, with respect to the Trial Chamber, the most critical analysis of the evidence of the witness Seferovic; it was, in truth, no more than a recitation of the effect of what he said .... And the unlikelihood is obviously a reflection of the inherent improbability of anybody with any regard to their own safety willingly entering a town

[26] This is not, alas, a completely fanciful accusation. Another witness who testified against Tadic was exposed as a perjurer seeking revenge on Serbs: see *Decision on Prosecution Motion to Withdraw Protective Measures for Witness L*, 5 December 1996, where the Trial Chamber observed that '[W]itness L had admitted ... that he had lied about the death of his father while under oath. Witness L asserted that he had done this at the behest of the Bosnian government authorities who had allegedly "trained" him to give evidence against the accused, Dusko Tadic .... Consequently, the Prosecution advised the Trial Chamber that it could no longer support witness L as a witness of truth and invited the Trial Chamber to disregard his evidence entirely.' Also see Nancy Combs, *Fact-Finding Without Facts: The Uncertain Evidentiary Foundations of International Criminal Convictions* (CUP, 2010) ch 5.

[27] *Prosecutor v Tadic*, IT-94-1-A (Appeals Chamber), 15 July 1999; (2002) 9 IHRR 1051, [58].

> currently occupied by Serb paramilitaries when they were in the process of actively deporting the Muslims to concentration camps in order to feed a pet bird. It is, we would submit, such an unlikely and improbable story that any Tribunal would want to reflect on whether it could possibly be true.[28]

Expressed in such stark terms, the proposition that a person would risk enemy bombardment and possible capture and internment in a concentration camp 'in order to feed a pet bird' does seem rather unlikely. Yet the ICTY Appeals Chamber remained unimpressed:

> The Appeals Chamber does not accept as inherently implausible the witness' claim that the reason why he returned to the town where the Serbian paramilitary forces had been attacking, and from which he had escaped, was to feed his pet pigeons. It is conceivable that a person may do such a thing, even though one might think such action to be an irrational risk. The Trial Chamber, after seeing the witness, hearing his testimony, and observing him under cross-examination, chose to accept his testimony as reliable evidence. There is no basis for the Appeals Chamber to consider that the Trial Chamber acted unreasonably in relying on that evidence for its finding that the Appellant killed the two men.[29]

Tadic's appeal against his convictions of these two murders was accordingly dismissed, although his overall sentence was subsequently reduced to 20 years (including time served).[30] Having obtained Serbian citizenship whilst still in custody, Tadic was granted provisional release after serving two-thirds of his sentence and deported to Serbia in 2008, where he resumed civilian life.

IV. Analysis[31]

The tale of Mr Seferovic's pigeons is worthy of extended commentary and analysis for the valuable light it sheds on issues of evidence, proof, legal process and adjudication. In the first instance, this memorable vignette constitutes an instructive study in fact-finding by international criminal tribunals. However, the resonances of this case-study extend far beyond its peculiar institutional context. Indeed, the brief cameo appearance of Mr Seferovic's pigeons in the litigation histories of the ICTY would repay close study by any legal scholar with an interest in questions of evidence and proof, in domestic as much as international proceedings.

A first striking feature of this aspect of Tadic's case is the extent to which the facts discussed on appeal are at variance with the testimony actually given by witness Seferovic at trial. For although Seferovic was asked several questions

[28] *Prosecutor v Tadic*, IT-94-1-A (Appeals Chamber), Transcript of Proceedings, 385–89 (20 April 1999).

[29] *Prosecutor v Tadic*, IT-94-1-A (Appeals Chamber), 15 July 1999, [66].

[30] R Norton-Taylor, 'War Crimes Court Sentence Slashed', *The Guardian*, 27 January 2000.

[31] For methodological tools and context, see Terence Anderson, David Schum and William Twining, *Analysis of Evidence* 2nd edn (CUP, 2005).

about feeding his pigeons under cross-examination, bird-feeding did not feature in his testimony-in-chief as Seferovic's overriding motivation for venturing back into Kozarac during the bombardment. In this exchange, for example, prosecution counsel tries to establish the day of the week when Seferovic came back into town:[32]

A [Seferovic]. No, I do not remember at all what day it was.

Q. Was it within a -----

A. I know that it was a very nice day in the morning.

Q. Was it within approximately three days after the shelling began?

A. I think so. I do not remember because I went through a terrible catastrophe myself.

Q. In any event, whatever day of the week it was or whatever the date was, did you go into Kozarac? Did you leave Besici and go into Kozarac on the first day that people began to surrender?

A. Yes, I did. I was looking for my brother, for my family members, friends, relatives.

And in the following two passages, prosecution counsel is trying to establish witness Seferovic's precise location at the material time:

Q. Can you point out on this map where your brother's house was?

A. (Indicated) Here, somewhere here, yes.

Q. That would be the street between the hospital and the church?

A. Yes.

Q. Was your brother at his home when you got there?

A. No, I did not find anyone at home.

Q. After that, did you move to a point a little bit closer to the Prijedor/Banja Luka highway?

A. Yes, yes. I saw what was happening around the church ….

Q. Mr. Seferovic, can you show us on this map where your brother's house was and the position you moved to after leaving your brother's house?

A. (Indicated) I think here. This is where my brother's house, and I then went through the gardens, through the back yards and then I came to this house, the last house here.

Q. What is across the street from that spot?

A. There is a church yard and a church.

Having established his position just across from the churchyard, Seferovic then gave a graphic account of the murders:

A. I could see clearly everything …

Q. Did you continue to observe this scene for some period of time?

[32] Passages of verbatim witness examination reproduced in this chapter are excerpted from ICTY Case No IT-94-1-T, Transcript of Hearing, 2651–2706 (14 June 1996).

A. Yes, yes. Those paramilitaries provoked the civilians no end. At a certain point, Dule Tadic came, dragged Osman from the group, shouted, 'Follow me', got him by his neck, and cut his throat and then stabbed him below that several times … and then he proceeded to Edin Besic, and with the same – and he hit him in the same way as he did Osman; and this was followed by incredible fire, and I then ran away. I followed the same path and I cut through and ran to Besici.

The first reference to birdlife in Seferovic's examination-in-chief appears by way of volunteered incidental detail, in answer to a question about why he needed to return to town to recover some possessions:

Q. What did you do when the attack [i.e. the shelling of Kozarac] started?

A. I ran out into the road … and then I went into the hills, into Besici.

Q. Did you stop to change your clothes or to pack any belongings?

A. No, no. No, I just left ….

Q. Did you go back to Kozarac at any point to retrieve some belongings?

A. Yes, yes. I did go back later. In the evening I went back home. I had a lot of birds and I fed the birds. I took my backpack and I went back into the hills.

It is only *after* Seferovic has already witnessed the murders that we hear anything about pigeons being a motivating factor in his return to the scene:

Q. Within a few days did you return to Kozarac?

A. Yes, I kept coming back to Kozarac because I had many birds, I felt the need to feed them. The last time, unfortunately, I was hit in the leg by a bullet, I do not know where from, was it a stray bullet or whether it was on purpose but I was fired [on] all the time, non-stop around the clock.

Q. After you were struck by that bullet did you manage to make your way back to Besici?

A. Yes, yes. I did manage to get back to Besici with the help of a stick, on a stick, yes.

For a time, Seferovic hid in a natural hollow by a stream and tried to dress his wound with plum brandy. He was later apprehended by Serb militias on the road back to Kozarac and sent to Omarska concentration camp. By this time, he seems to have had much more on his mind than feeding pigeons:

Q. Did you finally leave the hole and attempt to go back to Kozarac in an effort to find your family or friends?

A. Yes, I do not remember how many days I spent in the hole, but the pain was excruciating. I fainted several times and when the swelling receded I stood up. I somehow found superhuman strength to stand up, to pull myself up, with the help of that stick, and move and go and try to find my brother because I knew he had stayed in Kozarac …

Seferovic's sorties into Kozarac were also explored in cross-examination. Again, plausible reasons were stated with no initial mention of avian mercy missions:

Q. Did you stay in that basement, the first night, the Sunday, that the shelling started?

A. No, I did not. I went back to Kozarac. I took some personal belongings that I needed the most, my underwear, my shirts – and I really needed them when I was wounded because I used that to tie my leg. I did not have any bandages or anything like that.

Q. So, although the shelling was taking place on Kozarac on the Sunday night, you went back into Kozarac to get some of your personal belongings, is that right?

A. Yes, yes, the mortars were falling and I went to get my personal belongings.

When pigeon-feeding crops up again, it seems to be – at most – a secondary consideration in risking the shelling in Kozarac, mainly in order to retrieve essential provisions:

Q. The next day, which would be the Tuesday, after you had spent the night in the basement, did you remain in Besici?

A. No, in the morning I came home. I fed my birds. That was at dawn. I do not remember what hour exactly, but it was dawn. I fed my birds. I poured a lot of water for them, gave them a lot of seeds because I realised that I could not come back every day to feed the birds. Then I went back to Besici again, naturally with bread and blankets and other necessities because the houses were just filled with things ….

Q. So, having fed your birds at dawn, you left Kozarac and you went back up into the hills and again gave out some of the blankets and supplies that you had been able to take?

A. Yes.

There then appears the following passage of cross-examination, which does place greater stress on witness Seferovic's concern for his pigeons' welfare:

Q. So when you fed your birds in the early hours of Tuesday morning, presumably, you had fed them so that they would have enough for a few days, would that be right?

A. Yes.

Q. Did you return to those birds again to see that they were fed and watered?

A. No, but I did go back constantly to the house to see the birds. Even after Kozarac surrendered, I did that and afterwards. I always went back home and paid attention to the birds, not just mine alone, but also my neighbour's.

It should be stressed, however, that in these exchanges defence counsel was not trying to suggest that Seferovic was fabricating his evidence because nobody would be so idiotic as to enter a town under bombardment in order to feed pet birds. Rather, counsel was trying to demonstrate that Seferovic was confused about the relevant dates in an attempt to provide some substantiation for Tadic's alibi. This strategy proved largely fruitless, however. Seferovic just kept repeating that he could not really be sure what day it was; it might have been a Tuesday or possibly another day, but in any case, he was absolutely certain that he had watched his old classmate Dusko Tadic murder two unarmed Bosnian policemen in front of the Orthodox church on one of the days when the town of Kozarac surrendered to the Serbs:

[Defence counsel]: So when you say you went back into Kozarac to your brother's house which was near the hospital, was that on the Wednesday, the day after you had fed

> your birds in the morning, or was it on the same day that you had fed them at dawn on Tuesday?
>
> A. No, I do not remember what day it was when Kozarac surrendered, but when Kozarac surrendered I went to see my brother.
>
> Q. When you went to your brother's house, did you go alone or were you with anyone else?
>
> A. No, I was alone .... I just do not remember what day it was because, as I said, Kozarac could not have surrendered in one day. It took several days for it to surrender. I do not remember how many days because I was wounded and I do not remember.

On a close reading of the trial transcripts, therefore, it is apparent that Seferovic's desire to find food and additional clothes and to locate his brother were mentioned as significant – and on their face, much more plausible – reasons for forsaking the comparative safety of his hillside bolthole for the perils of a town under hostile occupation than any supposed preoccupation with pigeon-feeding.

Not only does the witness's evidence in-chief deflate defence counsel's ridicule of the notion that Seferovic would have risked death or capture 'to feed a pet bird' (a tendentious, if forensically unremarkable, adversarial distortion), it also significantly qualifies the Appeals Chamber's bald assertion that '*the* reason why he returned to the town where the Serbian paramilitary forces had been attacking, and from which he had escaped, was to feed his pet pigeons'.[33] The welfare of his pigeons was, at most, only one factor amongst several prompting Seferovic to steal back through the streets of Kozarac, where he would become witness to a double murder. Taking advantage of this – for an Evidence scholar – unusual opportunity to compare trial transcripts against the facts recited on appeal, and uncovering such material discrepancies between them, inevitably prompts the uncomfortable speculation that similar factual distortions might be creeping into domestic criminal appeals in England and Wales, and with very little prospect of detection after the event. Similar distortions may arise in judicial fact-finding in other adjudicative fora, including the European Court of Human Rights.[34] Socio-legal scholars have for many decades explored the institutional dynamics of 'case construction'[35] and we are familiar with the ways in which police interview technique[36] or incomplete prosecution disclosure,[37] for example, can distort the factual narratives presented

[33] *Prosecutor v Tadic*, IT-94-1-A (Appeals Chamber), 15 July 1999, [66] (emphasis supplied).

[34] Compare the ECtHR Chamber's factual analysis in *Al-Khawaja and Tahery v United Kingdom* (2009) 49 EHRR 1 with the Grand Chamber's subsequent treatment (of ostensibly the same facts and evidence) in *Al-Khawaja and Tahery v United Kingdom* (2012) 54 EHRR 23.

[35] Mike McConville, Andrew Sanders and Roger Leng, *The Case for the Prosecution: Police Suspects and the Construction of Criminality* (Routledge, 1991).

[36] Saul M Kassin et al, 'Police-Induced Confessions: Risk Factors and Recommendations' (2010) 34 *Law and Human Behavior* 3; David Dixon, 'Integrity, Interrogation and Criminal Injustice' in Jill Hunter, Paul Roberts, Simon N M Young and David Dixon (eds), *The Integrity of Criminal Process* (Hart Publishing, 2016).

[37] Tom Smith, 'The "Near Miss" of Liam Allan: Critical Problems in Police Disclosure, Investigation Culture and the Resourcing of Criminal Justice' [2018] *Criminal Law Review* 711.

at trial. Less attention has been devoted to potential discrepancies between trial proceedings and factual claims or assumptions on appeal.[38]

A second intriguing dimension of forensic analysis concerns the nature of the prosecution's response to the defence argument challenging Seferovic's evidence on appeal. Ms Brenda Hollis, appearing for the prosecution, adopted what might be termed a 'confession and avoidance' strategy. She conceded that Seferovic's actions might not appear very rational by normal standards, but insisted that people often do irrational things – especially where pet animals are concerned:

> The appellant seemed to argue that because this witness, Nihad Seferovic, would say that he would go into a town where the Serbs were taking it over to feed his birds, that his testimony is inherently incredible. Now, is this a decision many people would think is rational? Of course, it is not. But how many times have we heard stories of people going into burning buildings to rescue pets, of doing other things that subject them to a very real and immediate threat of death to save a pet? Are these rational acts? No, they're not. Are these acts that people do engage in? Yes, they are.[39]

There is nothing inherently wrong with the prosecution's strategy of locking horns with the defence on the issue of contextual rationality and its implications for witness credibility. It is difficult to argue with the general proposition that people sometimes behave irrationally, or that one person's rational errand is another person's folly. A more culturally sensitive analysis might nonetheless have provided greater assistance to the Court. On the one hand, western perceptions of animals are notoriously sentimental. In a culture where every deer calf is Bambi and even ants and fish can become CGI-conjured Hollywood stars, small wonder that people anthropomorphise their pets! The story of Mr Seferovic's pigeons is almost inevitably viewed through these popular cultural filters by western English speakers, but I wonder just how much of this urban sentimentality can legitimately be projected onto the still predominantly agrarian Balkans of the early 1990s. Is it possible, in other words, that the prosecutor's burning-building pet rescue analogy sounds more plausible to *us* than it would to the average Bosnian as a rationalisation of Mr Seferovic's return to Kozarac at such a dangerous – and, as it turned out, evidentially vital – moment in time?

Then again, it does not take much imagination to appreciate that attitudes towards animals are highly culturally divergent. Vivid examples immediately spring to mind, in the reverence for cattle displayed by Hindus and the Jewish disdain for pork,[40] to say nothing of some Buddhists' aversion to crushing insects underfoot. As a Yorkshireman, I know from personal observation that pigeon-fanciers derive long hours of enjoyment and entirely unsentimentalised peer-group

[38] Note that the point at issue here is *what facts were actually found* at first instance rather than appeal judges consciously second-guessing trial court determinations (which common law appellate courts are generally reluctant to do, especially regarding jury verdicts).

[39] Submissions of Prosecuting Counsel to the Appeals Chamber, Transcript, 20 April 1999, at 419.

[40] *Cf* David Fraser, *Anti-Shechita Prosecutions in the Anglo-American World, 1855–1913* (Academic Studies Press, 2018).

status and prestige from breeding champion racing birds. 'My pigeons are my life', or similar extravagant sentiments, would not astonish hardcore members of the pigeon-fancying fraternity.[41] Pigeons may well have originated from the Middle East,[42] and seem to have a special place in regional history and cultural life. It is claimed that keeping and training homing pigeons dates back to the Egyptian pharaohs. The Sultan of Baghdad set up a pigeon-post system in 1150, but in Beirut, Damascus and Cairo today, 'it is a working-class pastime'.[43] Enthusiasts in Yemen reportedly continue to organise races in the midst of brutal civil war, whilst a particularly prized Iraqi specimen sold for $180,000.[44] Do any of these cultural traditions and practices resonate with Mr Seferovic's situation,[45] and, by extension, help to illuminate the issue of his credibility as a witness? Since nobody took it upon themselves during the course of these lengthy proceedings to explore the local cultural context of Seferovic's wartime pigeon-feeding, we will presumably never really know.

A third noteworthy feature of the treatment of witness Seferovic's evidence concerns defence counsel's attempt to invoke academic commentary in order to attack Seferovic's testimonial credibility before the ICTY Appeals Chamber. In a case-note on *Tadic* published in the *American Journal of International Law*, Michael Scharf described Tadic's convictions of the murders of Besic and Didovic as 'curious', and characterised Nihad Seferovic as 'a Muslim who told the Tribunal the unlikely story that he had witnessed the murders when he returned to Kozarac to feed his pet pigeons after the Serb takeover of the town'.[46] This remark – almost a

[41] If you doubt my testimonial credibility, consider this corroboration: D Higgens, 'Return of Pigeon Racing "Like Putting Oxygen" back into Communities', *PA Yorks and Humber*, 1 June 2020: 'Retired miner Mr Greenshield, 72, said … "This is a very strong ex-mining area … So many people have lost people in the mines or are living with illnesses. The whole current situation has got people down and there are a lot of mental problems. The racing is something for people to get out of bed for. People are really looking forward to it. I think it would have killed some off if there hadn't been racing until next year. It's like putting oxygen back into the area".'

[42] Michael D Shapiro et al, 'Genomic Diversity and Evolution of the Head Crest in the Rock Pigeon' (2013) 339 *Science* 1063.

[43] Hugh Levinson, 'In Jordan, The Gentle Art of Keeping Pigeons is Seen as Dangerously Sexy', *The Independent*, 17 December 2000.

[44] France 24, 'Passion for Pigeons Persists in Arab World', 10 March 2021; BBC News, 'Turkey Lockdown: Pigeon-keeping in Istanbul on the Rise', 31 August 2021 www.bbc.co.uk/news/av/world-europe-58344157 (accessed 17 December 2025).

[45] *Cf* Ed Vulliamy, 'Bosnia Allies Fight Out New War', *The Guardian*, 24 October 1992 (reporting '[a]n old man lies dead, shot on the way to feed his pigeons. Another day in Sarajevo'). More hopefully, see Nick Hawton, 'Army Chiefs Look to a Secure Future as Former Foes Unite', *The Times*, 6 October 2003: 'Ten years ago, Hamza Visca was involved in hand-to-hand fighting in the blown out suburbs of Sarajevo. These days he sits behind his desk in the grand army cultural centre in the Bosnian capital and talks happily about his hobbies of pigeon-fancying … "Well, I guess I've always liked pigeons," the 44-year-old brigadier said, smiling under his brown-tinted John Lennon-style glasses. "Whenever I go abroad, I take photographs of them. So far, I've taken pictures of pigeons in 37 capitals. Since the war, it's had a greater significance for me. They remind me of doves, of symbols of peace".'

[46] Michael P Scharf, 'Prosecutor v Tadic, Case No IT-94-1-T' (1997) 91 *American Journal of International Law* 718, 719.

throwaway line in a Note mainly devoted to discussing the Trial Chamber's ruling on the (non)applicability of the Geneva Conventions to the conflict in Bosnia after 19 May 1992 (the date on which the Yugoslav National Army formally withdrew from hostilities) – was seized on by appellate counsel:[47]

> In our submission, the evidence of that witness [Seferovic] was implausible when analysed and has been described by distinguished commentators as 'curious'... The evidence has been the subject of consideration and analysis by commentators, and if I could draw the Court's attention to just one, and it is … commentary on International Decisions by Michael Scharf of the New England School of Law, who says – the article beginning on page 718 – at page 719: 'The most important Prosecution victory was the trial chamber's determination that Tadic had stabbed and cut the throats of two Muslim policemen outside a church after they were taken into custody by a group of Serb paramilitary forces. This is the only killing for which Tadic was found guilty by the trial chamber and was the key reason he received a twenty-year sentence. The finding is curious for two reasons'. I underline the word 'curious'. 'First, the only evidence to support it was the testimony of a single witness Nihad Seferovic, a Muslim who told the Tribunal the unlikely story that he had witnessed the murders when he had returned to Kozarac to feed his pet pigeons after the Serb take-over of the town. Second, nowhere in the indictment, which was amended twice by the prosecutor before trial, is there any reference to this murder'... I take no point on the drafting criticism. It is the evidential position that we say should exercise the minds of this Tribunal.

At this point Judge Shahabuddeen interrupted defence counsel's flow with the following perceptive and plain-speaking interrogatory:

> Why did Mr. Scharf say that the witness told an 'unlikely story'? Did he give any reasons to make out that proposition, that the witness told an 'unlikely story'? Perhaps he did. I don't know.

The paucity and faltering tone of counsel's response unintentionally speak volumes:

> The words 'unlikely story' are followed by the assertion that the witness had returned to Kozarac to feed his pet pigeons after the Serb take-over, and I think that, as I read the commentary of Mr. Scharf, is what he was saying was unlikely … And the unlikelihood is obviously a reflection of the inherent improbability of anybody with any regard to their own safety willingly entering a town currently occupied by Serb paramilitaries when they were in the process of actively deporting the Muslims to concentration camps in order to feed a pet bird. It is, we would submit, such an unlikely and improbable story that any Tribunal would want to reflect on whether it could possibly be true.

To which Judge Shahabuddeen indulgently replied: 'I understand. Thank you'.

What should be understood from this passage of argument? Michael Scharf has been one of the most well-informed and – as this passage intimates – influential commentators writing in English on the ICTY.[48] However, Scharf's offhand

[47] These passages are excerpted from ICTY Case No. IT-94-1-A, Transcript of Appellant's Submissions, 385–89 (20 April 1999).

[48] Michael P Scharf, *Balkan Justice* (Carolina Academic Press, 1997).

dismissal of witness Seferovic's evidence must have been based on the summary reproduced by the ICTY Trial Chamber which – as we have seen – bears only passing resemblance to the testimony Seferovic actually presented in the courtroom and his answers in cross-examination.[49] Thus, defence counsel on appeal was effectively invoking the authority of Scharf's academic commentary to dignify the appellant's submissions, but Scharf's opinion does not appear to have been particularly considered or supported by the trial record. Here, then, is a nice illustration of counsel's strategic attempt to rely upon expert (academic) authority for drawing factual inferences which: (i) on the defence's own argument, were supposedly self-evident, and thus presumably not in need of expert authority anyway; and (ii) rested upon no more than the Tribunal's own evidentiary analysis at first instance.

One does not need to be an adherent of autopoiesis[50] to detect a (viciously) circular self-referentiality in the sequence of inferences underpinning counsel's argument. Reducing Seferovic's motivation to an avian mercy mission is the very definition of an institutionally constructed fact, which was then deployed forensically to suggest the inherent implausibility of his eyewitness account. Inherent implausibility is a familiar basis for impeaching the credibility of a witness,[51] but its epistemic legitimacy is predicated on the witness actually having made the claims attributed to them. A fair reading of the trial record would not make pigeon-feeding the predominant, much less the exclusive, explanation for Seferovic's presence at the scene. Moreover, common law courts would generally exclude expert testimony of witness credibility (falling short of a clinical diagnosis) as an impermissible incursion on the trier of fact's primary institutional responsibility for resolving contested issues of fact.[52] Although there is no need to worry about protecting the lay jury in international criminal trials, which are always staffed by professional adjudicators, expert opinion of witness credibility is usually irrelevant and sometimes prejudicial to truth-seeking. Scharf's editorialising opinion that Seferovic told an 'unlikely story' would appear to exhibit both vices.[53]

[49] Scharf, ibid 143 and 211, repeats his summary dismissal of Seferovic's testimony in his book-length account of the Tadic trial: 'When the attack began on Kozarac in May 1992, Seferovic said that he fled to the hills seeking safety. Two days later, he snuck back into town to feed his pet pigeons, he said'; 'The other witness was Nihad Seferovic who had told the unlikely story that he had seen the defendant slit the throats of two Muslim policemen when he snuck back into Kozarac after the Serb takeover to feed his pigeons.'

[50] *Cf* Richard Nobles and David Schiff, *Understanding Miscarriages of Justice* (OUP, 2000).

[51] For empirical elucidation, see Paul Roberts and C Saunders, 'Piloting PTWI – A Socio-Legal Window on Prosecutors' Assessments of Evidence and Witness Credibility' (2010) 30 *Oxford Journal of Legal Studies* 101, 116–120.

[52] See, eg, *R v B* [2019] 1 WLR 2550, [2018] EWCA Crim 2733, [14]; *R v S;R v W* [2006] EWCA Crim 1404, [26]. For contextual discussion, see Paul Roberts and Tony Ward. 'Expert Evidence in Trials of Sexual Offences' in Pamela Radcliffe, Gisli Gudjonsson, Anthony Heaton-Armstrong and David Wolchover (eds), *Witness Testimony in Sexual Cases: Evidential, Investigative and Scientific Perspectives* (OUP, 2016).

[53] Might it be said that invoking Scharf's assessment was strictly argument rather than evidence? This looks like a distinction without a difference in this forensic context, but if one were forced to choose for the sake of conceptual purity, the inherent credibility of Seferovic's story was surely a question of fact rather than a proposition of law.

V. Leveraging the Critical Resources of International Criminal Trials

Beyond its intrinsic narrative appeal and vital role in securing two murder convictions, the tale of Mr Seferovic's pigeons was recounted in this chapter in order to exemplify the range and richness of the critical resources which international criminal adjudication offers to the student of evidence and proof. These resources are both material and intellectual. The following five exemplars and illustrations are by no means exhaustive.

(1) The websites of the UN's two ad hoc Tribunals, the ICTY[54] and ICTR,[55] house the most extensive collection of primary documents and ancillary information about contemporary international criminal trials currently available to the public. Although these Tribunals had ceased operation by 2017,[56] all the Courts' records and databases have been preserved 'as a monument to th[eir] accomplishments, and provid[ing] access to the wealth of resources that the Tribunal[s] produced over the years'.[57] The ICC has followed their lead and, at the time of writing, has 33 cases on foot.[58] These unique, and for the ICC still accumulating, archives contain not merely appellate decisions, but full transcripts of first-instance trial proceedings, rulings and judgments – materials of a type which cannot be obtained easily, if at all, for domestic criminal trials. Running to millions of pages,[59] keyword-searchable transcripts of hearings and trials involving more than 250 accused offer a fascinating window into the world of international criminal adjudication. It is a vantage point which Evidence scholars and teachers might readily exploit, not least as a partial corrective to the disproportionate influence of appellate judgments on the pedagogic emphasis and popular conceptions of our subject.

Even if transcripts of English criminal trials could be obtained more easily, they would not necessarily provide much indication of how the jury arrived at its peremptory general verdict of 'guilty' or 'not guilty'. Case analysis, for us, largely equates to dissecting what appellate courts have said about evidentiary norms or aspects of trial procedure, rather than having the opportunity to scrutinise evidence-taking and fact-finding processes. The proceedings and judgments of the ICTY, ICTR and ICC therefore contribute a source of valuable insights which are generally absent from English criminal jurisprudence; and, it might be added,

[54] www.icty.org/ (accessed 17 December 2025).

[55] unictr.irmct.org/ (accessed 17 December 2025).

[56] Legacy functions are discharged by the UN's International Residual Mechanism for Criminal Tribunals: see www.irmct.org/ (accessed 17 December 2025).

[57] ICTY Homepage, www.icty.org/ (accessed 17 December 2025).

[58] As of 29 August 2025: www.icc-cpi.int/cases.

[59] The ICTY's own estimate is 2.5 million pages of transcripts. The ultimately abortive four-year trial of former Yugoslav president Slobodan Milosevic alone filled almost 50,000 pages of transcript: *Prosecutor v Slobodan Milosevic* (IT-02-54).

from the judgments of the ECtHR, which tend to adopt formulaic language and rarely explain how any factual conclusion has been proven or inferred.

(2) The transcripts of Seferovic's testimony allow us to study the micro-dynamics of the evidential narratives 'constructed' through counsel's examination-in-chief and cross-examination at trial. Here we can trace the intersection between the applicable normative framework for presenting and testing witnesses' evidence and strategies for developing one's case in an adversarial trial setting. Seferovic's testimony presented Tadic's defence with several acute difficulties. Most obviously, Seferovic claimed to have witnessed the entire crime with no room for errors of interpretation. It was not as if (on Seferovic's account) Besic or Didovic had provoked Tadic or been killed in a fight in circumstances where Tadic might plausibly claim self-defence or lack of mens rea. Moreover, Seferovic and Tadic had known each other all their lives: this was a 'recognition', rather than the more common identification of a stranger, eyewitness scenario, and there was consequently little room for suggesting that Tadic had been misidentified as the cold-blooded assassin. Well-rehearsed forensic scripts for emphasising the weaknesses of eyewitness identification evidence[60] and playing up its role in producing miscarriages of justice[61] were consequently largely redundant. Prosecution counsel had concluded witness Seferovic's examination-in-chief with the classic dock-identification routine:

> [Counsel] You have told us about knowing Dule Tadic since you were a child and he was a child. Can you look around the courtroom, please, and tell us if Mr. Tadic is here?
>
> A. Yes.
>
> Q. Can you point him out, please?
>
> A. Yes, the gentleman up there. (Indicated).
>
> Q. Is that the man with the dark hair wearing the blue jacket and tie?
>
> A. Yes, that is it.
>
> Q. Mr. Seferovic, are you absolutely certain that this is the man you saw at the church slaughtering Osman and Edin?
>
> A. Yes, I am certain. Yes, I am certain that this is the man.[62]

Defence cross-examination of Seferovic was therefore largely confined to whittling away at his account of the precise location and sightlines of his hiding place, with the implication that either: (i) Seferovic had been further away from the incident than he had led the Court to believe when examined in-chief, so that he cannot have had

[60] Richard A Wise, Clifford S Fishman and Martin A Safer, 'How to Analyze the Accuracy of Eyewitness Testimony in a Criminal Case' (2009) 42 *Connecticut Law Review* 435.

[61] Criminal trial judges in England and Wales are instructed to tell juries that 'there is a need for caution to avoid the risk of injustice' and that even witnesses who are honest, convinced and convincing may still misidentify perpetrators: Judicial College, *The Crown Court Compendium Part I: Jury and Trial Management and Summing Up* (2025 update) 15-1.

[62] This passage and following excerpted from ICTY Case No IT-94-1-T, Transcript of Hearing, 2651–2706 (14 June 1996).

a completely unobscured view of the murders as he claimed; or (ii) – defence counsel's principal line of attack – that Seferovic had made the whole thing up: he was never in Kozorac at the material time, or at any rate never witnessed any murders:

> Q. When you were going through the back yards and gardens down to the orchard after you had been to your brother's house, you said that you could see the church clearly from where you were in the orchard?
>
> A. Yes, yes. I could see the church clearly, all too clearly, because there were leaves all over. The grass was a metre, a metre-and-a-half, tall. The hedge around the ground, the branches of plum trees, bending down to the ground. So that I could move as I liked and nobody, nobody could really see me.
>
> Q. Those things would also stop you seeing clearly if you have to look through grass or trees, branches, hedges?
>
> A. No, no. No, I was not moving then. I had found a spot and I had a good view. Nobody was paying attention to me, but to the police.
>
> Q. How long did you remain then in this position in the orchard?
>
> A. Not long, the incident happened perhaps a few minutes after I arrived. I did not have a watch so ….
>
> Q. After the incident happened did you leave straightaway?
>
> A. Yes, straightaway because there was very intensive fire and bullets were whistling by.
>
> Q. Bullets were whistling by where you were in the orchard?
>
> A. Yes, yes, when this incredible fire started, then I beat a retreat. …
>
> Q. Did you say that your brother's house was about 100 metres from the Serbian orthodox church in the centre of Kozarac?
>
> A. I may have and maybe it is that far. I said I never measured the distance; it could be.
>
> Q. Did you say that you only moved some 30 metres from your brother's house to a small orchard?
>
> A. No, I said that the house, that is, was about 30 metres or more from the orchard to the church. That is what I said.
>
> Q. Did you say that you were walking closer to a collection point?
>
> A. No, no, I did not.
>
> Q. Because what I am suggesting to you is that you have made up this story about seeing this incident in the afternoon in Kozarac in front of the Serbian orthodox church?
>
> A. No, I did not invent it. I saw it with my own eyes ….
>
> Q. Again so it is clear, what I suggest to you is that you have made this up; you did not see this at all?
>
> A. No, I did not make this up. I saw this with my own eyes and this is what I claim.

As may be inferred from these passages of cross-examination, Seferovic was a model witness from the prosecution's point of view. He stuck tenaciously to the basic outline of his story, provided considerable contextual detail, rarely appeared to contradict himself even on peripheral matters, and readily admitted that he could not remember certain significant facts, such as the day of the week on which the murders had occurred or precisely how far the church was from his brother's house in Kozarac.

We can further compare this trial record against findings of fact made at first instance, and the subsequent handling of disputed points of evidence on appeal. In this instance, striking discrepancies emerged between what the prosecution's star witness actually said at trial, and what counsel and the ICTY Appeals Chamber later assumed he had said. One can only speculate as to the frequency with which similar discrepancies might occur during the course of litigation generally. It is right to say that international criminal trials are atypical in many important respects: proceedings like those in *Tadic* are far more complex, lengthy and controversial than garden-variety domestic criminal prosecutions. On the other hand, we frequently read anecdotal reports that testifying in court is a frustrating and often distressing experience for lay witnesses.[63] They do not get to tell their story in their own words, and they sometimes leave with the impression that the court has not really heard what they came to say. Set in this institutional context, it does not seem fanciful to suggest that the corruption of testimony on appeal may be another way in which 'lay truth' is (mis)translated into 'lawyers' truth'[64] through further layers of reinterpretation. This is not to relativise the concept of truth,[65] but only an attempt to elucidate more fully the epistemological conditions and complexities of institutionally mediated truths (facts).[66]

(3) Seferovic's testimony also demonstrates how examining trials and appeals conducted by international tribunals can bring into sharper focus the extent to which justice depends on a shared cultural background of norms, assumptions, and expectations. We might think of this style of inquiry as a form of comparative institutional anthropology.[67] Wittgenstein memorably declared that 'if a lion could talk, we could not understand him'.[68] This was a striking

[63] See, eg, O Boycott, 'Courtrooms to Beef Up Protective Measures for Witnesses and Victims – Witnesses and Victims to be Better Protected after Survey Uncovers Widespread Dissatisfaction with Courtroom Experience', *The Guardian*, 11 September 2015.

[64] J D Jackson, 'Law's Truth, Lay Truth and Lawyers' Truth: The Representation of Evidence in Adversary Trials' (1992) III *Law and Critique* 29.

[65] For a concise conceptual primer, see Susan Haack, 'Truth, Truths, "Truth", and "Truths" in the Law' (2003) 17 *Harvard Journal of Law and Public Policy* 17. Note, in particular, Haack's elementary caution that, 'scare quotes … turn an expression meaning "X" into an expression meaning "so-called 'X'". So scare-quotes "truth", as distinct from truth, is what is taken to be truth; and scare-quotes "truths", as distinct from truths, are claims, propositions, or beliefs, which are taken to be truths – many of which are not really truths at all': ibid 18.

[66] See further, Susan Haack, 'Of Truth, in Science and in Law' (2008) 73 *Brooklyn Law Review* 985; Robert S Summers, 'Formal Legal Truth and Substantive Truth in Judicial Fact-Finding – Their Justified Divergence in Some Particular Cases' (1999) 18 *Law and Philosophy* 497.

[67] Robert Burns, Marianne Constable, Justin Richland and Winnifred Sullivan, 'Analysing the Trial: Interdisciplinary Methods' (2008) 31 *Political and Legal Anthropology Review* 303.

[68] Ludwig Wittgenstein, *Philosophical Investigations*, 3rd edn (Blackwell, 1967 [1953]) 223: for elucidation, see Marie McGinn, *Wittgenstein and the Philosophical Investigations* (London, Routledge, 1997) 51–60.

way of expressing the thought that communication is rooted in a shared 'life-world' of meaning, not in the sounds we utter in speech or the abstract symbols which we use to commit our experience to writing. Criminal trials of animals are, literally speaking, a thing of the past.[69] However, if international criminal adjudication figuratively exemplifies Wittgenstein's conundrum of communicating with 'lions', its study might also reasonably be expected to illuminate the dynamics of domestic trials, in which the beguiling familiarity of a common language may serve to conceal the divisions of cultural experience. In this way, international criminal proceedings may help to make explicit what is often relatively opaque at the domestic level.

The cultural conditioning of experience can hardly be ignored when trial participants do not even speak the same language (a situation also sometimes encountered in domestic criminal trials in England and Wales,[70] and an increasingly likely scenario in multicultural societies).[71] In extreme cases, international criminal proceedings involve participants, as accused, victims and witnesses, whose cultural experience and world-view are so divergent that their nations, tribes, parties or factions have recently resorted to genocidal violence and 'ethnic cleansing'. In these desperate circumstances, the capacity of any model of criminal procedure to deliver justice founded on secure inferences of fact is truly tested to the limit.

(4) The use of Scharf's article by appellate counsel in *Tadic* might be considered a mixed blessing. It is encouraging to know that academic literature is read by practitioners and may even be cited in court and influence adjudicative outcomes. The law and practice of international criminal tribunals developed at an extraordinary pace, but relatively few scholars – especially during the first decades – commented on 'nuts-and-bolts' procedural issues, or even on major points of evidentiary principle. In this evolutionary institutional environment, there is plenty of opportunity for scholars to make their mark and to contribute, in very tangible ways, to promoting the goals and serving the ideals of international criminal justice. But this kind of power carries with it a measure of responsibility. I do not know what basis Scharf had for branding Seferovic's testimony an 'unlikely story' leading to 'curious' convictions, but the tendentious use of these remarks by appellate counsel in *Tadic* might stand as a cautionary tale for commentators. In international criminal adjudication, the old cliché rings true: loose talk can cost lives.

(5) Tadic's convictions of the murders of Besic and Didovic shed valuable light on the question of sufficiency of proof and the related issue of the scope of

[69] William Ewald, 'Comparative Jurisprudence (I): What Was it Like to Try a Rat?' (1995) 143 *University of Pennsylvania Law Review* 1889, Part I; E P Evans, *The Criminal Prosecution and Capital Punishment of Animals: The Lost History of Europe's Animal Trials* (Faber & Faber, 1987 [1906]).

[70] *Cf* R Gwynedd Parry, 'The Language of Evidence' [2004] *Criminal Law Review* 1015.

[71] See, eg, *Erlam v Rahman* [2015] EWHC 1215 (QB); *Bielecki v DPP* [2011] EWHC 2245 (Admin), [2012] Crim LR 785; *R v B* [2007] EWCA Crim 374.

appellate review of findings of fact by first instance tribunals. On appeal, defence counsel complained:

> The evidence [given by Seferovic] was identified in the judgement of the Trial Chamber at paragraph 393, and it merely recounts there the evidence that the witness gave; and at 394, it sets out the case for the Defence, that he was not in the town at the time those two people were killed. It was not, with respect to the Trial Chamber, the most critical analysis of the evidence of the witness Seferovic; it was, in truth, no more than a recitation of the effect of what he said.[72]

Read strictly in terms of the reasons actually stated in the Trial Chamber's judgment for finding Tadic guilty on these counts, this complaint has some merit and plausibility. The conclusion that Seferovic's testimony was sufficiently compelling to prove the charges against Tadic beyond reasonable doubt is delivered *ex cathedra* without context or explicit rationalisation. The ICTY Appeals Chamber nonetheless concluded that: 'There is no basis for the Appeals Chamber to consider that the Trial Chamber acted unreasonably in relying on that evidence for its finding that the Appellant killed the two men.'[73]

Common lawyers will not be surprised to find an appellate court refusing to overturn first-instance findings of fact, especially where assessments of witness credibility are crucial to the factual determination and the original fact-finder had the advantage of observing the witness testify and undergo cross-examination. Recall, however, that there are no lay juries at the ICTY: fact-finding is undertaken by professional judges, who must then, in the Continental fashion,[74] write authoritative judgments justifying their factual conclusions as well as setting out the law they have applied to the facts thus found.[75] The example of witness Seferovic's testimony is revealing on this score in at least two respects. First, even with professional fact-finders, appellate tribunals are likely to be reluctant to intervene for as long as demeanour and live cross-examination are felt to be significant in judging witness credibility. Put another way, introducing more non-jury trials in domestic criminal proceedings would not necessarily open up appellate review to the extent that might be imagined.[76]

[72] ICTY Case No. IT-94-1-A, Transcript of Appellant's Submissions, 386–87 (20 April 1999).

[73] ICTY Case No. IT-94-1-A, Appeals Chamber Judgment, 15 July 1999, [66].

[74] Of course, common law judges in non-jury trials write such judgments, too. Also see John Jackson and Sean Doran, *Judge Without Jury: Diplock Trials in the Adversary System* (OUP, 1995).

[75] See, eg, Stephen R Levitt, 'The Life and Times of a Local Court Judge in Berlin' (2009) 10 *German Law Journal* 169; Antoinette Perrodet and Elena Ricci, 'The Italian System' in Mireille Delmas-Marty and John R Spencer (eds), *European Criminal Procedures* (CUP, 2002) 370 ('the judge must set out in a reasoned judgment the elements of the facts and of the law which form the basis of his judgment, stating the evidence he has accepted and the reasons for rejecting evidence to the contrary').

[76] A prediction tested, and substantially confirmed, in relation to Canadian bench trials in Paul Roberts, 'Reasonable Doubts? Rationalising Appellate Review of Witness Credibility in Criminal Trials' (2025) 28 *Canadian Criminal Law Review* 21.

Second, this aspect of the *Tadic* judgment shows that the discipline of requiring reasons for verdicts may not amount to a very great deal in practice. The prosaic challenges of encapsulating the inferential processes of fact-finding in a reasonably concise yet still appropriately informative summary deserve more careful consideration when critics of unreasoned jury verdicts extol the virtues of the Continental model of reasoned judgment-giving.[77] In this particular instance, however, much of the apparent mystery surrounding the evidentiary significance of Mr Seferovic's pigeons in the Judgments of the ICTY Trial and Appeals Chambers can easily be dispelled simply by reading the transcripts of witness Seferovic's testimony, which directly and quite unequivocally implicated Dusko Tadic in the murders of Edin Besic and Osman Didovic.

VI. Inconclusive Thoughts on Methodological Work in Progress

Much has changed over the two decades since I started thinking, teaching and writing about evidence and proof in the context of international criminal adjudication.[78] The trial practice and appellate jurisprudence of the ICTY and ICTR, interpreting serial iterations of the tribunals' Rules of Procedure and Evidence,[79] have been reinforced by the ICC and the 'internationalised' tribunals,[80] producing rapid normative development in both substantive and procedural international criminal law.[81] This has, in turn, generated a critical secondary literature, spanning technical procedural and doctrinal issues,[82]

[77] For discussion, see John D Jackson, 'Unbecoming Jurors and Unreasoned Verdicts: Realising Integrity in the Jury Room' in Jill Hunter, Paul Roberts, Simon N M Young and David Dixon (eds), *The Integrity of Criminal Process* (Hart Publishing, 2016); Paul Roberts, 'Does Article 6 of the European Convention on Human Rights Require Reasoned Verdicts in Criminal Trials?' (2011) 11 *Human Rights Law Review* 213.

[78] Paul Roberts, 'Why International Criminal Evidence?' in Paul Roberts and Mike Redmayne (eds), *Innovations in Evidence and Proof* (Hart Publishing, 2007).

[79] Between the original 1994 draft and the final 2015 iteration the ICTY's RPE underwent 50 published revisions.

[80] Cesare P R Romano, André Nollkaemper and Jann K Kleffner (eds), *Internationalized Criminal Courts: Sierra Leone, East Timor, Kosovo and Cambodia* (OUP, 2004).

[81] For overviews, see Robert Cryer, Darryl Robinson and Sergey Vasiliev, *An Introduction to International Criminal Law and Procedure*, 4th edn (CUP, 2019); Antonio Cassese and Paola Gaeta, *International Criminal Law*, 3rd edn (OUP, 2013).

[82] See, eg, John D Jackson and Yassin M Brunger, 'Witness Preparation in the ICC: An Opportunity for Principled Pragmatism' (2015) 13 *Journal of International Criminal Justice* 601; Robert Cryer, 'A Message From Elsewhere: Witnesses Before International Criminal Tribunals' in Paul Roberts and Mike Redmayne (eds), *Innovations in Evidence and Proof* (Hart Publishing, 2007); Richard May, David Tolbert, John Hocking, Ken Roberts, Bing Bing Jia, Daryl Mundis and Gabriel Oosthuizen (eds), *Essays on ICTY Procedure and Evidence in Honour of Gabrielle Kirk McDonald* (Kluwer, 2001); Rod Dixon, 'Developing International Rules of Evidence for the Yugoslav and Rwanda Tribunals' (1997) 7 *Transnational Law and Contemporary Problems* 81.

broader theorisation of evidentiary norms,[83] synthetic comparisons of procedural models,[84] and even some exploration of the epistemological practices[85] and inferential logic of fact-finding in international criminal trials[86] – exemplars of the interdisciplinary scholarship advocated in this book as a methodological foundation-stone of criminal jurisprudence. But one thing that has not changed much, on my reading, is the comparative neglect of evidence and procedure[87] relative to the oceans of ink devoted to commentary on other aspects of international criminal justice, such as the politics of international prosecutions and trials (will any more Great Powers ever sign up to the ICC Statute? Is the Court an unwitting instrument of neo-colonialism?), questions of jurisdiction and institutional dynamics (eg, the contested roles of the ICC Prosecutor and UN Security Council), theoretical tensions between retributive and restorative ideals (notably implicating victims' rights), and major developments in substantive criminal law. Besides, compared with domestic systems of criminal procedure and evidence evolved over centuries, international criminal procedure is still in its formative youth.

The story of Mr Seferovic's pigeons struck a chord and has stayed with me down the years. Though merely one tiny droplet in an ocean of pain and suffering and unspeakable atrocities prosecuted before the ICTY, Nihad Seferovic evidently cared about these small details – for him, pivotal life-events – and Dusko Tadic was made to care.[88] Beyond the fact that human beings are

[83] Michael Bohlander, 'Paradise Postponed? For a Judge-Led Generic Model of International Criminal Procedure and an End to "Draft-as-You-Go"' in Monika Ambrus and Ramses A Wessel (eds), *Netherlands Yearbook of International Law 2014* (TMC Asser Press, 2015); John D Jackson and Yassin M Brunger, 'Fragmentation and Harmonisation in the Development of Evidentiary Practices in International Criminal Tribunals' in Elies van Sliedregt and Sergey Vasiliev (eds), *Pluralism in International Criminal Law* (OUP, 2014); Paul Murphy, 'No Free Lunch, No Free Proof: The Indiscriminate Admission of Evidence is a Serious Flaw in International Criminal Trials' (2010) 8 *Journal of International Criminal Justice* 539; Richard May and Marieke Wierda, 'Trends in International Criminal Evidence: Nuremberg, Tokyo, The Hague, and Arusha' (1999) 37 *Columbia Journal of Transnational Law* 725.

[84] Kai Ambos, *Treatise on International Criminal Law Volume III: International Criminal Procedure* (OUP, 2016); Mireille Delmas-Marty, 'Reflections on the "Hybridisation" of Criminal Procedure' in John D Jackson, Máximo Langer and Peter Tillers (eds), *Crime, Procedure and Evidence in a Comparative and International Context* (Hart Publishing, 2008); Christoph J M Safferling, *Towards an International Criminal Procedure* (OUP, 2001).

[85] Yvonne McDermott, 'Strengthening the Evaluation of Evidence in International Criminal Trials' (2017) 17 *International Criminal Law Review* 1; Nancy Combs, *Fact-Finding Without Facts: The Uncertain Evidentiary Foundations of International Criminal Convictions* (CUP, 2010).

[86] Yvonne McDermott and Colin Aitken, 'Analysis of Evidence in International Criminal Trials using Bayesian Belief Networks' (2017) 16 *Law, Probability & Risk* 111; Yvonne McDermott, 'Inferential Reasoning and Proof in International Criminal Trials' (2015) 13 *Journal of International Criminal Justice* 507.

[87] Paul Roberts, 'The Priority of Procedure and the Neglect of Evidence and Proof: Facing Facts in International Criminal Law' (2015) 13 *Journal of International Criminal Justice* 479.

[88] At least according to a thin conception of 'made to care': Tadic was forced to listen to Seferovic's testimony and was condemned and punished for the crimes that testimony established. Confession, remorse, repentance, apology – these are more ambitious, and elusive, goals, that may be beyond the institutional competence of public trials to deliver: *cf* R A Duff, *Punishment, Communication and Community* (OUP, 2001); Alan Norrie, 'Albert Speer, Guilt, and "The Space Between"' in Matt Matravers (ed), *Punishment and Political Theory* (Hart Publishing, 1999).

hard-wired to love a good story,[89] perhaps it is the capacity of witness testimonies to render justice on a human scale that makes such narratives so memorable and compelling – the more so when the 'bigger picture' presents an invidious choice between abstracted summaries and generalisations or an accumulation of details too awful to contemplate and almost, literally, beyond comprehension.[90] Now, it is notoriously perilous to generalise from a single case; or more accurately regarding the case-study presented in this chapter, from a single testimonial strand of one part of one case. But I think this standard objection to non-statistical inference misfires when targeted at methodological inquiries of this kind. A method is not a theory, just as a tool is not a blueprint and a brick is not a house. If methodological inquiries are always, in this (methodological) sense, work in progress and may seem unsatisfactorily preliminary and incomplete (even to those undertaking them!), they are also essential precursors to robust theory construction, well-grounded substantive analyses, effective policy-making and responsible curation of the disciplines. Since ideas, concepts and research methods – unlike their progenitors and popularisers – never retire, the intellectual and practical legacies of methodological scholarship are both unknown and potentially unlimited.

This chapter employed the case-study of Mr Seferovic's pigeons to illustrate numerous ways in which the critical resources of international criminal adjudication might be leveraged to enrich scholarship on evidence, proof and procedure. In broader disciplinary contemplation, much of the potential value of these materials for Evidence scholars and teachers is encapsulated in a distinctive brand of comparativism. International criminal tribunals are an object lesson in sui generis comparative institutional design and procedural transplants. The ICTY, ICTR and ICC have all combined characteristic features of adversarial and inquisitorial process in novel and imaginative ways.[91] In an era of expanding and deepening legal cosmopolitanism, international criminal proceedings might be looked upon as laboratories of juridical innovation and potential models for domestic legal reform. Moreover, on a broad view of 'international criminal evidence' – one which embraces relevant aspects of international human rights law, in particular – it might be said that the old rigid distinction between 'domestic' and 'international' legal proceeding is already breaking down and heading for obsolescence. Supra-national and foreign legal norms are increasingly applicable

[89] Christopher Brooker, *The Seven Basic Plots: Why We Tell Stories* (Continuum, 2004); William Twining, *Rethinking Evidence: Exploratory Essays*, 2nd edn (CUP, 2006) chs 9–13; Nancy Pennington and Ried Hastie, 'A Cognitive Theory of Juror Decision Making: The Story Model' (1991) 13 *Cardozo Law Review* 519.

[90] *Cf* Lawrence Douglas, *The Memory of Judgment: Making Law and History in the Trials of the Holocaust* (Yale University Press, 2001); Hannah Arendt, *Eichmann in Jerusalem: A Report on the Banality of Evil* (Penguin, 1994 [1963]).

[91] Kai Ambos, 'International Criminal Procedure: "Adversarial," "Inquisitorial" or "Mixed"?' (2003) 3 *International Criminal Law Review* 1. For theoretical challenges and complexities, see Chapter 4. Also see Máximo Langer, 'The Long Shadow of the Adversarial and Inquisitorial Categories' in Markus D Dubber and Tatjana Hörnle (eds), *The Oxford Handbook of Criminal Law* (OUP, 2014).

in national legal process – as persuasive authority or examples of state practice, if not technically as legal precedents.[92] Of course, there are counter-trends and reactionary forces threatening to balkanise the globe, erode the international rule of law, and take us back to the hair-trigger Great Power diplomacy of the nineteenth century. The ideal of cosmopolitan legality is only one possible vision of humanity's future: nothing is guaranteed or taken for granted in this analysis.

Meanwhile, the notion of the 'domestic' Evidence lawyer has been reduced to anachronism. For some years now, I have been advising my Criminal Evidence students that in order to get to grips with criminal procedure in England and Wales, they need to become proficient in human rights jurisprudence and argumentation alongside mastering the intricacies of traditional common law evidence.[93] The right to a fair trial in international human rights law supplies a flexible normative framework for a new generation of evidentiary studies seamlessly integrating domestic criminal jurisprudence, comparative criminal procedure, and international criminal law.[94] International criminal trials, and in particular the permanent ICC, were invested with such high hopes and – to some extent contradictory – expectations that they were almost bound to disappoint their supporters and allow their critics to claim vindication. It is said that the honeymoon is over for international criminal justice as a project of global accountability for the worst of humanity's crimes.[95] From the institutional and disciplinary perspectives of cosmopolitan criminal jurisprudence, however, proceduralists' brief encounters with international criminal adjudication kindle the promise of a lasting affair.

[92] See further, Paul Roberts, 'Normative Evolution in Evidentiary Exclusion: Coercion, Deception and the Right to a Fair Trial' in Paul Roberts and Jill Hunter (eds), *Criminal Evidence and Human Rights* (Hart Publishing, 2012); Anne-Marie Slaughter 'A Global Community of Courts' (2003) 44 *Harvard International Law Journal* 191; Elaine Mak, *Judicial Decision-Making in a Globalised World: A Comparative Analysis of the Changing Practices of Western Highest Courts* (Hart Publishing, 2013).

[93] To similar effect, see John D Jackson, 'Common Law Evidence and the Common Law of Human Rights: Towards a Harmonic Convergence?' (2019) 27 *William & Mary Bill of Rights Journal* 689.

[94] Exemplars include Dimitrios Giannoulopoulos, *Improperly Obtained Evidence in Anglo-American and Continental Law* (Hart Publishing, 2019); Kelly Pitcher, *Judicial Responses to Pre-Trial Procedural Violations in International Criminal Proceedings* (Springer, 2018); Yvonne McDermott, *Fairness in International Criminal Trials* (OUP, 2016); Alexander Heinze, *International Criminal Procedure and Disclosure* (Dunker & Humblot, 2014); John D Jackson and Sarah J Summers, *The Internationalisation of Criminal Evidence* (CUP, 2012).

[95] David Luban, 'After the Honeymoon: Reflections on the Current State of International Criminal Justice' (2013) 11 *Journal of International Criminal Justice* 505.

10

Thinking Through Critical Criminology

BioNote: The year I spent in Cambridge as an MPhil student at the Institute of Criminology (then still accommodated in an old house on West Road, with a prefab extension for a seminar room) was an important period in my intellectual formation. I had already acquired a taste for theorising at Oxford, but this was mostly confined to conceptions of law (old-style analytical 'Jurisprudence') and justificatory theories of punishment. It was in Cambridge that I first really got to grips with sociology and social theory, which inevitably spilled over into metaphysics, epistemology, and moral and political philosophy. Although I was reading Marx, Durkheim, Foucault, and Frankfurt School critical theory, the philosophical foundations of their ideas were communicated through historical and sociological exegesis. It was energising and, after three years of a predominantly doctrinal undergraduate Law degree, somewhat liberating to read books like *The New Criminology*.[1] I soon began to wonder, however, just how sound their philosophical foundations really were.

With some undergraduate priming from Nicola Lacey, Andrew Ashworth and Andrew Rutherford at Oxford, I was ready to absorb Nigel Walker's seminars on penal theory, Loraine Gelsthorpe's classes on crime and 'minorities' and feminist criminology,[2] David Thomas' anecdote-fuelled monologues on sentencing law and practice, and Tony Bottoms and Richard Sparks' updates on contemporary developments in criminological theory and practice, amongst many other instructional occasions. There was real intellectual energy and excitement about the place, with regular guest lectures and academic visitors constantly passing through. As well as attending the lecture by Andreas von Hirsch mentioned in Chapter 2, I also heard a very thought-provoking seminar presentation by Antony Duff,[3]

[1] Ian Taylor, Paul Walton and Jock Young, *The New Criminology: For a Social Theory of Deviance* (Routledge & Kegan Paul, 1973).

[2] Loraine Gelsthorpe and Allison Morris (eds), *Feminist Perspectives in Criminology* (Open University Press, 1990). This is an opportunity, albeit very belated, to express my gratitude for Loraine Gelsthorpe, 'Approaching the Topic of Racism' in Dee Cook and Barbara Hudson (eds), *Racism and Criminology* (Sage, 1993).

[3] This was Duff's more Kantian period, but he was already starting to distance himself from some of the formulations advanced in R A Duff, *Trials and Punishments* (CUP, 1986). I recall that Bill McWilliams was a little disappointed by these oral concessions, having found the book's arguments compelling.

who would subsequently become another major influence and sponsor of my academic progress, extending serial invitations to participate in workshops and book projects over three decades (happily, with no indication of slowing down after many years' notional retirement). In truth, I wasn't particularly interested in Tony Bottoms' current research on prison sociology,[4] but his casual recommendations for reading material left a lasting impression.[5] Outside the classroom, I learnt as much again from my student contemporaries, many of whom would go on to forge successful careers as professional criminologists or criminal justice practitioners: Steve Bailey,[6] Helen Codd,[7] Mark Fenwick,[8] Sarah Goom,[9] Gerry Kearns,[10] Vicky Kemp,[11] Gary Trotter,[12] Andrew Yip.[13]

My most influential teacher during that year in Cambridge was undoubtedly Colin Sumner. Having graduated with a law degree, Sumner wrote a fairly hard-core technical PhD on Marxian conceptions of ideology,[14] and subsequently developed a distinctive theoretical conception of crime as social censure.[15] I encountered

[4] Richard Sparks, Anthony E Bottoms and Will Hay, *Prisons and the Problem of Order* (OUP, 1996).

[5] Two titles recommended by Tony were especially influential: John Braithwaite, *Crime, Shame and Reintegration* (CUP, 1989); and Primo Levi, *The Drowned and the Saved* (Abacus, 2013).

[6] 'Steven Bailey sees successful drugs conviction case end in £1.3m POCA confiscation order', *The Lawyer*, 26 May 2019.

[7] Helen Codd, 'Older People in Prison' in Sue Westwood and Nancy J Knauer (eds), *Research Handbook on Law, Society and Ageing* (Edward Elgar, 2024); David Scott and Helen Codd, *Controversial Issues in Prisons* (Open University Press, 2010).

[8] Mark Fenwick and Erik P M Vermeulen, 'Banking and Regulatory Responses to Fintech Revisited – Building the Sustainable Financial "Ecosystems" of Tomorrow' [2020] *Singapore Journal of Legal Studies* 165; Mark Fenwick, '"Penal populism" and Penological Change in Contemporary Japan' (2013) 17 *Theoretical Criminology* 215; Mark Fenwick, 'New Directions in Cultural Criminology' (2004) 8 *Theoretical Criminology* 377.

[9] Director General, Commercial with Trade and International (Civil Service Lawyer), www.gov.uk/government/people/sarah-goom#biography (accessed 17 December 2025).

[10] R D Mackay and Gerry Kearns, 'More Fact(s) about the Insanity Defence' [1999] *Criminal Law Review* 714; R D Mackay and Gerry Kearns, 'The Trial of the Facts and Unfitness to Plead' [1997] *Criminal Law Review* 644.

[11] Vicky Kemp, 'Authorising and Reviewing Detention: PACE Safeguards in a Digital Age' [2020] *Criminal Law Review* 572; Vicky Kemp, 'Whose Time is it Anyway? Factors Associated with Duration in Police Custody' [2012] *Criminal Law Review* 736; Pascoe Pleasence, Vicky Kemp and Nigel J Balmer, 'The Justice Lottery? Police Station Advice 25 Years on From PACE' [2011] *Criminal Law Review* 3.

[12] 'Former Queen's criminal law professor appointed to Ontario Court of Appeal', *Queen's Law News*, 24 November 2016: www.law.queensu.ca/news/Former-Queen-s-criminal-law-professor-appointed-to-Ontario-Court-of-Appeal (accessed 17 December 2025) (rather enviably saluted as 'A lawyer's lawyer, then a professor's professor, then a judge's judge').

[13] Andrew Kam-Tuck Yip and Alex Toft (eds), *Bisexuality, Religion and Spirituality: Critical Perspectives* (Routledge, 2020); Sharon Smith, Sally R Munt and Andrew Kam-Tuck Yip, *Cosmopolitan Dharma: Race, Sexuality, and Gender in British Buddhism* (Brill, 2016).

[14] Colin Sumner, *Reading Ideologies: Investigation into the Marxist Theory of Ideology and Law* (Academic Press, 1979).

[15] David Moxon, *Colin Sumner: Criminology Through the Looking-Glass* (Palgrave, 2020); Anthony Amatrudo (ed), *Social Censure and Critical Criminology: After Sumner* (Palgrave, 2017) (for which I organised a book-launch at Nottingham: www.nottingham.ac.uk/law/news/2017/seminar-and-book-launch-social-censure.aspx (accessed 17 December 2025)); Colin Sumner (ed), *The Blackwell Companion to Criminology* (Blackwell, 2004).

Colin in one of his most productive periods[16] and, in particular, observed the evolution of what would shortly be presented to the world as his 'respectful obituary' for the sociology of deviance[17] in its final performative drafts.[18] Colin's seminars on 'History of Criminological Thought' and 'The Sociology of Deviance and Social Censure', and their impromptu break-out sessions in The Granta, were consistently weekly highlights of that academic year. Colin included his students in teaching and research activity on almost equal terms and encouraged publication and wider engagement.[19] He was an early exponent of what we might today call comparative criminology.[20] I was amazed when Colin told me that he still had a load of unpublished fieldwork notes from his interviews in Africa. I still think it is a shame when qualitative fieldwork data never see the light of day, but now with my own collection of unpublished interview material, the contingencies of academic research and publishing are no longer a source of amazement.

Overall, my time in Cambridge equipped me with a firm foundation in sociology and social theory, which would prove to be a major intellectual asset, not only in undertaking socio-legal work on expert evidence as a researcher at Bristol during the following year,[21] but also in further explorations in moral and political philosophy when I subsequently returned to Oxford for the BCL and the last of my student days.

I. Introduction: A Dose of Criminology

When I arrived in Nottingham in 1993, there was no organised criminological presence in Sociology and Social Policy, and so Criminology teaching fell to the Law Department. I joined the teaching team led by Ralph Sandland and Rob Canton (then a part-time lecturer in SSP),[22] and spent four enjoyable and educational years co-teaching criminological theory, sentencing and punishment before redirecting my energies to developing the postgraduate programmes described in Chapter 8. Although I no longer teach Criminology[23]

[16] Colin Sumner (ed), *Censure, Politics and Criminal Justice* (Open University Press, 1990), the first volume of the 'New Directions in Criminology Series' which Sumner edited, was published during my first term in Cambridge.

[17] Colin Sumner, *The Sociology of Deviance: An Obituary* (Open University Press, 1994).

[18] See Paul Roberts, 'From Deviance to Censure: A "New" Criminology for the Nineties' (1996) 59 *Modern Law Review* 125.

[19] Colin Sumner (ed), *Violence, Culture, and Censure* (Routledge, 1997); Paul Roberts, 'Social Control and the Censures of Sex' (1993) 19 *Crime, Law and Social Change* 171.

[20] Colin Sumner (ed), *Crime, Justice and Underdevelopment* (Heinemann, 1982); Roberto Bergalli and Colin Sumner (eds), *Social Control and Political Order* (Sage, 1997).

[21] Paul Roberts, 'Science in the Criminal Process' (1994) 14 *Oxford Journal of Legal Studies* 469 [reprinted in Roberts (ed), *Expert Evidence and Scientific Proof in Criminal Trials* (Ashgate, 2014)].

[22] Rob subsequently moved to Leicester DeMontfort, where he flourished as Professor in Community and Criminal Justice. See Rob Canton and Jane Dominey, *Probation*, 2nd edn (Routledge, 2018); Rob Canton, *Why Punish? An Introduction to the Philosophy of Punishment* (Bloomsbury, 2017).

[23] Here and *passim*, when subject areas are capitalised as proper nouns, I refer to the organised academic discipline of that name.

to undergraduates and would not today hold myself out as a professional criminologist of any description, this chapter is not an aimless amble down Memory Lane. Revisiting some old criminological haunts will open up questions of disciplinary constitution and interdisciplinary interfaces which, hand-in-hand with meta-theoretical reflection on these topics, have been recurrent themes in my published work in criminal jurisprudence,[24] evidence and proof,[25] international and comparative criminal justice[26] and, lately, forensic science.[27] Returning to some of the pioneering texts of British critical criminology, and thinking through their methodological (and ethical) implications, will demonstrate the continuing vitality and heuristic value of engaging with these influential ideas, irrespective of disciplinary politics. Thinking 'through', in the sense intended by my title, encompasses both analytical thinking *about* critical criminology as an object of (critical) inquiry and appreciative engagement *with* critical criminological thinking as a rich, varied and still vibrant set of intellectual resources.

Before focusing specifically on 'critical criminology' – an instance of what I will be calling 'adjectival criminologies' – in Section III of this chapter, there is scene-setting and path-clearing work to be done. Section II begins by posing some existential questions for Criminology in general, leading to discussion of the institutional anchors of disciplinary formation and differentiation, and finally, to deeper exploration of the pivotal relationship (on my account) between Criminology and Criminal Justice. Section III opens with a conceptual reappraisal of 'critical' criminology, before elucidating some of its principal theoretical virtues and methodological limitations, as I now perceive them. Section III closes with a fundamental question of disciplinary method

[24] Paul Roberts (ed), *Theoretical Foundations of Criminal Trial Procedure* (Ashgate, 2014); Paul Roberts, 'Groundwork for A Jurisprudence of Criminal Procedure' in R A Duff and Stuart Green (eds), *Philosophical Foundations of Criminal Law* (OUP, 2011); Paul Roberts, 'Penal Offence in Question: Some Reference Points for Interdisciplinary Conversation' in Andrew Simester and Andrew von Hirsch (eds), *Incivilities: Regulating Offensive Behaviour* (Hart Publishing, 2006).

[25] Chapters 5–7. Also see Paul Roberts, 'The Priority of Procedure and the Neglect of Evidence and Proof: Facing Facts in International Criminal Law' (2015) 13 *Journal of International Criminal Justice* 479; Paul Roberts and Mike Redmayne (eds), *Innovations in Evidence and Proof* (Hart Publishing, 2007); Paul Roberts, 'Rethinking the Law of Evidence: A Twenty-first Century Agenda for Teaching and Research' (2002) 55 *Current Legal Problems* 297.

[26] Chapters 4, 8 and 9. Also see Paul Roberts, 'From Extradition to Surrender: EU Criminal Law and Comparative Legal Method' (2014) 53 *Howard Journal of Criminal Justice* 547; Paul Roberts, 'Comparative Criminal Justice Goes Global' (2008) 28 *Oxford Journal of Legal Studies* 369; Paul Roberts, 'Comparative Law for International Criminal Justice' in Esin Örücü and David Nelken (eds), *Comparative Law – A Handbook* (Hart Publishing, 2007); Paul Roberts, 'Restoration and Retribution in International Criminal Justice: An Exploratory Analysis' in Andrew von Hirsch et al (eds), *Restorative Justice and Criminal Justice* (Hart Publishing, 2003).

[27] Paul Roberts, 'Making Sense of Forensic Science Evidence' in Paul Roberts and Michael Stockdale (eds), *Forensic Science Evidence and Expert Witness Testimony: Reliability Through Reform?* (Edward Elgar, 2018); Paul Roberts, 'The New Interdisciplinary Forensic Science' (2016) 43 *Journal of Law and Society* 647; Paul Roberts, 'Renegotiating Forensic Cultures: Between Law, Science and Criminal Justice' (2013) 44 *Studies in the History and Philosophy of Biological and Biomedical Sciences* 47.

and professional ethics that should be familiar to (critical) criminologists; Section IV provides the critical resources to answer it, insofar as any satisfactory answers can be given.

II. Disciplining Criminology: Existential Questions

What is Criminology? This is a question to which criminologists have often returned.[28] It is also a question that many find irritating and unproductive, in part because it is by no means clear what kind of response should qualify as an answer. Certainly, no consensus emerges from previous discussions, and sceptics might doubt whether any real progress has ever been made by becoming entangled in such debates. This may be a general characteristic of all profound existential questions, disciplinary or otherwise. One is caught between the irrepressible human desire to wonder – What am I? *For* what am I? What will become of me? Do I even exist? – and the dawning realisation that there are probably no certain or entirely satisfactory answers to be had, at least if reason rather than faith is the measure of success. In relation to Criminology, the existential questions may seem unavailing, and ultimately pointless. Rather than worrying about what Criminology is, just do it! There would be a deep, tragic, irrationality in allowing searching self-scrutiny and reflection on the meaning of life (Criminology) to become a kind of paralysis sapping the will and stealing the time to live (or do criminological work). And yet, and yet …

Following through this train of thought, and to the horror of more practically minded colleagues who see their worst suspicions palpably materialising, questions of disciplinary constitution force second-order questions at the meta-theoretical level.[29] In other words, for example, why do you want to know what Criminology is? To what end, and in service of which values, is such a question being posed and investigated? What difference, if any, would adopting alternative definitions have ('in the real world', if you must)? This is the stuff of Stanley Cohen's 'third order of reality' involving 'reflection about the nature of the whole enterprise itself'.[30]

[28] See, eg, Mary Bosworth and Carolyn Hoyle (eds), *What is Criminology?* (OUP, 2011). Also see Ian Loader and Richard Sparks, 'Situating Criminology: On the Production and Consumption of Knowledge about Crime and Justice' in Mike Maguire, Rod Morgan and Robert Reiner (eds), *The Oxford Handbook of Criminology*, 5th edn (OUP, 2012); Kevin Carrington and Russell Hogg (eds), *Critical Criminology: Issues, Debates, Challenges* (Willan, 2002); Simon Holdaway and Paul Rock (eds), *Thinking About Criminology* (UCL Press, 1998).

[29] For parallel debates in legal theory, see Paweł Banaś, Adam Dyrda and Tomasz Gizbert-Studnicki (eds), *Metaphilosophy of Law* (Hart Publishing, 2016).

[30] Stanley Cohen, *Against Criminology* (Transaction Books, 1988) ix. Cohen characterised the first order of reality as 'the "thing" itself (crime and the apparatus for its control)'; the second order being 'research and speculation about this thing'.

A. The Eternal Triangle of Intellectual Inquiry, Applied to Criminology

In thinking through such theoretical conundrums, I have found it useful to employ a device I call The Eternal Triangle of Intellectual Inquiry (ET). Figure 10.1 presents ET in graphical form.

Fig 10.1 The Eternal Triangle of Intellectual Inquiry

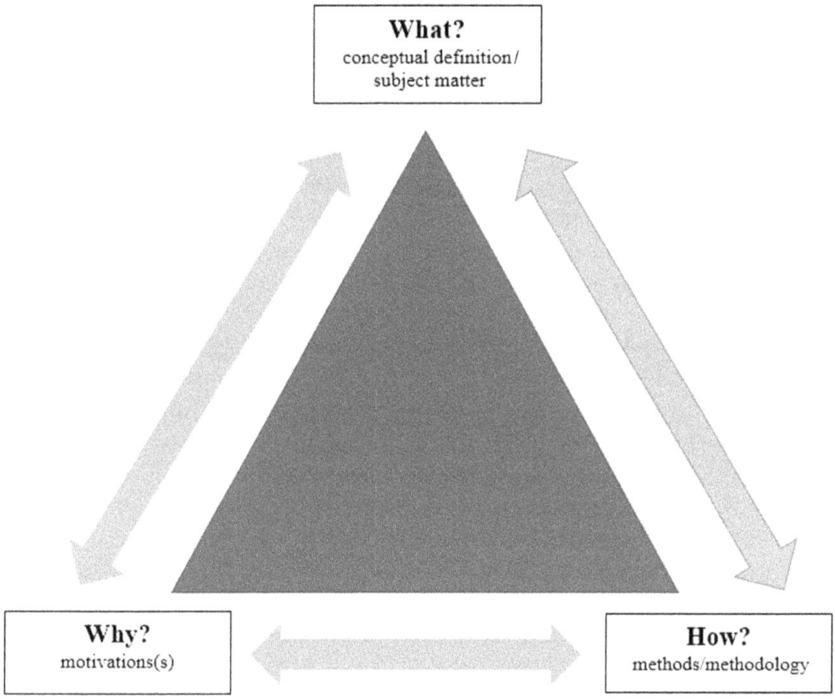

ET comprises three 'eternal' questions. First, there is the question of subject-matter definition, often requiring conceptual clarification or elucidation. Simply put, *what* is the research project or inquiry about? Second is the question of motivation. This concerns the justification for embarking upon any particular intellectual inquiry. *Why* is the proposed research question important or interesting? Answers to the question of motivation supply the rationale for selecting *these* particular research topics and questions from the virtually limitless universe of potential alternative inquiries. Third are questions of method and methodology. It is not enough only to know *what* the question is and *why* it is being posed; there is also the matter of means, that is, *how* the inquiry will be conducted. The significance of methodological possibilities and constraints is often under-appreciated, relative to considerations of subject-matter and motivation. The overall point, and value, of ET is not simply to identify the three eternal questions, which could just as easily have been presented in a list, but to highlight their 'triangular' relationships with each other. Crucially, the 'what', 'why' and 'how' dimensions of any intellectual inquiry are *interdependent*, and their answers are *mutually conditioning*. None can be answered satisfactorily without providing collectively coherent answers to all three. The challenge is to bring all three points on ET – the *what?*, the *why?* and the *how?* of any research project or question – into mutually supportive and self-adjusting reflective equilibrium.

ET immediately solves one apparent puzzle dogging theoretical reflection on the disciplinary constitution of Criminology. If definition is partly conditioned by motivation (and method), one should not expect to find general agreement even on basic questions of disciplinary constitution. To the contrary, definitions of 'Criminology' will, in part, reflect the purposes and interests of those doing the defining. We should, to elaborate, think of 'a discipline' as the outcome of an active, partly conscious and programmatic enterprise – discipline as an active verb, rather than a passive noun. There is nothing inherently wrong or unusual in any of this, so long as the process of naming and claiming is transparent and disciplinary choices are intellectually and methodologically defensible. This conceptualisation necessarily relativises the value of disciplinary definitions. A definition of 'Criminology', in answer to ET's subject-matter question, is not good or bad *tout court*, but only more or less functional or symbolically salient or ethically sound with respect to certain, specified or specifiable, objectives. One is led to adopt a pluralistic approach to disciplinary definition, but not without normative purchase. The ethical value, if any, of any particular disciplinary specification will reflect its intended objectives and uses, and possibly also its methods. As a characteristically modernist science with myriad practical applications, Criminology is intimately associated with 'useful knowledge', and – as is well known – not all of its specifications or applications in history have been either ethically neutral or socially progressive.[31]

The purpose and value of questioning Criminology's identity can be brought into sharper focus through the lens of ET. Starting with the question of motivation, previous attempts to define or conceptualise 'Criminology' are replete with intellectual puzzles, over and above their number and variety. Tim Newburn suggests that 'Criminology is a strange beast … the study of the making of laws, the breaking of laws, and of society's reaction to the breaking of laws.'[32] This is

[31] Consider, for example, Criminology's historical associations with eugenics, noted by Terence Morris, 'British Criminology: 1935-48' (1988) 28 *British Journal of Criminology* 20, 26–27. As one early enthusiast put it, 'the penal code is *par excellence* a group of eugenic measures … [a]nd following the results of eugenic science, it can tomorrow widen or narrow the circle of crimes in the end of conducing to the physical and psychic improvement of the race': Giulio Q Battaglini, 'Eugenics and the Criminal Law' (1914) 5 *Journal of the American Institute of Criminal Law and Criminology* 12, 15.

[32] Tim Newburn, *Criminology* (Willan, 2007) 4–5 (adopting the approach of Edwin Sutherland).

not a bad starting point for further exploration and reflection, as far as it goes, but two, contradictory features of this characterisation are immediately apparent. First, it is extraordinarily broad in encompassing topics – eg, detailed studies of the legislative process or doctrinal analysis of criminal law and procedure – that most scholars describing themselves as practising criminologists would not regard as part of Criminology. Second, it is too narrow in specifying legalistic parameters which seemingly exclude topics generally regarded as falling squarely within the criminological canon – eg, general studies of social deviancy, personality traits, public policy, social attitudes or crime in the media – that are not obviously or directly related to making or breaking *laws*. To stretch the definition to encompass every well-established sub-field or research tradition within contemporary Criminology, one would seemingly have to accommodate all aspects of modern life, and every dimension of policymaking and governance, in both the public and the private spheres – which is hardly any kind of serviceable definition or tractable programme. Criminology would be the study, or 'science',[33] of all aspects of human existence. The observation, routinely attributed to David Downes,[34] that Criminology is 'a *rendezvous* subject' is similarly suggestive and perplexing. It hints at a peculiar affinity or aspiration towards interdisciplinarity, without specifying what Criminology's constituent elements might be, or why or how they come together. A crossroads may present enticing new directions of travel,[35] but it is rarely a final, or especially desirable, destination.

Criminology may be unusual, if not unique, in the breadth of its disciplinary scope and methodological pluralism, and this is one reason for criminologists to be concerned with meta-theoretical questions of disciplinary constitution. Generalisations about Criminology are likely to be problematic at the very least, if not entirely *incomprehensible*, unless some effort is made to specify definitional parameters. Consider the claim that, 'Academic criminology … is engaging with human rights, and in a wider range of areas and ways than ever

[33] Let's not get hung up on definitional quibbles about the meaning of 'science', not least because much of the perceived problem with that term is actually just a peculiarity of modern vernacular English. 'Legal scientist', 'criminal scientist', etc, *sound* odd in English, but are standard usage in many other (European) languages. Suffice it to say that my understanding is not naively empiricist, narrowly positivistic or in thrall to scientism. See further, Susan Haack, *Defending Science – Within Reason: Between Scientism and Cynicism* (Prometheus Books, 2003); Paul Boghossian, *Fear of Knowledge: Against Relativism and Constructivism* (OUP, 2006); Tom Sorrell, *Scientism* (Routledge, 1994).

[34] See, eg, Simon Holdaway and Paul Rock, 'Thinking about Criminology: A Reflection on Theory within Criminology' in Holdaway and Rock (eds), *Thinking About Criminology* (UCL Press, 1998) 180; David Garland and Richard Sparks, 'Criminology, Social Theory and the Challenge of Our Times' in Garland and Sparks (eds), *Criminology and Social Theory* (OUP, 2000) 7; Mary Bosworth and Carolyn Hoyle, 'What Is Criminology? An Introduction' in Bosworth and Hoyle (eds), *What Is Criminology?* (OUP, 2011) 6. *Cf* Jock Young, 'In Praise of Dangerous Thoughts' (2003) 5 *Punishment & Society* 97 (rendering 'rendezvous discipline'); Jean Hine, 'Applied Criminology: Research, Policy and Practice' in Brian Stout, Joe Yates and Brian Williams (eds), *Applied Criminology* (Sage, 2008) 20 (same). Whatever Downes actually said, or Rock says he said, I'm damned if I can find the original source.

[35] *Cf* Kathleen Daly and Lisa Maher (eds), *Criminology at the Crossroads: Feminist Readings in Crime and Justice* (OUP, 1988).

before. But, to a remarkable degree … these engagements are characterized by the absence of – or disinterest in – enquiry into criminology's history with rights discourse.'[36] This thesis strikes me as a highly situated set of propositions, turning crucially on what one takes 'academic criminology' (and 'human rights') to mean. Certainly, large swathes of criminological research and publication, particularly those primarily concerned with the aetiology of offending behaviour and typically employing quantitative research methods, have little if any engagement with human rights. Rights discourse tends to be confined to those sub-parts of Criminology focused on public policy-making, policing and penal process – the 'reacting to crime' panel of Newburn's triptych. The extent to which this disciplinary subpart can legitimately stand in for 'academic Criminology' as a whole is a function of time and place. It is an extrapolation that would be more plausible in relation to British Criminology today,[37] for example, than it would have been 50 or 100 years ago, or in relation to contemporary US Criminology. Conversely, *some* criminologists were addressing issues of rights and justice before 'human rights' became popular currency, even amongst legal scholars.[38] There may then be an element of anachronism in looking for historical evidence of engagement with 'human rights' before that topic really existed in its modern sense as a tangibly recognisable object of inquiry. Finally, the further contention that 'it is only by enquiring into its history that academic criminology can make sense of the choices about human rights it faces today'[39] is puzzling on several levels. Granted that history (ie, accumulated human experience) has much to teach posterity, the value of its lessons can be assessed only in relation to some specified purpose or objective. Historical knowledge might be intrinsically valuable, but a history of criminological engagement with human rights, if produced as its own reward, would more naturally be characterised as History (of ideas and institutions) rather than Criminology. It cannot be excluded that historical self-awareness might profitably inform Criminology's meta-theoretical reflections

[36] Thérèse Murphy and Noel Whitty, 'Making History: Academic Criminology and Human Rights' (2013) 53 *British Journal of Criminology* 568, 571. Thirty years earlier, Cohen remarked on (then) contemporary criminologists' 'sustained attempt to translate the human rights agenda into the creation of new criminal offences by the state against its citizens …. [T]hese are potentially powerful sources of criminalization, and to my knowledge, no criminologist has begun to study their history, social base, and possible effects': Stanley Cohen, *Against Criminology* (Transaction Books, 1988) 265, 266.

[37] Murphy and Whitty concede in a footnote, ibid 568, that their analysis 'draws primarily on trends in UK academic criminology, but there is also reference to pertinent Australian, Canadian and US scholarship'.

[38] Notably, Herman Schwendinger and Julia Schwendinger, 'Defenders of Order or Guardians of Human Rights?' in Ian Taylor, Paul Walton and Jock Young (eds), *Critical Criminology* (Routledge & Kegan Paul, 1975). There was also early criminological interest in aspects of international criminal justice that would today be characterised, inter alia, as human rights issues: see John Hagan and Scott Greer, 'Making War Criminal' (2002) 40 *Criminology* 231; Sheldon Glueck, 'By What Tribunal Shall War Offenders Be Tried?' (1943) 56 *Harvard Law Review* 1059. Now see, generally, Anthony Amatrudo and Leslie William Blake, *Human Rights and the Criminal Justice System* (Routledge, 2014); Leanne Weber, Elaine Fishwick and Marinella Marmo (eds), *The Routledge International Handbook of Criminology and Human Rights* (Routledge, 2017).

[39] Murphy and Whitty (n 36) 569.

on its own disciplinary constitution and activity, but it is not obvious why historical inquiry should merit any methodological priority over, say, conceptual analysis, normative speculation or sociological investigations of practical effects. And why should Criminology's historical enlightenment be circumscribed by *its own* disciplinary engagement with human rights, rather than learning more comprehensively from general histories of human rights struggles, institutions and jurisprudence?

In short, generalisations about Criminology are likely to be *both* true *and* false, deeply puzzling or tantamount to meaningless, without careful attention to definitional questions. This realisation places a premium on meta-theoretical awareness, not only for those who want to make general statements about Criminology but also for anybody interpreting or evaluating such statements. The price of meaningful assertion will often be diminished generality, the more so when one is speaking of 'a polymath, hydra-headed discipline addressed to different audiences and diffusely focused'.[40] What is true of Criminology in particular times and places is unlikely to be true of Criminology always and everywhere.

B. Institutional Discipline

In addition to resolving intellectual puzzles, clarifying thought and facilitating meaningful communication, meta-theoretical questions of disciplinary constitution also have more programmatic and instrumental connotations. The project of disciplining Criminology is a particularised instance of disciplining academic disciplines in general. Academic disciplines are dynamic institutionalised intellectual constructs rather than static natural kinds. Academic disciplines and their sub-disciplinary taxonomies come and go in response to scientific innovation and in accordance with prevailing intellectual fashions. They emerge, evolve, grow, change, shrink and die, sometimes permanently (not too many alchemists or phrenologists around these days), sometimes only to remerge with renewed vitality, as classical scholarship of all kinds did during and after the western European Enlightenment. Having read the last rites over the sociology of deviance, Sumner was still prepared to concede it a zombified afterlife.[41]

Disciplines are functional conduits of disciplinary knowledge in at least two important senses. First, disciplines *organise* knowledge according to intelligible schemas which enhance disciplinary knowledge's accessibility, coherence and usefulness, and leverage its impact through effective interpretational and epistemic frameworks. Knowledge classified as 'criminological' is advertised

[40] Paul Rock, 'The Public Faces of Public Criminology' (2014) 14 *Criminology & Criminal Justice* 412.

[41] '[E]ver respectful and gentle ... who am I to dispute reincarnation, or the value of talking in words that don't speak, or the value of talking to the dead, or the role of dead sciences in reactionary epochs in need of new justifications?': Sumner (n 17) ix, x.

as especially salient for criminologists and is classified in this way precisely for that reason. Criminologists know where to look in the library, and which search terms to employ when interrogating digital databases, which academic journals to read, which professional associations to join, and which conferences to attend (at least partly) by reference to the sub-disciplinary taxonomies developed within criminological scholarship and the broader conceptual structures transcribing the contours of the discipline. Second, disciplines *reproduce* knowledge through institutionalisation, broadly conceived. University departments are configured, predominantly, along disciplinary lines. Teachers transmit disciplinary knowledges to students, some of whom graduate to higher-level studies and, in time, become the next generation of researchers and teachers. Physical concentration (and nowadays, remotely connected networks) of like-minded scholars pursuing overlapping research agendas facilitates, through dialogue and collaboration, the production of specialist textbooks, innovative degree programmes, new journals and more academic conferences, reinforcing, enriching and entrenching existing disciplinary structures. Supply – of students, of teachers and researchers, of publications – expands to fill capacity, fuelling further expansion. Institutional scaffolding projects disciplinary knowledges into the future, enabling each successive generation of scholars to build upon and refine what has gone before without constantly having to retrace steps or reinvent the disciplinary wheel.

At a time when the total sum of human knowledge is expanding with mind-boggling geometry, and the ability to mine, interrogate and utilise data is beginning to take priority over generating ever more data to the point of (mental and digital) saturation, the capacity of academic disciplines to organise knowledge effectively should not be underestimated as a practical virtue. Indeed, effective organisation might be regarded as a robust criterion for evaluating the quality of particular disciplinary frameworks. Of course, intensifying disciplinary specialisation in a world of exponentially increasing information poses the countervailing risk of a downward spiral into disaggregated insular silos, of knowing more and more about less and less in ever-decreasing circles. Stan Cohen confessed that '[f]or those of us in the strange business of criminology … the problem of insulation has been endemic, chronic, and the subject of much rumination'.[42] Meta-theoretical reflection on disciplinary constitution has another practical function at this juncture, in promoting interdisciplinary collaborations across conventional disciplinary boundaries. For such collaborations to be methodologically sound and mutually beneficial (and thus, plausibly sustainable), however, requires astute appreciation of disciplinary parameters and methodological commitments and careful attention to their effective trans-disciplinary integration. ET is offered up as a useful general heuristic to facilitate sensitive interdisciplinary engineering. Moreover, Criminology boasts exceptional potential for productive interdisciplinary collaboration, for example,

[42] Stanley Cohen, *Against Criminology* (Transaction Books, 1988) 277.

in relation to Genocide and Holocaust Studies,[43] International Criminal Justice,[44] War, Terrorism and Security[45] and Forensic Science.[46]

By any robust measure of disciplinary propagation and institutional entrenchment (eg, numbers of students, scholars, journals, or publications propagating the field), British Criminology has enjoyed several decades of sustained success. Whether this golden period of continuous expansion can be expected to continue into the future depends on a multitude of factors, prominently including UK higher education policy, the graduate jobs market, access to and integration within global networks of scholarship, and the sustainability of research grant funding, all of which will be agitated, possibly for a decade or more, by the unfathomable contingencies of Brexit. If the economy contracts, higher education will feel the pinch.[47] As recent electoral history amply confirms, there are few votes in raising taxes to plug funding shortfalls in higher education, and this is hardly surprising once post-compulsory education has been ideologically repositioned as a privatised consumer good for which its primary beneficiaries – those consumers of educational 'experience' formerly known as students – should be expected to stump up by way of down-payment on their own future prosperity. If there is any public money to spare for pre-election sweeteners, higher education will be found languishing low down on government departments' wishlists of funding priorities, alongside other electoral liabilities such as prisons and legal aid. Beyond economic considerations, erecting any further legal, institutional or cultural barriers to the free movement of ideas (which are enmeshed with and transmitted by the EU's four headline 'fundamental freedoms' covering goods, services, capital and labour) can never be a positive development for education or science, with their inherently borderless, universalistic and unifying aspirations.

On the positive side of the balance, however, it might be thought that Criminology is somewhat better placed to respond to current pressures within the higher education sector than, in particular, arts and humanities disciplines

[43] Alex Alvarez, *Genocidal Crimes* (Routledge, 2010); Joachim J Savelsberg, *Crime and Human Rights: Criminology of Genocide and Atrocities* (Sage, 2010); L Edward Day and Margaret Vandiver, 'Criminology and Genocide Studies: Notes on What Might Have Been and What Still Could Be' (2000) 34 *Crime, Law & Social Change* 43; George S Yacoubian Jr, 'The (In)significance of Genocidal Behavior to the Discipline of Criminology' (2000) 34 *Crime, Law & Social Change* 7.

[44] Mark A Drumbl, *Atrocity, Punishment, and International Law* (CUP, 2007); Wayne Morrison, *Criminology, Civilisation and the New World Order* (Cavendish, 2006). *Cf* Rob Watts, Judith Bessant and Richard Hil, *International Criminology – A Critical Introduction* (Routledge, 2008).

[45] Ruth Jamieson (ed), *The Criminology of War* (Routledge, 2014); George P Fletcher, 'The Law of War and its Pathologies' (2007) 38 *Columbia Human Rights Law Review* 517; Steven R Ratner, 'The Schizophrenias of International Criminal Law' (1998) 33 *Texas International Law Journal* 237; Lucia Zedner and Benjamin Goold (eds), *Crime and Security* (Routledge, 2006); Eugene McLaughlin, 'Political Violence, Terrorism and States of Fear' in John Muncie and Eugene McLaughlin (eds), *The Problem of Crime*, 2nd edn (Sage, 2001).

[46] Andy Williams, *Forensic Criminology* (Routledge, 2015); Christopher Lawless, *Forensic Science: A Sociological Introduction* (Routledge, 2016).

[47] I am deliberately leaving these 2016 predications unedited, so that readers may judge the accuracy of my prognosis for themselves.

(encompassing the greater part of legal scholarship as traditionally conceived and conducted). As a pre-eminently policy-relevant science, Criminology is relatively well-endowed with intellectual and practical resources to address the government's 'impact' agenda, emphasising the instrumental value of scholarly research in 'the real world' beyond the academy.[48] Concurrently, as a discipline closely associated with empirical research methodologies, Criminology is better adapted than humanistic scholarship to chase large research grants and develop international networks, partnerships and collaborations, all of which are increasingly being utilised as proxies for 'quality' in performance 'metrics', affecting funding and institutional reputation (which in turn drive student and staff recruitment and retention) and which are largely modelled on the methodological protocols, priorities and working practices of the 'hard' physical sciences.[49] Especially in its quantitative, behavioural science and social psychology variations, Criminology is better able to play the game of maximising grant income, multi-author publications, bolstering citation indexes, and demonstrating global 'significance', 'reach and 'impact' than the single-author, library-based scholarship typical of history, philosophy, languages or jurisprudence or even of mainstream, theoretically ambitious Sociology.[50] To point out Criminology's marginal disciplinary advantages in coping with REFs, TEFs, and the whole kit and caboodle of metrics-obsessed bureaucratic audits to which British higher education is now subjected[51] is not to overlook the ever-present risks to any self-respecting science which hitches its wagon to the policy-making caravan. What kind of 'science' allows its research agenda to be dominated by instrumental, and predictably short-term, political priorities? What if those in power do not like the truths that methodologically rigorous research findings speak back to them? How can scholarship avoid, or insulate itself from, the corruption of evidence-based policymaking into policy-based 'evidence-making'? These are not merely abstract worries in the recent annals of criminological research.[52] Moreover, it is barely possible to calculate the

[48] See UKRI, 'How Research England Supports Research Excellence', www.ukri.org/who-we-are/research-england/research-excellence/ref-impact/ (accessed 17 December 2025); Marta Natalia Wróblewska, 'Research Impact Evaluation and Academic Discourse' (2021) 8 *Humanities and Social Sciences Communications* Article 58.

[49] Chapter 11 returns to these themes.

[50] *Cf* John Holmwood, 'Sociology's Misfortune: Disciplines, Interdisciplinarity and the Impact of Audit Culture' (2010) 61 *British Journal of Sociology* 639, 646 (bemoaning the precariousness of critically reflexive Sociology and its gradual displacement by institutionally adaptive applied social sciences; '[t]hus, "sociologists" become "criminologists", "social policy" analysts and the like').

[51] Stefan Collini, *What Are Universities For?* (Penguin, 2012).

[52] See Will McMahon (ed), *Critical Thinking about the Uses of Research* (CCJS, 2008); Paddy Hillyard, Joe Sim, Steve Tombs and Dave Whyte, 'Leaving a "Stain Upon the Silence": Contemporary Criminology and the Politics of Dissent" (2004) 44 *British Journal of Criminology* 369. 'The discernible shift away from Home Office funding', Zedner et al suggest, 'is perhaps indicative of a fear of being pushed too far down the road of policy-led research towards projects that may, in any case, be hidden on a high shelf in government if the findings do not meet with the approval of whichever Justice Secretary holds the power on the day of publication': Lucia Zedner, Carolyn Hoyle and Mary Bosworth, 'Introduction' in Mary Bosworth, Carolyn Hoyle, and Lucia Zedner (eds), *Changing Contours of Criminal Justice* (OUP, 2016) xxiii.

longer-term damage that may be inflicted on the integrity of the research base and through the (possibly irreversible) erosion of academic collegiality across the sector by reductively market-driven approaches to teaching and scholarship.

So far, we have been exploiting the potential of meta-theoretical reflection on disciplinary constitution, and employing ET, to elucidate the epistemic significance of organising and transmitting knowledge through institutionalised academic disciplines, to clarify the meaning of general statements within and about Criminology, and to assess Criminology's disciplinary prospects against the backdrop of current UK educational policy and the broader political context. Recognising the active, programmatic nature of 'disciplining' disciplines opens up further opportunities for strategic deployment by criminological entrepreneurs, and for reflexive critical re-examination of such discipline-forming activity. From its self-conscious origins in nineteenth-century scientific positivism, Criminology has been promoted, and sold to policymakers, as instrumentally useful knowledge. In later, more institutionally secure and self-confident phases, Criminology has expanded its horizons to offer advice and assistance, and strike up new interdisciplinary partnerships, in areas of contiguous and overlapping research interests with anthropologists, economists, historians, legal scholars, political scientists and psychologists, amongst others. I have previously argued for the necessity of criminological contributions to the fledgling discipline of International Criminal Justice.[53] Concluding this part of the discussion by revisiting a more elemental relationship between Criminology and Criminal Justice will further illuminate both the epistemic and the programmatic dimensions of disciplining disciplines.

C. Criminology and Criminal Justice

Is Criminal Justice a subpart of Criminology, one chapter in its compendious volume? Or is Criminal Justice a separate discipline, intersecting with Criminology without being subsumed by it? My impression is that British criminologists tend to assume the former relation. Their mental Venn diagram of disciplinary constitution imagines Criminal Justice as a small circle entirely encompassed within the much larger circle of Criminology, which simultaneously incorporates, as additional subsets, reasonably well-articulated, institutionally rooted disciplinary sub-specialisms such as Penology and Victimology. The inclusion of topics such as 'policing', 'criminal process', 'trials', 'sentencing', 'prisons' and 'the penal system' in standard Criminology textbooks and reference works reinforces, what I take to be, a largely unselfconscious and theoretically lax, if mostly benign, disciplinary imperialism. Observing, uncontroversially, that Criminal Justice concerns itself

[53] Paul Roberts and Nesam McMillan, 'For Criminology in International Criminal Justice' (2003) 1 *Journal of International Criminal Justice* 315. To similar effect, see Mark A Drumbl, 'Toward a Criminology of International Crime' (2003) 19 *Ohio State Journal on Dispute Resolution* 263.

with institutional responses to crime (recall the third panel of Newburn's disciplinary triptych), criminologists easily presume that Criminal Justice must be, in disciplinary terms, 'one of us'. Indeed, criminologists have been taken to task, from within their own ranks, for being 'curiously unwilling to acknowledge th[e] fact' that 'much of what is done under the banner of criminology is in fact criminal justice'.[54] Yet it strikes me that observations along these lines are bedevilled by a terminological confusion, which, by extension, and viewed in the light of ET, translates into a missed opportunity for smart disciplinary constitution.

Terminological confusion can be traced to this central ambiguity: 'Criminal Justice' might refer to the institutions and practices of the criminal justice *process*, or it might refer to a distinctive normative ideal and consolidating value structure, for example, an ideal of *retributive* or *penal* justice. Conceivably, references to 'criminal justice' might straddle both meanings; though it has to be said, and emphatically, that failure to distinguish which and when is when and which is a pervasive source of confusion and theoretical incontinence and vacuity across this entire field of scholarship. Working predominantly within a social science paradigm, British criminologists tend to interpret 'Criminal Justice' sociologically, as referring to 'the study of policing, probation, criminal process, the trial, sentencing, and punishment'.[55] But a legal scholar or, even more so, a philosopher would more naturally associate 'Criminal Justice' with normative debates in moral and political philosophy centred on 'justice' as an organising ideal of human flourishing and peaceful coexistence, and with specifically penal applications stretching back (at least) to Homer and Plato.[56] Modern Penology represents an interesting study in intellectual hybridity, because it undoubtedly incorporates philosophical speculation as well as sociological and socio-legal commentaries on penal process, though not – as I say – always in the most methodologically coherent or pellucid terms.

Drawing the 'semantic sting'[57] from terminological confusions surrounding 'Criminal Justice' is a key insight of meta-theoretical reflection on Criminology's disciplinary constitution; and possibly a job for life for enterprising theoreticians, given the frequency with which such terminological confusions arise and their apparent resilience to permanent correction. Beyond terminological clarification, at least two further methodological lessons may be drawn from this exercise. First, the normative dimensions of Criminal Justice have been a notably active field of scholarly research and publication over the preceding three decades, but this expanding corpus has been produced by, predominantly, legal theorists and philosophers under the banner of Criminal Law Theory or criminal

[54] Lucia Zedner, Carolyn Hoyle and Mary Bosworth, 'Introduction' in Mary Bosworth, Carolyn Hoyle and Lucia Zedner (eds), *Changing Contours of Criminal Justice* (OUP, 2016) xxii.

[55] ibid. This discussion is later linked to '[t]he question of how any *social science discipline* develops and changes': ibid xxvi (emphasis supplied).

[56] See Trevor J Saunders, *Plato's Penal Code: Tradition, Controversy, and Reform in Greek Penology* (OUP, 1994).

[57] Ronald Dworkin, *Law's Empire* (Fontana, 1986) 45–46.

jurisprudence,[58] and largely outside the disciplinary parameters of Criminology as conventionally apprehended. Not badged as 'Criminology' and often appearing in specialist journals and book series, it is doubtful whether much of this normative criminal jurisprudence seeps into criminologists' consciousness or makes it onto Criminology students' or researchers' reading lists. This is a pertinent illustration of the cramped intellectual horizons and insularity to which disciplinary taxonomies are prone. Second, there is a tendency for criminologists working within an essentially descriptive, sociological paradigm to assert, or presuppose, normative positions that a philosopher would say must be 'earned' through competent normative argument. British Criminology, specifically, is characterised by a general inclination to be sociologically strong but normatively weak; albeit Penology, and in particular penal theory (insofar as this is plausibly categorised as Criminology), represents a partial exception.[59] Here one should recall that not every judgement expressed, or tendentious claim advanced, by an academic expert is properly described as expert academic opinion.

It is essentially for these reasons that I argued, many years ago, for regarding Criminology and Criminal Justice as essentially 'distinct but overlapping' disciplinary endeavours. This was my first pass at disciplinary taxonomy and differentiation:

> The fundamental, discipline-defining question for Criminology, I shall stipulate, is: 'What is crime?' Some criminologists understand themselves to be trying to answer a differently-framed question, namely 'What causes crime?'. However, this second question is merely a derivative of the first, since to look for the causes of something one must have a conscious or at least implicit idea of what that something is – in this case, 'crime' …. The enterprise of Criminal Justice, by contrast, is ultimately referable to a different foundational question, *viz* 'What shall we do about crime?', where 'we' is a placeholder for 'the state', 'society', 'the community', or some other relevant unit of social or political organization. On this view, Criminology stands to Criminal Justice as action stands to reaction.[60]

The article in which this argument was originally advanced discussed complexities surrounding the action/reaction dynamic that it is not necessary to reprise. Plainly, social reactions, both informal and official, partly *define* crime in the very act of responding to it. In retrospect, it was probably too narrow and reductive to stipulate 'What is Crime?' as Criminology's definitive question, not only because criminologists, then as now, are concerned with a broader range of social and

[58] See, in particular, Chapters 2 and 3. For other entry points into a burgeoning literature, see R A Duff and Stuart P Green (eds), *Philosophical Foundations of Criminal Law* (OUP, 2011); Douglas Husak, *The Philosophy of Criminal Law* (OUP, 2010); George P Fletcher (ed), *New Voices in Criminal Theory* (1998) 1 *Buffalo Criminal Law Review* Special Issue.

[59] Penology and Criminal Law Theory have shared ancestry, notably H L A Hart, *Punishment and Responsibility* (OUP, 1968; 2nd edn, Gardner ed 2008); and Herbert L Packer, *The Limits of the Criminal Sanction* (Stanford University Press, 1969).

[60] Paul Roberts, 'On the Preconditions and Possibilities of Criminal Law Theory' (1998) 11 *South African Journal of Criminal Justice* 285, 293.

policy issues than is fairly represented by any preoccupation with the concept of 'crime'; but also because this way of characterising Criminology credits criminologists with greater sensitivity to conceptual analysis than is sometimes merited. Nonetheless, the core of the original disciplinary taxonomy has withstood the test of time and further reflection, in ultimately resting on the motivational and, as I would now more strongly stress, methodological points of the Eternal Triangle:

> Criminology and Criminal justice have been differentiated, not by reference to distinct objects of inquiry, but in terms of distinctive disciplinary *objectives*. Criminology, as I have defined it, is an essentially descriptive enterprise. The answers it proposes to the question (I say) it is designed to address are 'scientific' reports produced from within the disciplinary paradigms of, in particular, Sociology, Economics, Politics, History, Biology, Psychology, Physiology and Neuroscience .... Where Criminology is descriptive, Criminal Justice is normative. Where criminological inquiry posed the question 'what *is* crime?', Criminal Justice asks 'what *should* we do about it?' The perspective is that of a system-insider – who could be a lawyer, a judge, a police officer or some other criminal justice professional, a researcher or any ordinary member of the public – who asks, or answers, a crime-related question of the appropriate form: What harms should be criminal offences? Should insane offenders be punished? Is provocation a good excuse? Who should go to gaol? How much punishment should be meted out to *this* offender? And so on .... [T]hese questions are raised by us, about us, and for us. They are a fractal of the supreme ethical question framed by Socrates: how shall we live? That being so, it should come as no surprise, on the view presented here, that Criminal Justice comprises a sub-part of moral and political philosophy.[61]

I hope that, in light of what has already been said, no reader will object that my disciplinary taxonomy is motivated by programmatic objectives. Of course it is! One lesson of ET is that there are no entirely innocent definitions of academic disciplines, only good – or bad – conceptualisations with respect to particularised objectives. Treating external description/internal prescription as the fault line differentiating Criminology from Criminal Justice is intended to promote a more scrupulous, methodologically sound approach to matching up research questions and modes of inquiry with well-warranted inferential conclusions, in conducting one's own research as well as in the consumption of research produced by others. For example, it is not generally appropriate to derive 'ought' (normative) conclusions from 'is' (descriptive) inquiries – an elementary (method)logical reasoning error known to philosophers as 'the naturalistic fallacy'. In terms of effective disciplinary signposting, recognising that Criminal Justice is applied political morality should incline scholarship in Criminal Justice and its various possible subdivisions (eg, policing, criminal procedure, criminal adjudication, criminal evidence, sentencing, etc) towards productive engagement with philosophical literature, concepts and methods.

[61] ibid 296–97. The original footnote elucidated: 'It is not a trivial question, Socrates said: what we are talking about is how one should live': Bernard Williams, *Ethics and the Limits of Philosophy* (Fontana, 1985) 1.

One response to this argument has been that I am trying to steal away all the interesting questions from Criminology and leave its exponents toiling in the residual dross. Being boring is perhaps the criminologist's ultimate *bête noire* and a fearful imprecation to cast around.[62] However, there is nothing in my argument to imply the intellectual, methodological, ethical, or any other priority of normative over descriptive research questions or agendas. I am making a point about *difference*, not priority; which principally concerns research *methods*, not professional identities. Whilst scholars are naturally entitled to present and associate themselves with whatever disciplinary traditions they choose, Criminology (and Criminal Justice) for the purposes of my disciplinary taxonomy are really just sets of tools in scholarship's comprehensive methodological toolbox. Choosing a hammer or a saw as the best tool for the job in hand does not preclude the use of other tools for different jobs, much less does hammering or sawing turn you into a hammer or a saw (or even a joiner). In fact, many important research questions require *both* descriptive *and* normative inquiries and methods to produce methodologically competent answers. Armchair philosophising devoid of salient empirical facts can be just as intellectually deficient, not to mention politically dangerous, as sociological description masquerading as normative argument.

In *Against Criminology*, published in 1988, Stan Cohen suggested that '[t]he great unwritten book in criminology is a serious examination of the basic principles of liberalism', seeing as how:

> Criminology was born of post-Enlightenment liberalism, and every significant attempt to define its scope and purpose, every major twist in its convoluted inner dialogue, have been made within or in reaction to that original discourse.[63]

'This', he promptly confessed, 'is not such a book'. There are doubtless many reasons why that great book still remains unwritten, starting with the conceptual slipperiness and disputed morality of 'liberalism'.[64] But the arrested development of meta-theoretical reflection on disciplinary constitution may well be another factor. A few pages later Cohen proposes that '[t]he stuff of criminology consists of only three questions: Why are laws made? Why are they broken? What do we do or what should we do about this?'[65] It is striking that a scholar as perceptive, learned and reflexive as Cohen apparently failed to notice that his discipline-defining questions number four, not three; and moreover, his 'third' question elides and thereby submerges the very methodological distinction between

[62] *Cf* Jeff Ferrell, 'Boredom, Crime and Criminology' (2004) 8 *Theoretical Criminology* 287, 295: '[T]he evolution of modern criminology has produced a stale commonality of boredom between its practitioners, its students and its prisoners .... As a result, the majority of mainstream criminological scholarship today can only be described as .... boring.'

[63] Stanley Cohen, *Against Criminology* (Transaction Books, 1988) x.

[64] See Chapter 2. A sense of the astonishing breadth of scholarship claiming to describe, or to denounce, 'liberalism' might be gleaned by comparing Larry Siedentop, *Inventing the Individual: The Origins of Western Liberalism* (Allen Lane, 2014) with Jonah Goldberg, *Liberal Fascism* (Penguin, 2009). And *cf* Stanley Fish, 'Liberalism Doesn't Exist' [1987] *Duke Law Journal* 997.

[65] Stanley Cohen, *Against Criminology* (Transaction Books, 1988) 9.

'ought' and 'is' that I have suggested should be brought to the fore in demarcating Criminology from Criminal Justice. In my disciplinary taxonomy, well-known texts such as Ashworth and Redmayne's *Criminal Process*[66] and Sanders, Young and Burton's *Criminal Justice*[67] are appropriately classified as works of Criminal Justice rather than Criminology, not by identification with their authors' disciplinary backgrounds[68] or the closer association of these texts with law schools and law teaching than with social science departments, still less because their titles settle the issue. The hallmark of Criminal Justice scholarship is that it attempts to structure its descriptions of criminal proceedings within a normative framework of ideals and values, as both of these texts do, with varying degrees of theoretical ambition, intensity and success.

Let me stress that *talking about* norms, as sociologists have done since Durkheim, must not be confused with *participating in* normative theorising. Concepts such as legitimacy, for example, can be interpreted as social phenomena and investigated sociologically without taking any position on what actually is or is not legitimate, normatively speaking.[69] This methodological stricture generalises to social constructionist, psychoanalytic, genealogical and historicist perspectives. Jurisprudential theorising has isolated normative statements 'from a point of view',[70] ie, statements containing a 'thin ought' expressed without deeper moral endorsement. For example, I can, in good faith, remind my observant friends that they 'ought not' to eat non-kosher food without myself endorsing or observing any such dietary restriction; we can intelligibly speak of the obligations imposed by long-dead normative systems such as Roman Law, etc. Criminology can, and does, engage with normativity in a descriptive sense without in any way compromising its credentials as (positivistic) social science. The question famously posed by Howard Becker to sociologists,[71] then, is rather more pertinently addressed to Criminal Justice scholars engaged in committed normative theorising from the internal point of view: whose side are we on? If criminal justice scholarship is appropriately characterised as being, in some broad sense, continuous with the institutional practices it evaluates, its own legitimacy must be bound up with the legitimacy of those practices. The extent to which well-placed criticism of institutional practices carries over to associated Criminal Justice research, and to the scholars who produce it, then becomes a live, and possibly urgent, question for academic scholarship.

[66] Andrew Ashworth and Mike Redmayne, *The Criminal Process*, 4th edn (OUP, 2010). Now see Liz Campbell, Andrew Ashworth and Mike Redmayne, *The Criminal Process*, 5th edn (OUP, 2019).

[67] Andrew Sanders, Richard Young and Mandy Burton, *Criminal Justice*, 4th edn (OUP, 2010). Now see Layla Skinns, Lucy Welsh and Andrew Sanders, *Sanders and Young's Criminal Justice*, 5th edn (OUP, 2021).

[68] *Cf* Andrew Ashworth, 'Criminal Justice, Not Criminology?' in Mary Bosworth and Carolyn Hoyle (eds), *What Is Criminology?* (OUP, 2011) ('When I am asked whether I am a criminologist, I always say no .... I would not want to pretend to be a criminologist when I am not one').

[69] See, eg, Mike Hough, Jonathan Jackson, Ben Bradford, Andy Myhill and Paul Quinton, 'Procedural Justice, Trust, and Institutional Legitimacy' (2010) 4 *Policing* 203.

[70] Joseph Raz, *The Authority of Law*, 2nd edn (OUP, 2009) 140–3, 306–8.

[71] Howard S Becker, 'Whose Side Are We On?' (1967) 14 *Social Problems* 239.

III. Adjectival Criminologies and 'Critical' Scholarship

Contemporary criminological scholarship is awash with what might be described as 'adjectival criminologies', that is to say, strands of Criminology qualified by one or more adjectival descriptors. In this vein we have seen marxist (not to be confused with Marxian!) criminology, socialist criminology, working-class criminology, conservative criminology, feminist criminology, alternative criminology, green (or environmental) criminology, southern criminology, peacemaking criminology, public criminology, administrative criminology, positivist criminology, left realist criminology, liberal criminology, neo-liberal criminology, postmodern criminology, cultural criminology, comparative criminology, international criminology – and not forgetting the variation to which this section's discussion now turns, *critical* criminology.

The impetus towards qualifying 'criminology' with adjectives doubtless partly stems from the desire to provide more informative descriptions of research questions and programmes, given that the scope of research on crime, policing, criminal process and penal policy is potentially so vast and protean that any *general* definition of the field must be so abstract and bland as to be almost vacuous.[72] There is also, it seems to me, a good deal of programmatic disciplining and scholarly entrepreneurship to be found in these descriptions. Sometimes, the aim is to promote Criminology in new(er) fields, such as war/peace studies or international relations, or to emphasise particular, possibly overlooked or underappreciated methodological approaches, such as comparative scholarship.[73] Often, there is a desire to associate research with broader political or social programmes, as in feminist or socialist criminology. Many of the adjectives are self-descriptions, badges of honourable affiliation displayed with pride, but some are principally argumentative constructs applied to label, and distance and sometimes vilify, intellectual or political opponents, occasionally bordering on verbal abuse. These adjectival criminologies police academic boundaries by credentialising theoretical orthodoxy whilst 'othering' intellectual immaturity or heresy, an interesting and

[72] Terms such as 'total social fact' (David Garland, *Punishment and Modern Society* (OUP, 1990) 287) or 'social ordering practice' (Nicola Lacey, 'Introduction: Making Sense of Criminal Justice' in Nicola Lacey (ed), *A Reader on Criminal Justice* (OUP, 1994) 28) purchase accuracy at some cost to clarity and illumination.

[73] A tradition pioneered by Hermann Mannheim, *Comparative Criminology* (Routledge & Kegan Paul, 1965). Now see, Katja Franko Aas, *Globalization and Crime*, 2nd edn (Sage, 2013); David Nelken (ed), *Comparative Criminal Justice and Globalization* (Ashgate, 2011); David Nelken, *Comparative Criminal Justice* (Sage, 2010); James Sheptycki and Ali Wardak (eds), *Transnational and Comparative Criminology* (Glasshouse Press, 2005); Paul Roberts, 'On Method: The Ascent of Comparative Criminal Justice' (2002) 22 *Oxford Journal of Legal Studies* 539; Vincenzo Ruggiero, Nigel South and Ian Taylor (eds), *The New European Criminology: Crime and Social Order in Europe* (Routledge, 1998); Lucia Zedner, 'Comparative Research in Criminal Justice' in Lesley Noaks, Mike Maguire and Mike Levi (eds), *Contemporary Issues in Criminology* (University of Wales Press, 1995).

little commented upon instance of Sumner's 'social censures' at the heart of the criminological enterprise itself. In addition to, or irrespective of, these grander ambitions, adjectival criminologies may reflect fascination with currently modish theories or theorists or represent attempts to extract some academic dividend from (self-proclaimed) novelty and innovation. *The New Criminology*[74] set the tone in this regard and has spawned many imitators and would-be successors. In a minority of instances, adjectival criminologies are lower-level explanatory constructs rather than entire schools of thought or broad theoretical perspectives and derive whatever power and credibility they are able to muster from their own heuristic resources rather than piggybacking on wider associations. A good illustration would be Garland's highly effective contrast between criminologies of the self and criminologies of the other.[75] 'Public criminology' functions in a similar fashion in the more expansive ruminations of Loader and Sparks.[76]

A. What's Really 'Critical' in Criminology

How does 'critical criminology' fit into this disciplinary landscape? To begin with, we may note that 'critical' criminology tends to be an elective badge of honour, rather than an academic social censure deployed for purposes of strategic exclusionary othering. Critical is something that (some) criminologists want to be and to advertise themselves as, like membership of a fashionable club or academic fraternity/sorority.[77] When Jock Young and colleagues decided to strike out on their own 'realist' path, it was 'left idealism' they explicitly rejected not, *nota bene*, the aspiration to be the authentic voice of the critical Left.[78] Critical criminology has been a self-conscious adjectival variant of British Criminology since the mid-1970s,[79] and it achieved a notable landmark of institutionalisation in 1990 with the creation of its own specialist academic periodical. *Critical Criminology* is the official journal of the American Society of Criminology Division on Critical Criminology & Social Justice, dedicated to exploring 'social, political and economic justice from alternative perspectives, including anarchistic, cultural, feminist, integrative,

[74] Ian Taylor, Paul Walton and Jock Young, *The New Criminology: For a Social Theory of Deviance* (Routledge & Kegan Paul, 1973).

[75] David Garland, 'The Limits of the Sovereign State: Strategies of Crime Control in Contemporary Society' (1996) 36 *British Journal of Criminology* 445.

[76] Ian Loader and Richard Sparks, *Public Criminology?* (Routledge, 2011).

[77] *Cf* Mark Kelman's depiction of the origins of Critical Legal Studies (CLS) as a loose coalition of scholars 'who have identified themselves with this organization (come to meetings, put themselves on a mailing list, engaged heavily in the incestuous mutual citation practices toward which "schools" of academic lawyers tend) .... Yet it was still a fair question whether anyone knew what "critical legal studies" meant': Mark Kelman, *A Guide to Critical Legal Studies* (Harvard University Press, 1987) 2.

[78] Jock Young, 'Incessant Chatter: Recent Paradigms in Criminology' in Mike Maguire, Rod Morgan and Robert Reiner (ed), *The Oxford Handbook of Criminology*, 1st edn (OUP, 1994); Jock Young and Roger Matthews (eds), *Rethinking Criminology: The Realist Debate* (Sage, 1992); Ian Taylor, *Crime in Context: A Critical Criminology of Market Societies* (Polity, 1999).

[79] Taylor, Walton and Young (eds) (n 38).

Marxist, peace-making, postmodernist and left-realist criminology'.[80] Feminist criminology is, to my knowledge, the only other adjectival criminology allied to broad social movements or political programmes[81] to attain this marker of institutional recognition and continuity;[82] and feminist criminology is often regarded as another variant of critical criminology.

If only certain criminologies are qualified as 'critical', others must be unqualified or disqualified. The adjective 'critical', the *OED* informs us,[83] means 'Given to judging; *esp*. given to adverse or unfavourable criticism; fault-finding, censorious'; or alternatively, 'Involving or exercising careful judgement or observation; nice, exact, accurate, precise, punctual' and 'Occupied with or skilful in criticism.' To the extent that the latter qualities are suggested, it would seem that all careful scholarship should aspire to be critical, and that being *un*critical would be a failure of methodological technique. In some areas and traditions of theorising, 'critical' means precisely that, and is best grasped as 'an attitude and a willingness to continuously question and to be put into question'[84] rather than subscription to any more substantive theoretical commitments or particular policy agendas. It has long been my view that 'critical thinking', also known as Philosophy, is just another way of characterising thinking done properly.[85] Understood in this way, no serious scholar or researcher would want to be, or to describe themselves as, 'uncritical'. Perhaps 'non-critical' would be a neutral and more accurate designation, though I have admittedly never heard anybody use it to differentiate criminological genres. These initial observations on linguistic usage call attention to the sheer

[80] www.divisiononcriticalcriminology.com/publications/journal/ (accessed 17 December 2025).

[81] I am not overlooking *Theoretical Criminology*, of which Colin Sumner was a founding co-editor. However, the porosity, if not complete incontinence, of the concept of 'theory' together with *Theoretical Criminology*'s inclusive mandate to 'create an international forum for the advancement of the theoretical aspects of criminology' embracing 'scholarship from all the disciplines which currently constitute criminology, notably sociology, history, anthropology, law, politics, psychology, jurisprudence, philosophy, psychiatry, economics, geography and development studies' (Piers Beirne and Colin Sumner, 'Editorial Statement' (1997) 1 *Theoretical Criminology* 5) resist categorisation as a distinctive adjectival strand. Theorising must be integral to any truly scholarly activity; but 'theory' is not necessarily 'critical' in the conventional sense. In short, *Theoretical Criminology* was always self-consciously pluralistic and engaged with the disciplinary mainstream, as its founding editors stressed, ibid 10: 'We are interested in any theoretical analysis which engages with existing thinking and moves it forward .... We welcome contributions from the best work of *all* perspective and traditions ....'

[82] *Feminist Criminology* was launched in 2006 as the official journal of the ASC's Division on Women and Crime, 'dedicated to research related to women, girls, and crime within the context of a feminist critique of criminology'. It operates as 'a venue for articles that place women in the center of the research question', whether as offenders, victims or criminal justice professionals: www.uk.sagepub.com/en-gb/hkg/journal/feminist-criminology (accessed 17 December 2025). Note that regionally or nationally-based criminology journals deploy adjectives to advertise the place of production not to qualify their criminological subject-matter; that is to say, for example, it is the *British Journal* of Criminology, not the Journal of *British Criminology*.

[83] www.oed.com/view/Entry/44592?redirectedFrom=critical#eid (accessed 17 December 2025).

[84] Panu Minkkinen, 'Critical Legal "Method" as Attitude' in Dawn Watkins and Mandy Burton (eds), *Research Methods in Law* (Routledge, 2013) 135.

[85] This is a fairly standard view amongst professional philosophers, see, eg, Lord Quinton, 'Philosophy' in Ted Honderich (ed), *The Oxford Companion to Philosophy* (OUP, 2005; online 2012).

brass-necked effrontery of proclaiming exclusivity in the 'critical' branding of one's own scholarship, should anybody be tempted to assert sole proprietorship in critical method.

The first dictionary definition is suggestive of a prominent connection between self-consciously critical scholarship and opposition to the status quo. First-wave critical criminologists certainly regarded themselves as reacting against what they labelled (not always very transparently or helpfully) 'orthodox criminology', 'traditional correctionally-oriented criminology', 'utilitarian criminology', 'Fabian criminology', 'exposé criminology', and so forth.[86] Although the ostensible project was for 'a thoroughly critical criminology' grounded in a 'fully social'[87] conception of criminality to sublimate and transcend its intellectual and institutional precursors, it might be more enlightening, in retrospect, to consider the ways in which the critique only properly makes sense in relation to its real and imagined targets and in light of the contextually-framed concerns of the day. Which is only to invoke the truism that ideas, intellectual trends and disciplinary reconfigurations are themselves socially and historically situated. Thus, as Stan Cohen ruefully reflected after 20 years' existential struggle with professional identity,[88] what began as a determinedly anti-Criminology was soon either largely absorbed into mainstream disciplinary debates or else rendered anachronistic by changing social and political landscapes: 'To be against criminology, it seems, one has to be part of it.'[89]

Commitment to historical authenticity, no less than professional good manners, demand that critics strive to avoid anachronism or trading on the wisdom of hindsight. The original critical criminologists knew nothing of the impending assault on the welfare state unleashed by neo-conservative economics in the 1980s; still less could they have anticipated the politics of global (in)security in a post-9/11 world. Our twenty-first-century folk devils and moral panics look very different to theirs. Yet the challenge of sympathetically reimagining the intellectual habitus of times gone by should not be underestimated. Re-reading pioneering works of critical criminology from the 1970s, with their unselfconscious references to hippies, beat culture, bohemian lifestyles, and the Women's Liberation Movement, transports me back to a barely remembered world of *Starsky and Hutch* (the original TV series, not the movie), *Serpico*, *The Deer Hunter*, and *Town Bloody Hall*. There is naturally no mention of 'the second plane'[90] or torture teams[91] or fundamentalist terrorism; of paedophiles,[92] sexting, revenge porn or trolling; of

[86] Ian Taylor, Paul Walton and Jock Young, 'Critical Criminology in Britain: Review and Prospects' in Taylor, Walton and Young (eds) (n 38).

[87] ibid 8, 20.

[88] Stanley Cohen, 'Against Criminology' in Cohen, *Against Criminology* (Transaction Books, 1988).

[89] ibid 8.

[90] Martin Amis, *The Second Plane* (Vintage, 2008).

[91] Philippe Sands, *Torture Team* (Allen Lane, 2008); Jeremy Waldron, *Torture, Terror, and Trade-Offs: Philosophy for the White House* (OUP, 2010).

[92] Richard Collier, 'Dangerousness, Popular Knowledge and the Criminal Law: A Case Study of the Paedophile as Sociocultural Phenomenon' in Peter Alldridge and Chrisje Brants (eds), *Personal Autonomy, The Private Sphere and Criminal Law* (Hart Publishing, 2001).

the surveillance society and the security state; of the appalling human tragedy and disturbing social and political fallout of late twentieth-century genocides[93] or twenty-first-century wars. For readers much younger than me, I imagine the cultural milieu of *Critical Criminology* must be about as personally accessible as histories of the General Strike, or the Battle of Agincourt. Still, my sense is that, both intellectually and ethically, critical criminology needed its orthodox counterpart, just as Foucault should be read in dialogue with Marxism,[94] and the inherited tradition of philosophical scepticism is parasitic on Plato's mainstream legacy. For one thing, studying the critique divorced from its target is liable to convey exaggeration and over-reaction. For another, whilst negative criticism can be positively productive when it corrects subsisting errors, exposes corruption, agitates complacency or inspires social reform or self-improvement, left to feed only on itself, 'adverse or unfavourable criticism, fault-finding, censorious[ness]' can become an evil-tempered, half-blind old jackal gnawing off its own legs.

B. Politics and Morality

Critical criminology positions itself in dialogue with the slightly older tradition of psychoanalytically inspired Frankfurt School *kritische Theorie*; which is also name-checked by the OED's entry for 'critical'. This literature exerted some influence in critical criminology's formative years (Sumner has a good line about the popularity of Marcuse's *One Dimensional Man*, in spite of its rebarbative prose, being proof of the indomitability of the human spirit!).[95] However, it is clear that Marxism and Marx (in that order) were the primary referents for critical criminologists trying to reconstruct a politically astute, 'thoroughly materialist' and 'fully social theory of deviance' committed to 'socialist diversity' and 'the abolition of inequalities in wealth and power'.[96] Earlier iterations of Sumner's account of social censures were presented as 'a distinctively Marxist position' rooted in 'the dynamics of class formation, struggle, alliance and demise which reflect the development of the dominant mode of production'.[97] Hard to believe now,[98] but Marxism was

[93] Philip Gourevitch, *We Wish to Inform You that Tomorrow We Will be Killed with Our Families* (Picador, 2000); Roméo Dallaire, *Shake Hands with the Devil* (Arrow Books, 2004); Richard J Goldstone, *For Humanity: Reflections of a War Crimes Investigator* (Yale University Press, 2000); Michael Ignatieff, *Blood and Belonging* (Vintage, 1994).

[94] As clearly emerges from Michel Foucault, *Power/Knowledge*, ed Colin Gordon (Harvester, 1980).

[95] Sumner (n 17) 280.

[96] Taylor, Walton and Young (n 86) 28, 44, 54.

[97] Colin Sumner, 'Rethinking Deviance: Towards A Sociology of Censure' in Sumner (ed), *Censure, Politics and Criminal Justice* (Open University Press, 1990) 30. Note that the original version of this essay was published in 1983, based on a 1981 conference paper.

[98] When I first started teaching in the early 1990s, my colleagues and I lectured on Marxist Criminology as one prominent strand of contemporary criminological theorising. Before long it became apparent, from a sea of blank faces staring back at us with bemusement and incomprehension, that we might as well have been talking about the theological beliefs of the ancient Egyptians. Thatcher's children!

all the theoretical rage way back then, so it is understandable that, having apprehended the necessity of interpreting crime and penality in social context, critical criminologists found themselves 'forced, logically, to turn for such an analysis (and such a criminology) to Marx'.[99] Subsequent history demonstrates, with impeccable irony, how this turning led up a blind alley. It is not only that energy was dissipated on pointless exegetical debates concerning the authentic authorial intent or ideological purity of this or that more or less obscure statement in Marx's scattered, unsystematic musings on crime, law and judicial process.[100] The credibility of this kind of knockabout has never really recovered from the 'People's Front of Judea'/'Judean People's Front' sketches in Monty Python's *Life of Brian*. Nor is the problem only that the Marxist theoretical apparatus fuelled denunciation of 'positivist' criminologies as bourgeois science, in a way that choked off other legitimate avenues of inquiry and arguably retarded the development of specialist subfields such as forensic criminology.[101] It is not even simply that Marx's theory of history is evidently useless as predictive science, and for much the same reasons as Nostradamus' prognostications, albeit at greater length and less entertainingly. Even if Determinism is true (and perhaps it isn't), I think we can be fairly confident that the universe doesn't dance to the tune of historical materialism or turn on the fulcrum of nineteenth-century conceptions of social class. The more fundamental, methodological and intellectual objection to the Marxist turn in critical criminology is that it involves the sacrifice of scholarly judgement to ideological dogma, an elementary betrayal of genuinely critical thought. If '[a] precondition for a radical criminology is the separation of the essential from the inessential, the historically-specific from the historically-inevitable',[102] the project was – yes, inevitably – still-born.

Critical criminologists have often taken their 'orthodox' counterparts to task for failing to address the political context of crime and punishment. Perhaps this connection was not as clear in criminologists' minds in 1975 as it would be today, but it seems to me self-evident that criminality and the administration

[99] Taylor, Walton and Young (n 86) 45.

[100] See, eg, Paul Q Hirst, 'Marx and Engels on Law, Crime and Morality' in Taylor, Walton and Young (eds) (n 38) (categorically denying the possibility of any 'Marxist theory of deviance'); with a reply by Taylor and Walton ('idiosyncratic … polemic … assertive … contentious … caricature … illusion'), followed by Hirst's rejoinder ('internally contradictory … misreading … inadequate and erroneous … fetishism'). Generally, see Hugh Collins, *Marxism and Law* (OUP, 1982); Maureen Cain and Alan Hunt (eds), *Marx and Engels on Law* (Academic Press, 1979); Roger Cotterrell, *The Sociology of Law: An Introduction*, 2nd edn (Butterworths, 1992) chs 4–5; David Garland, *Punishment and Modern Society* (OUP, 1990) chs 4–5; Douglas Hay, Peter Linebaugh, John G Rule, EP Thompson and Cal Winslow (eds), *Albion's Fatal Tree: Crime and Society in Eighteenth-Century England* (Penguin, 1975). The epitome of Marxism-inspired criminology remains Stuart Hall et al, *Policing the Crisis: Mugging, the State, and Law and Order* (Macmillan, 1978).

[101] The way Andy Williams tells it, in ch 3 of *Forensic Criminology* (Routledge, 2015), you can almost see the scars on his back ('sociological explanations tend […] to be dismissive or, worse, engage in vitriolic attacks on anything remotely scientific … a disdain for general positivistic methods, which is usually transmitted from academic generation to generation without any true critical reflection').

[102] Taylor, Walton and Young (n 86) 46.

of criminal justice are thoroughly *political* processes, whatever else they are, and that criminalisation, both in conception and in actuality, is the outcome of political choices, institutions and culture. How else to explain the variability of concepts of crime and punishment through history and between different national jurisdictions? It should then hardly be considered a blinding revelation that hierarchies of 'wealth, power and ideology' will tend to be reflected 'in the legal and moral discourses of the day'.[103] Indeed, 'the ideological and political character of moral censures is … open to view'.[104] It is difficult to comprehend how criminologists could have overlooked these obvious sociological truths (to the extent that they did). Aristotle's ancient conception of politics, as a discursive site of contested conceptions of justice centred on (in Rawls' neat encapsulation) 'the basic structure of society',[105] might have provided some useful guidance in this regard. Still, critical criminologists should be credited with popularising this realisation amongst subsequent generations of criminologists, to the point where it has become orthodox disciplinary common sense. Three further points are worth making.

First, the development and implementation of criminal law and the administration of criminal justice are very complex activities requiring technical expertise of various sorts for their effective practical operation. Policymaking is mediated by the discretionary judgements of criminal justice professionals at every stage of the process. Whilst these myriad operational decisions are constrained by institutional structures and cultures, and they may well produce predictably patterned outcomes, the idea that criminal justice is some kind of bourgeois conspiracy cannot withstand reasonably detailed appraisal of the socio-legal facts. Perhaps policymakers wished they could exert that kind of hydraulic impact on process outcomes, and perhaps this has been achieved in some highly authoritarian societies. But it is simply not possible in open liberal societies, in which government policy is filtered through professional judgement and constrained by institutional values, some of which were explicitly adopted to curtail governmental power. Recognising the complexity and contingency of criminal process opens up a vast array of institutional practices and operational ('discretionary') decision-making to sociological inquiry and jurisprudential analysis.[106]

Second, it is one thing to say that crime and penality are expressions of politics, quite another to claim that all criminologists should make this connection the fulcrum of their research programme. The range of legitimate research questions in Criminology is vast and diverse. For example, it is not necessary to analyse political economy in order to design better penal regimes for sex offenders or to

[103] Sumner (n 97) 27.
[104] Sumner (n 17) 310.
[105] John Rawls, *A Theory of Justice* (OUP, 1972) §1.2.
[106] See further, Jill Hunter, Paul Roberts, Simon NM Young and David Dixon (eds), *The Integrity of Criminal Process* (Hart Publishing, 2016).

assess whether criminalising drivers' use of mobile phones improves road safety. These questions might not be especially interesting to many criminologists, but that hardly disqualifies them as policy-relevant science or turns them into objects of ridicule. Seasoned participants in academic conferences are well-acquainted with the tactic of ignoring the presenter's paper and asking a question related to their own research instead. This is the tactic of *changing the subject*, and there may be more than faint echoes of it in the critical criminologist's objection to 'mainstream' criminological research agendas. Nor is it legitimate to accuse colleagues of 'overlooking' or 'ignoring' certain issues or research questions when, in truth, they were simply never interested in them, or claiming to say anything about them, in the first place. Engaging with the politics of crime and justice should, in my view, open up new research questions and opportunities in the spirit of disciplinary pluralism and in accordance with a sensible division of academic labour. It should not be a criterion for regulating disciplinary membership or peremptorily disqualifying plausible research questions or methods well-suited to answering them.

One needs to distinguish carefully between different strands of methodological critique. In particular, there is a world of difference between arguing that particular research questions or methods are categorically invalid on ideological grounds, and pointing out that particular research strategies are incompetent or deficient *on their own terms*, and therefore incapable of providing the right kind of information ('data') to answer the specified research questions or to support particularised inferential conclusions ('research findings'). To the extent that causal explanations (aka 'positivist social science') rest on indefensible conceptual assumptions or parameters, deny their own theoretical preconditions, fall into a 'fetishism of data'[107] or abandon epistemic rigour – where they reach the 'point at which positivism can be seen as the lazy option'[108] – criticism is surely well-warranted. Bad science is objectionable because it is bad, not because it is science.[109] Moreover, it is central to Criminology's mission to explain, and keep on repeating, to policymakers that faulty diagnosis is liable to produce disappointing, if not counterproductive and possibly even disastrous, policy prescriptions. Yet it is no less erroneous to mock basic tools of rationality, such as formal logic or algebra,[110] to presuppose the automatic superiority of particularistic context over abstracted generalisation, or to apply a single set of criteria to judge the quality of all criminological research, irrespective of professed methods or objectives. If your only model of good Criminology is a fully social theory of deviance, you can be sure that the greater part of criminological research is going to fall short of that very ambitious and exacting (and skewed) standard. And if this is your principal basis for asserting that '[c]riminological research is replete with findings which

[107] Jock Young, *The Criminological Imagination* (Polity, 2011) 35.
[108] ibid 48.
[109] Ben Goldacre, *Bad Science* (Fourth Estate, 2008).
[110] *Cf* Young (n 107) 10–13.

range from the very unlikely to the ridiculous',[111] you had better be prepared to be petard hoisted.[112]

My third point goes to the heart of critical criminology's methodological protocols and presuppositions. I argued in the previous section that Criminology can usefully be conceptualised as a fundamentally descriptive enterprise, whereas Criminal Justice is essentially normative in orientation. Scholarship focusing on the politics of crime and punishment could be sociological description, or normative theorising, or some mixture of the two. To the extent that critical criminologists share Marx's ambition to 'change the world', however, they are engaged in Criminal Justice (rather than Criminology) on my terms; and this implies wholehearted engagement with normative philosophy. To be sure, one might try to pre-empt this conclusion through various theoretical manoeuvres, such as appealing, with the later Marx, to a supposedly 'scientific' historical materialism or travelling, with Nietzsche, to an aesthetic 'beyond good and evil'. Neither of these theoretical gambits has a shred of credibility for anybody well-read in the history of ideas (or in twentieth-century political history, for that matter). What remains is normative philosophy, in which any substantial ethical position has to be earnt through convincing rational argument. The same rationalist precept applies to sceptical or relativist meta-ethical propositions, which are sometimes elided to the 'critical', as it does to any positive normative contention. Scepticism and relativism are not default assumptions which somehow prevail whenever other arguments are found wanting, as philosophical arguments nearly always are in some dimension or degree. To the contrary, the positive case for sceptical or relativist conclusions is often the weakest of all plausible alternatives.[113]

When Criminology shades into Criminal Justice, normative philosophising is inescapable, or research is methodologically inept. Partisanship is no substitute for normative argument, neither is intuitive moral outrage nor the projection of unexamined subjective preferences. The process of criminalisation

[111] ibid 32.

[112] One illustration may suffice here. Young, ibid 190–91, presents a graphic designed to illustrate the 'selective vision' of 'positivist criminology'. It is a funnel or inverted triangle, with 'social harms' at the top, proceeding through narrowing strata of 'criminal laws', 'crimes', 'suspicions', 'arrests', and finally, the small apex of 'prisoners' at the bottom. Viewed sympathetically, in the manner advocated in the first part of this essay, the graphic does a decent job of illustrating the – hardly novel or controversial – point that populations of prisoners or arrestees are only a small and highly selective subset of those who have actually broken criminal laws or engaged in socially harmful behaviour that, for one reason or another, is not currently criminalised, in law or fact. From the reflex perspective of a criminal justice scholar, however, Young has completely 'overlooked' or 'forgotten' every stage of criminal investigation, prosecution, trial, sentencing, appeals and post-conviction remedies (not to mention all forms of diversion and non-custodial penalties) between arrest and imprisonment. What a bizarre and woefully incomplete depiction of criminological subject-matter that omits most of what criminal justice scholars and penologists study! *Tu quoque*.

[113] This argument is well-made by Ronald Dworkin, 'Objectivity and Truth: You'd Better Believe It' (1996) 25 *Philosophy and Public Affairs* 87. For a good illustration of contemporary philosophical scepticism, see Bryan Frances, *Scepticism Comes Alive* (OUP, 2005); or more approachably, see Christopher Grau (ed), *Philosophers Explore The Matrix* (OUP, 2005).

is 'small-p' political through and through, but the (normative) questions to which we require answers include: what conduct *should* be proscribed by criminal law? What *should* be the grounds of criminal responsibility and liability? How *should* criminal trials be conducted? How, and how much, *should* offenders be punished? Substituting other concepts, such as replacing 'crime' with 'harm',[114] simply begs the question (to what extent should *harm* be the criterion of criminal prescription?) and defers the central normative issue (which setbacks to interests should qualify as 'harms' in the relevant sense?). Critical criminology, in short, frequently strays onto the methodological territory of Criminal Law Theory, where questions of criminalisation are keenly debated with growing theoretical sophistication.[115] There may well be greater scope for productive dialogue and mutual instruction.[116]

IV. Conclusions: Who's Critical Now?

This chapter began by revisiting some existential questions about the disciplinary constitution of Criminology. Section II introduced an heuristic device, the Eternal Triangle of Intellectual Inquiry (ET), to facilitate meta-theoretical reflection on the institutional character, significance, and techniques of actively 'disciplining' Criminology as an academic discipline. Methodological considerations were central to this exposition and were decisive in differentiating Criminology from Criminal Justice. Section III extended this general discussion to critical criminology, characterised as one prominent variant of contemporary 'adjectival criminologies', which was then itself subjected to critical re-examination. Compressed into one short chapter, the argument may appear less decisive, or respectful, than Sumner's obituary for the sociology of deviance, but there is a parallelism of method in our thinking through, thinking about, and thinking with distinctive theoretical traditions.

Learning is interactional, and always at some level biographical. This is no less true for entire academic disciplines than it is for individual scholars and researchers,

[114] *Cf* Danny Dorling, Dave Gordon, Paddy Hillyard, Christina Pantazis, Simon Pemberton and Steve Tombs, *Criminal Obsessions: Why Harm Matters More than Crime*, 2nd edn (CCJS, 2008); Paddy Hillyard, Christina Pantazis, Steve Tombs and Dave Gordon (eds), *Beyond Criminology: Taking Harm Seriously* (Pluto Press, 2004), incisively reviewed by Jeffrey Reiman (2006) 46 *British Journal of Criminology* 362.

[115] R A Duff, Lindsay Farmer, S E Marshall, Massimo Renzo and Victor Tadros (eds), *Criminalization: The Political Morality of the Criminal Law* (OUP, 2014); A P Simester and Andreas von Hirsch, *Crimes, Harms and Wrongs: On the Principles of Criminalisation* (Hart Publishing, 2011); Douglas Husak, *Overcriminalization: The Limits of the Criminal Law* (OUP, 2008); Michael Moore, *Placing Blame: A Theory of Criminal Law* (OUP, 1997); Joel Feinberg, *The Moral Limits of the Criminal Law*, vols I-IV (OUP, 1984–1988).

[116] For methodological exemplars, see Robert Reiner, *Crime* (Polity, 2016); Barbara Hudson, *Justice in the Risk Society* (Sage, 2004); Nicola Lacey, Celia Wells and Dirk Meure, *Reconstructing Criminal Law* (Weidenfeld & Nicolson, 1990).

and all of us are equally blessed and cursed with the task of 'educating oneself in public'.[117] There is a natural tendency to associate ideas with where we heard or read them first, rather than necessarily with who first entertained the thought or best expressed it. This realisation ought to stimulate wider, especially interdisciplinary reading, as well as perhaps a measure of diffidence and humility in the realisation that not everything that is fun to do is equally fun to watch or read about. The fact that crime is inherently political (in the broadest sense),[118] or that any comprehensive explanation of offending behaviour must inevitably appeal to aspects of social structure as well as personal agency, are not unique insights of critical criminology, but critical criminologists have done much to popularise these disciplinary axioms. Likewise, although attention to 'elite deviance'[119] and the crimes of the powerful has been part of the criminological canon for over a century (Sutherland and Bonger feature alongside Lombroso and Durkheim in standard histories), critical criminologists since the 1970s have massively expanded the literature on these topics, both in scope and quantity.[120] Even at 40 years' distance, there is still much to admire, and even envy, in the excitement and élan of first-wave British critical criminology. Progressive in intent, socially tolerant by inclination and pluralistic in research methods, its pioneers advocated 're-examination of the ways in which … legal norms are constructed, their function, and the extent to which they are appropriate'[121] and many scholars have subsequently taken up and developed these research agendas within and beyond academic Criminology. Critical criminologists simultaneously announced their intention to 'encroach upon "academic" divisions'[122] in order to claim the politics of crime as legitimate subject-matter for criminological inquiry. These methodological innovations have lost none of their salience or significance during the ensuing decades.

In one sense, the successful popularisation of critical criminological themes has made much of the original project redundant: the fate of all radical thought, *when vindicated because correct*, is to become subsumed and sublimated within the mainstream. It is easy to forget, when fully immersed in the sensual pleasures of positivism-bashing, that Enlightenment figures such as Bentham, Kant, Newton and Galileo were once the radical, anti-establishment thinkers. As Jock

[117] Attributed to Hegel's sideswipe at 'his former friend' Schelling: *cf* Michael S Moore, *Educating Oneself in Public: Critical Essays in Jurisprudence* (OUP, 2000).

[118] Stanley Cohen, 'Crime and Politics: Spot the Difference' (1996) 47 *British Journal of Sociology* 1.

[119] David R Simon, *Elite Deviance*, 10th edn (Routledge, 2011).

[120] Formative texts include Carol Smart, *Law, Crime and Sexuality* (Sage, 1995); Dee Cook and Barbara Hudson (eds), *Racism and Criminology* (Sage, 1993); Phil Scraton (ed), *Law, Order and the Authoritarian State* (Open University Press, 1987); Steven Box, *Power, Crime, and Mystification* (Routledge, 1983). Generally, see David Whyte, *Crimes of the Powerful: A Reader* (Open University Press, 2008); Penny Green and Tony Ward, *State Crime* (Pluto Press, 2004); David Nelken (ed), *White-Collar Crime* (Dartmouth, 1994); James W Messerschmidt, *Crime as Structured Action: Gender, Race, Class and Crime in the Making* (Sage, 1997); Wayne Morrison, *Theoretical Criminology: From Modernity to Post-Modernism* (Cavendish, 1995).

[121] Taylor, Walton and Young (n 86) 46.

[122] ibid 54.

Young himself asked, albeit rhetorically: 'What after all is the point of talking about critical criminology if all criminology worth its name is critical?'.[123] One might reasonably apprehend a healthy dose of good sense in a literal reading of that question, whilst still recognising the value of work being produced from within a self-consciously 'critical' tradition. Another major intellectual bequest to posterity of critical criminologists' pioneering efforts is more in the nature of a cautionary tale, not least for adjectival criminologies of the present and the future.

There is nothing inherently problematic in generating or utilising academic research within a personal or collective framework of political and ethical commitment. Indeed, in a way that those in thrall to a reductive – and currently, more's the pity, imperialistic – conception of scientific objectivity will never fully appreciate, *the absence* of such ethical commitments in social science (or legal) scholarship may often represent more of a problem than ostensibly neutral, detached, 'objective' (as opposed to objective) stances.[124] Political programmes may identify hitherto neglected issues and open up rewarding new avenues of inquiry for research, as, for example, feminist criminology has done with such conspicuous success since the 1970s.[125] But all of this presupposes that knowledge in the service of politics is actually *knowledge*, and not merely a convenient projection of one's ideological preferences. Good faith error is one thing and may be excusable and corrigible. When it comes to the crunch, however, scholars must put scholarship before politics or get out of the scholarship business. Because knowledge, expertise and sound judgement are the only qualities that separate professional criminologists (or legal scholars, etc) from any self-opinionated celebrity or taxi-driver with an internet connection and a Twitter feed.[126]

In a 'post-truth' world of segmented echo-chamber media and game show politicians, in which opinion-formers advise voters to ignore experts and trust instead to their own intuitions, however uninformed or unexamined (think with your blood!), scholarship had better stand up for its own epistemological integrity, or history will not judge us kindly for our dereliction. Having reflected on some enduring lessons of critical criminological experience, my answer to Becker's pointed question about the ethics of partisanship ought to be clear: the integrity of scholarship must be *our* lodestar. Some pockets of contemporary critical criminology still

[123] Young (n 107) 184. Jock Young's own reply, ibid 217, is that 'critical criminology in this age of the Gulag and the punitive turn is massively needed, it is the counter-voice to neo-liberalism and conservativism. And what is more critical criminology is flourishing'. I want to agree but am thrown back on the conceptual indeterminacy and disciplinary elusiveness of the 'critical'.

[124] A point that really shouldn't have to be repeated to sociologists after Zygmunt Bauman, *Modernity and the Holocaust* (Polity, 1989); or to legal scholars after Nuremberg: *cf* David Fraser, *Law After Auschwitz: Towards a Jurisprudence of the Holocaust* (Carolina Academic Press, 2005).

[125] Generally, see Loraine Gelsthorpe and Allison Morris (eds), *Feminist Perspectives in Criminology* (Open University Press, 1990); and overlapping with legal scholarship, Nicola Lacey, *Unspeakable Subjects: Feminist Essays in Legal and Social Theory* (Hart Publishing, 1998); Carol Smart, *Feminism and the Power of Law* (Routledge, 1989).

[126] Again, I am leaving this remark intact as a sign of the times, before anybody had heard of Elon Musk's X, let alone the presidential Truth Social.

harbour the aspiration of speaking for alienated youth and marginalised populations.[127] As a legal scholar, I wouldn't myself claim to be speaking 'for' anybody (other than myself), though I do take very seriously the methodological injunction that appreciative sociological research should endeavour to present the authentic voices of observed fieldwork communities and research interviewees. This precept, moreover, applies as much to the poor bloody infantry on the front line of criminal justice administration as it does to the 'nuts, sluts and preverts'[128] of 1960s and 1970s radical criminology or the working-class victims of criminal violence, discrimination and abuse rediscovered by left realist criminology in the 1980s and 1990s. Beyond that, if speaking truth to power sometimes feels like a hopelessly naïve and utopian disciplinary mission, we may have to settle for speaking as much truth as we can muster to anybody who will listen; since, when all is said and done, '[c]riminology's job is to inform'.[129]

[127] See, eg, Young (n 107) 180 ('There are two criminologies: one grants meaning to crime and deviance, one that takes it away … one that is the voice of those below and the investigator of the powerful, the other which echoes the white noise of the criminal justice system'). Reducing the entire diverse pluralistic spectrum of criminological research and theorising to just two, diametrically opposed mirror-images was presumably only a rhetorical flourish rather than a serious contribution to disciplinary taxonomy or critical evaluation.

[128] Alexander Liazos, 'The Poverty of the Sociology of Deviance: Nuts, Sluts and Preverts' (1972) 20 *Social Problems* 103. The deliberate misspelling of 'perverts' is one of Criminology's enduringly delicious in-jokes.

[129] Colin Sumner, 'Introduction: Contemporary Socialist Criminology' in Sumner (ed), *Censure, Politics and Criminal Justice* (Open University Press, 1990) 10.

11

Can UK Legal Scholarship Survive?

I. An Existential Question

An unorthodox collection of essays merits an unconventional conclusion. We draw to a close with meditations on this stark question: can legal scholarship survive in UK law schools? The question is posed in general terms, because criminal jurisprudence is not distinctive in this conversation. Its survival and flourishing are bound up with the fate of university-based legal scholarship in general. So in order to assess the prospects for criminal jurisprudence in the coming years and decades, we must attend to the shared intellectual and material infrastructure of scholarship in UK law schools, set against the backdrop of higher education (HE) policy and funding. This chapter offers more systematic reflection on themes merely hinted at in isolated remarks scattered throughout the preceding chapters.

It might seem unduly pessimistic, alarmist almost, perhaps even faintly ridiculous to entertain the possibility of a credible existential threat to UK-based legal scholarship. But my experience over the last 30 years, and especially during the last decade, drives me to the conclusion that this is a conversation we need to be having, and sooner rather than too much later when the time for effective remedies might already have passed and decline could be irreversibly terminal. Before immersing ourselves in a litany of depressing details, let me repeat Chapter 1's anticipatory warning of the vital importance of retaining a sense of perspective and proportion in this discussion. The HE sector experiences peaks and troughs over time. The early 1990s, when I joined the profession, was a period of reform, expansion and widespread optimism. The last ten years have been a period of decline and enveloping gloom. Finances are universally acknowledged to be tight. Universities have been forced into a faux-market place in which tuition fees are capped whilst costs rise relentlessly. UK immigration policy has restricted access to foreign students as a supplementary source of income, on which many institutions had become increasingly reliant. Some HE institutions (HEIs) may be effectively insolvent and in immediate peril of closure or forced merger. Across the sector voluntary redundancy schemes are sliding ineluctably into compulsory lay-offs. Meanwhile, education unions call strikes in the forlorn hope[1] of reversing

[1] Alas, this is my honest assessment of the current situation. The medics formerly known as 'junior doctors' are closer to the front of the queue for public money than academics, and I seriously doubt that their strike demands for a reversal of historic wage erosion are going to be met, either. If everybody thought this way, prediction would be self-fulfilling prophecy. So I hope you dissent from my pessimism and ultimately prove me wrong.

a decade's deterioration in pay, pensions and employment conditions. At times like these, when nobody thinks that the UK HE sector is thriving, it is important to remember that the wheel will probably turn again at some point in the future. The market will bottom out and there will be some upside to the natural business cycle, at least for those institutions that can batten down the hatches and weather the storm for long enough to survive mostly intact.

Whilst macro-economic and national policy drivers inevitably constrain or enable legal scholarship, this chapter focuses on matters closer to home and over which HEIs, academic associations and even individual scholars exert more direct influence. Universities are central players in the formulation of HE policy and bear primary responsibility for its interpretation and implementation. And this is where I would locate the most immediate existential threats to legal scholarship, including criminal jurisprudence. I anticipate that engaging with these issues will strike many legal scholars as another unwelcome distraction, leeching away time that would be better devoted to the central business of legal research and publication. I am trying to balance this frustration, which I share, against the realisation that, if you don't want to go extinct with the dinosaurs, time spent scanning the horizon for asteroids is probably a sound investment.

Time is the essential resource for scholarship. Time to read, to write, to think, to test first thoughts and develop research programmes in discussion with other scholars engaged in the same or related inquiries. Unfortunately, time for scholarship has shrunk dramatically in my time as a UK university-based scholar. There are many factors and drivers. Massively increased student numbers, alongside far more onerous requirements for assessment, monitoring and pastoral support, are part of the picture. Whereas the three summer months between mid-June and mid-September used to be more or less ring-fenced for research,[2] assessment processes are now in train year-round. There is no longer any guaranteed respite from university bureaucracy, enabled by a digital infrastructure that never sleeps. Universities have been transformed into centralised managerial bureaucracies organised to facilitate effective implementation of top-down policy agendas. In this institutional set-up, individual scholars (and teachers) become entirely fungible nodes of production regulated

[2] Provoked by a leader in *The Independent* newspaper (19 August 1996) declaring that '[i]t looks as though the nation's academics are reluctant to give up their research, trips to foreign universities or just their month in the Dordogne for the sake of … a post A-level admissions system that will secure fairness and peace of mind for thousands of young people', I replied in a letter published under the editorial headline 'No Apology for a Summer of Research': *The Independent*, 21 August 1996. 'I am not embarrassed', I protested, 'to refuse to "give up on my research", partly because that would be tantamount to giving up on my students, too. Research is what I am paid (not much) to do …. The summer recess … is now the only period in which conferences, networking with colleagues in institutions abroad and substantial research projects may be undertaken.' Whilst I still broadly endorse the sentiment, this now sounds like a voice from a distant universe, lost in time.

by uniform organisational structures calibrated through big data analysis. Growing bureaucratisation and audit culture in HE policy and practice have been observed internationally and have been underway for many years.[3] It seems to me, however, that we have reached a critical juncture at which existential questions for the future of UK legal scholarship can no longer be postponed. The right moment to pose the question and debate the issues is now, whilst there is still time and opportunity to preserve what remains and avert potentially irreversible damage to the intellectual and material infrastructure of UK legal scholarship.

This chapter focuses, selectively, on three, interweaving strands of UK legal scholarship's complex institutional environment which, in their different ways, can be seen as primary causal agents. They are: (i) the Research Excellence Framework (REF); (ii) an increasingly aggressive Open Access (OA) agenda in academic publishing; and (iii) changes in the institutional structures and cultures of universities, responsive to broader shifts in UK HE policy, including (i) and (ii). In concert, this triple threat has fostered an environment distinctly inhospitable to legal scholarship as traditionally understood. The claim is not that anybody is *intending* to harm legal scholarship. We are, instead, in the realms of unfortunate side-effects, negative externalities and unforeseen consequences. Those who are deliberately pursuing the policies and consciously driving the institutional changes which threaten to hobble and perhaps ultimately destroy UK legal scholarship are doing so, by and large, for intelligible and even laudable reasons of national, sectoral or institutional wellbeing. They are trying to persuade Government to invest in UK research capacity and infrastructure and to secure the financial viability of their universities. The logic of collective institutional welfare entails that university leaders will do whatever is best for the institution as a whole, and if that means that individual disciplines must suffer so that the majority may thrive (or just survive), so be it. The problem for the discipline of Law is that it is extremely, possibly even uniquely,[4] vulnerable to being thrown under the managerial juggernaut for the sake of the greater institutional good.

[3] See, eg, Margaret Thornton, 'Gothic Horror in the Legal Academy' (2005) 14 *Social and Legal Studies* 267; Susan B Boyd, 'Corporatism and Legal Education in Canada' (2005) 14 *Social and Legal Studies* 287; Anthony Bradney, 'The Quality Assurance Agency and the Politics of Audit' (2001) 28 *Journal of Law and Society* 430.

[4] Departments that don't recruit many students or attract mega-research grants can simply be closed and staff made redundant. This may be the fate of modern languages and classics departments, for example: Poppy Wood, 'Modern Languages and Ancient History Degrees Face Axe at Russell Group University', *The Telegraph* 28 January 2025 (reporting plans to make 400 staff redundant at Cardiff University). The uniqueness of Law lies in the fact that it is relatively strong in student recruitment, but relatively weak in research grant capture. This means that law schools have better survival prospects than most other arts, humanities and social sciences departments, which is good news for job retention. However, turning law schools into undergraduate degree factories does nothing to support legal scholarship and may well turn out to be the most effective strategy for administering its *coup de grace*.

II. Legal Scholarship, Research and Teaching

Before tackling this chapter's central diagnostic task, the first order of business is conceptual clarification. For the claim that UK legal scholarship faces existential threats is clouded by conceptual obscurity. Different conceptions of 'legal scholarship' may be defensible for particular purposes, but without a clear and reasonably consensual conception of legal scholarship, it will not be possible to talk sensibly about its current condition or future viability or to assess what might be at stake in its survival or extinction. One way of getting to the pith of the notion is to think about the relationship of legal scholarship to related activities such as research and teaching.

Scholarship has embraced teaching since the birth of western philosophy and the foundation of its rival 'schools'.[5] Just as plainly, not all teachers are scholars. Whereas teachers teach, scholars communicate their scholarship through teaching (amongst other mechanisms and media). This model of scholarship fits the discipline of Law very well. Even at first-year undergraduate level, and right up through undergraduate and postgraduate curricula, students are taught the latest legislation, cases and commentaries. If it is possible to bring in aspects of the teacher's own research into related lectures and seminars, so much the better. Law teachers are used to revising their teaching materials, if not day by day, then often week by week, and certainly on an annual basis. Last year's lectures will almost certainly be out-of-date in many topical specialisms, and even in areas such as Land Law where doctrinal development may be relatively slow and incremental, conscientious teachers must search for relevant new developments and satisfy themselves that there are none before recycling last year's handouts. The university-based discipline of Law has a relationship with legal institutions and legal practice that is, to my knowledge, uniquely symbiotic. Of course, all disciplines develop over time – we are still learning new things about the Romans, after all – and some areas of science and technology, for example, are subject to rapid development and constant innovation. I am not aware of any other discipline, however, in which a set of social institutions routinely and pervasively makes deliberate determinations which alter what is taught to university students. Self-evidently, Parliament and appellate courts do not have this pedagogic objective in mind when enacting legislation or handing down judgments and thereby developing – and changing – the law. Besides, as I understand it, much undergraduate STEM teaching is so far removed from cutting-edge scientific research that it cannot really be characterised as scholarly activity, just as STEM textbooks are not generally regarded as works of scholarship. This perhaps explains why slogans such as 'research-led teaching' seem to have fallen out of fashion, even though they precisely encapsulate what Law teaching, at all levels, is, or should be. Textbooks such as Smith and Hogan

[5] Betrand Russell, *History of Western Philosophy* (Routledge, 1991 [1946]) (commencing in the sixth century BC with 'the Milesian School').

on Criminal Law,[6] Treitel on Contract,[7] Winfield and Jolowicz on Tort,[8] Cross on Evidence,[9] and Wade on Administrative Law[10] were instrumental in defining the content and delineating the parameters of particular topical sub-specialisms and continue to shape their respective fields through successive new editions. They are indisputably works of legal scholarship.

It follows from what has already been said that (good) law teaching cannot be offered unless it is grounded in sound, up-to-date legal research; and it further follows that legal research is only a necessary, and not a sufficient, criterion of legal scholarship. Any legal teacher worth their salt must be a competent legal researcher, but this does not mean that every teacher of law is also engaged in scholarship. If that remark sounds controversial, consider: every legal practitioner worth their salt must also be a competent legal researcher, but this truism plainly does not imply that every legal practitioner is engaged in legal scholarship. So where does this leave the triangular relationship between legal scholarship, research and teaching?

Research is the common root. For whilst legal scholars may teach, and most university-based legal scholars do so, legal scholarship may be pursued independently of teaching or supervising postgraduate students. Research is essential to scholarship (as well as teaching), because if you do not know the law, you cannot analyse, criticise or teach it. And since law is constantly changing, scholars (and teachers) must constantly be engaged in researching the latest legal developments to know what the law is. To be sure, the amount of time and effort that must be invested in legal research varies from topic to topic, and by subdisciplinary specialism. But the investment may be very substantial. Criminal Law, as the doctrinal component of criminal jurisprudence, produces literally thousands of new appellate decisions annually, not to mention frequent major legislative developments, constant tinkering with the Criminal Procedure Rules, new practice directions and judicial guidance, etc. One could probably spend every waking hour researching and writing about new developments and never run out of new material. Secondary literature addressing doctrinal developments in criminal law, much of it straddling academia and legal practice, is a flourishing cottage industry in its own right.

[6] J C Smith and Brian Hogan, *Criminal Law* (Butterworths, 1965); now David Ormerod, Karl Laird and Matthew Gibson, *Smith, Hogan & Ormerod's Criminal Law*, 17th edn (OUP, 2024).

[7] G H Treitel, *The Law of Contract* (Stevens, 1962); now Edwin Peel, *Treitel on the Law of Contract*, 16th edn (Sweet & Maxwell, 2025).

[8] P H Winfield, *A Text-Book on the Law of Tort* (Sweet & Maxwell, 1937). J A Jolowicz became a coauthor (with T Ellis Lewis) from the seventh to the ninth editions (1963–1971) and was in turn succeeded from the tenth to the eighteenth editions (1975–2010) by W V H (Horton) Rogers. Now see James Goudkamp and Donal Nolan, *Winfield & Jolowicz on Tort*, 21st edn (Sweet & Maxwell, 2025).

[9] Rupert Cross, *Evidence* (Butterworths, 1958); now Roderick Munday, *Cross & Tapper on Evidence*, 13th edn (OUP, 2018).

[10] H W R Wade, *Administrative Law* (OUP, 1961); now C F Forsyth and I J Ghosh, *Wade & Forsyth's Administrative Law*, 12th edn (OUP, 2022).

This substrate of legal research is elevated to legal scholarship, I suggest, when it is combined with an analytical method and critical scholarly attitude. Primary legal sources and secondary materials form a vast, disorganised, unwieldy corpus. Even in an age of digital repositories and computer-generated keyword searches, the law on a particular issue may be disparate, disjointed and difficult to locate, such that simply saying what the law is may involve considerable skill and expertise in searching for legal materials, engineering their logical reconstruction and interpreting legal meaning. This practical activity indubitably qualifies as legal research, but it is not yet legal scholarship whilst it remains at the level of essentially descriptive reportage. Predominantly practitioner-orientated legal summaries and digests of new cases and legislation are essentially legal journalism. Their practical utility and influence could be enormous – as with journalism generally – but the virtues of such activity are primarily journalistic rather than scholarly, as are the institutional constraints under which they operate. For example, timeliness of publication is much more significant in journalism than it is in scholarship.

Analytical method combined with a critical attitude are necessary for transforming descriptive legal reportage into scholarship. This transformation involves a variety of intellectual skills, techniques and attributes, prominently including contextualisation, classification, comparison, analysis, criticism, evaluation, reinterpretation, restructuring, reimagining and normative prescription. Of course, legal scholars routinely criticise positive law and advocate doctrinal correctives and legislative reforms (Bentham's 'censorial jurisprudence'),[11] by reference to normative models and ideals endorsed as prescriptively superior. Normative criticism probably more or less equates with extending 'a critical attitude to law' in the popular imagination. However, there is much greater depth to legal scholarship than this surface reform-orientated activity. Especially in a common law system, in which convention and legal tradition enjoy special jurisprudential status, scholarly engagement with the law requires intimate knowledge of legal institutional history and practices. Legal scholarship involves 'thinking like a lawyer',[12] and this is reflected – for example – in an appreciation of which kinds of argument might work, and why, in relation to particular legal issues arising before particular tribunals in particular jurisdictions; and conversely, which arguments will not run. (It is often said

[11] 'A book of jurisprudence can have but one or the other of two objects: 1. To ascertain what *law* is: 2. to ascertain what it ought to be. In the former case it may be styled a book of *expository* jurisprudence; in the latter, a book of *censorial* jurisprudence …': Jeremy Bentham, 'Of the Limits of the Penal Branch of Jurisprudence' § 21, reproduced in J H Burns and H L A Hart (eds), *An Introduction to the Principles of Morals and Legislation* (OUP, 1996) 293–94. Also see David Baumgardt, 'Bentham's "Censorial" Method' (1945) 6 *Journal of the History of Ideas* 456 (contending at 462 that '[i]n the whole literature of ethics … there is perhaps nowhere to be found a clearer account of the fundamental distinction between "censorial" and "expository" inquiry than the account given by Bentham').

[12] Frederick Schauer, *Thinking Like a Lawyer* (Harvard University Press, 2009); Joel P Trachtman, *The Tools of Argument: How the Best Lawyers Think, Argue, and Win* (CreateSpace Independent Publishing, 2013).

that law is a system of rules[13] or principles,[14] but it is barely less illuminating to conceptualise law as a system of *arguments*.) Law is distinctively, and perhaps amongst the university disciplines uniquely, jurisdictional. English law is plainly not French law; it is not even Scottish law, or UK law for that matter. Nobody is – or should be – surprised when the positive law of one jurisdiction differs from the positive law of another jurisdiction. Yet it is absurd – or sinister – to imagine that scientific knowledge could be subject to geographical variation, as though English Chemistry, Engineering or Maths could be any different from Indian or Chinese Chemistry, Engineering or Maths, etc. Here again, however, the common law is complex. English lawyers must learn how precedents generated in other common law jurisdictions (and according to a rather indistinct hierarchy) may exert *persuasive authority* in English law without being strictly *binding* precedents. This is just one, relatively mild, respect in which legal research and scholarship need to be comparative in the modern world.

I have so far been concentrating on the more *doctrinal* dimensions of legal scholarship, where the interface between university-based scholarly activity and legal practice is most intense and fruitful. One might fairly describe this mode as 'traditional legal scholarship',[15] with the important caveat that 'traditional' in this context does not mean 'outdated'. It remains as true today as it ever was that before law can be exposed to the full rigours of scholarship, it is necessary to be able to find and state the relevant law correctly. With that essential criterion granted, contemporary legal scholarship aspires to apply the full gamut of intellectual tools, processes and methods to the tasks of investigating, understanding, criticising and improving law, legal institutions, legal processes, and legal policy. Paradigmatic scholarly activity includes: investigating the socio-legal reality of the 'law in action',[16] utilising empirical methods; developing jurisprudential analyses of legal concepts, problems and issues, ranging from macroscopic questions of political authority and social order to minutely technical points of legal engineering, and often drawing on philosophical resources (especially epistemology, moral and political philosophy, and practical ethics); undertaking historical (including archival) research into the development of law and legal ideas and institutions over time; testing current law (or law reform proposals) against regulatory models, including economic modelling; comparative analyses of laws and practices in other jurisdictions, sometimes with an eye to appropriation ('legal transplants', 'policy transfers', 'judicial dialogue'), and

[13] H L A Hart, *The Concept of Law* (OUP, 1961); Joseph Raz, *The Authority of Law*, 2nd edn (OUP, 2009).

[14] Ronald Dworkin, *A Matter of Principle* (OUP, 1985); Ronald Dworkin, *Taking Rights Seriously* (Duckworth, revsd 1978).

[15] Terry Hutchinson and Nigel Duncan, 'Defining and Describing What We Do: Doctrinal Legal Research' (2012) 17 *Deakin Law Review* 83.

[16] Roscoe Pound, 'Law in Books and Law in Action' (1910) 44 *American Law Review* 12; Karl N Llewellyn, 'Law and the Social Sciences – Especially Sociology' (1949) 62 *Harvard Law Review* 1286.

nowadays with a significantly cosmopolitan twist;[17] and exploring the limits of existing disciplinary boundaries, occasionally reinventing new subdisciplines (environmental law, human rights law, international criminal law,[18] law and technology, etc) and remodelling the disciplinary landscape. In this broader register, legal scholarship is involved in types of activity with obvious parallels and resonances with research conducted in other university departments. Much of this work is at least implicitly interdisciplinary, and some of it is self-consciously boundary-transcending. Legal scholars do not directly make law, in the way that judges and legislators do, but they do make the *discipline* of Law, as an institutionally curated space for concentrated scholarly inquiry. Responsibility for the ongoing curation and vitality of legal scholarship also naturally falls to legal scholars.

Notice that, on this account, *publication* is not part of the definition of legal scholarship. Doubtless, the *impact* of legal scholarship is largely a function of its publication and wider dissemination. And of course, most legal scholars do and should publish their research, arguments, analyses and criticisms, and recommendations.[19] However, I cannot see why the activity of scholarship should be equated with its dissemination. A legal scholar who only communicates her scholarship through her teaching is still a scholar, I think, although she might well find herself being shunted onto a teaching-only contract in the modern British university (more on this later). A person who writes poetry is still writing poetry, even if he puts all his scribblings in a drawer and never shows his poems to anybody. But is such a person nonetheless a poet? I am not sure. What about the person who puts all their legal writings in a drawer and never shows them to anybody, and never uses them to inform her teaching? Although such research activity might qualify as legal scholarship, on my account, perhaps we would be hard-pressed to describe this secret scribbler as a legal scholar, with its implicit suggestion of participation in wider collective scholarly endeavours.

Having sketched out what I hope will be a recognisable and tolerably uncontroversial conception of legal scholarship, we may return to and finesse our original question. Further exegesis will sharpen this conception, but also – necessarily – make it more contentious, since thickening concepts always

[17] See, eg, Paul Roberts, 'Normative Evolution in Evidentiary Exclusion: Coercion, Deception and the Right to a Fair Trial' in Paul Roberts and Jill Hunter (eds), *Criminal Evidence and Human Rights* (Hart Publishing, 2012). My (unpublished) inaugural lecture at the University of Nottingham, delivered on 10 September 2010 (seven years after my appointment to a personal chair in Criminal Jurisprudence), was titled: 'Confronting the Challenges of Cosmopolitan Criminal Jurisprudence'. If I don't write this book before I die, somebody else can have this well-honed title, with my blessing (but not until then).

[18] See Chapters 8 and 9.

[19] Yale Kamisar, 'Why I Write (And Why I Think Law Professors Generally Should Write)' (2004) 41 *San Diego Law Review* 1747.

increases their contestability. Why should one believe that this model of legal scholarship currently faces mortal peril? My answer targets the 'unholy trinity' of REF, OA and HE institutional policy. It will be convenient to consider each strand in turn, with the proviso that it is their *cumulative* (and largely unplanned, perhaps unanticipated) combined effects that present existential challenges to legal scholarship.

III. REF – Thin End of the Wedge

The Research Excellence Framework (REF) is not directly concerned with legal scholarship, but only with legal *research*. The clue is in the name. But since legal scholarship is necessarily rooted in legal research, the salience of REF for legal scholarship can hardly be doubted. Having been through seven cycles of REF or its predecessor – the Research Assessment Exercise (RAE) – since its introduction in 1986, it is by now possible to discern some longer-term themes and trends, alongside elements of institutional entrenchment. At the time of writing, preparations for REF 2029 have been paused[20] and the precise shape and formal requirements of the exercise have yet to be finalised. Judging by past experience, however, previous iterations – culminating most proximately with REF 2021 – are likely to be reliable guides to the general evaluative framework and its policy direction of travel.

REF defines 'research' as 'a process of investigation leading to new insights, effectively shared'.[21] The REF definition expressly encompasses 'research that is published, disseminated or made publicly available in the form of assessable research outputs, and confidential reports'.[22] This conception of research emphasises the instrumental value of research 'outputs', which are primarily conceived in STEM[23] terms as discrete 'findings' with practical social utility, as the following more detailed elucidation clearly signals:

> [Research] includes work of direct relevance to the needs of commerce, industry, culture, society, and to the public and voluntary sectors; scholarship; the invention and generation of ideas, images, performances, artefacts including design, where these lead

[20] 'Pause to REF 2029 Criteria Setting and Publication of Final Guidance', 4 September 2025: 2029.ref.ac.uk/news/pause-to-ref-2029-criteria-setting-and-publication-of-final-guidance/. Now see 'REF 2029 Publishes Updates and Resumes Criteria Setting Following Pause', 10 December 2025: 2029.ref.ac.uk/news/ref-2029-publishes-updates-and-resumes-criteria-setting-following-pause/ (accessed 16 February 2026).

[21] REF2021, *Guidance on Submissions*, Annex C: Definitions of research and impact for the REF, [1]: 2021.ref.ac.uk/publications-and-reports/guidance-on-submissions-201901/index.html (accessed 17 December 2025).

[22] ibid [3].

[23] That is, Science, Technology, Engineering, Mathematics – sometimes rendered STEMM when medical and biological sciences are included. Economists are supposedly prone to STEM-envy, whilst business schools envy economists' relative proximity to STEM. Lesson: the Green-eyed Monster's appetite is insatiable, and if you entertain him, he may consume you.

> to new or substantially improved insights; and the use of existing knowledge in experimental development to produce new or substantially improved materials, devices, products and processes, including design and construction.[24]

Research, then, paradigmatically involves producing (1) useful, (2) new (3) *stuff* (including ideas, images, designs and performances). Conversely, stuff that is old and/or not useful is not research, thus excluding:

> routine testing and routine analysis of materials, components and processes such as for the maintenance of national standards, as distinct from the development of new analytical techniques. It also excludes the development of teaching materials that do not embody original research.[25]

Scholarship by express definition *is* research within REF's conception. However, 'scholarship' on my conception will not be scholarship for the purposes of REF unless it is 'effectively shared'. Whether legal scholarship that is not published could qualify as REF scholarship turns, as a matter of definition, on whether law teaching is regarded as 'embody[ing] original research'. On my understanding, routine law teaching must always be founded on the teacher's 'original research' in primary materials and secondary literature. But it may be overly optimistic to expect this capacious interpretation to be widely endorsed, in particular by non-lawyers – and more especially by those working in disciplines in which it is normal to expect an intellectual gulf between undergraduate education and cutting-edge research.

Initial doubts are fuelled by REF's own definition of 'scholarship' as 'the creation, development and maintenance of the intellectual infrastructure of subjects and disciplines, in forms such as dictionaries, scholarly editions, catalogues and contributions to major research databases'. Strikingly, from a legal perspective, 'scholarship' is conceived self-referentially as the maintenance of a discipline's own material and intellectual resources, rather than as encompassing direct contributions to public institutions, intellectual heritage and the social fabric. Dictionaries, catalogues and databases are taken to exemplify contributions to scholarship, but textbooks – let alone practitioner-orientated works – are not mentioned. Besides, these definitional issues are largely eclipsed by another, pragmatic, factor: only published 'outputs' can feature in what still remains[26] the centrepiece of REF, the individual pieces of research nominated by the 'unit' (law school) for REF assessment. Insofar as scholarship constitutes research within REF, therefore, it must for nearly all practical purposes produce discretely identifiable, itemised output-stuff.

[24] Annex C: Definitions of research and impact for the REF, [2].

[25] ibid.

[26] Outputs used to dominate the RAE; in REF they sit alongside 'impact' and 'environment', but in REF2021 still accounted for the lion's share (60%) of a unit's overall assessment. Current policy thinking indicates that the significance of outputs will diminish further in future exercises, which will prioritise institutional infrastructure and research culture over the contributions of individual scholars.

REF's metric of output quality comprises three primary assessment criteria, namely 'originality, significance and rigour'.[27] I have heard previous RAE Law Subpanel members paraphrase OSR as equating to 'new and exciting' research. Rigour is an indispensable foundation of quality in research, since many very bad ideas have been strikingly original[28] and enormously influential (think about eugenics[29] or Soviet agronomy[30]) and that which is new and exciting may also be claptrap. Research outputs are scored on a five-point scale, running from 'four stars' at the top down to 'unclassified' at the bottom. Four-star work achieves 'world leading' OSR; three-star work must demonstrate 'internationally excellent' OSR, which, however, 'falls short of the highest standards of excellence'. For a two-star rating, the OSR must be 'recognised internationally', whereas one-star outputs are 'recognised nationally' in OSR terms. An unclassified quality rating is awarded to outputs judged to 'fall[] below the standard of nationally recognised work'. There is an important rider to these definitions, providing an early hint that REF terminology sometimes takes on an Orwellian flavour:

> 'World-leading', 'internationally' and 'nationally' in this context refer to quality standards. They do not refer to the nature or geographical scope of particular subjects, nor to the locus of research nor its place of dissemination. For example, research which is focused within one part of the UK might be of 'world-leading' standard. Equally, work with an international focus might not be of 'world-leading, internationally excellent or internationally recognised' standard.[31]

This significant qualification is an important, and intelligent, concession to the practical difficulties of trying to design a generic set of quality standards for *all* academic disciplines, characterised by enormous diversity of size, scope, geographical reach and methodological conventions. In the context of Law, for example, it would plainly be absurd if all outputs addressing international law were *eo ipso* judged to be higher quality, and were automatically awarded more stars, than all outputs concerned with domestic law (an irony only intensified by the fact that international law has traditionally not been regarded as 'proper law' by many legal

[27] Annex C: Definitions of research and impact for the REF, [26].

[28] Admittedly, many *apparently* novel ideas are just historical junk repackaged and flogged to undiscerning new consumers. *Cf* Daniel Goldhagen, *Hitler's Willing Executioners: Ordinary Germans and the Holocaust* (Abacus, 1997) (noting the recycling of established anti-Semitic tropes in Nazi ideology).

[29] See, eg, Terence Morris, 'British Criminology: 1935-48' (1988) 28 *British Journal of Criminology* 20, 26–27 (quoting one enthusiast's suggestion that 'the elimination of crime can be effected only by the extirpation of the physically, mentally and morally unfit, or by their complete segregation in a socially asceptic environment'); Giulio Q Battaglini, 'Eugenics and the Criminal Law' (1914) 5 *Journal of the American Institute of Criminal Law and Criminology* 12, 15.

[30] Nils Rolls-Hansen, 'The Lysenko Effect: Undermining the Autonomy of Science' (2005) 29 *Endeavour* 143. Mao's determination to implement crackpot scientific notions and impossible engineering projects is said to have contributed to the deaths by starvation of 38 million Chinese people during the Great Leap Forward (1958–61): Jung Chang and Jon Halliday, *Mao: The Unknown Story* (Vintage, 2007) 522–35.

[31] Annex A: Assessment criteria and level definitions, [8].

scholars and practitioners).[32] But consistent commitment to this sensible precept will on occasion entail some stretching of ordinary linguistic meanings. For example, an article on, say, some obscure point of Scots property law could be four-star 'world leading' in REF terms, even though only a handful of Scottish legal scholars and specialist practitioners will ever read it (or, perhaps, understand it). It is worth underlining this point, because when REF definitions and assessments are extrapolated to other contexts (as they increasingly are, in both HE policy and public debate), it is essential that these subtleties of meaning, some of which defy conventional linguistic usage, are not lost in translation.

Although RAE/REF was originally supposed to be a periodic assessment of subsisting research activity as a mechanism for distributing grant income to its most productive (and deserving?) end-users, it quickly became a regulative mechanism influencing research agendas and activity. In its current manifestation, REF cannot realistically be regarded as an innocent measuring tool. Rather, it proactively drives research policy and practice. In relation to legal research and scholarship specifically, REF places a premium on longer, more developed, extensively researched (and footnoted), and overtly theoretically informed outputs typically published in academic journals or as full-length topical monographs. Some, but not all, varieties of book chapters and edited collections are also favoured. Empirical socio-legal research generating new data is also well placed to meet REF expectations, because it usually involves generating new and potentially useful stuff (research findings) on the standard scientific model underpinning nearly all STEM research. These are the styles of output most likely to score the coveted three- and four-star ratings, whereas shorter, less fully developed and/or practitioner focused pieces are far less likely to be considered 'world leading' or 'internationally excellent', even on the extended REF definitions. This dichotomy is largely blind to an important distinction within legal research methodology between journalistic reportage of new legal developments and doctrinal legal scholarship which is analytical and critical in the traditional vein.

One predictable concern with this revised incentive structure for legal research is that it might lead to the production of much 'academic' legal writing (with pejorative undertones) and the institutionalised downgrading and neglect of other forms of legal scholarship, including practitioner-orientated writing and contributions to law reform. There is a view in some quarters that the professorial tenure system has produced this kind of effect in US legal scholarship, driving an unhealthy, mutually impoverishing wedge between law schools and legal practice.[33] Regardless of the truth of this local tension, in general the decisive factor is more likely to be found

[32] H L A Hart, *The Concept of Law* (Clarendon, 1961) 231; *cf* Rosalyn Higgins, *Problems & Process: International Law and How We Use It* (OUP, 1994).

[33] See, eg, Richard A Posner, 'Legal Scholarship Today' (2002) 115 *Harvard Law Review* 1314; Harry T Edwards, 'The Growing Disjunction Between Legal Education and the Legal Profession' (1992) 91 *Michigan Law Review* 34; Brian Leiter, 'Intellectual Voyeurism in Legal Scholarship' (1992) 4 *Yale Journal of Law and Humanities* 79; Richard A Posner, 'The Decline of Law as an Autonomous Discipline: 1962-1987' (1987) 100 *Harvard Law Review* 761.

in broader career incentive structures for university-based legal scholars rather than anything specifically pertaining to national research assessment exercises. My own view is that RAE/REF has not, thus far, tangibly eroded productive relationships between legal scholarship and legal practice in the UK, and that three factors have operated as important binding agents in this regard. Firstly, the Subpanel covering Law has consistently taken a robust position on recognising the value of all forms of legal research outputs, including those resulting from traditional legal scholarship.[34] Coupled with functional rather than literal interpretations of quality standard descriptors, this well-advertised policy reassures legal scholars that outputs principally addressed to legal practice can still achieve 'world leading' or 'internationally excellent' ratings provided that they meet the OSR thresholds. Secondly, the emergence of 'impact' as a new set of desiderata for research, which accompanied the transition from RAE2008 to REF2014, administers a corrective to any tendency to steer legal research in an excessively 'academic' direction. Traditional legal scholarship addressed to practising lawyers and courts has always pursued 'impact', in terms of offering new arguments to counsel, rival analyses to appellate courts and normative rationales for policymakers to change and develop the law.[35] Marx could never have said of *lawyers* that, whilst academicians[36] have only described the world, the point is to change it!

The third factor that seems to me important in preserving a healthy dialogue between legal scholarship and legal practice is that REF's *direct* demands on individual scholars for research output are relatively modest when considered, in isolation, as discrete temporal cycles. RAE required each active scholar to submit four pieces, produced over five or six years (with graduated reductions for 'early career researchers' (ECRs) and those undertaking voluntary, or enforced, career breaks or interruptions). REF2021 demanded an average of 2.5 outputs per researcher, with individual contributions capped at five pieces. REF2029 dispenses with any minimum (or maximum) number of outputs for individual researchers,[37]

[34] 'Unit of Assessment 18: Law … includes all doctrinal, theoretical, empirical, comparative, critical, historical or other studies of law and legal phenomena including criminology, and socio-legal studies …. Research in law may intersect with or draw upon a variety of disciplines and methodologies': *Panel Criteria and Working Methods*, REF2019/02, [104]–[105].

[35] It has been suggested that 'the inclusion of impact as a criterion of measurement since REF2014 is having an effect on how and what legal academics research': Joanne Conaghan, 'Legal Research and the Public Good: The Current Landscape' (2023) 43 *Legal Studies* 569, 579. Whilst I don't dissent from the general proposition, Conaghan's anonymised quotation from 'by far the most expansive mission statement in the [REF2021] environmental narratives' as demonstrable proof is unintentionally ironic. I know, because I wrote it. We used exactly the same wording in our previous School submission to REF2014 and it was originally composed as an attempt to encapsulate the research Nottingham colleagues *were already doing*, prior to the introduction of 'impact' as a formal criterion of REF assessment.

[36] Marx actually said 'philosophers', rather begging the question as to which philosophers he had been reading. The entire western Socratic tradition is orientated towards practical reasoning and decision-making.

[37] 'In a change from REF 2021 there will … be no minimum or maximum output requirements for individual staff members': REF2029, *Guidance* (12 July 2025), 2029.ref.ac.uk/guidance/section-4-contributions-to-knowledge-and-understanding-cku-guidance/#ss, para 3.4.1. This significant

but it is likely that HEIs will maintain their own internal performance expectations broadly in line with historical REF practice. Whilst it would be unwise to generalise too confidently over large and diverse cohorts of legal scholars with different career stages, trajectories and ambitions, suffice it to say that many legal scholars are able to produce far more than four or five high-quality pieces within a single REF period. Inevitably, only part of this scholarly activity is reflected in REF (and some REF pieces may be low-hanging fruit compared to more ambitious scholarly projects with fewer guaranteed 'outputs'). Analogously to that notional day every year when we stop earning money to pay the Chancellor of the Exchequer and start accumulating income for ourselves, legal scholars can pay their dues to REF within the first few years of the REF cycle, proportionally (rather than temporally) speaking, after which they are free to employ their scholarship to whatever activities they desire. For many legal scholars, at least part of this 'REF-free time' will be devoted to addressing practitioner audiences and engaging in practical law reform of one kind or another.

Some readers may consider this benign assessment of RAE/REF dangerously complacent, naïve or self-satisfied.[38] My view is that REF is not *directly* to blame for the majority of ills frequently laid at its door. Rather, most problems arise from the way in which REF results have been (mis)used for other purposes (eg, in the construction of 'league tables' of institutions or law school performance) or through institutional adaptations to REF pressures, perceived and real. For example, most of the staggeringly disproportionate workload now associated with REF arises, not from the assessment itself, but from the bureaucratic procedures put in place by individual HEIs in order to prepare for REF – preparations that are now effectively permanently ongoing rather than episodic, and almost amount to 90 mini-REFs in individual law schools preceding the main, actual, one. I return to this ratchet effect later. For now, I want to emphasise a more profound, if diffuse and somewhat intangible, sense in which REF's model of research as the production of discrete units of useful new stuff cuts across traditional conceptions of (legal) scholarship.

I have suggested that legal scholarship is primarily characterised by expert knowledge, analytical method and critical attitude. It also requires professional commitment to certain ethical ideals, such as prioritising truth over ideology in intellectual inquiries and speaking truth to power in scholarly communication.

rule revision extends the logic of the flexible model proposed in advance of REF2021 by Lord Nicholas Stern, *Building on Success and Learning from Experience: An Independent Review of the Research Excellence Framework* (2016), [67]–[68]. (Stern tentatively suggested 'a prescribed maximum, say six' and 'a prescribed minimum, potentially none'.) However, the latest updated Guidance (10 December 2025) announces an 'expectation … that no more than 5 outputs are associated with a single substantive link', ie author: para 7.2.3 Exceeding this expected limit will require explicit justification: para 7.2.5.

[38] There is no question that many individual scholars have benefitted personally from REF, principally through accelerated promotions as a reward for high productivity in publications. Having progressed within the same institution from junior lecturer on the lowest salary grade to full professor within ten years, I am one of that fortunate cohort.

Scholarship involves participation in the life of the mind, and this is a form of professional (and personal) *life* rather than temporary employment in the Fordist production of research widgets or patentable inventions. This identity-based conception of legal scholarship is quite at odds with a REF model of discrete research 'outputs' produced within an identifiable temporal period, in which the output counter goes back to zero at the start of each new REF cycle. In scholarship, *the scholar* is the primary product of research, as well as being the author of particular publications produced along the way, and self-education is always part of the point of the enterprise.[39] The scholar's main tool is his or her mind, and this muscle acquires more power as it is fed and cultivated. Like fine wine, scholarship matures with age (but can also go rancid if kept beyond its shelf-life). These features of scholarship not merely differ from much of the research activity conducted within the STEM paradigm; they are fundamentally antithetical to it. For one thing, the authority of scholarship partly rests on the personal (ie, professional)[40] authority of the scholar. In legal practice, the opinions of particular academic writers are afforded greater respect on account of their expertise, and the most eminent may become de facto legal authorities. In science, by contrast, the validity of research is wholly detached from the personality of the researcher, and replicability of findings is regarded as an essential precondition of sound scientific knowledge. Another point of sharp contrast is that, whilst scientists certainly need to develop skills of clear and concise written communication, there is no sense in which the medium is *part of* the message. Scientific writing tends to be short, impersonal and functional, because the only objective is to communicate 'the findings' and explain their significance to the intended lay or scientific audience. The individual scholar must be abstracted from the equation to ensure that objective scientific knowledge is conveyed successfully, unpolluted by the taint of subjectivity.[41] Legal argument is something else. It employs a range of stylistic tropes, rhetorical manoeuvres, interpretational conventions and forms of argumentation, fusing logical analysis with literary flair and tradecraft. To say that these aspects of legal scholarship are 'merely presentational' would completely misrepresent and understate their importance. An argument expressed in a different way, or by a different person, will sometimes be a *different argument* at

[39] *Cf* Michael S Moore, *Educating Oneself in Public* (OUP, 2000).

[40] To be clear, I refer to the professional expertise of individual scholars rather than to a simple projection of subjective preferences, as might be implied by unfocused invocations of 'the personal is political'. Unless some version of this distinction can be maintained, legal scholarship is just another ideological rhetoric. But in that event, why should anybody credit *progressive* legal scholarship? Moral: be careful what you wish for, because what goes around comes around.

[41] This characterisation describes a professional ideology of disciplinary self-justification. The sociological reality of real science, in which personalities loom large, experiments frequently fail to replicate expected results, and rival teams compete to win the race to Nobel prizes, may be another matter entirely: *cf* Bruno Latour and Steve Woolgar, *Laboratory Life: The Construction of Scientific Facts* (Sage, 1979).

law. In legal scholarship, it may be misguided and ultimately unavailing to try to extricate the dancer from the dance.[42]

These essential characteristics of legal scholarship diverge from the STEM model of research (broadly reflected in REF) in ways highly salient to the present discussion. Papers in STEM subjects tend to be short, and they are often co-authored by teams: it doesn't really seem to matter who actually 'writes up' the research, since the writing is merely the final task of communicating the results of a collaborative research effort mostly conducted in the laboratory. In law, the writing *constitutes* a significant portion of the research, and it cannot generally be farmed out to anybody else (because then it would be *their* research). Co-authorship is commonplace, but generally confined to two or three co-authors, not least because legal scholarship is riven with normative controversies and you cannot really write successfully with anybody who doesn't share your normative (jurisprudential and/or ethical) commitments or agree with your analytical conclusions. Traditional legal scholarship embraces short-form publications, notably the doctrinal 'case note' typically pitched as a fast response to recent legal developments and often aimed at influencing the outcome of future appeals (potentially including a further appeal from the noted case itself). Even when it would be a stretch to describe all of these publications as *scholarly works* in their own right – some are more in the nature of legal journalism, as I have said[43] – the best are invariably informed by the author's scholarship.[44] In REF terms, however, legal scholarship is skewed towards long-form articles and monographs; and increasing concentration on '(four) star quality' both for REF-returnable outputs and for internal staff appraisal is only likely to reinforce the dominance of extended doctrinal exegesis, the generation of new empirical findings (on the STEM model), and works of theoretical speculation.

So far as individual scholars are concerned, two further implications are noteworthy. First, legal scholars (and presumably most scholars across the arts, humanities and social sciences) will generally take far longer to produce their (REF)-'best' outputs than their peers in STEM disciplines. It is certainly not unusual to spend two or three years of almost constant activity in producing a monograph,[45] and the best articles can take scarcely less time from conception to publication, once the often-lengthy process of peer review and editorial revision is factored into the equation. Concomitantly, legal scholars are unlikely to match the total number of outputs coauthored by their STEM peers during a REF period

[42] *Cf* Jerry H Gill, 'On Knowing the Dancer from the Dance' (1975) 34 *Journal of Aesthetics and Art Criticism* 125.

[43] I am reliably informed that this is how Sir John Smith regarded his enormously influential *Criminal Law Review* commentaries. But it should be added that these commentaries were frequently first drafts of text, ideas and arguments that would later be incorporated into full-blown articles or new editions of *Smith and Hogan*.

[44] See, eg, J R Spencer, *Noted, But Not Invariably Approved* (Hart Publishing, 2014).

[45] My first proper book, Roberts and Zuckerman, *Criminal Evidence* (OUP, 2004), actually took seven years to complete.

or over the course of a career. This is one reason – there are many others – why AHSS scholars across the board should resist comparative quantitative measures of research performance, whether as proxies for 'value for money' or for any other supposed purpose. Such exercises are guaranteed to show that STEM researchers are massively more productive in terms of the sheer quantity of papers they author (or, stated more precisely, papers on which they are credited as a coauthor[46]). Certainly, there is no conceivable way in which individual legal scholars could meaningfully compete in quantitative terms with teams of STEM researchers pumping out scores of short research papers with ten, 100 or even 1,000[47] or more 'co-authors'.

A second implication concerns the nature of academic careers over a working lifetime. Until comparatively recently, most legal scholars would produce one or two books over the course of their entire careers, and many produced none at all: being content to disseminate their scholarship through articles, case notes, essays, reviews and lectures. Under a REF regime, in which the counter goes back to zero every six or so years, to be consistently at the top of their research output game, a legal scholar would need to produce *at least* six or seven major new monographs (or the equivalent in weighty articles) at regular intervals over their working life. In fraught discussions of research productivity, it is often remarked that a scholar such as Ludwig Wittgenstein, indisputably one of the most influential philosophers of the twentieth century but who only ever wrote two books (the second of which is barely a book in the conventional sense, and didn't appear until two years after his death),[48] might have been fired or forced onto a teaching-only contract under REF. Mine is a slightly different point. I am not convinced that any but the most exceptionally imaginative and productive legal scholars could have seven substantial works of legal scholarship in them. This would, at any rate, be a model of Herculean achievement, and there has never been a generation of legal scholars anywhere in the world which has ever come close to matching it. One suspects that most ordinary mortals would burn out or lose motivation and give up some way short of the magic seven. In contrast to colleagues in STEM disciplines, there is no avenue to move into grant proposal writing and 'research management', whilst sustaining a heavy-hitting publications batting average by co-authoring with junior colleagues and postdoctoral researchers who do all or most of the actual research and writing. Even if one takes a brutally instrumental view, according to

[46] The ethics of co-authorship plainly differ substantially across disciplines. It is simply a fact, that I record without implied criticism, that co-authorship is routinely claimed and credited in STEM subjects in circumstances that would be regarded as plagiarism and/or exploitation in legal scholarship.

[47] This is not hyperbole. *Cf* Davide Castelvecchi, 'Physics Paper Set Record with more than 5,000 Authors' (2015) 522 *Nature* (15 May) (reporting that a paper published in *Physical Review Letters* had 5,154 authors; listing their names consumed 24 of the article's 33 pages. An earlier 2012 paper boasted only 2,932 authors, 21 of whom were deceased).

[48] Ludwig Wittgenstein, *Philosophical Investigations* (Blackwell, 1973 [1953]). Most of the many books bearing Wittgenstein's name were edited notes published posthumously by his student, Elizabeth (GEM) Anscombe.

which burnt-out performers are best pensioned off to make way for fresh talent, I doubt whether this model of an academic career will be especially enticing for new recruits. Besides, who would still be in post to provide guidance and mentorship for developing scholars coming through the ranks?[49]

To summarise, REF itself is not directly responsible for reducing diversity in the forms of published legal scholarship. It did not set out to alienate academic law from legal practice, or to impose unrealistic demands on productivity across academic careers consistent with a rounded conception of the responsibilities of academic leadership and disciplinary curation. Nonetheless, REF has been a central component in an emergent HE policy framework, inducing predictable adaptations by HEIs which in chain reaction tend to produce all three unintended consequences, each of them injurious to the health of legal scholarship. A second causal agent, to which we now turn, is the campaign for 'open access' in academic research and publishing.

IV. Open Access – Too Much of a Good Thing?

The drive towards 'open access' (OA), which has rapidly become a pillar of HE policy, has multiple strands and rationales. Part of the OA agenda concerns promoting research integrity through making primary data more accessible to scrutiny and verification (recalling the importance of replication in STEM research). The part more salient to the present discussion relates to the accessibility of published research outputs, especially those that are funded by UK research councils. On a simplistic – but nonetheless broadly accurate – view, commercial academic publishers are parasitic rentier capitalists par excellence. On the traditional model, research in public universities is funded by the public purse. Academic researchers supply their written manuscripts to publishers *for free* (or small royalties for books, typically 5–10 per cent of the cover price), which commercial publishers run through fairly cheap production processes (further streamlined by digital publishing software, and increasingly contracted out to India for cut-price copyediting), and then sell the published 'outputs' as books or journal articles back to university libraries, academic associations and personal subscribers at vastly inflated prices, raking in huge profits. The journals, moreover, are edited by scholars *for free* (or minor benefits in kind), and article submissions are refereed by editorial boards and wider pools of scholars who are expert in the field, again gratis vis-à-vis publishers. Academics freely participate in these editorial and refereeing activities, which can be intellectually onerous

[49] My impression is that much of this mentoring is currently undertaken by formally retired emeritus professors, many of whom are also remarkably productive in published scholarship. In a world of early retirement and reduced pensions, this cohort of Boomer professors may never be replaced. In the meantime, the productivity of the sector is being artificially inflated, in effect by liquidating the capital of its past investments, and with a looming cliff-edge of mortality on the horizon.

and significantly time-consuming, partly owing to the personal esteem associated with being recognised as an expert or leader in the field,[50] partly because they promise deferred gratification through promotion and other academic appointments, and partly because this activity contributes to the wellbeing and development of one's discipline and it's the right thing to do.

From the point of view of HE institutions and UK government funding bodies, however, all of this freely contributed academic labour is not 'free' at all. Rather, to the extent that it is done on their dollar (a somewhat moot point, since UK academics perform a lot of this work in their evenings, weekends and holidays outside their contracted hours), universities are paying *twice* for this research, and they are evidently paying through the nose. OA aims at a fundamental reset to break the stranglehold, once and for all, of this exploitative pattern of academic publishing. The ideal open access model is that all outputs from academic research should be available, immediately and without charge, to anybody in the world with a working internet connection.

Here is one simple remedial model. HEIs could instruct all academic researchers employed in UK public universities that, from a stated date, all future research publications must be placed in full text on a free-to-download, publicly accessible institutional repository; or alternatively, HEIs might individually subscribe to a collective database shared by all UK institutions. Given the scale of the undertaking, this mega-repository would probably have to be organised on a disciplinary basis, and the categories currently used by REF to map research activity onto 34 'units of assessment' would seem to supply a ready-made, reasonably plausible multidisciplinary taxonomy. It is instructive to consider why this simple solution is a non-starter, given the existing landscape of academic publishing.

It might be objected that HEIs telling independent scholars where they should publish is simply incompatible with academic freedom, a legal value acknowledged in UK legislation,[51] or contravenes more basic principles of freedom of expression.[52] There may well be an academic freedom objection to the OA agenda, but it does not gain any traction here. There is no reason why HEIs should, or would, instruct scholars that they may *only* publish in OA institutional repositories.

[50] Robert Maxwell reputedly fanned academic vanities and wooed editors with fancy dinners at his Oxfordshire pile in order to build up his vast journal publishing empire Pergamon Press: Stephen Buranyi, 'Is the Staggeringly Profitable Business of Scientific Publishing Bad for Science?' *The Guardian*, 27 June 2017.

[51] See, eg, Higher Education and Research Act 2017, s 36 (duty of Office of Students to protect academic freedom in the performance of its functions); Counter-Terrorism and Security Act 2015, s 31 (ministerial guidance issues to universities must 'have particular regard to the importance of academic freedom'). By s 202(2)(a) of the Education Reform Act 1988 the University Commissioners are charged 'to ensure that academic staff have freedom within the law to question and test received wisdom, and to put forward new ideas and controversial or unpopular opinions, without placing themselves in jeopardy of losing their jobs or privileges they may have at their institutions'.

[52] ECHR Art 10; Education (No 2) Act 1986, s 43 (freedom of speech in universities, polytechnics and colleges); *R (Butt) v Home Secretary* [2019] 1 WLR 3873, [2019] EWCA Civ 256.

Rather, the disincentive to do so is that, once published, such material would probably[53] be of no further interest to commercial publishers. Who is going to buy a book or article that they can already immediately access on-line free of charge? Certainly not university libraries, since no longer having to pay commercial publishers to buy back material generated by their own research community is a central rationale of OA. So universities will say that it is perfectly reasonable to request, or instruct, their academics to publish in institutional repositories, and that any knock-on implications for the commercial value of the research are hardly their business or concern. Academics are already being paid to research and publish. Whilst existing custom and practice may tolerate (modest) author royalties, it is hard to see how academic writers have a strong *moral*[54] claim to double-dip (again, with the vital provisos that particular outputs are in fact referable to contracted labour, and that non-economic moral rights of authorship[55] are properly respected and protected).

One vision of the OA long game is that academic publishers are put out of business entirely. There is no technological reason why this should not happen, given the power of already existing publication repositories (such as RIS,[56] SSRN[57] and ResearchGate[58]) and the simplicity of desktop digital publishing software. Yet there are at least two sets of reasons for doubting that this extinction scenario will eventuate anytime soon. First, there are largely pragmatic transitional considerations obstructing the route to final obliteration from where we are now. Those who regard commercial academic publishers as predatory bloodsuckers need only worry about the practical means for plotting their extinction. The second set of reasons sees commercial publishers in a more positive light,

[53] I am told that there are known exceptions to this generalisation, which is encouraging, but I cannot believe that publishers will widely adopt a practice that seems to defy commercial logic. If events prove me wrong, so much the better.

[54] The legal position depends on the details of academic contracts. The better view is that copyright resides in academic authorship, so that as things currently stand academic authors are entitled to exploit their rights commercially: see *Stephenson Jordan & Harrison v MacDonald & Evans* (1952) 69 RPC 10, 28 (suggesting that it was 'both just and commonsense' that academics own copyright in their lectures, and a fortiori in written publications); Justine Pila, 'Who Owns the Intellectual Property Rights in Academic Work?' (2010) 32 *European Intellectual Property Review* 609. But the position could change in future. In Hohfeldian idiom, there is a subsisting legal claim right, but it is underpinned by a bare moral liberty.

[55] Encompassing rights concerning attribution, false attribution, derogatory treatment and privacy: Copyright, Designs and Patents Act 1988, ss 77–89; pithily summarised by Robin Jacob, Matthew Fisher and Lynne Chave, *Guidebook to Intellectual Property*, 7th edn (Hart Publishing, 2022) ch 23.

[56] The University of Nottingham's 'Research Information System': www.nottingham.ac.uk/dts/researcher/applications-and-tools/research-information-system.aspx is one version of information management digital architecture prevalent across the HE sector. It is provided by a commercial supplier called Worktribe, which claims to have 77 institutional clients and some 540,000 individual users: www.worktribe.com/about-us/clients/ (accessed 23 December 2025).

[57] Social Science Research Network, www.ssrn.com/index.cfm/en/ (advertising '1,763,778 preprints and research papers from 2,525,924 researchers in over 69 disciplines') (accessed 23 December 2025).

[58] www.researchgate.net/about (claiming to host publications generated by 20 million researchers from 190 countries) (accessed 23 December 2025).

as adding value and making tangible contributions to the ecology of academic publishing.[59] Unless such valuable contributions can be replicated in-house by universities at similar or cheaper cost, commercial publishers should have a long-term future as partners in academic publishing. In my view, this scenario is especially (not necessarily uniquely) salient for the discipline of Law and for legal scholarship.

Suppose that by demanding immediate full-text publication in on-line institutional repositories, UK HEIs de facto precluded UK-based academics from publishing books with commercial publishers and from submitting papers to run-for-profit journals. What would follow? What would *not* happen is that journals and publishers would be starved of content. This is because many academic journals, and most of the best, are international operations, with multinational editorial boards and global readerships. What would most likely happen is that UK-based scholars would be de facto excluded from international scientific communication and research collaboration, followed in short order by UK HEIs tumbling in global league table rankings and haemorrhaging scientific researchers to other jurisdictions. The lesson of this simple thought experiment is that unilateral action in OA policy is not a realistic option. International cooperation and coordinated action on OA are essential to the future vitality and sustainability of UK science.

Might it be possible, over time, for universities to set up their own publishing operations and journals to rival those of commercial publishers? This is conceivable, but consider: how will universities acquire the technical competence to produce academic books and journals, at volume, other than by hiring more staff with relevant publishing skills, presumably at commercial rates? And why would academic scholars resign prestigious journal editorships or board memberships in order to edit university-based journal start-ups without any established reputations or readership? Why would any scholar submit their manuscript to a parochial UK university-based journal or publishing house, rather than going with an established international market-leader in the field? Perhaps the new university presses and journals could publish manuscripts and articles that failed to get accepted anywhere else? That would hardly conduce to promoting quality in scholarship. Then again, cyberspace is already very well served by predatory journals – real, virtual or robotic – that will publish just about anything for a (so they advertise, discounted!) fee. I am invited by email to publish with or to edit scores of these journals annually. I only need to read as far as 'Dear Doctor Roberts' before pressing delete.[60]

[59] An argument that publishers increasingly advance on their own account: see The Publishers Association, 'The Value of UK Publishing', www.publishers.org.uk/influence/value-of-uk-publishing/ (asserting that '[a]cademic publishing plays an integral role in the research and innovation ecosystem … [W]ithout the highly specialised and time-intensive tasks carried out by UK academic publishers, innovation may be less effective').

[60] Not having a doctorate turns out to be an excellent device for filtering out time-wasters.

We are now beginning to touch on the deeper problems of OA, which are encapsulated in terms of social epistemology,[61] authority, trust, curation and information management. The open internet contains mind-bogglingly vast oceans of information accumulating daily at an exponential rate. The problem with the internet is not so much *accessing* information, as figuring out how to organise, interpret and use the information that we can already (too) easily access. A major challenge, arising precisely from the anarchic openness of the internet, is that a very great deal of the information it contains is false or unreliable, some of it deliberately pernicious lies. We can already see that generative AI, though still in its technological childhood, is going to accentuate the global proliferation of digital misinformation. The essence of the epistemological problem is: how can you trust what you read? On what basis does *this* search engine-generated information supply epistemic warrant for rational belief? Doubtless, much of the ostensible information contained on the internet is designed for amusement, diversion or titillation, and its truth-claims – if it makes any – should be seasoned with a large pinch of salt. The best way to take a 'fun fact' is probably to treat it as a bit of fun, even though it may not be a fact. Scientific research publications, by contrast, are utterly worthless – or worse – unless their contents are true (reading academic papers is unlikely to be very entertaining, after all). Reliable epistemic warrant is a sine qua non of published academic research. This is where the established academic journals and publishing houses make their most tangible positive contribution. Journals, book series and reputable publishers curate, organise and validate content through peer review and editorial interventions. Many submitted manuscripts are rejected; the acceptance rate for the leading generalist law journals may be of the order of 1:20, and I have never been involved in a journal that did not reject at least half of the article submissions it receives. No less importantly, papers (and many book manuscripts) accepted for publication routinely undergo extensive revisions in response to referees' comments and significant editorial improvements and rewriting. Again, in somewhat literary disciplines like Law, this process of revision is not simply a question of cosmetic beautification or enhancing clarity of expression to communicate content more effectively. The 'outputs' published in leading journals and book series, which for the purposes of UK legal scholarship are nearly all commercial ventures, are materially improved through the publication process, and their inclusion in established titles is a dependable badge of quality. In this tangible fashion, commercial publishers contribute significantly to the quality of UK legal scholarship.

Academic peer review undoubtedly has its own quirks and imperfections. The system is not robust against scientific fraud (eg, 'dry labbing', reporting fake data) or deliberate subversion,[62] partly because peer review mechanisms presuppose

[61] Alvin I Goldman, *Knowledge in a Social World* (OUP, 1999).

[62] Yascha Mounk, 'What an Audacious Hoax Reveals About Academia', *The Atlantic*, 5 October 2018; Editors of *Lingua Franca*, *The Sokal Hoax: The Sham that Shook the Academy* (University of Nebraska Press, 2000).

scientific competence and a commitment to scholarly integrity on the part of all serious researchers. There are also allegations of systematic bias, personal feuds, intra-disciplinary spats, backscratching and mutual citation circles, which are all the more problematic in fields characterised by deep normative and methodological disputes about what qualifies as sound research. STEM subjects tend towards agreed experimental protocols, such as the 'double blind' drug trial in medical research; not so Arts and Humanities. As Chapter 3 observed, a philosophical paper could be original, rigorous, significant and excellent in every way, save for being utterly wrong. Traditional legal scholarship straddles these worlds, inasmuch as the legislature did what it did and the court said whatever it said and you have to get those basic facts right (like equations in an economics paper), but this still leaves significant room for differences of interpretation and normative evaluation with regard to any legal issue or development interesting enough to be worth writing about. For all that, it seems to me that existing systems of peer reviewing and publication work tolerably well for UK legal scholarship. Anybody who feels shut out by the existing journals on methodological or political – as opposed to quality – grounds is free, in a commercial marketplace, to pitch new ideas to publishers and set up their own journals and book series if there is a research community or wider audience to support them. UK legal scholarship has witnessed prodigious growth in new journal titles over the last several decades in specialist sectors such as human rights, international law and feminist legal writing, in addition to many niche areas,[63] partly incentivised by REF. Anybody who doubts the efficacy of quality enhancement and curation through existing publication arrangements should consider what would be left if commercial publishers suddenly departed, or were driven out of, the academic publishing market. What do you think would happen to the global visibility, reach and impact of your work if you were reduced to publishing only on institutional repositories and personal websites? What would be the practical implications of your best published work no longer appearing on LexisNexis,[64] Westlaw[65] or HeinOnline,[66] commercial legal databases that service (international) legal practice as well as legal scholarship and which UK funders are powerless to force into an open access environment? It is no answer to reply that your papers would be keyword searchable on GoogleScholar, because that model of scholarly communication presupposes that your potential audience is already looking for your work. Whilst that proactive premiss might hold for, say,

[63] Eg *Law, Probability & Risk*, created in 2002; and *Criminal Law and Philosophy*, published from 2007 (Full disclosure: I am a founding editorial board member of both titles).

[64] 'The all-in-one platform for legal research, guidance you can trust and legal AI solutions built for how legal work really happens', according to its owner Thomson Reuters: www.lexisnexis.co.uk/.

[65] More 'legal solutions' from Thomson Reuters, including a generative AI 'CoCounsel' enabling 'research tasks like never before': legalsolutions.thomsonreuters.co.uk.

[66] '[A] premier online research platform that provides more than 242 million pages of multidisciplinary periodicals, essential government documents, international resources, case law, and much more', offered by William S Hein & Co: home.heinonline.org/.

specialist teams of cancer researchers, it does not apply to judges or practising lawyers or most (Anglophone) academic legal research communities, which rely on, for example, in criminal jurisprudence, the latest issue of the *Criminal Law Review* to filter the world of events and flag up significant recent developments and ongoing scholarly debates. What about social media networks? Would quality in published legal scholarship become a function of how many followers you have on Twitter?[67]

These sorts of considerations apply broadly across the arts, humanities and social sciences (AHSS or SHAPE[68]) disciplines and are unique to Law only in their finer-grained institutional manifestations. The extent of potential disruption presumably explains why advocates of OA have hitherto adopted a gradualist approach. Current policy essentially involves a shift from backend 'consumer pays' (through journal subscriptions and book purchases) to frontend 'producer pays', whereby open access is purchased from commercial publishers through the levy of what are (euphemistically?) described as 'article processing charges' (APCs). Commercial publishers continue to make their profit in this flipped economic model of academic publishing, but who is the 'producer' who pays? It is presumably not individual researchers, since the APCs in question run to high hundreds or thousands of pounds/dollars per article, and as much as £10,000 for a book manuscript. Academics are not wealthy by professional standards, but most of us need to make a living at it, and a 'scholar pays' model would entail that the most productive legal scholars would quickly become bankrupt.[69] Nor will readers and users of research be charged, since the whole point of OA is that research becomes freely accessible at the point of use (which is also, incidentally, a massive positive externality for the rest of the world, and either something we can all celebrate as promoting scholarship in developing countries and contributing to global social justice; or – depending on your point of view – constitutes a subsidy to foreign business to undercut British industry and workers). So UK HEIs and funding councils continue to pay, but now upfront to publish open access rather than post-publication to buy academic books and journals for their libraries.

The economic rationality of this strategy hinges on the total cost of APCs being smaller, at least in the long run, than the existing costs of buying books and journals from commercial publishers (assuming that nobody in government has discovered a magic money tree earmarked for HE). It is vulnerable to commercial publishers simply ramping up APCs in order to preserve, or improve, their existing profit margins (which indeed appears to be happening). Setting aside questions of purely economic rationality, this is where the academic freedom worry returns

[67] Leaving unaltered what I wrote before 'academic Twitter' was unceremoniously Xed may serve to amplify my original point. Billionaire ownership of these platforms is merely symptomatic of a medium fundamentally corrosive to scholarship.

[68] 'Social Sciences, Humanities and the Arts for People and the Economy (SHAPE) is a collective name for the social sciences, humanities and the arts': thebritishacademy.ac.uk/this-is-shape/.

[69] Personally, in addition, I associate author payment with vanity publishing, and would never pay to publish on principle.

with a vengeance for legal scholarship. Upfront APCs may not be too threatening for STEM researchers who are used to needing big research grants and/or major institutional financial support to buy kit and consumables to do any meaningful research at all. The obvious strategy for them is to factor APC costs into grant proposals as particularised items of expenditure. It is a contingent matter whether this manoeuvre will result in a reduction in the total number of research projects, or the amount of research activity within particular projects, that can be funded from a fixed pot of grant money.[70] But it is unlikely, given the comparative scale of the sums involved, that APCs would make a significant dent in grant proposal costings or budgets for scientific research (especially if the money saved from not having to purchase books and journals at the backend of the research process is sensibly re-vired to cover APCs). But what happens in a discipline like Law, where there is little tradition of securing grant money to fund legal scholarship and correspondingly restricted opportunities for obtaining such funding? I have already mentioned my own dismal record of grant capture failure.[71] Moreover, insofar as dedicated funding is available, the sums involved tend to be paltry by STEM standards, because they are only needed to cover such things as replacement teaching (to buy the time to think, read and write), research visits to libraries and archives, and conference travel and subsistence. One APC could easily cost as much as the entirety of a travel grant to present a paper at an overseas conference. In this context, 'producer pays' could effectively mean that publication in the leading outlets for legal scholarship resides in the gift of HEIs rather than individual scholars.

It is not advertised HE policy to muzzle legal scholars and pre-vet their publications; if it were, the policy would be illegal. But recall that our concern is with unfortunate side-effects and unintended consequences rather than putative conspiracies to silence legal scholars. REF is a key tool for leveraging policy implementation. The OA requirements for REF2021 were fairly relaxed. Only *articles* published after 2016 were even 'in scope', and the preferred model of 'green' OA permitted a one-year embargo on full-text publication so long as indexing requirements (eg, in institutional repositories) were met. Publication in books and book chapters remained uninhibited, subject only to toothless exhortations to greater compliance with the spirit of OA: anything published before 2016 was automatically compliant with the rules, and there was even a 5 per cent non-compliance allowance for each unit's submitted outputs, reflecting the transitional nature of the new OA framework mid-REF cycle. Besides, once individual scholars have 'paid their dues' to REF by publishing three or four high-quality pieces compliant with OA requirements, they remain free to publish other material commercially that may be held behind paywalls forever (and also probably hosted by one of the

[70] A partial precedent might be seen in the introduction some years ago of 'full economic costing' (fec) for external grant awards. When universities could charge for 'central services', the unit cost of research projects rose 30% or more, so that proportionately fewer awards could be allocated from a fixed budget for government-funded research.

[71] BioNote to Chapter 6.

major legal databases, such as Westlaw, which are paid-for subscription services beyond the reach of OA policy governance). It would have been alarmist to start trumpeting the academic freedom of legal scholars if this had been the highwater mark of REF-mandated OA. In fact, this transitional arrangement was merely a staging post en route to more radical policy transformation.

UK Research and Innovation (UKRI), the umbrella organisation[72] for the UK's government-funded research councils, laid out its incipient policy agenda in a consultation document issued prior to the completion of the last REF cycle.[73] Looking forward to what it quaintly styled 'the REF-after-REF 2021' (REF being now so all-encompassing that the new cycle begins *before* the current one is completed), UKRI lamented that, although significant progress had been achieved,[74] the impetus towards OA had stalled. Part of the problem was that commercial publishers were – it must be said, entirely predictably – increasing *both* subscription charges and APCs to drive profit margins.[75] In truth, APCs may be financially unsustainable on any plausible model, because so much of the work of journal refereeing and editing is consumed by papers that are *rejected*. So what authors must actually pay for is not merely all the editorial work on *their* article submissions, but a proportionate cost of the entire refereeing and editorial operation. The sums involved for leading journals like *Science* and *Nature* are said to imply APCs north of $40,000 per article.[76] A consortium of European-led governments and research funders, under the banner of Plan S and its offshoot cOAlition S, has resolved 'to make full and immediate OA a reality'.[77] This would seem to require comprehensive mandatory regulation that cannot easily be outflanked by the commercial sector. The policy proposals put out for consultation by UKRI were duly adopted in 2021,[78] and now stipulate:[79]

- immediate OA for all 'in scope' peer-reviewed journal articles with no embargo period;
- OA within 12 months of publication for all 'in scope' books, book chapters and edited collections published after 1 January 2024;

[72] Technically, a 'non-departmental public body sponsored by the Department for Science, Innovation and Technology (DSIT)'.

[73] UK Research and Innovation, *UKRI Open Access Review: Consultation* (UKRI, 13 February 2020).

[74] 'The proportion of UK-authored articles available immediately on publication rose from 20% to 37% between 2014 and 2016 (compared with 25% globally) and over half can be read online for free, one year after publication': ibid [17].

[75] '[A]nalysis by the Universities UK Open Access Coordination Group found that between 2013 and 2016 the average OA article processing charge (APC) increased by 16% (compared with a rise of 5% in the Consumer Price Index), alongside a 20% increase in expenditure on journal subscriptions': ibid [19].

[76] Richard Van Noorden, 'Open Access: The True Cost of Science Publishing' (2013) 495 *Nature* 426, 427 (observing that 'Philip Campbell, editor-in-chief of *Nature*, estimates his journal's internal costs at £20,000–30,000 ($30,000–40,000) per paper. Many publishers say they cannot estimate what their per-paper costs are because article publishing is entangled with other activities').

[77] UKRI (n 73) [33].

[78] UKRI, *UKRI Open Access Policy – Explanation of Policy Changes*, 6 August 2021.

[79] UKRI, *UK Research and Innovation Open Access Policy*, updated 15 November 2023.

- imposition of mandatory licensing requirements under the Creative Commons attribution (CC BY) template;[80] and conversely,
- publication in journals, 'hybrid' platforms or repositories which fail to meet OA access and discovery standards is forbidden.

OA means, in this context, that 'the final Version of Record or the Author's Accepted Manuscript' must be free to view and download via an online publication platform, publishers' website, or institutional or subject repository'.[81] Although UKRI policy is not coterminous with REF, the intention to forge a shared approach and present a united front is clearly signalled:

> UKRI's review will also inform the development of the OA policy for research outputs submitted to the UK-wide REF-after-REF 2021. UKRI and the UK HE funding bodies share the view that the outputs of publicly funded research should be widely and freely accessible as soon as possible. As far as possible, they are seeking commonality between the UKRI and REF-after-REF 2021 OA policies, including a common policy position for outputs that fall within the scope of both policies.[82]

Therein lies the rub. From the broader perspective of the continued health and vitality of UK legal scholarship, REF policy is largely a sideshow. UKRI is pursuing a determinedly coercive approach designed to change where and how researchers publish, primarily – but not exclusively[83] – where government provides research funding. This applies to *all* 'in scope' publications, whether or not they are returned to a future REF. It could mean, for example, that legal researchers were forbidden from publishing in North American, Australasian, African or South Asian legal journals unless these publications were fully OA compliant themselves – which is unlikely to be the case where overseas jurisdictions do not subscribe to parallel OA policies or requirements.[84] Concerted action at the European level provides little reassurance for legal scholars, given the primacy of the Anglosphere to common law jurisprudence.

Before getting too carried away, it is important to stress that 'in scope' means 'funded by UKRI affiliated research councils'.[85] On the face of it, this means externally grant-funded research, and does not include the block grant 'QR' funding

[80] UKRI wisely avoids wading into the legal quagmire of who actually owns copyright in works of scholarship. The policy position is that 'it is good practice for researchers and research organisations to retain the copyright to their work'.

[81] ibid [17].

[82] UKRI (n 73) [29].

[83] More comprehensive policy aims include 'providing sustainable support for open access and better value for money; encouraging the development of new models of open access publishing; and supporting the adoption of open access in the UK and internationally'. As the major provider of UK research funding, UKRI can leverage its market dominance to drive change across the sector.

[84] Might it be possible to argue that US and Australian law school reviews are exempt because they are student-run and not 'peer reviewed' in the STEM sense? Perhaps: but this tactic could backfire, since it invites the retort that, absent peer review, legal publications are not 'research' for REF purposes.

[85] These being the seven broadly disciplinary research councils (AHRC, BBSRC, ESRC, EPSRC, MRC, NERC, STFC), plus Innovate UK and Research England.

distributed to HEIs through REF. So it could be argued that these proposals do not reach the bulk of published legal scholarship, which is not directly grant-funded. I cannot see how this defensive line could be held long term. After all, QR is still public money, and legal scholars would be using it to evade OA policies across HE and possibly eroding the disciplinary efficacy of OA by propping up a commercial publishing sector committed to exploiting legal scholarship for profit. I foresee, at the very least, a rule that says that all submissions to REF must be OA compliant – implying that legal scholars would not be able to publish their presumptively best work in the leading journals unless they can find the money to pay hefty APCs. For monographs the situation is both clearer and more uncertain. Those monographs completed either as revisions of research council-funded PhD theses or with direct UKRI support for sabbatical terms are definitely in-scope. Whether it will still be possible to publish such monographs with leading commercial publishers, in the UK or overseas, will depend on assessments of commercial viability by individual publishers or, again, substantial upfront APC charges. Will a one-year embargo period be sufficient to reassure a publisher that a particular manuscript can recoup its costs and possibly even turn a healthy profit? Quite possibly not, especially when university libraries are not going to fork out for books that they know they will be able to access for free within twelve months or less.

One dimension of OA policy that tends to be skated over is that 100 per cent open access can be achieved in either one of two directions, or with a pincer movement in both directions simultaneously. One could alter the mode of dissemination for existing research; and/or one could eliminate non-compliant publications.[86] A world in which precisely one legal journal article is published annually, and made freely available on the open internet, is a world of 100 per cent open access legal research publishing. This *reductio ad absurdum* is not a facile debating point. One of the stated objectives of OA is to 'improve the efficiency of research and of scholarly communication by reducing duplication and enabling easier access to research and identification of past findings'.[87] This desideratum evidently presupposes the now-familiar STEM model, according to which findings are findings, and provided that they remain accessible, they don't need repeating once reported.[88] Recalling the old saw that the entire corpus of western philosophy is merely a footnote to Plato, it is just as well that this model of once-and-for-always publication of 'findings' does not apply across the arts, humanities and (much) social science.

[86] Some EDI initiatives are vulnerable to similar 'levelling down' dilution. One way of eliminating the professorial 'gender pay gap', for example, would be to select a figure in the lower reaches of the professorial scale and to pay all professors that same salary – robbing Peter to pay Paula, so to speak.

[87] UKRI (n 73) [16].

[88] However, STEM researchers might well object that this contention seriously underestimates the importance of validation of scientific knowledge through replication. Indeed, there is an acknowledged 'replication crisis' in some areas of experimental science, such as behavioural psychology: see, eg, Jason M Chin, Bethany Growns and David T Mellor, 'Improving Expert Evidence: The Role of Open Science and Transparency (2019) 50 *Ottawa Law Review* 369. This is a whole other can of worms, since the concept of 'replication' is far from straightforward in theory or practice: see NAS, *Reproducibility and Replicability in Science* (National Academies Press, 2019).

Every legal scholar's new take on an old case is a novel contribution to scholarship. Questions of justice, legal form, legislative technique and the legitimacy of political authority that vexed Plato are very much still with us today.[89] Unfortunately, the commercial realities of publishing may entail that UK-based legal scholars' contributions to these timeless debates will be fewer and less influential in the future. Edited collections would appear especially vulnerable under the rule of OA. It is likely that if these books cannot be sold commercially at a profit, they will not be written. Without the prospect of a – potentially REF-able – publication at the end of the process, it may well be that the academic conferences and workshops that often precede such collaborations will not take place, either. Although edited collections are often regarded as variable in quality, my own experience of participating in a score or more of such projects, as contributing author, editor or discussant, over 30 years is that they have involved some of the most energising, instructive and productive meetings of my career, leading to major, even landmark publications.[90] I would greatly regret the demise of this genre, not merely as published works of scholarship, but as catalysts and facilitators of scholarly discourse and debate, intellectual innovation, networking, collaboration, mutual education and long-lasting academic friendships.

Where do legal textbooks fit into this new publishing paradigm? Generically, 'textbooks' are beyond the scope of UKRI's OA policy.[91] I suspect that this is because

[89] Richard O Brooks (ed), *Plato and Modern Law* (Ashgate, 2007).

[90] Including Paul Roberts and Michael Stockdale (eds), *Forensic Science Evidence and Expert Witness Testimony: Reliability Through Reform?* (Edward Elgar, 2018); John D Jackson and Sarah J Summers (eds), *Obstacles to Fairness in Criminal Proceedings* (Hart Publishing, 2018); Anthony Amatrudo (ed), *Social Censure and Critical Criminology: After Sumner* (Palgrave Macmillan, 2017); Jill Hunter, Paul Roberts, Simon N M Young and David Dixon (eds), *The Integrity of Criminal Process: From Theory into Practice* (Hart Publishing, 2016); A P Simester, Anjte du Bois-Pedain and Ulfrid Neumann (eds), *Liberal Criminal Theory: Essays for Andreas von Hirsch* (Hart Publishing, 2014); Carmen Vázquez (ed), *Estandares de prueba y prueba cientifica* (Marcial Pons, 2013); Paul Roberts and Jill Hunter (eds), *Criminal Evidence and Human Rights: Reimagining Common Law Procedural Traditions* (Hart Publishing, 2012); R A Duff and Stuart Green (eds), *Philosophical Foundations of Criminal Law* (OUP, 2011); John Jackson, Maximo Langer and Peter Tillers (eds), *Crime, Procedure and Evidence in A Comparative and International Context – Essays in Honour of Professor Mirjan Damaška* (Hart Publishing, 2008); Paul Roberts and Mike Redmayne (eds), *Innovations in Evidence and Proof: Integrating Theory, Research and* Teaching (Hart Publishing, 2007); Antony Duff, Lindsay Farmer, Sandra Marshall and Victor Tadros (eds) *The Trial on Trial, Volumes I-III* (Hart Publishing, 2004–2007); Andrew Simester (ed), *Appraising Strict Liability* (OUP, 2005); Andrew von Hirsch et al (eds), *Restorative Justice and Criminal Justice* (Hart Publishing, 2003); Peter Alldridge and Chrisje Brants (eds), *Personal Autonomy, The Private Sphere and the Criminal Law: A Comparative Study* (Hart Publishing, 2001); Andrew von Hirsch, David Garland and Alison Wakefield (eds), *Ethical and Social Perspectives on Situational Crime Prevention* (Hart Publishing, 2000).

[91] UKRI (n 73) [98]. 'Trade books' are also excluded, presenting the difficulty of borderline cases. Most academic legal publishing involves short print runs reaching only academic (including student) audiences, but books on topics such as forensic science, miscarriages of justice or criminal justice policy may enjoy somewhat broader appeal and better sales. The bind for both textbooks and trade books is the same: if such publications are not scholarship, they are outside the OA requirements, but will probably not be supported by UKRI funding or returned to REF. If they *are* scholarship, they can be supported by UKRI funding and returned to REF, but no commercial publisher is likely to risk publishing them (unless paid thousands in upfront processing fees) owing to OA requirements.

the idea that a book intended for teaching (undergraduate) students could simultaneously be a discipline-defining contribution to scholarship is not cognisable from within the STEM paradigm. Any prospect of legal textbooks being able to fly under the radar, however, would presumably be limited by REF eligibility, which will almost certainly treat material[92] presented as scholarship as within scope for OA purposes. Any legal textbook with scholarly ambitions would be equated with a monograph in terms of OA compliance. But this is completely at odds with the business model for producing legal textbooks, which are perhaps the only kind of academic legal publishing capable of generating real money through volume sales to students. Legal textbook publishing as we know it would be killed off by a requirement for full-text OA availability within one year of publication. Apart from anything else, it is inconceivable that authors would be able to turn around new editions every year.[93] It seems more likely, then, that legal textbooks will be driven in the direction of servicing undergraduate modules, with simplified treatments, 'further reading' lists rather than full citation and documentation, practice exam questions, coloured text boxes and the like. Textbooks like this may be pedagogically excellent, but they will not be contributing much, if anything, to legal scholarship. It is legitimate to ask whether iconic titles such as *Smith and Hogan's Criminal Law* or *Cross on Evidence* would have been written in this publishing environment. It will not do to insist that driven scholars like John Smith and Rupert Cross would have written their pioneering books, come what may, because scholars of their generation did not have to produce four or five REF pieces every six or so years, nor were they told that many leading (international) journals and publishing houses are off-limits because they are not OA-compliant. The real question today is why would a legal scholar invest many years of their time writing a *scholarly* textbook, which cannot be supported by UKRI-funded research leave (because it would then be in-scope) and will not in any case be eligible for REF? Somebody might do it anyway – legal scholars can be a pretty headstrong, obdurate bunch – but all the institutional drivers and career incentives are ranged against it.

This discussion cannot conclude without noticing the elephant in the room. As far as I know, there has never been any historic problem of access to UK-based legal scholarship. Nor is there any credible case for saying that OA will 'enhance the integrity and rigour of [*legal*] research through greater openness, transparency and increased opportunity for findings to be scrutinised'.[94] There are several

Caught in this Catch 22, the book might not be written at all, or if written it might not be read. In this scenario OA policy triumphs by diminishing the quantity, quality and impact of UK legal scholarship.

[92] Expressly including 'trade books' when they are 'the *only* output from UKRI-funded research': ibid.

[93] Compare practitioner-focused works such as *Blackstone's Criminal Practice*, which *are* produced annually. The value of these encyclopaedic works depends on their being both reasonably comprehensive and bang up-to-date. Practitioners will pay handsomely for the new edition every single year, old editions becoming instantly practically worthless. Such works are produced by teams of authors, many of whom are not (full-time) academics; and although they are certainly rigorous and influential, such practitioner books are not works of great scholarly imagination or disciplinary innovation.

[94] UKRI (n 73) [16].

salient factors differentiating legal research and publication from what might be the norm in STEM and other related subjects. First, much legal scholarship is addressed to lawyers, courts and legal scholars within a particular jurisdiction. It is a professional literature of little or no interest to lay readers, who would not be able to understand most of its terminology or technical significance even if they tried to read it. Second, insofar as legal arguments, conclusions or policy recommendations *are* of interest to more generalist readers, legal scholars routinely publish them in a range of accessible formats, from Law Commission reports and (published) submissions to parliamentary inquiries, through research briefing notes and NGO policy papers, to institutional press releases and media op-ed pieces, lately augmented by blog-posts, tweets and the rest. If a legal scholar has a decent argument to make or any interesting research findings to report, you can be pretty confident that the word will get out and the world will know, if it cares to. Third, insofar as UK-based scholars want to address scholars – or indeed, lawyers, courts or policymakers – beyond their jurisdiction, they will choose to publish in journals with relevantly regional or international readerships, including those produced overseas and sponsored by scholarly associations.

Fourth, Anglophone legal scholarship is readily available to all scholars and students in institutions subscribing to the major proprietary legal databases, principally LexisNexis and Westlaw. These are paid-for services, but a chunk of the running costs and commercial profit are contributed by legal practitioners. In reality, it is difficult to see how any modern law school could operate credibly without these subscriptions, even if it were exclusively devoted to teaching law and produced no scholarship whatever. So this is really a sunk cost for any HEI wanting to retain a law school; and the massive benefits it confers on faculty members using these resources to produce scholarly publications are effectively a positive externality for UK legal scholarship. HEIs have already paid for this facility, and largely through student fees rather than research grant income.[95]

Fifth, subscriptions to legal journals are not, generally speaking, expensive. Many legal scholars have, or have had, multiple personal subscriptions to specialist journals in their field, which generally cost around £50 (tax deductible), and sometimes come as part of a package with subscriptions to learned societies.[96] One of the consequences of OA, however, is that publishers have driven up subscription costs to replace 'lost' sales revenue, especially for journals marketed to legal practitioners (who presumably pass on these rising costs to clients). In my field, the cost of subscribing to the *Criminal Law Review* rapidly escalated, to the point

[95] I note, without exploring, an ethical issue. Law teachers train their students to use these proprietary legal tools which students then rely on later in practice, and they – or their firms – have to keep paying for in perpetuity. Is this akin to pedalling legal crack, and making lifelong addicts of our students? A different thought, more pertinent to the present discussion: since law teachers are in a unique position to induct students into the use of proprietary databases, why do we not leverage our gatekeeper status to drive down the price of institutional subscriptions to the databases? In fact, why is this not an argument for *free* HEI access for educational use?

[96] Most prominently, members of the Society of Legal Scholars get *Legal Studies* thrown in.

where I could no longer justify continuing a personal subscription I had found very useful and maintained for almost two decades. So the most tangible impact of OA that I have personally experienced to date is that my access to published legal material has *diminished*, albeit marginally, inasmuch as *Crim LR* is accessible electronically on Westlaw. Perhaps one might extrapolate a more general lesson from this personal anecdote, about the potential for OA to impact negatively on UK legal scholarship, even though nobody means us any harm.

V. Institutional Rationality, from Toxic Interdisciplinarity to the Tragedy of Metrics

Most legal scholarship produced in the UK is the output of scholars employed by public universities, so it naturally follows that the policies, practices and cultures of individual HEIs and across the sector will be amongst the most direct, and potentially profound, influences on the production of legal scholarship. Many aspects of institutional environments are highly salient, not least the inverse relationship between burgeoning university bureaucracy and shrinking time left over for legal scholarship mentioned in the introduction. The discussion in this section focuses, selectively, on the structural dynamics of interactions between HEIs and wider HE policy initiatives such as REF and OA. It elucidates one way in which HE policy, as interpreted and implemented by individual HEIs, represents an ongoing existential threat to UK legal scholarship.

Research England (formerly HEFCE) and UKRI (incorporating RCUK) are not well disposed towards taking responsibility for the internal policies and practices of HEIs, or indeed for other consequential features of the HE landscape. If newspapers print misleading league tables based on crude REF GPA scores, or individual universities create disproportionately onerous bureaucratic systems for preparing their REF returns, Research England will say that this has nothing to do with them. But equally, HEIs will say that they are obliged to create large bureaucracies to deal effectively with all the policy changes and additional demands on the sector emanating from central government, not only REF, but also TEF,[97] Widening Participation, OFFA,[98] EDI and all the rest. So the amount of time, effort and financial resource universities invest in 'management' constantly spirals, but nobody is to blame or even, one suspects, really in control. This is a variant of a

[97] 'The Teaching Excellence Framework (TEF) is a national scheme run by the Office for Students (OfS) that aims to encourage higher education providers to improve and deliver excellence in the areas that students care about the most: teaching, learning and achieving positive outcomes from their studies': www.officeforstudents.org.uk/for-providers/quality-and-standards/about-the-tef/ (accessed 17 December 2025).

[98] RIP. 'The Office for Fair Access has ceased operation, and responsibility for regulating fair access to higher education in England sits with the Office for Students', www.offa.org.uk/. Now see Office for Students (OfS): www.officeforstudents.org.uk/ (accessed 17 December 2025).

scenario known to game theorists as the Prisoners' Dilemma,[99] and to economists and political theorists as the Tragedy of the Commons.[100] Everybody is behaving perfectly rationally according to their situation, but the overall outcome is decidedly sub-optimal. Nobody is responsible for tending to the common property (in our case, the UK's rich and proud history of world-leading legal scholarship), with the result that this collective asset, owned by nobody, is left to degenerate and fall into rack and ruin.

Now let's play a game I like to call Fantasy Vice Chancellor. You are the vice chancellor of a large public university with a law school. You don't know very much about law schools or the nature of legal teaching or scholarship, and you certainly do not feel any special professional responsibility for its disciplinary flourishing, over and above the general level of concern and goodwill that you extend to all the other, say, 34[101] schools and departments in your university. You know that Law sits within Social Sciences,[102] and reasonably presume that its disciplinary norms and methods are, broadly speaking, social scientific.[103] You secretly hope that you can rely on your Head of College to brief you about Law (but she is in fact an economist,[104] and neither knows nor cares more than you do about legal scholarship). One of your main tasks as vice chancellor is to distribute a finite global pot of research funding to support research activity across the university. Professors in STEM subjects inform you that they cannot do their research without major funding. On the upside, however, they will be able, with your pump-priming assistance, to pursue and hopefully capture major external funding from charities or the research councils to match or exceed institutional financial backing; REF publications galore are almost guaranteed, and they might even bag you a Nobel Prize or two into the bargain. This looks like an excellent investment. At the same time, you want to help all faculties in the university to ensure that research is thriving across the institution. After all, you are not trying to turn your university into Imperial College London. Happily, researchers in the Arts and Social Sciences faculties don't need nearly as much money as STEM researchers; albeit their scope for attracting significant matching funding is correspondingly limited. You are spending less; the returns are likely to be comparatively modest, but the

[99] Martin Peterson (ed), *The Prisoner's Dilemma* (CUP, 2015).

[100] Garrett Hardin, 'The Tragedy of the Commons' (1968) 162 *Science* 1243; Garrett Hardin, 'Extensions of "The Tragedy of the Commons"' (1998) 280 *Science* 682. Hardin's own application to population growth is only one extension of a general, arguably not very novel idea. *Cf* Brett M Frischmann, Alain Marciano and Giovanni Battista Ramello, 'Retrospectives: Tragedy of the Commons after 50 Years' (2019) 33 *Journal of Economic Perspectives* 211.

[101] This being the number of discrete units of assessment in REF2021.

[102] Not true of all university law schools, but this seems to be the majority position, and coheres with the REF classification of Law within Main Panel C.

[103] Which, for the avoidance of doubt, is false: see Christopher McCrudden, 'Legal Research and the Social Sciences' (2006) 122 *Law Quarterly Review* 632; Geoffrey Samuel, 'Is Law Really A Social Science? A View From Comparative Law' (2008) 67 *Cambridge Law Journal* 288; David Nelken, 'Blinding Insights? The Limits of a Reflexive Sociology of Law' (1998) 25 *Journal of Law and Society* 407.

[104] Or substitute the disciplinary affiliation of the faculty bosses least likely to be sympathetic to Law in your institution.

investment in AHSS research – to be cashed out partly in REF outputs, impact and associated institutional esteem – still looks solid.

So you sit down with your Head of College to consider how to distribute funds amongst researchers in the social sciences. Your decisions must naturally be evidence-based and fair, so you turn to metrics, the ubiquitous tool of twenty-first-century university management. Unfortunately, it strikes you on consulting these data that your law school is not doing so well. Grant income per capita is disappointingly low, as is the quotient of PhD students. You are vaguely aware that the law school has a popular and lucrative LLM programme, but that does not seem relevant to *research*. When you examine publication metrics, the picture only becomes worse. Members of the law school score poorly on SciVal,[105] *h*-index[106] and other standard measures of publication activity and research influence. Indeed, it appears as though many of the most prolific producers of heavily cited legal research papers in the university are not even law professors but are rather to be found in the business school, politics department, psychology or elsewhere! You do not know that most online legal publications are stored behind paywalls and so are not counted by citation algorithms – either as outputs in their own right or as the primary vehicle for citing other legal scholarship. Alternative criteria of research impact at which legal scholars excel, such as citations in higher courts or (published) contributions to law reform, are too discipline-specific to appear in generic algorithms, and nobody ever mentions or considers them. Thankfully, researchers in the business school, political science and sociology departments seem to be doing quite well in attracting grant funding for empirical projects of various kinds. And they are producing well-cited, eminently REF-able outputs. We have now reached the crux of Fantasy Vice Chancellor: how would you distribute the (modest) pot of institutional research funding across your social sciences faculty? And what would you do with your (f)ailing law school?

This is what I might be inclined to do as FVC. The most demonstrable institutional asset of the law school is that it attracts very large numbers of well-qualified undergraduates. This money can be utilised to subsidise research and teaching in other departments which are academically strong but which, through no fault of their own, are not nearly as successful as law schools at recruiting students. If the law school had more teachers, it could take even more students, make

[105] An Elsevier product, 'SciVal provides access to the research performance of over 24,700 research institutions and their associated researchers, from 234 nations worldwide': www.scival.com/.

[106] Providing a geometric score for citations of published work: a score of 1 means one output cited once, 2 means two outputs each cited twice, 3 means three outputs each cited three times, and so on. According to ResearchGate, my *h*-index score is 16, and this places me in the top 3% of researchers in Criminal Law and the top 13% of all ResearchGate members. These rankings make such strong appeals to personal vanity that it takes a conscious effort to remember that they are all deeply flawed and essentially meaningless. And yet they are routinely employed as proxies for research quality and impact, because they are administratively convenient and appear objective to busy people with limited curiosity.

more money, and do even more good across the university. In fact, the undergraduate in-take could literally be doubled almost at a stroke, because there are (currently[107]) sufficient numbers of applicants, and once the capacity of the largest lecture theatre is exceeded, primary teaching will have to be doubled up anyway – or, better still, beamed by remote technologies to theoretically unlimited class sizes anywhere in the world. The best, most economical way of finding more law teachers is to shift existing 'under-performing' staff onto teaching-only contracts and double their teaching loads. Many will not like this, and some will retire or leave, but the supply of recently qualified PhD students in Law is buoyant, and malcontents can easily be replaced by eager young teachers, often on significantly lower salaries than departing staff. Best of all, the REF problem posed by 'unproductive' law professors is completely solved, because staff on teaching-only contracts are not returnable to REF. There is no significant OA issue either, as teaching staff do not need to publish legal scholarship (even if universities properly accommodate the need for quality law teaching to be grounded in legal *research*, and teaching-related publications are required for career progression along 'teaching and learning' pathways).

A credible public law school must still undertake research and produce influential, including four-star 'world leading', publications and impact case studies. This task will now fall to a residual group of the law staff cohort (mis)identified as 'research active'. Proportions would vary across institutions, but research-active staff would probably account for no more than half of the faculty in most UK law schools. Researchers' teaching loads will not *directly*[108] increase, though the practicalities of covering diverse legal specialisms across the law school curriculum entail that their teaching loads would probably not decrease noticeably either. In response to institutional pressures to secure external finance, legal researchers would be well-advised to undertake projects that require major grant funding, such as socio-legal empirical studies. Certain kinds of law reform projects, such as those seeking to promote social justice, may be attractive to charities such as the Nuffield Foundation. Resources will be devoted to 'horizon-scanning' for emergent funding opportunities, which in much law reform activity means trying to catch the eye of relevant government departments and aligning research agendas with temporary policy enthusiasms (themselves hostage to the ministerial merry-go-round). In the past, I have

[107] This market is not a birthright. There are various perceptible threats to its continuation, including increasingly fierce competition for students from law schools in other jurisdictions (Australia, Hong Kong, the Netherlands) and the prospect of technology (especially AI) eliminating many of the jobs that law graduates have traditionally done. HEI policy is also significant, as anything that harms the international reputation of UK law schools for excellence in legal education – eg, rapid over-recruitment, leading to tangible depreciation in 'the student experience' – could throttle the Golden Goose.

[108] Nominal teaching loads account for only part of the actual burden of teaching, which also encompasses assessment, pastoral care, and informal discussions and instruction. These additional elements are hard to quantify and tend to fall on whoever happens to be available at the time. 'Research active' staff would not be immune.

forged productive research partnerships with the Crown Prosecution Service,[109] but after a decade of austerity, there is nothing in the CPS budget for these (to them) optional extras. There is no dedicated UK funding stream to support doctrinal or theoretical legal research, so legal scholars must swell the ranks of arts and humanities researchers competing for smaller slices of the same funding pie. Interdisciplinary research will be favoured, partly because this impresses the Research Councils,[110] but also because publishing in non-law journals will more easily comply with OA requirements and is more likely to attract citation and boost the researcher's personal metrics. There is a great deal to be said in favour of interdisciplinary research,[111] but there are also downsides, two of which are potentially toxic for the health of legal scholarship. First, a fair amount of interdisciplinary effort on the part of legal scholars goes into educating non-lawyers about law. This is important work, but it tends not to be the acme of legal scholarship in terms of originality, intellectual rigour or significance. To the extent that legal scholars become preoccupied with teaching law to scholars in other disciplines, primary research questions and writing more consequential for the health and development of law, legal institutions and the discipline of Law may be neglected.

Second, whereas genuinely interdisciplinary collaboration involves a merging of disciplinary questions, methods, and materials facilitating mutual learning and co-constructed research programmes, there is another mode of superficially interdisciplinary encounter that is more accurately described as external colonisation. In this mode, a researcher from another discipline notices that a legal scholar is trying their hand at economics, political science, sociology, statistics or whatever, but infers that because the legal scholar's approach does not fully endorse the other discipline's research agenda or adopt all of its methodological assumptions and protocols, the legal scholar's work is fundamentally deficient. 'Full marks for curiosity and effort', thinks Disciplinary Observer, 'but Legal Scholar is barking up the wrong tree here. I will put her right, and she

[109] Paul Roberts and Candida Saunders, 'Piloting PTWI – A Socio-Legal Window on Prosecutors' Assessments of Evidence and Witness Credibility' (2010) 30 *Oxford Journal of Legal Studies* 101; Paul Roberts and Candida Saunders, *Interviewing Prosecution Witnesses: A Socio-Legal Evaluation of the Pre-Trial Witness Interview Pilot* (CPS, 2008); Paul Roberts, Debbie Cooper and Sheelagh Judge, 'Monitoring Success, Accounting for Failure: The Outcome of Prosecutors' Applications for Special Measures under the Youth Justice and Criminal Evidence Act 1999' (2005) 9 *International Journal of Evidence & Proof* 269; Debbie Cooper and Paul Roberts, *Special Measures for Vulnerable and Intimidated Witnesses: An Analysis of Crown Prosecution Service Monitoring Data* (CPS, 2005).

[110] Lord Nicholas Stern, *Building on Success and Learning from Experience: An Independent Review of the Research Excellence Framework* (2016) 28–29 (affirming 'the essential role of interdisciplinary research in addressing complex problems and research questions posed by global social, economic, ecological and political challenges'); British Academy, *Crossing Paths: Interdisciplinary Institutions, Careers, Education and Applications* (2016), www.britac.ac.uk/interdisciplinarity.

[111] Paul Roberts, 'Interdisciplinarity in Legal Research' in Mike McConville and Wing Hong Cui (eds), *Research Methods for Law*, 3rd edn (Edinburgh University Press, 2024); Douglas W Vick, 'Interdisciplinarity and the Discipline of Law' (2004) 31 *Journal of Law and Society* 163; Arthur Allen Leff, 'Law and' (1978) 87 *Yale Law Journal* 989.

will thank me for it!'[112] Needless to say, legal scholarship will *not* be grateful for such patronising interventions, which involve hijacking Law's disciplinary-constituting questions, methods and materials and turning them into something else. Interdisciplinarity only works *for legal scholarship* if it involves collaboration rather than colonisation. Writing economics, or political science, or sociology papers with some reference to law might win you friends in other departments and faculties and secure more citations, but it won't produce better *legal* scholarship.

VI. Concluding with Questions: Please Discuss

As befits a volume dedicated to inspiring scholarship in criminal jurisprudence, the last words of this final chapter are more concerned with future possibilities than with nostalgia for times past. In the midst of a fiscal crisis, it is difficult to be optimistic about the immediate prospects for the UK's HE sector, but – to reiterate a message from the introduction – we need to take the longer view with an eye to more favourable institutional circumstances at some future point in time. If UK legal scholarship is to survive largely intact to reach those once and future sunny uplands, we also need to understand the dynamics of our current institutional circumstances and develop a shrewd appreciation of the acute challenges they pose, particularly if not uniquely for legal scholarship. I have suggested that their cumulative impact is nothing short of existential.

There are many interweaving threads in this multilayered tapestry, and they may in future combine or knot together in complex, unpredictable ways. Yet whatever patterns they may weave, it is difficult to see how traditional legal scholarship, in particular, fares well under current policies and institutional arrangements. One overdetermined consequence is a discernible drift towards reducing the autonomy of legal scholars to choose their own research programmes and the location and format of their publications. This does not bode well for independent thought or critical voices sometimes at odds with university central planning or prevailing government policy. Lap dogs know better than to bite the hand that feeds them.

[112] If tempted to dismiss this imagined dialogue as Music Hall pantomime, consider a real-life exhibit, curtesy of Lee Epstein and Gary King, 'The Rules of Inference' (2002) 69 *University of Chicago Law Review* 1,11, 15, 17: '[T]he complete list of all law review articles devoted to improving, understanding, explicating, or adapting the rules of inference is as follows: none …. Our purpose was to identify where the problems were. Our answer? Everywhere. We find that serious problems of inference and methodology abound everywhere we find empirical research in the law reviews and in articles written by members of the legal community … [E]very one we have read thus far – every single one – violates at least one of the rules we discuss … Since all – every single one – have the potential to find their way into a court case, an administrative proceeding, or a legislative hearing, we can only imagine the serious consequences for public policy (not to mention for the development of knowledge) that may have already resulted – or still may result.' For a measured riposte, see Jack Goldsmith and Adrian Vermeule, 'Empirical Methodology and Legal Scholarship' (2002) 69 *University of Chicago Law Review* 153.

Law does not attract big money grants; it is unlikely to garner many citations by STEM publication standards (especially when concerned with technical points of domestic law); and OA policy is likely to make it increasingly difficult to publish doctrinal scholarship in places where its readership and practical influence would be greatest.[113] Meanwhile, shallow, trendy or sensationalist research could be incentivised. All this propelled by the seductive logic of policy initiatives and institutional structures, where everybody is simply trying to do their professional best to respond to operational imperatives with the information and resources at their disposal. If even only half of the risks and perverse incentives canvassed in this chapter fully eventuate, the prognosis for UK legal scholarship on its current trajectory seems bleak. Unless legal scholars now take seriously the question of legal scholarship's continuing viability, within a decade we may be confronting a different, altogether gloomier question, viz: whatever happened to UK legal scholarship?

At this juncture, it is wise to heed Bohr's sagacious aphorism about the perils of making predictions, especially when they concern the future.[114] Structural arguments identify tendencies and generate plausible hypotheses rather than affording firm grounds for prognostication, pessimistic or otherwise. The primary aim of this chapter is to stimulate, or provoke, a debate regarding the existential condition of UK legal scholarship today. In one sense, something called 'legal scholarship' will almost certainly survive. But to regard that as a satisfactory answer to the existential question posed in this chapter would be a glaring semantic fallacy,[115] like thinking that any institution with 'university' in its name actually is one purely on that nominal basis.[116] Major reductions in the quantity, scope and influence of legal scholarship, coupled with palpable qualitative deteriorations in the rigour and ambition of published material, might still be a form of intellectual life, Jim, but not as we know it. Fully-fledged legal scholarship as life of the mind might soon be confined to small coteries of legal monks in their cloistered collegiate scriptoriums.[117] We are concerned with upholding a thriving tradition of scholarship and transmitting its disciplinary wisdom to future generations. Of course, legal scholarship must change and adapt to meet the new social, technological

[113] *Cf* Andrew Ashworth and Ian Dennis, 'Fifty Years of the *Criminal Law Review*' in *The Criminal Law Review: 50th Anniversary Edition* (Sweet & Maxell, 2004).

[114] *Cf* Ehud Guttel and Alon Harel, 'Uncertainty Revisited: Legal Prediction and Legal Postdiction' (2008) 107 *Michigan Law Review* 467.

[115] I was first alerted to the ontological distinction between the thing and the name-for-the-thing by Ronald Dworkin's memorably entertaining illustrations of 'the semantic sting', but my favourite aphoristic encapsulation is this: *you can call a cat a fish, if you want to, but it still won't swim under water*!

[116] Anyone for the 'University of Law'? Search for 'scholarship' or 'research' on its glossy brochure website, www.law.ac.uk/, and then compare the results to the conception of legal scholarship sketched in section II of this chapter.

[117] But what is the optimally 'right' amount of legal scholarship that the UK should sustain? Might a strategic cull prove regenerative and promote more cost-efficient productivity? Suffice it to say that I don't see anybody currently advancing this argument explicitly or owning its implications. A new Dark Age in legal scholarship would be the diametric opposite of what the RAE originally promised to deliver.

and institutional demands of the day. Stasis means entropy and death, not vitality. So we honour the past by living up to it, not by freezing tradition in amber and turning legal scholarship into a museum piece. In the end, it comes down to preserving core values, professional integrity,[118] institutional resilience and disciplinary identity.

The discussion and arguments presented in this chapter are idiosyncratic and incomplete, as well as inconclusive. On the assumption that the majority of my intended audience has already internalised legal scholarship's virtues and value, there was no concerted attempt to justify its existence or to expound its instrumental contribution to sustaining healthy liberal democracy and the rule of law.[119] My approach was essentially diagnostic of current institutional arrangements and policies. Publicising the issues and attempting to get a better grip on the size and shape of the problem might hopefully inspire more imaginative solutions than any I could offer. Preservation of what remains, let alone remedial action, will require collective disciplinary responses, and the burdens – of success or failure – will fall mainly on the coming generations.

Having presented throughout the volume snapshots of 'ten academic lives in nine festschriften', this final chapter draws most directly and extensively on my own personal experience concentrated in one part of the wider UK HE and law school ecosystems. Readers must judge for themselves how far this partial vision can safely be extrapolated into reliable generalisations with wider applicability across the sector. Plainly, there are important differences between institutions, not least in terms of reputation, resources and mission, and these will be compounded by personal factors pertaining to individual scholars. Nonetheless, it is both my intention and my impression that the picture I paint will be familiar, at least in its primary pigments and general contours, to colleagues based in a variety of institutions and at different stages of their academic careers. This working hypothesis (which if falsified would reduce much of the foregoing discussion to autobiographical self-indulgence) is reinforced by this chapter's focus on the structural logic of REF, open access, and HEI institutional responses to HE policy, framed by the broader social, economic, and political landscape which modern universities must navigate. Many of the tendencies, implications and potential consequences of this structural logic will foreseeably affect scholarship across the arts, humanities and social sciences, but there are additional reasons for thinking that legal scholarship is especially vulnerable to the corrosive effects of recent HE policy and prevailing university management theory and technique.

The discipline of Law does not fit comfortably within macro-disciplinary templates and methodological schemas, which may partly explain why Law has

[118] Also see Anthony T Kronman, 'Living in the Law' (1987) 54 *University of Chicago Law Review* 835.

[119] *Cf* Martha C Nussbaum, 'The Use and Abuse of Philosophy in Legal Education' (1993) 45 *Stanford Law Review* 1627; Douglas Husak, 'What Moral Philosophers Might Learn from Criminal Theorists' (2004) 36 *Rutgers Law Journal* 191; Allen Buchanan, 'Philosophy and Public Policy: A Role for Social Moral Epistemology' (2009) 26 *Journal of Applied Philosophy* 276.

traditionally occupied its own faculty in universities around the world – not merely in common law jurisdictions. Academic law's intimate relationship with legal practice, legal institutions and law reform infuses legal pedagogy and scholarship in ways that are not replicated in other disciplines, and which provide unique disciplinary opportunities for influence and impact, alongside some special disciplinary responsibilities and challenges. If universities are serious about their law schools being more than just degree factories, they need to think again about how to get the best out of them. Judged by generic standards for 'social science', however, Law is virtually guaranteed to be found wanting, as though legal scholarship were just a second-rate, amateurish, pale imitation of sociology, economics or political science – a fallacy of toxic interdisciplinarity.

Legal scholarship is undertaken by legal scholars. This conceptual fusion goes beyond HR sloganising to insist that legal scholarship's chief assets *are* its people; no less than the corpus of learning we cultivate, not as owners, but as trustees. In true scholarship, there is no hard-and-fast separation between the producer and the product. Nurturing and appropriately exploiting this human resource will require HEIs to recognise models of academic careers in which performance is judged, and rewarded, holistically over a working lifetime, rather than being forced into a REF hothouse cycle that disrupts and distorts intellectual labour with a punishing sequence of arbitrary Year Zeros and will tend to incentivise safe productivity over truly ground-breaking (and consequently more risky) scholarship. A rational staffing policy for law schools would not demote or freeze out experienced scholars at the height of their intellectual powers and professional influence and authority, possibly before they have had full opportunity to make their best, career-defining contributions. Nor can law schools thrive without experienced scholars' essential contributions to mentoring the next generation of legal academics, including through research collaboration and co-authorship.

Can UK legal scholarship survive? We need to take this existential question seriously. Consider the arguments canvassed in the preceding pages. Why or how is the foregoing diagnosis of prevailing institutional conditions mistaken? If its diagnosis is (broadly) correct, why are the suggested logical implications not foreseeable or even likely? And if you did not appreciate (in either sense) this chapter's depressing prognosis, what are you going to do about it? Few people outside the sector really have much awareness of what is currently taking place in universities. I suspect that many legal professionals would be astounded – and perhaps dismayed – by how much things have changed since they were (law) students. At all events, it can hardly be doubted that legal scholars care more than anybody else about the health, vitality and resilience of legal scholarship, and nobody is better placed than us to assess its current, fragile condition. If we do not speak up for legal scholarship, nobody will. If we do not sound the alarm in the face of impending danger or fight our institutional corner when our vital interests are imperilled, nobody else is coming to save us.

INDEX

www.ingramcontent.com/pod-product-compliance
Ingram Content Group UK Ltd.
Pitfield, Milton Keynes, MK11 3LW, UK
UKHW020235290926
15470UKWH00002B/564

9 781509 986187